For current pricing information,
or to learn more about this or any Nextext title,
call us toll-free at **1-877-4NX-TEXT**
or visit our website at www.nextext.com.

A NEXTEXT ANTHOLOGY

WORLD TRADITIONS IN THE
Humanities

nextext

World Traditions in the Humanities

CHAPTER 3: CHINA AND JAPAN

CHAPTER 4: AFRICA

CHAPTER 5: NATIVE AMERICAN CULTURES

CHAPTER 6: GREECE AND ROME

CHAPTER 7: CHRISTIANITY AND BYZANTINE CULTURE

CHAPTER 9: THE MIDDLE AGES

CHAPTER 10: THE RENAISSANCE

CHAPTER 11: THE SEVENTEENTH AND EIGHTEENTH CENTURIES

CHAPTER 13: THE EARLY TWENTIETH CENTURY

CHAPTER 14: THE LATER TWENTIETH CENTURY

Throughout the anthology, vocabulary words appear in boldface type and are footnoted. Specialized or technical words and phrases appear in lightface type and are footnoted.

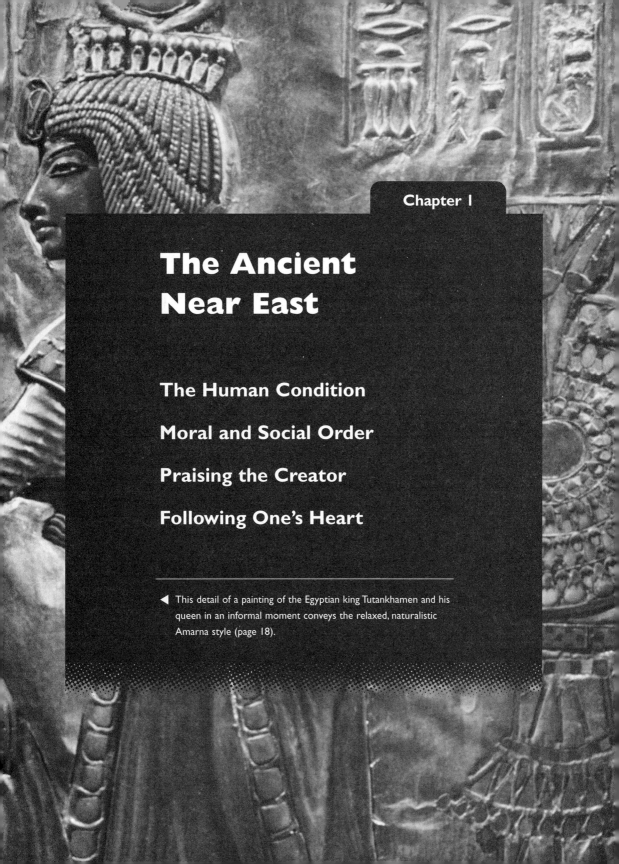

Chapter 1

The Ancient Near East

The Human Condition

Moral and Social Order

Praising the Creator

Following One's Heart

◀ This detail of a painting of the Egyptian king Tutankhamen and his queen in an informal moment conveys the relaxed, naturalistic Amarna style (page 18).

from

The Epic of Gilgamesh

Mesopotamia was the ancient region of the Tigris and Euphrates rivers, which flow through what is now Iraq and empty into the Persian Gulf. The first great work of world literature, The Epic of Gilgamesh, *was composed in Mesopotamia around 2000 B.C. The hero Gilgamesh and his friend Enkidu have angered the gods, who curse Enkidu so that he falls ill. In the first of the following passages, Enkidu dreams of the world of the dead. In the second passage, Gilgamesh, terrified by his friend's death and in search of the secret of everlasting life, encounters the wine-goddess Siduri.*

As Enkidu slept alone in his sickness, in bitterness of spirit he poured out his heart to his friend. "It was I who cut down the cedar, I who levelled the forest, I who slew Humbaba[1] and now see what has become of me. Listen, my friend, this is the dream I dreamed last night. The heavens roared, and earth rumbled back an answer; between them stood I before an awful being, the somber-faced man-bird; he had directed on me his purpose. His was a vampire face, his foot was a lion's foot, his hand was an eagle's talon. He fell on me and his claws were in my hair, he held me fast and I smothered; then he transformed me so that my arms became wings covered with feathers. He turned his stare towards me, and he led me away to the palace of Irkalla, the Queen of Darkness, to the house from which none who enters ever returns, down the road from which there is no coming back.

"There is the house whose people sit in darkness; dust is their food and clay their meat. They are clothed like birds with wings for covering, they see no light, they sit in darkness. I entered the house of dust and I saw the kings of the earth, their crowns put away forever; rulers and princes, all those who once wore kingly crowns and ruled the world in the days of old. They who had stood in the place of the gods like Anu and Enlil, stood now like servants to fetch baked meats in the house of dust, to carry cooked meat and cold water from the water-skin. In the house of

---

[1] Humbaba—giant slain by Gilgamesh and Enkidu.

dust which I entered were high priests and **acolytes**,[2] priests of the incantation and of ecstasy; there were servers of the temple, and there was Etana, that king of Kish whom the eagle carried to heaven in the days of old. I saw also Samuqan, god of cattle, and there was Ereshkigal the Queen of the Underworld; and Belit-Sheri squatted in front of her, she who is recorder of the gods and keeps the book of death. She held a tablet from which she read. She raised her head, she saw me and spoke: 'Who has brought this one here?' Then I awoke like a man drained of blood who wanders alone in a waste of rushes; like one whom the **bailiff**[3] has seized and his heart pounds with terror."

Gilgamesh had peeled off his clothes, he listened to his words and wept quick tears, Gilgamesh listened and his tears flowed. He opened his mouth and spoke to Enkidu: "Who is there in strong-walled Uruk[4] who has wisdom like this? Strange things have been spoken, why does your heart speak strangely? The dream was marvellous but the terror was great; we must treasure the dream whatever the terror; for the dream has shown that misery comes at last to the healthy man, the end of life is sorrow." And Gilgamesh lamented, "Now I will pray to the great gods, for my friend had an ominous dream."

* * *

Beside the sea she lives, the woman of the vine, the maker of wine; Siduri sits in the garden at the edge of the sea, with the golden bowl and the golden vats that the gods gave her. She is covered with a veil; and where she sits she sees Gilgamesh coming towards her, wearing skins, the flesh of the gods in his body, but despair in his heart, and his face like the face of one who has made a long journey. She looked, and as she scanned the distance she said in her own heart, "Surely this is some **felon**;[5] where is he going now?" And she barred her gate against him with the cross-bar and shot home the bolt. But Gilgamesh, hearing the sound of the bolt, threw up his head and lodged his foot in the gate; he called to her, "Young woman, maker of wine, why do you bolt your door; what did you see that made you bar your gate? I will break in your door and burst in your gate, for I am Gilgamesh who seized and killed the Bull of Heaven, I killed the watchman of the cedar forest, I overthrew Humbaba who lived in the forest, and I killed the lions in the passes of the mountain."

Then Siduri said to him, "If you are that Gilgamesh who seized and killed the Bull of Heaven, who killed the watchman of the cedar forest, who overthrew Humbaba that lived in the forest, and killed the lions in the passes of the mountain, why are your cheeks so starved and why is your face so drawn? Why is despair in your heart and your face like the face of one who has made a long journey? Yes,

---

[2] **acolytes**—attendants to a priest.
[3] **bailiff**—officer of a court who makes arrests.
[4] **Uruk**—city ruled by Gilgamesh.
[5] **felon**—criminal.

why is your face burned from heat and cold, and why do you come here wandering over the pastures in search of the wind?"

Gilgamesh answered her, "And why should not my cheeks be starved and my face drawn? Despair is in my heart and my face is the face of one who has made a long journey, it was burned with heat and with cold. Why should I not wander over the pastures in search of the wind? My friend, my younger brother, he who hunted the wild ass of the wilderness and the panther of the plains, my friend, my younger brother who seized and killed the Bull of Heaven and overthrew Humbaba in the cedar forest, my friend who was very dear to me and who endured dangers beside me, Enkidu my brother, whom I loved, the end of **mortality**[6] has overtaken him. I wept for him seven days and nights till the worm fastened on him. Because of my brother I am afraid of death, because of my brother I stray through the wilderness and cannot rest. But now, young woman, maker of wine, since I have seen your face do not let me see the face of death which I dread so much."

She answered, "Gilgamesh, where are you hurrying to? You will never find that life for which you are looking. When the gods created man they allotted to him death, but life they retained in their own keeping. As for you, Gilgamesh, fill your belly with good things; day and night, night and day, dance and be merry, feast and rejoice. Let your clothes be fresh, bathe yourself in water, cherish the little child that holds your hand, and make your wife happy in your embrace; for this too is the **lot**[7] of man."

---

[6] **mortality**—condition of being subject to death.

[7] **lot**—fate.

QUESTIONS TO CONSIDER

1. What did the ancient Mesopotamians believe about how people's conduct in life affected their fate after death?

2. What view of the Mesopotamian gods is conveyed by this selection?

3. The mood of a literary work is the overall emotional feeling it creates. What words would you choose to describe the mood of the *Epic of Gilgamesh*?

Pre
what's in future?

The Harper's Song for Inherkhawy

This poem, found on the wall of an ancient Egyptian tomb, is an example of the widespread literary motif known as carpe diem (Latin for "seize the day"). Carpe diem literature recommends the enjoyment of the pleasures of the moment, because the future is uncertain.

I

All who come into being as flesh
    pass on, and have since God walked the earth;
      and young blood mounts to their places.

The busy fluttering souls and bright transfigured spirits
    who people the world below
      and those who shine in the stars with Orion.[1]
They built their mansions, they built their tombs—
    and all men rest in the grave.

Name — remembered

So set your home well in the sacred land
    that your good name last because of it;

Care for your works in the realm under God
    that your seat in the West be splendid.

The waters flow north, the wind blows south,
    and each man goes to his hour.

---

[1] Orion—"the Hunter," a constellation.

[Handwritten margin note top left: Indulgences today? (Bath + Body works)]

II

So, seize the day! Hold holiday!
    Be unwearied, unceasing, alive,
        you and your own true love;
Let not your heart be troubled during your **sojourn**[2]
        on earth,
    but seize the day as it passes!

[Handwritten margin note: What @ valued time]

Put incense and sweet oil upon you,
    garlanded[3] flowers at your breast,
While the lady alive in your heart forever
    delights, as she sits beside you....

Let your heart be drunk on the gift of Day
    until that day comes when you anchor.

[Handwritten margin note: Why cap.? meaning? (connotations?)]

---

[2] **sojourn**—temporary stay.
[3] **garlanded**—woven into a wreath.

QUESTIONS TO CONSIDER

1. Does the speaker in this poem present the fact of death as a result of supernatural forces or as part of a natural cycle? Refer to specific lines in your answer.

2. Would you describe the morality reflected in this poem as selfish? Why or why not?

3. How would you describe the vision of the human condition presented in this poem?

[Handwritten note: Optimistic or pessimistic?]

Adam and Eve

One of the greatest contributions of the Jews to civilization is the literature contained in the Bible. The Bible begins with the Book of Genesis, which gives an account of the creation of heaven and earth and of the early history of the Jews. In this passage from Genesis, God creates the first man and woman, Adam and Eve.

When the Lord God made Earth and Heaven, there was neither shrub nor plant growing wild upon the earth, because the Lord God had sent no rain on the earth; nor was there any man to **till**[1] the ground. A flood used to rise out of the earth and water all the surface of the ground. Then the Lord God formed a man from the dust of the ground and breathed into his nostrils the breath of life. Thus the man became a living creature. Then the Lord God planted a garden in Eden away to the east, and there he put the man whom he had formed. The Lord God made trees spring from the ground, all trees pleasant to look at and good for food; and in the middle of the garden he set the tree of life and the tree of the knowledge of good and evil. . . .

The Lord God took the man and put him in the garden of Eden to till it and care for it. He told the man, "You may eat from every tree in the garden, but not from the tree of the knowledge of good and evil; for on the day that you eat from it, you will certainly die." Then the Lord God said, "It is not good for the man to be alone. I will provide a partner for him." So God formed out of the ground all the wild animals and all the birds of heaven. He brought them to the man to see what he would call them, and whatever the man called each living creature, that was its name. Thus the man gave names to all cattle, to the birds of heaven, and to every wild animal; but for the man himself no partner had yet been found. And so the Lord God put the man into a **trance,**[2] and while he slept, he took one of his ribs and closed the flesh over the place. The Lord God then built up the rib, which he had taken out of the man, into a

---

[1] **till**—cultivate.

[2] **trance**—sleep, state of unconsciousness.

woman. He brought her to the man, and the man said:

Now this, at last—
bone from my bones,
flesh from my flesh!—
this shall be called woman,
for from man was this taken.

That is why a man leaves his father and mother and is united to his wife, and the two become one flesh. Now they were both naked, the man and his wife, but they had no feeling of shame towards one another.

The serpent was more crafty than any wild creature that the Lord God had made. He said to the woman, "Is it true that God has forbidden you to eat from any tree in the garden?" The woman answered the serpent, "We may eat the fruit of any tree in the garden, except for the tree in the middle of the garden; God has forbidden us either to eat or to touch the fruit of that; if we do, we shall die." The serpent said, "Of course you will not die. God knows that as soon as you eat it, your eyes will be opened and you will be like gods knowing both good and evil." When the woman saw that the fruit of the tree was good to eat, and that it was pleasing to the eye and tempting to contemplate,[3] she took some and ate it. She also gave her husband some and he ate it. Then the eyes of both of them were opened and they discovered that they were naked; so they stitched fig-leaves together and made themselves loincloths.[4]

The man and his wife heard the sound of the Lord God walking in the garden at the time of the evening breeze and hid from the Lord God among the trees of the garden. But the Lord God called to the man and said to him, "Where are you?" He replied, "I heard the sound as you were walking in the garden, and I was afraid because I was naked, and I hid myself." God answered, "Who told you that you were naked? Have you eaten from the tree which I forbade you?" The man said, "The woman you gave me for a companion, she gave me fruit from the tree and I ate it." Then the Lord God said to the woman, "What is this that you have done?" The woman said, "The serpent tricked me, and I ate." Then the Lord God said to the serpent:

Because you have done this you
     are accursed
more than all cattle and all wild
     creatures.
On your belly you shall crawl, and
     dust you shall eat
all the days of your life.
I will put enmity[5] between you and
     the woman,
between your brood[6] and hers.
They shall strike at your head,
and you shall strike at their heel.

---

[3] **contemplate**—look at, behold.
[4] **loincloths**—coverings worn around the waist and hips.
[5] **enmity**—hatred.
[6] **brood**—offspring, descendants.

To the woman he said:

> I will increase your labor and your
>   groaning,
> and in labor you shall bear children.
> You shall be eager for your husband,
> and he shall be your master.

And to the man he said:

> Because you have listened to your wife
> and have eaten from the tree which I
>   forbade you,
> accursed shall be the ground on
>   your account.
> With labor you shall win your food
>   from it

> all the days of your life.
> It will grow thorns and thistles for you,
> none but wild plants for you to eat.
> You shall gain your bread by the sweat
>   of your brow
> until you return to the ground;
> for from it you were taken.
> Dust you are, to dust you shall return.

QUESTIONS TO CONSIDER

1. Was it fair of God to test human beings in this way? Why or why not?

2. In your view, who bears the greatest responsibility for Adam and Eve's fall?

3. How would you describe the character of God as he appears in Genesis?

Mesopotamian Law

About 1750 B.C. Mesopotamia was conquered by Hammurabi, who established his capital at Babylon on the Euphrates. To help unify his empire, he collected existing Mesopotamian laws into a single code of around 300 specific laws. The code regulated not only crime but also a variety of other areas. He engraved this Code of Hammurabi on stone pillars (or stelas) and placed them throughout his empire. The following regulations from Hammurabi's Code deal with marriage and the family, personal injury, and trade.

129. If the wife of a man is found lying with another male, they shall be bound and thrown into the water. If the husband lets his wife live, then the king shall let his servant live. . . .

138. If a man has decided to divorce . . . a wife who has presented him with children, then he shall give back to that woman her **dowry,**[1] and he shall give her the use of field, garden, and property, and she shall bring up her children. After she has brought up her children, she shall take a son's portion of all that is given to her children, and she may marry the husband of her heart.

141. If a man's wife, dwelling in his house, has decided to leave, has been guilty of **dissipation,**[2] has wasted her house, and has neglected her husband, then she shall be prosecuted. If her husband says she is divorced, he shall let her go her way; he shall give her nothing for divorce. If her husband says she is not divorced, her husband may marry another woman, and that [first] woman shall remain a slave in the house of her husband.

142. If a woman hates her husband, and says "You shall not possess me," the reason for her dislike shall be inquired into. If she is careful, and has no fault, but her husband takes himself away and neglects her, then that woman is not to blame. She shall take her dowry and go back to her father's house. . . .

---

[1] **dowry**—property brought by a woman to her husband at marriage.

[2] **dissipation**—misuse.

This is the top of a stela of Hammurabi's Code discovered in Iran in 1901. Hammurabi stands on the left; seated on the right is the Mesopotamian sun-god Shamash.

148. If a man has married a wife, and sickness has seized her, and he has decided to marry another, he may marry; but his wife whom the sickness has seized he shall not divorce. She shall dwell in the house he has built, and he shall support her while she lives. . . .

168. If a man has decided to **disinherit**[3] his son, and has said to the judge, "I **disown**[4] my son," then the judge shall look into his reasons. If the son has not been guilty of a serious offense which would justify his being disinherited, then the father shall not disown him.

169. If the son has committed a serious offense against his father which justifies his being disinherited, still the judge shall overlook this first offense. If the son commits a grave offense a second time, his father may disown him. . . .

195. If a son has struck his father, his hands shall be cut off.

196. If a man has destroyed the eye of another free man, his own eye shall be destroyed.

197. If he has broken the bone of a free man, his bone shall be broken.

198. If he has destroyed the eye of a peasant, or broken a bone of a peasant, he shall pay one mina[5] of silver.

199. If he has destroyed the eye of a man's slave, or broken a bone of a man's slave, he shall pay half his value.

200. If a man has knocked out the teeth of a man of the same rank, his own teeth shall be knocked out.

201. If he has knocked out the teeth of a peasant, he shall pay one-third of a mina of silver.

202. If a man strikes the body of a man who is superior in status, he shall publicly receive sixty lashes with a cowhide whip. . . .

206. If a man has struck another man in a dispute and wounded him, that man shall swear, "I did not strike him knowingly"; and he shall pay for the physician.

---

[3] **disinherit**—deprive of an inheritance.
[4] **disown**—deny responsibility for.
[5] mina—500 grams.

209. If a man strikes the daughter of a free man, and causes her **fetus**[6] to abort, he shall pay ten shekels[7] of silver for her fetus.

210. If that woman dies, his daughter shall be slain.

215. If a physician has treated a man with a metal knife for a severe wound, and has cured the man, or has opened a man's tumor with a metal knife, and cured a man's eye, then he shall receive ten shekels of silver.

216. If the son of a peasant, he shall receive five shekels of silver. . . .

218. If a physician has treated a man with a metal knife for a severe wound, and has caused the man to die, or has opened a man's tumor with a metal knife, and destroyed the man's eye, his hands shall be cut off. . . .

229. If a builder has built a house for a man, and his work is not strong, and if the house he has built falls in and kills the householder, that builder shall be slain.

230. If the child of the householder is killed, the child of that builder shall be slain.

231. If the slave of the householder is killed, he shall give slave for slave to the householder.

232. If goods have been destroyed, he shall replace all that has been destroyed; and because the house that he built was not made strong, and it has fallen in, he shall restore the fallen house out of his own personal property.

---

[6] **fetus**—unborn child.
[7] shekels—units equal to one sixtieth of a mina or 8⅓ grams.

QUESTIONS TO CONSIDER

1. What general moral principle underlies many of the specific regulations in the Code of Hammurabi?

2. How fair or unfair does Hammurabi's Code seem to women? Explain.

3. What class system is indicated in Hammurabi's Code? How does this structure affect the law?

4. Why do you think Hammurabi's stela was topped by a carving of him and the sun-god Shamash?

Sim. to Law today

from

The Book of the Dead

The ancient Egyptians pictured a person's judgment after death as taking place before the god Osiris, ruler of the world of the dead. Papyrus scrolls of spells were placed in the wrappings of mummified bodies to advise the deceased about what they needed to say to Osiris in order to attain immortality. The most famous of these is known as The Book of the Dead. *This confession from* The Book of the Dead *lists all the misdeeds an individual had avoided during life.*

To be said on reaching the Hall of the Two Truths[1] so as to purge (the deceased) of
any sins committed and to see the face of every god:

> Hail to you, Great God, Lord of the Two Truths!
> I have come to you, my Lord,
> I was brought to see your beauty.
> I know you, I know the names of the forty-two gods,
> Who are with you in the Hall of the Two Truths.
> Who live by warding off evildoers,
> Who drink of their blood,
> On that day of judging characters before Wennofer.[2]
> Lo, your name is "He-of-Two-Daughters,"
> (And) "He-of-Maat's-Two-Eyes."
> Lo, I come before you,
> Bringing Maat to you,
> Having repelled evil for you.
> I have not done crimes against people,
> I have not mistreated cattle,
> I have not sinned in the Place of Truth.

---

[1] Two Truths—Maat ("truth") embodied in two goddesses: Isis, goddess of right, and Nephthys, goddess of truth.

[2] Wennofer—one of the names of Osiris.

In this judgment scene from *The Book of the Dead*, the jackal-headed god Anubis weighs the heart of a deceased man against a feather representing truth. If Osiris decides against the deceased, the man's heart will be devoured by Ammit, the composite monster (part crocodile, part lion, part hippo) crouching under the scale.

> I have not known what should not be known,
> I have not done any harm.
> I did not begin a day by exacting more than my due,
> My name did not reach the bark of the mighty ruler.[3]
> I have not **blasphemed**[4] a god,
> I have not robbed the poor.
> I have not done what the god **abhors,**[5]
> I have not **maligned**[6] a servant to his master.
> I have not caused pain,
> I have not caused tears.
> I have not killed,
> I have not ordered to kill,
> I have not made anyone suffer.
> I have not damaged the offerings in the temples,
> I have not **depleted**[7] the loaves of the gods,
> I have not stolen the cakes of the dead.[8]

---

[3] **bark of the mighty ruler**—boat in which the sun god Re sails across the sky.

[4] **blasphemed**—spoke irreverently about sacred persons or things.

[5] **abhors**—hates, detests.

[6] **maligned**—spoke harmful untruths about.

[7] **depleted**—taken away.

[8] **cakes of the dead**—food left for the dead.

economics

I have not increased nor reduced the measure, . . .
I have not cheated in the fields.
I have not added to the weight of the balance,
I have not falsified the plummet[9] of the scales.
I have not taken milk from the mouth of children,
I have not deprived cattle of their pasture.
I have not snared birds in the reeds of the gods,
I have not caught fish in their ponds.
I have not held back water in its season,
I have not dammed a flowing stream,
I have not **quenched**[10] a needed fire.
I have not neglected the days of meat offerings,
I have not detained cattle belonging to the god,
I have not stopped a god in his procession.

customs/relig.?
beliefs?

I am pure, I am pure,
I am pure, I am pure! . . .
No evil shall befall me in this land,
In this Hall of the Two Truths;
For I know the names of the gods in it,
The followers of the great God!

positive

import. of names

more have not than have

---

[9] **plummet**—weight.
[10] **quenched**—extinguished, put out.

QUESTIONS TO CONSIDER

1. Create some general categories of misdeeds (religious offenses, offenses against other people, mistreatment of animals, unfair business practices, and so on). Organize the misdeeds listed in the confession according to your categories. What does the pattern that emerges suggest about Egyptian society?

2. Using this list as evidence, was religion in ancient Egypt more concerned with beliefs or with behaviors?

3. Using both the confession and the judgment scene as evidence, does the religion of the ancient Egyptians seem to have been largely defined by fear? Why or why not?

The Ten Commandments

According to the Book of Exodus in the Bible, the Jews were rescued from slavery in Egypt by their leader Moses with God's help. Afterwards Moses led them through the desert to Mount Sinai to meet with God. In this passage from Exodus, God uses Moses as an intermediary to give the Jews the Ten Commandments, the core of their religious law.

Chapter 19

In the third month, when the children of Israel were gone forth out of the land of Egypt, the same day came they into the wilderness of Sinai.

For they were departed from Rephidim, and were come to the desert of Sinai, and had pitched in the wilderness; and there Israel camped before the mount.

And Moses went up unto God, and the Lord called unto him out of the mountain, saying, "Thus shalt thou say to the house of Jacob, and tell the children of Israel;

Ye have seen what I did unto the Egyptians, and how I bear you on eagles' wings, and brought you unto myself.

Now therefore, if ye will obey my voice indeed, and keep my **covenant,**[1] then ye shall be a peculiar treasure unto me above all people: for all the earth is mine:

And ye shall be unto me a kingdom of priests, and an holy nation. These are the words which thou shalt speak unto the children of Israel." . . .

So Moses went down unto the people, and spake unto them.

Chapter 20

And God spake all these words, saying, "I am the Lord thy God, which have brought thee out of the land of Egypt, out of the house of **bondage.**[2]

Thou shalt have no other gods before me.

Thou shalt not make unto thee any graven[3] image, or any likeness of any thing that is in heaven above, or that is in the earth beneath, or that is in the water under the earth:

---

[1] **covenant**—agreement.

[2] **bondage**—slavery.

[3] graven—carved.

Thou shalt not bow down thyself to them, nor serve them: for I the Lord thy God am a jealous God, visiting the **iniquity**[4] of the fathers upon the children unto the third and fourth generation of them that hate me;

And showing mercy unto thousands of them that love me, and keep my commandments.

Thou shalt not take the name of the Lord thy God in vain; for the Lord will not hold him guiltless that taketh his name in vain.

Remember the sabbath day, to keep it holy.

Six days shalt thou labor, and do all thy work:

But the seventh day is the sabbath of the Lord thy God: in it thou shalt not do any work, thou, nor thy son, nor thy daughter, thy manservant, nor thy maid-servant, nor thy cattle, nor thy stranger that is within thy gates:

For in six days the Lord made heaven and earth, the sea, and all that in them is, and rested the seventh day: wherefore the Lord blessed the sabbath day, and **hallowed**[5] it.

Honor thy father and thy mother: that thy days may be long upon the land which the Lord thy God giveth thee.

Thou shalt not kill.

Thou shalt not commit adultery.

Thou shalt not steal.

Thou shalt not bear false witness against thy neighbor.

Thou shalt not **covet**[6] thy neighbor's house, thou shalt not covet thy neighbor's wife, nor his manservant, nor his maid-servant, nor his ox, nor his ass, nor any thing that is thy neighbor's."

---

[4] **iniquity**—evil.
[5] **hallowed**—made holy.
[6] **covet**—desire wrongfully.

QUESTIONS TO CONSIDER

1. How are the Ten Commandments organized? What types of behavior are dealt with in different sections?

2. What does this passage from Exodus indicate about God's character and standards of justice?

3. The first commandment forbids the making of a "graven image." What is being prohibited?

4. In general, is it a good or bad thing to attempt to depict spiritual beings in art? Why or why not?

Mesopotamian and Egyptian Sculpture

Like many cultures throughout history, ancient Mesopotamia and Egypt devoted much of their art to images of the ruling class. The basic purpose of the Mesopotamian sculptures on pages 18 and 19 was propaganda— glorification of the power and ruthlessness of the king. Early Egyptian sculptures, such as the statue on page 20 of King Mycerinus and his queen, were often stiffly formal and idealized portraits expressing stability and timelessness. Under the rule of the religious revolutionary Akhenaton (page 24), a more relaxed, naturalistic style of art flowered briefly. The images on pages 19 and 20 of Queen Nefertiti and of Akhenaton and his family reflect this style (called the Amarna style from the modern name of the site of Ahkenaton's capital).

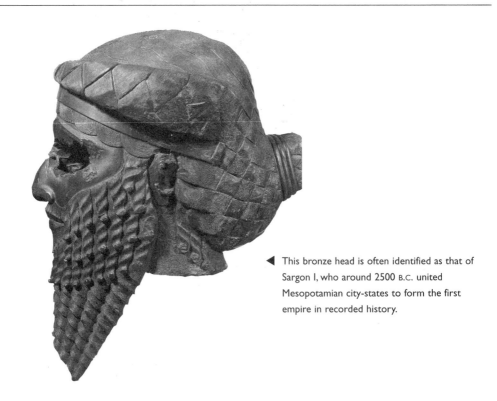

◀ This bronze head is often identified as that of Sargon I, who around 2500 B.C. united Mesopotamian city-states to form the first empire in recorded history.

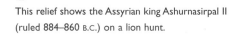

This relief shows the Assyrian king Ashurnasirpal II (ruled 884–860 B.C.) on a lion hunt.

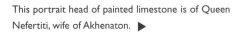

The Assyrians were the most ruthless empire-builders of Mesopotamia. This relief shows an Assyrian attack on a walled city.

This portrait head of painted limestone is of Queen Nefertiti, wife of Akhenaton. ▶

This relief shows Akhenaton, Queen Nefertiti, and their children receiving radiant blessings from the divine sun. ▶

This relief depicts the Egyptian ruler Mycerinus (ruled c. 2525 B.C.) between two goddesses. ▼

QUESTIONS TO CONSIDER

1. How would you compare the ideas of kingship conveyed by the bronze head of a Mesopotamian ruler and the statue of Mycerinus?

2. How do the goddesses with Mycerinus and the portrait of Nefertiti differ as ideals of female beauty?

3. What ruling class values does each of the sculptural reliefs convey?

Psalms

The religious poems in the Book of Psalms in the Bible are the hymns of the Jewish religion. Nearly half of the 150 psalms were traditionally ascribed to David (ruled c. 1010–970 B.C.), the famous hero-king of ancient Israel; however, modern scholars date them to hundreds of years after his reign. Psalms 8 and 19 celebrate God's power and goodness as manifested in the created world.

Psalm 8

O Lord our Lord, how excellent is thy name in all the earth!
Who hast set thy glory above the heavens.
Out of the mouth of babes and sucklings[1] hast thou ordained
  strength because of thine enemies,
That thou mightest still the enemy and the avenger.
When I consider thy heavens, the work of thy fingers,
The moon and the stars, which thou hast ordained;
What is man, that thou art mindful of him?
And the son of man, that thou visitest him?
For thou hast made him a little lower than the angels,
And hast crowned him with glory and honor.
Thou madest him to have **dominion**[2] over the works of thy hands;
Thou hast put all things under his feet:
All sheep and oxen,
Yea, and the beasts of the field;
The fowl of the air, and the fish of the sea,
And whatsoever passeth through the paths of the seas.
O Lord our Lord, how excellent is thy name in all the earth!

[1] sucklings—nursing infants.
[2] **dominion**—rule.

Psalm 19

The heavens declare the glory of God
And the firmament[3] showeth his handywork.
Day unto day uttereth speech,
And night unto night showeth knowledge.
There is no speech or language where their voice is not heard.
Their line[4] is gone out through all the earth,
And their words to the end of the world.
In them he hath set a **tabernacle**[5] for the sun,
Which is as a bridegroom coming out of his chamber,
And rejoiceth as a strong man to run a race.
His going forth is from the end of the heaven,
And his circuit unto the ends of it:
And there is nothing hid from the heat[6] thereof.
The law of the Lord is perfect, converting the soul:
The testimony of the Lord is sure, making wise the simple.
The **statutes**[7] of the Lord are right, rejoicing the heart:
The commandment of the Lord is pure, enlightening the eyes.
The fear of the Lord is clean, enduring forever:
The judgments of the Lord are true and righteous altogether.
More to be desired are they than gold, yea, than much fine gold:
Sweeter also than honey and the honeycomb.
Moreover by them is thy servant warned:
And in keeping of them there is great reward.
Who can understand his errors?
Cleanse thou me from secret faults.
Keep back thy servant also from **presumptuous**[8] sins;
Let them not have dominion over me:

---

[3] firmament—curved expanse of the sky.

[4] line—rule of conduct.

[5] **tabernacle**—structure used as a place of worship.

[6] heat—qualifying trial in a race.

[7] **statutes**—laws.

[8] **presumptuous**—overly bold.

Then shall I be upright,
And I shall be innocent from the great **transgression.**[9]
Let the words of my mouth, and the meditation of my heart,
Be acceptable in thy sight, O Lord, my strength, and my redeemer.

---

[9] **transgression**—misdeed.

QUESTIONS TO CONSIDER

1. What qualities of the material world seem to impress the speakers of these psalms most? Beauty? strength? order? variety?

2. What reflection does the speaker in Psalm 8 derive from examining creation?

3. To what is the sun compared in Psalm 19? What feelings are created by these comparisons?

[handwritten annotations: "Seen - free thinking association" ... "Pre" "what give praise + thanks for?"]

Hymn to Aton

Amenhotep IV, who ruled Egypt from around 1375 to 1357 B.C., attempted to replace the many gods of traditional Egyptian religion in favor of the worship of a single god, Aton ("disk"), the sun. He changed his name to Akhenaton ("It is well with Aton") and wrote hymns in praise of the sun god. After Akhenaton's death, the official priesthood regained control and his sun cult was forgotten.

[handwritten: "Praise"]

[handwritten: "the sun"]

Thou appearest beautifully on the horizon of heaven,
Thou living Aton, the beginning of life!
When thou art arisen on the eastern horizon,
Thou has filled every land with thy beauty.

[handwritten: "what specific compliments?"]

Thou art gracious, great, glistening, and high over every land;
Thy rays encompass the lands to the limit of all that thou hast made:
As thou art Re,[1] thou reachest to the end of them;
Thou subduest them for thy beloved son.[2]
Though thou art far away, thy rays are on earth;
Though thou art in their faces, no one knows thy going.

[handwritten: "not completely (they had "seen the light")"]

[handwritten: "sun. ?"]

When thou settest in the western horizon,
The land is in darkness, in the manner of death.
They sleep in a room, with heads wrapped up,
Nor sees one eye the other.
All their goods which are under their heads might be stolen,
But they would not perceive it.
Every lion is come forth from his den;
All creeping things, they sting.

[handwritten: "archetype"]

[handwritten: "Seems to have doubts"]

---

[1] Re—another name for the sun god.
[2] beloved son—Akhenaton.

Darkness is a shroud, and the earth is in stillness,
For he who made them rests in his horizon.

At daybreak, when thou arisest on the horizon,
When thou shinest as the Aton by day,
Thou drivest away the darkness and givest thy rays.
The Two Lands[3] are in festivity every day,
Awake and standing upon their feet,
For thou hast raised them up.
Washing their bodies, taking their clothing.
Their arms are raised in praise at thy appearance.
All the world, they do their work. . . .

Creator of seed in women,
Thou who makest fluid into man,
Who maintainest the son in the womb of his mother,
Who soothest him with that which stills his weeping,
Thou nurse even in the womb,
Who givest breath to sustain all that he has made!
When he descends from the womb to breathe
On the day when he is born,
Thou openest his mouth completely,
Thou suppliest his necessities.
When the chick in the egg speaks within the shell,
Thou givest him breath within it to maintain him.
When thou hast made him his fulfillment within the egg, to break it,
He comes forth from the egg to speak at his completed time;
He walks upon his legs when he comes forth from it. . . .

How manifold it is, what thou hast made!
They are hidden from the face of man.
O sole god, like whom there is no other!
Thou didst create the world according to thy desire,
Whilst thou wert alone:
All men, cattle, and wild beasts,
Whatever is on earth, going upon its feet,
And what is on high, flying with its wings. . . .

[3] Two Lands—Upper and Lower Egypt.

Thou art in my heart,
And there is no other that knows thee
Save thy son,
For thou hast made him well-versed in thy plans and in thy strength.
The world came into being by thy hand,
According as thou hast made them.
When thou hast risen they live,
When thou settest they die.
Thou art lifetime thy own self,
For one lives only through thee.

Eyes are fixed on beauty until thou settest.
All work is laid aside when thou settest in the west.
But when thou risest again,
Everything is made to flourish for the king. . . .

QUESTIONS TO CONSIDER

1. What qualities does Akhenaton attribute to Aton?

2. How does Akhenaton describe his relationship to Aton?

3. How is evil presented in Akhenaton's hymn? Is Aton responsible for evil?

Love Poems

The literatures of ancient Mesopotamia and Egypt include a small quantity of love poetry. The Mesopotamian poem below deals with the loves of Inanna, a goddess; the speaker is the sister of Inanna's beloved, the god Dumuzi. In the Egyptian poem on page 28 another young woman speaks, expressing mixed feelings when she sees a man she likes.

The Sister as Matchmaker

"The fair Inanna gives you (this) gift;
She has met you, my beloved one,
When I was away on an errand,
And is charmed with you and delighted in you,
And—my brother—she had me come into her house
And she lay down on the quilt of the bed
And when the sweet darling was lying next to my heart
And we were chatting one to the other, one to the other,
She began moaning about my good-looking brother
And sighed for him like one who is faint,
And she was overcome with trembling
  from the ground up, exceedingly,
And—my brother—**smiting**[1] her hips (in anguish)
Does the sweet darling pass the time of day."

---

[1] **smiting**—striking.

I Was Simply Off to See Nefrus My Friend

I was simply off to see Nefrus my friend,
    Just to sit and chat at her place (about men),
When there, hot on his horses, comes Mehy
    (Oh god, I said to myself, it's Mehy!)
Right over the crest of the road
      wheeling along with the boys.

O Mother Hathor,[2] what shall I do?
    Don't let him see me! Where can I hide?
Make me a small creeping thing
    to slip by his eye (sharp as Horus')[3] unseen.
Oh, look at you, feet—(this road is a river!)
    you walk me right out of my depth!
Someone, silly heart, is exceedingly ignorant here—
    aren't you a little too easy near Mehy?
If he sees that I see him, I know he will know
    how my heart flutters (Oh, Mehy!)

I know I will blurt out,
    "Please take me!" (I mustn't)
No, all he would do is brag out my name,
    just one of the many . . . (I know) . . .
Mehy would make me just one of the girls
    for all of the boys in the palace (oh Mehy).

---

[2] Hathor—Egyptian goddess.
[3] Horus—Egyptian god.

QUESTIONS TO CONSIDER

1. Each of these poems was written more than 3,000 years ago. Which elements in them seem ancient? Which seem modern?

2. What qualities do the speakers in these poems share?

3. What fear is the speaker in "I Was Simply Off to See Nefrus My Friend" expressing with her metaphor "this road is a river"?

Ruth

After the Jews conquered the land of Israel, they were first governed by a series of tribal military leaders known as judges. The Jews were frequently at war with the peoples around them, including the inhabitants of Moab, a country beyond the Dead Sea that formed Israel's eastern border. Set in this distant period, the Book of Ruth in the Bible is a simple, eloquent story of love and loyalty that tells how a woman of Moab became the great-grandmother of David, Israel's greatest king.

Chapter 1

Now it came to pass in the days when the judges ruled that there was a famine in the land. And a certain man of Bethlehem-Judah[1] went to **sojourn**[2] in the country of Moab, he, and his wife, and his two sons.

And the name of the man was Elimelech, and the name of his wife Naomi, and the name of his two sons Mahlon and Chilion, Ephrathites of Bethlehem-Judah. And they came into the country of Moab and continued there.

And Elimelech, Naomi's husband died; and she was left, and her two sons.

And they took them wives of the women of Moab; the name of the one was Orpah, and the name of the other Ruth; and they dwelled there about ten years.

And Mahlon and Chilion died also, both of them; and the woman was left of her two sons and her husband.

Then she arose with her daughters-in-law, that she might return from the country of Moab: for she had heard in the country of Moab how that the Lord had visited his people in giving them bread.

Wherefore she went forth out of the place where she was, and her two daughters-in-law with her; and they went on the way to return unto the land of Judah.

And Naomi said unto her two daughters-in-law, "Go, return each to her mother's house: the Lord deal kindly with you, as ye have dealt with the dead and with me. The Lord grant you that ye may find rest, each of you in the house of her husband."

Then she kissed them; and they lifted up their voice and wept.

---

[1] Bethlehem-Judah—town in the southern part of Israel.

[2] **sojourn**—stay for a time.

And they said unto her, "Surely we will return with thee unto thy people."

And Naomi said, "Turn again, my daughters: why will ye go with me? Are there yet any more sons in my womb, that they may be your husbands?

"Turn again, my daughters, go your way; for I am too old to have a husband. If I should say I have hope, if I should have a husband also tonight and should also bear sons, would ye **tarry**[3] for them till they were grown? Would ye stay for them from having husbands? Nay, my daughters; for it grieveth me much for your sakes that the hand of the Lord is gone out against me."

And they lifted up their voice and wept again: and Orpah kissed her mother-in-law, but Ruth clave[4] unto her.

And she said, "Behold, thy sister-in-law is gone back unto her people and unto her gods: Return thou after thy sister-in-law."

And Ruth said, "**Entreat**[5] me not to leave thee or to return from following after thee: for whither thou goest, I will go; and where thou lodgest, I will lodge: thy people shall be my people, and thy God my God: where thou diest, will I die, and there will I be buried: the Lord do so to me,[6] and more also, if ought but death part thee and me."

When she saw that she was steadfastly minded to go with her, then she left speaking unto her.

So they two went until they came to Bethlehem. And it came to pass, when they were come to Bethlehem, that all the city was moved about them, and they said, "Is this Naomi?"

And she said unto them, "Call me not Naomi, call me Mara:[7] for the Almighty hath dealt very bitterly with me. I went out full, and the Lord hath brought me home again empty: why then call ye me Naomi, seeing the Lord hath testified against me, and the Almighty hath afflicted me?"

So Naomi returned, and Ruth the Moabitess, her daughter-in-law, with her, which returned out of the country of Moab: and they came to Bethlehem in the beginning of barley harvest.

Chapter 2

And Naomi had a kinsman of her husband's, a mighty man of wealth, of the family of Elimelech; and his name was Boaz.

And Ruth the Moabitess said unto Naomi, "Let me now go to the field and glean[8] ears of corn after him in whose sight I shall find grace." And she said unto her, "Go, my daughter."

And she went, and came, and gleaned in the field after the reapers: and her hap[9] was to light on a part of the field belonging unto Boaz, who was of the kindred of Elimelech.

---

[3] **tarry**—wait, delay.

[4] clave—clung.

[5] **entreat**—beg.

[6] do so to me—punish me.

[7] Mara—Hebrew word meaning "bitter." Naomi means "my sweetness."

[8] glean—gather grain left by reapers.

[9] hap—fortune.

And, behold, Boaz came from Bethlehem and said unto the reapers, "The Lord be with you." And they answered him, "The Lord bless thee."

Then said Boaz unto his servant that was set over the reapers, "Whose damsel[10] is this?"

And the servant that was set over the reapers answered and said, "It is the Moabitish damsel that came back with Naomi out of the country of Moab. And she said, 'I pray you, let me glean and gather after the reapers among the sheaves': so she came, and hath continued even from the morning until now, that she tarried a little in the house."

Then said Boaz unto Ruth, "Hearest thou not, my daughter? Go not to glean in another field, neither go from hence, but abide here fast by my maidens. Let thine eyes be on the field that they do reap, and go thou after them: have I not charged the young men that they shall not touch thee? And when thou art athirst, go unto the vessels, and drink of that which the young men have drawn."

Then she fell on her face and bowed herself to the ground and said unto him, "Why have I found grace in thine eyes, that thou shouldest take knowledge of me, seeing I am a stranger?"

And Boaz answered and said unto her, "It hath fully been showed me all that thou hast done unto thy mother-in-law since the death of thine husband: and how thou hast left thy father and thy mother, and the land of thy nativity and art come unto a people which thou knewest not heretofore. The Lord recompense thy work, and a full reward be given thee of the Lord God of Israel, under whose wings thou art come to trust."

Then she said, "Let me find favor in thy sight, my lord; for that thou hast comforted me, and for that thou hast spoken friendly unto thine handmaid, though I be not like unto one of thine handmaidens."

And Boaz said unto her, "At mealtime come thou hither, and eat of the bread, and dip thy morsel in the vinegar." And she sat beside the reapers: and he reached her parched corn, and she did eat, and was sufficed, and left.

And when she was risen up to glean, Boaz commanded his young men, saying, "Let her glean even among the sheaves, and reproach her not. And let fall also some of the handfuls on purpose for her, and leave them, that she may glean them, and rebuke her not."

So she gleaned in the field until even, and beat out that she had gleaned: and it was about an ephah[11] of barley.

And she took it up and went into the city: and her mother-in-law saw what she had gleaned: and she brought forth and gave to her what she had reserved after she was sufficed.

And her mother-in-law said unto her, "Where hast thou gleaned today? and where wroughtest thou? Blessed be he that did take knowledge of thee." And she showed her mother-in-law with whom she had wrought, and said, "The man's name with whom I wrought today is Boaz."

---

[10] damsel—young woman.

[11] about an ephah—approximately a bushel.

And Naomi said unto her daughter-in-law, "Blessed be he of the Lord, who hath not left off his kindness to the living and to the dead." And Naomi said unto her, "The man is near of kin unto us, one of our next kinsmen."

And Ruth the Moabitess said, "He said unto me also, 'Thou shalt keep fast by my young men, until they have ended all my harvest.'"

And Naomi said unto Ruth her daughter-in-law, "It is good my daughter, that thou go out with his maidens, that they meet thee not in any other field."

So she kept fast by the maidens of Boaz to glean unto the end of barley harvest and of wheat harvest; and dwelt with her mother-in-law.

Chapter 3

Then Naomi her mother-in-law said unto her, "My daughter, shall I not seek rest for thee, that it may be well with thee? And now is not Boaz of our **kindred,**[12] with whose maidens thou wast? Behold, he winnoweth barley tonight in the threshing-floor. Wash thyself therefore, and anoint thee, and put thy **raiment**[13] upon thee, and get thee down to the floor: but make not thyself known unto the man, until he shall have done eating and drinking. And it shall be, when he lieth down, that thou shalt mark the place where he shall lie, and thou shalt go in and uncover his feet and lay thee down; and he will tell thee what thou shalt do."

And she said unto her, "All that thou sayest unto me I will do."

And she went down unto the floor and did according to all that her mother-in-law bade her.

And when Boaz had eaten and drunk and his heart was merry, he went to lie down at the end of the heap of corn: and she came softly and uncovered his feet and laid her down.

And it came to pass at midnight, that the man was afraid and turned himself: and, behold, a woman lay at his feet.

And he said, "Who art thou?" And she answered, "I am Ruth thine handmaid: spread therefore thy skirt over thine hand-maid; for thou art a near kinsman."

And he said, "Blessed be thou of the Lord, my daughter: for thou hast showed more kindness in the latter end than at the beginning, inasmuch as thou followedst not young men, whether poor or rich. And now, my daughter, fear not; I will do to thee all that thou requirest: for all the city of my people doth know that thou art a virtuous woman. And now it is true that I am thy near kinsman: howbeit,[14] there is a kinsman nearer than I. Tarry this night, and it shall be in the morning that if he will perform unto thee the part of a kinsman,[15] well; let him do the kinsman's part: but if he will not do the part of a kinsman to thee, then will I

---

[12] **kindred**—relations, extended family, clan.

[13] **raiment**—dress, clothing.

[14] **howbeit**—however.

[15] part of a kinsman—If a married man died without a son, Jewish law required his nearest male relative to marry his widow and provide him with a male heir.

do the part of a kinsman to thee, as the Lord liveth: lie down until the morning."

And she lay at his feet until the morning: and she rose up before one could know another. And he said, "Let it not be known that a woman came into the floor."

Also he said, "Bring the vail[16] that thou hast upon thee, and hold it." And when she held it, he measured six measures of barley and laid it on her: and she went into the city.

And when she came to her mother-in-law, she said, "Who art thou, my daughter?" And she told her all that the man had done to her.

And she said, "These six measures of barley gave he me; for he said to me, 'Go not empty unto thy mother-in-law.'"

Then said she, "Sit still, my daughter, until thou know how the matter will fall: for the man will not be in rest until he have finished the thing this day."

Chapter 4

Then went Boaz up to the gate[17] and sat him down there: and, behold, the kinsman of whom Boaz spake came by; unto whom he said, "Ho, such a one! turn aside, sit down here." And he turned aside and sat down.

And he took ten men of the elders of the city and said, "Sit ye down here." And they sat down.

And he said unto the kinsman, "Naomi, that is come again out of the country of Moab, selleth a parcel of land, which was our brother Elimelech's. And I thought to advertise thee, saying, Buy it before the inhabitants and before the elders

of my people. If thou wilt redeem it, redeem it: but if thou wilt not redeem it, then tell me, that I may know: for there is none to redeem it beside thee; and I am after thee." And he said, "I will redeem it."

Then said Boaz, "What day thou buyest the field of the hand of Naomi, thou must buy it also of Ruth the Moabitess, the wife of the dead, to raise up the name of the dead upon his inheritance."

And the kinsman said, "I cannot redeem it for myself, lest I mar mine own inheritance: redeem thou my right to thyself; for I cannot redeem it."

Now this was the manner in former time in Israel concerning redeeming and concerning changing, for to confirm all things; a man plucked off his shoe, and gave it to his neighbor: and this was a testimony in Israel.

Therefore the kinsman said unto Boaz, "Buy it for thee." So he drew off his shoe.

And Boaz said unto the elders and unto all the people, "Ye are witnesses this day, that I have bought all that was Elimelech's, and all that was Chilion's and Mahlon's, of the hand of Naomi. Morover, Ruth the Moabitess, the wife of Mahlon, have I purchased[18] to be my wife, to raise up the name of the dead upon his inheritance, that the name of

---

[16] vail—cloak.

[17] gate—town gate where legal agreements were made before witnesses.

[18] Ruth . . . purchased—that is, obtained the right to marry Ruth by purchasing the property of Naomi's dead husband and sons.

the dead be not cut off from among his brethren and from the gate of his place: ye are witnesses this day."

And all the people that were in the gate and the elders said, "We are witnesses. The Lord make the woman that is come into thine house like Rachel and like Leah,[19] which two did build the house of Israel: and do thou worthily in Ephratah, and be famous in Bethlehem. And let thy house be like the house of Pharez, whom Tamar bare unto Judah,[20] of the seed which the Lord shall give thee of this young woman."

So Boaz took Ruth, and she was his wife: and when he went in unto her, the Lord gave her conception, and she bore a son.

And the women said unto Naomi, "Blessed be the Lord, which hath not left thee this day without a kinsman, that his name may be famous in Israel. And he shall be unto thee a restorer of thy life and a nourisher of thine old age: for thy daughter-in-law, which loveth thee, which is better to thee than seven sons, hath born him."

And Naomi took the child and laid it in her bosom and became nurse unto it.

And the women her neighbors gave it a name, saying, "There is a son born to Naomi"; and they called his name Obed: he is the father of Jesse, the father of David.

Now these are the generations of Pharez: Pharez begat Hezron, and Hezron begat Ram, and Ram begat Amminadab, and Amminadab begat Nahshon, and Nahshon begat Salmon, and Salmon begat Boaz, and Boaz begat Obed, and Obed begat Jesse, and Jesse begat David.

---

[19] Rachel . . . Leah—wives of the Jewish patriarch Jacob.

[20] Pharez . . . Tamar . . . Judah—Judah's son Pharez was an ancestor of Boaz, born to Tamar, a widow who, like Ruth, claimed the right of kinship.

QUESTIONS TO CONSIDER

1. Do you think that Ruth is right to value the ties of affection more than those of nationality? Why or why not?

2. How would you describe the feelings that Ruth and Boaz have for each other?

3. A theme is the underlying meaning of a literary work. What is the theme of the story of Ruth?

Life, Death, and Destiny in Mesopotamia

GEORGES ROUX

The first great civilization developed more than 5,000 years ago in Mesopotamia, "the land between the rivers." This refers to the region of the Tigris and Euphrates rivers, which flow through what is now Iraq to empty into the Persian Gulf. In this area a long series of civilizations rose and fell—Sumerian, Akkadian, Babylonian, Assyrian. In his book Ancient Iraq, *the French scholar Georges Roux summarizes the Mesopotamian view of the human condition.*

Sumerians, Babylonians and Assyrians looked up to their gods as servants look to their good masters: with submission and fear, but also with admiration and love. For kings and commoners alike, obedience to divine orders was the greatest of qualities, as the service of the gods was the most **imperative**[1] of duties. While the celebration of the various festivals and the performance of the complicated rituals of the cult were the task of priests, it was the duty of every citizen to send offerings to the temples, to attend the main religious ceremonies, to care for the dead, to pray and make penance, and to observe the innumerable rules and taboos that marked nearly every moment of his life. A sensible man "feared the gods" and scrupulously followed their prescriptions. To do otherwise was not only foolish but sinful, and sin—as everyone knew—brought on man's head the most terrible punishments. Yet it would be wrong to think of the Mesopotamian religion as a purely formal affair, when hymns and prayers disclose the most delicate feelings and burst with genuine emotion. The Mesopotamians put their confidence in their gods; they relied upon them as children rely upon their parents, they talked to them as to their "real fathers and mothers," who could be offended and punish, but who could also be **placated**[2] and forgive.

---

[1] **imperative**—absolutely necessary.
[2] **placated**—pacified.

Offerings, sacrifices and the observance of religious prescriptions were not all that the Mesopotamian gods required from their worshippers. To "make their hearts glow with libation,"[3] to make them "exultant with succulent meals" was certainly deserving, but it was not enough. The favors of the gods went to those who led "a good life," who were good parents, good sons, good neighbors, good citizens, and who practiced virtues as highly esteemed then as they are now: kindness and compassion, righteousness and sincerity, justice, respect of the law and of the established order. Every day worship your god, says a Babylonian "Counsel of Wisdom," but also:

> To the feeble show kindness,
> Do not insult the downtrodden,
> Do charitable deeds, render service all
>   your days . . .
> Do not utter libel, speak what is of
>   good report,
> Do not say evil things, speak well
>   of people . . .

As a reward for piousness and good conduct the gods gave man help and protection in danger, comfort in distress and bereavement, good health, honorable social position, wealth, numerous children, long life, happiness. This was perhaps not a very noble ideal by Christian standards, but the Sumerians and Babylonians were contented with it, for they were practical, down-to-earth people who loved and enjoyed life above everything. To live for ever was the dearest of their dreams, and a number of their myths—in particular Adapa and the Gilgamesh cycle—aimed at explaining why man had been denied the privilege of immortality.

But only the gods were immortal. For men death was ineluctable[4] and had to be accepted:

> Only the gods live for ever under
>   the sun,
> As for mankind, numbered are
>   their days,
> Whatever they achieve is but wind.

What happened after death? Thousands of graves with their funerary[5] equipment testify to a general belief in an after-life where the dead carried with them their most precious belongings and received food and drink from the living. But such details of the Mesopotamian eschatology[6] as we can extract from the myth "Inanna's descent to the Netherworld" or the Sumerian cycle of Gilgamesh are scanty and often contradictory. The "land of no return" was a vast space somewhere underground, with a huge palace where reigned Ereshkigal, the

The favors of the gods went to those who led "a good life."

---

[3] libation—pouring out wine or another drink as an offering to the gods.

[4] ineluctable—inescapable.

[5] funerary—relating to a burial.

[6] eschatology—religious beliefs concerning the end of the world, the last judgment, and the afterlife.

Sumerian Persephone,[7] and her husband Nergal, the god of war and **pestilence**,[8] surrounded by a number of deities and guards. To reach this palace the spirits of the dead had to cross a river by ferry, as in the Greek Hades,[9] and take off their clothes. Thereafter, they lived a wretched and dreary life in a place

> Where dust is their food, clay their
> sustenance;
> Where they see no light and dwell
> in darkness,
> Where they are clad like birds with
> garments of wings,
> Where over door and bolt dust
> has spread.

Yet we learn from other sources that the sun lit the Netherworld on its way round the earth, and that the sun-god Utu pronounced judgment on the dead, so that they were probably not all treated with the same severity. It would seem that the Sumerian idea of hell was as vague as ours, and that a great deal of this literature is just poetical embroidery on a loose theme.

Death, however, was not the Mesopotamians' sole preoccupation. They had, like us, their share of disease, poverty, frustration and sorrow, and like us they wondered: how could all this happen when the gods ruled the world? How could Evil prevail over Good? To be sure, it was often possible to put the blame on man himself. So tight was the network of rules and prohibitions that surrounded him that to sin and offend the gods was the easiest thing to do. Yet there were occasions when the irreproachable had nevertheless been punished, when the gods seemed to behave in the most incomprehensible way. A Babylonian poem called *Ludlul bêl nemeqi*, "I will praise the Lord of Wisdom," pictures the feelings of a man, once noble, rich and healthy, now ruined, hated by all and afflicted with the most terrible diseases. As it turns out, in the end the god Marduk takes pity on him and saves him; but our Babylonian Job[10] had had time to doubt the wisdom of Heaven. Bitterly he exclaimed:

> Who knows the will of the gods in
> heaven?
> Who understands the plan of the
> underworld gods?
> Where have mortals learnt the way of
> a god?
> He who was alive yesterday is dead
> today.
> For a minute he was dejected,
> suddenly he is exuberant.
> One moment people are singing in
> exaltation,
> Another they groan like professional
> mourners . . .
> I am appalled at these things; I do not
> understand their significance.

But the famous Babylonian "pessimism" was much more than a temporary outburst of despair. It was metaphysical[11] in essence,

---

[7] Persephone—Greek goddess who was queen of the Underworld.

[8] **pestilence**—epidemic disease.

[9] Hades—Underworld.

[10] Job—biblical figure who God allowed to be tested with many misfortunes.

[11] metaphysical—concerned with views about the fundamental nature of the universe.

not ethical, and had its roots in the natural conditions which prevailed in Mesopotamia itself. The Tigris-Euphrates valley is a country of violent and unexpected changes. The same rivers that bring life can also bring disaster. The winters may be too cold or rainless, the summer winds too dry for the ripening of the dates. A cloudburst can in a moment turn a parched and dusty plain into a sea of mud, and on any fine day a sandstorm can suddenly darken the sky and blow devastation. Confronted with these manifestations of supernatural forces, the Mesopotamian felt bewildered and helpless. He was seized with frightful anxiety. Nothing, he believed, was ever sure. His own life, the life of his family, the produce of his fields and of his cattle, the rhythm and measure of the river floods, the cycle of seasons and indeed the very existence of the universe were constantly at stake. If the cosmos did not revert to confusion, if the world order was none the less maintained, if the human race survived, if life came again to the fields after the scorching heat of the summer, if the moon and the sun and the stars kept revolving in the sky, it was by an act of will of the gods. But the divine decision had not been pronounced once and for all at the origin of all things; it had to be repeated again and again, particularly at the turn of the year, just before that terrible oriental summer when nature seems to die and the future appears loaded with uncertainty. The only thing man could do in these critical circumstances was to provoke the decision of the gods and

secure their goodwill by performing the age-old rites that ensured the maintenance of order, the revival of nature and the permanence of life. Each spring, therefore, a great and poignant ceremony took place in many cities and especially in Babylon: the *akîtu* or New Year Festival, which combined the great drama of Creation and the annual reinstatement of the king, and culminated in the gathering of all the gods who solemnly "decreed the Destinies." Only then could the king go back to his throne, the shepherd to his flock, the peasant to his field. The Mesopotamian was reassured: the world would exist for another year.

QUESTIONS TO CONSIDER

1. From this passage, do you think the Mesopotamian view of the human condition was basically positive or negative? Explain.

2. How did the Mesopotamians view their relationship with their gods?

3. How did climate affect Mesopotamian culture?

4. Imagine you are an administrator of a Mesopotamian city-state. What are three things that will help improve the lives of the people you govern?

Education in Ancient Egypt

MARGARET A. MURRAY

Education in both Egypt and Mesopotamia was rigorous but very narrow in scope, being intended largely to provide the writing and mathematical skills needed by government clerks and officials. Only boys received even this rather restricted schooling; girls remained at home and were taught domestic skills by their mothers. In her book The Splendor That Was Egypt, *archaeologist Margaret A. Murray describes the training received by boys being prepared for the "learned professions."*

The education of the children, especially of the boys, was considered to be of great importance. They appear to have been sent to boarding-school at the age of four, but food does not seem to have been supplied by the school, for the mothers went every day carrying bread and beer for their little sons. The subjects taught at school were chiefly reading, writing, and arithmetic. Great pains were taken that the boys should be well trained as they were all being educated to be clerks in government offices, or priests, or artists; reading and writing were essential for these three professions, and for the government service arithmetic was of great practical value on account of the complicated system of taxation. Each department of the government service had its own school, to which the members of that department had the right to send their sons. In the upper forms[1] a boy was given some of the work of that department, so that he was partially trained by the time he was old enough to enter the service. There was, however, no compulsion on a boy to enter the department in which his father served; he could strike out a new line for himself if he wished, but usually he followed his father in the department where the paternal influence would be of use to him.

Good handwriting was considered essential, and copies were set for this purpose. Composition was also important, as a good scribe often had to write letters in which style was of more consequence than

---

[1] forms—grades.

matter. A scribe might have to write petitions for illiterate persons, and if these were couched in beautiful language and flowing periods,[2] the great man to whom the petition was addressed would be more influenced by them than by the urgency of the grievance. The document known as *The Eloquent Peasant* gives models of different forms of petitions, from the fulsomely[3] flattering to the subtly threatening. This document belongs to the 12th dynasty, and shows that the petition-scribe was making a handsome living at that early time.

Writing had to be practiced on cheap materials until the budding scribe could be trusted with papyrus.[4] Like the artist the scribe began on pieces of limestone picked up on the desert, or on broken potsherds from the village dust-heap. And again like the artist he used a brush made of a slip of reed with the fibers of one end a little teased out. Arithmetic was taught on severely practical lines. Much of the work in the government offices dealt with taxation which was in kind, chiefly corn; and this was complicated by the estimate that must be made on the corn-fields before they were sown. Each year this estimate had to be made, and it was based on the height of the previous **inundation**[5] which often removed the previous land-marks. Thus every scribe had to be able to calculate the cultivable area of a field and the cubic contents of a heap of corn. The method would have been simple but that the Egyptian never seems to have mastered the multiplication table; he did everything

by addition. On the few arithmetical problems which survive, the scribe has written out at the top his version of the multiplication table to help him to the solution. The method was by counting first the left-hand column, and then counting the opposite numbers. The example given below is the twice-times table.

1.........................2
2.........................4
4.........................8
8.......................16
16.....................32

Thus to find the multiple of five, count on the left hand column 4 and 1, then count the opposite numbers, 8 and 2, which gives the answer. Of the method of training in the higher forms of mathematics there is no trace, though a few mathematical papyri are known.

Lessons in the schools began early in the morning before the heat of the day, and were over at noon, when the "children rush out, shouting for joy." Punishments were much the same as in all schools, impositions and caning.[6] Some of the impositions have survived and show that they were the same as the "lines" of the present day; that is a certain number of lines from some classic written over and over again. These

---

[2] periods—sentences.

[3] fulsomely—excessively.

[4] papyrus—paper made from reeds.

[5] **inundation**—flood; in this case, the annual rising of the Nile.

[6] impositions and caning—punishment exercises and beating.

are perhaps the most tantalizing of all the documents which have been preserved, for they are invariably of some exciting story of which only the beginning has been transcribed, and of which this wretched child's imposition is the only copy. Beating was, of course, the chief punishment for idleness, and was freely used. Some of the grim old teachers seem to have taken a delight in applying it, and say, "The ears of a boy are on his back, he hears when he is beaten."

Royal children, of whom there must have been a considerable number in the Pharaoh's harem, were taught by private tutors, but as the children of great nobles were admitted to share the lessons, there was formed a sort of royal school. There are several records of boys who had their education in the palace. As early as the 4th dynasty Ptah-shepses records that he "was born in the time of Men-kau-Rê, and was educated among the royal children in the King's palace, in the private apartments and the royal harem; he was more honored by the King than any child." This last remark shows that there were other children of non-royal rank, sharing the education with the little princes. When they grew older, the young princes were put to some profession and were not allowed to be idle.

There were many moral books written "for the young," full of copybook **maxims.**[7] They are painfully like some of those which afflict youth in all countries and in all periods. Some of the maxims are very sound, as when a boy is told always to love his mother because of what she has done for him. "Always to mother be loving and tender; God will be angry if love you don't render." Good manners were always insisted upon, and it is interesting to find that even in the time of Herodotus[8] the manners of the young Egyptian men impressed him very favorably: "The young men when they meet their elders give way and turn aside; and when they approach, rise up from their seats." This carries out the **injunction**[9] of the moral writer: "Manners, remember, will make people love you. Rise for your elders and those set above you."

An inscription of the 6th dynasty shows how a man gradually rose from one office to another. This was a man called Nekhebu who in the end held the highest office of his profession. "His Majesty found me a common builder, and his Majesty appointed me to the offices of Inspector of Builders, then Overseer of Builders and Superintendent of a Guild. And his Majesty placed me as King's Architect and Builder, then Royal Architect and Builder under the

Even in the time of Herodotus the manners of the young Egyptian men impressed him very favorably.

---

[7] **maxims**—wise sayings.

[8] Herodotus—Greek historian (484?–425? B.C.).

[9] **injunction**—advice.

King's Supervision. And his Majesty appointed me Sole Companion, King's Architect and Builder in the Two Houses." Nekhebu's brother had held all these appointments previously, and Nekhebu had his early training under his brother: "When I was in the service of my brother, the Overseer of Works, I used to do the writing, I used to carry his palette.[10] When he was appointed Inspector of Buildings I used to carry his measuring rod. When he was appointed Overseer of Builders, I used to be his companion. When he was appointed King's Architect and Builder, I used to rule the city for him, and did everything excellently. When he was appointed Sole Companion, King's Architect and Builder in the Two Houses, I used to take charge of all his possessions for him. When he was appointed Overseer of Works, I used to report to him concerning everything about which he had spoken."

As the priestly training was the highest form of education, the career of Bak-en-Khonsu is of interest. He says, "I passed four years as a little child; I passed twelve years as a youth as chief of the training stables of Men-Maot-Rê" (Setekhy I of the 19th dynasty). He went direct from the training stables to the temple, where he became a libation[11] priest, being then sixteen. He held that office for four years, and at the age of twenty he became a "divine father," and remained in that position for twelve years; he then held the post of third prophet of Amon[12] for fifteen years, then second prophet of Amon for twelve years, and finally when nearly sixty he obtained the highest office of all, the first prophet or High-priest of Amon, and died at the age of eighty-seven. All the Pharaohs had a priestly training, and therefore were highly educated according to the standards of the time. They were great travellers also, and had a considerable knowledge of other countries besides their own. The queens were certainly able to read and write, and appear to have been often well-educated.

---

[10] palette—small flat slab used to carry the pigments used by an Egyptian scribe in writing.

[11] libation—pouring out wine or another drink as an offering to the gods.

[12] Amon—Egyptian god.

QUESTIONS TO CONSIDER

1. A society's educational system provides evidence of basic cultural values. On the basis of this passage, what was important to the ancient Egyptians?

2. Which aspects of education in ancient Egypt are most like American education today? Which aspects are least like contemporary education?

3. Egyptian education was very job-oriented. Do you agree with this direction for education? Why or why not?

Sinai

THOMAS CAHILL

Sinai is the arid wilderness in which the Jews wandered after their escape from slavery in Egypt, a story told in the Book of Exodus (page 16). In The Gifts of the Jews, *Thomas Cahill discusses the significance of the story of the Exodus and how it differs from mythic narratives such as the Mesopotamian* Epic of Gilgamesh *(page 2).*

The story of the Exodus—of Israel's escape from Egypt—has been told and retold so many times down the ages in literature, song, and art that it brings us up short to realize that the story does not belong to history proper, but to the prehistoric lore of a minor Semitic tribe that had not yet learned to read and write, a tribe so unimportant that it makes virtually no appearance in the contemporary history of its powerful—and literate—neighbors. When we examine the considerable extant literatures of Mesopotamia and Egypt, we find no obvious mention of the Israelites. If, as the majority of scholars have provisionally concluded, Israel escaped from Egypt in the reign of Rameses II about midway through the thirteenth century

B.C., why is there no record of this marvelous defeat in any Egyptian text or inscription? Of course, the defeat may have been so embarrassing to Egypt that, like many great powers, it could not allow itself to record honestly what happened. Alternatively, the story of the drowning of Pharaoh's army may have been inflated over time by Hebrew oral tradition, and what had been a minor **skirmish**[1] in Egyptian eyes (we know, for instance, that Rameses II died not in a watery grave but in his bed) was eventually puffed up beyond all recognition. Most radically: the Exodus may never have taken place, but may be just a story concocted, like *Gilgamesh,* by **nomadic**[2] herdsmen in need of an evening's entertainment.

---

[1] **skirmish**—battle between small groups of fighters.
[2] **nomadic**—wandering.

This last hypothesis, though temptingly unambiguous, can be maintained only by ignoring certain undeniable aspects of the actual text of the Bible. There are real differences—literary differences, differences of tone and taste, but, far more important, differences of substance and approach to material—between *Gilgamesh* and Exodus, and even between *Gilgamesh* and Genesis. The anonymous authors of *Gilgamesh* tell their story in the manner of a myth. There is no attempt to convince us that anything in the story ever took place in historical time. At every point, rather, we are reminded that the action is taking place "once upon a time"—in other words, in that **pristine**[3] Golden Time outside meaningless earthly time. The story of Gilgamesh, like the gods themselves, belongs to the realm of the stars. It is meant as a model for its hearers, who believed, in any case, that everything important, everything **archetypal**,[4] happened, had happened, was happening—it is impossible to fix this occurrence clearly in one tense, since it occurs outside time— beyond the earthly realm of unimportant instances. For all the ancients (except the Israelites, the people who would become the Jews), time as we think of it was unreal; the Real was what was heavenly and archetypal. For us, the heirs of Jewish perception, the exact opposite is true: earthly time is real time; Eternity, if we think of it at all, is the end of time (or simply an illusion).

The text of the Bible is full of clues that the authors are attempting to write history of some sort. Of course, as we read the patriarchal narratives of Genesis or the escape-from-Egypt narrative of Exodus, we know we are not reading anything with the specificity of a history of FDR's administration. The people who constructed these narratives did not, like Doris Kearns Goodwin,[5] have access to the card catalogue of the Library of Congress or the resources of the Internet. They had heard the story they were writing down, had received it from an oral culture, had in fact received it in two or three variant forms—in the varieties we would expect from tales told over and over down the centuries at one caravan site after another. They did their best to be faithful to their tradition, even if one strand of that tradition occasionally contradicted another. But there is in these tales a kind of specificity—a concreteness of detail, a concern to get things right—that convinces us that the writer has no doubt that each of the main events he chronicles happened. More than this, that they happened—that God spoke to Avraham and told him to leave Sumer[6] for the unknown, that God spoke to Moshe[7] and told him to lead the Israelites out of Egypt—is the

---

[3] **pristine**—uncorrupted.

[4] **archetypal**—serving as a model or pattern.

[5] Doris Kearns Goodwin—American historian of the career of Franklin D. Roosevelt.

[6] Sumer—region in southern Mesopotamia that according to the Bible was Abraham's original home.

[7] Avraham . . . Moshe—Abraham and Moses.

whole point. These are not, like *Gilgamesh*, archetypal tales with a moral at the end: they share nothing essential with other ancient myths from *Gilgamesh* to Aesop to Grimms' fairy tales. If the stories of Cupid and Psyche or Beauty and the Beast never happened in real time, no one is the poorer for that. But if Avraham and Moshe never existed, or if they did not receive their commissions from God, their stories have no point at all—nor does the genetic collection known as "the Jewish people," nor do Christians or Muslims, who also count themselves heirs of Avraham.

We are looking here at one of the great turning points in the history of human sensibility—at an enormous value shift. What was real for the Sumerians (and for all other peoples but the Jews) was the Eternal. What was to become gradually real for the Jews and remains real for us is the here and now and the there and then. The question that springs constantly to our lips—"Did that *really* happen?"—had little meaning in any ancient civilization. For the ancients, nothing new ever did happen, except for the occasional monstrosity. Life on earth followed the course of the stars; and what had been would, in due course, come around again. What was peculiar or unique, like Oedipus's union with his mother,[8] was of necessity monstrous. Surprise was to be eschewed;[9] the wise man looked for the predictable, the repeatable, the archetypal, the eternal. One came to inner peace by coming to terms with the Wheel.[10]

In the two great narratives of the first two books of the Bible, Israel invents not only history but the New as a positive value. It may seem trivial to remark that we could not even have advertising campaigns for soap commercials without the Jews (since soap commercials are always flogging "new" and "revolutionary" improvements). But no "commercial" of the ancient world flogged the New. The beer of the Sumerians was good because of its associations with the eternal, with the archetypal goddess who took care of such things. If the brewer had announced his product as new—as singular and never-before-known—he would have been committing entrepreneurial suicide, for no one would have drunk it. The Israelites, by becoming the first people to live—psychologically—in real time, also became the first people to value the New and to welcome Surprise. In doing this, they radically subverted all other ancient worldviews.

> *What was to become gradually real for the Jews and remains real for us is the here and now and the there and then.*

---

[8] Oedipus's union with his mother—The Greek myth of Oedipus tells the story of a man who unknowingly kills his father and marries his mother.

[9] eschewed—avoided.

[10] Wheel—the Cosmic Wheel, a world-view in which there is an ever-returning cycle of events.

The past is no longer important just because it can be mined for exemplars[11] but because it has brought us to the present: it is the first part of our journey, the journey of our ancestors. So in retelling their life stories, we have a serious obligation to get their histories straight. We are not merely creating literature: we are retelling a personal story that really happened and that has helped to make us the people that we are.

This is what impelled the Israelites to take such care with genealogies—whose son was whom, the names of even such normally unimportant people as wives. And though we cannot expect that the literate redactors[12]—the authors of the Books of Genesis and Exodus, who finally set down this grand jumble of oral material some centuries after the events described— were academic historians, checking and rechecking their facts against the surviving documents of antiquity, we should not doubt that their intention was to write a chronicle of real events, essentially faithful to their sources.

We, reading their work in a wholly different age, surrounded as we are by linguistic and documentary assistance that would have astonished the authors of the Bible, are able to detect many mistakes. We know, for instance, that the name Moshe or Moses, which the authors of Exodus took for a Hebrew name, is actually Egyptian. But this only shows their faithfulness. Though they mis-guidedly tried to interpret the name as

a Hebrew one, they have left us uninten-tional proof that the man they are writing about was indeed raised as an Egyptian and could have been named by Pharaoh's daughter. This constitutes circumstantial evidence that the story of Moses is true (or at least that he is not a fictional char-acter), for how else could such indirect evidence have been planted in the Bible by authors who could not have meant to put it there? . . .

Of course, for us, with our superior tools of textual analysis, the inconsisten-cies, the jarringly awkward **juxtapositions**[13] of one strand of tradition against another, the outright errors all stand out in ways they could have done for no age before our own. But our ability to see how this narrative was constructed over time should not blind us to its immense achievement: mankind's first attempt to write history, a history that mattered deeply because one's whole identity was bound up with it.

For the ancients, the future was always to be a replay of the past, as the past was simply an earthly replay of the drama of the heavens: "History repeats itself"—that is, false history, the history that is not history but myth. For the Jews, history will be no less replete with moral lessons. But the moral is not that history repeats itself but that it is always some-thing new: a process unfolding through

---

[11] exemplars—models.

[12] redactors—editors, compilers.

[13] **juxtapositions**—combinations.

time, whose direction and end we cannot know, except insofar as God gives us some hint of what is to come. The future will not be what has happened before; indeed, the only reality that the future has is that it has not happened yet. It is unknowable; and what it will be cannot be discovered by **auguries**[14]—by reading the stars or examining **entrails**.[15] We do not control the future; in a profound sense, even God does not control the future because it is the collective responsibility of those who are bringing about the future by their actions in the present. For this reason, the concept of the

future—for the first time—holds out promise, rather than just the same old thing. We are not doomed, not bound to some predetermined fate; we are free. If anything can happen, we are truly liberated—as liberated as were the Israelite slaves when they crossed the Sea of Reeds.[16]

---

[14] **auguries**—methods of predicting the future from various signs.

[15] **entrails**—internal organs of an animal.

[16] Sea of Reeds—literal translation of the Hebrew name for the Red Sea, body of water crossed by the Jews in the biblical story of their flight from slavery in Egypt.

QUESTIONS TO CONSIDER

1. What is the "circumstantial evidence" Thomas Cahill offers to explain that the story of Moses actually happened?

2. What, according to Cahill, distinguishes mythic narratives like *Gilgamesh* that take place "once upon a time" from basically historical accounts like the story of the Exodus?

3. Do you agree with Cahill that if the biblical accounts of Abraham and Moses are not historical "their stories have no point at all"? Why or why not?

Chapter 2

India

The Search for Enlightenment

A Woman's Place

The Paths of Glory

◀ The wealth of sculpture covering the Kesava Temple suggests the richness of Hindu mythology.

The Sermon at Benares

In the 6th century B.C., *Siddhartha Gautama, a prince from a small kingdom in northern India, preached a doctrine of the renunciation of desire as the key to human salvation. Called the Buddha ("Enlightened One") by his followers, he founded what became one of the world's great spiritual traditions, Buddhism. The following is the Buddha's first sermon, preached at the city of Benares.*

"There are two extremes, O bhikkhus,[1] which the man who has given up the world ought not to follow—the habitual practice, on the one hand, of self-indulgence which is unworthy, vain and fit only for the worldly-minded—and the habitual practice, on the other hand, of self-mortification, which is painful, useless and unprofitable.

"Neither **abstinence**[2] from fish or flesh, nor going naked, nor shaving the head, nor wearing matted hair, nor dressing in a rough garment, nor covering oneself with dirt, nor sacrificing to Agni,[3] will cleanse a man who is not free from delusions.

"Reading the Vedas,[4] making offerings to priests, or sacrifices to the gods, self-mortification by heat or cold, and many such penances performed for the sake of immortality, these do not cleanse the man who is not free from delusions.

"Anger, drunkenness, **obstinacy,**[5] **bigotry,**[6] deception, envy, self-praise, disparaging others, **superciliousness**[7] and evil intentions constitute uncleanness; not verily[8] the eating of flesh.

"A middle path, O bhikkhus, avoiding the two extremes, has been discovered by the Tathagata[9]—a path which opens the eyes, and bestows understanding, which leads to peace of mind, to the higher wisdom, to full enlightenment, to Nirvana![10]

"What is that middle path, O bhikkhus, avoiding these two extremes, discovered

---

[1] bhikkhus—people who practice self-denial; ascetics.

[2] **abstinence**—refraining.

[3] Agni—ancient Indian god of fire.

[4] Vedas—ancient Indian hymns.

[5] **obstinacy**—stubbornness.

[6] **bigotry**—intolerance.

[7] **superciliousness**—contempt.

[8] verily—truly.

[9] Tathagata—one of the Buddha's titles, sometimes interpreted as "He who has arrived at the truth."

[10] Nirvana—total enlightenment.

by the Tathagata—that path which opens the eyes, and bestows understanding, which leads to peace of mind, to the higher wisdom, to full enlightenment, to Nirvana?

"Let me teach you, O bhikkhus, the middle path, which keeps aloof from both extremes. By suffering, the **emaciated**[11] devotee produces confusion and sickly thoughts in his mind. Mortification is not conducive even to worldly knowledge; how much less to a triumph over the senses!

"He who fills his lamp with water will not dispel the darkness, and he who tries to light a fire with rotten wood will fail. And how can anyone be free from self by leading a wretched life, if he does not succeed in quenching the fires of lust, if he still hankers after either worldly or heavenly pleasures. But he in whom self has become extinct is free from lust; he

met.

This statue of Buddha seated in meditation shows a Greek influence that may have reached India through the conquests of Alexander the Great or trade with the Roman Empire.

will desire neither worldly nor heavenly pleasures, and the satisfaction of his natural wants will not defile him. However, let him be moderate, let him eat and drink according to the needs of the body.

"Sensuality is **enervating;**[12] the self-indulgent man is a slave to his passions, and pleasure-seeking is degrading and vulgar.

"But to satisfy the necessities of life is not evil. To keep the body in good health is a duty, for otherwise we shall not be able to trim the lamp of wisdom, and keep our mind strong and clear. Water surrounds the lotus-flower, but does not wet its petals.

"This is the middle path, O bhikkhus, that keeps aloof from both extremes. . . ."

Now the Blessed One[13] set the wheel of the most excellent law rolling, and he began to preach to the five bhikkhus, opening to them the gate of immortality, and showing them the bliss of Nirvana.

The Buddha said:

"The spokes of the wheel are the rules of pure conduct: justice is the uniformity of their length; wisdom is the tire; modesty and thoughtfulness are the hub in which the immovable axle of truth is fixed.

"He who recognizes the existence of suffering, its cause, its remedy, and its **cessation**[14] has fathomed the four noble truths. He will walk in the right path.

---

[11] **emaciated**—abnormally thin.

[12] **enervating**—weakening.

[13] Blessed One—the Buddha.

[14] **cessation**—ending.

Perscriptive

"Right views will be the torch to light his way. Right aspirations will be his guide. Right speech will be his dwelling-place on the road. His gait[15] will be straight, for it is right behavior. His refreshments will be the right way of earning his livelihood. Right efforts will be his steps: right thoughts his breath; and right contemplation will give him the peace that follows in his footprints.

"Now, this, O bhikkhus, is the noble truth concerning suffering:

"Birth is attended with pain, decay is painful, disease is painful, death is painful. Union with the unpleasant is painful, painful is separation from the pleasant; and any craving that is unsatisfied, that too is painful. In brief, bodily conditions which spring from attachment are painful.

"This, then, O bhikkhus, is the noble truth concerning suffering.

"Now this, O bhikkhus, is the noble truth concerning the origin of suffering:

"Verily, it is that craving which causes the renewal of existence, accompanied by sensual delight, seeking satisfaction now here, now there, the craving for the gratification of the passions, the craving for a future life, and the craving for happiness in this life.

"This, then, O bhikkhus, is the noble truth concerning the origin of suffering.

"Now this, O bhikkhus, is the noble truth concerning the destruction of suffering:

"Verily, it is the destruction, in which no passion remains, of this very thirst; it is the laying aside of, the being free from, the dwelling no longer upon this thirst.

"This, then, O bhikkhus, is the noble truth concerning the destruction of suffering.

"Now this, O bhikkhus, is the noble truth concerning the way which leads to the destruction of sorrow. Verily! it is this noble eightfold path; that is to say:

"Right views; right aspirations; right speech; right behavior; right livelihood; right effort; right thoughts; and right contemplation.

"This, then, O bhikkhus, is the noble truth concerning the destruction of sorrow. "By the practice of loving kindness I have attained liberation of heart, and thus I am assured that I shall never return in renewed births. I have even now attained Nirvana."

---

[15] gait—manner of walking.

QUESTIONS TO CONSIDER

1. Do you agree with the Buddha's view that there is no spiritual value in suffering? Why or why not?

2. Buddha is addressing himself here to "those who have given up the world." Do you think Buddha's doctrine of the Middle Path would be valuable for people still "in the world"? Why or why not?

3. What qualities conveyed by the statue of Buddha are similar to the values expressed in his sermon?

from

The Bhagavad Gita

One of the most revered of all Hindu religious texts is The Bhagavad Gita *("Song of the Lord"). This text is a philosophical dialogue between a prince named Arjuna and the Hindu god Krishna, who is serving as the prince's charioteer in a great battle that is about to take place. Arjuna's forces are going to fight an army that includes many of his kinsmen and friends. The prince is grief-stricken by the prospect of killing them and tells Krishna he will not fight. Krishna responds with the following speech.*

Thy tears are for those beyond tears; and are thy words words of wisdom? The wise grieve not for those who live; and they grieve not for those who die—for life and death shall pass away.

Because we all have been for all time: I, and thou, and those kings of men. And we all shall be for all time, we all for ever and ever.

As the Spirit of our mortal body wanders on in childhood, and youth and old age, the Spirit wanders on to a new body: of this the **sage**[1] has no doubts.

From the world of the senses, Arjuna, comes heat and comes cold, and pleasure and pain. They come and they go: they are **transient.**[2] Arise above them, strong soul.

The man whom these cannot move, whose soul is one, beyond pleasure and pain, is worthy of life in Eternity. The unreal never is: the Real never is not. This truth indeed has been seen by those who can see the true.

Interwoven in his creation, the Spirit is beyond destruction. No one can bring to an end the Spirit which is everlasting.

For beyond time he dwells in these bodies, though these bodies have an end in their time; but he remains immeasurable, immortal. Therefore, great warrior, carry on thy fight.

If any man thinks he slays, and if another thinks he is slain, neither knows the ways of truth. The Eternal in man cannot kill: the Eternal in man cannot die.

He is never born, and he never dies. He is in Eternity: he is for evermore. Never-born

---

[1] **sage**—wise man.

[2] **transient**—short-lived, passing.

This statue of the Hindu god Siva as Nataraja ("Lord of the Dance") shows him atop a figure symbolizing self and ignorance. Siva is surrounded by a circle of flames representing the cycle of destruction leading to creation.

and eternal, beyond times gone or to come, he does not die when the body dies.

When a man knows him as never-born, everlasting, neverchanging, beyond all destruction, how can that man kill a man, or cause another to kill?

simile

As a man leaves an old garment and puts on one that is new, the Spirit leaves his mortal body and then puts on one that is new.

Weapons cannot hurt the Spirit and fire can never burn him. Untouched is he by drenching waters, untouched is he by **parching**[3] winds.

Beyond the power of sword and fire, beyond the power of waters and winds, the Spirit is everlasting, omnipresent, never-changing, never-moving, ever One.

Invisible is he to mortal eyes, beyond thought and beyond change. Know that he is, and cease from sorrow.

But if he were born again and again, and again and again he were to die, even then, victorious man, cease thou from sorrow.

For all things born in truth must die, and out of death in truth comes life. Face to face with what must be, cease thou from sorrow.

Invisible before birth are all beings and after death invisible again. They are seen between two unseens. Why in this truth find sorrow?

One sees him in a vision of wonder, and another gives us words of his wonder. There is one who hears of his wonder; but he hears and knows him not.

The Spirit that is in all beings is immortal in them all: for the death of what cannot die, cease thou to sorrow.

Think thou also of thy duty and do not waver. There is no greater good for a warrior than to fight in a righteous war.

There is a war that opens the doors of heaven, Arjuna! Happy the warriors whose fate is to fight such war.

But to forgo this fight for righteousness is to forgo thy duty and honor: is to fall into **transgression.**[4]

Men will tell of thy dishonor both now and in times to come. And to a man who is in honor, dishonor is more than death.

The great warriors will say that thou hast run from the battle through fear; and those who thought great things of thee will speak of thee in scorn.

And thine enemies will speak of thee in contemptuous words of ill-will and **derision,**[5] pouring scorn upon thy courage. Can there be for a warrior a more shameful fate?

In death thy glory in heaven, in victory thy glory on earth. Arise therefore, Arjuna, with thy soul ready to fight.

Prepare for war with peace in thy soul. Be in peace in pleasure and pain, in gain and in loss, in victory or in the loss of a battle. In this peace there is no sin.

---

[3] **parching**—drying.

[4] **transgression**—violation of moral law; sin.

[5] **derision**—mockery, ridicule.

QUESTIONS TO CONSIDER

1. What is Krishna's argument that it is impossible to kill or be killed?

2. Does Krishna justify war in general or only Arjuna's duty to fight this battle? Explain.

3. How does the image of Nataraja embody some of the ideas presented in *The Bhagavad Gita*?

Poems of Kabir

Over the centuries, social conflict in India has often been based in differences of religion or caste (a hereditary system of classes and occupations). One reformer who urged people to overcome religious and caste prejudices was the poet Kabir (c. 1450–1518 A.D.). Drawing on both the Hindu and Muslim traditions, Kabir preached devotion to a personal God.

O servant, where dost thou seek Me?
Lo! I am beside thee.
I am neither in temple nor in **mosque:**[1]
    I am neither in Kaaba[2] nor in Kailash:[3]
Neither am I in rites and ceremonies, nor in Yoga[4] and renunciation.
If thou art a true seeker, thou shalt at once see Me:
    thou shalt meet Me in a moment of time.
Kabir says, "O Sadhu![5] God is the breath of all breath."

It is needless to ask of a saint the caste to which he belongs;
For the priest, the warrior, the tradesman,
    and all the thirty-six castes, alike are seeking for God.
It is but folly to ask what the caste of a saint may be;
The barber has sought God, the washerwoman, and the carpenter—
Even Raidas was a seeker after God.

---

[1] **mosque**—Islamic house of worship.
[2] Kaaba—holiest shrine of Islam; located at Mecca.
[3] Kailash—mountain in Tibet regarded by Hindus as the paradise of the god Siva and the holiest place on earth.
[4] Yoga—Hindu system of spiritual discipline.
[5] Sadhu—Hindu holy man.

The Rishi Swapacha was a **tanner**[6] by caste.
Hindus and Moslems alike have achieved that End,
   where remains no mark of distinction.

O brother! when I was forgetful, my true Guru[7] showed me the Way.
Then I left off all rites and ceremonies,
   I bathed no more in the holy water:
Then I learned that it was I alone who was mad,
   and the whole world beside me was sane;
   and I had disturbed these wise people.
From that time forth I knew no more how to roll in the dust in **obeisance:**[8]
I do not ring the temple bell:
I do not set the idol on its throne:
I do not worship the image with flowers.
It is not the **austerities**[9] that mortify the flesh which are pleasing to the Lord,
When you leave off your clothes and kill your senses,
   you do not please the Lord:
The man who is kind and who practices righteousness,
   who remains passive amidst the affairs of the world,
   who considers all creatures on earth as his own self,
He attains the Immortal Being, the true God is ever with him.
Kabir says: "He attains the true Name whose words are pure,
   and who is free from pride and conceit."

---

[6] **tanner**—worker who processes animal hides into leather.
[7] **Guru**—Hindu spiritual guide.
[8] **obeisance**—bodily movement expressing respect.
[9] **austerities**—practices of self-denial, such as fasting.

Why not God dwell in house of worship holy place?

If God be within the mosque, then to whom does this world belong?
If Ram[10] be within the image which you find upon your pilgrimage,
    then who is there to know what happens without?
Hari[11] is in the East: Allah[12] is in the West. Look within your heart,
    for there you will find both Karim[13] and Ram;
All the men and women of the world are His living forms.
Kabir is the child of Allah and of Ram: He is my Guru, He is my Pir.[14]

---

[10] Ram—or Rama, one of the incarnations of the Hindu god Vishnu.

[11] Hari—title of Vishnu.

[12] Allah—name of God in Islam.

[13] Karim—"the Bountiful," a title of Allah.

[14] Pir—saint or teacher in Sufism, the Islamic mystical tradition.

QUESTIONS TO CONSIDER

1. Do you agree with Kabir's views about the unimportance of formal religion in the quest for God? Why or why not?

2. What is Kabir's attitude toward the caste system?

3. What does Kabir see as the essential elements of religious life?

*What agree
w/? What offensive?*

again - caste

The Duties of Women

The Hindu ethical tradition is based on dharma, the duty of virtuous action. A Hindu's duty is defined by caste (the hereditary system of classes and occupations), by stage of life, and by sex. The oldest surviving code of Hindu sacred law based on dharma is the Laws of Manu. (According to Hindu mythology, Manu was the first human being.) The following passages from the Laws of Manu deal with the nature and duties of women.

= Adam

what make of this?

It is the nature of women to seduce men in this world; for that reason the wise are never unguarded in the company of females. . . .

For women no rite is performed with sacred texts, thus the law is settled; women who are **destitute**[1] of strength and destitute of the knowledge of Vedic[2] texts are as impure as falsehood itself, that is a fixed rule.

Where women are honored, there the gods are pleased; but where they are not honored, no sacred rite yields rewards.

Where the female relations live in grief, the family soon wholly perishes; but that family where they are not unhappy ever prospers.

keep them happy, put on pedestal

In childhood a female must be subject to her father, in youth to her husband, when her lord is dead to her sons; a woman must never be independent.

?!

She must not seek to separate herself from her father, husband, or sons; by leaving them she would make both her own and her husband's families contemptible. . . .

Familiar

Him to whom her father may give her, or her brother with the father's permission, she shall obey as long as he lives, and when he is dead, she must not insult his memory.

No father who knows the law must take even the smallest **gratuity**[3] for his daughter; for a man who, through avarice, takes a gratuity, is a seller of his offspring. . . .

[1] **destitute**—lacking.

[2] Vedic—relating to the Vedas, a body of ancient Indian hymns.

[3] **gratuity**—gift.

Three years let a damsel[4] wait, though she be marriageable, but after that time let her choose for herself a bridegroom of equal caste and rank.

If, being not given in marriage, she herself seeks a husband, she incurs no guilt, nor does he whom she weds.

To be mothers were women created, and to be fathers men; religious rites, therefore, are ordained in the Veda to be performed by the husband together with the wife. . . .

No sacrifice, no vow, no fast must be performed by women apart from their husbands; if a wife obeys her husband, she will for that reason alone be exalted in heaven. . . .

Let the husband employ his wife in the collection and expenditure of his wealth, in keeping everything clean, in the fulfilment of religious duties, in the preparation of his food, and in looking after the household utensils. . . .

Drinking spirituous liquor, associating with wicked people, separation from the husband, rambling abroad, sleeping at unseasonable hours, and dwelling in other men's houses, are the six causes of the ruin of women. . . .

Offspring, religious rites, faithful service, highest **conjugal**[5] happiness and heavenly bliss for the ancestors and oneself, depend on one's wife alone. . . .

"Let mutual fidelity continue until death," . . . may be considered as the summary of the highest law for husband and wife.

Let man and woman, united in marriage, constantly exert themselves, that they may not be disunited and may not violate their mutual fidelity.

For one year let a husband bear with a wife who hates him; but after a year let him deprive her of her property and cease to cohabit with her. . . .

A barren[6] wife may be **superseded**[7] in the eighth year, she whose children all die in the tenth, she who bears only daughters in the eleventh, but she who is quarrelsome without delay. But a sick wife who is kind to her husband and virtuous in her conduct, may be superseded only with her own consent and must never be disgraced.

---

[4] damsel—young woman.

[5] **conjugal**—relating to marriage.

[6] barren—infertile.

[7] **superseded**—replaced; here, by another wife.

QUESTIONS TO CONSIDER

1. What assumptions about women underlie the Laws of Manu?

2. What protections for women do the Laws of Manu include?

3. Would any of the ideals and prescriptions of the Laws of Manu be useful in modern marriages? Explain.

Literature about Courtship

The following two works present very different views of courtship in India. The first is a story from a collection called The Tales of the Ten Princes *by the Sanskrit writer Dandin (6th century A.D.); the second is a poem from the Tamil language of South India.*

from *The Tales of the Ten Princes*
Dandin

In the land of the Dravidians[1] is a city called Kanci. Therein dwelt the very wealthy son of a merchant, by name Saktikumara. When he was nearly eighteen he thought: "There's no pleasure in living without a wife or with one of bad character. Now how can I find a really good one?" So, dubious of his chance of finding wedded bliss with a woman taken at the word of others, he became a fortune-teller, and roamed the land with a measure of unhusked rice tied in the skirts of his robe; and parents, taking him for an interpreter of birthmarks, showed their daughters to him. Whenever he saw a girl of his own class, whatever her birthmarks, he would say to her: "My dear girl, can you cook me a good meal from this measure of rice?" And so, ridiculed and rejected, he wandered from house to house.

One day in the land of the Sibis, in a city on the banks of the Kaveri, he examined a girl who was shown to him by her nurse. She wore little jewelry, for her parents had spent their fortune and had nothing left but their **dilapidated**[2] mansion. As soon as he set eyes on her he thought: "This girl is shapely and smooth in all her members. Not one limb is too fat or too thin, too short or too long. Her fingers are pink; . . . her palms are marked with signs which promise corn, wealth, and sons; her nails are smooth and polished like jewels; her fingers are straight and tapering and pink; her arms curve sweetly from the shoulder, and are smoothly jointed; her slender neck is curved like a conch-shell; her lips are rounded and of even red; her pretty chin does not recede; her cheeks are round, full and firm; her eyebrows do not

---

[1] Dravidians—peoples of South India.

[2] **dilapidated**—falling apart, ruinous.

join above her nose, and are curved, dark, and even; her nose is like a half-blown sesamum flower; her wide eyes are large and gentle and flash with three colors, black, white, and brown; her brow is fair as the new moon; her curls are lovely as a mine of sapphires; her long ears are adorned doubly, with earrings and charming lotuses,[3] hanging limply; her abundant hair is not brown, even at the tips, but long, smooth, glossy, and fragrant. The character of such a girl cannot but correspond to her appearance, and my heart is fixed upon her, so I'll test her and marry her. For one regret after another is sure to fall on the heads of people who don't take precautions!" So, looking at her affectionately, he said, "Dear girl, can you cook a good meal for me with this measure of rice?"

Then the girl glanced at her old servant, who took the measure of rice from his hand and seated him on the veranda, which had been well sprinkled and swept, giving him water to cool his feet. Meanwhile the girl bruised the fragrant rice, dried it a little at a time in the sun, turned it repeatedly, and beat it with a hollow cane on a firm, flat spot, very gently, so as to separate the grain without crushing the husk. Then she said to the nurse, "Mother, goldsmiths can make good use of these husks for polishing jewelry. Take them, and, with the coppers you get for them, buy some firewood, not too green and not too dry, a small cooking pot, and two earthen dishes."

When this was done she put the grains of rice in a shallow, wide-mouthed, round-bellied **mortar,**[4] and took a long and heavy **pestle**[5] of acacia-wood, its head shod with a plate of iron. . . . With skill and grace she exerted her arms, as the grains jumped up and down in the mortar. Repeatedly she stirred them and pressed them down with her fingers; then she shook the grains in a winnowing basket to remove the beard, rinsed them several times, worshiped the hearth, and placed them in water which had been five times brought to the boil. When the rice softened, bubbled, and swelled, she drew the embers of the fire together, put a lid on the cooking pot, and strained off the gruel.[6] Then she patted the rice with a ladle and scooped it out a little at a time; and when she found that it was thoroughly cooked she put the cooking pot on one side, mouth downward. Next she damped down those sticks which were not burnt through, and when the fire was quite out she sent them to the dealers to be sold as charcoal, saying, "With the coppers that you get for them, buy as much as you can of green vegetables, ghee,[7] curds, sesamum oil, myrobalans[8] and tamarind."[9]

When this was done she offered him a few savories. Next she put the rice-gruel in a new dish immersed in damp sand, and

---

[3] lotuses—water lilies.

[4] **mortar**—bowl in which substances are ground.

[5] **pestle**—tool for grinding substances in a mortar.

[6] gruel—thin cooked cereal.

[7] ghee—clarified butter.

[8] myrobalans—edible seeds from an Indian tree.

[9] tamarind—pungent spice.

cooled it with the soft breeze of a palm-leaf fan. She added a little salt, and flavored it with the scent of the embers; she ground the myrobalans to a smooth powder, until they smelt like a lotus; and then, by the lips of the nurse, she invited him to take a bath. This he did, and when she too had bathed she gave him oil and myrobalans (as an **unguent**).[10]

After he had bathed he sat on a bench in the paved courtyard, which had been thoroughly sprinkled and swept. She stirred the gruel in the two dishes, which she set before him on a piece of pale green plantain leaf, cut from a tree in the courtyard. He drank it and felt rested and happy, relaxed in every limb. Next she gave him two ladlefuls of the boiled rice, served with a little ghee and condiments. She served the rest of the rice with curds, three spices (mace, cardamom, and cinnamon), and fragrant and refreshing buttermilk and gruel. He enjoyed the meal to the last mouthful.

When he asked for a drink she poured him water in a steady stream from the spout of a new pitcher—it was fragrant with incense, and smelt of fresh trumpet-flowers and the perfume of full-blown lotuses. He put the bowl to his lips, and his eyelashes sparkled with rosy drops as cool as snow; his ears delighted in the sound of the trickling water; his rough cheeks thrilled and tingled at its pleasant contact; his nostrils opened wide at its sweet fragrance; and his tongue delighted in its lovely flavor, as he drank the pure water in great gulps. Then, at his nod, the girl gave him a mouthwash in another bowl. The old woman took away the remains of his meal, and he slept awhile in his ragged cloak, on the pavement plastered with fresh cowdung.

Wholly pleased with the girl, he married her with due rites, and took her home. Later he neglected her awhile and took a mistress, but the wife treated her as a dear friend. She served her husband indefatigably,[11] as she would a god, and never neglected her household duties; and she won the loyalty of her servants by her great kindness. In the end her husband was so enslaved by her goodness that he put the whole household in her charge, made her sole mistress of his life and person, and enjoyed the three aims of life—virtue, wealth, and love. So I maintain that virtuous wives make their lords happy and virtuous.

What She Said to Her Girl Friend
Uruttiran

"Friend,
like someone who gets drunk secretly
on hard liquor
till his body begins to ooze with it,
and goes on to brag shamelessly
till listeners shiver,
and then gets caught
with the stolen liquor in his hand,

---

[10] **unguent**—ointment.
[11] indefatigably—tirelessly.

I too got caught
with my secret in my hands:
my goatherd lover's
string of jasmine[12]
that I'd twined in my hair
fell before my foster-mother[13]
as she loosened my hair
to smear it with butter,[14]

and embarrassed her
before Father, Mother,
and others in the house.

And she
didn't ask a thing about it,
or get angry,
but like someone
shaking off a live coal
she shook it off
and moved into the backyard.

Then I
dried my hair perfumed with sandal,[15]
knotted it,
and picking up the end
of my blue flower-border dress
   that comes down to the floor.

I tiptoed in fear
and hid
in the thick of the forest."

"O you got scared because of that?
No fears. Even as you wore
your young man's garlands,
they too have conspired
to give you to him.

They'll pour soft sand
in the wide yard,
put curtains all around,
and make a wedding there
very soon.

Not only all day today,
but all night yesterday,
we've been scheming
to do just that."

---

[12] jasmine—fragrant flower.

[13] foster-mother—either her personal servant or her father's second wife.

[14] butter—typically used to oil hair in South Asia.

[15] sandal—sandalwood, a fragrant Indian tree.

QUESTIONS TO CONSIDER

1. From Dandin's story, what qualities does an ideal woman possess?

2. One meaning of irony is the contrast between what is expected and what actually occurs. How is the Tamil poem ironic?

3. What are the similarities and differences between the views of courtship presented in Dandin's story and the Tamil poem?

from

The Baburnama

The Mughal empire of India was founded by a Central Asian adventurer called Babur who conquered northern India in the 1520s. Babur's Mughal ("Mongol") dynasty would last for over 300 years. He also left a frank, vigorous account of his life, The Baburnama *("Book of Babur"). In the first of the following passages from his autobiography, Babur tells of his father's sudden death; in the second he describes an attempt by Indians to assassinate him.*

The Year 1494

In the month of Ramzan,[1] in the year fourteen hundred and ninety-four, and in the twelfth year of my age, I became King of Ferghana.[2]

The country of Ferghana is situated on the extreme boundary of the habitable world. It is of small extent, and is surrounded with hills on all sides except the west.

The country abounds in grains and fruits, its grapes and melons are excellent and plentiful, and it is noted for pomegranates and apricots. The people have a way of taking the stones out of the apricot and putting in almonds in their place, which is very pleasant.

It is abundantly supplied with running water, and is extremely pleasant in spring.

There are many gardens overlooking the rivers where tulips and roses grow in great **profusion,**[3] and there are meadows of clover, sheltered and pleasant, where travellers love to rest. They are called the mantle[4] of lambskins.

It abounds in birds and beasts of game; its pheasants are so fat that four persons may dine on one and not finish it, and the game and venison[5] are excellent.

It is a good sporting country; the white deer, mountain goat, stag, and hare are found in great plenty, and there is good hunting and hawking.

---

[1] Ramzan—Ramadan, Islamic month of fasting.

[2] Ferghana—region in what is now Uzbekistan.

[3] **profusion**—abundance.

[4] mantle—loose, sleeveless cloak.

[5] venison—deer meat.

In the hills are mines of turquoises, and in the valleys people weave cloth of a purple color.

The revenues of Ferghana suffice to maintain 4,000 troops.

My father, Omer-Sheikh-Mirza, was a prince of high ambition and magnificent **pretensions,**[6] and was always bent on some scheme of conquest. He several times led an army against Samarkand,[7] and was repeatedly defeated.

At this time, 1494, the Sultan Mahomed Khan and the Sultan Ahmed Mirza, having taken offense at his conduct, concluded an alliance, and one marched an army from the north, the other from the south, against his dominions.

At this crisis a singular incident occurred. The Fort of Akhsi is situated on a steep precipice, on the edge of which some of its buildings are raised.

On the fourth day of Ramzan, 1494, my father was engaged in feeding his pigeons, when the platform slipped, **precipitating**[8] him from the top of the rock, and with his pigeons and pigeon-house he took his flight to the other world.

My father was of low stature, had a short bushy beard, and was fat. He used to wear his tunic extremely tight, insomuch that as he was wont to contract his waist when he tied the strings; when he let himself out again the strings often burst. He was not particular in food or dress, and wore his turban without folds, allowing the ends to hang down. His generosity was large, and so was his whole soul, yet brave withal and manly. He was only a middling shot with the bow, but had uncommon force with his fists, and never hit a man without knocking him flat to the ground.

He was a humane man, and played a great deal at backgammon.

He had three sons and five daughters. Of the sons, I, Muhammed Babur, was the eldest.

My mother was Kutlak Khanum.

The Year 1526

A very important incident happened on Friday, the 16th of Rabia-ul-Awal,[9] in this year. The circumstances are these:— The mother of Ibrahim,[10] an ill-fated lady, had heard that I had eaten some things from the hand of natives of Hindustan.[11] It happened in this way. Three or four months ago, never having seen any of the dishes of Hindustan, I desired Ibrahim's cooks to be called, and out of fifty or sixty cooks, four were chosen and retained. The lady, having heard the circumstance, sent a person to Etaweh to call Ahmed, the taster,[12] and delivered into the hands of a female slave an ounce of poison, wrapped up in a folded paper, desiring it to be given to the taster Ahmed. Ahmed gave it to a Hindustani cook who was in my kitchen, seducing him with the promise of four districts, and desiring him, by some means

---

[6] **pretensions**—claims.

[7] Samarkand—city in Turkestan.

[8] **precipitating**—hurling down.

[9] Rabia-ul-Awal—third month of the Islamic year.

[10] Ibrahim—Indian ruler defeated and killed by Babur.

[11] Hindustan—India.

[12] taster—servant who samples food for a ruler to test for poison.

or other, to throw it into my food. She sent another female slave after the one whom she had desired to carry the poison to Ahmed, in order to observe if the first slave delivered the poison or not. It was fortunate that the poison was not thrown into the pot, it was thrown into the tray. He did not throw it into the pot, because I had strictly enjoined the tasters to watch the Hindustanis, and they had tasted the food in the pot while it was cooking. When they were dishing the meat, my graceless tasters were inattentive, and he threw it upon a plate of thin slices of bread; he did not throw above one half of the poison that was in the paper upon the bread, and put some meat fried in butter upon the slices of bread. If he had thrown it above the fried meat, or into the cooking pot, it would have been still worse; but in his confusion, he spilt the better half of it on the fireplace.

On Friday, when afternoon prayers were past, they dished the dinner. I was very fond of hare, and ate some, as well as a good deal of fried carrot. I was not, however, sensible of any disagreeable taste; I likewise ate a morsel or two of smoke-dried meat, when I felt nausea. The day before, while eating some smoke-dried flesh, I had felt an unpleasant taste in a particular part of it. I ascribed my nausea to that incident. The nausea again returned, and I was seized with so violent a retching, two or three times while the tray was before me, that I had nearly vomited. At last, perceiving that I could not check it, I went out. While on the way

my heart rose, and I had again nearly vomited. When I had got outside I vomited a great deal.

I had never before vomited after my food, and not even after drinking wine. Some suspicions crossed my mind. I ordered the cooks to be taken into custody, and desired the meat to be given to a dog, which I directed to be shut up. Next morning about the first watch, the dog became sick, his belly swelled, and he seemed distressed. Although they threw stones at him, and shoved him, they could not make him rise. He remained in this condition till noon, after which he rose and recovered. Two young men had also eaten of this food. Next morning they too vomited much, one of them was extremely ill, but both in the end escaped.

> A calamity fell upon me, but I escaped
>   in safety,
> Almighty God bestowed a new life
>   upon me,—
> I came from the other world,—
> I was again born from my mother's
>   womb.

> I was broken and dead, but am again
>   raised to life;
> Now, in the salvation of my life, I
>   recognize the hand of God.

I ordered Muhammed Bakhshi to guard and examine the cooks, and at last all the particulars came to light, as they have been detailed.

On Monday, being a court day, I directed all the grandees and chief men, the Begs and Vazirs,[13] to attend the Diwan.[14] I brought in the two men and the two women, who, being questioned, detailed the whole circumstances of the affair in all its particulars. The taster was ordered to be cut to pieces. I commanded the cook to be **flayed**[15] alive. One of the women was ordered to be trampled to death by an elephant; the other I commanded to be shot with a matchlock.[16] The lady I directed to be thrown into custody. She too, pursued by her guilt, will one day meet with due **retribution.**[17] On Saturday I drank a bowl of milk. I also drank some of the makhtum flower, brayed[18] and mixed in spirits. The milk scoured my inside extremely. Thanks be to God, there are now no remains of illness! I did not fully comprehend before that life was so sweet a thing. The poet says,

Whoever comes to the gates of death,
knows the value of life.

Whenever these awful occurrences pass before my memory, I feel myself involuntarily turn faint. The mercy of God has bestowed a new life on me, and how can my tongue express my gratitude? Having resolved with myself to overcome my repugnance, I have written fully and circumstantially everything that happened. Although the occurrences were awful, and

not to be expressed by the tongue or lips, yet by the favor of Almighty God, other days awaited me, and have passed in happiness and health.

---

[13] Begs and Vazirs—court officials.

[14] Diwan—council meeting.

[15] **flayed**—skinned.

[16] matchlock—early type of gun.

[17] **retribution**—reward.

[18] brayed—crushed finely.

QUESTIONS TO CONSIDER

1. Both of these passages deal with death. How does the tone of Babur's account of his father's death compare with that of his account of the attempt on his own life?

2. Babur was a warrior and had often faced danger. Why do you think this particular brush with death so impressed him with the value of life?

3. Do you see an inconsistency between Babur's new sense of the value of life and the terrible punishments that he gives to those guilty of the assassination attempt? Why or why not?

Mughal Art

The Mughal emperors were great patrons of the arts. The art of book illustration flourished in Persia, and many Persian painters were attracted to the Mughal court. They created a style of painting marked by vivid, lifelike depictions of a wide range of subject matter, from palace life to the natural world. The following examples of Mughal painting all deal with the subject of mortality. Another example of Mughal art associated with death is the Taj Mahal. This masterpiece of Mughal architecture was built by the emperor Shah Jahan (ruled 1628–1658 A.D.) as a tomb for his beloved wife, Mumtaz Mahal, who died in childbirth.

▲

In his memoirs, the Mughal emperor Jahangir (ruled 1605–1627) describes this image of his attendant 'Inayat Khan on his deathbed: "Though painters have striven much in drawing an emaciated face, yet I have never seen anything like this, or even approaching to it. Good God, can a son of man come to such a shape and fashion?"

▲

This painting portrays Babur's grandson, the Mughal emperor Akbar, in old age, probably shortly before his death in 1605 at the age of sixty-four. Behind him are his grandsons Khurram (later Shah Jahan) and Khusrau.

▲

In this painting Akbar's son Jahangir is depicted enthroned on an hourglass. The European depicted in the lower left is King James I of England. Immediately above him is the Ottoman sultan.

Although built as a memorial to the Shah Jahan's enduring sorrow over a tragic death, the Taj Mahal expresses grace and elegance rather than gloom.

QUESTIONS TO CONSIDER

1. Both the paintings of Akbar and of 'Inyat Khan depict men near death. How do the attitudes toward death expressed by these two works differ?

2. What symbolism is reflected in Jahangir's hourglass throne?

3. The Taj Mahal has been criticized as being "too feminine." Do you agree or disagree? Explain.

4. If you were designing a memorial for a loved one, what effect(s) would you want to create?

5. "Few civilizations confronted death as coolly as the Mughals," observes art historian Stuart Cary Welch. From the evidence of *The Baburnama,* the Mughal paintings, and the Taj Mahal, do you agree or disagree with this estimate?

Indian Art and Culture

STUART CARY WELCH

The civilization of India has had a largely unbroken cultural tradition from ancient times to the present. "To this day," observes one historian, "legends known to the humblest Indian recall the names of shadowy chieftains who lived nearly a thousand years before Christ, and the orthodox Brahmin in his daily worship repeats hymns composed even earlier." In this essay, art historian Stuart Cary Welch describes some of the most important features of what he calls "the Great Tradition" of Indian civilization.

The bounty of the Indian subcontinent, a triangular peninsula 2,000 miles long suspended beneath the vast Central Asian land mass, has since ancient times attracted horde after horde of immigrants and ambitious seekers of empire. The Bay of Bengal forms India's eastern border; the Arabian Sea lies to the west, the Indian Ocean to the south. Across the top of the wedge-shaped peninsula, 1,600 miles of mountain ranges—the Hindu Kush, Karakoram, and Himalaya—barricade India from the rest of Asia. Migrants from Turkistan and the Central Asian steppes began to scramble through the Khyber and Bolan passes in India's northwest corner during the second millennium B.C. and continued to pour in until as late as the seventeenth century.

After struggling through the hazardous mountain passes, each family, tribe, or army usually faced another epic test in "the cockpit of India," the narrow corridor between the Indus and Ganges river basins: angry settlers determined to protect the lands they had in turn wrested from earlier arrivals. But in India the bitter and the sweet often blossom from a single stem. Within the seductive walled paradise, as hard to leave as it is to enter, a culture of cultures was nurtured, ever gaining in intensity and savor over the centuries as wave upon wave of ethnically and linguistically varied people eventually laid down their arms, settled, and were **assimilated.**[1]

Geography and climate contribute to the form and substance of culture and art. In the north of the Indian subcontinent rise

---

[1] **assimilated**—absorbed.

the world's highest peaks, and below them stretch some of the most luxuriant valleys and arid deserts, flattest plains and densest jungles. The monsoon[2] winds contribute to the pattern of extremes, scorching the land for part of the year, then from June to October bringing essential, cooling rains up from the south that wash the mountainsides, crumbling the rich loam the holy Ganges River carries to one of the world's lushest plains. But the monsoon is **capricious,**[3] sometimes bringing floods with an excess of bounty, sometimes withholding its liquid blessing for so long that parts of the fertile paradise become hells of drought and famine. It is not surprising that in the ancient religions of India such **erratic**[4] behavior was attributed to deities who personified the forces and spirits of nature. When the gods smiled, the monsoon was good; if their wrath was not appeased, it brought floods or drought.

In the face of such extremes, it is also not surprising that the flavors of Indian art are so pronounced—even her classicism is excessive in its restraint—or that Indians developed the metaphysical concepts of maya and karma. Hindus see the physical world as a form of maya, or illusion, from which man's greatest hope is to escape and to become one with the Supreme Soul, the only true reality, beyond which nothing exists. Only through liberation from the continuous cycle of creation and destruction can man transcend karma, the inevitable consequences of his every action, either in this life or in the ones that follow.

The ancient Aryans[5] were probably the last of the invaders and immigrants of the early period whose ways were not gradually absorbed, or Indianized, entirely beyond recognition. The Vedas (literally, knowledge), the four sacred books of the Aryans, written in Sanskrit, are fundamental to Indian thought and are still revered by Hindus. The earliest of the Vedas, the *Rig Veda*, which was probably compiled sometime between 1500 and 1000 B.C., contains the oldest hymns in the world, songs of praise to Indra, Lord of the Heavens, and to other Aryan gods. The Vedas are also a rich source of historical information, if one allows for their bias.

The Vedic texts describe the Aryans' attacks on the fortified towns of dark-skinned, "broad-nosed, and bull-lipped" barbarians, hostile cattle breeders who were terrified by the unfamiliar horse-drawn chariots of the militant and efficiently organized conquerors. In the nineteenth century, however, archeologists uncovered evidence at the pre-Aryan sites of Mohenjo-Daro and Harappa in the Indus Valley that presents quite a different view, implying that in fact the Aryans were the barbarians and their victims were peaceful, prosperous people who lived in highly organized communities with wide streets and advanced drainage systems and were in contact with

---

[2] monsoon—rainy season in India.

[3] **capricious**—unpredictable.

[4] **erratic**—changeable, unpredictable.

[5] Aryans—nomadic peoples of Central Asia who invaded and settled northern India.

nations in western and Central Asia. Among the many objects excavated at Mohenjo-Daro are a dancing girl or goddess cast in bronze and a steatite[6] bust of a bearded man, which could be a royal portrait, that date to the late third or early second millennium B.C.. They rank among the masterpieces of Indian art. . . .

Although some elements of the caste system may have existed before they came, the Aryans are usually credited with this specifically Indian concept, which has become less influential in modern times. By about 900 to 600 B.C., when the three later Vedas were compiled, Aryan society was led by priests whose complex rituals had become accepted as indispensable to tribal prosperity. Aryan priests divided humankind into four still familiar major social classes, each further subdivided into many castes and subcastes. The scholars and priests who devised and perpetuated the system constituted the highest class, the Brahmins. Warriors and rulers made up the second, the Kshatriyas. The third class, the Vaishyas, was composed of farmers and merchants, and the laborers and serfs who worked the land were the fourth class, the Shudras. The English word *caste* comes from *casta*, Portuguese for lineage. The Aryans used the Sanskrit word *varna*, which means "color." The darker, "uncivilized" aboriginals whom the fair-skinned Aryans had defeated were relegated to a fifth group, the Panchama, outside the caste system.

Despite its diversity, Indian culture is composed of interlocking cells. In India each separate part of the whole, each element of life, each idea or thing, is relegated to its own niche, either in the phenomenal world or in the realm of soul and mind. However rigid the order might seem, much of its strength lies in its flexibility. Within the caste system, for instance, new categories have evolved for those who do not fit into earlier schemes: outlaws, foreigners, practitioners of new occupations. Furthermore, each segment of the community is linked to and often depends on the others, and the hierarchy is in constant flux, varying not only in time but in space and in the mind. Many tribal people, heedless of the caste system, see themselves as the mighty rulers of their domains. And however deep India's divisions along religious lines, Muslim prime ministers were often employed at Hindu courts, and Hindu officials at Muslim courts. Hindu painters worked for Muslim patrons, and Muslim artists painted Hindu subjects for Hindu employers.

India's many religions—Hinduism, Jainism, Islam, Christianity, Zoroastrianism—reflect her racial, linguistic, and cultural variety. Hinduism and Islam, the major religions, are divided into many sects and branches, whose teachings over the centuries have blended with the timeless beliefs, often ecstatic and magical, of animists who worship the spirits of trees, rivers, animals, or ancestors. In all likelihood many of the highly evolved rituals, sacrifices, and spiritual disciplines, such as yoga, pranayama (breath control),

---

[6] steatite—soapstone.

mantras (words of power), and trance, were adapted from the practices of animists. India's exploration of spiritual techniques—meditation, yantras and mandalas (psychocosmograms, or sacred diagrams of the cosmos), ecstatic dance, numerology, the use of mind-expanding herbs and mushrooms—has been sustained and profound. All that is "good" and all that is "bad" and every shade between—from focusing on points of light to firewalking, to over- and under-indulgence in almost everything from foods and liquids to the senses of sight, sound, smell, and touch—has been analyzed, codified, and tested.

After the fourteenth century, as Hindu literature and religious texts were increasingly written in or translated into the vernacular dialects, Hinduism underwent a revival. Bhakti, or devotional, cults grew in popularity and achieved respectability under the influence of such mystics as Chaitanya (1485–1534) and Kabir (1440–1518), who sought to abolish caste and taught that the way to salvation was through bhakti-marga, the road of fervent devotion to God, rather than through knowledge or asceticism. Chaitanya, a poet who was born a Brahmin in Bengal, revered Krishna and his divine consort Radha. Kabir, who was born a Muslim, allowed his followers a choice of worshiping the Hindu gods or Allah. At his death, according to legend, Kabir's Hindu followers were determined to cremate his body; the Muslims insisted upon burial. But when they drew back the sheet that covered the corpse they found it had turned to flowers. Half the blossoms were burned, the rest were buried.

Most Indians are Hindus, followers of a religion as hard to define as the shape and texture of sunlight. Penetrating every chink, its brilliance dazzles but also casts deep shadows. In keeping with India's diversity, Hinduism adjusts to time, place, and personality. Like the land it is all-welcoming and all-transforming. Even Christians and Muslims have been touched by its influences. An evolved and evolving faith, without set creeds, dogmas, or practices, with no church, no standardized worship, no single prophet or holy book, Hinduism could be described as a nonreligion that has absorbed every stage of Indian cultural and doctrinal belief, from animism to Brahminism, to the sectarianism of the Shaivites and Vaishnavites, on through reformed Hinduism and the more recent phase, which **amalgamates**[7] metaphysics with patriotism. It could be argued that every Hindu creation is imbued with devotional spirit. Many Hindus follow a guru,[8] and they tend to be guided by what they regard as their moral duty, or dharma, determined by their caste and stage of life: student, the time of **celibacy**[9] and learning; householder, the years of marriage, parenthood, and worldly responsibility; hermit or ascetic, the phase of gradual

---

[7] **amalgamates**—merges.
[8] guru—Hindu spiritual teacher.
[9] **celibacy**—unmarried state.

withdrawal to the forest for meditation; or pilgrim, the stage of renunciation, when one breaks all ties with the world and prepares one's soul for dissolution into the universal spirit.

Inasmuch as life is but illusion to Hindus, neither worldly phenomena, including works of art, nor the hours or weeks required to make them, matter as much as in the West. Infinite amounts of time and skill are often expended on **ephemera**,[10] especially when they are related to religion. In Bengal, for instance, extraordinary marriage **pavilions**[11] of jute—as intricate as they are impermanent—are prepared for brides and grooms. Painstakingly detailed images of the goddess Kali are modeled in clay, polychromed,[12] adorned with finery, and then, after a brief puja (worship), borne in procession to the riverbank and immersed. Holy earth reverts to mud. Perhaps because damaged images lose potency, damaged objects are not highly regarded. A Westerner or a Japanese might repair a fine but broken teacup; an Indian, reared in a tropical climate where deterioration is swift and immaculate cleanliness essential, would throw it away. Similarly, patinations[13] on bronzes that would delight Western or Far Eastern connoisseurs are often cleaned in India. Indians are also less apt to **venerate**[14] "old-fashioned" designs; a

> *The extended family is the nest of Indian culture, a legacy from pre-Aryan times.*

prince's inherited jewels are as likely as a villager's silver ornaments to be sent to the jeweler for redoing in celebration of tomorrow's wedding.

The extended family is the nest of Indian culture, a legacy from pre-Aryan times. Family members share a residence, whether a hut or a palace complex, eat food from the same kitchen, hold property in common, and join together in worship. Within the family, which usually includes several generations as well as those adopted into it, seniority is strictly observed, and everyone, from the male elder in charge to the most junior of wives, carries out his or her assigned tasks. If privacy is rare, the family provides security and companionship in high degree. Villages, where most families live, are the modules of existence. Village life is regulated by nature, by the sun and moon, by the cycle of seasons, by birth and death, and by human needs. Houses, usually built of mud and thatch, conform to the land and are scaled to people and domestic animals. Walls are soft-edged and curved as human arms, legs, or bellies. In such congenial settings, villagers gather by lamplight for storytelling and dramatic performances of ancient myths and legends. . . .

Muslims first came to India in 712, less than a hundred years after the death of the Prophet, when Arab traders reached

---

[10] **ephemera**—artifacts intended to be short-lived.

[11] **pavilions**—tents.

[12] polychromed—painted in many colors.

[13] patinations—films or coatings on bronze produced by oxidation.

[14] **venerate**—revere.

Sind in what is now Pakistan. Over the next three centuries, the teachings of Muhammad spread throughout Central Asia, and the armies of Islam gathered strength. In the eleventh and twelfth centuries, far greater forces led by rugged Turks and Afghans raided India through the northwestern mountain passes, destroying as they pushed eastward and southward magnificent medieval Brahminical and Buddhist temples and monuments, erasing forever part of the legacy of India's Great Tradition. The Muslim invasions dealt the final blow to Buddhist culture in North India, and at the outset of the fourteenth century, as now, most Indians were Hindus, Muslims, or animists whose tribal and folk traditions, always fundamental to Indian culture, flowed on almost **impervious**[15] to distracting change. As the conquerors adjusted to their new surroundings, Islam's cultural heritage enriched and blended with India's, and by 1300 truly Indo-Muslim idioms were emerging in the art and architecture of the sultanates of North India and the Deccan.

Another, far more vigorous Muslim invasion began in 1525, when Babur, from the kingdom of Fergana in Russian Turkistan, marched his army into northern India and occupied the Punjab. A year later, Babur defeated the last sultan of the weakened Lodi dynasty at Panipat and founded the Mughal empire. Babur was not only a mighty prince, descended from Timur (Tamerlane) and Chinghiz Khan,[16] he was also a scholar and a poet, and we know from his autobiography that he considered life in his newly acquired territories inferior in many ways to the cultivated society he had left behind. Babur died in 1530, but his four-year reign initiated one of the most creative periods in India's cultural history, during which **indigenous**[17] and foreign ideas intertwined in fresh patterns of great beauty and profundity.

---

[15] **impervious**—resistant.

[16] Timur . . . Chinghiz Khan—Timur (1336?–1405) and Chinghiz or Genghis Khan (1162–1227) were Central Asian military rulers.

[17] **indigenous**—native.

QUESTIONS TO CONSIDER

1. Stuart Cary Welch briefly sketches Indian family life. Which qualities in his description do you find appealing? Which do you find unappealing?

2. Welch characterizes Hinduism as a "nonreligion." What does he mean and how has this characteristic enabled Hinduism to be particularly representative of the Indian cultural tradition?

3. How does the Hindu belief that life is an illusion influence attitudes toward works of art?

Chapter 3

China and Japan

Finding the Way

Women's Worlds

Thoughts in Solitude

 This wood block print by the Japanese artist Hokusai (1760–1849) transforms powerful forces of wind and water into a pattern that is beautiful rather than threatening.

Confucianism and Taoism

Tradition holds that the two great founders of Chinese philosophy, Confucius and Lao Tzu, were contemporaries who lived at the end of the sixth century B.C. Confucius was a reformer who taught that the practice of moderation, benevolence, and respect for tradition was necessary to sustain the moral order of society. His thought is preserved in **The Analects,** *a collection of his sayings made soon after his death. By contrast, Lao Tzu's philosophy, expressed in the mystical, paradoxical* **Tao Te Ching** *("Classic of the Way and Its Power"), bases social reform in simplicity, passivity, and harmony with the* **tao** *("way"), a mysterious, all-powerful cosmic order. An elegant literary expression of Taoist philosophy appeared several hundred years after Lao Tzu's time in the witty fables of his follower Chuang-tzu.*

from *The Analects*

The Master[1] said, He who rules by moral force is like the pole-star, which remains in its place while all the lesser stars do **homage**[2] to it.

The Master said, Govern the people by regulations, keep order among them by **chastisements,**[3] and they will flee from you, and lose all self-respect. Govern them by moral force, keep order among them by ritual[4] and they will keep their self-respect and come to you of their own accord.

Mêng Wu Po asked about the treatment of parents. The Master said, Behave in such a way that your father and mother have no anxiety about you, except concerning your health.

The Master said, High office filled by men of narrow views, ritual performed without reverence, the forms of mourning observed without grief—these are the things I cannot bear to see!

Wealth and rank are what every man desires; but if they can only be retained to the **detriment**[5] of the Way he professes, he must relinquish them. Poverty and obscurity are what every man detests; but if they can only be avoided to the detriment of the Way he professes, he must accept them. The gentleman who ever parts company

---

[1] Master—Confucius.

[2] **homage**—reverence.

[3] **chastisements**—punishments.

[4] ritual—traditional religious practices.

[5] **detriment**—loss, damage.

with Goodness does not fulfil that name. Never for a moment does a gentleman quit the way of Goodness. He is never so **harried**[6] but that he cleaves[7] to this; never so tottering but that he cleaves to this.

The Master said, Mêng Chih-fan is no boaster. When his people were routed he was the last to flee; but when they neared the city-gate, he whipped up his horses, saying, It was not courage that kept me behind. My horses were slow.

Chi Wen Tzu used to think thrice before acting. The Master hearing of it said, Twice is quite enough.

The Master said, Learn as if you were following someone whom you could not catch up, as though it were someone you were frightened of losing.

Jan Jung asked about Goodness. The Master said, Behave when away from home as though you were in the presence of an important guest. Deal with the common people as though you were officiating at an important sacrifice. Do not do to others what you would not like yourself. Then there will be no feelings of opposition to you, whether it is the affairs of a State that you are handling or the affairs of a Family.[8] Jan Jung said, I know that I am not clever; but this is a saying that, with your permission, I shall try to put into practice.

Tzu-kung asked about government. The Master said, Sufficient food, sufficient weapons, and the confidence of the common people. Tzu-kung said, Suppose you had no choice but to dispense with one of these three, which would you forgo? The Master said, Weapons. Tzu-kung said, Suppose you were forced to dispense with one of the two that were left, which would you forgo? The Master said, Food. For from of old death has been the lot of all men; but a people that no longer trusts its rulers is lost indeed.

from *Tao Te Ching*

3

By not exalting the talented you will cause
   the people to cease from rivalry and
   contention.
By not prizing goods hard to get, you will
   cause the people to cease from robbing
   and stealing.
By not displaying what is desirable, you
   will cause the people's hearts to remain
   undisturbed.

Therefore, the Sage's way of governing
   begins by

   Emptying the heart of desires,
   Filling the belly with food,
   Weakening the ambitions,
   Toughening the bones.

---

[6] **harried**—bothered, annoyed.
[7] cleaves—clings.
[8] Family—ruling clan.

In this way he will cause the people to
   remain without knowledge and without
   desire, and prevent the knowing ones
   from any ado.
Practice Non-Ado, and everything will be
   in order.

4

The Tao is like an empty bowl,
Which in being used can never be filled up.
Fathomless, it seems to be the origin of
   all things.
It blunts all sharp edges,
It unties all tangles,
It harmonizes all lights,
It unites the world into one whole.
Hidden in the deeps,
Yet it seems to exist for ever.
I do not know whose child it is;
It seems to be the common ancestor of all,
   the father of things.

5

Heaven-and-Earth is not sentimental;
It treats all things as straw-dogs.[9]
The Sage is not sentimental;
He treats all his people as straw-dogs.

Between Heaven and Earth,
There seems to be a Bellows:
It is empty, and yet it is inexhaustible;
The more it works, the more comes out
   of it.
No amount of words can fathom it:
Better look for it within you.

11

Thirty spokes converge upon a single hub;
It is on the hole in the center that the use
   of the cart hinges.

We make a vessel from a lump of clay;
It is the empty space within the vessel that
   makes it useful.

We make doors and windows for a room;
But it is these empty spaces that make the
   room livable.

Thus, while the **tangible**[10] has advantages,
It is the intangible that makes it useful.

from *Chuang-tzu*

Once Chuang Chou[11] dreamt he was a
butterfly, a butterfly flitting and fluttering
around, happy with himself and doing as
he pleased. He didn't know he was Chuang
Chou. Suddenly he woke up and there he
was, solid and unmistakable Chuang Chou.
But he didn't know if he was Chuang
Chou who had dreamt he was a butterfly,
or a butterfly dreaming he was Chuang
Chou. Between Chuang Chou and a butterfly there must be some distinction! This is
called the Transformation of Things.

   Hui Tzu[12] said to Chuang-tzu, "Your
teachings are of no practical use."

---

[9] straw-dogs—figures used as offerings in rituals and
then burned.

[10] **tangible**—touchable.

[11] Chuang Chou—Chuang-tzu.

[12] Hui Tzu—a logician and friend of Chuang-tzu.

Chuang-tzu said, "Only those who already know the value of the useless can be talked to about the useful. This earth we walk upon is of vast extent, yet in order to walk a man uses no more of it than the soles of his two feet will cover. But suppose one cut away the ground round his feet till one reached the Yellow Springs,[13] would his patches of ground still be of any use to him for walking?" Hui Tzu said, "They would be of no use!" Chuang-tzu said, "So then the usefulness of the useless is evident!"

Hui Tzu recited to Chuang-tzu the rhyme:

"I have got a big tree
That men call the *chü*.
Its trunk is knotted and **gnarled**,[14]
And cannot be fitted to plumb-line
    and ink,
Its branches are bent and twisted,
And cannot be fitted to compass or
    square.
It stands by the road-side,
And no carpenter will look at it."

"Your doctrines," said Hui Tzu, "are **grandiose**,[15] but useless, and that is why no one accepts them." Chuang-tzu said, "Can it be that you have never seen the pole-cat, how it crouches waiting for the mouse, ready at any moment to leap this way or that, high or low, till one day it lands plump on the spring of a trap and dies in the snare? Again there is the yak, 'huge as a cloud that covers the sky.' It can maintain this great bulk and yet would be quite incapable of catching a mouse. . . .

As for you and the big tree which you are at a loss how to use, why do you not plant it in the realm of Nothing Whatever, in the wilds of the Unpastured Desert, and aimlessly tread the path of Inaction by its side, or vacantly lie dreaming beneath it?"

What does not invite the axe
No creature will harm.
What cannot be used
No troubles will befall.

---

[13] Yellow Springs—world of the dead.

[14] **gnarled**—twisted.

[15] **grandiose**—pompous.

QUESTIONS TO CONSIDER

1. What are the differences between Confucius's ideal of good government and those of Lao Tzu?

2. Is Confucius's formula, "Do not do to others what you would not like yourself," wiser than the Golden Rule, "Do unto others as you would have them do unto you"? Why or why not?

3. What are some of the characteristics that contribute to Confucius's ideal of "the gentleman"?

4. A paradox is an apparently contradictory statement that points to a truth. Emily Dickinson's lines, "Success is counted sweetest/By those who ne'er succeed," are an example of a paradoxical statement. What are some paradoxes in the passages from Lao Tzu and Chuang-tzu?

Confucianism and Government

Confucian teaching held that a just ruler had divine approval, known as the "Mandate of Heaven." If an emperor set an example of virtue, officials would govern honestly and the people would obey willingly. If an emperor were wicked and unjust, the Mandate of Heaven and the right to rule could be lost. The Moral Power of the Ruler *and* The Deep Significance of the Spring and Autumn Annals *express this classic Chinese view of the significance of the emperor. Confucian teaching also influenced Japanese ideas of government, as reflected in a code of laws for Japan's military aristocracy drawn up in 1615 by the ruling Tokugawa dynasty.*

---

from *The Moral Power of the Ruler*

The power to achieve success or failure lies with the ruler. If the measuring-line is true, then the wood will be straight, not because one makes a special effort, but because that which it is "ruled" by makes it so. In the same way if the ruler is sincere and upright, then honest officials will serve in his government and scoundrels will go into hiding, but if the ruler is not upright then evil men will have their way and loyal men will retire to **seclusion**.[1] Why is it that people often scratch melons or gourds with their fingernails, but never scratch stones or jewels? Because no matter how hard they scratch stones or jewels they can never make an impression. In the same way if the ruler can be made to adhere to right, maintain fairness, and follow a measuring-line, as it were, in measuring high and low, then even though his ministers come to him with evil designs it will be the same as **dashing**[2] eggs against a rock or throwing fire into water. King Ling loved slim waists and all the women went on diets and starved themselves. The King of Yüeh admired bravery and all the men outdid each other in dangerous feats defying death. From this we may see that he who wields authority can change the customs and transform the manners of his people.

---

[1] **seclusion**—solitude.

[2] **dashing**—throwing violently so as to break; smashing.

from *The Deep Significance of the Spring and Autumn Annals*

The ruler is the basis of the state. In administering the state, nothing is more effective for educating the people than reverence for the basis. If the basis is revered then the ruler may transform the people as though by supernatural power, but if the basis is not revered then the ruler will have nothing by which to lead his people. Then though he employ harsh penalties and severe punishments the people will not follow him. This is to drive the state to ruin, and there is no greater disaster. What do we mean by the basis? Heaven, earth, and man are the basis of all creatures. Heaven gives them birth, earth nourishes them, and man brings them to completion. Heaven provides them at birth with a sense of filial[3] and brotherly love, earth nourishes them with clothing and food, and man completes them with rites[4] and music. The three act together as hands and feet join to complete the body and none can be dispensed with. . . . If all three are lacking, then the people will become like deer, each person following his own desires, each family its own ways. Fathers cannot employ their sons nor rulers their ministers, and though there be walls and battlements[5] they will be called an "empty city.". . . But the enlightened and worthy ruler, being of good faith, is strictly attentive to the three bases. His sacrifices are conducted with utmost reverence; he makes offerings to and serves his ancestors; he advances brotherly affection and encourages filial conduct. In this way he serves the basis of Heaven. He personally grasps the plow handle and plows a furrow, plucks the mulberry himself and feeds the silkworms, breaks new ground to increase the grain supply and open the way for a sufficiency of clothing and food. In this way he serves the basis of earth. He sets up schools for the nobles and in the towns and villages to teach filial piety and brotherly affection, reverence and humility. He enlightens the people with education and moves them with rites and music. Thus he serves the basis of man. If he rightly serves these three, then the people will be like sons and brothers, not daring to be unsubmissive. . . . This is called a spontaneous reward, and when it comes, though he **relinquish**[6] his throne, give up his kingdom and depart, the people will take up their children on their backs, follow him, and keep him as their lord, so that he can never leave them. . . .

Those who in ancient times invented writing drew three lines and connected them through the middle, calling the character "king." The three lines are Heaven, earth, and man, and that which passes through the middle joins the principles of all three. Occupying the center of Heaven,

---

[3] filial—befitting a son or daughter.

[4] rites—traditional religious practices.

[5] battlements—fortifications on top of the wall of a castle.

[6] **relinquish**—give up claim to.

earth, and man, passing through and joining all three—if he is not a king, who can do this? . . .

Therefore the great concern of the ruler lies in diligently watching over and guarding his heart, that his loves and hates, his angers and joys may be displayed in accordance with right, as the mild and cool, the cold and hot weather come forth in proper season. If the ruler constantly practices this without error, then his emotions will never be at fault, as spring and autumn, winter and summer are never out of order. Then may he form a trinity with Heaven and earth. If he holds these four passions deep within him and does not allow them recklessly to come forth, then may he be called the equal of Heaven.

Laws Governing the Military Households

1. The study of literature and the practice of the military arts, archery and horsemanship, must be cultivated diligently. . . .

From of old the rule has been to practice "the arts of peace on the left hand, and the arts of war on the right"; both must be mastered. Archery and horsemanship are indispensable to military men. Though arms are called instruments of evil, there are times when they must be resorted to. In peacetime we should not be **oblivious**[7] to the danger of war. Should we not, then, prepare ourselves for it?

2. Drinking parties and wanton revelry should be avoided.

In the codes that have come down to us this kind of **dissipation**[8] has been severely proscribed. Sexual indulgence and habitual gambling lead to the downfall of a state.

3. Offenders against the law should not be harbored or hidden in any domain.

Law is the basis of social order. Reason may be violated in the name of the law, but law may not be violated in the name of reason. Those who break the law deserve heavy punishment.

4. Great lords, the lesser lords, and officials should immediately expel from their domains any among their retainers or henchmen who have been charged with treason or murder.

Wild and wicked men may become weapons for overturning the state and destroying the people. How can they be allowed to go free?

5. Henceforth no outsider, none but the inhabitants of a particular domain, shall be permitted to reside in that domain.

Each domain has its own ways. If a man discloses the secrets of one's own country to another domain or if the secrets of the other domain are disclosed to one's own, that will sow the seeds of deceit. . . .

6. Whenever it is intended to make repairs on a castle of one of the feudal domains, the [government] should be

---

[7] **oblivious**—unconscious, unaware.

[8] **dissipation**—waste.

notified. The construction of any new castles is to be halted and **stringently**[9] prohibited.

"Big castles are a danger to the state." Walls and moats are the cause of great disorders.

7. Immediate report should be made of innovations which are being planned or of factional conspiracies being formed in neighboring domains.

Men all incline toward **partisanship;**[10] few are wise and impartial. There are some who refuse to obey their masters, and others who feud with their neighbors. Why, instead of abiding by the established order, do they **wantonly**[11] embark upon new schemes?

8. Do not enter into marriage privately [that is, without notifying the government authorities].

Marriage follows the principle of harmony between yin and yang,[12] and must not be entered into lightly. In the *Book of Changes,* . . . it says, "Marriage should not be contracted out of enmity (against another). Marriages intended to effect an alliance with enemies [of the state] will turn out badly." The Peach Blossom ode in *The Book of Poetry* also says that "When men and women are proper in their relationships and marriage is arranged at the correct time; then throughout the land there will be no loose women." To form an alliance by marriage is the root of treason.

9. Visits of the daimyo[13] to the capital are to be in accordance with regulations.

The *Chronicles of Japan, continued* contains a regulation that "Clansmen should not gather together whenever they please, but only when they have to conduct some public business; and also that the number of horsemen serving as an escort in the capital should be limited to twenty. . . ." Daimyo should not be accompanied by a large number of soldiers. Twenty horsemen shall be the maximum escort for daimyo with an income of from one million to two hundred thousand koku of rice.[14] For those with an income of one hundred thousand koku or less, the escort should be proportionate to their income. On official missions, however, they may be accompanied by an escort proportionate to their rank.

10. Restrictions on the type and quality of dress to be worn should not be transgressed.

Lord and vassal, superior and inferior, should observe what is proper to their station in life. [Then follows an injunction against the wearing of fine white damask or purple silk by retainers without authorization.]

---

[9] **stringently**—strictly.

[10] **partisanship**—strong loyalty.

[11] **wantonly**—recklessly.

[12] yin and yang—cosmic principles in Chinese thought whose interaction defines all things; yin is negative, dark, and feminine; yang is positive, bright, and masculine.

[13] daimyo—great feudal lords.

[14] koku of rice—about five bushels. Rank was based on the amount of rice a landholder's estate produced.

11. Persons without rank shall not ride in palanquins.[15] From of old there have been certain families entitled to ride in palanquins without special permission, and others who have received such permission. Recently, however, even the ordinary retainers and henchmen of some families have taken to riding about in palanquins, which is truly the worst sort of presumption.[16] Henceforth permission shall be granted only to the lords of the various domains, their close relatives and ranking officials, medical men and astrologers, those over sixty years of age, and those ill or infirm. In the cases of ordinary household retainers or henchmen who willfully ride in palanquins, their masters shall be held accountable.

Exceptions to this law are the court families, Buddhist prelates, and the clergy in general.

12. The samurai[17] of the various domains shall lead a frugal and simple life.

When the rich make a display of their wealth, the poor are humiliated and envious. Nothing engenders corruption so much as this, and therefore it must be strictly curbed.

13. The lords of the domains should select officials with a capacity for public administration.

Good government depends on getting the right men. Due attention should be given to their merits and faults; rewards and punishments must be properly meted out. If a domain has able men, it flourishes; if it lacks able men it is doomed to perish. This is the clear admonition of the wise men of old.

The purport of the foregoing should be conscientiously observed.

---

[15] palanquins—enclosed litters carried on poles.

[16] presumption—boldness.

[17] samurai—warrior aristocracy.

QUESTIONS TO CONSIDER

1. What values are common to all three of these texts?

2. Which social order seems more stable, the one reflected in the Chinese texts or in the Japanese text? Explain.

3. How were "status symbols" approached in these documents?

4. In your opinion, how important is it that public officials and other leaders provide a good example for society?

Confucianism and Education

Early in Chinese history, education became based on the "Confucian Classics." These included ancient writings compiled by Confucius, as well as his own works and those of his followers. Candidates for the most desirable careers, which were positions in government service, were required to pass a series of examinations in which they showed a thorough knowledge of these works. In the 1600s, Confucianism also influenced education in Japan. The following works deal with education in China and Japan. The first is the journal of Matteo Ricci, an Italian priest who lived in China from 1583 to 1610. The second is Common Sense Teachings for Japanese Children *by Japanese Confucian scholar Kaibara Ekiken (1630–1714).*

from *Journals*
Matteo Ricci

Before discussing the question of the government of this wonderful empire, it will be helpful to give an outline of the progress the Chinese have made in literature and in the sciences, and of the nature of the academic degrees which they are accustomed to confer. The whole nature of the Chinese government is intimately bound up with these particular factors, and this government differs in form from that of any other in the world. . . .

It is evident to everyone here that no one will labor to attain proficiency in mathematics or in medicine who has any hope of becoming prominent in the field of philosophy. The result is that scarcely anyone devotes himself to these studies, unless he is deterred from the pursuit of what are considered to be the higher studies, either by reason of family affairs or by mediocrity of talent. The study of mathematics and that of medicine are held in low esteem, because they are not fostered by honors as is the study of philosophy, to which students are attracted by the hope of the glory and the rewards attached to it. This may be readily seen in the interest taken in the study of moral philosophy. The man who is promoted to the higher degrees in this field, prides himself on the fact that he has in truth attained to the **pinnacle**[1] of Chinese happiness.

The most renowned of all Chinese philosophers was named Confucius.

---

[1] **pinnacle**—topmost point.

This great and learned man . . . spurred on his people to the pursuit of virtue not less by his own example than by his writings. His self-mastery and **abstemious**[2] ways of life have led his countrymen to assert that he surpassed in holiness all those who in times past, in the various parts of the world, were considered to have excelled in virtue. Indeed, if we critically examine his actions and sayings as they are recorded in history, we shall be forced to admit that he was the equal of the pagan philosophers[3] and superior to most of them. He is held in such high esteem by the learned Chinese that they do not dare to call into question any pronouncement of his and are ready to give full recognition to an oath sworn in his name. . . .

Confucius . . . compiled four volumes[4] of the works of more ancient philosophers and wrote five books of his own. . . . The nine books of Confucius, making up the most ancient of Chinese libraries, of which all others are a development, . . . present a collection of moral precepts for the future good and development of the kingdom.

There is a law in the land, handed down from ancient kings and confirmed by the customs of centuries, stating that he who wishes to be learned, and to be known as such, must draw his fundamental doctrine from these same books. In addition to this it is not sufficient for him to follow the general sense of the text, but what is far more difficult, he must be able to write aptly and exactly of every particular doctrine contained in these books. . . . Contrary to what has been stated by some

of our writers, there are no schools or public academies in which these books are taught or explained by masters. Each student selects his own master by whom he is instructed in his own home and at his personal expense.

The number of such private teachers, of course, is great, partly because it would be hard for one master to teach many at a time, owning to the difficulty of handling the Chinese characters, and partly because it is an old custom here for each home to have a private school for its own children. . . .

In the field of philosophy there are three degrees, conferred upon those who pass the written examinations assigned for each degree. . . .

When the . . . candidates are admitted to the palace and the doors closed and sealed on the outside with a public seal, each of the two presiding officers, appointed by the emperor, explains in public three passages selected at will from the Four Books.[5] He then presents these passages as the general subject matter, and a separate paper must be written on the selection made by each examiner. Then four passages are selected from any one of the five Books of Doctrines[6] and assigned for additional matter for examination. . . . These seven written papers must show evidence

---

[2] **abstemious**—moderate in eating and drinking.

[3] pagan philosophers—Greek and Roman philosophers.

[4] four volumes—Confucius actually compiled five ancient classics.

[5] Four Books—works by Confucius and his followers, including *The Analects* (page 80).

[6] Books of Doctrines—works by Confucius and his followers.

not only of proper use of words but also of a proper appreciation of the ideas contained in the doctrines and a strict observance of the rules of Chinese **rhetoric**.[7] No **dissertation**[8] should exceed five hundred characters, corresponding to as many words in our usage.

On the second day of examination, after two days of rest, and behind closed doors, . . . topics are offered for examination relative to things that have happened in the past, to the annals of the ancients, and to events which may be expected to happen in the near future. These papers are written in triplicate,[9] in the form of an advisory document, addressed to the emperor as to what would seem to be the best course to follow for the good of the empire in certain **eventualities**.[10]

On the third day three difficulties or arguments are offered for examination, which are drawn from possibilities that might arise in planning the direction of public administration. Again, papers are written in triple copy, and each one explains the judgment he wishes to offer in settlement of the argument he has chosen to discuss. When each of the candidates has selected his argument for discussion and committed it to memory, he enters into the room assigned him by the one in charge and does his writing in silence. . . .

When the examinations are over and the ceremonies described at an end, the royal examiners publish a book which is distributed throughout the whole empire, containing the results of the examinations, the names of the new licentiates,[11] and the outstanding manuscripts on the various subjects treated in the examinations. The place of honor in this publication is assigned to the one who received the highest ranking.

from *Common Sense Teachings for Japanese Children*
Kaibara Ekiken

In January when children reach the age of six, teach them numbers one through ten, and the names given to designate 100, 1,000, 10,000 and 100,000,000. Let them know the four directions, East, West, North and South. Assess their native intelligence and differentiate between quick and slow learners. Teach them Japanese pronunciation from the age of six or seven, and let them learn how to write. . . . From this time on, teach them to respect their elders, and let them know the distinctions between the upper and lower classes and between the young and old. Let them learn to use the correct expressions.

When the children reach the age of seven, do not let the boys and girls sit together, nor must you allow them to dine together. . . .

For the eighth year.

This is the age when the ancients began studying the book *Little Learning*.[12]

---

[7] **rhetoric**—art of literary composition.

[8] **dissertation**—essay written by a candidate for a degree.

[9] triplicate—three identical copies.

[10] **eventualities**—possible events.

[11] licentiates—recipients of academic degrees.

[12] *Little Learning*—Confucian book of instruction for young children.

Beginning at this time, teach the youngsters etiquette befitting their age, and caution them not to commit an act of impoliteness. Among those which must be taught are: daily **deportment**,[13] the manners set for appearing before one's senior and withdrawing from his presence, how to speak or respond to one's senior or guest, how to place a serving tray or replace it for one's senior, how to present a wine cup and pour rice wine and to serve side dishes to accompany it, and how to serve tea. Children must also learn how to behave while taking their meals.

Children must be taught by those who are close to them the virtues of filial piety[14] and obedience. To serve the parents well is called filial piety, and to serve one's seniors well is called obedience. The one who lives close to the children and who is able to teach must instruct the children in the early years of their life that the first obligation of a human being is to revere the parents and serve them well. Then comes the next lesson which includes respect for one's seniors, listening to their commands and not holding them in contempt. One's seniors include elder brothers, elder sisters, uncles, aunts, and cousins who are older and worthy of respect. . . . As the children grow older, teach them to love their younger brothers and to be compassionate to the employees and servants. Teach them also the respect due the teachers and the behavior codes governing friends. The etiquette governing each movement toward important guests—such

as standing, sitting, advancing forward, and retiring from their presence—and the language to be employed must be taught. Teach them how to pay respect to others according to the social positions held by them. Gradually the ways of filial piety and obedience, loyalty and trustworthiness, right deportment and **decorum**,[15] and sense of shame must be inculcated[16] in the children's minds and they must know how to implement them. Caution them not to desire the possessions of others, or to stoop below one's dignity in consuming excessive amounts of food and drink. . . .

Once reaching the age of eight, children must follow and never lead their elders when entering a gate, sitting, or eating and drinking. From this time on they must be taught how to become humble and yield to others. Do not permit the children to behave as they please. It is important to caution them against "doing their own things."

At the age of ten, let the children be placed under the guidance of a teacher, and tell them about the general meaning of the five constant virtues[17] and let them understand the way of the five human relationships.[18] Let them read books by the

---

[13] **deportment**—conduct, behavior.

[14] filial piety—Confucian ideal of reverence toward parents and other elders.

[15] **decorum**—dignified behavior.

[16] inculcated—taught by frequent repetitions.

[17] five constant virtues—human heartedness, righteousness, propriety, wisdom, and good faith.

[18] five human relationships—those between rulers and subjects, fathers and sons, husbands and wives, older and younger brothers, and friends.

Sage[19] and the wise men of old and cultivate the desire for learning. . . . When not engaged in reading, teach them the literary and military arts. . . .

Fifteen is the age when the ancients began the study of the *Great Learning*.[20] From this time on, concentrate on the learning of a sense of justice and duty. The students must also learn to cultivate their personalities and investigate the way of governing people. . . .

Those who are born in the high-ranking families have the heavy obligations of becoming leaders of the people, of having people entrusted to their care, and of governing them. Therefore, without fail, a teacher must be selected for them when they are still young. They must be taught how to read and be informed of the ways of old, of cultivating their personalities, and of the way of governing people. If they do not learn the way of governing people, they may injure the many people who are entrusted to their care by the Way of Heaven. That will be a serious disaster. . . .

In olden days in China, when children reached the age of twenty, a capping ceremony was held to celebrate their coming of age. . . . In olden days, in Japan too, both the court nobles and samurai[21] placed ceremonial caps on those who reached the age of twenty. . . . Once the ceremony is completed, the children become adults. From that moment on, they must discard their former childish way, follow the virtues of the adult society, reach out everywhere for knowledge, and act in an exemplifying manner. . . .

---

[19] Sage—Confucius.

[20] *Great Learning*—basic Confucian treatise.

[21] samurai—members of the hereditary class of warriors in Japan.

QUESTIONS TO CONSIDER

1. From Matteo Ricci's account of Chinese education, what would you say was its chief advantage to Chinese society?

2. What was the major disadvantage of Chinese education?

3. In what ways did Chinese education differ significantly from higher education in modern America?

4. From Kaibara Ekiken's manual, what was the major emphasis in the education of Japanese children?

5. In your opinion, what personality traits would be encouraged by following Ekiken's educational program? What traits would be discouraged?

The Ballad of Mulan

Sometimes compared to the medieval French heroine Joan of Arc (page 336), the Chinese woman warrior Mulan was from the border regions of northern China. This famous ballad tells how she joins a force to fight off an attack by nomad raiders and goes on to serve in the army for twelve years without any of her fellow soldiers becoming aware she is a woman.

Click, click, forever click, click;
Mulan sits at the door and weaves.
Listen, and you will not hear the shuttle's sound,
But only hear a girl's sobs and sighs.
"Oh tell me, lady, are you thinking of your love,
Oh tell me, lady, are you longing for your dear?"
"Oh no, oh no, I am not thinking of my love,
Oh no, oh no, I am not longing for my dear.
But last night I read the battle-roll;
The Khan[1] has ordered a great levy[2] of men.
The battle-roll was written in twelve books,
And in each book stood my father's name.
My father's sons are not grown men,
And of all my brothers, none is older than me.
Oh let me to the market to buy saddle and horse,
And ride with the soldiers to take my father's place."
In the eastern market she's bought a gallant horse,
In the western market she's bought saddle and cloth.
In the southern market she's bought snaffle[3] and reins,

---

[1] Khan—emperor of China.
[2] levy—military draft.
[3] snaffle—bit for a horse.

In the northern market she's bought a tall whip.
In the morning she stole from her father's and mother's house;
At night she was camping by the Yellow River's[4] side.
She could not hear her father and mother calling to her by her name,
But only the song of the Yellow River as its hurrying waters hissed and
    swirled through the night.
At dawn they left the River and went on their way;
At dusk they came to the Black Water's side.
She could not hear her father and mother calling to her by her name,
She could only hear the muffled voices of Scythian horsemen[5] riding on
    the hills of Yen.
A thousand leagues[6] she tramped on the errands of war,
Frontiers and hills she crossed like a bird in flight.
Through the northern air echoed the watchman's tap;
The wintry light gleamed on coats of mail.[7]
The captain had fought a hundred fights, and died;
The warriors in ten years had won their rest.
They went home; they saw the Emperor's face;
The Son of Heaven[8] was seated in the Hall of Light.
To the strong in battle lordships and lands he gave;
And of prize money a hundred thousand strings.[9]
Then spoke the Khan and asked her what she would take.
"Oh, Mulan asks not to be made
    A Counsellor at the Khan's court;
She only begs for a camel that can march
    A thousand leagues a day,
    To take her back to her home."

When her father and mother heard that she had come,
They went out to the wall and led her back to the house.
When her little sister heard that she had come,
She went to the door and rouged her face afresh.

---

[4] Yellow River—major river of northern China.

[5] Scythian horsemen—Central Asian nomads.

[6] leagues—three-mile-long units of length.

[7] mail—armor formed of linked metal rings.

[8] Son of Heaven—title of the emperor.

[9] strings—cords strung with coins.

When her little brother heard that his sister had come,
He sharpened his knife and darted like a flash
Toward the pigs and sheep.

She opened the gate that leads to the eastern tower,
She sat on her bed that stood in the western tower.
She cast aside her heavy soldier's cloak,
And wore again her old-time dress.
She stood at the window and bound her cloudy hair;
She went to the mirror and fastened her yellow combs.
She left the house and met her messmates[10] in the road;
Her messmates were startled out of their wits.
They had marched with her for twelve years of war
And never known that Mulan was a girl.
For the male hare has a lilting, lolloping gait,[11]
And the female hare has a wild and roving eye;
But set them both scampering side by side,
And who so wise could tell you "This is he"?

---

[10] messmates—fellow soldiers.
[11] gait—manner of walking.

QUESTIONS TO CONSIDER

1. Is this ballad primarily a story of military adventure or a moral fable? Explain your answer.

2. In what ways does Mulan's behavior reflect Confucian values?

3. What is the significance of the last four lines?

The Death of Atsumori

The power of Japan's military rulers was based on the loyalty of their warriors, called samurai. Like the knights of the European Middle Ages, the samurai pledged complete loyalty to their lord. The following episode displays some of the values of these aristocratic warriors. It comes from The Tale of the Heike, *a cycle of ballads dealing with a vicious civil war (1156–1185) between two powerful landowning clans, the Minamoto and the Taira, or Heike.*

When the Heike were routed at Ichi no tani, and their nobles and courtiers were fleeing to the shore to escape in their ships, Kumagai Naozane came riding along a narrow path onto the beach, with the intention of intercepting one of their great captains. Just then his eye fell on a single horseman who was attempting to reach one of the ships in the offing. The horse he rode was dappled-gray, and its saddle glittered with gold mounting. Not doubting that he was one of the chief captains, Kumagai beckoned to him with his war fan,[1] crying out: "Shameful! to show an enemy your back. Return! Return!"

The warrior turned his horse and rode back to the beach, where Kumagai at once engaged him in mortal combat. Quickly hurling him to the ground, he sprang upon him and tore off his helmet to cut off his head, when he beheld the face of a youth of sixteen or seventeen, delicately powdered and with blackened teeth,[2] just about the age of his own son and with features of great beauty. "Who are you?" he asked. "Tell me your name, for I would spare your life."

"Nay, first say who you are," replied the young man.

"I am Kumagai Naozane of Musashi, a person of no particular importance."

"Then you have made a good capture," said the youth. "Take my head and show it to some of my side, and they will tell you who I am."

"Though he is one of their leaders," mused Kumagai, "if I slay him it will not turn victory into defeat, and if I spare him, it will not turn defeat into victory. When

---

[1] war fan—used in battle to signal subordinates.

[2] blackened teeth—In early Japan teeth blackened with dye were considered a sign of beauty.

my son Kojirō was but slightly wounded at Ichi no tani this morning, did it not pain me? How this young man's father would grieve to hear that he had been killed! I will spare him."

Just then, looking behind him, he saw Doi and Kajiwara coming up with fifty horsemen. "Alas! look there," he exclaimed, the tears running down his face, "though I would spare your life, the whole countryside swarms with our men, and you cannot escape them. If you must die, let it be by my hand, and I will see that prayers are said for your rebirth in Paradise."

"Indeed it must be so," said the young warrior. "Cut off my head at once."

Kumagai was so overcome by compassion that he could scarcely wield his blade. His eyes swam and he hardly knew what he did, but there was no help for it; weeping bitterly he cut off the boy's head. "Alas!" he cried, "what life is so hard as that of a soldier? Only because I was born of a warrior family must I suffer this affliction! How lamentable it is to do such cruel deeds!" He pressed his face to the sleeve of his armor and wept bitterly. Then, wrapping up the head, he was stripping off the young man's armor when he discovered a flute in a brocade bag. "Ah," he exclaimed, "it was this youth and his friends who were amusing themselves with music within the walls this morning. Among all our men of the Eastern Provinces I doubt if there is any one of them who has brought a flute with him. How gentle the ways of these courtiers!"

When he brought the flute to the Commander, all who saw it were moved to tears; he discovered then that the youth was Atsumori, the youngest son of Tsunemori,[3] aged sixteen years. From this time the mind of Kumagai was turned toward the religious life.

---

[3] Tsunemori—one of the Heike leaders.

QUESTIONS TO CONSIDER

1. Why is Kumagai reluctant to kill Atsumori?

2. How does he resolve his dilemma?

3. What values are displayed in this episode?

4. How does this episode reflect the traditional Japanese view that an aristocrat must practice "the arts of peace on the left hand, and the arts of war on the right"?

from

Lessons for Women

PAN CHAO

Member of a celebrated family of scholars and poets, Pan Chao (45–120? A.D.) became the most famous woman writer of ancient China. She is best known for her essay Lessons for Women, *in which she formulated guidelines for women's behavior based on Confucian values. Popularized by other writers, Pan Chao's ideas had a great influence on attitudes about women's roles in China.*

Humility

On the third day after the birth of a girl the ancients observed three customs: first to place the baby below the bed; second to give her a potsherd[1] with which to play; and third to announce her birth to her ancestors by an offering. Now to lay the baby below the bed plainly indicated that she is lowly and weak, and should regard it as her primary duty to humble herself before others. To give her potsherds with which to play **indubitably**[2] signified that she should practice labor and consider it her primary duty to be industrious. To announce her birth before her ancestors clearly meant that she ought to esteem as her primary duty the continuation of the observance of worship in the home.

These three ancient customs **epitomize**[3] a woman's ordinary way of life and the teachings of the traditional ceremonial rites and regulations. Let a woman modestly yield to others; let her respect others; let her put others first, herself last. Should she do something good, let her not mention it; should she do something bad, let her not deny it. Let her bear disgrace; let her even endure when others speak or do evil to her. Always let her seem to tremble and to fear. When a woman follows such **maxims**[4] as these, then she may be said to humble herself before others.

Let a woman retire late to bed, but rise early to duties; let her not dread tasks by day or by night. Let her not refuse to perform domestic duties whether easy or

---

[1] potsherd—broken pottery; used as a weight in spinning thread.

[2] **indubitably**—without doubt.

[3] **epitomize**—typify, summarize.

[4] **maxims**—rules of conduct.

difficult. That which must be done, let her finish completely, tidily, and systematically. When a woman follows such rules as these, then she may be said to be industrious.

Let a woman be correct in manner and upright in character in order to serve her husband. Let her live in purity and quietness of spirit, and attend to her own affairs. Let her love not gossip and silly laughter. Let her cleanse and purify and arrange in order the wine and the food for the offerings to the ancestors. When a woman observes such principles as these, then she may be said to continue ancestral worship.

No woman who observes these three fundamentals of life has ever had a bad reputation or has fallen into disgrace. If a woman fail to observe them, how can her name be honored; how can she but bring disgrace upon herself?

Husband and Wife

The Way of husband and wife is intimately connected with yin and yang,[5] and relates the individual to gods and ancestors. Truly it is the great principle of Heaven and Earth, and the great basis of human relationships. . . .

If a husband be unworthy, then he possesses nothing by which to control his wife. If a wife be unworthy, then she possesses nothing with which to serve her husband. If a husband does not control his wife, then the rules of conduct manifesting his authority are abandoned and broken. If a wife does not serve her husband, then the proper relationship between men and

women and the natural order of things are neglected and destroyed. As a matter of fact, the purpose of these two, the controlling of women by men and the serving of men by women, is the same.

Now examine the gentlemen of the present age. They only know that wives must be controlled and that the husband's rules of conduct manifesting his authority must be established. They therefore teach their boys to read books and study histories. But they do not in the least understand that husbands and masters must also be served, and that the proper relationship and the rites should be maintained.

Yet only to teach men and not to teach women—is that not ignoring the essential relation between them? According to the *Rites* it is the rule to begin to teach children to read at the age of eight years, and by the age of fifteen years they ought then to be ready for cultural training. Only why should it not be that girls' education as well as boys' be according to this principle?

Respect and Caution

As yin and yang are not of the same nature, so man and woman have different characteristics. The distinctive quality of the yang is rigidity; the function of the yin is yielding. Man is honored for strength; a woman is beautiful on account of her gentleness. Hence there arose the common saying: "A man though born like a wolf may, it is feared, become a weak

---

[5] yin and yang—cosmic principles in Chinese thought whose interaction defines all things; yin is negative, dark, and feminine; yang is positive, bright, and masculine.

monstrosity; a woman though born like a mouse may, it is feared, become a tiger."

Now for self-culture nothing equals respect for others. To counteract firmness nothing equals compliance. Consequently it can be said that the Way of respect and acquiescence is woman's most important principle of conduct. So respect may be defined as nothing other than holding on to that which is permanent; and acquiescence nothing other than being liberal and generous. Those who are steadfast in devotion know that they should stay in their proper places; those who are liberal and generous esteem others, and honor and serve them.

If husband and wife have the habit of staying together, never leaving one another, and following each other around within the limited space of their own rooms, then they will lust after and take liberties with one another. From such action improper language will arise between the two. This kind of discussion may lead to **licentiousness.**[6] Out of licentiousness will be born a heart of disrespect to the husband. Such a result comes from not knowing that one should stay in one's proper place.

Furthermore, affairs may be either crooked or straight; words may be either right or wrong. Straightforwardness cannot but lead to quarreling; crookedness cannot but lead to accusation. If there are really accusations and quarrels, then undoubtedly there will be angry affairs. Such a result comes not from esteeming others, and not honoring and serving them.

If wives suppress not contempt for husbands, then it follows that such wives rebuke and scold their husbands. If husbands stop not short of anger, then they are certain to beat their wives. The correct relationship between husband and wife is based upon harmony and intimacy, and conjugal love is grounded in proper union. Should actual blows be dealt, how could matrimonial relationship be preserved? Should sharp words be spoken, how could conjugal love exist? If love and proper relationship both be destroyed, then husband and wife are divided.

Womanly Qualifications

A woman ought to have four qualifications: 1. womanly virtue, 2. womanly words, 3. womanly bearing, and 4. womanly work. Now what is called womanly virtue need not be brilliant ability, exceptionally different from others. Womanly words need be neither clever in debate nor keen in conversation. Womanly appearance requires neither a pretty nor a perfect face and form. Womanly work need not be work done more skillfully than that of others.

To guard carefully her chastity, to control **circumspectly**[7] her behavior, in every motion to exhibit modesty, and to model each act on the best usage—this is womanly virtue.

To choose her words with care, to avoid vulgar language, to speak at appropriate times, and not to weary others with

---

[6] **licentiousness**—unrestrained sexuality.

[7] **circumspectly**—watchfully.

much conversation may be called the characteristics of womanly words.

To wash and scrub filth away, to keep clothes and ornaments fresh and clean, to wash the head and bathe the body regularly, and to keep the person free from disgraceful filth may be called the characteristics of womanly bearing.

With wholehearted devotion to sew and to weave, to love not gossip and silly laughter, in cleanliness and order to prepare the wine and food for serving guests may be called the characteristics of womanly work.

These four qualifications characterize the greatest virtue of a woman. No woman can afford to be without them. In fact they are very easy to possess if a woman only treasure them in her heart. The ancients had a saying: "Is Love far off? If I desire love, then love is at hand!" So can it be said of these qualifications.

QUESTIONS TO CONSIDER

1. In Pan Chao's view, what traits would an ideal woman possess?

2. What kind of independence does Pan Chao encourage for women?

3. Pan Chao's thought is based on a view of women as dependent on and subordinate to men, a view that has been fought in modern times by the women's rights movement. Would a contemporary feminist find anything to approve in Lessons for Women?

4. Who can you think of who most closely resembles the ideal of womanliness presented by Pan Chao? Explain your reasons.

Japanese Court Journals

Much of the best prose literature in early Japan was written by the women of the Japanese court, who produced diaries, letters, essays, and fiction. The most famous of these writers was Murasaki Shikibu (c. 928–1031?), whose long novel of court life, The Tale of Genji, *is one of the masterpieces of world literature. In addition to her fiction, Murasaki Shikibu also left a vivid record of her own life in her diary. The most brilliant of her contemporaries at court was Sei Shōnagon, who created a sharply observed picture of the world around her and a fascinating self-portrait in her journal,* The Pillow Book.

from *The Diary of Murasaki Shikibu*

Lady Sei Shōnagon. A very proud person. She values herself highly, and scatters her Chinese writings all about. Yet should we study her closely, we should find that she is still imperfect. She tries to be exceptional, but naturally persons of that sort give offence. She is piling up trouble for her future. One who is too richly gifted, who indulges too much in emotion, even when she ought to be reserved, and cannot turn aside from anything she is interested in, in spite of herself will lose self-control. How can such a vain and reckless person end her days happily! . . .

Having no excellence within myself, I have passed my days without making any special impression on any one. Especially the fact that I have no man who will look out for my future makes me comfortless. I do not wish to bury myself in dreariness. Is it because of my worldly mind that I feel lonely? On moonlight nights in autumn, when I am hopelessly sad, I often go out on the balcony and gaze dreamily at the moon. It makes me think of days gone by. People say that it is dangerous to look at the moon in solitude, but something impels me, and sitting a little withdrawn I muse there. In the wind-cooled evening I play on the koto,[1] though others may not care to hear it. I fear that my playing betrays the sorrow which becomes more intense, and I become disgusted with myself—so foolish and miserable am I.

---

[1] koto—Japanese stringed instrument.

My room is ugly, blackened by smoke. I play on a thirteen or six-stringed koto, but I neglect to take away the bridges[2] even in rainy weather, and I lean it up against the wall between the cabinet and the door jamb.[3] On either side of the koto stands a lute [Japanese biwa]. A pair of big bookcases have in them all the books they can hold. In one of them are placed old poems and romances. They are the homes of worms which come frightening us when we turn the pages, so none ever wish to read them. As to the other cabinet, since the person[4] who placed his own books there no hand has touched it. When I am bored to death I take out one or two of them; then my maids gather around me and say: "Your life will not be favored with old age if you do such a thing! Why do you read Chinese? Formerly even the reading of Sutras[5] was not encouraged for women." They **rebuke**[6] me in the shade [that is, behind my back]. I have heard of it and have wished to say, "It is far from certain that he who does no forbidden thing enjoys a long life," but it would be a lack of reserve to say it to the maids. Our deeds vary with our age and deeds vary with the individual. Some are proud to read books, others look over old cast-away writings because they are bored with having nothing to do. It would not be becoming for such a one to chatter away about religious thoughts, noisily shaking a rosary.[7] I feel this, and before my women keep myself from doing what otherwise I could do easily. But after all, when I was among the ladies of the court I did not say what I wanted to say either, for it is useless to talk with those who do not understand one and troublesome to talk with those who criticize from a feeling of superiority. Especially one-sided persons are troublesome. Few are accomplished in many arts and most cling narrowly to their own opinion.

Pretty and coy, shrinking from sight, unsociable, proud, fond of romance, vain and poetic, looking down upon others with a jealous eye—such is the opinion of those who do not know me, but after seeing me they say, "You are wonderfully gentle to meet with; I cannot identify you with that imagined one."

I see that I have been slighted, hated, and looked down upon as an old gossip, and I must bear it, for it is my destiny to be solitary. The Queen said once, "You were ever mindful not to show your soul, but I have become more intimate with you than others."

from *The Pillow Book*
Sei Shōnagon

In Spring It Is the Dawn
In spring it is the dawn that is most beautiful. As the light creeps over the hills, their outlines are dyed a faint red and wisps of purplish cloud trail over them.

---

[2] bridges—thin wedges that raise the strings of a musical instrument above the sounding board.

[3] jamb—vertical frame of a doorway.

[4] the person—Murasaki's dead husband.

[5] Sutras—Buddhist scriptures.

[6] **rebuke**—criticize sharply.

[7] rosary—string of beads used to count prayers.

In summer the nights. Not only when the moon shines, but on dark nights too, as the fireflies flit to and fro, and even when it rains, how beautiful it is!

In autumn the evenings, when the glittering sun sinks close to the edge of the hills and the crows fly back to their nests in threes and fours and twos; more charming still is a file of wild geese, like specks in the distant sky. When the sun has set, one's heart is moved by the sound of the wind and the hum of the insects.

In winter the early mornings. It is beautiful indeed when snow has fallen during the night, but splendid too when the ground is white with frost; or even when there is no snow or frost, but it is simply very cold and the attendants hurry from room to room stirring up the fires and bringing charcoal, how well this fits the season's mood! But as noon approaches and the cold wears off, no one bothers to keep the **braziers**[8] alight, and soon nothing remains but piles of white ashes.

When I Make Myself Imagine

When I make myself imagine what it is like to be one of those women who live at home, faithfully serving their husbands—women who have not a single exciting prospect in life yet who believe that they are perfectly happy—I am filled with scorn. Often they are of quite good birth, yet have had no opportunity to find out what the world is like. I wish they could live for a while in our society, even if it should mean taking service as

Attendants, so that they might come to know the delights it has to offer.

I cannot bear men who believe that women serving in the Palace are bound to be frivolous and wicked. Yet I suppose their prejudice is understandable. After all, women at Court do not spend their time hiding modestly behind fans and screens, but walk about, looking openly at people they chance to meet. Yes, they see everyone face to face, not only ladies-in-waiting like themselves, but even Their Imperial Majesties (whose **august**[9] names I hardly dare mention), High Court Nobles, senior courtiers, and other gentlemen of high rank. In the presence of such exalted personages the women in the Palace are all equally **brazen,**[10] whether they be the maids of ladies-in-waiting, or the relations of Court ladies who have come to visit them, or housekeepers, or latrine-cleaners, or women who are of no more value than a roof-tile or a pebble. Small wonder that the young men regard them as immodest! Yet are the gentlemen themselves any less so? They are not exactly bashful when it comes to looking at the great people in the Palace. No, everyone at Court is much the same in this respect. . . .

Hateful Things

One is in a hurry to leave, but one's visitor keeps chattering away. If it is someone of no importance, one can get rid of

---

[8] **braziers**—containers for holding hot coals to heat a room.

[9] **august**—majestic.

[10] **brazen**—bold.

him by saying, "You must tell me all about it next time"; but, should it be the sort of visitor whose presence commands one's best behavior, the situation is hateful indeed.

One finds that a hair got caught in the stone on which one is rubbing one's ink-stick, or again that gravel is lodged in the inkstick, making a nasty, grating sound.

Someone has suddenly fallen ill and one summons the exorcist.[11] Since he is not at home, one has to send messengers to look for him. After one has had a long fretful wait, the exorcist finally arrives, and with a sigh of relief one asks him to start his **incantations**.[12] But perhaps he has been exorcising too many evil spirits recently; for hardly has he installed himself and begun praying when his voice becomes drowsy. Oh, how hateful!

A man who has nothing in particular to recommend him discusses all sorts of subjects at random as though he knew everything.

An elderly person warms the palms of his hands over a brazier and stretches out the wrinkles. No young man would dream of behaving in such a fashion; old people can really be quite shameless. I have seen some dreary old creatures actually resting their feet on the brazier and rubbing them against the edge while they speak. These are the kind of people who in visiting someone's house first use their fans to wipe away the dust from the mat and, when they finally sit on it, cannot stay still but are forever spreading out the front of their hunting costume or even tucking it up under their knees. One might suppose that such behavior was restricted to people of humble station; but I have observed it in quite well-bred people, including a Senior Secretary of the Fifth Rank in the Ministry of Ceremonial and a former Governor of Suruga.

I hate the sight of men in their cups[13] who shout, poke their fingers in their mouths, stroke their beards, and pass on the wine to their neighbors with great cries of "Have some more! Drink up!" They tremble, shake their heads, twist their faces, and **gesticulate**[14] like children who are singing, "We're off to see the Governor." I have seen really well-bred people behave like this and I find it most distasteful.

To envy others and to complain about one's own lot; to speak badly about people; to be inquisitive about the most trivial matters and to resent and abuse people for not telling one, or, if one does manage to worm out some facts, to inform everyone in the most detailed fashion as if one had known all from the beginning—oh, how hateful!

One is just about to be told some interesting piece of news when a baby starts crying.

A flight of crows circle about with loud caws.

An admirer has come on a clandestine visit, but a dog catches sight of him and starts barking. One feels like killing the beast. . . .

---

[11] exorcist—healer who attempts to drive an evil spirit from an afflicted person.

[12] **incantations**—magic spells spoken or chanted.

[13] in their cups—intoxicated.

[14] **gesticulate**—gesture in an animated manner.

Things That Make One's Heart Beat Faster

Sparrows feeding their young. To pass a place where babies are playing. To sleep in a room where some fine incense has been burnt. To notice that one's elegant Chinese mirror has become a little cloudy. To see a gentleman stop his carriage before one's gate and instruct his attendants to announce his arrival. To wash one's hair, make one's toilet,[15] and put on scented robes; even if not a soul sees one, these preparations still produce an inner pleasure.

It is night and one is expecting a visitor. Suddenly one is startled by the sound of rain-drops, which the wind blows against the shutters.

Things That Arouse a Fond Memory of the Past

Dried hollyhock.[16] The objects used during the Display of Dolls.[17] To find a piece of deep violet or grape-colored material that has been pressed between the pages of a notebook.

It is a rainy day and one is feeling bored. To pass the time, one starts looking through some old papers. And then one comes across the letters of a man one used to love.

Last year's paper fan. A night with a clear moon.

A Preacher Ought To Be Good-Looking

A preacher ought to be good-looking. For, if we are properly to understand his worthy sentiments, we must keep our eyes on him while he speaks; should we look

away, we may forget to listen. Accordingly an ugly preacher may well be the source of sin. . . .

But I really must stop writing this kind of thing. If I were still young enough, I might risk the consequence of putting down such impieties, but at my present stage of life I should be less **flippant.**[18]

Some people, on hearing that a priest is particularly venerable and pious, rush off to the temple where he is preaching, determined to arrive before anyone else. They, too, are liable to bring a load of sin on themselves and would do better to stay away. . . .

Elegant Things

Pre: What are elegant thing?

A white coat worn over a violet waistcoat.
Duck eggs.
Shaved ice mixed with liana syrup and put in a new silver bowl.[19]
A rosary of rock crystal.
Wisteria blossoms. Plum blossoms covered with snow.
A pretty child eating strawberries.

Things That Cannot Be Compared

Summer and winter. Night and day. Rain and sunshine. Youth and age. A person's laughter and his anger. Black and

---

[15] make one's toilet—groom oneself.

[16] dried hollyhock—dried flowers used as decorations in a Japanese festival.

[17] Display of Dolls—Japanese festival.

[18] **flippant**—lacking in seriousness.

[19] shaved ice . . . silver bowl—used as a refreshment in summer.

white. Love and hatred. The little indigo plant and the great philodendron. Rain and mist.

When one has stopped loving somebody, one feels that he has become someone else, even though he is still the same person. In a garden full of evergreens the crows are all asleep. Then, towards the middle of the night, the crows in one of the trees suddenly wake up in a great flurry and start flapping about. Their unrest spreads to the other trees, and soon all the birds have been startled from their sleep and are cawing in alarm. How different from the same crows in daytime!

QUESTIONS TO CONSIDER

1. Why does Murasaki Shikibu seem to be suffering?

2. In her diary, Lady Murasaki criticizes Sei Shōnagon for being arrogant, overly emotional, and too enthusiastic in pursuit of her interests. Do you agree with this estimate of Shōnagon's character? Why or why not?

3. What is Sei Shōnagon's attitude toward domestic life?

4. Based on these two works, how much independence was exercised by the women of the Japanese court?

[handwritten annotations: Japanese/Asian - minimalism in art + poetry (nothing other - emotion w/ restraint) ✳ pick something - capture essence in 3 words]

Chinese and Japanese Poetry

Poetry in China tended to be brief lyrics written on a variety of themes, including the beauty of nature, rural life, family relationships, romantic love, and friendship. The two most highly regarded Chinese poets were Li Po (701–762) and Tu Fu (712–770). Although they were close friends, they represent opposite cultural tendencies in their verse: Li Po expresses a Taoist romanticism; Tu Fu a Confucian rationalism. Japanese poets also excelled in short lyric forms, the briefest being the haiku, in which seventeen syllables are arranged in three lines (5–7–5). The greatest master of the haiku form was Matsuo Munefusa (1644–1694), who used the pseudonym Bashō. The following poems by Li Po, Tu Fu, and Bashō all convey an intense sense of solitude—either that of the speaker or of the subject.

In the Quiet Night

LI PO

So bright a gleam on the foot of my bed—
Could there have been a frost already?
Lifting myself to look, I found that it was moonlight.
Sinking back again, I thought suddenly of home.

A Sigh from a Staircase of Jade

LI PO

Her jade-white staircase is cold with dew;
Her silk soles are wet, she lingered there so long . . .
Behind her closed **casement**,[1] why is she still waiting,
Watching through its crystal pane the glow of the autumn moon?

---

[1] **casement**—window.

Remembering My Brothers on a Moonlight Night

TU FU

A wanderer hears drums **portending**[2] battle.
By the first call of autumn from a wild-goose at the border,
He knows that the dews tonight will be frost.
. . . How much brighter the moonlight is at home!
O my brothers, lost and scattered,
What is life to me without you?
Yet if **missives**[3] in time of peace go wrong—
What can I hope for during war?

A Night Abroad

TU FU

A light wind is rippling at the grassy shore. . . .
Through the night, to my motionless tall mast,
The stars lean down from open space,
And the moon comes running up the river.
. . . If only my art might bring me fame
And free my sick old age from office!—
Flitting, flitting, what am I like
But a sand-snipe[4] in the wide, wide world!

Clouds

BASHŌ

Clouds come from time to time—
   and bring to men a chance to rest
   from looking at the moon.

---

[2] **portending**—foreshadowing.

[3] **missives**—messages, letters.

[4] sand-snipe—small shorebird.

The Poor Man's Son

BASHŌ

Poverty's child—
    he starts to grind the rice,
    and gazes at the moon.

Darkness

BASHŌ

On a withered branch
a crow has settled—
    autumn nightfall.

In a Wide Wasteland

BASHŌ

On the **moor**:[5] from things
    detached completely—
    how the skylark sings!

---

[5] **moor**—stretch of open wasteland.

QUESTIONS TO CONSIDER

1. What situation is presented in "A Sigh from a Staircase of Jade"?

2. What is the tone of the recollections of home in Li Po's "In the Quiet Night" and Tu Fu's "Remembering My Brothers on a Moonlight Night"?

3. What are the different ways in which imagery of the moon functions in these poems?

4. What is the difference between the feeling of solitude created by "Darkness" and "In a Wide Wasteland"?

Landscape Art

For the Chinese, painting or viewing landscape art was a spiritual act. Depictions of landscapes, such as the lovely scene in The Poet Lin Bu Walking in the Moonlight *by Chinese painter Du Jin (active late 1400s), express the harmony between natural things and the cosmic order. Japanese landscape art also aimed at evoking the beauty and serenity of nature, even with an unpromising subject, as in* Night Rain at Karasaki *by Ando Hiroshige (1797–1858).*

▲
Hiroshige explored the potential for beauty in bad weather in this print of a rain-soaked tree.

Du Jin used delicate but spontaneous brushwork to convey the outlines of tree and rock in this painting. ▶

QUESTIONS TO CONSIDER

1. Is the view of solitude taken by Du Jin's painting like that in Tu Fu's poem "A Night Abroad" (page 110)? Why or why not?

2. Is the mood created by Hiroshige's woodcut like that of Bashō's poem "Darkness" (page 111)? Why or why not?

3. Which artist seems more realistic in his depiction of landscape?

Chinese Literature and Its Characteristics

LIU WU-CHI

Testifying to the unbroken continuity of traditional Chinese culture, one historian has observed, "Every Chinese is born at least thirty-five hundred years old." While there have been challenges to this tradition—the most recent being the Cultural Revolution begun by the Communist government in the late 1960s—the basic patterns of Chinese culture remain remarkably constant. In this essay, Liu Wu-Chi examines how some of the fundamental characteristics of traditional culture are reflected in Chinese literature.

Cataclysmic[1] changes past and present notwithstanding, China is still a land which treasures its great traditions. Chinese culture, marked by antiquity, continuity, and constant renewal, has remained essentially **homogeneous**[2] for at least three thousand years. As early as 1400 B.C., archaeological evidence indicates, the Chinese people had already a remarkable civilization supported by a well-advanced writing system and a fine technology of bronze casting and sericulture.[3] During the incomparably long Chou dynasty, which lasted some eight hundred years—until the third century B.C.—much of ancient Chinese civilization, built upon a sociopolitical structure that closely resembled the feudal system[4] in medieval Europe, was firmly established. This was the period of classical Chinese philosophy, in which great thinkers from the newly risen intellectual class vied with each other to win the minds of the rulers and the people alike. The brilliance of this philosophy was matched only by that of the poetry which flourished at about the same time in the Yellow River and Yangtze[5] regions.

---

[1] **cataclysmic**—characterized by violent upheaval.

[2] **homogeneous**—composed of similar elements.

[3] sericulture—production of silk.

[4] feudal system—social system in which land is exchanged for military service.

[5] Yellow River and Yangtze—chief river systems of China.

Chinese culture continued to develop for another two thousand years from the Han through the T'ang and Sung eras to the modern period. During the centuries, this culture remained almost unchallenged and basically unimpaired in the face of political disruptions and civil wars, changing dynasties, and the conquest of the country by non-Chinese ethnic groups from beyond the Great Wall.[6] . . .

Other foreign influences also contributed to Chinese civilization. Buddhism,[7] which was first brought to China from Central Asia, not only offered the Chinese a new attitude toward life and thought, but also stimulated their creativity in painting, sculpture, and literature. In our own period, Western science and technology have increased man's knowledge of the world and the universe; they have also brought to the Chinese an awareness of the **inexorable**[8] laws of nature, the determining factors of social environment, and the need to cope with both. All these ideas are reflected in modern Chinese literature. Thus nourishment from abroad has sustained periodically the growth of Chinese culture, and prevented **stagnation**[9] and decadence. While absorbing foreign influences, the Chinese have been able to keep intact their own culture, which has been constantly expanding and thriving.

Whatever native ingredients and alien elements entered into the melting pot of Chinese civilization, its main component has been essentially Confucianism, which consists of the teachings of Confucius, Mencius, and their followers in subsequent ages. Especially important among later scholars were the Neo-Confucianists of the Sung and Ming periods, who, in the typical **eclectic**[10] manner in which Chinese thinkers formulated their teachings, instilled into Confucianism selected portions of Taoism[11] and Buddhism. After that time, the Neo-Confucian teachings and interpretations of the Confucian classics became standard works of reference for candidates in the state examination, which required a knowledge of the Confucian doctrines. Since successful scholars were appointed to offices in the government and could look forward, if they were ambitious and clever enough, to climbing the bureaucratic ladder to positions of power and influence, the Confucian classics, which formed the literary basis of the examinations, became the most immediate concern of the would-be scholar-officials.

A practicable moral philosophy that teaches the rules of personal cultivation and the virtues of human relationship, Confucianism has molded the Chinese national character and pervaded every aspect of Chinese society, the family, literature and the arts. In a broad sense, much of Chinese literature is Confucian literature.

---

[6] Great Wall—1,400-mile-long defensive barrier completed in the 3rd century B.C. to guard China's northern frontier.

[7] Buddhism—Indian philosophy based on the teachings of the Buddha (page 50).

[8] **inexorable**—unalterable.

[9] **stagnation**—sluggishness.

[10] **eclectic**—chosen from various sources.

[11] Taoism—Chinese philosophy based on the teachings of Lao Tzu (page 80).

The all-embracing influence of Confucianism worked in two ways: it affected the life and ideas of writers who followed the tradition, and of those who reacted against it. Generally speaking, Confucianism triumphed in times of peace and prosperity, but when the country was in disorder, Taoism and Buddhism took over, gaining a large following among the people.

> There is always a moral lesson in a work of Chinese literature.

Similarly in a man's personal life, success strengthened his belief in the Confucian orthodoxy while disappointments bred in him a desire to wander astray to the other-worldliness of Buddhism and Taoism. It was the rebels from Confucianism who deviated from the norm and carved out new paths in literary fields. They found their inspiration sometimes abroad but oftener among the common people, whose spring of native wit and emotion replenished constantly the dwindling **reservoir**[12] of literary sources and materials depleted by long periods of use.

The majority of Chinese writers, however, have been **conformists**[13] to the grand Confucian tradition. To them, literature has been a vehicle for the communication of the aim of Confucian doctrine: to teach and influence people to be good. Thus there is always a moral lesson in a work of Chinese literature. In literary criticism, aesthetic excellence was considered secondary to moral soundness. In the course of centuries there had been built up a large body of moral treatises, exhortations and admonitions, and though modern critics tend to **disparage**[14] them, their sway over the Chinese mind and conduct was great and lasting. Likewise, history was highly regarded for its moral and political import, the lessons of the past being held up as a mirror for the present and future. One of the four major divisions of a Chinese library, history ranked next to the Confucian classics in importance, above philosophy and belles-lettres.[15] Enriched by a vast bulk of historical materials, Chinese literary writings abound in allusions to historical figures and events, a knowledge of which is even now a criterion for Chinese scholarship.

Influenced by Confucian ethics, the Chinese were especially strong in their sense of right and wrong, which naturally found expression in literature. This moral concern gave rise to the concept of poetic justice, which is as much Chinese as Greek. The idea that virtue is to be rewarded and vice punished was propagated by Confucian philosophers and embodied in the heavens and hells of the Buddhist and Taoist religions. The three great Chinese doctrines merged in the common belief in retribution, a popular **tenet**[16] upheld by all and sundry whatever their philosophy or

---

[12] **reservoir**—stock.

[13] **conformists**—those who act in accord with group standards.

[14] **disparage**—belittle.

[15] belles-lettres—literature such as poetry, fiction, essays.

[16] **tenet**—belief, opinion.

religion. This belief, amply demonstrated in literature, deterred the growth of anything like the Western concept of tragedy. Though a man may fall victim to the snares of fate and suffer from tragedies in real life, it would be the Chinese writer's duty to see to it that in literature's make-believe world sorrows are toned down and virtues are praised and duly recompensed. From the Chinese point of view it would be a blemish in a literary work not to give its readers a sense of satisfaction in the ultimate vindication and triumph of the good and virtuous.

All these considerations strengthened the Chinese belief in the pragmatic view of literature. Instead of being the mysterious or **inscrutable**[17] Orientals represented by Westerners in their early reports on China, the Chinese were and are a practical people, have supported the down to earth teachings of Confucius, and created a literature whose main function is **utilitarian**[18] rather than **aesthetic**.[19] Brushing aside as worthless the concept of art for art's sake, Chinese writers pressed philosophy and history into the service of literature, not because of their contribution to knowledge and truth but because of their usefulness to humanity. . . .

The writing of poetry, which has been generally regarded in the West as the most imaginative and loftiest of all literary forms, was in China a common, everyday undertaking of the intellectuals. Chinese poets, unlike some of their Western compeers who happily built their castles in the air, were on the whole earthbound and **mundane**.[20] They were disturbed neither by poetic agonies and aesthetic aspirations, nor by the thrills of romantic excursions into the mind and the universe. Instead, they were content with weaving songs out of the materials of daily life and occupation. Almost every educated Chinese was a poet who turned out verses as fast as there was an occasion for them. And in China there were numerous occasions for poetry: court celebrations and religious festivities; weddings and funerals; garden parties, where the beauties of the peonies and chrysanthemums were **felicitated**;[21] convivial feasts during which, after a generous flow of wine, companies were promoted, merged and dissolved; trips to scenic spots, where even the latent poetic talent would burst into bloom—these and a thousand and one other occasions, on which, no matter how trivial they seemed, poetry was the language that spoke understandingly and pleasurably to the heart. . . .

One of the striking features of Chinese poetry is compactness, the most popular forms being four-line and eight-line poems, with five or seven words in each line. For the Chinese, brevity was the soul of poetry. Within this limited scope, fine workmanship became a major requirement for excellence, and each word was weighed carefully for artistic effect. There is an interesting though probably apocryphal story of the T'ang poet Li Po's making fun

---

[17] **inscrutable**—impossible to understand.

[18] **utilitarian**—concerned with usefulness.

[19] **aesthetic**—concerned with beauty.

[20] **mundane**—common, ordinary.

[21] **felicitated**—congratulated.

of his friend, Tu Fu, for the latter's painstaking efforts at writing poetry. One day, meeting Tu Fu on the top of a hill, Li Po was said to have accosted him in the following verse:

How thin, wretchedly thin you have
grown!
Have you been suffering from poetry
again?

Another story tells of the hard way in which Chia Tao, a later T'ang poet, settled a point of versification. Walking one day on the busy, crowded streets of metropolitan Ch'ang-an, Chia Tao was beating rhythm with a stick when he knocked down a front carrier of an official sedan.[22] He had been debating whether he should use the word "push" or "knock" in the line

The monk knocks at the moonlit door.

Thus, deeply immersed in thought, he began to push and knock until he inadvertently upset the official procession. Fortunately for Chia Tao, the great dignitary in the sedan chair was no other than the famous writer Han Yü. The latter not only forgave the distressed poet but also settled the poetic problem for him in favor of the word "knock." Since then the term "push and knock" has become synonymous with a writer's careful deliberation in literary compositions.

Music was another important asset of Chinese poetry. All its three major types, shih, tz'u, and ch'ü, were originally sung with accompaniment by music. Later, when music was **weaned**[23] from poetry, a complicated prosody was evolved with definite rhyming schemes and tonal patterns. Though no longer set to music, Chinese poems were written to be read aloud, probably in much the same way as the Greek were. It was quite an experience to watch an old fashioned scholar shaking his head and wagging his queue[24] with a great deal of gusto and relish as he recited a poem, intoning every word in such a way as to bring out the best musical qualities of the verse he declaimed. This kind of poetry recitation, however, has become a lost art today.

Basing their creativity upon brevity, artistry, and music, Chinese poets managed to bring into being with the magic of words a fairyland of poetry. The commonplace which is transformed into the wonderful is not far to seek, for its like is here in all our little worlds: on the hearths of our homes, warm with friendship and family love, in the moon that smiles and the flowers that beckon to us, in the landscape paintings that recreate the beauty of nature in a series of pictorial images. Poetry too can keep us company when we are traveling in distant lands. Extremely nostalgic, the frequently exiled Chinese poets were unconsolable in their yearnings for their native land, strong in their expressions of

---

[22] sedan—or sedan chair, enclosed litter carried on poles.
[23] **weaned**—separated from.
[24] queue—long braid of hair.

domestic attachment, and insistent in their reminiscences of the golden age that had slipped away. All these sentiments are natural and ordinary enough, but in the voices of the poets they become poignantly beautiful in rhythmic utterances. The Chinese writers have performed the miracle of transforming the homely into the beautiful, of investing the trivia of daily life with a halo of poetry, or, rather, they have proved, in the words of a critic, that common sense, the most salutary and the most nearly universal sense, is also at the heart of the sense of beauty itself, quickened and yet sobered by the wistful warmth of humanity.

QUESTIONS TO CONSIDER

1. How would you describe the role of Confucianism in both continuity and change in the Chinese cultural tradition?

2. According to Liu Wu-Chi, traditional Chinese literature is moral in purpose and characterized by the "triumph of the good and virtuous." Do you see a "happy ending" as essential to teaching a moral lesson? Why or why not?

3. How would you distinguish between the traditional Western and Chinese attitudes toward the writing of poetry? Which attitude seems more appropriate to you?

The Japanese Appreciation of Nature

YURIKO SAITO

Depictions of nature in many cultural traditions have stressed the strength and timelessness of natural phenomena; by contrast, Japanese depictions of nature have often emphasized such qualities as delicacy and transitoriness. In this essay, Yuriko Saito explores the Japanese attitudes towards nature that produce this tendency.

Many commentators have noted that the Japanese appreciation of nature is directed exclusively towards those objects and phenomena which are small, charming and tame. This characteristic becomes conspicuous especially when we compare it with the Western and other Oriental (such as Chinese and Korean) traditions which appreciate not only those small, tame objects of nature but also gigantic or frightful aspects of nature.

Citing various short ancient poems which are perhaps the best record of the traditional Japanese appreciation of nature, Hajime Nakamura points out that "the love of nature, in the case of the Japanese, is tied up with their tendencies to cherish **minute**[1] things and treasure delicate things." Even when a grand landscape is appreciated, it is not the grandeur or awesome scale of the scene but rather its composition compressed into a compact design that is praised. . . .

A graphic illustration of the Japanese appreciation of mountains as friendly and warm rather than hostile and formidable can be found in some of the wood block prints of the Edo period. Consider, for example, Ando Hiroshige's depiction of Mount Hakone from the *Fifty-Three Sceneries of Tōkaido*. While successfully conveying the difficulty of passing this steep mountain by fantastically exaggerating its profile, this print does not give the viewer an impression that the mountain is hostile, or that it challenges us to conquer it. Moreover, despite its steep shape, the size of the mountain relative to the size of men in procession is rather reduced, avoiding the

[1] **minute**—tiny.

impression that the mountain is overbearing. In addition, the color used for the men in procession and the mountain are almost indistinguishable, again avoiding a stark contrast between the two.

The same observation can be made of the Japanese depiction of the sea. . . .

Even when a rough sea is depicted in visual art (which is not frequent), it never gives the impression of ferociousness. Take, for example, the famous wood block print by Katsushika Hokusai of a gigantic wave almost swallowing boats, with Mount Fuji seen at a distance. While the represented state of affairs might be horrifying, the work does not convey such a feeling at all. Although highly evocative of dynamic movement, because of a fairly contrived and calculated composition with a distant Mount Fuji as a static focal point, this print gives us a feeling which is neither insecure nor dreadful.

Likewise, creatures depicted by the Japanese are often small, harmless ones such as butterflies, warblers, copper pheasants, cuckoos. On the other hand, ferocious, life-endangering animals such as tigers are frequently objects of appreciation in other traditions. Indeed, in the Japanese tradition we do not find a praise for "forests filled with wild beasts"; instead there is a constant appreciation of things which are "small, gentle and intimate."

Some thinkers ascribe this conspicuous absence of the sublime in the Japanese appreciation of nature wholly to Japan's relatively tame landscape and mild climate. Tall cliffs, unbounded landscapes and soaring mountains may indeed be lacking in Japanese **topography.**[2] However, the lack of appreciation of the sublime in the Japanese tradition cannot be wholly accounted for by reference to this factor. The fierce and awful aspects of nature such as annual autumn typhoons, earthquakes and rough seas are fully experienced by the Japanese, perhaps most eloquently documented by a mediaeval Buddhist **recluse,**[3] Kamo no Chōmei, in his *An Account of My Hut* (1212).

In spite of the frequent occurrences of devastating typhoons, however, it is noteworthy that the morning *after* a typhoon, not the typhoon itself, is praised for its aesthetic appeal in three major classics in the Japanese tradition: *The Pillow Book* (c. 1002), *The Tale of Genji* (c. 1004) and *Essays in Idleness* (c. 1340). For example, in *The Pillow Book*, a series of anecdotes and essays concerning the Heian period court life, Sei Shōnagon praises the beauty of the morning after the storm without describing her experience of the storm itself during the previous night. The only reference made to the storm is her amazement at recognizing the arrangement of leaves "one by one through the chinks of the lattice-window" is the work of "the same wind which yesterday raged so violently.". . .

The lack of appreciation of the sublime in the Japanese appreciation of nature . . . is explained by the Japanese view of nature in its relation to man. Rather than conceiving the relationship between man and nature as contrasting, I shall argue that the Japanese

---

[2] **topography**—surface features of a geographical area.
[3] **recluse**—hermit.

appreciate nature primarily for its identity with man. As Masaharu Anesaki observes:

> Both Buddhism and Shintoism[4] teach that the things of nature are not essentially unlike mankind, and that they are endowed with spirits similar to those of men. Accordingly awe and sublimity are almost unknown in Japanese painting and poetry, but beauty and grace and gentleness are visible in every work of art.

In what way then is nature considered to be essentially the same as man in the Japanese tradition? There are two ways in which the Japanese have traditionally identified with nature. One may be called emotional identification and the other is identification based upon the transience of both man and nature.

There is a long tradition in Japanese literature of emotional expression in terms of natural objects or phenomena. Lament and love, two strong emotions which constitute the major subject-matters of Japanese literature, are often expressed not directly but in terms of or by reference to nature. This tradition goes as far back as the oldest anthology of Japanese poems, *Manyōshu*, compiled in the eighth century. Shuichi Katō explains that this anthology indicates "the court poets of the *Manyōshu* expressed their profound feelings in terms of their daily natural surroundings.". . .

Some natural objects and phenomena are associated with certain emotive content in Japanese literature so frequently that they have been established as symbols for expressing particular emotions. For example, cherry blossoms (especially when they are falling) are often associated with sorrow in classical Japanese literature because they **epitomize**[5] the transience of beauty. The autumn evening is a favorite symbol among medieval poets for expressing desolation and loneliness. . . .

The Japanese appreciation of nature for its **affinity**[6] rather than contrast with man has another basis. In addition to appreciating the relatively small and gentle objects and phenomena of nature, the Japanese are also known for their appreciation of the transitory aspects of nature. This fact is most significantly reflected in the traditional phrase by which the Japanese refer to nature as an object of appreciation—*kachōfugetsū*, flower, bird, wind and moon. Flowers (most notably cherry blossoms) do not stay in bloom forever; the bird song is always changing and passing; wind is literally passing and transitory by definition; and the moon is constantly changing its appearance and location. Indeed these natural objects and phenomena form the favorite subjects for Japanese art. Other natural objects and phenomena frequently referred to in Japanese art are also short-lived: rain, dew, fog, insects, and various seasonal flowers.

The Japanese preoccupation with the change of seasons should be understood in this regard. In many instances of appreciation of nature from the earliest record, the

---

[4] **Buddhism and Shintoism**—Buddhism is an Indian philosophy based on the teachings of the Buddha (page 50); Shintoism is the traditional religion of Japan, combining nature and ancestor worship.

[5] **epitomize**—provide a perfect example.

[6] **affinity**—close relationship.

Japanese have been most sensitive to the characteristics of each season and the transition from one to the other. Consider the following examples. *The Pillow Book* begins with the famous description of the best of each season; . . . a famous passage in *Essays in Idleness* (a well-known series of essays by a fourteenth-century retired Buddhist monk, Yoshida Kenkō) also is directed towards appreciating the transition of seasons. . . .

What is the basis for this Japanese appreciation of the transitory nature of natural objects and phenomena? There is an immediate aesthetic appeal of something which does not last for long. Psychologically we tend to cherish and appreciate objects or events more if we know that they will never be the same. Hence, commentators discussing the notion of Japanese wisdom point out that the Japanese appreciation of the flower, moon and snow is based upon "regret for the transience of phenomena" which compels them to cherish "those rare occurrences fitting to each season and time."

A contemporary Japanese painter, Higashiyama Kaii, indicates that his experience of viewing the full moon in the spring against the foreground of drooping cherry blossoms in full bloom in the Maruyama district of Kyoto is intensified by the recognition of the transitory and non-recurring nature of the phenomenon.

> Flowers look up at the moon. The moon looks at the flowers. . . . This must be what is called an encounter. Flowers stay in their fullest bloom only for a short period of time and it is very difficult for them to encounter the moon. Moreover, the full moon is only for this one night. If cloudy or rainy, this view cannot be seen. Furthermore, I must be there to watch it. . . .
>
> If flowers are in full bloom all the time and if we exist forever, we won't be moved by this encounter. Flowers exhibit their glow of life by falling to the ground.

This frequent association between transience of nature and transience of human life stems from the conviction that nature and man are essentially the same, rooted in the same principle of existence. As Higashiyama remarks, referring to his discussion of viewing the full moon against the cherry blossoms at Maruyama.

> Nature is alive and always changing. At the same time, we ourselves, watching nature change, are also changing day by day. Both nature and ourselves are rooted in the same fated, ever-changing cycle of birth, growth, decline and death.

QUESTIONS TO CONSIDER

1. What central points does Yuriko Saito make about the Japanese appreciation of nature?

2. Do you agree with Saito that Hokusai's print (page 78) "gives us a feeling which is neither insecure nor dreadful"? Why or why not?

3. Would a view of nature emphasizing its affinity with human beings be the best way to protect the planet? Why or why not?

Linking Cultures

Sacred Places

Probably the earliest human art was an expression of concepts of the sacred. From the very beginning, storytelling, song, and dance were employed in sacred myth and ritual. The visual arts shaped the spaces dedicated to worship. These images of sacred places come from a variety of cultures and eras. As you examine them, reflect on these questions:

• What visual elements and themes appear in these monuments?
• What different moods do these monuments inspire?
• What do the monuments suggest about human ideas of the divine?

▲

Lascaux *(Paleolithic)*

In a sanctuary deep within a cave in southern France, hunters painted these magical images of the animals they pursued.

▲

Pyramids of Giza *(Egypt)*
Like artificial mountains, these colossal structures were built as a combination of temple and tomb for the kings of Egypt, who were worshipped as gods.

Stonehenge *(Neolithic)*
Erected by prehistoric peoples over centuries, this complex arrangement of standing stones and earthworks appears to be aligned to the movements of the sun and moon.

▼

Great Stupa at Sanchi *(India)*
Often enclosing relics of the Buddha, a stupa is a stone-covered mound of earth symbolizing the World Mountain.

Zen Garden *(Japan)*
The sand gardens of Zen Buddhism are intended only for contemplation—not to be entered. The sand with its carefully raked patterns represents water; the rocks are islands.
▼

▲

Qiyun Pagoda *(China)*
The Buddhist monument known as a pagoda had its origin in the stupa. Like the stupa,
the multi-storied tower of the pagoda was thought to represent the cosmos.

▲

Pyramid of Kukulkan (Maya)

Dedicated to the worship of Kukulkan, the feathered serpent god of the Maya, this pyramid was located in their city of Chichén Itzá.

The Parthenon (Greece)
Creating a dominant impression of grace and balance, this Athenian temple was dedicated to the city's patron, the goddess Athena Parthenos ("Virgin").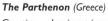

◀ **The Pantheon** (Rome)
Dedicated to "all the gods," this Roman temple had a vast, gilded dome symbolizing the vault of the sky.

Hagia Sophia *(Byzantine)*
An early admirer of this church observed that its dome, which is pierced by forty arched windows, seemed to float "like the radiant heavens."

The Dome of the Rock *(Islam)*
Erected in Jerusalem over the rock from which Muslims believe the Prophet Muhammad ascended to heaven, this shrine is the oldest surviving Islamic monument.

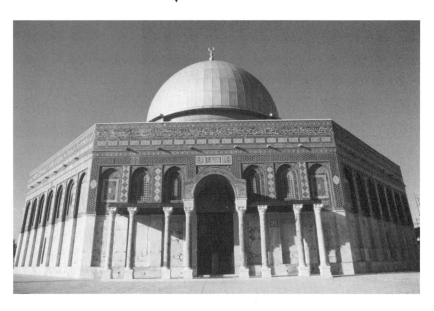

▲

Chartres Cathedral *(France)*

The keynote of the Gothic cathedrals of the Middle Ages is a structural "verticalism"
that draws the worshipper's eye upward.

▲

Church of the Sagrada Familia *(Spain)*
Both the Gothic cathedral and the curvilinear style of Art Nouveau inspired the Spanish architect Antonio Gaudí in creating this church.

▲

Unity Temple *(United States)*
American architect Frank Lloyd Wright's
Unitarian church is a monumental
abstract design that makes no references
to traditional religious structures.

◀ **Notre-Dame-du-Haut** *(France)*
Designed by the Swiss-born architect
Le Corbusier, this modern sanctuary
on a mountaintop has a timeless,
primeval quality.

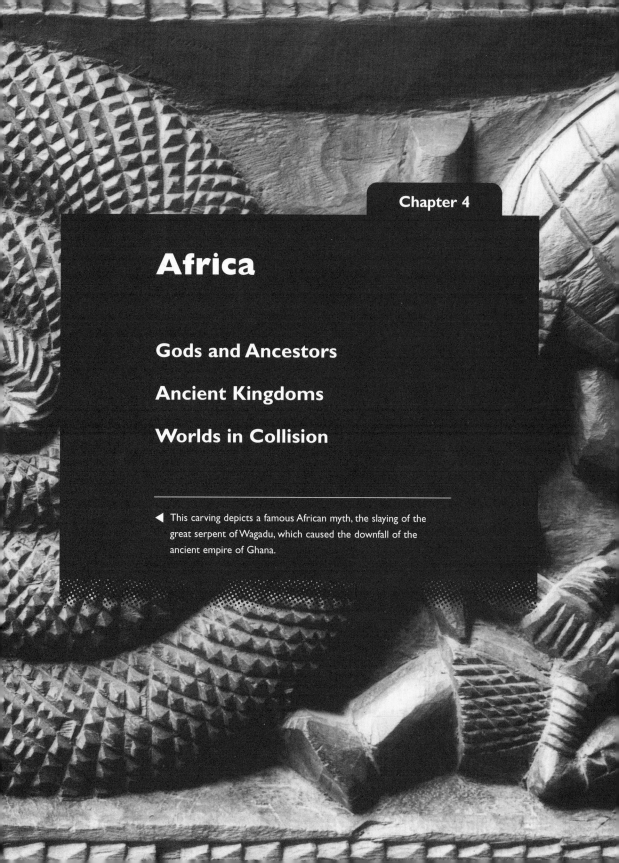

Chapter 4

Africa

Gods and Ancestors

Ancient Kingdoms

Worlds in Collision

◀ This carving depicts a famous African myth, the slaying of the great serpent of Wagadu, which caused the downfall of the ancient empire of Ghana.

Myths and Folk Tales

Much of oral literature of the peoples of Africa deals with their gods. It includes myths and folktales, praise songs and prayers. The traditional gods of the Yoruba people of western Nigeria are known as the orisha. The orisha form a large and elaborate hierarchy that includes some 400 gods and spirits. Notable among them are the supreme god Olorun, Obatala, a creator god, and Eshu, a trickster whose nature combines good and evil. The first text is from the Yoruba creation myth; the second is a folk tale about Eshu (here called Edju).

from Yoruba Creation Myth

In ancient days, at the beginning of time, there was no solid land here where people now dwell. There was only outer space and the sky, and, far below, an endless stretch of water and wild marshes. Supreme in the domain of the sky was the orisha, or god, called Olorun, also known as Olodumare and designated by many praise names. Also living in that place were numerous other orishas, each having attributes of his own, but none of whom had knowledge or powers equal to those of Olorun. Among them was Orunmila, also called Ifa, the eldest son of Olorun. To this orisha Olorun had given the power to read the future, to understand the secret of existence and to divine the processes of fate. There was the orisha Obatala, King of the White Cloth, whom Olorun trusted as

though he also were a son. There was the orisha Eshu, whose character was neither good nor bad. He was compounded out of the elements of chance and accident, and his nature was unpredictability. He understood the principles of speech and language, and because of this gift he was Olorun's linguist.[1] These and the other orishas living in the domain of the sky acknowledged Olorun as the owner of everything and as the highest authority in all matters. Also living there was Agemo, the chameleon,[2] who served Olorun as a trusted servant.

Down below, it was the female deity Olokun who ruled over the vast expanses

[1] linguist—spokesman, herald.

[2] chameleon—small lizard.

of water and wild marshes, a gray region with no living things in it, either creatures of the bush or vegetation. This is the way it was, Olorun's living sky above and Olokun's domain of water below. Neither kingdom troubled the other. They were separate and apart. The orishas of the sky lived on, hardly noticing what lay below them.

All except Obatala, King of the White Cloth. He alone looked down on the domain of Olokun and pondered on it, saying to himself: "Everything down there is a great wet **monotony**.[3] It does not have the mark of any inspiration or living thing." And at last he went to Olorun and said: "The place ruled by Olokun is nothing but sea, marsh and mist. If there were solid land in that domain, fields and forests, hills and valleys, surely it could be populated by orishas and other living things."

Olorun answered: "Yes, it would be a good thing to cover the water with land. But it is an ambitious enterprise. Who is to do the work? And how should it be done?"

Obatala said: "I will undertake it. I will do whatever is required."

He left Olorun and went to the house of Orunmila, who understood the secrets of existence, and said to him: "Your father has instructed me to go down below and make land where now there is nothing but marsh and sea, so that living beings will have a place to build their towns and grow their crops. You, Orunmila, who can divine the meanings of all things, instruct me further. How may this work be begun?"

Orunmila brought out his divining tray[4] and cast sixteen palm nuts on it. He read their meanings by the way they fell. He gathered them up and cast again, again reading their meanings. And when he had cast many times he added meanings to meanings, and said: "These are the things you must do: Descend to the watery wastes on a chain of gold, taking with you a snail shell full of sand, a white hen to disperse the sand, a black cat to be your companion, and a palm nut. That is what the divining figures tell us."

Obatala went next to the goldsmith and asked for a chain of gold long enough to reach from the sky to the surface of the water.

The goldsmith asked, "Is there enough gold in the sky to make such a chain?"

Obatala answered: "Yes, begin your work. I will gather the gold." Departing from the forge of the goldsmith, Obatala went then to Orunmila, Eshu and the other orishas, asking each of them for gold. They gave him whatever they had. Some gave gold dust, some gave rings, bracelets or **pendants**.[5] Obatala collected gold from everywhere and took it to the goldsmith.

The goldsmith said, "More gold is needed."

So Obatala continued seeking gold, and after that he again returned to the goldsmith, saying, "Here is more metal for your chain."

The goldsmith said, "Still more is needed."

---

[3] **monotony**—wearisome sameness.

[4] divining tray—board used to foretell the future.

[5] **pendants**—hanging ornaments.

Obatala said, "There is no more gold in the sky."

The goldsmith said, "The chain will not reach to the water."

Obatala answered: "Nevertheless, make the chain. We shall see."

The goldsmith went to work. When the chain was finished he took it to Obatala. Obatala said, "It must have a hook at the end."

"There is no gold remaining," the goldsmith said.

Obatala replied, "Take some of the links and melt them down."

The goldsmith removed some of the links, and out of them he fashioned a hook for the chain. It was finished. He took the chain to Obatala.

Obatala said, "Now I am ready." He fastened the hook on the edge of the sky and lowered the chain. Orunmila gave him the things that were needed—a snail shell of sand, a white hen, a black cat, and a palm nut. Then Obatala gripped the chain with his hands and feet and began the descent. The chain was very long. When he had descended only half its length Obatala saw that he was leaving the realm of light and entering the region of greyness. A time came when he heard the wash of waves and felt the damp mists rising from Olokun's domain. He reached the end of the golden chain, but he was not yet at the bottom, and he clung there, thinking, "If I let go I will fall into the sea."

While he remained at the chain's end thinking such things, he heard Orunmila's voice from above, saying, "The sand."

So Obatala took the snail shell from the knapsack at his side and poured out the sand.

Again he heard Orunmila call to him, saying this time, "The hen."

Obatala dropped the hen where he had poured the sand. The hen began at once to scratch at the sand and scatter it in all directions. Wherever the sand was scattered it became dry land. Because it was scattered unevenly the sand formed hills and valleys. When this was accomplished, Obatala let go of the chain and came down and walked on the solid earth that had been created. The land extended in all directions, but still it was barren of life.

Obatala named the place where he came down Ife. He built a house there. He planted his palm nut and a palm tree sprang out of the earth. It matured and dropped its palm seeds. More palm trees came into being. Thus there was vegetation at Ife. Obatala lived on, with only his black cat as a companion.

After some time had passed, Olorun the Sky God wanted to know how Obatala's expedition was progressing. He instructed Agemo the chameleon to descend the golden chain. Agemo went down. He found Obatala living in his house at Ife. He said: "Olorun instructed me this way: He said, 'Go down, discover for me how things are with Obatala.' That is why I am here."

Obatala answered, "As you can see, the land has been created, and palm groves are plentiful. But there is too much greyness. The land should be illuminated."

Agemo returned to the sky and reported to Olorun what he had seen and heard. Olorun agreed that there should be light down below. So he made the sun and set it moving. After that there was warmth and light in what had once been Olokun's exclusive domain.

Obatala lived on, with only his black cat for a companion. He thought, "Surely it would be better if many people were living here." He decided to create people. He dug clay from the ground, and out of the clay he shaped human figures which he then laid out to dry in the sun. He worked without resting. He became tired and thirsty. He said to himself, "There should be palm wine in this place to help a person go on working." So he put aside the making of humans and went to the palm trees to draw their inner fluid, out of which he made palm wine. When it was fermented he drank. He drank for a long while. When he felt everything around him softening he put aside his gourd cup and went back to modeling human figures. But because Obatala had drunk so much wine his fingers grew clumsy, and some of the figures were misshapen. Some had crooked backs or crooked legs, or arms that were too short. Some did not have enough fingers, some were bent instead of being straight. Because of the palm wine inside him, Obatala did not notice these things. And when he had made enough figures to begin the populating of Ife he called out

to Olorun the Sky God, saying, "I have made human beings to live with me here in Ife, but only you can give them the breath of life." Olorun heard Obatala's request, and he put breath in the clay figures. They were no longer clay, but people of blood, **sinews**[6] and flesh. They arose and began to do the things that humans do. They built houses for themselves near Obatala's house, and in this way the place Obatala named Ife became the city of Ife.

But when the effects of the palm wine had worn off Obatala saw that some of the humans he had made were misshapen, and remorse filled his heart. He said: "Never again will I drink palm wine. From this time on I will be the special protector of all humans who have deformed limbs or who have otherwise been created imperfectly." Because of Obatala's pledge, humans who later came to serve him also avoided palm wine, and the lame, the blind and those who had no pigment in their skin invoked his help when they were in need.

Edju and the Two Friends

Once upon a time, Olorun first created Enja, or mortal man, and, after that, Edju, the god. Once there were a pair of friends. When they went out they were always dressed alike. Everyone said, "These two men are the best of friends." Edju saw them and said, "These men are very dear to each other. I will make them differ and that will be a fine beginning for a very big

---

[6] **sinews**—tough tissues connecting muscles and bones; tendons.

Idja."[7] The fields of these friends adjoined. A path ran between and separated them. Edju used to walk on it of a morning and then wore a "filla" or black cap.

Now, when Edju wanted to start this quarrel, he made himself a cap of green, black, red, and white cloth, which showed a different color from whatever side it was looked at. He put it on one morning on his walk abroad. Then he took his tobacco pipe and put it, not, as usual, in his mouth, but at the **nape**[8] of his neck, as if he were smoking at the back of his head. And then he took his staff as usual, but, this time, carried it upside down, that is to say, so that it hung, not over his breast in front, but over his shoulder behind. Both the friends were at work in their fields. They looked up for a second. Edju called out, "Good morning!" They gave him the same and went on with their toil.

Then they went home together. One said to the other, "The old man (Edju) went the opposite road through the fields today. I noticed that by his pipe and his stick." The other said, "You're wrong. He went the same way as usual, I saw it by the way his feet were going." The first said, "It's a lie; I saw his pipe and his staff much too plainly; and, besides, he had on a white instead of a black cap." The second one retorted, "You must be blind or asleep; his cap was red." His friend said, "Then you must already have had some palm-wine this morning, if you could see neither the color of his cap, nor the way he was walking." The other one answered him,

"I haven't even seen a drop this morning, but you must be crazed." The other man said, "You are making up lies to annoy me." Then the other one said, "Liar yourself! And not for the first time by a good deal." One of them drew his knife and went for the other who got a wound. He also drew his knife and cut his **assailant**.[9] They both ran away bleeding to the town. The folk saw them and said, "Both these friends have been attacked. There will be war." One of them said, "No, this liar is no friend of mine." And the other one, "Don't believe a single word of his. When he opens his mouth, the lies swarm from it."

Meanwhile, Edju had gone to the King of the town. He said to the King, "Just ask the two friends what is the matter with them! They have cut each other's heads about with knives and are bleeding." The King said, "What, the two friends, who always wear clothes alike have been quarreling? Let them be summoned!" So it was done. The King asked them, "You are both in sad case. What made you fall out?" They both said, "We could not agree as to what it was that went through our fields this morning." Then the King asked, "How many people went along your footpath?" "It was a man who goes the same way everyday. Today he went in another direction, wearing a white cap instead of a black one," said one of the friends. "He lies," shouted the other; "the old man had on a

---

[7] Idja—lawsuit.

[8] **nape**—back of the neck.

[9] **assailant**—attacker.

red cap and walked along in the usual direction!" Then the King asked, "Who knows this old man?" Edju said, "It is I. These two fellows quarreled because I so willed it." Edju pulled out his cap and said, "I put on this cap, red on one side, white on the other, green in front, and black behind. I stuck my pipe in my nape. So my steps went one way while I was looking another. The two friends couldn't help quarreling. I made them do it. Sowing **dissension**[10] is my chief delight."

---

[10] **dissension**—discord.

QUESTIONS TO CONSIDER

1. Based on these two stories, would you say the Yoruba see the characteristics of their gods as chiefly divine or chiefly human? Explain.

2. In the Yoruba creation myth, what motivates the orisha to make the world?

3. What explanation for such evils as human deformities and strife are offered by these Yoruba tales?

4. Trickster figures such as Eshu seem to do evil without any real motive. What do you think such figures represent?

Folk Songs

Along with traditional African beliefs in gods and spirits exists the veneration of ancestors. The souls of the dead are believed to protect the community and to be reborn in the young. The following two folk songs both express traditional beliefs about the ancestors. The first is from the Sudan in East Africa; the second from the Khoi people of South Africa.

Song of a Mother to Her First-Born

Speak to me, child of my heart.
Speak to me with your eyes, your round laughing eyes,
Wet and shining as Lupeyo's bull-calf.

Speak to me little one,
Clutching my breast with your hand,
So strong and firm for all its littleness.
It will be the hand of a warrior, my son,
A hand that will gladden your father.
See how eagerly it fastens on me:
It thinks already of a spear.
O son, you will have a warrior's name and be a leader of men.
And your sons, and your sons' sons, will remember you long
    after you have slipped into darkness.
But I, I shall always remember your hand clutching me so.
I shall recall how you lay in my arms,
And looked at me so, and so,
And how your tiny hands played with my bosom.
And when they name you great warrior, then will my eyes be wet
    with remembering.

And how shall we name you, little warrior?
See, let us play at naming.
It will not be a name of despisal,[1] for you are my first-born.
Not as Nawal's son is named will you be named.
Our gods will be kinder to you than theirs.
Must we call you "Insolence" or "Worthless One"?

Shall you be named, like a child of ill fortune, after the dung of cattle?
Our gods need no cheating, my child:
They wish you no ill.
They have washed your body and clothed it with beauty.
They have set a fire in your eyes.
And the little puckering ridges of your brows—
Are they not the seal of their finger-prints when they fashioned you?
They have given you beauty and strength, child of my heart,
And wisdom is already shining in your eyes,
And laughter.

So how shall we name you, little one?
Are you your father's father, or his brother, or yet another?
Whose spirit is it that is in you, little warrior?
Whose spear-hand tightens round my breast?
Who lives in you and quickens to life, like last year's melon seed?
Are you silent, then?
But your eyes are thinking, thinking, and glowing like the eyes of
    a leopard in a thicket.
Well, let be.
At the day of the naming you will tell us.

O my child, now indeed I am happy.
Now indeed I am a wife—
No more a bride, but a Mother-of-one.
Be splendid and magnificent, child of desire.
Be proud as I am proud.
Be happy as I am happy.

---

[1] despisal—scorn.

Be loved as now I am loved.
Child, child, child, love I have had from my man.
But now, only now, have I the fullness of love.
Now, only now, am I his wife and the mother of his first-born.
His soul is safe in your keeping, my child, and it was I, I, I who
have made you.

Therefore am I loved.
Therefore am I happy.
Therefore am I a wife.
Therefore have I great honor.

You will tend his shrine when he is gone.
With sacrifice and oblation[2] you will recall his name year by year.
He will live in your prayers, my child,
And there will be no more death for him, but everlasting life
    springing from your loins.
You are his shield and his spear, his hope and redemption from
    the dead.
Through you he will be reborn, as the saplings[3] in the Spring.
And I, I am the mother of his first-born.
Sleep, child of beauty and courage and fulfilment, sleep.
I am content.

The Ancestors

The days have passed;
we are a wandering camp
brighter days before us
perhaps.

---

[2] oblation—offering.
[3] saplings—young trees.

Light fades
night becomes darker
Hunger tomorrow.

God is angry
the elders have gone
Their bones are far
their souls wander.
Where are their souls?

The passing wind
knows it perhaps.

Their bones are far
their souls wander.
Are they far away,
are they quite close?
Do they want sacrifice,
do they want blood?
Are they far,
are they near?

The passing wind
the spirit that whirls the leaf
knows it perhaps.

QUESTIONS TO CONSIDER

1. Why do you think someone would name a child "Worthless One"?

2. What belief in immortality is expressed in "Song of a Mother to Her First-Born"?

3. How does "The Ancestors" link the ancestors to the plight of the community?

Masks

Ancient African rock paintings of masked figures indicate that the masking tradition there is a very old one; however, the fact that many masks are constructed of perishable materials makes determining this tradition's origins difficult. While the few remaining examples of the use of masks in Western cultures—such as Halloween or Mardi Gras—are simply for amusement, African masks are generally part of serious religious rituals such as initiations.

◀ Made by the Guro people of the Ivory Coast, this mask was used in the ceremonies of men's societies.

This double-face mask expresses the duality of male and female; it was created by the Baule people of the Ivory Coast. ▶

◀ One of the few African masks to be used exclusively by women, this helmet mask is employed in female initiation ceremonies among the Mende people of Sierra Leone.

This carved head representing the link to the ancestors topped one of the bark reliquaries used among the Fang people of Gabon to hold the skulls of the dead.

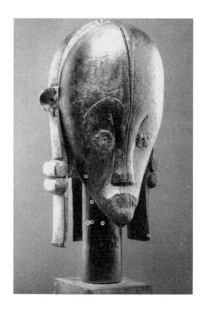

▲

This mask is used in the annual festivals of the Egungun, a secret society among the Yoruba people of Nigeria that is associated with the cult of the dead.

QUESTIONS TO CONSIDER

1. What do you think is the basic appeal of making and wearing masks?

2. How would you describe the basic emotion expressed by the Guro mask? the reliquary head? the Egungun mask?

3. Modern European artists such as the Cubists (who reduced natural forms to geometric shapes) and Expressionists (who distorted natural forms in pursuit of heightened emotion) found inspiration in African masks. Why do you think this was so?

Queen Magda's Journey

One of the most famous tales in the Bible describes the visit of the Queen of Sheba to Israel's King Solomon. According to the version of the tale told by the Ethiopian people of East Africa, the queen's name was Magda, and she returned to her country bearing Solomon's son, who grew up to become the first king of Ethiopia.

"Let my voice be heard by all of you, my people. I am going in quest of Wisdom and Learning. My spirit impels me to go and find them out where they are to be had, for I am smitten[1] with the love of Wisdom and I feel myself drawn as though by a leash toward Learning. Learning is better than treasures of silver and gold, better than all that has been created upon earth. And afterward what can be compared to Learning here below? . . ."

Thereupon the Queen set out with much state and majesty and gladness, for by the will of the Lord, she wished in her heart to make this journey to Jerusalem, to rejoice in the Wisdom of Solomon. They had loaded seven hundred and ninety boats, and mules without number. And the Queen set forth, her trust in God. . . .

After Queen Magda had remained six months in Jerusalem, she desired to return to her own country.

She sent unto Solomon messengers who said to him as follows: "My wish would be to stay with you; but because of those I have brought with me, I must return into my kingdom. God will grant that all I have learned from you may bear fruit in my soul and in the soul of those of my people who, like me, have heard you."

When the King received this message, he meditated in his heart, and he thought: "This woman full of beauty has come to me from the uttermost parts of the earth. Who knows if it be not the will of God that I should have seed[2] of her?"

And so he sent unto the Queen this response: "Since you have done as much as to come hither, will you leave without seeing the glory of my kingdom, the workings of my government, without admiring how my soldiers maneuver, and how I honor

---

[1] smitten—strongly affected.

[2] seed—offspring, children.

the dignitaries of my kingdom? I treat them like saints in Paradise. In each of these things you will find much Wisdom. So I beg of you that you will come and be present at these spectacles. You shall remain behind me, hidden by a curtain. I will show you the things which I tell you of now. You shall become acquainted with all the customs of my kingdom and this Learning which has pleased you shall remain with you until the end of your days."

Magda sent another messenger who brought back this response: "I was ignorant, and through you I have learned Wisdom. . . . That which you now ask of me is only so that my knowledge and my honor may increase. I will come as you desire."

Then was King Solomon satisfied. He bade his dignitaries array themselves in fine apparel. He made his table twice as large as it was. He ordered that the banquet hall and all the palace be got ready in splendor.

The supper of the King was as formal as the Law of the Kingdom. The Queen entered after the King, she was seated behind him with much honor and pomp. She witnessed all that was going on during the **repast**.[3] She was amazed at what she saw and at what she heard, and in her heart she gave thanks to the God of Israel.

Solomon had raised for her a throne covered with silken carpets bound with fringes of gold, of silver, of pearls, and of **brilliants**.[4] He had had his servants scatter

about the palace all sorts of perfumes. . . . When one entered one was satisfied without eating, because of these perfumes.

Now Solomon caused them to serve unto Magda a repast prepared expressly for her so that she might become very thirsty. . . . She partook of this repast and when Solomon had presided over the banquet until the guests, the stewards, the councilors, the great chiefs, the servitors had been seven times renewed, and had departed, the King rose.

He went in unto the Queen and finding her alone he said: "I beg you to rest here until tomorrow, out of love for me."

She answered: "Swear to me by your God, by the God of Israel, that you will not use of your strength against me? If in any way whatever I **transgress**[5] from the law of my country, I shall be plunged into sorrow, into sickness and suffering. . . ."

Solomon answered: "I swear to you that my force shall make no attack upon your honor. But now you in turn must swear that you will touch nothing within this palace." . . .

She answered: "Then swear that you will not lay hold with violence upon my honor, and I will promise with all my heart to touch nothing of what belongs to you."

He swore, and he made her swear.

Then he got upon his bed which was made ready in the next room to this one. And she remained where she was.

---

[3] **repast**—meal.

[4] **brilliants**—gems.

[5] **transgress**—violate a legal or moral code.

Immediately he gave orders to the servants in attendance to wash a vase and to fill it with very pure water, and to put it where it might be seen in the room of the Queen. Then the man was to close the doors and the outside windows. The servant did as Solomon had ordered him in a language which the Queen did not understand.

Solomon did not go to sleep but he feigned unconsciousness. As for the Queen, she dozed a little, then she roused herself, got up, and found that her mouth was dry, for the King had with **malice**[6] given her food which creates a thirst. She was tormented by this thirst. She tried to bring saliva to her lips to moisten them. But she found none. Then she wished to drink the water she had seen before she had fallen asleep. She looked toward Solomon, and she could see him. . . .

The King pretended to sleep heavily but he was awake and he was watching until the Queen should rouse herself to drink the water.

She got down from her bed, she walked **stealthily**,[7] she lifted with her hands the vase of pure water. But before she could drink he had seized her by the arm.

He said: "Why have you broken your vow? You promised that you would touch nothing in my palace."

She was trembling, she answered: "Is it breaking my vow to drink a little water?"

"And what more precious treasure than water have you known under the sun?"

She said: "I have sinned against myself. But you, you will be faithful to your vow and you will permit me to drink?"

He asked: "Do you free me of the oath which I have given?"

She said: "Be free of it but let me drink. . . ."

He let fall her arm, she drank. And after she had drunk he did as he would with her, and they slept together.

Now as the King was sleeping he had a vision. He saw a dazzling sun which came down from the heavens and shed its rays upon Israel. This brilliancy endured a certain length of time, then the sun moved away. It stopped in its course over Ethiopia and it seemed that it was shining there for centuries. The King waited for the return of this star to Israel, but it did not come back. . . .

While this vision was descending upon King Solomon in his sleep, his soul was troubled and his mind worked like lightning. He awoke trembling. Then he admired the courage, the force, the beauty, the innocence and the virginity of the Queen, for she had governed her country since her earliest youth and during this delightful time she had kept her body in purity.

Then Queen Magda said to King Solomon: "Send me back to my country."

He went within his palace, he opened his treasure, he gave splendid presents for Ethiopia and important riches, dazzling **raiment**,[8] and everything that is good.

---

[6] **malice**—evil intent.

[7] **stealthily**—secretly.

[8] **raiment**—clothing.

Then he got ready the caravan of the Queen: chariots, animals. The chariots numbered six thousand. They were laden with precious things. Some of them rolled upon the ground, others moved by the aid of the wind. The King had built them according to the learning which God had given him.

The Queen went away satisfied. She departed, and set out upon her way. Now Solomon accompanied her with much pomp and majesty.

When they had gone a certain distance he wished to speak alone with Queen Magda. He took from his finger a ring. He gave it to her and said: "Take this ring and keep it as a token of my love. If thou shouldst ever bear a child this ring will be the sign of recognition. If it should be a son send him to me. And in any case may the peace of God be with thee. While I was sleeping by thy side I had a vision. The sun which before my eyes was shining upon Israel, moved away. It went and soared above Ethiopia. It remained there. Who knows but that thy country may be blessed because of thee? Above all keep the truth which I have brought thee. Worship God. . . . May thy journey be a safe one."

QUESTIONS TO CONSIDER

1. Why would the Ethiopians preserve this story?

2. In the biblical tradition, Solomon is legendary for his wisdom. How wise does he seem in this story?

3. What effect does Solomon's dream have on him?

4. How does Queen Magda react emotionally to her experience?

The Traditions of the Griot

For hundreds of years, griots, or oral historians employed by the ruling class, preserved the ancient traditions of the peoples of West Africa. The following passages are from an oral epic dealing with Sundiata, founder of the West African empire of Mali, recorded in the 1950s. The first passage introduces the griot; the second presents Sundiata's chief opponent, the sorcerer-king Soumaoro; and the third describes an insult match between these two prior to a climactic battle.

I am a griot. It is I, Djeli Mamoudou Kouyaté, son of Bintou Kouyaté and Djeli Kedian Kouyaté, master in the art of eloquence. Since time immemorial the Kouyatés have been in the service of the Keita princes of Mali; we are vessels of speech, we are the **repositories**[1] which harbor secrets many centuries old. The art of eloquence has no secrets for us; without us the names of kings would vanish into **oblivion**,[2] we are the memory of mankind; by the spoken word we bring to life the deeds and exploits of kings for younger generations.

I derive my knowledge from my father Djeli Kedian, who also got it from his father; history holds no mystery for us; we teach to the **vulgar**[3] just as much as we want to teach them, for it is we who keep the keys to the twelve doors of Mali.[4]

I know the list of all the sovereigns who succeeded to the throne of Mali. I know how the black people divided into tribes, for my father bequeathed to me all his learning; I know why such and such is called Kamara, another Keita, and yet another Sibibé or Traoré; every name has a meaning, a secret import.

I teach kings the history of their ancestors so that the lives of the ancients might serve them as an example, for the world is old, but the future springs from the past.

My word is pure and free of all untruth; it is the word of my father; it is

---

[1] **repositories**—storage places.

[2] **oblivion**—forgetfulness.

[2] **vulgar**—common people.

[4] twelve doors of Mali—the twelve original provinces of which Mali was composed.

the word of my father's father. I will give you my father's words just as I received them; royal griots do not know what lying is. When a quarrel breaks out between tribes it is we who settle the difference, for we are the **depositaries**[5] of oaths which the ancestors swore.

Listen to my word, you who want to know; by my mouth you will learn the history of Mali.

By my mouth you will get to know the story of the ancestor[6] of great Mali, the story of him who, by his exploits, surpassed even Alexander the Great;[7] he who, from the East, shed his rays upon all the countries of the West.

Listen to the story of the son of the Buffalo, the son of the Lion. I am going to tell you of Maghan Sundiata, of Mari-Djata, of Sogolon Djata, of Naré Maghan Djata; the man of many names against whom sorcery could avail nothing.

* * *

At the time when Sundiata was preparing to assert his claim over the kingdom of his fathers, Soumaoro was the king of kings, the most powerful king in all the lands of the setting sun. The fortified town of Sosso was the **bulwark**[8] of **fetishism**[9] against the word of Allah.[10] For a long time Soumaoro defied the whole world. Since his accession to the throne of Sosso he had defeated nine kings whose heads served him as fetishes in his macabre chamber.[11] Their skins served as seats and he cut his footwear from human skin. Soumaoro was

not like other men, for the jinn[12] had revealed themselves to him and his power was beyond measure. So his countless sofas[13] were very brave since they believed their king to be invincible. But Soumaoro was an evil demon and his reign had produced nothing but bloodshed. Nothing was taboo for him. His greatest pleasure was publicly to flog venerable old men. He had defiled every family and everywhere in his vast empire there were villages populated by girls whom he had forcibly abducted from their families without marrying them.

The tree that the tempest will throw down does not see the storm building up on the horizon. Its proud head braves the winds even when it is near its end. Soumaoro had come to despise everyone. Oh! how power can pervert a man. If man had but a mithkal[14] of divine power at his disposal the world would have been annihilated long ago. Soumaoro arrived at a point where he would stop at nothing.

---

[5] **depositaries**—persons to whom something is given for safekeeping.

[6] ancestor—Sundiata.

[7] Alexander the Great—Macedonian conqueror (356–323 B.C.) whose empire stretched from Greece to India.

[8] **bulwark**—defense.

[9] **fetishism**—traditional religious beliefs and practices. A fetish is an object believed to possess magic power.

[10] word of Allah—religion of Islam.

[11] macabre chamber—weird room.

[12] jinn—spirits in Islamic folklore.

[13] sofas—warriors.

[14] mithkal—tiny Arabic unit of weight; the smallest fraction of something.

* * *

Sundiata went and pitched camp at Dayala in the valley of the Niger.[15] Now it was he who was blocking Soumaoro's road to the south. Up till that time, Sundiata and Soumaoro had fought each other without a declaration of war. One does not wage war without saying why it is being waged. Those fighting should make a declaration of their grievances to begin with. Just as a sorcerer ought not to attack someone without taking him to task for some evil deed, so a king should not wage war without saying why he is taking up arms.

Soumaoro advanced as far as Krina, near the village of Dayala on the Niger and decided to assert his rights before joining battle. Soumaoro knew that Sundiata also was a sorcerer, so, instead of sending an embassy, he committed his words to one of his owls.[16] The night bird came and perched on the roof of Djata's tent and spoke. The son of Sogolon in his turn sent his owl to Soumaoro. Here is the dialogue of the sorcerer kings:

"Stop, young man. Henceforth I am the king of Mali. If you want peace, return to where you came from," said Soumaoro.

"I am coming back, Soumaoro, to recapture my kingdom. If you want peace you will make amends to my allies and return to Sosso where you are the king."

"I am king of Mali by force of arms. My rights have been established by conquest."

"Then I will take Mali from you by force of arms and chase you from my kingdom."

"Know, then, that I am the wild yam of the rocks; nothing will make me leave Mali."

"Know, also that I have in my camp seven master smiths who will shatter the rocks. Then, yam, I will eat you."

"I am the poisonous mushroom that makes the fearless vomit."

"As for me, I am the ravenous cock, the poison does not matter to me."

"Behave yourself, little boy, or you will burn your foot, for I am the red-hot cinder."

"But me, I am the rain that extinguishes the cinder; I am the boisterous torrent[17] that will carry you off."

"I am the mighty silk-cotton tree that looks from on high on the tops of other trees."

"And I, I am the strangling creeper that climbs to the top of the forest giant."

"Enough of this argument. You shall not have Mali."

"Know that there is not room for two kings on the same skin, Soumaoro; you will let me have your place."

"Very well, since you want war I will wage war against you, but I would have you know that I have killed nine kings

---

[15] Niger—principal river of West Africa.

[16] owls—Sorcerers are believed to be aided by familiar spirits, demons who inhabit the bodies of animals.

[17] boisterous torrent—loud, fast-flowing river or stream.

whose heads adorn my room. What a pity, indeed, that your head should take its place beside those of your fellow **madcaps**."[18]

"Prepare yourself, Soumaoro, for it will be long before the calamity that is going to crash down upon you and yours comes to an end."

Thus Sundiata and Soumaoro spoke together. After the war of mouths, swords had to decide the issue.

---

[18] **madcaps**—reckless persons.

QUESTIONS TO CONSIDER

1. In traditional West African societies, what different functions did the griot perform?

2. What does Soumaoro represent in this account?

3. What do you think is the purpose of the insult match between Sundiata and Soumaoro?

Village Life in Benin

OLAUDAH EQUIANO

The son of a chief, Olaudah Equiano was born around 1745 in the West African kingdom of Benin. Kidnapped as a child and sold into slavery, he eventually obtained his freedom, became active in the antislavery movement, and published his autobiography. In this passage, he describes the life he knew in Benin before he was enslaved.

As our manners are simple, our luxuries are few. The dress of both sexes is nearly the same. It generally consists of a long piece of calico, or muslin, wrapped loosely round the body, somewhat in the form of a highland plaid. This is usually dyed blue, which is our favorite color. It is extracted from a berry, and is brighter and richer than any I have seen in Europe. Besides this, our women of distinction wear golden ornaments; which they dispose with some **profusion**[1] on their arms and legs. When our women are not employed with the men in tillage,[2] their usual occupation is spinning and weaving cotton, which they afterwards dye, and make it into garments. They also manufacture earthen vessels, of which we have many kinds. Among the best are tobacco pipes, made after the same fashion, and used in the same manner, as those in Turkey.

Our manner of living is entirely plain; for as yet the natives are unacquainted with those refinements in cookery which **debauch**[3] the taste: bullocks, goats, and poultry supply the greatest part of their food. These constitute likewise the principal wealth of the country, and the chief articles of its commerce. The flesh is usually stewed in a pan; to make it savory we sometimes use also pepper, and other spices, and we have salt made of wood ashes. Our vegetables are mostly plantains, eadas, yams, beans, and Indian corn. The head of the family usually eats alone; his wives and slaves have also their separate tables. Before we taste food we always wash our hands: indeed our cleanliness on all occasions is extreme; but on this it is an

---

[1] **profusion**—abundance.

[2] **tillage**—cultivation, farming.

[3] **debauch**—corrupt.

indispensable ceremony. After washing, libation[4] is made, by pouring out a small portion of the food, in a certain place, for the spirits of departed relations, which the natives suppose to preside over their conduct, and guard them from evil. They are totally unacquainted with strong or spirituous liquors; and their principal beverage is palm wine. This is gotten from a tree of that name by tapping it at the top, and fastening a large gourd to it; and sometimes one tree will yield three or four gallons in a night. When just drawn it is of a most delicious sweetness; but in a few days it acquires a tartish[5] and more spirituous flavor: though I never saw any one intoxicated by it. The same tree also produces nuts and oil. Our principal luxury is in perfumes; one sort of these is an odoriferous[6] wood of delicious fragrance. the other a kind of earth; a small portion of which thrown into the fire diffuses a most powerful odor. We beat this wood into powder, and mix it with palm oil; with which both men and women perfume themselves.

In our buildings we study convenience rather than ornament. Each master of a family has a large square piece of ground, surrounded with a moat, fence, or enclosed with a wall made of red earth tempered; which, when dry, is as hard as brick. Within this are his houses to accommodate his family and slaves; which, if numerous, frequently present the appearance of a village. In the middle stands the principal building, appropriated to the sole use of the master, and consisting of two apartments; in one of which he sits in the day

with his family, the other is left apart for the reception of his friends. He has besides these a distinct apartment in which he sleeps, together with his male children. On each side are the apartments of his wives, who have also their separate day and night houses. The habitations of the slaves and their families are distributed throughout the rest of the enclosure. These houses never exceed one story in height. They are always built of wood, or stakes driven into the ground, crossed with wattles,[7] and neatly plastered within, and without. The roof is thatched with reeds. Our day-houses are left open at the sides; but those in which we sleep are always covered, and plastered in the inside, with a composition mixed with cowdung, to keep off the different insects, which annoy us during the night. The walls and floors also of these are generally covered with mats. Our beds consist of a platform, raised three or four feet from the ground, on which are laid skins, and different parts of a spongy tree called plantain. Our covering is calico or muslin, the same as our dress. The usual seats are a few logs of wood; but we have benches, which are generally perfumed, to accommodate strangers: these compose the greater part of our household furniture. Houses so constructed and furnished require but little

---

[4] libation—ritual offering to the gods or spirits of the dead.

[5] tartish—bitter, sour.

[6] odoriferous—strong-smelling.

[7] wattles—sticks.

skill to erect them. Every man is a sufficient architect for the purpose. The whole neighborhood afford their **unanimous**[8] assistance in building them and in return receive, and expect no other recompense than a feast.

As we live in a country where nature is prodigal of her favors, our wants are few and easily supplied; of course we have few manufactures. They consist for the most part of calicoes, earthern ware, ornaments, and instruments of war and husbandry. But these make no part of our commerce, the principal articles of which, as I have observed, are provisions. In such a state money is of little use; however we have some small pieces of coin, if I may call them such. They are made something like an anchor; but I do not remember either their value or denomination.[9] We have also markets, at which I have been frequently with my mother. These are sometimes visited by stout mahogany-colored men from the south west of us: we call them Oye-Eboe which term signifies red men living at a distance. They generally bring us firearms, gunpowder, hats, beads, and dried fish. The last we esteemed a great rarity, as our waters were only brooks and springs. These articles they barter with us for odoriferous woods and earth, and our salt of wood ashes. They always carry slaves through our land; but the strictest account is exacted of their manner of procuring them before they are suffered to pass. Sometimes indeed we sold slaves to them, but they were only prisoners of war, or such among us as had been convicted of kidnapping, or adultery, and some other

crimes, which we esteemed **heinous.**[10] This practice of kidnapping induces me to think, that, notwithstanding all our strictness, their principal business among us was to trepan[11] our people. I remember too they carried great sacks along with them, which not long after I had an opportunity of fatally seeing applied to that infamous purpose.

Our land is uncommonly rich and fruitful, and produces all kinds of vegetables in great abundance. We have plenty of Indian corn, and vast quantities of cotton and tobacco. Our pineapples grow without culture; they are about the size of the largest sugar-loaf, and finely flavored. We have also spices of different kinds, particularly pepper; and a variety of delicious fruits which I have never seen in Europe; together with gums of various kinds, and honey in abundance. All our industry is exerted to improve those blessings of nature. Agriculture is our chief employment; and every one, even the children and women, are engaged in it. Thus we are all **habituated**[12] to labor from our earliest years. Every one contributes something to the common stock; and as we are unacquainted with idleness, we have no beggars. . . .

Our tillage is exercised in a large plain or common,[13] some hours walk from our dwellings, and all the neighbors resort thither in a body. They use no beasts of

---

[8] **unanimous**—complete.

[9] denomination—amount.

[10] **heinous**—evil.

[11] trepan—trap.

[12] **habituated**—accustomed.

[13] common—open land owned by a community together.

husbandry; and their only instruments are hoes, axes, shovels, and beaks, or pointed iron to dig with. Sometimes we are visited by locusts, which come in large clouds, so as to darken the air, and destroy our harvest. This however happens rarely, but when it does a famine is produced by it, I remember an instance or two wherein this happened. This common is often the theater of war; and therefore when our people go out to till their land, they not only go in a body, but generally take their arms with them for fear of a surprise; and when they apprehend[14] an invasion they guard the avenues to their dwellings, by driving sticks into the ground, which are so sharp at one end as to pierce the foot, and are generally dipped in poison. From what I can recollect of these battles, they appear to have been irruptions[15] of one little state or district on the other, to obtain prisoners or booty. Perhaps they were incited to this by those traders who brought the European goods I mentioned amongst us. Such a mode of obtaining slaves in Africa is common; and I believe more are procured this way and by kidnapping, than any other. When a trader wants slaves, he applies to a chief for them, and tempts him with his wares. It is not extraordinary, if on this occasion he yields to the temptation with as little firmness, and accepts the price of his fellow creatures' liberty with as little reluctance as the enlightened merchant. Accordingly he falls on his neighbors, and a desperate battle ensues. If he prevails and takes prisoners, he gratifies his avarice[16] by selling them; but, if his party

be vanquished, and he falls into the hands of the enemy, he is put to death: for, as he has been known to foment[17] their quarrels, it is thought dangerous to let him survive, and no ransom can save him, though all other prisoners may be redeemed. We have firearms, bows and arrows, broad two-edged swords and javelins: we have shields also which cover a man from head to foot. All are taught the use of these weapons; even our women are warriors, and march boldly out to fight along with the men. Our whole district is a kind of militia: on a certain signal given, such as the firing of a gun at night, they all rise in arms and rush upon their enemy. It is perhaps something remarkable, that when our people march to the field a red flag or banner is borne before them. I was once a witness to a battle in our common. We had been all at work in it one day as usual, when our people were suddenly attacked. I climbed a tree at some distance, from which I beheld the fight. There were many women as well as men on both sides; among others my mother was there, and armed with a broad sword. After fighting for a considerable time with great fury, and after many had been killed our people obtained the victory, and took their enemy's chief prisoner. He was carried off in great triumph, and, though he offered a large ransom for his life, he was put to

---

[14] apprehend—fear.

[15] irruptions—sudden attacks.

[16] **avarice**—greed.

[17] foment—encourage.

death. A virgin of note among our enemies had been slain in the battle, and her arm was exposed in our market-place, where our trophies were always exhibited. The spoils were divided according to the merit of the warriors. Those prisoners which were not sold or redeemed we kept as slaves: but how different was their condition from that of the slaves in the West Indies! With us they do no more work than other members of the community, even their masters; their food, clothing and lodging were nearly the same as theirs, (except that they were not permitted to eat with those who were free-born); and there was scarce any other difference between them, than a superior degree of importance which the head of a family possesses in our state, and that authority which, as such, he exercises over every part of his household. Some of these slaves have even slaves under them as their own property, and for their own use.

As to religion, the natives believe that there is one Creator of all things, and that he lives in the sun, and is girted round with a belt that he may never eat or drink; but, according to some, he smokes a pipe, which is our own favorite luxury. They believe he governs events, especially our deaths or captivity; but, as for the doctrine of eternity, I do not remember to have ever heard of it: some however believe in the transmigration of souls[18] in a certain degree. Those spirits, which are not transmigrated, such as our dear friends or relations, they believe always attend them,

and guard them from the bad spirits or their foes. For this reason they always before eating, as I have observed, put some small portion of the meat, and pour some of their drink, on the ground for them; and they often make oblations of the blood of beasts or fowls at their graves.

---

[18] transmigration of souls—passage of souls after death to rebirth in other bodies.

QUESTIONS TO CONSIDER

1. Do you think Olaudah Equiano romanticized his picture of West African village life? Why or why not?

2. What was the position of woman in the society Equiano describes?

3. How did Equiano distinguish between slavery in his village and slavery as he later experienced it in the Americas?

4. According to an African proverb, "It takes a village to raise a child." What values would a child have received in Equiano's village?

Letters to the King of Portugal

NZINGA MEMBA

Beginning in the early 1400s, the Portuguese began to explore the coast of Africa, establishing fortified trading posts and dealing in gold, ivory, and slaves. In the 1480s they established close contacts with the West African kingdom of Kongo, resulting in the introduction of the Christian religion and European goods into the country. The following passages come from several letters sent in 1526 to the king of Portugal by Nzinga Memba, ruler of Kongo, describing the problems that have been created by the presence of Europeans in his country.

Sir, Your Highness should know how our Kingdom is being lost in so many ways that it is convenient to provide for the necessary remedy, since this is caused by the excessive freedom given by your agents and officials to the men and merchants who are allowed to come to this Kingdom to set up shops with goods and many things which have been prohibited by us, and which they spread throughout our Kingdoms and Domains in such an abundance that many of our vassals,[1] whom we had in obedience, do not comply because they have the things in greater abundance than we ourselves; and it was with these things that we had them content and subjected under our vassalage and jurisdiction, so it is doing a great harm not only to the service of God, but the security and peace of our Kingdoms and State as well.

And we cannot reckon how great the damage is, since the mentioned merchants are taking every day our natives, sons of the land and the sons of our noblemen and vassals and our relatives, because the thieves and men of bad conscience grab them wishing to have the things and wares of this Kingdom which they are ambitious of; they grab them and get them to be sold; and so great, Sir, is the corruption and **licentiousness**[2] that our country is being completely depopulated, and Your Highness should not agree with this nor

---

[1] vassals—subordinates in a feudal system who swear loyalty to an overlord in exchange for land use.

[2] **licentiousness**—lawlessness.

accept it as in your service. And to avoid it we need from those (your) Kingdoms no more than some priests and a few people to teach in schools, and no other goods except wine and flour for the holy sacrament.[3] That is why we beg of Your Highness to help and assist us in this matter, commanding your factors that they should not send here either merchants or wares, because it is *our will that in these Kingdoms there should not be any trade of slaves nor outlet for them.* Concerning what is referred [to] above, again we beg of Your Highness to agree with it, since otherwise we cannot remedy such an obvious damage. Pray Our Lord in His mercy to have Your Highness under His guard and let you do forever the things of His service. I kiss your hands many times.

Moreover, Sir, in our Kingdoms there is another great inconvenience which is of little service to God, and this is that many of our people, keenly desirous as they are of the wares and things of your Kingdoms, which are brought here by your people, and in order to satisfy their **voracious**[4] appetite, seize many of our people, freed and exempt men, and very often it happens that they kidnap even noblemen and the sons of noblemen, and our relatives, and take them to be sold to the white men who are in our Kingdoms; and for this purpose they have concealed them; and others are brought during the night so that they might not be recognized.

And as soon as they are taken by the white men they are immediately ironed[5] and branded with fire, and when they are carried to be embarked, if they are caught by our guards' men the whites **allege**[6] that they have bought them but they cannot say from whom, so that it is our duty to do justice and to restore to the freemen their freedom, but it cannot be done if your subjects feel offended, as they claim to be.

And to avoid such a great evil we passed a law so that any white man living in our Kingdoms and wanting to purchase goods in any way should first inform three of our noblemen and officials of our court whom we rely upon in this matter, and these are Dom Pedro Manipanza and Dom Manuel Manissaba, our chief usher, and Gonçalo Pires our chief freighter, who should investigate if the mentioned goods are captives or free men, and if cleared by them there will be no further doubt nor **embargo**[7] for them to be taken and embarked. But if the white men do not comply with it they will lose the aforementioned goods. And if we do them this favor and concession it is for the part Your Highness has in it, since we know that it is in your service too that these goods are taken from our Kingdom, otherwise we should not consent to this. . . .

---

[3] holy sacrament—Christian worship service of the Mass.

[4] **voracious**—greedy.

[5] ironed—put in chains.

[6] **allege**—claim without proof.

[7] **embargo**—prohibition.

Sir, Your Highness has been kind enough to write to us saying that we should ask in our letters for anything we need, and that we shall be provided with everything, and as the peace and the health of our Kingdom depend on us, and as there are among us old folks and people who have lived for many days, it happens that we have continuously many and different diseases which put us very often in such a weakness that we reach almost the last extreme; and the same happens to our children, relatives and natives owing to the lack in this country of physicians and surgeons who might know how to cure properly such diseases. And as we have got neither **dispensaries**[8] nor drugs which might help us in this forlornness, many of those who had been already confirmed and instructed in the holy faith of Our Lord Jesus Christ perish and die; and the rest of the people in their majority cure themselves with herbs and breads and other ancient methods, so that they put all their faith in the mentioned herbs and ceremonies if they live, and believe that they are saved if they die; and this is not much in the service of God.

And to avoid such a great error and inconvenience, since it is from God in the first place and then from your Kingdoms and from Your Highness that all the good and drugs and medicines have come to save us, we beg of you to be agreeable and kind enough to send us two physicians and two **apothecaries**[9] and one surgeon, so that they may come with their drugstores

and all the necessary things to stay in our kingdoms, because we are in extreme need of them all and each of them. We shall do them all good and shall benefit them by all means, since they are sent by Your Highness, whom we thank for your work in their coming. We beg of Your Highness as a great favor to do this for us, because besides being good in itself it is in the service of God as we have said above.

---

[8] **dispensaries**—places where medicines are distributed.
[9] **apothecaries**—druggists.

QUESTIONS TO CONSIDER

1. What was the chief problem resulting from the Portuguese presence in Kongo?

2. The king would like to limit the Europeans in Kongo to priests and teachers and to limit goods to the wine and flour needed in the Christian worship service. In the king's place, what would you have proposed?

3. Do you think Nzinga Memba considered himself the equal of the king of Portugal? Why or why not?

Benin Art

Formed in the late 1100s, the West African kingdom of Benin was ruled by an oba, or divine king, and a hierarchy of chiefs. Most of the people of Benin lived in farming villages such as the one described by Olaudah Equiano in his autobiography (page 157). At its height Benin was a center for the arts, with sculptors producing beautiful works in ivory and bronze. After the arrival of the Portuguese in 1485, the works of the artists of Benin begin reflecting the European presence.

◀ This ivory saltcellar, or container for salt, depicts Portuguese officials accompanied by their servants.

▲

The central figure on this bronze plaque is the oba; three of his chiefs appear below. The figures flanking his head represent the Portuguese.

In this bronze plaque a Portuguese soldier is shown holding a matchlock, an early type of gun. ▶

▲

This ivory mask of the oba shows him wearing a headdress
fringed with tiny figures of Portuguese soldiers.

QUESTIONS TO CONSIDER

1. A caricature is a representation that
   exaggerates one or more features
   of the subject it depicts. Do any of the
   representations of the Portuguese in the
   Benin art seem to be caricatures? Explain.

2. What do these images suggest about the
   way in which the artists of Benin viewed
   their own society?

3. From these works, what words would you
   choose to characterize the overall attitude of
   the people of Benin toward the Portuguese—
   *respectful, fearful, amused, cautious, admiring,
   interested, contemptuous?*

The Mask, Masking, and Masquerade Arts in Africa

HERBERT M. COLE

"Of all the varied arts of Africa," claims Herbert Cole, "it is the mask that is preeminent. Masks are known from all cultures and continents, but those of Africa come to mind first for many people." In this article, Cole identifies some of the basic factors that shape the art of the African mask.

Clearly the mask, masking, and masquerade are interlocking aspects of one of Africa's most significant artistic phenomena. A physical object of specific materials, shape, and size, the *mask* is normally designed to cover the face or head. *Masking* is the active presence of one or more fully costumed character(s). *Masquerades* are important events involving varied masked dancers, musicians, and their audiences. Each character, its attributes, songs, and dances, has many meanings usually expressed in no other manner.

Of all the varied arts of Africa wrought in gold, ivory, brass, terra-cotta, and other materials, especially wood and fiber, it is the mask that is preeminent. Masks are known from all cultures and continents, but those of Africa come to mind first for many people.

How did African masking originate? Were animal skins and heads first used to embody, and then to deceive, sought-after prey and/or to **placate**[1] their spirits? We cannot know, despite the logic that suggests ancient hunting and its rituals as early motivations for such transforming disguises. . . .

Mythology on the origins of masking survives. Many such myths collected in different parts of Africa share a single and rather puzzling theme: that women first had the secrets of masks. Sometimes, too, women are said to have been the first masked dancers, after which the masks and their rituals were taken over entirely by men, who then normally excluded women from all such rites except as onlookers. . . .

---

[1] **placate**—appease.

In regard to the history of masking, we must also note that masquerades have long been and continue to be subject to change. Some of the masks discussed below may not still exist in Africa; most do. Masquerades are probably Africa's most **resilient**[2] art form, continually evolving to meet new needs. In some areas, too, urban masquerades have sprung up, based in part on earlier forms yet reflecting modern social realities and employing plastic, aluminum, and other new products. Masking is sufficiently deeply embedded in African cultures for us to predict with some certainty that it will continue with vitality—and more changes—in the years to come.

The arts of transformation in Africa range along a continuum[3] from slight modifications of a visible face and body to wholesale alteration of the human form through its enclosure in a "costume" of nonhuman character. Our concern here, of course, is with these latter, spirit-associated transformations which cancel or obliterate the wearer's personality, even his humanity, by superimposing a wholly new form. The change is often into another human character—a pretty girl, old man, mother, hunter, or stranger—but something essential has happened; this being is also *a spirit*. Its visible face—the mask—is inanimate, with immobile features. This *is* and *is not* a human being. So transformed, the new being is saying: "I am not myself.". . .

Masking arts may also quite drastically *alter* human forms. Under a disguise the bodily armature[4] can be bulked out to nonhuman shapes and sizes with hoops or pads; it may be armless and extended upward on a frame or pole, its face amplified with exaggerated quasi-human, zoomorphic,[5] or bizarre features. Appearance and behavior are also extraordinary, otherworldly. The being glides, walks on (spits fire, speaks in a foreign or nonsensical tongue. The masker neither talks nor act like a true human and, as he careens wildly through the village, seems to be outside human laws.

The masker neither talks nor acts like a true human.

Mask-carvers and costume-makers (only occasionally the same person) have over the centuries evolved thousands of imaginative spirit beings, invoking many disparate materials in creative and striking ensembles. The overwhelming majority of masks are wood, carved by professional carvers or blacksmiths who normally serve long apprenticeships learning their skills by studying, copying, and improving upon the corpus[6] of locally admired mask types and forms. Other materials are also used for making masks, and quite a number are composite, multimedia constructions. Often, too, the substances used to make or decorate masks have local symbolic values and thus contribute to the "message-system" of a masquerade. . . .

---

[2] **resilient**—flexible.

[3] continuum—series without internal divisions.

[4] armature—framework.

[5] zoomorphic—imitating the form of an animal.

[6] corpus—collection.

Masquerading is the province of males of all ages, and artists themselves are also participants in these activities. Elaborate performances must, of course, be organized, choreographed, and rehearsed by members of the masking cults. In some cases artists even dance masks, or masked characters are named for them. Carvers, tailors, and other mask-makers may become quite famous locally, and their names have occasionally become well-known to the world beyond. Scholars of the Yoruba, for example, have been recognizing specific artists for years in an effort to take the "anonymity" out of African art—a **laudable**[7] pursuit. From the view of most African peoples, on the other hand, such emphasis on a carver's individuality is misplaced. Africans are most concerned with the entire costumed character, including its dances and songs, not just the mask or headpiece. Many people besides the professional carver are involved in successful masked theater. In many cases, too, non-professional cult members carve masks or headdresses or fabricate costumes from cloth or vegetal fibers. . . .

It is worthwhile to set forth some of the principles underlying the forms and styles of masks and headpieces. First, nearly all African sculptors work with an *idea* when carving rather than re-creating the face of a particular individual. This idea is a local convention—the expected form— of a particular character's mask. Thus the heads and facial features (and costumes) of masks are strongly conventionalized to conform with a culturally specific ideal for any given character. In formal terms these conventions include simplification, distortion, and exaggeration. The idea behind some characters requires the artist to combine several creatures in the same carving: antelope, bird, warthog, and human. Explicit animal masks too are often distorted; they conform to the accepted *convention* for an antelope or elephant rather than imitating exact natural forms. In most cases this is because the intention is to represent a *spirit* rather than a real antelope or a flesh-and-blood Mrs. Jones. Portraiture in the sense Americans and Europeans know it is therefore almost entirely absent. A few masks, it is true, are locally designated as representations of Mrs. Jones, but she will be recognized from her facial markings or favorite hairstyle rather than subtle physiognomic details and idiosyncrasies.[8] If African sculptors wanted to make highly naturalistic, fleshy, and realistic masks, they most certainly would have done so. Usually they chose not to. . . .

The dramatic art of African masking brings the essentially mysterious world of nature and the supernatural into the known and more predictable community of humans. Many African belief systems require men (very rarely women) to materialize spirits by impersonating them so that these spirits may act upon the human realm and, equally, so that people may respond to—thank, placate, entertain—the forces upon which life depends.

---

[7] **laudable**—praiseworthy.

[8] physiognomic . . . idiosyncrasies—personal facial characteristics.

Regardless of mask or costume type or style, the artistic transformations that create "spirit dancers" (maskers) are a major unifying force among the myriad arts of sub-Saharan Africa, from the western savanna and forests to the East African coast. A number of cultures, however, make marginal use of masks, and some have none at all.

Spirit transformations are complex phenomena, especially when compared to the minor and **vestigial**[9] roles played by masks and masking in the modern Western world. Western masks, although they hint at a banished sacred era since they appear at holidays-holy days— Halloween and Mardi Gras, for example, are largely playful and secular today, mere disguises. Rarely are they taken very seriously. To this day in much of Africa, however, spirit impersonation is highly serious despite industrialization, bureaucratic government, Christianity, Islam, school education, modern medicine, and the like. Masqueraders certainly entertain African people still, as they have done in the past. In contrast to those in the West, however, African spirit dancers may also intervene forcefully and mysteriously in human affairs, redirecting social action, punishing wrongdoers, educating the young, or helping to raise a man to a higher status by dramatizing timeless moral and ethical values. Not all African masks have powerful and "heavy" spiritual roles. In fact they range along a continuum from these to more lighthearted beings whose primary purpose is entertainment. In the

1980s maskers may no longer have the legal sanction to execute people and burn houses, yet in many places they are still highly regarded and everywhere they still have the power to affect the quality of life.

---

[9] **vestigial**—as a slight trace.

QUESTIONS TO CONSIDER

1. Why do you think that women might have been the first human beings to create masks?

2. According to Herbert Cole, do masks represent individuals or types?

3. In creating a mask, what strategies does a carver use?

4. Why is masking a collaborative art?

5. What are the differences between the roles of masking in traditional African cultures and in modern Western society?

Chapter 5

Native American Cultures

In the Beginning

The Circle of Life

Peace and War

_____

◀ This huge serpent coiling across a hillside in southern Ohio is a sacred image created by the Adena people more than 2,000 years ago.

from

Popul Vuh

When Europeans began to explore the Western Hemisphere, it was already the home of hundreds of distinct Native American cultures, from nomadic hunter-gatherers to complex urban civilizations. These cultures possessed rich oral literatures, including both sacred traditions preserved in mythology and folktales told for entertainment. The following example of Native American myth is a creation story from Popul Vuh, *a book that preserves the traditions of the Quiché Maya people of Guatemala.*

This is the account of how all was in suspense, all calm, in silence; all motionless, still, and the expanse of the sky was empty.

This is the first account, the first narrative. There was neither man, nor animal, birds, fishes, crabs, trees, stones, caves, ravines, grasses, nor forests; there was only the sky.

The surface of the earth had not appeared. There was only the calm sea and the great expanse of the sky.

There was nothing brought together, nothing which could make a noise, nor anything which might move, or tremble, or could make noise in the sky.

There was nothing standing; only the calm water, the placid sea, alone and tranquil. Nothing existed.

There was only immobility and silence in the darkness, in the night. Only the Creator, the Maker, Tepeu, Gucumatz,[1] the Forefathers, were in the water surrounded with light. They were hidden under green and blue feathers, and were therefore called Gucumatz. By nature they were great sages and great thinkers. In this manner the sky existed and also the Heart of Heaven, which is the name of God and thus He is called.

Then came the word. Tepeu and Gucumatz came together in the darkness, in the night, and Tepeu and Gucumatz talked together. They talked then, discussing and deliberating; they agreed, they united their words and their thoughts. Then while they mediated, it became clear to them that when dawn would break, man must appear. Then they planned the creation, and the growth of the trees and the thickets and the birth of life and the

---

[1] Gucumatz—this Quiché god's name means "the feathered serpent."

creation of man. Thus it was arranged in the darkness and in the night by the Heart of Heaven who is called Huracán. . . .

First the earth was formed, the mountains and the valleys; the currents of water were divided, the rivulets were running freely between the hills, and the water was separated when the high mountains appeared. . . .

Then they made the small wild animals, the guardians of the woods, the spirits of the mountains, the deer, the birds, pumas, jaguars, serpents, snakes, vipers, guardians of the thickets.

And the Forefathers asked: "Shall there be only silence and calm under the trees, under the vines? It is well that hereafter there be someone to guard them."

So they said when they meditated and talked. Promptly the deer and the birds were created. Immediately they gave homes to the deer and the birds. . . .

And the creation of all the four-footed animals and the birds being finished, they were told by the Creator and the Maker and the Forefathers: "Speak, cry, warble, call, speak each one according to your variety, each, according to your kind." So was it said to the deer, the birds, pumas, jaguars, and serpents.

"Speak, then, our names, praise us, your mother, your father. . . ."

But they could not make them speak like men; they only hissed and screamed and cackled; they were unable to make words, and each screamed in a different way.

When the Creator and the Maker saw that it was impossible for them to talk to each other, they said: "It is impossible for them to say our names, the names of us, their Creators and Makers. This is not well," said the Forefathers to each other. . . .

They wished to give them another trial; they wished to make another attempt; they wished to make [all living things] adore them.

But they could not understand each other's speech; they could succeed in nothing, and could do nothing. For this reason they were sacrificed, and the animals which were on earth were condemned to be killed and eaten.

For this reason another attempt had to be made to create and make men by the Creator, the Maker, and the Forefathers.

"Let us try again! Already dawn draws near: Let us make him who shall nourish and sustain us! What shall we do to be invoked, in order to be remembered on earth? We have already tried with our first creations, our first creatures; but we could not make them praise and venerate us. So, then, let us try to make obedient, respectful beings who will nourish and sustain us." Thus they spoke.

Then was the creation and the formation. Of earth, of mud, they made [man's] flesh. But they saw that it was not good. It melted away, it was soft, did not move, had no strength, it fell down, it was limp, it could not move its head, its face fell to one side, its sight was blurred, it could not look behind. At first it spoke, but had no mind. Quickly it soaked in the water and could not stand.

And the Creator and the Maker said: "Let us try again because our creatures will not be able to walk nor multiply. Let us consider this," they said.

Then they broke up and destroyed their work and their creation. And they said: "What shall we do to perfect it, in order that our worshipers, our invokers, will be successful?". . .

Then they spoke to those soothsayers, the Grandmother of the day, the Grandmother of the Dawn, as they were called by the Creator and the Maker, and whose names were Xpiyacoc and Xmucané.

And said Huracán, Tepeu, and Gucumatz when they spoke to the soothsayer, to the Maker, who are the diviners:[2] "You must work together and find the means so that man, whom we shall make, man, whom we are going to make, will nourish and sustain us, invoke and remember us. . . ."

"Cast the lot with your grains of corn and the *tzité*.[3] Do it thus, and we shall know if we are to make, or carve his mouth and eyes out of wood." Thus the diviners were told.

They went down at once to make their divination, and cast their lots with the corn and the *tzité*. "Fate! Creature!" said an old woman and an old man. . . .

Beginning the divination, they said: "Get together, grasp each other! Speak, that we may hear." They said, "Say if it is well that the wood be got together and that it be carved by the Creator and the Maker, and if this [man of wood] is he who must nourish and sustain us when there is light when it is day!" . . .

Then they talked and spoke the truth: "Your figures of wood shall come out well; they shall speak and talk on earth."

"So may it be," they answered when they spoke.

And instantly the figures were made of wood. They looked like men, talked like men, and populated the surface of the earth.

They existed and multiplied; they had daughters, they had sons, these wooden figures; but they did not have souls, nor minds, they did not remember their Creator, their Maker; they walked on all fours, aimlessly.

They no longer remembered the Heart of Heaven and therefore they fell out of favor. It was merely a trial, an attempt at man. At first they spoke, but their face was without expression; their feet and hands had no strength; they had no blood, nor substance, nor moisture, nor flesh; their cheeks were dry, their feet and hands were dry, and their flesh was yellow.

Therefore, they no longer thought of their Creator nor their Maker, nor of those who made them and cared for them.

These were the first men who existed in great numbers on the face of the earth.

---

[2] diviners—persons skilled in foretelling the future.

[3] *tzité*—hard, red seeds of the coral tree, used by the Quiché in divination.

QUESTIONS TO CONSIDER

1. How do the Quiché gods relate to one another in the process of creating the world?

2. Based on this Quiché myth, what is the essential function of created beings?

Trickster Tales

In addition to sacred myths, Native American oral tradition is also rich in folk tales told for entertainment. A common hero of these tales is the trickster, a folklore figure displaying elements of both cunning and stupidity. The first of the following trickster tales is an origin story told by the Caddo people of the Great Plains; the second is a Cherokee folk tale.

Coyote and the Origin of Death

In the beginning of this world there was no such thing as death. Everyone continued to live until there were so many people that there was no room for any more on the earth. The chiefs held a council to determine what to do. One man arose and said that he thought it would be a good plan to have the people die and be gone for a little while, and then return. As soon as he sat down Coyote[1] jumped up and said that he thought that people ought to die forever, for this little world was not large enough to hold all of the people, and if the people who died came back to life, there would not be food enough for all. All of the other men objected, saying that they did not want their friends and relatives to die and be gone forever, for then people would grieve and worry and there would not be any happiness in the world. All except Coyote decided to have the people die and be gone for a little while, and then to come back to life again.

The medicine men built a large grass house facing the east, and when they had completed it they called the men of the tribe together and told them that they had decided to have the people who died come to the medicine house and there be restored to life. The chief medicine man said they would sing a song that would call the spirit of the dead to the grass house, and when the spirit came they would . . . restore it to life again. All of the people were glad, for they were anxious for the dead to be restored to life and come again and live with them.

After a time—when the first man had died—the medicine men assembled in the grass house and sang. In about ten days a whirlwind blew from the west and circled about the grass house. Coyote saw it. And as the whirlwind was about to enter the house, he closed the door. The spirit in the whirlwind, finding the door closed, whirled on by. Death forever was then

---

[1] Coyote—the principal trickster figure in the mythology of the Native Americans of the Great Plains.

introduced, and people from that time on grieved about the dead and were unhappy.

Now whenever anyone meets a whirlwind or hears the wind whistle he says: "There is someone wandering about." Ever since Coyote closed the door, the spirits of the dead have wandered over the earth, trying to find some place to go, until at last they find the road to Spirit Land.

Coyote jumped up and ran away and never came back, for when he saw what he had done he was afraid. Ever after that he ran from one place to another, always looking back first over one shoulder and then over the other, to see if anyone was pursuing him, and ever since then he has been starving, for no one will give him anything to eat.

The Rabbit and the Tar Wolf

Once upon a time there was such a severe drought that all streams of water and all lakes were dried up. In this emergency the beasts assembled together to devise means to **procure**[2] water. It was proposed by one to dig a well. All agreed to do so except the hare. She refused because it would soil her tiny paws. The rest, however, dug their well and were fortunate enough to find water. The hare beginning to suffer and thirst, and having no right to the well, was thrown upon her wits to procure water. She determined, as the easiest way, to steal from the public well. The rest of the animals, surprised to find that the hare was so well supplied with water, asked her where she got it. She replied that she arose betimes[3] in the morning and gathered the dewdrops. However the wolf and the fox suspected her of theft and hit on the following plan to detect her:

They made a wolf of tar and placed it near the well. On the following night the hare came as usual after her supply of water. On seeing the tar wolf she demanded who was there. Receiving no answer she repeated the demand, threatening to kick the wolf if he did not reply. She receiving no reply kicked the wolf, and by this means adhered to the tar and was caught. When the fox and wolf got hold of her they consulted what it was best to do with her. One proposed cutting her head off. This the hare protested would be useless, as it had often been tried without hurting her. Other methods were proposed for dispatching[4] her, all of which she said would be useless. At last it was proposed to let her loose to perish in a thicket. Upon this the hare affected great uneasiness and pleaded hard for life. Her enemies, however, refused to listen and she was accordingly let loose. As soon, however, as she was out of reach of her enemies she gave a whoop, and bounding away she exclaimed: "This is where I live."

---

[2] **procure**—obtain.

[3] betimes—early.

[4] dispatching—killing.

QUESTIONS TO CONSIDER

1. From the stories of the coyote and the hare, what are some of the main qualities of a mythological trickster?

2. The coyote story explains the origin of death. What else does it explain?

3. A folk tale such as "The Rabbit and the Tar Wolf" was told primarily for entertainment. Do you think it also teaches? Why or why not?

4. What do you think a figure such as the trickster represents?

Sacred Songs

Much of the oral poetry of the Native American peoples expresses a religious feeling that combines spirituality with a deeply rooted reverence for the natural world. These songs are both from Pueblo Indian peoples.

Song of the Sky Loom

Mother Earth   Father Sky
we are your children

With tired backs we bring you gifts you love

Then weave for us a garment of brightness,
its warp the white light of morning,
weft[1] the red light of evening,
fringes the falling rain,
its border the standing rainbow.

Thus weave for us a garment of brightness
so we may walk fittingly where birds sing,
so we may walk fittingly where grass is green.

Mother Earth   Father Sky

---

[1] warp . . . weft—The lengthwise threads in woven cloth are the warp; the crosswise threads are the weft.

I Have Killed the Deer

I have killed the deer.
I have crushed the grasshopper
And the plants he feeds upon.
I have cut through the heart
Of trees growing old and straight.
I have taken fish from water
And birds from the sky.
In my life I have needed death
So that my life can be.
When I die I must give life
To what has nourished me.
The earth receives my body
And gives it to the plants
And to the caterpillars
To the birds
And to the coyotes
Each in its own turn so that
The circle of life is never broken.

QUESTIONS TO CONSIDER

1. What relationships are expressed between human beings and nature in "Song of the Sky Loom" and "I Have Killed the Deer"?

2. In "Song of the Sky Loom" natural phenomena are compared to woven cloth; in "I Have Killed the Deer" they are described as a "circle of life." What is similar about these images?

3. What is the attitude toward death in "I Have Killed the Deer"?

The Sun Dance

LUTHER STANDING BEAR

The Sun Dance, an annual sacrificial ritual lasting several days, was the most important religious event of the year for the Sioux people. Held each summer, it brought different bands of the Sioux together to perform religious rituals intended to preserve their physical and spiritual well-being. Between 1881 and 1935, in an attempt to suppress Indian religious practices, the U.S. government prohibited the Sun Dance and other Native American forms of worship. In the following account, Luther Standing Bear describes the last performance of the Sun Dance held before the government ban went into effect.

It was about the middle of the summer of 1879 that I saw the last great Sun Dance of the Sioux. The Brules[1] were holding the dance about six miles southwest of Rosebud Agency, on the place where old Chief Two Strikes's band now have their **allotments**.[2] As I started for Carlisle Indian School in the fall of 1879, I cannot say whether this was the last dance held or not.

I have read many descriptions of this dance, and I have been to different tribes which claimed they did the "real thing," but there is a great difference in their dances from the Sun Dance of the Sioux.

The Sun Dance started many years before Christopher Columbus drifted to these shores. We then knew that there was a God above us all. We called God "Wakan Tanka," or the "Big Holy," or sometimes "Grandfather." You call God "Father." I bring this before you because I want you to know that this dance was our religious belief. According to our legend, the red man was to have this dance every summer, to fulfill our religious duty. It was a sacrificial dance.

During the winter if any member of the tribe became ill, perhaps a brother or a cousin would be brave enough to go to the medicine man and say, "I will sacrifice my body to the Wakan Tanka, or Big Holy, for the one who is sick." Or if the buffalo were beginning to get scarce, some one would sacrifice himself so that the tribe might have something to eat.

The medicine man would then take this brave up to the mountain alone, and announce to the Great Spirit that the young

---

[1] Brules—one of the bands of the Sioux.

[2] **allotments**—grants of land.

man was ready to be sacrificed. When the parents of this young man heard that he was to go through the Sun Dance, some of his brothers or cousins would sacrifice themselves with him as an honor.

If some young man of another band had the desire to go through the Sun Dance, some of his friends or relatives might offer to dance with him. Sometimes as many as thirty or forty braves went into the dance.

As soon as the women heard that there was to be a Sun Dance in their band, they began making all the things which were necessary for the ceremony. They placed beautiful porcupine-quill-work[3] on the eagle bone whistles which the men carried in their mouths during the dance, as well as the beautiful head-dresses for the dancers. These were made from porcupine-quill-work. The dancer wore a piece of buckskin around the waist, hanging down like a skirt. This also had pretty quill-work decorations. Soon all the things were ready for the dance.

When the chiefs learned this dance was coming, they called a meeting and selected a place they thought as best suited to hold it. They then sent word to the other bands to get ready. . . .

The first day all the people collected at the center of the camp and some scouts were selected to go out and look for the cottonwood pole which was to be used in the dance. . . .

One of the old-timers would then relate how they had found a pole which was considered good enough to be used in

the dance. Then everybody got ready to go to the place where the pole had been found.

All the various lodges[4] of the tribe now gathered in the timber near the place where the pole was located. . . .

After all had finished their ceremonies, some one cut the tree down. There were about twenty men to carry this pole. They had long sticks which they put under it, and two men to a stick to carry it. Everybody was carrying something. Some carried forked branches, others limbs of the tree, etc. They had no one to order them around, but every one did his share toward this religious dance.

As the twenty men lifted the pole, they walked slowly toward the camp. The rest of the tribe trailed along behind. They stopped three times, and each time a medicine man howled like a wolf. . . .

At last the men came in with the pole. Then the lodges had some more ceremonies to be gone through with, while some of the men started to dig the hole in which to set the pole. Others would get busy arranging forked poles in a circle. This circle was to serve as our hall.

When the hole was ready, all the men from the different lodges got together to help erect the pole, which was sometimes sixty or seventy feet long. They tied two braided rawhide ropes about the middle of the pole, on which some brave was to hang. Other ropes were to be used to hoist the pole into place. . . .

When all was ready, some of the men used forked poles, some held on to the

---

[3] procupine-quill-work—ornaments made from the stiff outer spines of the porcupine.

[4] lodges—subdivisions within the tribe.

ropes, and others got hold of the pole. It required about forty men to do this work properly. The pole must be raised and dropped in the hole at one operation, and with no second lifting. Some pushed, others pulled, while the men with the forked sticks lifted. As the pole dropped in to the hole, everybody cheered.

There was a strong superstition regarding this pole. It was believed that if the pole dropped before it was set into the hole, all our wishes and hopes would be shattered. There would be great thunderstorms and high winds; our shade or council hall would be blown away, and there would be no Sun Dance. On top of this, it was believed that the whole tribe would have a run of bad luck.

Consequently, when this pole was being erected, every man used all his strength to ward off any accident or **mishap**.[5] We were taught to believe that if all minds worked together, it helped a great deal. We were taught this by our parents, and we had strong faith in it.

The pole was always a cottonwood tree, as I have previously stated. No other tree would do. It was not always a straight tree, but there was always a branch which extended out from the main trunk. This would be about thirty or forty feet up. This branch would be cut off about four feet from the trunk. On the top of the pole, branches with leaves on would be left. . . .

They made a bundle of branches from the tree which were wrapped in bark and tied together. This bundle was placed in the branch which had been cut off about four feet from the trunk. When this bundle

was in place, it looked not unlike a huge cross, when viewed from a distance.

From this cross-piece hung something which resembled a buffalo and a man. These **effigies**[6] were cut from rawhide and were tied up with rawhide rope. . . .

When the main big pole was all completed, the men bent their energies toward the dancing hall, or shade, as it should rightfully be called. All the forked poles were placed in a double circle, about fifteen feet apart, with an opening left toward the east. Long sticks were laid from one forked pole to another in the inner circle as well as the outside circle. We used no nails in those days, and anything that was to be fastened must be bound with rawhide or tied with bark. In this case, we peeled off the bark of the willow trees and used that to fasten the poles together. Then the longest tipi[7] poles would be brought in, and laid from the inner to the outer circle. The outside wall was made from **entwined**[8] branches, and on top would be laid the largest tipi coverings, which made a fine shade. This "shade" was about one hundred and fifty feet in diameter, with a depth of about fifteen feet. It was considered a great honor to have one's tipi covering chosen for this purpose. . . .

While this dance was in progress, different medicine men were in the tipis with the young men who were to do the Sun Dance. From each tipi came six, eight, and

---

[5] **mishap**—unfortunate accident.

[6] **effigies**—images or representations.

[7] tipi—conical, hide-covered dwelling of many of the Plains Indians; also *tepee*.

[8] **entwined**—twisted together.

sometimes ten from a band to dance. There was a leader, who carried a pipe of peace; the others followed one by one. They wore buffalo robes with the hair outside, and quite resembled a band of buffalo coming to a stream to drink.

After these Sun Dance candidates reached the shade from their tipis, they did not go in immediately, but marched around the outside three times. After the fourth time, they went in and took their places. Then the medicine man came forward and took charge of four or eight of the dancers. Four of them must be painted alike. They put on beautiful head-dresses richly ornamented with porcupine quills. Their wrists were wound around with sagebrush, and the eagle-bone whistles they used were likewise decorated.

This was a very solemn affair. These men were to dance for three or four days, without food or water. Some of their relatives cried; others sang to praise them and made them feel courageous.

The singers were now in their places. They used no tom-tom, but sat around a large buffalo hide which lay flat on the ground, using large sticks to beat upon the dried skin.

The braves started dancing as soon as the sun started to rise. They stood facing the sun with both hands raised above their heads, the eagle-bone whistles in their mouths, and they blew on these every time the singers hit the skin with their sticks. All day long they stood in one position, facing the sun, until it set. . . .

The dance would be kept up until one of the participants fainted, then he was laid out on one of the sagebrush beds. On the second day of the dance a young man who had started it would come into the shade. First he would walk all around the hall so that all could see him. Then he went straight to the pole. He was giving himself for a living sacrifice. Two medicine men would lift the young man and lay him down under the pole. An old man would then come forward with a very sharp-pointed knife. He would take hold of the breast of the young brave, pull the skin forward, and pierce it through with his knife. Then he would insert a wooden pin (made from the plum tree) through the slit and tie a strong buckskin thong to this pin.

From the pole two rawhide ropes were suspended. The candidate would now be lifted up and the buckskin string tied to the rawhide rope. The candidate was now hanging from his breasts, but the rope was long enough for him to remain on the ground. Although the blood would be running down from the knife **incision**,[9] the candidate would smile, although every one knew he must be suffering intense pain.

At this point the friends or relatives of the young brave would sing and praise him for his courage. Then they would give away ponies or make other presents. The singers now began to sing and the young brave to dance. The other dancers were behind him, four in a line, and they accompanied his dancing. These dancers always stood in one spot while they danced, but the candidate danced and at the same time

---

[9] **incision**—cut.

pulled at the rope, trying to tear out the wooden pin fastened through his breasts.

If he tried very hard and was unsuccessful, his friends and relatives possibly could not bear to see him suffer any longer; so they would give away a pony to some one who would help him tear loose. This party would stand behind the dancer and seize him around the waist, while the candidate at the same time would throw himself backward, both pulling with all their strength. If they could not yet tear the candidate loose, an old man with a sharp knife would cut the skin off, and the dancer would fall beneath the pole. Then he would be picked up and carried to a sagebrush bed. Occasionally a man with a very strong constitution, after tearing loose, would get off his bed and resume the dancing. I have often seen these braves with their own blood dried to their bodies, yet going on with the dance.

This brave candidate fasted three or four days; taking no food or water during that time, instead of the forty days the Savior[10] did. The candidate had his body pierced beneath the cross. I learned all about this religion in the natural way, but after learning how to read the white man's books I compared your religion with ours; but religion, with us Indians, is stronger.

Many things were done during this dance which were similar to what I have read about Christ. We had one living sacrifice, and he fasted three or four days instead of forty. This religious ceremony was not always held in the same place. We did not commercialize our belief. Our medicine men received no salary. Hell was unknown

to us. We trusted one another, and our word was as good as the white man's gold of today. We were then true Christians.

After the dance was over, everybody moved away, going where he pleased. It was a free country then. But afterward, if we ever returned to that sacred spot where the pole was yet standing, with the crosspiece attached, we stood for a long time in reverent attitude, because it was a sacred place to us.

But things have changed, even among the white people. They tear down their churches and let playhouses be built on the spot. What can be your feeling of reverence when you think of the house of God, in which you worshipped, being used to make fun in?

As I have many times related in my story, I always wanted to be brave, but I do not think I could ever have finished one of these Sun Dances.

---

[10] Savior—Jesus Christ.

QUESTIONS TO CONSIDER

1. What characteristics did the Sun Dance share with religious ceremonials with which you are familiar?

2. In concluding his account, Luther Standing Bear made several implicit criticisms of Christianity. What did he object to? Do you agree with him?

3. Do you think the U.S. government was justified in prohibiting the Sun Dance? Why or why not?

Native American Art

Like their poetry, much Native American visual art dealt with sacred themes. Most of the following artifacts depict gods or other supernatural beings. Through the creation of such objects, Native Americans sought power to control their environment. Even everyday objects, such as the Mimbres pot below, might possess power. When the Mimbres buried the dead, they covered their heads with a pot that had been symbolically "killed" by piercing it with a hole.

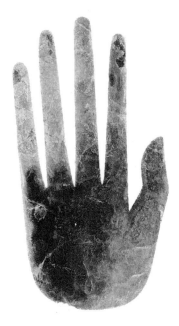

▲
This image of a hand was carved from mica by the Hopewell people, a Mound Builder culture of southern Ohio.

▲
The Mimbres of the American Southwest produced this pot decorated with a design of a bat between 1000 and 1150 A.D.

▲
This statue of Xilonen, Aztec goddess of the young corn, was created by the Huastecs, a Maya people conquered by the Aztecs in the 1400s.

This Aztec ornament depicts a serpent, a symbol associated with their god Huitzilopochtli.
▼

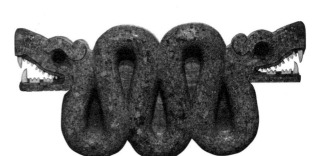

Painted by Short Bull, a leader of the Oglala Sioux in the late 1800s, this image depicts the Sun Dance, the central religious ritual of the Sioux (page 181).
▼

▲
A wall decoration from the Nootka culture of the Northwest Coast shows highly stylized representations of animals—a thunder bird, a killer whale, a lightning snake, and a wolf.

Kachinas are believed by the Hopi and other Pueblo Indians of the American Southwest to be the mythical ancestors of human beings. ▶

QUESTIONS TO CONSIDER

1. What do you feel are some of the dominant qualities expressed by these artifacts?

2. Although Native American artists did not aim at realism in art but rather to capture the essence of something, their work still reflects careful observation. What are some realistic details in the stylized images on the Mimbres pot and Nootka wall decoration?

3. What artifacts in modern society function as images of power?

Tribal Government

Founded in the late 1500s, the Iroquois Confederacy was originally a union of five related tribes—Mohawks, Oneidas, Onondagas, Cayugas, and Senecas—who lived in upper New York State. "The Origin of the Long House" is a Seneca legend of the founding of the Confederacy by two peacemakers, Hiawatha of the Onandagas and Deganawida of the Mohawks. The Incas ruled an extensive empire in western South America until conquered by the Spanish in the 1530s. The passage from The Royal Commentaries of the Incas, by Garcilaso de la Vega (1539–1616), deals with Inca law.

The Origin of the Long House

Where the Mohawk river empties into the Hudson in ancient times there was a Mohawk village. The people there were fierce and warlike and were continually sending out war parties against other settlements and returning would bring back long strings of scalps to number the lives they had destroyed. But sometimes they left their own scalps behind and never returned. They loved warfare better than all other things and were happy when their hands were slimy with blood. They boasted that they would eat up all other nations, and so they continued to go against other tribes and fight with them.

Now among the Mohawks was a chief named Deganawida, a very wise man, and he was very sad of heart because his people loved war too well. So he spoke in council and implored them to desist lest they perish altogether, but the young warriors would not hear him and laughed at his words; but he did not cease to warn them until at last despairing of moving them by ordinary means, he turned his face to the west and wept as he journeyed onward and away from his people. At length he reached a lake whose shores were fringed with bushes, and being tired he lay down to rest. Presently, as he lay meditating, he heard the soft spattering of water sliding from a skillful paddle and peering out from his hiding place, he saw in the red light of sunset a man leaning over his canoe and dipping into the shallow water with a basket. When he raised it up it was full of shells, the shells of the periwinkles that live in shallow pools. The man pushed his canoe toward the shore and sat down on the beach, where he kindled a fire. Then he began to string his shells and, finishing a string, would touch the shells and talk. Then, as if satisfied, he would lay it down and make another until he had a large number. Deganawida watched the strange proceeding with wonder. The sun had long since set, but Deganawida still watched the man with the shell strings sitting in the flickering light of the fire that shadowed the bushes and shimmered over the lake.

After some deliberation he called out, "Kwē, I am a friend!" and stepping out upon the sand stood before the man with the shells. "I am Deganawida," he said, "and come from the Mohawk."

"I am Hiawatha of the Onondaga," came the reply.

Then Deganawida inquired about the shell strings for he was very curious to know their import and Hiawatha answered, "They are the rules of life and laws of good government. This all white string is a sign of truth, peace and good will; this black string is a sign of hatred, of war and of a bad heart; the string with the alternate beads, black and white, is a sign that peace should exist between the nations. This string with white on either end and black in the middle is a sign that wars must end and peace be declared." And so Hiawatha lifted his strings and read the laws.

Then said Deganawida, "You are my friend indeed, and the friend of all nations. Our people are weak from warring and weak from being warred upon. We who speak one tongue should combine against the Hadiondas[1] instead of helping them by killing one another, but my people are weary of my advising and would not hear me."

"I, too, am of the same mind," said Hiawatha, "but Tatodaho[2] slew all my brothers and drove me away. So I came to the lakes and have made the laws that should govern men and nations. I believe that we should be as brothers in a family instead of enemies."

"Then come with me," said Deganawida, "and together let us go back to my people and explain the rules and laws."

So when they had returned, Deganawida called a council of all the chiefs and warriors and the women, and Hiawatha set forth the plan he had devised. The words had a marvelous effect. The people were astonished at the wisdom of the strange chief from the Onondaga, and when he had finished his **exposition**[3] the chiefs promised obedience to his laws. They delegated Deganawida to go with him to the Oneida and council with them, then to go onward to Onondaga and win over the arrogant erratic Tatodaho, the tyrannical chief of the Onondaga. Thus it was that together they went to the Oneida country and won over their great chief and made the people promise to support the proposed league. Then the Oneida chief went with Hiawatha to the Cayugas and told them how by supporting the league they might preserve themselves against the fury of Tatodaho. So when the Cayuga had promised allegiance, Deganawida turned his face toward Onondaga and with his comrades went before Tatodaho. Now when Tatodaho learned how three nations

---

[1] Hadiondas—enemies of the Iroquois.

[2] Tatodaho—brutal chief of the Onandagas.

[3] **exposition**—detailed explanation.

had combined against him he became very angry and ran into the forest where he gnawed at his fingers and ate grass and leaves. His evil thoughts became serpents and sprouted from his skull and waving in a tangled mass hissed out venom. But Deganawida did not fear him and once more asked him to give his consent to a league of peace and friendship; but he was still wild until Hiawatha combed the snakes from his head and told him that he should be the head chief of the confederacy and govern it according to the laws that Hiawatha had made. Then he recovered from his madness and asked why the Seneca had not been visited, for the Seneca outnumbered all the other nations and were fearless warriors. "If their jealousy is aroused," he said, "they will eat us."

Then the delegations visited the Seneca and the other nations to the west but only the Seneca would consider the proposal. The other nations were exceedingly jealous.

Thus a peace pact was made and the Long House built, and Deganawida was the builder, but Hiawatha was its designer.

Now moreover, the first council of Hiawatha and Deganawida was in a place now called Albany at the mouth of a small stream that empties into the Hudson.

from *Royal Commentaries of the Incas*

Garcilaso de la Vega

They had no **pecuniary**[4] fines or **confiscation**[5] of property, saying that to punish the offender's possessions and leave him alive was not the way to rid the state of evil-doing, but merely to rid the evildoer of his responsibilities and leave him the freer to commit greater misdeeds. If any *curaca*[6] rebelled—and this was the crime the Incas punished most severely— or committed any other crime that merited the death penalty, even though the latter was inflicted, the victim's successor was not deprived of his estate, but entrusted with it with a warning about the guilt and punishment of his father so that he should beware of a similar fate. . . . The judge had no discretion about the penalties required by law, but was obliged to apply them in their **integrity**,[7] under pain of death for infringement of the royal command. They held that if the judge had discretion the majesty of the law, established by the king with the opinion and consent of the gravest and most experienced men of the Council, would be diminished. Moreover such gravity and experience was wanting in single judges, and the use of discretion would make them **venal**[8] and open the door to the purchase of justice by bribery or **importunity**,[9] leading to utter confusion in the state, since each judge would do as he thought fit and it was not right that anyone should constitute himself a legislator, when his duty was to execute what the law prescribed, however rigorous.

---

[4] **pecuniary**—consisting of money.

[5] **confiscation**—seizure.

[6] *curaca*—local ruler.

[7] **integrity**—wholeness.

[8] **venal**—corrupt.

[9] **importunity**—persistent urging.

Of course, when one considers how severe the laws were and that the usual penalty for even a small infraction was, as has been said, death, it may be maintained that they were the laws of barbarians. Yet, if we ponder on the benefit received by the commonwealth from this very severity, we may on the contrary affirm that they were the laws of wise people who wished to **extirpate**[10] evil-doing from their state. The infliction of the legal penalties with such severity and the love of life and hatred of death natural in men caused them to detest the crimes that led to death. Consequently there was hardly any crime to punish the whole year through in the empire of the Incas, the whole thirteen hundred leagues[11] of it and all its various tribes with their different languages being governed by the same laws and ordinances, as if it were of one house. The fact that the laws were regarded as divine was also important in securing that they were kept with love and respect, for as in their vain faith they held the kings to be children of the Sun and the Sun to be God, they considered any ordinary command of the king to be a divine commandment, and the special laws for the common good even more so. So they said the Sun ordered the laws to be made and revealed them to his child the Inca.[12] Hence lawbreaking was held to be sacrilegious and **anathema**,[13] even if the crime were committed in ignorance. . . .

There were no appeals from one court to another in any suit, whether civil or criminal, for as the judge had no latitude, the law applicable to the case was enforced simply at the first instance and the case was closed, though indeed, owing to the government of those kings and the way of life of their subjects, there were in any case few civil cases. Each town had a judge for the cases that might occur, and he was obliged to carry out the law within five days after hearing the parties. If any case of more importance or greater **atrocity**[14] than usual occurred, for which a higher judge was required, they would go to the capital of the province there to have it settled, for in the chief town of each province there was a higher governor in case of need, so that no **plaintiff**[15] need leave his own town or province to seek justice. For the Inca kings understood that the poor, because of their **penury**,[16] could not be expected to seek justice outside their provinces or in many courts because of the expense involved and the inconvenience they would suffer, which often exceed the value of the object of the case. Thus justice perishes, especially if the poor sue the rich and powerful, who crush the justice of the poor with their might. Wishing to remedy these wrongs, the Inca princes gave no occasion for the judges to exercise **discretion**[17] or for many courts to exist, or for plaintiffs to have to travel beyond their

---

[10] **extirpate**—destroy completely.

[11] leagues—measures of distance equal to three miles.

[12] the Inca—ruler of the Inca Empire.

[13] **anathem**a—accursed.

[14] **atrocity**—brutality, viciousness.

[15] **plaintiff**—person who brings a legal action in a court.

[16] **penury**—poverty.

[17] **discretion**—independent judgment.

own provinces. The ordinary judges had to report the sentences they gave each moon[18] to superior judges, and these reported to higher judges, for at court there were judges of various ranks, according to the kind and seriousness of the business. Indeed in all the ministries of the Inca state there was a hierarchy from the lower to the higher and so up to the supreme officers, who were presidents or viceroys of the four quarters of the empire. The reports were made to show that due justice had been administered so that the lower judges should not neglect it, or if they did neglect it, that they should be severely punished. This was a kind of secret investigation made every month. The manner of making such reports to the Inca and the members of his Supreme Council was by means of knots tied in strings of various colors which they read as figures. Knots of certain colors meant the crimes punished, and small threads of various colors attached to the thicker strings showed the penalty meted out and the law that had been applied. Thus they made themselves understood without the use of writing. . . .

It certainly often amazed the Spaniards that their own best accountants went astray in their calculations while the Indians were perfectly accurate in dividing and reckoning, and the more difficult the operation the easier it seemed. Those who operated the system did nothing else day or night, and thus became perfect and highly skilled in it.

If any dissension[19] arose between two kingdoms or provinces about boundaries or grazing rights, the Inca would send one of the judges of the blood royal, who enquired, and saw with his own eyes what the two parties claimed, and tried to reconcile[20] them: the decision was given as a judgment in the Inca's name and became an inviolable law, as if pronounced by the king himself. If the judge failed to reconcile the parties, he reported what had happened to the Inca with his recommendation about the claims of each party and the obstacles. The Inca then pronounced sentence, or if the judge's report did not satisfy him, ordered the case to be suspended until he should next visit the district so that he could see for himself and decide accordingly. Their subjects regarded this as a great grace and favor on the part of the Inca.

---

[18] moon—month.

[19] dissension—discord.

[20] reconcile—pacify.

QUESTIONS TO CONSIDER

1. In "The Origin of the Long House," what seems to be the reason for the continual tribal warfare?

2. Why does Tatodaho decide to join the peace pact promoted by Hiawatha and Deganawida?

3. According to Garcilaso de la Vega, what contributed to the peacefulness of the Inca Empire?

4. Neither the Iroquois or the Incas developed a writing system. How did their non-written methods of record-keeping help in maintaining peace?

Narratives of Encounter

From the moment that Europeans and Native Americans first encountered one another in the Western Hemisphere, the destruction of the Indian way of life began through war, disease, economic exploitation, religious prejudice, and other factors. The following two narratives picture the beginning and end of that sad process. The first is an Aztec account of the arrival of the Spanish under Hernán Cortés, who between 1519 and 1521 conquered the Aztec Empire. The second is a Kiowa folktale telling of the final departure of the buffalo herds upon which their way of life had depended.

from *Codex Florentino*

The year 13-Rabbit[1] now approached its end. And when it was about to end, they appeared, they were seen again. The report of their coming was brought to Motecuhzoma,[2] who immediately sent out messengers. It was as if he thought the new arrival was our prince Quetzalcoatl.[3]

This is what he felt in his heart: He has appeared! He has come back! He will come here, to the place of his throne and canopy, for that is what he promised when he departed!

Motecuhzoma sent five messengers to greet the strangers and to bring them gifts. . . .

He said to them: "Come forward, my Jaguar Knights,[4] come forward. It is said that our lord has returned to this land. Go

to meet him. Go to hear him. Listen well to what he tells you; listen and remember."

Motecuhzoma also said to the messengers: "Here is what you are to bring our lord. This is the treasure of Quetzalcoatl." This treasure was the god's finery: a serpent mask inlaid with turquoise, a decoration for the breast made of quetzal[5] feathers, a collar woven in the petatillo style with a gold disk in the center, and a shield decorated with gold and mother-of-pearl

---

[1] year 13-Rabbit—corresponding to 1519.

[2] Motecuhzoma—ruler of the Aztecs; also known as Montezuma.

[3] Quetzalcoatl—divine ruler of the Toltecs, predecessors of the Aztecs; tradition held that he had sailed eastward, promising to return.

[4] Jaguar Knights—elite warriors among the Aztecs.

[5] quetzal—brightly colored bird of the rain forests of Mexico and Central America.

and bordered with quetzal feathers with a **pendant**[6] of the same feathers. . . .

Then Motecuhzoma gave them the finery of Quetzalcoatl. This finery was: a **diadem**[7] made of jaguar skin and pheasant feathers and adorned with a large green stone, round turquoise earrings with curved pendants of shell and gold, a collar of *chalchihuites*[8] in the petatillo style with a disk of gold in the center, a cloak with red borders, and little gold bells for the feet.

There was also a golden shield, pierced in the middle, with quetzal feathers around the rim and a pendant of the same feathers, the crooked staff of Ehecatl with a cluster of white stones at the crook, and his sandals of fine soft rubber.

These were the many kinds of adornments that were known as "divine adornments." They were placed in the possession of the messengers to be taken as gifts of welcome along with many other objects, such as a golden snail shell and a golden diadem. All these objects were packed into great baskets; they were loaded into **panniers**[9] for the long journey.

Then Motecuhzoma gave the messengers his final orders. He said to them: "Go now, without delay. Do reverence to our lord the god. Say to him: 'Your deputy, Motecuhzoma, has sent us to you. Here are the presents with which he welcomes you home to Mexico.'"

When they arrived at the shore of the sea, they were taken in canoes to Xicalanco. They placed the baskets in the same canoes in which they rode, in order to keep them under their personal vigilance. From Xicalanco they followed the coast until they sighted the ships of the strangers.

When they came up to the ships, the strangers asked them: "Who are you? Where are you from?"

"We have come from the City of Mexico."

The strangers said: "You may have come from there, or you may not have. Perhaps you are only inventing it. Perhaps you are mocking us." But their hearts were convinced; they were satisfied in their hearts. They lowered a hook from the bow of the ship, and then a ladder, and the messengers came aboard.

One by one they did reverence to Cortés by touching the ground before him with their lips. They said to him: "If the god will **deign**[10] to hear us, your deputy Motecuhzoma has sent us to render you homage. He has the City of Mexico in his care. He says: 'The god is weary.'"

Then they arrayed the Captain in the finery they had brought him as presents. With great care they fastened the turquoise mask in place, the mask of the god with its crossband of quetzal feathers. A golden earring hung down on either side of this mask. They dressed him in the decorated vest and the collar woven in the petatillo style—the collar of *chalchihuites*, with a disk of gold in the center.

---

[6] **pendant**—hanging ornament.

[7] **diadem**—crown.

[8] *chalchihuites*—green stones such as jade.

[9] **panniers**—baskets.

[10] **deign**—be willing.

Next they fastened the mirror to his hips, dressed him in the cloak known as "the ringing bell" and adorned his feet with the greaves[11] used by the Huastecas, which were set with *chalchihuites* and hung with little gold bells. In his hand they placed the shield with its fringe and pendant of quetzal feathers, its ornaments of gold and mother-of-pearl. Finally they set before him the pair of black sandals. As for the other objects of divine finery, they only laid them out for him to see.

The Captain asked them: "And is this all? Is this your gift of welcome? Is this how you greet people?"

They replied: "This is all, our lord. This is what we have brought you."

Then the Captain gave orders, and the messengers were chained by the feet and by the neck. When this had been done, the great cannon was fired off. The messengers lost their senses and fainted away. They fell down side by side and lay where they had fallen. But the Spaniards quickly revived them: they lifted them up, gave them wine to drink and then offered them food.

The Captain said to them: "I have heard that the Mexicans are very great warriors, very brave and terrible. If a Mexican is fighting alone, he knows how to retreat, turn back, rush forward and conquer, even if his opponents are ten or even twenty. But my heart is not convinced. I want to see it for myself. I want to find out if you are truly that strong and brave."

Then he gave them swords, spears and leather shields. He said: "It will take place very early, at daybreak. We are going to fight each other in pairs, and in this way we will learn the truth. We will see who falls to the ground!"

They said to the Captain: "Our lord, we were not sent here for this by your deputy Motecuhzoma! We have come on an exclusive mission, to offer you rest and repose and to bring you presents. What the lord desires is not within our **warrant**.[12] If we were to do this, it might anger Motecuhzoma, and he would surely put us to death."

The Captain replied: "No, it must take place. I want to see for myself, because even in Castile they say you are famous as brave warriors. Therefore, eat an early meal. I will eat too. Good cheer!"

With these words he sent them away from the ship. They were scarcely into their canoes when they began to paddle furiously. Some of them even paddled with their hands, so fierce was the anxiety burning in their souls. They said to each other: "My captains, paddle with all your might! Faster, faster! Nothing must happen to us here! Nothing must happen . . . !"

They arrived in great haste at Xicalanco, took a hurried meal there, and then pressed on until they came to Tecpantlayacac. From there they rushed ahead and arrived in Cuetlaxtlan. As on the previous journey, they stopped there to rest. When they were about to depart, the village official said to them: "Rest for at least a day! At least catch your breath!"

---

[11] greaves—leg armor.

[12] **warrant**—authorization.

They said: "No, we must keep on! We must report to our king, Motecuhzoma. We will tell him what we have seen, and it is a terrifying thing. Nothing like it has ever been seen before!" Then they left in great haste and continued to the City of Mexico. They entered the city at night, in the middle of the night.

While the messengers were away, Motecuhzoma could neither sleep nor eat, and no one could speak with him. He thought that everything he did was in vain, and he sighed almost every moment. He was lost in despair, in the deepest gloom and sorrow. Nothing could comfort him, nothing could calm him, nothing could give him any pleasure.

He said: "What will happen to us? Who will outlive it? Ah, in other times I was contented, but now I have death in my heart! My heart burns and suffers, as if it were drowned in spices . . . ! But will our lord come here?"

Then he gave orders to the watchmen, to the men who guarded the palace: "Tell me, even if I am sleeping: 'The messengers have come back from the sea.'" But when they went to tell him, he immediately said: "They are not to report to me here. I will receive them in the House of the Serpent. Tell them to go there." And he gave this order: "Two captives are to be painted with chalk."

The messengers went to the House of the Serpent, and Motecuhzoma arrived. The two captives were then sacrificed before his eyes: their breasts were torn open, and the messengers were sprinkled with their blood. This was done because the messengers had completed a difficult mission: they had seen the gods, their eyes had looked on their faces. They had even conversed with the gods!

When the sacrifice was finished, the messengers reported to the king. They told him how they had made the journey, and what they had seen, and what food the strangers ate. Motecuhzoma was astonished and terrified by their report, and the description of the strangers' food astonished him above all else.

He was also terrified to learn how the cannon roared, how its noise resounded, how it caused one to faint and grow deaf. The messengers told him: "A thing like a ball of stone comes out of its **entrails**:[13] it comes out shooting sparks and raining fire. The smoke that comes out with it has a pestilent[14] odor, like that of rotten mud. This odor penetrates even to the brain and causes the greatest discomfort. If the cannon is aimed against a mountain, the mountain splits and cracks open. If it is aimed against a tree, it shatters the tree into splinters. This is a most unnatural sight, as if the tree had exploded from within."

The messengers also said: "Their trappings and arms are all made of iron. They dress in iron and wear iron casques[15] on their heads. Their swords are iron; their bows are iron; their shields are iron; their

---

[13] **entrails**—internal organs.

[14] pestilent—deadly.

[15] casques—helmets.

spears are iron. Their deer carry them on their backs wherever they wish to go. These deer, our lord, are as tall as the roof of a house.

"The strangers' bodies are completely covered, so that only their faces can be seen. Their skin is white, as if it were made of lime. They have yellow hair, though some of them have black. Their beards are long and yellow, and their moustaches are also yellow. Their hair is curly, with very fine strands.

"As for their food, it is like human food. It is large and white, and not heavy. It is something like straw, but with the taste of a cornstalk, of the pith of a cornstalk. It is a little sweet, as if it were flavored with honey; it tastes of honey, it is sweet-tasting food.

"Their dogs are enormous, with flat ears and long, dangling tongues. The color of their eyes is a burning yellow; their eyes flash fire and shoot off sparks. Their bellies are hollow, their flanks long and narrow. They are tireless and very powerful. They bound here and there, panting, with their tongues hanging out. And they are spotted like an ocelot."[16]

When Motecuhzoma heard this report, he was filled with terror. It was as if his heart had fainted, as if it had shriveled. It was as if he were conquered by despair.

The Buffalo Go
Old Lady Horse

Everything the Kiowas had came from the buffalo. Their tipis[17] were made of buffalo hides, so were their clothes and moccasins.

They ate buffalo meat. Their containers were made of hide, or of bladders or stomachs. The buffalo were the life of the Kiowas.

Most of all, the buffalo was part of the Kiowa religion. A white buffalo calf must be sacrificed in the Sun Dance.[18] The priests used parts of the buffalo to make their prayers when they healed people or when they sang to the powers above.

So, when the white men wanted to build railroads, or when they wanted to farm or raise cattle, the buffalo still protected the Kiowas. They tore up the railroad tracks and the gardens. They chased the cattle off the ranges. The buffalo loved their people as much as the Kiowas loved them.

There was war between the buffalo and the white men. The white men built forts in the Kiowa country, and the woolly-headed buffalo soldiers[19] shot the buffalo as fast as they could, but the buffalo kept coming on, coming on, even into the post cemetery at Fort Sill. Soldiers were not enough to hold them back.

Then the white men hired hunters to do nothing but kill the buffalo. Up and down the plains those men ranged, shooting sometimes as many as a hundred buffalo a day. Behind them came the skinners with their wagons. They piled the hides

---

[16] ocelot—spotted wildcat.

[17] tipis— conical, hide-covered dwelling of many of the Plains Indians; also *tepees*.

[18] Sun Dance—annual sacrificial ritual of some of the Plains Indian peoples (page 181).

[19] buffalo soldiers—Tenth Cavalry, made up of African American troops.

and bones into the wagons until they were full, and then took their loads to the new railroad stations that were being built, to be shipped east to the market. Sometimes there would be a pile of bones as high as a man, stretching a mile along the railroad track.

The buffalo saw that their day was over. They could protect their people no longer. Sadly, the last remnant of the great herd gathered in council, and decided what they would do.

The Kiowas were camped on the north side of Mount Scott, those of them who were still free to camp. One young woman got up very early in the morning. The dawn mist was still rising from Medicine Creek, and as she looked across the water, peering through the haze, she saw the last buffalo herd appear like a spirit dream.

Straight to Mount Scott the leader of the herd walked. Behind him came the cows and their calves, and the few young males who had survived. As the woman watched, the face of the mountain opened.

Inside Mount Scott the world was green and fresh, as it had been when she was a small girl. The rivers ran clear, not red. The wild plums were in blossom, chasing the red buds up the inside slopes. Into this world of beauty the buffalo walked, never to be seen again.

QUESTIONS TO CONSIDER

1. Why did the Aztecs initially welcome the arrival of the Spaniards?

2. Why did Cortés fire cannon in the presence of the Aztec messengers and propose that they fight with his troops?

3. What common qualities do the white men possess in both the Aztec and Kiowa accounts?

4. Which of these two accounts seems the more tragic?

The Aztecs

JANE MCLAREN WALSH AND YOKO SUGIURA

The Aztecs were the last of a series of great civilizations that flourished in Mexico and Central America. Arriving in central Mexico in the 1200s, the Aztecs controlled a large empire by the early 1500s, when they were conquered by a Spanish force under Hernán Cortés (page 194). This article describes the structure of Aztec society and glimpses life in their great cities.

In the fourteenth century A.D., when the Aztecs, along with other ethnic groups, arrived at the shores of the lakes in the central Valley of Mexico, according to their own history and legend, their primary god Huitzilopochtli, "Left-handed Humming-bird," ordered them to settle on an island where they would find an eagle perched on a cactus devouring a serpent. The eagle is the emblem of the war god, Huitzilopotchli, and the serpent is that of the old god Quetzalcoatl. The symbolism is clear. After numerous battles with already established states that, despite Aztec legend, had actually forcibly **relegated**[1] the newcomers to the small island in the lake, the Aztecs defeated the Tepanecs of Atzcapotzalco and became the main power in the Valley of Mexico. In less than two hundred years they built the most power-ful and extensive empire in Mesoamerica.[2] They demanded tribute from their conquered neighbors in the valley and took control over the surrounding *chinampas*, the famous "floating gardens" of Mexico.

Aztec society was tightly **stratified**[3] and contained many hereditary classes, such as the priesthood, the nobility, the military, certain classes of merchants, commoners, and slaves. There were, however, means for achieving some class mobility, chiefly through the military. The social structure was organized around the *calpulli*, twenty corporate groups probably derived from the community's original clans. Each calpulli appointed one chief for civil and religious affairs and, almost always, a sec-ond chief for war. Since agriculture was the basis of life in ancient Mexico, the calpulli controlled the land that supported its

[1] **relegated**—sent to an inferior condition.
[2] Mesoamerica—region including Mexico and Central America.
[3] **stratified**—arranged in levels.

members. Warfare brought new lands and riches in the form of goods and slaves. Successful warriors were granted lands and people to work them. This system of rewards was much like that of the Spaniards, who gained land in Spain at approximately the same period through the reconquest from the Moors.[4] The Spaniards would eventually repeat this tradition in Mexico. In fact, a century before the *encomienda*, the Spanish system of land grants and indentured servitude,[5] was initiated in Mexico, the Aztecs were in the habit of appropriating entire village populations, moving them into more controllable regions, and forcing them to work on state construction projects. Conquered peoples were forced to pay tribute to the Aztec overlords in quantities of finished goods, such as textiles, pottery, and other craft articles. They also paid in raw materials — jade, gold, and silver and other items considered precious, such as tropical bird feathers. In addition, tribute payers were required to supply human beings for slavery or sacrifice. Considering the enormous payments extracted from conquered peoples, it is not difficult to imagine the resentment that groups like the Tlaxcalans must have harbored toward the Aztecs.

The two main Aztec temples in the center of Tenochtitlán were dedicated to the ancient rain god, Tlaloc, and the tribal god, Huitzilopochtli. The latter, according to Aztec belief, demanded continual **sustenance**[6] in the form of human hearts. The sacrifice of living beings, cruelly dispatched by having their hearts cut out of their chests, was a constant in Aztec daily life. The blood of sacrificial victims was thought to be a means of feeding the gods and thus sustaining all creation. According to legend, more than five thousand people were sacrificed at the coronation of Montezuma II to mark the event. Some say the main pyramid was inaugurated with the sacrifice of twenty thousand.

Aside from territorial expansion, sacrifice was one of the main motivations for warfare, which was carried out for the purpose of obtaining victims. "Flower wars," as they were called (blood and flowers seem to be metaphorically the same in Aztec writing), were completely staged, choreographed[7] events. Usually they were fought with subjugated cities, although occasionally defensive allies were the combatants. The duration was agreed upon beforehand and the purpose was to gain captives. Once the requisite captives were obtained, both sides would call a truce.

. . . Tenochtitlán, which covered an area of some ten square miles, several times larger than sixteenth-century London, was one of the wonders of the world. The high towers and painted buildings sparkled in the sunlight. The city was situated on an island in the center of a lake, connected to the mainland by a series of broad causeways, supplied with fresh water by means of a huge aqueduct and surrounded by chinampas, in a valley teeming with wildlife. In these extraordinarily productive chinampas,

---

[4] Moors—North African Arabs and Berbers who ruled parts of Spain and Portugal in the Middle Ages.

[5] indentured servitude—service for a period of time specified in a contract.

[6] **sustenance**—nourishment, food.

[7] choreographed—carefully managed.

the Aztecs cultivated an enormous variety of vegetables and flowers. They only appeared to float, however. The Aztecs formed their gardens artificially by digging ditches in the marshy lakeshore to drain the water and piling up the fertile mud to form the field. Some archaeological evidence indicates that this highly productive agricultural technique may have originated at a much earlier time, but it was during the Aztec reign that the chinampa system became the principal source of their food supply. It is thus easy to understand that the production of chinampas was carefully planned and controlled by the central government. In addition to the chinampas, the surrounding mountains were covered with agricultural terraces, which were irrigated by fresh water brought by the aqueduct. They supplied the city with other varieties of fruits and vegetables.

. . . Tenochtitlán was situated on one of two islands, the other was occupied by its sister city Tlatelolco, with causeways connecting the two cities to the mainland and other surrounding towns like Tláhuac, Texcoco, and Xochimilco. A huge dike,[8] constructed during the rule of Montezuma I, under the guidance of Netzahualcoyotl, the poet-king of Texcoco, separated the brackish[9] water of the largest lake from those surrounding the islands. The writer Francisco de Garáy described in detail the effect of the masterfully engineered dike. "As the lakes of fresh water to the south poured their surplus water into the lake of Mexico through the narrows of Culhuacan and Mexicaltzingo, those waters spread through the western lake, the Lake of Mexico, and completely filled it. . . . In this way the basin of fresh water was converted into a fish pond and a home for all sorts of aquatic fowl. Chinampas covered its surface, separated by **limpid**[10] spaces which were furrowed by swift canoes, and all the suburbs of this enchanting capital became flowery orchards."

The central sacred precinct of Tenochtitlán was larger and more grandiose than that of Tlatelolco. The square was the religious and administrative center of the empire. It was dominated by the enormous pyramid with twin temples dedicated to Huitzilopochtli and Tlaloc, with smaller pyramids to Quetzalcoatl and his rival Tezcatlipoca. A series of wooden racks filled with the skulls of sacrificial victims stood to one side of the round pyramid to the god of wind, Ejecatl. In all there were more than seventy buildings within the enormous court. . . .

Bernal Díaz[11] could not contain his amazement when he described Tenochtitlán's sister city, Tlatelolco. Here he was especially impressed by the great market. "We were astounded at the number of people and the quantity of merchandise that it contained, and at the good order and control that was maintained, for we had never seen such a thing before. The chieftains who accompanied us acted as guides. Each kind of merchandise was kept by itself and had its fixed place marked out. Let us begin with the dealers in gold, silver, and precious

---

[8] dike—embankment used to hold back water.

[9] brackish—slightly salty.

[10] **limpid**—clear.

[11] Bernal Díaz—Spanish officer with Cortés and historian of the conquest of the Aztecs.

stones, feathers, mantles, and embroidered goods. Then there were other wares consisting of Indian slaves both men and women. . . . Next there were other traders who sold great pieces of cloth and cotton, and articles of twisted thread and there were cacahuateros who sold cacao." He goes on to list the merchandise: ropes and sandals, skins of wild animals, vegetables and herbs, fowls, rabbits, deer and young dogs, "every sort of pottery made in a thousand different forms from great water jars to little jugs, these also had a place to themselves." He also remarked upon the honey, lumber, blocks and benches, firewood, *amatl* (bark) paper, tobacco, ointments, dyes, salt and stone knives, axes of copper, brass, and tin, and gourds and painted jars. "I could wish that I had finished telling of all the things which are sold there, but they are so numerous and of such different quality and the great marketplace with its surrounding arcades was so crowded with people, that one would not have been able to see and inquire about it all in two days."

The market with its carefully marked divisions, its "fixed places," speaks volumes about Aztec society, its complexity, sophistication, centralized polity,[12] the enormous variety of craft specialists it produced, and the division of the society into classes of nobility, commoners, and slaves. The market was in a sense an Aztec **discourse**,[13] the means by which this society defined and talked about itself. The variety of goods sold in the market also reflects the many and diverse regions with which Tenochtitlán traded. Trade networks had been established throughout the empire for many years, and long-distance trade sent merchants far outside the imperial domain. They traveled as far south as Central America and as far north as the Pueblos of the American Southwest. The son of an Aztec feather merchant, who had accompanied his father on journeys, was the first to tell the Spaniards tales of the seven cities of Cíbola.[14] Aztec trade was carried out by a hereditary class of merchants, called *pochteca*, who often traveled in long caravans protected by soldiers and the power of the emperor. During Montezuma's reign the pochteca had become rich and powerful. Some trade was state supported and, therefore, had definite political overtones, since pochteca often served as spies, ambassadors, and agents of the emperor. Apparently pochteca always traded at market places within towns. Because they often traveled great distances they usually dealt in high-value, low-bulk items. Many historians believe that trade preceded tribute in the formation of this empire. Traders in search of more varied merchandise traveled farther and farther afield. They were often followed by conquering armies.

---

[12] polity—system of government.

[13] **discourse**—formal discussion.

[14] seven cities of Cíbola—legendary cities of fabulous wealth believed to exist in the American Southwest.

QUESTIONS TO CONSIDER

1. On the basis of this article, what condition in the Aztec Empire might have contributed to the success of the Spanish in conquering it?

2. How did the Aztecs' need for sacrificial victims affect their military policy?

3. How was the great market of Tlatelolco a mirror of Aztec society?

Chapter 6

Greece and Rome

Heroism

Women's Values

The Good Life

◀ This relief from the Ara Pacis ("Altar of Peace") at Rome depicts
a procession of the emperor Augustus and his family.

from

The Iliad

HOMER

The earliest works of Greek literature are Homer's epic poems, The Iliad *and* The Odyssey, *which were written down around 725 B.C.* The Iliad *narrates episodes from near the close of the Trojan War, which the Greeks thought had occurred some 500 years before Homer's time. According to their traditions, this ten-year siege by Greek forces of the city of Troy (located near the northwest coast of what is now Turkey) was undertaken because a Trojan prince had kidnapped the wife of a Greek king. In Book 6 of* The Iliad, *the chief Trojan hero, Hector, who has returned from the battlefield to his home in the city, is asking the servants where his wife, Andromache, has gone.*

A busy, willing servant answered quickly,
"Hector, seeing you want to know the truth,
she hasn't gone to your sisters, brothers' wives
or Athena's shrine[1] where the noble Trojan women
gather to win the great grim goddess over.
Up to the huge gate-tower of Troy she's gone
because she heard our men are so hard-pressed,
the Achaean[2] fighters coming on in so much force.
She sped to the wall in panic, like a madwoman—
the nurse went with her, carrying your child."

At that, Hector spun and rushed from his house,
back by the same way down the wide, well-paved streets
throughout the city until he reached the Scaean Gates,
the last point he would pass to gain the field of battle.
There his warm, generous wife came running up to meet him,

---

[1] Athena's shrine—shrine of Athena, goddess of wisdom and war, who favors the Greeks in their struggle with the Trojans.
[2] Achaean—Greek.

Andromache the daughter of gallant-hearted Eetion
who had lived below Mount Placos rich with timber,
in Thebe below the peaks, and ruled Cilicia's people.
His daughter had married Hector **helmed**[3] in bronze.
She joined him now, and following in her steps
a servant holding the boy against her breast,
in the first flush of life, only a baby,
Hector's son, the darling of his eyes
and radiant as a star . . .
Hector would always call the boy Scamandrius,
townsmen called him Astyanax, Lord of the City,
since Hector was the lone defense of Troy.
The great man of war breaking into a broad smile,
his gaze fixed on his son, in silence. Andromache,
pressing close beside him and weeping freely now,
clung to his hand, urged him, called him: "Reckless one,
my Hector—your own fiery courage will destroy you!
Have you no pity for him, our helpless son? Or me,
and the destiny that weighs me down, your widow,
now so soon. Yes, soon they will kill you off,
all the Achaean forces massed for assault, and then,
bereft[4] of you, better for me to sink beneath the earth.
What other warmth, what comfort's left for me,
once you have met your doom? Nothing but torment!
I have lost my father. Mother's gone as well. . . .
You, Hector—you are my father now, my noble mother,
a brother too, and you are my husband, young and warm and strong!
Pity me, please! Take your stand on the **rampart**[5] here,
before you orphan your son and make your wife a widow.
Draw your armies up where the wild fig tree stands,
there, where the city lies most open to assault,
the walls lower, easily overrun. Three times
they have tried that point, hoping to storm Troy,
their best fighters led by the Great and Little Ajax,
famous Idomeneus, Atreus' sons, valiant Diomedes.

---

[3] **helmed**—helmeted.
[4] **bereft**—deprived.
[5] **rampart**—fortification.

Perhaps a skilled prophet revealed the spot
or their own fury whips them on to attack."

And tall Hector nodded, his helmet flashing:
"All this weighs on my mind too, dear woman.
But I would die of shame to face the men of Troy
and the Trojan women trailing their long robes
if I would shrink from battle now, a coward.
Nor does the spirit urge me on that way.
I've learned it all too well. To stand up bravely,
always to fight in the front ranks of Trojan soldiers,
winning my father great glory, glory for myself.
For in my heart and soul I also know this well:
the day will come when sacred Troy must die,
Priam[6] must die and all his people with him,
Priam who hurls the strong ash spear . . .

                                        Even so,
it is less the pain of the Trojans still to come
that weighs me down, not even of Hecuba[7] herself
or King Priam, or the thought that my own brothers
in all their numbers, all their gallant courage,
may tumble in the dust, crushed by enemies—
That is nothing, nothing beside your agony
when some brazen Argive[8] **hales**[9] you off in tears,
wrenching away your day of light and freedom!
Then far off in the land of Argos you must live,
laboring at a loom, at another woman's beck and call,
fetching water at some spring, Messeis or Hyperia,
resisting it all the way—
the rough yoke of necessity at your neck.
And a man may say, who sees you streaming tears,
'There is the wife of Hector, the bravest fighter
they could field, those stallion-breaking Trojans,
long ago when the men fought for Troy.' So he will say

---

[6] Priam—Hector's father, king of Troy.

[7] Hecuba—Hector's mother, queen of Troy.

[8] Argive—Greek; from Argos, a region of southern Greece.

[9] **hales**—drags.

and the fresh grief will swell your heart once more,
widowed, robbed of the one man strong enough
to fight off your day of slavery.
                                        No, no,
let the earth come piling over my dead body
before I hear your cries, I hear you dragged away!"

In the same breath, shining Hector reached down
for his son—but the boy recoiled,
cringing against his nurse's full breast,
screaming out at the sight of his own father,
terrified by the flashing bronze, the horsehair crest,
the great ridge of the helmet nodding, bristling terror—
so it struck his eyes. And his loving father laughed,
his mother laughed as well, and glorious Hector,
quickly lifting the helmet from his head,
set it down on the ground, fiery in the sunlight,
and raising his son he kissed him, tossed him in his arms,
lifting a prayer to Zeus and the other deathless gods:
"Zeus, all you immortals! Grant this boy, my son,
may be like me, first in glory among the Trojans,
strong and brave like me, and rule all Troy in power
and one day let them say, 'He is a better man than his father!'—
when he comes home from battle bearing the bloody gear
of the mortal enemy he has killed in war—
a joy to his mother's heart."
                                        So Hector prayed
and placed his son in the arms of his loving wife.
Andromache pressed the child to her scented breast,
smiling through her tears. Her husband noticed,
and filled with pity now, Hector stroked her gently,
trying to reassure her, repeating her name: "Andromache,
dear one, why so desperate? Why so much grief for me?
No man will hurl me down to Death, against my fate.
And fate? No one alive has ever escaped it,
neither brave man nor coward, I tell you—
it's born with us the day that we are born.

So please go home and tend to your own tasks,
the **distaff**[10] and the loom, and keep the women
working hard as well. As for the fighting,
men will see to that, all who were born in Troy
but I most of all."

                                    Hector aflash in arms
took up his horsehair-crested helmet once again.
And his loving wife went home, turning, glancing
back again and again and weeping live warm tears.

---

[10] **distaff**—rod for holding wool, flax, etc., in the process of spinning.

QUESTIONS TO CONSIDER

1. For the Greeks, the Homeric epics were a source of moral teaching. What moral values are conveyed in this passage?

2. How does Hector's view about the fate of his city affect his heroic determination?

3. How do Hector's and Andromache's ideas of heroism differ?

4. The Homeric epics are typically impersonal, presenting characters and events objectively. Is that true here? Why or why not?

from

The Trojan Women

EURIPIDES

The Greeks of the city-state of Athens began European theater around 500 B.C. For the Greeks, theater was not simply entertainment; it helped them confront current religious, moral, or political problems. At the time the playwright Euripides (c. 480–406? B.C.) wrote The Trojan Women, *the Athenians were troubled by the growing brutality of their war with another Greek city-state, Sparta, and his play echoed recent atrocity stories. The setting is Troy after its capture by the Greeks (page 206). The city's men are either dead or have fled; among the survivors are the Trojan queen, Hecuba, and her daughter-in-law Andromache, widow of Troy's greatest hero, Hector.*

Andromache. Polyxena lies dead upon Achilles' tomb,[1]
    a gift to a corpse, to a lifeless thing.

Hecuba. My sorrow! That is what Talthybius meant—
    I could not read his riddle.[2] Oh, too plain.

Andromache. I saw her there and left the chariot
    and covered her dead body with my cloak,
    and beat my breast.

Hecuba. Murdered—my child. Oh, wickedly!
    Again I cry to you. Oh, cruelly slain!

Andromache. She has died her death, and happier by far
    dying than I alive.

---

[1] Polyxena . . . Achilles' tomb—The Greeks sacrificed Hecuba's daughter, Polyxena, at the tomb of their greatest hero, Achilles, who had been killed during the final days of the Trojan War.

[2] Talthybius . . . riddle—The Greek messenger Talthybius, unwilling to tell Hecuba the truth, reported that her daughter was free from trouble.

Hecuba. Life cannot be what death is, child.
Death is empty—life has hope.

Andromache. Mother, O Mother, hear a truer word.
Now let me bring joy to your heart.
I say to die is only not to be,
and rather death than life with bitter grief.
They have no pain, they do not feel their wrongs.
But the happy person who has come to wretchedness,
his soul is a lost wanderer,
the old joys that were once, left far behind.
She is dead, your daughter—to her the same
as if she never had been born.
She does not know the wickedness that killed her.
While I—I aimed my shaft at good **repute.**[3]
I gained full measure—then missed happiness.
For all that is called virtuous in a woman
I strove for and I won in Hector's house.
Always because we women, whether right or wrong,
are spoken ill of
unless we stay within our homes, my longing
I set aside and kept the house.
Light talk, **glib**[4] women's words,
could never gain an entrance there.
My own thoughts were enough for me,
best of all teachers to me in my home.
Silence, a tranquil eye, I brought my husband,
knew well in what I should rule him,
and when to give him obedience.
And this report of me came to the Greeks
for my destruction. When they captured me
Achilles' son would have me.
I shall be a slave to those who murdered—
O Hector, my beloved—shall I thrust him aside,
open my heart to the man that comes to me,

---

[3] **repute**—reputation.
[4] **glib**—spoken easily or lightly.

and be a traitor to the dead?
And yet to shrink in **loathing**[5] from him
and make my masters hate me—
One night, men say, one night in a man's bed
will make a woman tame—
Oh, shame! A woman throw her husband off
and in a new bed love another—
Why, a young colt will not run in the yoke
with any but her mate—not a dumb beast
that has not reason, of a lower nature.
O Hector, my beloved, you were all to me,
wise, noble, mighty, in wealth, in manhood, both.
No man had touched me when you took me,
took me from out my father's home
and yoked a girl fast to you.
And you are dead, and I, with other plunder,
am sent by sea to Greece. A slave's yoke there.
Your dead Polyxena you weep for,
what does she know of pain like mine?
The living must have hope. Not I, not anymore.
I will not lie to my own heart. No good will ever come.
But oh, to think it would be sweet.

A Woman.[6] We stand at the same point of pain. You
mourn your ruin,
and in your words I hear my own calamity.

Hecuba. Those ships—I never have set foot on one,
but I have heard of them, seen pictures of them.
I know that when a storm comes which they think
they can ride out, the sailors do their best,
one by the sail, another at the helm, and others **bailing**.[7]
But if great ocean's raging overwhelms them,
they yield to fate.
They give themselves up to the racing waves.

---

[5] **loathing**—disgust, repulsion.

[6] **Woman**—This character is one of the women of Troy who form the chorus, typical of Greek drama. In Greek theater the chorus often commented on the words and actions of the principal characters.

[7] **bailing**—getting water out of a boat.

So in my many sorrows I am dumb.
I yield, I cannot speak.
The great wave from God has conquered me.
But, O dear child, let Hector be,
and let be what has come to him.
Your tears will never call him back.
Give honor now to him who is your master.
Your sweet ways—use them to **allure**[8] him.
So doing you will give cheer to your friends.
Perhaps this child, my own child's son,
you may rear to manhood and great aid for Troy,
and if ever you should have more children,
they might build her again. Troy once more be a city!
Oh—one thought leads another on.
But why again that servant of the Greeks?
I see him coming. Some new plan is here.

(*Enter Talthybius with soldiers. He is troubled and
advances hesitatingly.*)

Talthybius. Wife of the noblest man that was in Troy,
    O wife of Hector, do not hate me.
    Against my will I come to tell you.
    The people and the kings have all resolved—

Andromache. What is it? Evil follows words like those.

Talthybius. This child they order—Oh, how can I say it—

Andromache. Now that he does not go with me to the
    same master—

Talthybius. No man in Greece shall ever be his master.

Andromache. But—leave him here—all that is left of Troy?

Talthybius. I don't know how to tell you. What is bad,
    words can't make better.

Andromache. I feel you kind. But you have not good news.

---

[8] **allure**—attract, tempt.

Talthybius. Your child must die. There, now you know
the whole, bad as it is.

Andromache. Oh, I have heard an evil worse than a slave in her
master's bed.

Talthybius. It was Odysseus[9] had his way. He spoke to all
the Greeks.

Andromache. O God. There is no measure to my pain.

Talthybius. He said a hero's son must not grow up—

Andromache. God, on his own sons may that counsel fall.

Talthybius. —but from the towering wall of Troy be thrown.
Now, now—let it be done—that's wiser.
Don't cling so to him. Bear your pain
the way a brave woman suffers.
You have no strength—don't look to any help.
There's no help for you anywhere.
Think—think.
The city gone—your husband too. And you
a captive and alone, one woman—how
can you do battle with us? For your own good
I would not have you try, and draw
hatred down on you and be shamed.
Oh, hush—never a curse upon the Greeks.
If you say words that make the army angry
the child will have no burial, and without pity—
Silence now. Bear your fate as best you can.
So then you need not leave him dead without a grave,
and you will find the Greeks more kind.

Andromache. Go die, my best beloved, my own, my treasure,
in cruel hands, leaving your mother comfortless.
Your father was too noble. That is why
they kill you. He could save others,
he could not save you for his nobleness.
My bed, my bridal—all for misery—

---

[9] Odysseus—one of the Greek leaders, known for his cunning and ruthlessness.

when long ago I came to Hector's halls
to bear my son—oh, not for Greeks to slay,
but for a ruler over a teeming Asia.
Weeping, my little one? There, there.
You cannot know what waits for you.
Why hold me with your hands so fast, cling so fast to me?
You little bird, flying to hide beneath my wings.
And Hector will not come—he will not come,
up from the tomb, great spear in hand, to save you.
Not one of all his kin, of all the Trojan might.
How will it be? Falling down—down—oh, horrible.
And his neck—his breath—all broken.
And none to pity. You little thing,
curled in my arms, you dearest to your mother,
how sweet the fragrance of you.
All nothing then—this breast from where
your baby mouth drew milk, my **travail**[10] too,
my cares, when I grew wasted watching you.
Kiss me—Never again. Come, closer, closer.
Your mother who bore you—put your arms around my neck.
Now kiss me, lips to lips.
O Greeks, you have found out ways to torture
that are not Greek.
A little child, all innocence of wrong—
you wish to kill him. . . .
Quick! Take him—seize him—cast him down—
if so you will. Feast on his flesh.
God has destroyed me, and I cannot—
I cannot save my child from death.
Oh hide my head for shame and fling me into the ship.

(She falls, then struggles to her knees.)

My fair bridal—I am coming—
Oh, I have lost a child, my own.

---

[10] **travail**—pain; here, of childbirth.

A Woman. O wretched Troy, tens of thousands lost
    for a woman's sake,[11] a hateful marriage bed.

Talthybius. *(drawing the child away)* Come, boy, let go. Unclasp
    those loving hands,
    poor mother.
    Come now, up, up, to the very height,
    where the towers of your fathers crown the wall,
    and where it is decreed that you must die.

(To the soldiers) Take him away.
    A **herald**[12] who must bring such orders
    should be a man who feels no pity,
    and no shame either—not like me.

---

[11] a woman's sake—Helen, wife of Menelaus, king of Sparta; her abduction by Paris, a prince of Troy, was the cause of the Greek expedition against the city.

[12] **herald**—messenger.

QUESTIONS TO CONSIDER

1. How is Hector's son destroyed by his father's heroism?

2. How has Andromache's virtue contributed to her misfortune?

3. What is the only type of heroism that remains for the captive women of Troy?

4. Greek leaders of the Trojan War such as Odysseus were great heroic models for the Greeks. What do you think is Euripides' view of them in this play?

Lyric Poetry

The Homeric epics are impersonal. In the century after they were written down, a new type of poetry appeared in which the poet's feelings become the subject. Some of the most beautiful of these Greek lyrics were by women. The most famous of these women poets was Sappho (c. 620–c. 565 B.C.), who wrote with passion and grace about the beauty of the world, about love, and about art. The following are some of her lyrics, along with those of three other women poets, Korinna, Praxilla, and Anyte.

To Anaktoria

SAPPHO

Some say cavalry and others claim
infantry or a fleet of long oars
is the supreme sight on the black earth.
I say it is

the one you love. And easily proved.
Did not Helen[1] who far surpassed all
mortals in beauty desert the best
of men, her king,

and sail off to Troy and forget
her daughter and dear kinsmen? Merely
the Kyprian's gaze[2] made her bend and led
her from her path;

---

[1] Helen—wife of Menelaus, king of Sparta; her abduction by—or elopement with—Paris, a prince of Troy, was the cause of the war between the Greeks and Trojans.

[2] Kyprian's gaze—The Kyprian was Aphrodite, goddess of love, who was born near the island of Cyprus.

these things remind me now
of Anaktoria who is far,
and I
for one

would rather see her warm supple step
and the sparkle of her face—than watch
all the dazzling chariots and armored
       hoplites of Lydia.[3]

To an Uneducated Woman

SAPPHO

When dead you will lie forever forgotten,
for you have no claim to the Pierian[4] roses.
Dim here, you will move more dimly in Hell,
flitting among the undistinguished dead.

Kleïs

SAPPHO

I have a small daughter who is beautiful
like a gold flower. I would not trade
my darling Kleïs for all Lydia[5] or even
for lovely Lesbos.[6]

---

[3] hoplites of Lydia—heavily armed foot soldiers of an ancient country located in what is now Turkey.

[4] Pierian—Pieria was birthplace of the Muses, the nine goddesses who were patrons of the various branches of learning and the arts.

[5] Lydia—an ancient country known for its great wealth.

[6] Lesbos—island home of Sappho.

Age and Light

SAPPHO

Here are fine gifts, children,
O friend, singer on the clear tortoise lyre,

all my flesh is wrinkled with age,
my black hair has faded to white,

my legs can no longer carry me,
once nimble like a fawn's,

but what can I do?
It cannot be undone,

no more than can pink armed Dawn
not end in darkness on earth,

or keep her love for Tithonos,[7]
who must waste away;

yet I love refinement, and beauty and light
are for me the same as desire for the sun.

Her Wealth

SAPPHO

The golden Muses[8] gave me
true riches: when dead
I shall not be forgotten.

---

[7] Dawn . . . Tithonos—In love with the mortal Tithonos, the goddess of dawn made him immortal but not eternally youthful, so that he grew ever older but could not die.

[8] Muses—nine goddesses who were believed to inspire artists and scholars.

On Herself

KORINNA

I Korinna am here to sing the courage
of heroes and heroines in old myths.

To daughters of Tanagra[9] in white robes,
I sing. And all the city is delighted
with the clean water of my **plaintive**[10] voice.

Of the Sensual World

PRAXILLA

Most beautiful of things I leave is sunlight;
then come glazing stars and the moon's face;
then ripe cucumbers and apples and pears.

Repose

ANYTE

Lounge in the shade of the luxuriant laurel's
beautiful foliage. And now drink sweet water
from the cold spring so that your limbs weary
with summer toil will find rest in the west wind.

---

[9] Tanagra—town in central Greece, possibly Korinna's home.

[10] **plaintive**—mournful.

QUESTIONS TO CONSIDER

1. Both Sappho's "To Anaktoria" and Praxilla's "Of the Sensual World" offer different examples of "most beautiful" things. What would your list include?

2. Judging by "To an Uneducated Woman" and "Her Wealth," what did Sappho want from poetry?

3. In her own time, Praxilla was criticized for putting "cucumbers and the like on a par with the sun and the moon." Do you see this as a fault in her poem? Why or why not?

4. The tone of a literary work reflects the writer's attitude toward the subject and the audience. Select your favorite of these poems. What is the tone?

Images of Women

The chief goal of Greek sculpture was the creation of ideal human forms. Beginning in the 7th century B.C., there was an evolution of styles from rigid postures through a carefully balanced realism to an emphasis on exaggerated movement. Although the Romans imitated many of the forms of Greek art, they also independently developed a highly naturalistic style of portraiture. The following images of women display characteristic styles of Greek and Roman art.

◀ This stiffly posed statue of a young woman (called a kore, "maiden") is an example of the earliest, or Archaic, period of Greek sculpture.

A relief of the goddess Athena, shown mourning for those killed in battle, marks the transitional phase between the Archaic and Classical periods. ▶

This relief of the goddess Nike ("Victory") untying her sandal displays the strength and grace of the Classical period. ▶

This bronze statuette of a dancer displays another aspect of Hellenistic sculpture—small-scale works produced for private ownership depicting everyday subjects. ▶

◀ A masterpiece of the final, or Hellenistic, period of Greek art, the *Nike of Samothrace* appears as if advancing against the force of a powerful wind.

▲

The carefully detailed hairstyle of this portrait bust of a woman conveys the emphasis in Roman art on accurate observation.

Another example of Roman taste for realism is this detail of a Roman wall painting that shows a young woman in the everyday act of writing. ▶

QUESTIONS TO CONSIDER

1. Which Greek sculpture seems most beautiful to you? What qualities contribute most to this impression?

2. Does the Roman portrait bust seem idealized to you? Why or why not?

3. What personal qualities are conveyed by the Roman mural of the young woman writing?

The Funeral Oration of Pericles

THUCYDIDES

Greek geography, with its mountains and islands, encouraged development of small independent "city-states." In the 5th century B.C., Greece was dominated by two very different city-states—Athens and Sparta. These city-states fought two lengthy conflicts, the Peloponnesian Wars, which ended in Athenian defeat. In The History of the Peloponnesian War *by the Greek historian Thucydides (c. 460–c. 400 B.C.), the Athenian leader Pericles (c. 495–c. 429 B.C.) delivers a funeral oration for the city's war dead at the beginning of the Second Peloponnesian War.*

I have no wish to make a long speech on subjects familiar to you all: so I shall say nothing about the warlike deeds by which we acquired our power or the battles in which we or our fathers gallantly resisted our enemies, Greek or foreign. What I want to do is, in the first place, to discuss the spirit in which we faced our trials and also our constitution and the way of life which has made us great. After that I shall speak in praise of the dead, believing that this kind of speech is not inappropriate to the present occasion, and that this whole assembly, of citizens and foreigners, may listen to it with advantage.

Let me say that our system of government does not copy the institutions of our neighbors. It is more the case of our being a model to others, than of our imitating anyone else. Our constitution is called a democracy because power is in the hands not of a minority but of the whole people. When it is a question of settling private disputes, everyone is equal before the law; when it is a question of putting one person before another in positions of public responsibility, what counts is not membership of a particular class, but the actual ability which the man possesses. No one, so long as he has it in him to be of service to the state, is kept in political **obscurity**[1] because of poverty. And, just as our political life is free and open, so is our day-to-day life in our relations with each other. We do not get into a state with our next-door neighbor if he enjoys himself in his own way, nor do we give him the kind of black looks which,

---

[1] **obscurity**—position of being unknown or without prominence.

though they do no real harm, still do hurt people's feelings. We are free and tolerant in our private lives; but in public affairs we keep to the law. This is because it commands our deep respect.

We give our obedience to those whom we put in positions of authority, and we obey the laws themselves, especially those which are for the protection of the oppressed, and those unwritten laws which it is an acknowledged shame to break.

And here is another point. When our work is over, we are in a position to enjoy all kinds of recreation for our spirits. There are various kinds of contests and sacrifices regularly throughout the year; in our own homes we find a beauty and a good taste which delight us every day and which drive away our cares. Then the greatness of our city brings it about that all the good things from all over the world flow in to us, so that to us it seems just as natural to enjoy foreign goods as our own local products.

Then there is a great difference between us and our opponents, in our attitude toward military security. Here are some examples: Our city is open to the world, and we have no periodical deportations[2] in order to prevent people observing or finding out secrets which might be of military advantage to the enemy. This is because we rely, not on secret weapons, but on our real courage and loyalty. There is a difference, too, in our educational systems. The Spartans, from their earliest boyhood, are submitted to the most laborious training in courage; we pass our lives without all these restrictions, and yet are just as ready to face the same dangers as they are. Here is a proof of this: When the Spartans invade our land, they do not come by themselves, but bring all their allies with them; whereas we, when we launch an attack abroad, do the job by ourselves, and, though fighting on foreign soil, do not often fail to defeat opponents who are fighting for their own hearths and homes. As a matter of fact none of our enemies has ever yet been confronted with our total strength, because we have to divide our attention between our navy and the many missions on which our troops are sent on land. Yet, if our enemies engage a detachment of our forces and defeat it, they give themselves credit for having thrown back our entire army; or, if they lose, they claim that they were beaten by us in full strength. There are certain advantages, I think, in our way of meeting danger voluntarily, with an easy mind, instead of with a laborious training, with natural rather than with state-induced courage. We do not have to spend our time practicing to meet sufferings which are still in the future; and when they are actually upon us we show ourselves just as brave as these others who are always in strict training. This is one point in which, I think, our city deserves to be admired. There are also others:

Our love of what is beautiful does not lead to **extravagance**;[3] our love of the things of the mind does not make us soft. We

---

[2] deportations—expulsions of aliens.

[3] **extravagance**—excess.

regard wealth as something to be properly used, rather than as something to boast about. As for poverty, no one need be ashamed to admit it: the real shame is in not taking practical measures to escape from it. Here each individual is interested not only in his own affairs but in the affairs of the state as well: even those who are mostly occupied with their own business are extremely well-informed on general politics—this is a peculiarity of ours: we do not say that a man who takes no interest in politics is a man who minds his own business; we say that he has no business here at all. We Athenians, in our own persons, take our decisions on policy or submit them to proper discussions: for we do not think that there is an **incompatibility**[4] between words and deeds; the worst thing is to rush into action before the consequences have been properly debated. And this is another point where we differ from other people. We are capable at the same time of taking risks and of estimating them beforehand. Others are brave out of ignorance; and, when they stop to think, they begin to fear. But the man who can most truly be accounted brave is he who best knows the meaning of what is sweet in life and of what is terrible, and then goes out undeterred to meet what is to come.

Again, in questions of general good feeling there is a great contrast between us and most other people. We make friends by doing good to others, not by receiving good from them. This makes our friendship all the more reliable, since we want to keep alive the gratitude of those who are in our debt by showing continued goodwill to them: whereas the feelings of one who owes us something lack the same enthusiasm, since he knows that, when he repays our kindness, it will be more like paying back a debt than giving something spontaneously. We are unique in this. When we do kindnesses to others, we do not do them out of any calculations of profit or loss: we do them without afterthought, relying on our free **liberality**.[5] Taking everything together then, I declare that our city is an education to Greece, and I declare that in my opinion each single one of our citizens, in all the manifold aspects of life, is able to show himself the rightful lord and owner of his own person, and do this, moreover, with exceptional grace and exceptional versatility. And to show that this is no empty boasting for the present occasion, but real **tangible**[6] fact, you have only to consider the power which our city possesses and which has been won by those very qualities which I have mentioned. Athens, alone of the states we know, comes to her testing time in a greatness that surpasses what was imagined of her. In her case, and in her case alone, no invading enemy is ashamed at being defeated, and no subject can complain of being governed by people unfit for their responsibilities. Mighty indeed are the marks and monuments of our empire

---

[4] **incompatibility**—disharmony.

[5] **liberality**—generosity.

[6] **tangibile**—not imaginary.

which we have left. Future ages will wonder at us, as the present age wonders at us now. We do not need the praises of a Homer,[7] or of anyone else whose words may delight us for the moment, but whose estimation of facts will fall short of what is really true. For our adventurous spirit has forced an entry into every sea and into every land; and everywhere we have left behind us everlasting memorials of good done to our friends or suffering inflicted on our enemies.

This, then, is the kind of city for which these men, who could not bear the thought of losing her, nobly fought and nobly died. It is only natural that every one of us who survive them should be willing to undergo hardships in her service. And it was for this reason that I have spoken at such length about our city, because I wanted to make it clear that for us there is more at stake than there is for others who lack our advantages; also I wanted my words of praise for the dead to be set in the bright light of evidence. . . .

I could tell you a long story (and you know it as well as I do) about what is to be gained by beating the enemy back. What I would prefer is that you should fix your eyes every day on the greatness of Athens as she really is, and should fall in love with her. When you realize her greatness, then reflect that what made her great was men with a spirit of adventure, men who knew their duty, men who were ashamed to fall below a certain standard. . . .

Perhaps I should say a word or two on the duties of women to those among you who are now widowed. I can say all I have to say in a short word of advice. Your great glory is not to be inferior to what God has made you, and the greatest glory of a woman is to be least talked about by men, whether they are praising you or criticizing you.

---

[7] Homer—Greek epic poet (page 206).

QUESTIONS TO CONSIDER

1. How would you describe the Athenian ideal of "the good life"?

2. According to Pericles, the Athenian concept of citizenship emphasized both liberty and equality. Which do you think was the more valuable element?

3. How did the Athenians maintain their military strength?

4. How did Pericles present the position of women in Athens?

5. Do you think Athens would have been a good environment for an artist? Why or why not?

The Reforms of Lycurgus

PLUTARCH

According to Greek tradition, Sparta was founded by a lawgiver named Lycurgus, who may have lived in the 9th century B.C. In his Life of Lycurgus, *the Greek biographer Plutarch (c. 46–c. 120 A.D.) describes some of his reforms.*

Among the many changes and alterations which Lycurgus made, the first and of greatest importance was the establishment of the senate, which, having a power equal to the kings' in matters of great consequence, and, as Plato[1] expresses it, allaying and qualifying the fiery genius of the royal office, gave steadiness and safety to the commonwealth. For the state, which before had no firm basis to stand upon, but leaned one while towards an absolute monarchy, when the kings had the upper hand, and another while towards a pure democracy, when the people had the better, found in this establishment of the senate a central weight, like ballast in a ship, which always kept things in a just **equilibrium**;[2] the twenty-eight[3] always adhering to the kings so far as to resist democracy, and, on the other hand, supporting the people against the establishment of absolute monarchy. . . .

After the creation of the thirty senators, his next task, and, indeed, the most hazardous he ever undertook, was the making a new division of their lands. For there was an extreme inequality among them, and their state was overloaded with a multitude of indigent and necessitous[4] persons, while its whole wealth had centered upon a very few. To the end, therefore, that he might expel from the state arrogance and envy, luxury and crime, and those yet more **inveterate**[5] diseases of want and **superfluity**,[6] he obtained of them to renounce their properties, and to consent

---

[1] Plato—Greek philosopher (page 233).

[2] **equilibrium**—balance.

[3] the twenty-eight—the Spartan senate.

[4] indigent and necessitous—poor and needy.

[5] **inveterate**—chronic.

[6] **superfluity**—overabundance.

to a new division of the land, and that they should live all together on an equal footing; merit to be their only road to eminence, and the disgrace of evil, and credit of worthy acts, their one measure of difference between man and man.

Upon their consent to these proposals, proceeding at once to put them into execution, he divided the country of Laconia[7] in general into thirty thousand equal shares, and the part attached to the city of Sparta into nine thousand; these he distributed among the Spartans, as he did the others to the country citizens. A lot was so much as to yield, one year with another, about seventy bushels of grain for the master of the family, and twelve for his wife, with a suitable proportion of oil and wine. And this he thought sufficient to keep their bodies in good health and strength; superfluities they were better without. . . .

Not contented with this, he resolved to make a division of their movables too, that there might be no **odious**[8] distinction or inequality left among them; but finding that it would be very dangerous to go about it openly, he took another course, and defeated their avarice by the following stratagem: he commanded that all gold and silver coin should be called in, and that only a sort of money made of iron should be current, a great weight and quantity of which was but very little worth; so that to lay up [even moderate savings] required a pretty large closet, and, to remove it, nothing less than a yoke of oxen. With the diffusion of this money, at once a number of vices were banished from Lacedaemon;[9] for who would

rob another of such a coin? Who would unjustly detain or take by force, or accept as a bribe, a thing which it was not easy to hide, nor a credit to have, nor indeed of any use to cut in pieces? For when it was just red hot, they quenched it in vinegar, and by that means spoiled it, and made it almost incapable of being worked.

In the next place, he declared an outlawry of all needless and superfluous arts; but here he might almost have spared his proclamation; for they of themselves would have gone after the gold and silver, the money which remained being not so proper payment for curious[10] work; for, being of iron, it was scarcely portable, neither, if they should take the pains to export it, would it pass among the other Greeks, who ridiculed it. So there was now no more means of purchasing foreign goods and small wares; merchants sent no shiploads into Laconian ports; no rhetoric-master,[11] no itinerant fortune-teller, or gold or silversmith, engraver, or jeweler, set foot in a country which had no money; so that luxury, deprived little by little of that which fed and fomented[12] it, wasted to nothing, and died away of itself. For the rich had no advantage here over the poor, as their wealth and abundance had no road

---

[7] Laconia—region of Greece in which Sparta is located.

[8] **odious**—hateful.

[9] Lacedaemon—Sparta.

[10] curious—skillful (an archaic meaning).

[11] rhetoric-master—speech-teacher.

[12] fomented—encouraged.

to come abroad by, but were shut up at home doing nothing. And in this way they became excellent artists in common, necessary things; bedsteads, chairs, and tables, and such like staple utensils in a family, were admirably well made there. Their cup, particularly, was very much in fashion, and eagerly bought up by soldiers, as Critias reports; for its color was such as to prevent water, drunk upon necessity and disagreeable to look at, from being noticed; and the shape of it was such that the mud stuck to the sides, so that only the purer part came to the drinker's mouth. For this, also, they had to thank their lawgiver, who, by relieving the artisans of the trouble of making useless things, set them to show their skill in giving beauty to those of daily and indispensable use.

The third and most masterly stroke of this great lawgiver, by which he struck a yet more effectual blow against luxury and the desire of riches, was the **ordinance**[13] he made, that they should all eat in common, of the same bread and same meat, and of kinds that were specified, and should not spend their lives at home, laid on costly couches at splendid tables, delivering themselves up into the hands of their tradesmen and cooks, to fatten them in corners, like greedy brutes. . . .

But to return to their republic repasts; they met by companies of fifteen, more or less, and each of them stood bound to bring in monthly a bushel of meal, eight gallons of wine, five pounds of cheese, two pounds and a half of figs, and some very small sum of money to buy flesh or fish

with. Besides this, when any of them made sacrifice to the gods, they always sent a **dole**[14] to the common hall; and, likewise, when any of them had been a hunting, he sent thither a part of the venison[15] he had killed; for these two occasions were the only excuses allowed for supping at home.

They used to send their children to these tables as to schools of temperance; here they were instructed in state affairs; by listening to experienced statesmen; here they learned to converse with pleasantry, to make jests without scurrility,[16] and take them without ill humor. In this point of good breeding, the Lacedaemonians excelled particularly, but if any man were uneasy under it, upon the least hint given there was no more to be said to him. It was customary also for the eldest man in the company to say to each of them, as they came in, "Through this" (pointing to the door), "no words go out."

In order to ensure the good education of their youth (which, as I said before, he thought the most important and noblest work of a lawgiver), he went so far back as to take into consideration their very conception and birth, by regulating their marriages. For Aristotle[17] is wrong in saying that, after he had tried all ways to reduce the women to more modesty and sobriety, he was at last forced to leave them as they were, because that, in the absence of their

---

[13] **ordinance**—law, regulation.

[14] **dole**—portion.

[15] venison—deer meat.

[16] scurrility—coarseness, obscenity.

[17] Aristotle—Greek philosopher (384–322 B.C.).

husbands, who spent the best part of their lives in the wars, their wives, whom they were obliged to leave absolute mistresses at home, took great liberties and assumed the superiority; and were treated with overmuch respect and called by the title of lady or queen. The truth is, he took in their case, also, all the care that was possible; he ordered the maidens to exercise themselves with wrestling, running, throwing the quoit,[18] and casting the dart, to the end that the fruit they conceived might, in strong and healthy bodies, take firmer root and find better growth, and withal[19] that they, with this greater vigor, might be the more able to undergo the pains of childbearing. And to the end he might take away their over-great tenderness and fear of exposure to the air, and all acquired womanishness, he ordered that the young women should go naked in the processions, as well as the young men, and dance, too, in that condition, at certain solemn feasts, singing certain songs, whilst the young men stood around, seeing and hearing them. On these occasions, they now and then made, by jests, a befitting reflection upon those who had misbehaved themselves in the wars; and again sang encomiums[20] upon those who had done any gallant action, and by these means inspired the younger sort with an emulation of their glory. Those that were thus commended went away proud, elated, and gratified with their honor among the maidens; and those who were rallied[21] were as sensibly touched with it as if they had been formally reprimanded; and so

much the more, because the kings and the elders, as well as the rest of the city, saw and heard all that passed. Nor was there anything shameful in this nakedness of the young women; modesty attended them, and all wantonness was excluded. It taught them simplicity and a care for good health, and gave them some taste of higher feelings, admitted as they thus were to the field of noble action and glory. Hence it was natural for them to think and speak as Gorgo, for example, the wife of Leonidas,[22] is said to have done, when some foreign lady, as it would seem, told her that the women of Lacedaemon were the only women of the world who could rule men; "With good reason," she said, "for we are the only women who bring forth men."

---

[18] quoit—ring tossed over an upright peg in a game.

[19] withal—besides.

[20] encomiums—songs of praise.

[21] rallied—ridiculed.

[22] Leonidas—one of the kings of Sparta.

QUESTIONS TO CONSIDER

1. How would you describe the Spartan ideal of "the good life"?

2. How did Lycurgus encourage the equality of all Spartan citizens?

3. How did the Spartans ensure their military strength?

4. What was the position of women in Sparta?

5. Do you think Sparta would have been a good environment for an artist? Why or why not?

from

Crito

PLATO

One of the most influential thinkers in history, the Greek philosopher Plato (427–347 B.C.) wrote a series of dialogues featuring his teacher Socrates (469?–399 B.C.). A self-styled moral "gadfly" who wandered the streets of Athens, Socrates urged people to question accepted values and ideas. Brought to trial on a charge of "introducing new gods" and "corrupting the young," Socrates was condemned to death by drinking poison. In this dialogue with his friend Crito (who urged him to flee), Socrates explains his reasons for accepting the decision of the court and refusing offers to escape his punishment.

Socrates: In leaving the prison against the will of the Athenians, do I wrong any? or rather do I not wrong those whom I ought least to wrong? Do I not desert the principles which were acknowledged by us to be just—what do you say?

Crito: I cannot tell Socrates; for I do not know.

Socrates: Then consider the matter in this way:—Imagine that I am about to play truant (you may call the proceeding by any name which you like), and the laws and the government come and **interrogate**[1] me: "Tell us Socrates," they say, what are you about? Are you not going by an act of yours to overturn us— the laws, and the whole state, as far as in you lies? Do you imagine that a state can subsist and not be overthrown, in which the decisions of law have no power, but are set aside and trampled upon by individuals?" What will be our answer, Crito, to these and the like words? Any one, and especially a rhetorician,[2] will have a good deal to say on behalf of the law which requires a sentence to be carried out. He will argue that this law should not be set aside; and shall we reply, "Yes, but the state has injured us and gives an unjust sentence." Suppose I say that?

Crito: Very good, Socrates.

Socrates: "And was that our agreement with you?" the law would answer, "or were you to abide by the sentence of the state?" And if I were to express my astonishment

[1] **interrogate**—question formally.

[2] rhetorician—expert on the use of language.

at their words, the law would probably add: "Answer, Socrates, instead of opening your eyes—you are in the habit of asking and answering questions. Tell us, —What complaint have you to make against us which justifies you in attempting to destroy us and the state? In the first place did we not bring you into existence? Your father married your mother by our aid and begat[3] you. Say whether you have any objection to urge against those of us who regulate marriage?" None, I should reply. "Or against those of us who after birth regulate the nurture and education of children, in which you also were trained? Were not the laws which have the charge of education, right in commanding your father to train you in music and gymnastic?" Right, I should reply. "Well then, since you were brought into the world and nurtured and educated by us, can you deny in the first place that you are our child and slave, as your fathers were before you? And if this is true you are not on equal terms with us; nor can you think that you have a right to do to us what we are doing to you. Would you have any right to strike or **revile**[4] or do any other evil to your father or your master, if you had one, because you have been struck or reviled by him, or received some other evil at his hands?—you would not say this? And because we think right to destroy you, do you think that you have any right to destroy us in return, and your country as far as in you lies? Will you, O professor of true virtue, pretend that you

are justified in this? Has a philosopher like you failed to discover that our country is more to be valued and higher and holier far than mother or father or any ancestor, and more to be regarded in the eyes of the gods and of men of understanding? also to be soothed, and gently and reverently **entreated**[5] when angry, even more than a father, and either to be persuaded, or if not persuaded, to be obeyed? And when we are punished by her, whether with imprisonment or stripes,[6] the punishment is to be endured in silence; and if she lead us to wounds or death in battle, thither we follow as is right; neither may any one yield or retreat or leave his rank, but whether in battle or in a court of law, or in any other place, he must do what his city and his country order him; or he must change their view of what is just: and if he may do no violence to his father or mother, much less may he do violence to his country." What answer shall we make to this, Crito? Do the laws speak truly, or do they not?

Crito: I think they do.

Socrates: Then the laws will say: "Consider, Socrates, if we are speaking truly that in your present attempt you are going to do us an injury. For, having brought you into the world, and nurtured and educated you, and given you and every other citizen a share in every good which we had to give,

---

[3] begat—produced offspring.

[4] **revile**—speak abusively.

[5] **entreated**—begged.

[6] stripes—whipping.

we further proclaim to any Athenian by the liberty that we allow him, that if he does not like us when he has become of age and has seen the ways of the city, and made our acquaintance, he may go where he pleases and take his goods with him. None of us laws will forbid him or interfere with him. Any one who does not like us and the city, and who wants to emigrate to a colony or to any other city, may go where he likes, retaining his property. But he who has experience of the manner in which we order justice and administer the state, and still remains, has entered into an implied contract that he will do as we command him. And he who disobeys us is, as we maintain, thrice wrong; first, because in disobeying us he is disobeying his parents; secondly, because we are the authors of his education; thirdly, because he has made an agreement with us that he will duly obey our commands; and he neither obeys them nor convinces us that our commands are unjust; and we do not rudely impose them, but give him the alternative of obeying or convincing us;—that is what we offer, and he does neither.

"These are the sort of accusations to which as we were saying, you, Socrates, will be exposed if you accomplish your intentions; you, above all other Athenians." Suppose now I ask, why I rather than anybody else? They will justly retort upon me that I above all other men have acknowledged the agreement. "There is clear proof," they will say, "Socrates, that we and the city were not displeasing to you. Of all Athenians you have been the most constant resident in the city, which, as you never leave, you may be supposed to love. For you never went out of the city either to see the games, except once when you went to Isthmus,[7] or to any other place unless when you were on military service; nor did you travel as other men do. Nor had you any curiosity to know other states or their laws. Your affections did not go beyond us and our state; we were your special favorites, and you **acquiesced**[8] in our government of you; and here in this city you begat your children, which is proof of your satisfaction. Moreover, you might in the course of the trial, if you had liked, have fixed the penalty at banishment; the state which refuses to let you go now would have let you go then. But you pretended that you preferred death to exile and that you were not unwilling to die. And now you have forgotten these fine sentiments, and pay no respect to us the laws, of whom you are the destroyer; and are doing what only a miserable slave would do, running away and turning your back upon the compacts and agreements which you made as a citizen. And first of all answer this very question: Are we right in saying that you agreed to be governed according to us in deed, and not in word only? Is that true or not?" How shall we answer, Crito? Must we not assent?

---

[7] games . . . Isthmus—Athletic contests were often a part of Greek religious festivals. The Isthmian Games honoring the sea god Poseidon took place at Corinth, a city on the isthmus connecting central Greece to the Peloponnesus, the peninsula of southern Greece.

[8] **acquiesced**—submitted without protest.

Crito: We cannot help it, Socrates.

Socrates: Then will they not say: "You, Socrates, are breaking the **covenants**[9] and agreements which you made with us at your leisure, not in any haste or under any compulsion or deception, but after you have had seventy years to think of them, during which time you were at liberty to leave the city, if we were not to your mind, or if our covenants appeared to you to be unfair. You had your choice, and might have gone either to Lacedaemon[10] or Crete, both which states are often praised by you for their good government, or to some other Hellenic[11] or foreign state. Whereas you, above all other Athenians, seemed to be so fond of the state, or, in other words, of us her laws (and who would care about a state which has no laws?), that you never stirred out of her; the halt, the blind, the maimed were not more stationary in her than you were. And now you run away and forsake your agreements. Not so, Socrates, if you will take our advice; do not make yourself ridiculous by escaping out of the city.

"For just consider, if you transgress and err in this sort of way, what good will you do either to yourself or to your friends? That your friends will be driven into exile and deprived of citizenship, or will lose their property, is tolerably certain; and you yourself, if you fly to one of the neighboring cities, as, for example, Thebes or Megara, both of which are well governed, will come to them as an enemy, Socrates, and their government will be against you, and all patriotic citizens will cast an evil eye upon you as a subverter[12] of the laws, and you will confirm in the minds of the judges the justice of their own condemnation of you. For he who is a corrupter of the laws is more than likely to be a corrupter of the young and foolish portion of mankind. Will you then flee from well-ordered cities and virtuous men? And is existence worth having on these terms? Or will you go to them without shame, and talk to them, Socrates? And what will you say to them? What you say here about virtue and justice and institutions and laws being the best things among men? Would that be decent of you? Surely not. But if you go away from well-governed states to Crito's friends in Thessaly, where there is great disorder and license,[13] they will be charmed to hear the tale of your escape from prison, set off with ludicrous particulars of the manner in which you were wrapped in a goatskin or some other disguise, and metamorphosed[14] as the manner is of runaways; but will there be no one to remind you that in your old age you were not ashamed to violate the most sacred laws from a miserable desire of a little more life? Perhaps not, if you keep them in good temper; but if they are out of temper you will hear many degrading things; you will live, but how?—as the flatterer of all men, and the servant of all

---

[9] **covenants**—agreements.

[10] Lacedaemon—Sparta.

[11] Hellenic—Greek.

[12] subverter—overthrower.

[13] license—lawlessness.

[14] metamorphosed—changed in appearance.

men; and doing what?—eating and drinking in Thessaly, having gone abroad in order that you may get a dinner. And where will be your fine sentiments about justice and virtue? Say that you wish to live for the sake of your children—you want to bring them up and educate them—will you take them into Thessaly and deprive them of Athenian citizenship? Is this the benefit which you will confer upon them? Or are you under the impression that they will be better cared for and educated here if you are still alive, although absent from them; for your friends will take care of them? Do you fancy that if you are an inhabitant of Thessaly they will take care of them, and if you are an inhabitant of the other world that they will not take care of them? Nay; but if they who call themselves friends are good for anything, they will—to be sure they will.

"Listen then, Socrates, to us who have brought you up. Think not of life and children first, and of justice afterwards, but of justice first, that you may be justified before the princes of the world below. For neither will you nor any that belong to you be happier or holier or juster in this life, or happier in another, if you do as Crito bids. Now you depart in innocence, a sufferer and not a doer of evil; a victim, not of the laws but of men. But if you go forth, returning evil for evil, and injury for injury, breaking the covenants and agreements which you have made with us, and wronging those whom you ought least of all to wrong, that is to say, yourself, your friends, your country, and us, we shall be angry with you while you live, and our brethren, the laws in the world below, will receive you as an enemy; for they will know that you have done your best to destroy us. Listen, then, to us and not to Crito."

This, dear Crito, is the voice which I seem to hear murmuring in my ears, like the sound of the flute in the ears of the mystic; that voice, I say, is humming in my ears, and prevents me from hearing any other. And I know that anything more which you may say will be vain. Yet speak, if you have anything to say.

Crito: I have nothing to say, Socrates.

Socrates: Leave me then, Crito, to fulfill the will of God, and to follow whither he leads.

QUESTIONS TO CONSIDER

1. How do you think Socrates would define "the good life"?

2. If Socrates were practicing his role of social "gadfly" in modern America, would he be brought to trial? Why or why not?

3. Are you persuaded by Socrates' arguments that he should not flee his punishment? Why or why not?

4. Should there be limits on free speech? If so, what limits?

Roman Wisdom

The Roman poets Lucretius (97?–54 B.C.) and Horace (65–8 B.C.) were both rationalists and moralists. Lucretius's long philosophical poem On the Nature of Things presents a materialist vision of the universe defined by the random motion of atoms. Death is final, so fears of punishment in an afterlife are groundless. The wise person uses the power of reason to achieve a serene detachment. In his masterpiece, the Odes, Horace also frequently addresses moral questions, urging moderation and a refined enjoyment of the good things of life.

from *On the Nature of Things*

Lucretius

What joy it is, when out at sea the storm-winds are lashing the waters, to gaze from the shore at the heavy stress some other man is enduring! Not that anyone's afflictions are in themselves a source of delight; but to realize from what troubles you yourself are free is joy indeed. What joy, again, to watch opposing hosts **marshaled**[1] on the field of battle when you have yourself no part in their peril! But this is the greatest joy of all: to stand **aloof**[2] in a quiet citadel, stoutly fortified by the teaching of the wise, and to gaze down from that elevation on others wandering aimlessly in a vain search for the way of life; pitting their wits one against another, disputing for precedence, struggling night and day with unstinted effort to scale the **pinnacles**[3] of wealth and power. O joyless hearts of men! O minds without vision! How dark and dangerous the life in which this tiny span is lived away! Do you not see that nature is clamoring for two things only: a body free from pain, a mind released from worry and fear for the enjoyment of pleasurable sensations?

So we find that the requirements of our bodily nature are few indeed, no more than is necessary to banish pain. To heap pleasure upon pleasure may heighten men's enjoyment at times. But what matter if there are no golden images of youths about the house, holding flaming torches in their right hands to illumine banquets prolonged into the night? What matter if the hall does not sparkle with silver and gleam with gold, and

---

[1] **marshaled**—arrayed.

[2] **aloof**—apart.

[3] **pinnacles**—topmost points.

no carved and gilded rafters ring to the music of the lute? Nature does not miss these luxuries when men recline in company on the soft grass by a running stream under branches of a tall tree and refresh their bodies pleasurably at small expense. Better still if the weather smiles upon them and the season of the year **stipples**[4] the green **herbage**[5] with flowers. Burning fevers flee no swifter from your body if you toss under figured counterpanes and coverlets of crimson than if you must lie in rude home-spun.

If our bodies are not profited by treasures or titles or the majesty of kingship, we must go on to admit that neither are our minds. . . . The fears and anxieties that dog the human breast do not shrink from the clash of arms or the fierce rain of missiles. They stalk unabashed among princes and **potentates**.[6] They are not awestruck by the gleam of gold or the bright sheen of purple robes.

Can you doubt then that this power rests with reason alone? All life is a struggle in the dark. As children in blank darkness tremble and start at everything, so we in broad daylight are oppressed at times by fears as baseless as those horrors which children imagine coming upon them in the dark. This dread and darkness of the mind cannot be dispelled by the sunbeams, the shining shafts of day, but only by an understanding of the outward form and inner workings of nature.

Odes, Book One, II
Horace

Dare not ever to ask, knowledge is
    wrong, what fate the gods have
    wrought
Both for me and for you, Leuconoë,[7]
    neither attempt to learn
Babylonian stars.[8] Better endure
    whate'er the fate which Jove[9]
Has allotted to us, whether it be many
    more winters, or
Whether this one which breaks
    Tuscany's sea 'gainst the wave-
    hollowed rocks
Be the last. So be wise, strain now your
    wines;[10] let us cut down long hope
To our life's little span. While yet we
    speak, jealously flees now our
Lifetime. Seize then today, trusting
    tomorrow no more than we must.

---

[4] **stipples**—speckles.

[5] **herbage**—plants.

[6] **potentates**—rulers.

[7] Leuconoë—a fictional name.

[8] Babylonian stars—predictions of the future by Mesopotamian astrologers.

[9] Jove—Jupiter, chief of the gods.

[10] strain now your wines—Horace advises immediately enjoying one's wines (which are prepared for drinking by being strained) rather than letting them age.

Odes, Book Two, 10

Horace

Wiser shall you live, O Licinius,[11] by
Neither pressing always toward open
  water,
Nor, though heeding storms, hugging
  too close to the
Uneven shore line.
Whosoever chooses the golden mean,
  that
Man is safe and free from a **squalid**[12]
  roof, and
Soberly is free of a courtly mansion
Apt to rouse envy.

Oftener by winds is the mighty pine
  tree
Shaken, lofty palaces fall with harder
Crash, and bolts of lightning more
  often strike the
Tops of the mountains.

Still the heart, the well-prepared heart
  keeps hoping
Change of **lot**[13] will come to the troubled,
  fears it
For the fortunate. Jupiter again brings
Hideous winter,

And removes it. Not, if things now go
  badly,
Thus will they continue; Apollo sometimes
Wakes the silent Muse with his lute,
  not always
Bends he his curved bow.[14]

---

[11] Licinius—person to whom this ode is addressed.
(Licinius was an official later executed for conspiring
against the emperor Augustus.)

[12] **squalid**—filthy.

[13] **lot**—fortune.

[14] Apollo . . . bow—With his lyre (a stringed instrument
here translated lute), the god Apollo inspired poetry; with
his bow he caused disease. The Muse refers to a personi-
fication of poetic inspiration.

QUESTIONS TO CONSIDER

1. Does Lucretius' philosophy seem cold and
   unfeeling to you? Why or why not?

2. How does Lucretius' picture of the human
   condition compare with that of Horace?

3. According to these two writers, what values
   contribute to a good life?

The Greek Mind

H. D. F. KITTO

The complicated nature of modern life encourages people to categorize: family, friends, sex, work, recreation, education, culture, religion, politics. According to historian H. D. F. Kitto, this fragmented sense of life was not typical of the ancient Greeks. In his book The Greeks, *Kitto discusses different aspects of what he sees as the central characteristic of ancient Greek thinking—"a sense of the wholeness of things."*

A sense of the wholeness of things is perhaps the most typical feature of the Greek mind. . . . The modern mind divides, specializes, thinks in categories: the Greek instinct was the opposite, to take the widest view, to see things as an organic whole. . . .

Let us now try to illustrate this "wholeness" a little further, beginning with that very Greek thing, the Greek language.

He who is beginning Greek is in constant difficulties with certain words which, he thinks, ought to be simple, and in fact are, but at first seem unexpectedly difficult. There is the word *kalos* and its opposite *aischros*. He is told that the former means "beautiful." He knows the Latin equivalent, *pulcher,* and is quite happy. He reads of a *kalê polis,* "a beautiful city"; Homer calls Sparta *kalligynaikos,* "city of beautiful women"; all is well. But then he reads that Virtue is "beautiful," that it is a "beautiful" thing to die for one's country, that the man of great soul "strives to attain the beautiful"; also that a good weapon or a commodious[1] harbor is "beautiful." He concludes that the Greek took an essentially aesthetic[2] view of things; and the conclusion is confirmed when he finds that the word *aischros,* the Latin *turpis,* the English *base* or *disgraceful,* also means, "ugly," so that a man can be "base" not only in character but also in appearance. How charming of the Greeks to turn Virtue into Beauty and Vice into Ugliness!

[1] commodious—spacious.

[2] aesthetic—concerned with beauty.

But the Greek is doing nothing of the sort. It is we who are doing that, by dividing concepts into different, though perhaps parallel categories, the moral, the intellectual, the aesthetic, the practical. The Greek did not: even the philosophers were reluctant to do it. When Plato makes Socrates[3] begin an argument by saying, "You will agree that there is something called the Kalon," we may be sure that he is going to bamboozle the other man by sliding gently from *kalon*, "beautiful," to *kalon*, "honorable." The word really means something like "worthy of warm admiration," and may be used indifferently in any of these categories—rather like our word "fine." We have words like this in English: the word *bad* can be used of conduct, poetry or fish, in each case meaning something quite different, but in Greek this refusal to specialize the meaning is habitual.

The word *hamartia* means "error," "fault," "crime" or even "sin"; literally, it means "missing the mark," "a bad shot." We exclaim, "How intellectualist these Greeks were! Sin is just 'missing the mark'; better luck next time!" Again we seem to find confirmation when we find that some of the Greek virtues seem to be as much intellectual as moral—a fact that makes them untranslatable, since our own vocabulary must distinguish. There is *sophrosyne*, literally "whole-mindedness" or "unimpaired-mindedness." According to the context it will mean "wisdom," "prudence," "temperateness," "chastity," "sobriety," "modesty," or "self-control," that is,

something entirely intellectual, something entirely moral, or something intermediate.

Our difficulty with the word, as with *hamartia*, is that we think more in departments. *Hamartia*, "a bad shot," does not mean "Better luck next time"; it means rather that a mental error is as blameworthy, and may be as deadly, as a moral one.

And then, to complete our education we find that in regions where we should use intellectual terms, in political theory for example, Greek uses words heavily charged with a moral content. "An aggressive policy" is likely to be *adikia*, "injustice," even if it is not *hybris*, "wanton wickedness"; while "aggrandizement" or "profiteering" is *pleonexia*, "trying to get more than your share," which is both an intellectual and a moral error, a defiance of the laws of the universe.

Let us turn back to Homer[4] for a moment. The poet of the *Iliad* had what some misguided people today think the most necessary qualification for the artist: he was class-conscious. He writes only of kings and princes; the ordinary soldier plays no part in the poem. Moreover, these kings and princes are portrayed sharply with all the limitations of their class and time; they are proud, fierce, vengeful, glorying in war though at the same time hating it. How could it happen then that such heroes could become **exemplars**[5] and a

---

[3] Plato . . . Socrates—Greek philosophers (page 233).
[4] Homer—Greek epic poet (page 206).
[5] **exemplars**—models.

living inspiration to the later **bourgeoisie**?[6] Because, being Greeks, they could not see themselves in any context but the widest possible, namely as men. Their ideal was not a specifically knightly ideal, like Chivalry or Love: they called it *aretê*—another typically Greek word. When we meet it in Plato we translate it "Virtue" and consequently miss all the flavor of it. "Virtue," at least in modern English, is almost entirely a moral word; *aretê* on the other hand is used indifferently in all the categories and means simply "excellence." It may be limited of course by its context; the *aretê* of a race-horse is speed, of a cart-horse strength. If it is used, in a general context, of a man it will connote excellence in the ways in which a man can be excellent—morally, intellectually, physically, practically. Thus the hero of the *Odyssey*[7] is a great fighter, a wily schemer, a ready speaker, a man of stout heart and broad wisdom who knows that he must endure without too much complaining what the gods send; and he can both build and sail a boat, drive a furrow as straight as anyone, beat a young braggart at throwing the discus, challenge the Phaeacian youth at boxing, wrestling or running; flay, skin, cut up and cook an ox, and be moved to tears by a song. He is in fact an excellent all-rounder; he has surpassing *aretê*. So too has the hero of the older poem, Achilles[8]—the most formidable of fighters, the swiftest of runners, and the noblest of soul; and Homer tells us, in one notable verse, how Achilles was educated. His father entrusted the lad to old Phoenix, and told Phoenix to train him to be "A maker of speeches and a doer of deeds." The Greek hero tried to combine in himself the virtues which our own heroic age divided between the knight and the churchman.

That is one reason why the epic survived to be the education of a much more civilized age. The heroic ideal of *aretê*, though firmly rooted in its own age and circumstances, was so deep and wide that it could become the ideal of an age that was totally different. . . .

[There is] another aspect of this wholeness of mind, one in which the Greeks contrasted sharply with the "barbarians"[9] and with most modern peoples. The sharp distinction which the Christian and the Oriental world has normally drawn between the body and the soul, the physical and the spiritual, was foreign to the Greek—at least until the time of Socrates and Plato. To him there was simply the whole man. That the body is the tomb of the soul is indeed an idea which we meet in certain Greek mystery-religions, and Plato, with his doctrine of immortality, necessarily distinguished sharply between body and soul; but for all that, it is not a typical Greek idea. The Greek made physical training an important part of education, not because he said to himself, "Look here, we mustn't forget the body," but because it could never occur to him to train anything but

---

[6] **bourgeoisie**—the middle class.

[7] *Odyssey*—epic poem by Homer concerning the wanderings of one of the Greek heroes of the Trojan War.

[8] Achilles—greatest hero of the Greeks in the Trojan War.

[9] "barbarians"—The Greeks distinguished between Greek-speaking peoples and all others, who were "barbarians" ("stammerers").

the whole man. It was as natural for the polis[10] to have gymnasia[11] as to have a theater or warships, and they were constantly used by men of all ages, not only for physical but also for mental exercise.

But it is the Games, local and international, which most clearly illustrate this side of the Greek mind. Among us it is sometimes made a reproach that a man "makes a religion of games." The Greek did not do this, but he did something perhaps more surprising: he made games part of his religion. To be quite explicit, the Olympian Games, the greatest of the four international festivals, were held in honor of Zeus of Olympia, the Pythian Games in honor of Apollo, the Panathenaic Games in honor of Athena.[12] Moreover, they were held in the sacred precinct. The feeling that prompted this was a perfectly natural one. The contest was a means of stimulating and displaying human *aretê*, and this was a worthy offering to the god. In the same way, games were held in honor of a dead hero, as to Patroclus in the *Iliad*. But since *aretê* is of the mind as well as of the body, there was not the slightest incongruity or affection in combining musical contests with athletic; a contest in flute-playing was an original fixture in the Pythian Games—for was not Apollo himself "Lord of the Lyre"?

It was *aretê* that the games were designed to test—the *aretê* of the whole man, not a merely specialized skill. The usual events were a sprint, of about 200 yards, the long race (1½ miles), the race in armor, throwing the discus, and the javelin, the long jump, wrestling, boxing (of a very dangerous kind), and chariot-racing. The great event was the pentathlon: a race, a jump, throwing the discus, and the javelin, and wrestling. If you won this, you were a man. Needless to say, the Marathon race was never heard of until modern times: the Greeks would have regarded it as a monstrosity. As for the skill shown by modern champions in games like golf or billiards, the Greeks would certainly have admired it intensely, and thought it an admirable thing—in a slave, supposing that one had no better use for a slave than to train him in this way. Impossible, he would say, to acquire skill like this and at the same time to live the proper life of a man and a citizen. It is this feeling that underlies Aristotle's[13] remark that a gentleman should be able to play the flute—but not too well.

---

[10] polis—Greek city-state.

[11] gymnasia—plural of *gymnasium*.

[12] Zeus . . . Apollo . . . Athena—three of the chief Greek gods.

[13] Aristotle—Greek philosopher (384–32 B.C.).

QUESTIONS TO CONSIDER

1. What does the way the ancient Greeks used language convey about their way of thinking?

2. What would an ancient Greek have thought of the traditional educational ideal, "A sound mind in a sound body"?

3. Kitto uses Odysseus as an example of the Greek ideal of the "excellent all-rounder," capable of doing all things well. Would such an ideal make sense today? Why or why not?

The Social Status of Women in Republican Rome

EVA CANTARELLA

"By our standards at least," observes historian Eva Cantarella, "the conditions of Roman women's lives were ample reason for discontent." In her book Pandora's Daughters, *Cantarella examines various aspects of the lives of women in Rome during the time of the Republic.*

Roman citizens had three names: a first name, *praenomen*, which was the individual's name; a second, *nomen*, which was the name of the *gens*;[1] and a third, *cognomen*, which indicated the particular family group. Women, however, had only the gentile name[2] and the family name. They had no individual names.

Cornelia, Caecilia, Tullia—these are gentile, not personal names. When there was more than one woman in a group and confusion might arise, designations such as Maior and Minor (elder and younger) or Prima, Seconda, and Tertia were added. This peculiarity of the naming system prompts us to ask whether Roman women really did not have names or whether they had names that were never used. . . .

If, for Pericles,[3] great was "the glory of the woman who is talked about the least,

whether in praise or blame," for the Romans the glory of women required that their names never be pronounced. It was said of the Bona Dea[4] that no man (except her husband) ever heard her name as long as she lived. In the fifth century, Macrobius[5] praises the modesty of a woman whose name nobody knew. It is difficult not to share the observation made by Moses Finley. By not indicating women with *praenomina*, he writes, "it is as if the Romans wished to suggest that women were not, and ought not be genuine individuals, but only fractions of a family. Anonymous and passive fractions at that. . . ."

---

[1] *gens*—clan.
[2] gentile name—clan name.
[3] Pericles—Athenian leader (page 225).
[4] Bona Dea—Roman goddess worshipped solely by women.
[5] Macrobius—Roman philosopher (5th century A.D.).

By our standards at least, the conditions of Roman women's lives were ample reason for discontent. A unique and difficult-to-interpret episode narrated by Livy[6] reveals a certain tension in relations between the sexes.

A trial for poisoning was held in 331 B.C. at Rome. During the consulship of M. Claudius Marcellus and C. Valerius Potitus, many illustrious persons died mysteriously. Reported by a female slave, certain *matronae*[7] were accused of having poisoned them. *Venena*, poisons, were found in their houses but the women said they were medicines. Challenged to drink them, the *matronae* did so and died. At the end of the trial, 160 women had been condemned. However one interprets this disturbing episode, it and other signs indicate the definite existence of a problem.

Around the second century B.C., the status of women deteriorated. Women who lived in the country deeply resented the loss of privileges involved in the female role in the peasant family. Women of the better-off classes had seen their chances to enjoy the privileges of wealth diminish. A series of sumptuary laws[8] *(leges sumptuariae)* had established rigorous limitations on female luxury.

The *lex Oppia* in 215 B.C. had forbidden women to wear excessive quantities of jewelry or colored clothing. Twenty years later, in 195, demonstrations of discontent brought about the repeal of this law. But in 169 a new provision, the *lex Voconia* . . . established that women (with the exceptions of Vestal Virgins[9] and the Flaminica Dialis[10]) could not inherit more than 200,000 asses,[11] which greatly

irritated the women of the wealthier classes. Furthermore, women of all social classes had to endure the inconvenience caused by the absence of the men, who were occupied in continual wars.

It is no wonder that in this context Bacchic cults[12] asserted themselves increasingly. Our best information comes from Livy. At first limited to women, these cults spread thanks to the intervention and innovations of the Campanian priestess Paculla Annia and were opened to men as well. After orgiastic dances in the woods of Stimula (the goddess of madness in whose woods, *lucus Stimulae*, at the foot of the Aventine the Maenads[13] had taken refuge), the participants in the rite ran toward the Tiber, into which they threw lit torches. . . .

The Bacchic rites indicate a social reality that was the exact opposite of what one might think at first sight. They actually reveal the sexual repression of the Roman woman. Such repression was, of course, perfectly functional for the purpose of procreation, where there was no room for eroticism and love. Every display of emotion, in the context of family life in general and conjugal life in particular, was

---

[6] Livy—Roman historian (59 B.C.–17 A.D.).

[7] *matronae*—married women.

[8] sumptuary laws—regulations controlling personal expense.

[9] Vestal Virgins—priestesses of Vesta, Roman goddess of the hearth.

[10] Flaminica Dialis—priestesses of Jupiter, chief Roman god.

[11] asses—plural of *as*, ancient Roman coin.

[12] Bacchic cults—worshippers of Bacchus, Roman god of wine, whose rites included drunken, frenzied dancing.

[13] Maenads—goddesses who were companions of Bacchus and celebrated his rites.

vigorously reproved. Very significant in this regard is the story (it does not matter whether it is real or imaginary—what is important is that it was retold for didactic purposes) that the senator Manilius risked being expelled from the Senate for kissing his wife in public.

The enormous spread of the Bacchic cults—celebrated primarily by women and at first only by them—must be placed in this context. The ritual was the only moment in which women could express a part of themselves that had been suppressed—only then could they experience eroticism. It was a moment in which they found compensation for the dissatisfaction of an ungratifying emotional and erotic life.

Altogether understandable, then, are the reasons for the enormous spread of the Bacchanalia. Just as understandable are the reasons for the fierce repression with which they were stopped, in the course of which the accusations were again brought against women for using poisons. In the wake of the Bacchanalian scandal, another trial for poisoning was held that made the trial of 331 B.C. appear **negligible**.[14] Again there were mysterious deaths and a special investigation. The subsequent trial concluded with more than 2,000 women condemned. One of these was the widow of a consul who wanted to get rid of her husband, so went the accusation, so that her son by her first marriage might have access to the consulship. But despite these, let us say, **pathological**[15] episodes, new and troubling social *phenomena* pointed to a crisis at hand.

The birth rate began to fall during the Republic. It fell in massive proportions in the centuries to follow. One **hypothesis**[16] posits mass lead poisoning. The **conduits**[17] of the aqueducts that brought water to Rome were made of lead; Roman women used cosmetics that contained large amounts of lead; vessels for food and drink were often made of lead. The theory is not unreasonable; indeed traces of lead have been found in Roman skeletons. But lead poisoning alone, no matter how widespread, cannot account for all the circumstances that contributed to making a declining birth rate a serious social problem.

Contraception was in use by this time. Apart from utterly ineffective measures (spells and **amulets**,[18] such as a cat's liver tied to the left foot or a spider bound in the skin of a stag and held in contact with the body), some methods, although rudimentary, were certainly more effective, such as a piece of soft wool saturated with substances that prevented fertilization. Furthermore, abortion was widely practiced.

Decline in the birth rate was due in part to external causes, but it was certainly also partly due to women's life-choices. For women of the lower classes the motivation to use contraception was economic; for the privileged, it was the desire to enjoy the advantages that their new status allowed. They hoped to find an identity that was not exclusively tied to motherhood.

But this could not be allowed, because it conflicted with the need to reproduce a

---

[14] **negligible**—small, unimportant.

[15] **pathological**—reflecting a diseased condition.

[16] **hypothesis**—possible explanation.

[17] **conduits**—pipes.

[18] **amulets**—good luck charms.

social body and transmit a family and political ideology. Actions against the worrisome phenomenon were taken as soon as it appeared. . . .

So far what has interested us are the general conditions of Roman women's life. Now we will look at some female figures who managed to emerge from anonymity to become celebrated models and exemplars of behavior. The first observation to make about these women is that, other than their "heroic" moment, usually linked to some political event, we know almost nothing of their lives. Apart from the exemplary deed to which they owe their immortality, all is shadow and silence.

Of the women chosen to be remembered in the history of Rome written by men (again, it is not important whether their recorded actions are real or legendary), we begin with Lucretia and Virginia.

Wife of Collatinus, Lucretia killed herself after being raped by Sextus, son of Tarquinius Superbus. The people reacted by rising against the foreign kings and throwing them out of the city.

Virginia, object of the desires of the decemvir[19] Appius Claudius, did not kill herself but was killed by her father. In her case too, the popular reaction led to the ouster of the decemvir.

The syntactic structure of the two legends is almost identical. Object of illicit desire, a woman dies to affirm the supreme value of **conjugal**[20] fidelity (Lucretia) and virginity (Virginia). The people find in the outrage the strength to react against power and reconfirm this value, sanctioning the fundamental importance of a law of family morality, evidently one of the pillars on

which the social and political organization was based.

Equally predictable and instructive are the stories of Veturia, Volumnia, and Cornelia. Veturia and Volumnia, respectively mother and wife of Coriolanus,[21] went to his camp as he was leading the Volscians against Rome and obtained from him what ambassadors, magistrates, and priests had been unable to obtain. They convinced Coriolanus to abandon arms.

The hagiography[22] of Cornelia, second daughter of Scipio Africanus[23] and mother of the tribunes Tiberius and Gaius Gracchus, is well known. She had twelve children (only three of whom lived to adulthood); her daughter Sempronia married Scipio Aemilianus. After the death of her husband, Cornelia would not remarry and refused even the proposal of Ptolemy VII Physcon.[24] She was the exemplary image of the *univira*, a woman who had only one man in her entire life. Cornelia remained the ideal model of womanly behavior, despite the evident contradiction with a strong population policy. What is more, Cornelia was educated and intellectually polished: Even Cicero[25] admired the style of her letters. But Cornelia owes her fame to her reply when asked why she did not wear jewels. "These," she said, pointing to her

---

[19] decemvir—member of one of a number of permanent boards, each composed of ten men (the meaning of *decemvir*) that were part of the government of Rome.

[20] **conjugal**—relating to marriage.

[21] Coriolanus—legendary Roman hero (late 5th century B.C.).

[22] hagiography—writing about a saint.

[23] Scipio Africanus—Roman general (237–183 B.C.) who defeated Hannibal.

[24] Ptolemy VII Physcon—king of Egypt from 145 to 116 B.C.

[25] Cicero—Roman statesman, orator, and writer (106–43 B.C.).

children, "are my jewels." And on the statue erected in her honor she was remembered with the inscription "Cornelia, mother of the Gracchi." . . .

There were also women who refused the role of the model woman. Among these, Clodia is famous. She was loved by Catullus[26] and celebrated by him with the name Lesbia. Clodia was a free woman: we are in the first century B.C., when a new type of woman appears on the scene in Rome. Some Roman women were inspired by actresses or Greek hetaerae,[27] and tried to imitate them. In 61 B.C., at age thirty-three, Clodia met Catullus, then twenty-seven. In 59, at the death of her husband, she left Catullus for the even younger Caelius. Few facts are recorded, but they are more than sufficient to understand that Clodia was far from the example propagandized by the women discussed previously; she was a woman who chose and left her lovers, who refused to be an object of possession. When, later abandoned by Caelius, she accuses him of not having returned money she lent him, of having stolen her jewelry, and, finally, of having tried to poison her, the oration written by Cicero in defense of Caelius does not spare her image: "Clytemnestra,"[28] he calls her, and worse, *quandrantaria*—a two-bit Clytemnestra. He dwells not so much on the facts contested by Caelius as on Clodia herself, a woman whose conduct alone makes her accusations unreliable.

As soon as she was widowed, said Cicero (not missing the chance to **insinuate**[29] that Clodia had poisoned her husband), she gave herself to a dissolute life of orgiastic parties both in Rome and at her villa in Baiae on the Bay of Naples. The slaves who testified in her favor had no credibility: they too participated in their mistress's debauchery, and she had not hesitated to free them in order to obtain their complicity. As if that were not enough, Clodia was the incestuous lover of Clodius, her brother, the bitter enemy of Cicero.

That was essentially Caelius' defense, and he was acquitted. The case is symptomatic: Clodia's accusations could not have any grounds. She was "different," and as such could not possibly be telling the truth.

Despite the clear signs of malcontent and rebellion that spread in the second century, despite the attempt at "liberation" sought in the Bacchanalia, despite the "Lesbias" (there must have been others, not loved by Catullus and thus not known), the average Roman woman, the anonymous woman, the woman not talked about, was probably not very different from Lucretia or Cornelia.

---

[26] Catullus—Roman poet (84?–54? B.C.).

[27] hetaerae—class of often highly cultured prostitutes in ancient Greece.

[28] Clytemnestra—wife of Agamemnon, leader of the Greeks in the Trojan War, who murdered him on his return from Troy.

[29] **insinuate**—hint, suggest.

QUESTIONS TO CONSIDER

1. What do Roman naming customs reflect about the identity of Roman women?

2. Why did the Bacchic cults become popular among some Roman women?

3. What does the existence of such heroines as Lucretia and Cornelia indicate about the behavior expected of Roman women?

Linking Cultures

The Human Face

Perhaps the most expressive of all subjects of art is the human face. It has been interpreted in a broad range of forms and styles, from heroic images of gods and rulers to naturalistic portraits of ordinary people. The following images of human faces come from a variety of cultures and eras. As you examine them, reflect on these questions:

• Which images seem idealized? Which seem realistic?
• What dominant emotions are expressed by these images?
• What do these images suggest about the human conception of the beautiful? of the heroic?

◀ **Head of Sesostris III** (Egypt)
Suggesting a highly self-conscious personality, this fragment of a sculpture depicts a powerful ruler of ancient Egypt.

◀ **Sharaku Toshusai**

Ichikawa Ebizo as Kwandayu *(Japan)*
This print depicts an actor costumed
as a villain in Kabuki, a form of
Japanese drama employing highly
stylized makeup and costume.

Abu'l Hasan

Shah Jahan Holding a
Turban Jewel *(India)*
The Mughal emperor Shah Jahan
(page 69) inscribed this painting,
"A good portrait of me in my
twenty-fifth year." ▶

"Mask of Agamemnon" *(Greece)*
Called by the name of the leader of the
Greek forces in the Trojan War (page 206),
this gold mask was found in an ancient
tomb covering the face of a dead king.

Bronze of Queen Mother *(Benin)*
This bronze head depicts the queen mother of the
West African kingdom of Benin (page 165) wearing
a woven crown symbolizing her power.

Portrait of a Boy *(Egypto-Roman)*
In the Roman colony of Egypt, a painting
depicting the dead person was often
attached to a mummified body. ▶

▲

Albrecht Dürer

Self-Portrait (Germany)
The first artist to record his fascination with his own image,
Dürer produced self-portraits throughout his career.

▲
Dance Headdress *(Haida)*
Fashioned by the Haida, a Native American people of the Northwest Coast region, this headdress represents a spirit face seen by shamans in their trances.

▲
Leonardo da Vinci

Ginevra de' Benci *(Italy)*
This depiction of a young woman from a wealthy family of Florence has been called "the first psychological portrait ever painted."

▲

William Hogarth

The Shrimp Girl _(England)_
This portrait of a street vendor displays
Hogarth's customary vigor of expression, but
not his characteristic satire (page 440).

▲

Julia Margaret Cameron

George Frederick Watts _(England)_
Cameron's photographs of her family and
friends, who included many cultural celebrities
such as the artist Watts, were modeled on
19th-century paintings.

▲

Bartolomé Esteban Murillo

A Girl and Her Duenna (Spain)
In the 1600s, the scenes of daily life known as "genre pictures," such as
this glimpse of a girl and her chaperon, became popular.

Pablo Picasso

Portrait of Ambroise Vollard *(Spain)*
The artistic movement known as Cubism portrayed objects as arrangements of geometrical planes, as in this portrait by Picasso of a Paris art dealer. ▶

Gwen John

Self-Portrait *(England)*
This artist's depiction of herself combines conflicting elements of gentleness and determination.
▼

▲

Andy Warhol

Marilyn (United States)
This artist based much of his work on familiar images from American
popular culture, such as this silkscreen print of actress Marilyn Monroe.

Chapter 7

Christianity and Byzantine Culture

The Law of Love

Choosing a Path

Power and Holiness

◀ In *The Lamentation*, a Byzantine wall painting, Jesus' mother Mary and his follower John mourn over his dead body.

The Teachings of Jesus

Christians divide the Bible into two sections, the Old Testament (the laws, history, and literature of the Jews) and the New Testament. The core of the New Testament is the four Gospels, biographies of Christianity's founder, Jesus. The Gospels are traditionally attributed to individuals called Matthew, Mark, Luke, and John, who were either early followers of Jesus or associates of these followers. The following passages are from the Gospels of Matthew and Luke.

from *The Sermon on the Mount*

Matthew

Seeing the crowds, he[1] went up on the mountain, and when he sat down his disciples came to him. And he opened his mouth and taught them, saying:

"Blessed are the poor in spirit, for theirs is the kingdom of heaven.

"Blessed are those who mourn, for they shall be comforted.

"Blessed are the **meek**,[2] for they shall inherit the earth.

"Blessed are those who hunger and thirst for righteousness, for they shall be satisfied.

"Blessed are the merciful, for they shall obtain mercy.

"Blessed are the pure in heart, for they shall see God.

"Blessed are the peacemakers, for they shall be called sons of God.

"Blessed are those who are persecuted for righteousness' sake, for theirs is the kingdom of heaven.

"Blessed are you when men **revile**[3] you and persecute you and utter all kinds of evil against you falsely on my account. Rejoice and be glad, for your reward is great in heaven, for so men persecuted the prophets who were before you."

---

[1] he—Jesus.

[2] **meek**—humble.

[3] **revile**—abuse verbally.

The Good Samaritan
Luke

And behold, a lawyer stood up to put him
to the test, saying, "Teacher, what shall I
do to inherit eternal life?" He said to him,
"What is written in the law? How do you
read?" And he answered, "You shall love
the Lord your God with all your heart,
and with all your soul, and with all your
strength, and with all your mind; and your
neighbor as yourself." And he said to him,
"You have answered right; do this, and
you will live."

But he, desiring to justify himself, said
to Jesus, "And who is my neighbor?" Jesus
replied, "A man was going down from
Jerusalem to Jericho, and he fell among
robbers, who stripped him and beat him,
and departed, leaving him half-dead. Now
by chance a priest was going down that
road; and when he saw him he passed by
on the other side. So likewise a Levite,[4]
when he came to the place and saw
him, passed by on the other side. But a
Samaritan,[5] as he journeyed, came to
where he was; and when he saw him, he
had compassion, and went to him and
bound up his wounds, pouring on oil and
wine; then he set him on his own beast
and brought him to an inn, and took care
of him. And the next day he took out two
denarii[6] and gave them to the innkeeper,
saying 'Take care of him; and whatever
more you spend, I will repay you when I
come back.' Which of these three, do you
think, proved neighbor to the man who fell
among the robbers?" He said, "The one
who showed mercy on him." And Jesus
said to him, "Go and do likewise."

The Prodigal Son
Luke

And he said, "There was a man who had
two sons; and the younger of them said
to his father, 'Father, give me the share of
property that falls to me.' And he divided
his living between them. Not many days
later, the younger son gathered all he had
and took his journey into a far country, and
there he **squandered**[7] his property in loose
living. And when he had spent everything,
a great famine arose in that country, and he
began to be in want. So he went and joined
himself to one of the citizens of that country, who sent him into his fields to feed
swine. And he would gladly have fed on
the pods that the swine ate; and no one
gave him anything. But when he came to
himself he said, 'How many of my father's
hired servants have bread enough and to
spare, but I perish here with hunger! I will
arise and go to my father and I will say to
him, "Father, I have sinned against heaven
and before you; I am no longer worthy to
be called your son; treat me as one of your
hired servants."'

---

[4] Levite—person who assisted the priests of the
Jewish temple.

[5] Samaritan—member of an ethnic group of ancient Israel
regarded with hostility by the Jewish majority.

[6] denarii—plural of denarius, a Roman coin.

[7] **squandered**—wasted.

"And he arose and came to his father. But while he was yet at a distance, his father saw him and had compassion, and ran and embraced him and kissed him. And the son said to him, 'Father, I have sinned against heaven and before you; I am no longer worthy to be called your son.' But the father said to his servants, 'Bring quickly the best robe, and put it on him; and put a ring on his hand, and shoes on his feet; and bring the fatted calf and kill it, and let us eat and make merry; for this my son was dead, and is alive again; he was lost, and is found.' And they began to make merry.

"Now his elder son was in the field; and as he came and drew near to the house, he heard music and dancing. And he called one of the servants and asked what this meant. And he said to him, 'Your brother has come, and your father has killed the fatted calf, because he has received him safe and sound.' But he was angry and refused to go in. His father came out and **entreated**[8] him, but he answered his father, 'Lo, these many years I have served you, and I never disobeyed your command; yet you never gave me a kid, that I might make merry with my friends. But when this son of yours came, who has devoured your living with harlots,[9] you killed for

him the fatted calf!' And he said to him, 'Son you are always with me, and all that is mine is yours. It was fitting to make merry and be glad, for this your brother was dead, and is alive; he was lost, and is found.'"

---

[8] **entreated**—begged.

[9] harlots—prostitutes.

QUESTIONS TO CONSIDER

1. In the passage from the Sermon on the Mount, what characterizes most of those to whom Jesus promises blessings?

2. In the story of the Good Samaritan, what point does Jesus make by having the priest and the Levite avoid the injured man?

3. What moral is common to both the stories of the Good Samaritan and the Prodigal Son?

from

First Epistle to the Corinthians

PAUL

The New Testament includes twenty-one Epistles, letters addressed to various individuals and communities. Paul (died c. 67 A.D.) was an early Christian missionary who wrote most of the Epistles. This epistle was directed to the Christians of the Greek city of Corinth, who were divided over the spiritual value of such phenomena as "speaking in tongues."

If I speak in the tongues of men and of angels, but have not love, I am a noisy gong or a clanging cymbal. And if I have prophetic powers, and understand all mysteries and all knowledge, and if I have all faith, so as to remove mountains, but have not love, I am nothing. If I give away all I have, and if I deliver my body to be burned, but have not love, I gain nothing.

Love is patient and love is kind; love is not jealous or boastful; it is not **arrogant**[1] or rude. Love does not insist on its own way; it is not irritable or resentful; it does not rejoice at wrong, but rejoices in the right. Love bears all things, believes all things, hopes all things, endures all things.

Love never ends; as for prophecy, it will pass away; as for tongues, they will cease; as for knowledge, it will pass away. For our knowledge is imperfect and our prophecy is imperfect; but when the perfect comes, the imperfect will pass away. When I was a child, I spoke like a child, I thought like a child, I reasoned like a child; when I became a man, I gave up childish ways. For now we see in a mirror dimly, but then face to face. Now I know in part; then I shall understand fully, even as I have been fully understood. So faith, hope, love abide, these three; but the greatest of these is love.

---

[1] **arrogant**—excessively proud.

QUESTIONS TO CONSIDER

1. What kinds of spiritual powers does Paul describe at the beginning of this passage?

2. What is Paul's view of the relationship of love to other spiritual virtues?

Persecution of the Christians

Many religious sects existed within the Roman Empire, and if they were also willing to worship the emperor and the gods of Rome, they were officially tolerated. Because Christians objected to these practices, they were persecuted from time to time by the Roman government. The following documents offer different views of these persecutions. The first two are an exchange of official letters on the Christians between the emperor Trajan (ruled 98–117 A.D.) and Pliny the Younger, who was governor of the Roman province of Bithynia (located in the northwest part of what is now Turkey). The final document comes from a history of the Church written by a Christian bishop, Eusebius (c. 263–339? A.D.). Eusebius describes a persecution in what is now south-central France in 177 A.D.

Letter to Emperor Trajan

Pliny the Younger

It is customary for me, Sir, to refer all matters to you concerning which I am in doubt. For who can better direct my uncertainty or instruct my ignorance?

I have never been present at the trials of Christians; hence, I do not know the extent nor the manner of their prosecution and punishment. I have been greatly puzzled by the question whether some distinction should be made on account of age, or even the very young should be treated like those of more mature years; whether pardon should be granted for repentance, or whether a man who has once been a Christian should have no advantage from giving up his faith; whether a person who merely bears the name of Christian, but is not guilty of any crime, should be punished, or only the crimes accompanying Christianity.

Meanwhile, in the cases of those who have been reported to me as Christians, I have pursued the following method: I asked them, whether they were Christians. If they confessed, I asked them a second and a third time, threatening them with death. If they persisted, I ordered them to be put to death. For, whatever their creed might be, I felt no doubt that their **perverseness**[1] and unyielding stubbornness ought to be punished. There were others **infatuated**[2] with a similar madness,

---

[1] **perverseness**—willfulness.
[2] **infatuated**—possessed with a foolish love or admiration.

but, since they were Roman citizens, I remanded[3] them to the city. So, because of the very handling of the matter, as usually happens, the accusations have spread and many kinds of cases have come up. A list was posted, without the author's signature, containing the names of many people. Those who denied that they were or had been Christians, and who repeated an **invocation**[4] to the gods, as I dictated it, and who offered wine and incense before your statue, which I had ordered to be brought in for this purpose along with the images of the gods, and who cursed Christ, none of which acts, it is said, true Christians can be **compelled**[5] to perform; these persons, I thought, should be dismissed. Others, whose names appeared on the list, said that they were Christians, but soon denied it, asserting that they had once been Christians, but had later ceased to be such, some three or more years ago and one man twenty years ago. All worshipped your statue and the images of the gods and **reviled**[6] Christ. They affirmed, however, that the full extent of their sin, or error, consisted of their habit of meeting on a fixed day before sunrise and singing a song antiphonally[7] to Christ, as a god, and binding themselves by an oath, not to do any evil deeds, but to commit no theft, robbery or adultery, nor to break their word, nor to refuse to return deposited moneys, when called upon. When these ceremonies had been performed, it was their custom, they said, to depart and later to reassemble

for the purpose of partaking of food of an ordinary and innocent sort. Even this they had ceased to do subsequent to my **edict**[8] in which, according to your orders, I had forbidden the existence of fraternal organizations. And so I thought it all the more necessary to determine the truth even by torture in the cases of two female servants, who were called deaconesses.[9] But I discovered nothing more than a base and excessive superstition.

Consequently, I have adjourned the inquiry and betaken myself to your counsels. For the matter appeared to me worthy of consultation, especially in view of the large number of those involved. Indeed, many of all ages and ranks, and even of both sexes are now and will be called to stand trial. For the **contagion**[10] of this superstition has spread not only through the cities, but also through the villages and the farms; it seems possible, however, to stop it and cure it. At any rate, it is certain that the temples which were almost deserted have begun to be crowded, and the religious festivals which have long been interrupted are being reestablished. Everywhere sacrificial victims are being

---

[3] remanded—sent to another court.

[4] **invocation**—prayer.

[5] **compelled**—forced.

[6] **reviled**—abused verbally.

[7] antiphonally—as a response.

[8] **edict**—decree.

[9] deaconesses—women in the early Church who performed certain priestly duties.

[10] **contagion**—transmission of a disease.

sold, of which very few buyers were found up to the present. From this fact it is easy to infer how many persons may be reclaimed, if an opportunity is left for repentance.

Letter to Pliny
Trajan

You have pursued the right method, my dear Pliny, in examining the cases of those who have been reported to you as Christians. No general rule having a fixed form, as it were, can be constituted. Christians should not be sought out, but if they are reported and proved to be such, they must be punished; yet, if anyone denies that he is a Christian and proves it in fact, by worshipping our gods, even though he has been suspected in the past, he shall obtain pardon because of his repentance. Lists drawn up without a signature ought not to receive consideration in any charge. Such procedure establishes a very bad precedent and is not in keeping with the spirit of our times.

from *The History of the Church*
Eusebius

There were also arrested certain **heathen**[11] slaves of our members, since the governor had publicly commanded that we should all be prosecuted, and these by the **snare**[12] of Satan, fearing the tortures which they saw the saints suffering, when the soldiers urged them, falsely accused us of . . .

things which it is not right for us either to speak of or to think of or even to believe that such things could ever happen among men.[13] When this rumor spread all men turned like beasts against us, so that even if any had formerly been **lenient**[14] for friendship's sake they then became furious and raged against us, and there was fulfilled that which was spoken by our Lord that "the time will come when whosoever killeth you will think that he doeth God service."

Maturus and Sanctus and Blandina and Attalus were led forth to the wild beasts, to the public, and to a common exhibition of the inhumanity of the heathen, for the day of fighting with beasts was specially appointed for the Christians. Maturus and Sanctus passed again through all torture in the amphitheater as though they had suffered nothing before, but rather as though, having conquered the opponent in many bouts, they were now striving for his crown. Once more they ran the gauntlet in the accustomed manner, endured the worrying of the wild beasts, and everything which the maddened public, some in one way, some in another, were howling for and commanding, finally, the iron chair on which the roasting of their own bodies clothed them with its reek. Their persecutors

---

[11] **heathen**—pagan.

[12] **snare**—trap.

[13] things . . . men—Eusebius probably refers to charges of cannibalism based on a misunderstanding of the sacrament of the Eucharist, in which Christians symbolically consumed the body and blood of Christ.

[14] **lenient**—tolerant.

did not stop even here, but went on growing more and more furious, wishing to conquer their endurance, yet gained nothing from Sanctus beyond the sound of the [Christian] confession which he had been accustomed to make from the beginning.

. . . Blandina was hung on a stake and offered as a prey to the wild beasts that were let in. She seemed to be hanging in the shape of a cross, and by her continuous prayer gave great zeal to the combatants, while they looked on during the contest, and with their outward eyes saw in the form of their sister him who was crucified for them, to persuade those who believe on him that all who suffer for the glory of Christ have forever fellowship with the living God. Then when none of the beasts would touch her she was taken down from the stake and brought back into the jail, and was thus preserved for another contest. . . .

In addition to all this, on the last day of the gladiatorial sports, Blandina was again brought in with Ponticus, a boy of about fifteen years old, and they had been brought in every day to see the torture of the others, and efforts were made to force them to swear by the idols, and the mob was furious against them because they had remained steadfast and disregarded them, so that there was neither pity for the youth of the boy nor respect for the sex of the woman. They exposed them to all the terrors and put them through every torture in turn, trying to make them swear, but not being able to do so. For Ponticus was

encouraged by the Christian sister, so that even the heathen saw that she was **exhorting**[15] and strengthening him, and after nobly enduring every torture he gave up his spirit. But the blessed Blandina, last of all, like a noble mother who had encouraged her children and sent them forth triumphant to the king, having herself endured all the tortures of the children, hastened to them, rejoicing and glad at her departure as though invited to a marriage feast rather than cast to the beasts. And after **scourging**,[16] after the beasts, after the gridiron, she was at last put in a net and thrown to a bull. . . . And so she too was sacrificed, and the heathen themselves confessed that never before among them had a woman suffered so much and so long.

---

[15] **exhorting**—encouraging.

[16] **scourging**—whipping.

QUESTIONS TO CONSIDER

1. From Pliny's account, of what are the Christians guilty?

2. How would you describe Trajan as a ruler?

3. What does Eusebius indicate about the motivation for the persecutions?

4. The early Christian theologian Tertullian observed, "The blood of martyrs is the seed of the church." Why do you think this might be true?

Fathers of the Church

The Fathers of the Church were a group of important theologians who defined the orthodox tradition of early Christianity. Among the Church fathers were Jerome and Augustine. Jerome (c. 347–419?A.D.) was a scholar who rejected classical learning—as he describes in the following letter—and devoted himself to creating the Church's official Latin version (or Vulgate text) of the Bible. Augustine (354–430 A.D..) summarized the Christian teaching of his time in his major work, The City of God.

The Christian and the Classics

Jerome

Many years ago for the sake of the kingdom of heaven I cut myself off from home, parents, sister, relations, and, what was harder, from the dainty food to which I had been used. But even when I was on my way to Jerusalem to fight the good fight there, I could not bring myself to forgo the library which with great care and labor I had got together at Rome. And so, miserable man that I was, I would fast, only to read Cicero[1] afterwards. I would spend long nights in vigil,[2] I would shed bitter tears called from my inmost heart by the remembrance of my past sins; and then I would take up Plautus[3] again. Whenever I returned to my right senses and began to read the prophets, their language seemed harsh and barbarous. With my blind eyes I could not see the light: but I attributed the fault not to my eyes but to the sun. While the old serpent was thus mocking me, about the middle of Lent[4] a fever attacked my weakened body and spread through my inmost veins. It may sound incredible, but the ravages it wrought on my unhappy frame were so **persistent**[5] that at last my bones scarcely held together.

Meantime preparations were made for my funeral: my whole body grew gradually cold, and life's vital warmth only lingered faintly in my poor throbbing breast.

---

[1] Cicero—Roman statesman, orator, and writer (106–43 B.C.).

[2] vigil—voluntary wakefulness as a spiritual practice.

[3] Plautus—Roman playwright (c. 254–c. 184 B.C.).

[4] Lent—season of penance in Christianity.

[5] **persistent**—continual.

Suddenly I was caught up in the spirit and dragged before the Judge's judgment seat: and here the light was so dazzling, and the brightness shining from those who stood around so radiant, that I flung myself upon the ground and did not dare to look up. I was asked to state my condition and replied that I was a Christian. But He who presided said: "Thou liest; thou art a Ciceronian, not a Christian. 'For where thy treasure is there will thy heart be also.'" Straightway I became dumb, and amid the strokes of the whip—for He had ordered me to be scourged—I was even more bitterly tortured by the fire of conscience, considering with myself the verse: "In the grave who shall give thee thanks?" Yet for all that I began to cry out and to bewail[6] myself, saying: "Have mercy upon me, O Lord, have mercy upon me": and even amid the noise of the lash my voice made itself heard. At last the bystanders fell at the knees of Him who presided, and prayed Him to pardon my youth and give me opportunity to repent of my error, on the understanding that the extreme of torture should be inflicted on me if ever I read again the works of Gentile[7] authors. In the stress of that dread hour I should have been willing to make even larger promises, and taking oath I called upon His name: "O Lord, if ever again I possess worldly books or read them, I have denied thee."

After swearing this oath I was dismissed, and returned to the upper world.

There to the surprise of all I opened my eyes again, and they were so drenched with tears, that my distress convinced even the **incredulous**.[8] That this experience was no sleep nor idle dream, such as often mocks us, I call to witness the judgment seat before which I fell and the terrible verdict which I feared. May it never be my lot again to come before such a court as that! I profess that my shoulders were black and blue, and that I felt the bruises long after I awoke from my sleep. And I acknowledge that henceforth I read the books of God with a greater zeal than I had ever given before to the books of men.

from *The City of God*
Augustine

Of the Two Contrary Courses Taken by the Human Race, from the Beginning
Of the place and **felicity**[9] of the local paradise,[10] together with man's life and fall therein, there are many opinions, many assertions, and many books, as several men thought, spoke, and wrote. What we held hereof, or could gather out of holy scriptures, correspondent unto their truth and authority, we related in some of the foregoing books. If they be farther looked into, they will give birth to more questions and longer disputations than we have now room for. Our time is not so large as to per

---

[6] bewail—lament.
[7] Gentile—pagan.
[8] **incredulous**—unbelieving.
[9] **felicity**—happiness.
[10] local paradise—Garden of Eden (page 7).

mit us to argue scrupulously upon every question that may be asked by busy heads that are more curious of inquiry than capable of understanding. I think we have sufficiently discussed the doubts concerning the beginning of the world, the soul, and mankind; which last is divided into two sorts, such as live according to man, and such as live according to God. These we mystically call two cities or societies, the one predestined to being eternally with God, the other condemned in perpetual torment with the devil. This is their end, of which hereafter. Now seeing we have said sufficient concerning their origin, both in the angels whose number we know not, and in the two first parents of mankind, I think it fit to pass on to their progression from man's first offspring until he cease to beget[11] anymore. All the time included between these two points, wherein the livers ever succeed the diers, is the progression of these two cities. Cain therefore was the first begotten of those two that were mankind's parents, and he belongs to the city of man; Abel[12] was the later, and he belongs to the city of God. For as we see that in an individual man (as the apostle[13] says) that which is spiritual is not first, but that which is natural first, and then the spiritual (whereupon all that comes from Adam's corrupted nature must needs be evil and carnal[14] at first, and then if a man be **regenerate**[15] by Christ, becomes good and spiritual afterward): so in the first propagation of man, and progression of the two cities of which we dispute, the carnal citizen was born first, and the pilgrim on earth or heavenly citizen afterwards, being by grace predestined, and by grace elected, by grace a pilgrim upon earth, and by grace a citizen in heaven. For as for his birth; it was out of the same corrupted mass that was condemned from the beginning; but God like a potter (for this **simile**[16] the apostle himself uses) out of the same lump, made "one vessel to honor and another to reproach." The vessel of reproach was made first, and the vessel of honor afterwards. For in each individual, as I said, there is first reprobation,[17] whence we must needs begin (and wherein we need not remain), and afterwards goodness, to which we come by profiting, and coming thither therein make our abode. Whereupon it follows that no one can be good that has not first been evil, though all that be evil become not good; but the sooner a man betters himself the quicker does this name follow him, abolishing the memory of the other. Therefore, it is recorded of Cain that he built a city, but Abel was a pilgrim, and built none. For the city of the saints is above, though it have citizens here

---

[11] beget—produce children.

[12] Cain . . . Abel—sons of Adam and Eve, the first humans, in the Bible; Cain, the first-born, killed his brother and was exiled by God.

[13] apostle—Paul (page 265).

[14] carnal—fleshly.

[15] regenerate—spiritually renewed.

[16] simile—likeness, comparison.

[17] reprobation—disapproval.

upon earth, wherein it lives as a pilgrim until the time of the kingdom come; and then it gathers all the citizens together in the resurrection of the body, and gives them a kingdom to reign in with their King for ever and ever.

Of the Sons of the Flesh and the Sons of Promise

The shadow and prophetical image of this city (not making it present but signifying it) served here upon earth, at the time when such a foreshadowing was needed; and was called the holy city, because it was a symbol of the city that was to be, though not the reality. Of this city serving as an image, and the free city herein prefigured, the apostle speaks thus unto the Galatians:[18] "Tell me, ye that desire to be under the law, do ye not hear the law? For it is written that Abraham[19] had two sons, one by a bondwoman, and the other by a free: but the son of the bondwoman was born of the flesh, and the son of the freewoman by promise. Which things are an **allegory**:[20] for these are the two Testaments, the one given from Mount Sinai, begetting man in servitude, which is Hagar; for Sinai is a mountain in Arabia, joined to the Jerusalem on earth, for it serves with her children. But our mother the **celestial**[21] Jerusalem is free, for it is written: Rejoice, thou barren that bearest not: break forth into joy, and cry out, thou that travailest[22] not with child, for the desolate hath many more children than the married wife. But we, brethren, are the sons of promise to Isaac. But as then he that was born of the flesh persecuted him that was born after the spirit, even so it is now. But what says the scripture? 'Cast out the bondwoman and her son, for the bondwoman's son shall not be heir with the freewoman's.' Then, brethren, we are not children of the bondwoman, but of the free." Thus the apostle authorizes us to conceive of the Old and New Testaments. For a part of the earthly city was made an image of the heavenly, not signifying itself but another, and therefore serving: for it was not ordained to signify itself but another, and itself was signified by another precedent type; for Hagar, Sarah's servant, and her son, were an image hereof. And because, when the light comes, the shadows must flee away, Sarah the freewoman signifying the free city (which that shadow of the earthly Jerusalem signified in another manner) said: "Cast out the bondwoman and her son: for the bondwoman's son shall not be heir with my son Isaac": whom the apostle calls the freewoman's son. Thus then we find this earthly city in two forms; the one presenting itself, and the other prefiguring the celestial city, and serving it.

---

[18] apostle. . . Galatians—Paul's epistle to the Galatians, a Christian community in what is now Turkey.

[19] Abraham—ancestor of the Jews. In the Bible he has two sons, Isaac, child of Abraham's wife Sarah, and Ishmael, child of Sarah's servant Hagar. Isaac becomes his father's heir; Ishmael and Hagar are exiled to the desert, where they become the ancestors of the Arabs.

[20] **allegory**—narrative in which various elements represent other meanings.

[21] **celestial**—heavenly.

[22] travailest—suffer the pains of childbirth.

Our nature corrupted by sin produces citizens of earth; and grace freeing us from the sin of nature makes us citizens of heaven: the first are called the vessels of wrath, the last of mercy. And this was signified in the two sons of Abraham, the one of whom being born of the bondwoman was called Ishmael, being the son of the flesh; the other, the freewoman's, Isaac, the son of promise. Both were Abraham's sons; but natural custom begot the first, and gracious promise the latter. In the first was a demonstration of man's use, in the second was a revelation of God's.

QUESTIONS TO CONSIDER

1. Both Jerome and Augustine see the necessity of choosing one of two paths. What, in your own words, are the two paths each describes?

2. What effect does his reading of the classical writers have on Jerome's response to the Bible?

3. How would you describe Jerome's conversion experience?

4. Augustine points out that Adam's first child, Cain, was evil, and his second, Abel, was good. What lesson does Augustine draw from this?

Byzantine and Russian Rulers

Based in Constantinople, the Byzantine Empire was the successor to the Roman Empire. One of the most notorious figures in Byzantine history was Theodora, an actress who became the wife of the emperor Justinian. The first document is an account by the Byzantine historian Procopius. He describes Justinian and Theodora during a violent rebellion in 532 A.D. known as the Nike Revolt, when much of Constantinople was burned by mobs. In the 800s, Byzantine culture began to penetrate into Russia. In 957 a Russian princess, Olga of Kiev, traveled to Constantinople, where she was baptized. The second document, from The Russian Primary Chronicle, *describes an episode several years earlier, when Olga also faced a challenge to her rule.*

from *The History*
Procopius

Meanwhile, all of the citizens who were sane-minded were fleeing to the opposite mainland, and fire was applied to the city as if it had fallen under the hand of an enemy. The sanctuary of Sophia and the baths of Zeuxippus, and the portion of the imperial residence from the propylea[1] as far as the so-called House of Ares were destroyed by fire, and besides these both the great **colonnades**[2] which extended as far as the marketplace which bears the name of Constantine,[3] in addition to many houses of wealthy men and a vast amount of treasure. During this time the emperor and his [wife] with a few members of the senate shut themselves up in the palace and remained quietly there. . . .

Now the emperor and his court were deliberating as to whether it would be better for them if they remained or if they took to flight in the ships. And many opinions were expressed favoring either course. And the Empress Theodora also spoke to the following effect: "As to the belief that a woman ought not to be daring among men or to assert herself boldly among those who are holding back from fear, I consider that the present crisis most certainly does

---

[1] propylea—gateway.

[2] **colonnades**—rows of columns.

[3] Constantine—Roman emperor who in 330 A.D. moved his capital to the ancient Greek city of Byzantium, which was renamed Constantinople.

not permit us to discuss whether the matter should be regarded in this or in some other way. For in the case of those whose interests have come into the greatest danger nothing else seems best except to settle the issue immediately before them in the best possible way. My opinion then is that the present time, above all others, is inopportune for flight, even though it bring safety. For while it is impossible for a man who has seen the light not also to die, for one who has been an emperor it is unendurable to be a fugitive. May I never be separated from this purple,[4] and may I not live that day on which those who meet me shall not address me as mistress. If, now, it is your wish to save yourself, O Emperor, there is no difficulty. For we have much money, and there is the sea, here the boats. However consider whether it will not come about after you have been saved that you would gladly exchange that safety for death. For as for myself, I approve a certain ancient saying that royalty is a good burial-shroud." When the queen had spoken thus, all were filled with boldness, and, turning their thoughts towards resistance, they began to consider how they might be able to defend themselves if any hostile force should come against them.

---

[4] purple—a color only royalty were allowed to wear.

This Byzantine mosaic shows Theodora among her attendants, offering a golden chalice to hold the wine used in Christian worship.

from *The Russian Primary Chronicle*

Olga was informed that the Derevlians[5] had arrived, and summoned them to her presence with a gracious welcome. . . . The Derevlians then announced that their tribe had sent them to report that they had slain her husband, because he was like a wolf, crafty and ravening, but that their princes, who had thus preserved the land of Dereva, were good, and that Olga should come and marry their Prince Mal. For the name of the Prince of Dereva was Mal.

Olga made this reply: "Your proposal is pleasing to me; indeed, my husband cannot rise again from the dead. But I desire to honor you tomorrow in the presence of my people. Return now to your boat, and remain there with an aspect of **arrogance**.[6] I shall send for you on the morrow, and you shall say, 'We will not ride on horses nor go on foot; carry us [on your shoulders] in our boat.' And you shall be carried in your boat." Thus, she dismissed them to their vessel.

Now Olga gave command that a large deep ditch should be dug in the castle. . . . Thus on the morrow, Olga as she sat in the hall sent for the strangers, and her messengers approached them and said, "Olga summons you to great honor." But they replied, "We will not ride on horseback nor in wagons, nor go on foot; carry us in our boat." The people of Kiev then lamented: "Slavery is our lot. Our prince is killed,

and our princess intends to marry their prince." So they carried the Derevlians in their boat. The latter sat on the cross-benches in great robes, puffed up with pride. They thus were borne into the court before Olga, and when the men had brought the Derevlians in, they dropped them into the trench along with the boat. Olga bent over and inquired whether they found the honor to their taste. They answered that it was worse than the death of Igor. She then commanded that they should be buried alive, and they were thus buried. . . .

Olga then sent to the Derevlians the following message: "I am now coming to you, so prepare great quantities of mead[7] in the city where you killed my husband, that I may weep over his grave and hold a funeral feast for him." When they heard these words, they gathered great quantities of honey, and brewed mead. Taking a small escort, Olga made the journey with ease, and upon her arrival at Igor's tomb, she wept for her husband. She bade her followers pile up a great mound, and when they had piled it up, she also gave command that a funeral feast should be held. Thereupon the Derevlians sat down to drink, and Olga bade her followers wait upon them.

---

[5] Derevlians—Slavic people who had killed Olga's husband Igor.

[6] **arrogance**—excessive pride.

[7] mead—alcoholic beverage brewed from honey.

The Derevlians inquired of Olga where the **retinue**[8] was which they had sent to meet her. She replied that they were following with her husband's bodyguard. When the Derevlians were drunk, she bade her followers fall upon them, and went about herself egging on her retinue to the Massacre of the Derevlians. So they cut down five thousand of them; but Olga returned to Kiev and prepared an army to attack the survivors.

---

[8] **retinue**—followers.

1. Theodora came from the lower classes. Do you think this influenced her determination not to flee?

2. Do the qualities conveyed by the mosaic portrait of Theodora match the person depicted by Procopius? Why or why not?

3. Do you think Olga was justified in taking the action she did? Explain.

Byzantine and Russian Icons

Early Christians debated the morality of depicting the sacred. Some people felt that images of Jesus, his mother, the saints, and other sacred subjects helped people focus their devotions and could even be a channel of divine grace. Those who opposed such depictions invoked the prohibition in the Ten Commandments against graven images, arguing that picturing the sacred encouraged idolatry. In the Byzantine Empire devotion to sacred images, called icons, was very strong—and opposition to them equally fierce. Below are examples of Byzantine icons, followed by two readings conveying different aspects of the devotion to sacred images.

This mosaic of Christ as Pantocrator ("All-Ruler") recalls the portrait of the Empress Theodora (page 276). ▶

Probably painted by a Byzantine artist in the 1100s, *The Virgin of Vladimir* is Russia's most revered icon.

Displaying the same tender melancholy as *The Virgin of Vladimir*, this Madonna is seated within an elaborate throne that suggests a miniature building.

This scene from Genesis of the three angels who visit Abraham to announce the birth of his son Isaac was painted around 1410 by Andrei Rublev, the finest Russian icon painter. ▶

On an Icon of the Virgin

Manuel Philes

What is this? How, and through what art, did you find yourself, a faint and shadowy picture, gripped in the weaving of a humble woof?[1] And how did the wax, melted by the flame, not burn the inflammable cloth upon which it fell, but skillfully paint this your image? Ah, Mary, you change the very nature of matter: you who once appeared in the **guise**[2] of a bush the flames could not consume now depict yourself by means of this strange fire; and here Christ himself pours from above a secret moisture on the flame of the torch so that the believer may look on this picture and escape the ghostly flame of suffering.

from *Chronographia*

Michael Psellus

Some men lose themselves in the contemplation of God; their whole being is directed to one perfect object, and on that object they depend entirely. Others, with still greater devotion, and truly inspired with the Divine Spirit, are even more identified with the object of their worship. So it was with Zoe.[3] Her passionate veneration for the things of God had really brought her into contact, so to speak, with the First and Purest Light. Certainly there was no

---

[1] woof—fabric.

[2] **guise**—appearance.

[3] Zoe—Byzantine empress (died 1050).

moment when the Name of God was not on her lips.

I will give an example of this piety of hers. She had made for herself an image of Jesus, fashioning it with as much accuracy as she could (if such a thing were possible). The little figure, **embellished**[4] with bright metal, appeared to be almost living. By changes of color it answered questions put to it, and by its various tints foretold coming events. Anyway, Zoe made several prophecies with regard to the future from a study of this image. So, when she had met with some good fortune, or when some trouble had befallen her, she would at once consult her image, in the one case to acknowledge her gratitude, in the other to beg its favor. I myself have often seen her, in moments of great distress, clasp the sacred object in her hands, contemplate it, talk to it as though it were indeed alive, and address it with one sweet term of endearment after another. Then at other times I have seen her lying on the ground; her tears bathing the earth, while she beat her breasts over and over again, tearing at them with her hands. If she saw the image turn pale, she would go away crestfallen,[5] but if it took on a fiery red color, its halo lustrous with a beautiful radiant light, she would lose no time in telling the emperor and prophesying what the future was to bring forth.

---

[4] **embellished**—adorned.

[5] crestfallen—dejected.

QUESTIONS TO CONSIDER

1. What qualities do these icons seem intended to convey?

2. How does the speaker in "On an Icon of the Virgin" use the imagery of flame to link the Virgin Mary through her portrait to an individual believer?

3. How did the Empress Zoe seem to view her image of Christ?

The Gospel According to Luke

ANNIE DILLARD

While the four Gospels share many features, each presents a different vision of Jesus. American writer Annie Dillard (1945–) explores some of the characteristics of Luke's account of Jesus and his ministry.

Historians of every school agree—with varying enthusiasm—that this certain Jewish man lived, wandered in Galilee and Judaea, and preached a radically spiritual doctrine of prayer, poverty, forgiveness, and mercy for all under the fathership of God; he attracted a following and was crucified by soldiers of the occupying Roman army. There is no reason to hate him, unless the idea of a God who knows, hears, and acts—which idea he proclaimed—is itself offensive.

In Luke, Jesus makes no claims to be the only Son of God. Luke is a **monotheist**:[1] Jesus is the Son of Man, and the Messiah,[2] but Jesus is not God's only-begotten Son, of one substance with the Father, who came down from heaven. Luke never suggests that Christ was begotten before all worlds, that he was very God of very God, that eternity interrupted time

with his coming, or that faith in his divinity is the sole path to salvation. The substance of his teaching is his way; he taught God, not Christ. The people in Luke are a rogues' gallery of tax collectors, innkeepers, fallen women, shrewd bourgeois owners, thieves, Pharisees,[3] and assorted unclean Gentiles. He saves them willy-nilly; they need not, and do not, utter creeds first.

Salvation in Luke, for the followers of Christ, consists in a life of prayer, repentance, and mercy; it is a life in the world with God. Faith in Christ's divinity has nothing to do with it. The cross as God's own sacrifice has nothing to do with it; the cross is Jesus' own sacrifice, freely and reluctantly chosen, and of supreme

---

[1] **monotheist**—believer in one God.

[2] Messiah—leader the Jews believed would be sent by God to deliver them from their enemies.

[3] Pharisees—members of a Jewish sect that practiced strict religious observance.

moment on that head. That Jesus was resurrected in flesh and blood means in Luke, I think, that he was indeed the Messiah whom God had promised to lead the people—now all people—by his teaching and example, back to prayerful and spiritual obedience to God their father and creator.

Still, his teachings are as surprising as his life. Their requirements are harsh. Do not ask your goods back from anyone who has taken them from you. Sell all that thou hast, and give it to the poor. Do not stop to perform a son's great duty, to bury a father. Divorce and remarriage is adultery. Forgive an enemy seven times in one day, without limit. Faith is not a gift but a plain duty. Take no thought for your life. Pray without ceasing. Unto everyone which hath shall be given; and from him that hath not, even that he hath shall be taken away.

> Religion is for outcasts and victims; Jesus made that clear.

The teachings that are not harsh are even more radical, and harder to swallow.

Consider the lilies how they grow: they toil not, they spin not; and yet I say unto you, that Solomon[4] in all his glory was not arrayed like one of these.

If then God so clothe the grass, which is today in the field, and tomorrow is cast into the oven; how much more will he clothe you, O ye of little faith? . . .

Your Father knoweth that you have need of these things.

But rather seek ye the kingdom of God; and all these things shall be added unto you.

Fear not, little flock. . . .

Ask, and it shall be given you; seek, and ye shall find; knock, and it shall be opened unto you.

For every one that asketh receiveth; and he that seeketh findeth; and to him that knocketh it shall be opened.

"O Fear not, little flock": this seems apt for those pious watercolor people so long ago, those blameless and endearing shepherds and fishermen, in colorful native garb, whose lives seem pure, because they are not our lives. They were rustics,[5] silent and sunlit, outdoors, whom we sentimentalize and ignore. They are not in our world. They had some nascent[6] sort of money, but not the kind to take seriously. They got their miracles, perhaps, but they died anyway, long ago, and so did their children. Salvation is obviously for them, and so is God, for they are, like the very young and the very old in our world, **peripheral**.[7] Religion is for outcasts and victims; Jesus made that clear. Religion suits primitives. They have time to work up their touching faith in unverifiable promises. . . .

Our lives are complex. There are many things we must consider before we go considering any lilies. There are many things we must fear. We are in charge; we are running things in a world we made; we are nobody's little flock.

---

[4] Solomon—king of ancient Israel famous for his wealth.

[5] rustics—country people.

[6] nascent—beginning to exist; rudimentary.

[7] **peripheral**—unimportant.

In Luke, Christ's ministry enlarges in awfulness—from the sunny Galilean[8] days of eating and drinking, preaching on lakesides, saying lovely things, choosing disciples, healing the sick, making the blind see, casting out demons, and raising the dead—enlarges in awfulness from this exuberant world, where all is possible and God displays his power and love, to the dark messianic journey which begins when Peter acknowledges him ("Who do you think I am?") as the Christ, and culminates in the eerie night-long waiting at the lip of the vortex[9] as Pilate and Herod[10] pass Jesus back and forth and he defends himself not.

Jesus creates his role and succumbs to it. He understands his destiny only gradually, through much prayer; he decides on it, foretells it, and sets his face to meet it. On the long journey to Jerusalem, which occupies many chapters of Luke, he understands more and more. The narrative builds a long sober sense of crushing demand on Jesus the man, and the long sober sense of his gradually strengthening himself to see it, to cause it, and to endure it. (The account of his ministry's closure parallels the account of its beginning three years previously; Jesus very gradually, and through prayer, chooses, creates, and assumes his tremendous and transcendent role. He chooses his life, and he chooses his death.)

In that final long journey to Jerusalem, the **austerity**[11] of Jesus deepens; his mystery and separateness magnify. The party is over. Pressure rises from crowds, pressure rises from the Jewish authorities.

His utterances become vatic[12] and Greekish. Behold, we go up to Jerusalem, he tells his disciples. If anyone wishes to follow me, let him deny himself, take up his cross day after day, and so follow me. For the Son of Man is coming into his glory. What awaits him is uncertain, unspecified, even unto the cross and upon it; but in the speeches of his last days, in this village and that, his awareness becomes stonily clearer. Privately, often, and urgently, he addresses his disciples in dire terms: When they call you before the magistrates, do not trouble yourself about what you are to say. I have a baptism to undergo. The days will come when ye shall desire to see one of the days of the Son of Man, and ye shall not see it. "And they understood none of these things."

On the way to Jerusalem he addresses the Pharisees, who bring him a message from Herod ("that fox"): "I must walk today, and tomorrow, and the day following: for it cannot be that a prophet perish out of Jerusalem." He adds an apostrophe:[13] "O Jerusalem, Jerusalem, which killest the prophets, and stonest them that are sent unto thee; how often

---

[8] Galilean—referring to Galilee, the region in the north of Palestine that was Jesus' home.

[9] vortex—whirling movement.

[10] Pilate and Herod—Pilate was Roman governor of Judea; Herod was ruler of Galilee.

[11] **austerity**—severity, strictness.

[12] vatic—prophetic.

[13] apostrophe—address to someone not present.

would I have gathered thy children together, as a hen doth gather her brood under her wings, and ye would not!"

And he does walk, that day, and the next day, and the day following, soberly, wittingly, and freely, going up to Jerusalem for the Passover in which he will not be passed over. There is little mingling with crowds, and only four healings, two of them provokingly on the Sabbath. His words are often harsh and angry. "Thou fool," he has God saying to a rich man. "Ye **hypocrites**,"[14] he calls his disciples. In one of his stories an outraged master says, "Depart from me, all ye workers of **iniquity**."[15] I am come to send fire on the earth. But those mine enemies . . . bring hither, and slay them before me.

He enters the city on a "colt" and is at once discovered driving the money changers out of the Temple. "Whosoever shall fall upon that stone shall be broken; but on whomsoever it shall fall, it will grind him to powder." As for the temple in which they stand, "there shall not be left one stone upon another. . . . These be the days of vengeance."

The crowds around Jesus are so great in Jerusalem that the Roman authorities must take him at night, as he quits the garden. There he has prayed in an agony, "Father, if thou be willing, remove this cup from me: nevertheless not my will, but thine, be done." Then he has prayed *more* earnestly, and his sweat fell down to the ground. Betrayed to the soldiers, he shuttles back and forth between Pilate and Herod all night; the cock crows; Peter denies him; and in the morning Pilate takes him— him supremely silent, magnificent, and vulnerable—before the chief priests and Jewish rulers, and before an unspecified crowd. They cry, "Release unto us Barabbas."[16] And their voices and those of the chief priests prevail. As Roman soldiers lead Jesus away, "there followed him a great company of people." Where were they a minute ago, that they could not outshout the claque[17] for Barabbas?

In Luke alone, after Jesus on the cross commends his spirit to the hands of God and dies, a Roman soldier is moved to say, "Certainly this was a righteous man." Luke alone recounts the incident on the road to Emmaus. Two disciples walking to Emmaus are talking about Jesus' crucifixion, which has occurred three days previously, when a stranger joins them and asks what they are talking about; the disciples, surprised, explain. The stranger interprets messianic prophecies in Scripture for them, beginning with Moses, which seems to surprise them not at all. In the village, they invite the stranger in. When at table he takes the loaf, gives thanks, and breaks it, then their eyes are opened, they recognize him, and he vanishes.

---

[14] **hypocrites**—persons who do not practice what they claim to believe.

[15] **iniquity**—evil.

[16] Barabbas—robber pardoned in place of Jesus to appease a Jewish crowd.

[17] claque—persons hired to applaud a performer.

Amazed, they walk that night all the way back to Jerusalem—another seven miles—and tell the others. And while they are speaking, Jesus appears yet again. They are "terrified," but Jesus says, "Why are ye troubled? and why do thoughts arise in your hearts?" He shows them his wounded hands and feet, and they are full of joy and wondering, and very far from recognizing that, among other things, ordinary hospitality is called for—so Jesus has to ask, "Have ye here any meat?" (They give him broiled fish and a piece of honeycomb.) Then the resurrected Jesus explains scriptural prophecies concerning the Messiah's death and his resurrection on the third day; charges them to preach to all nations; leads them out as far as Bethany (two miles east); blesses them; and is carried up to heaven. . . .

The Gospel of Luke ends immediately and abruptly after the Ascension outside Bethany, on that Easter Sunday when the disciples had walked so much and kept receiving visitations from the risen Christ. The skies have scarcely closed around Christ's heels when the story concludes on the disciples: "And [they] were continually in the temple, praising and blessing God. Amen."

What a pity, that so hard on the heels of Christ come the Christians. There is no breather. The disciples turn into the early Christians between one rushed verse and another. What a dismaying pity, that here come the Christians already, flawed to the core, full of wild ideas and hurried self-importance. They are already blocking, with linked arms, the howling gap in the weft[18] of things that their man's coming and going tore.

For who can believe in the Christians? They are, we know by hindsight, suddenly not at all peripheral. They set out immediately to take over the world, and they pretty much did it. They converted emperors, raised armies, lined their pockets with real money, and did evil things large and small, in century after century, including this one. They are smug and busy, just like us, and who could believe in them? They are not innocent, they are not shepherds and fishermen in rustic period costume, they are men and women just like us, in polyester. Who could believe salvation is for these rogues? That God is for these rogues? For they are just like us, and salvation's time is past.

Unless, of course—

Unless Christ's washing the disciples' feet, their dirty toes, means what it could, possibly, mean: that it is all right to be human. That God knows we are human, and full of evil, all of us, and we are his people anyway, and the sheep of his pasture.

> *The disciples turn into the early Christians between one rushed verse and another.*

---

[18] weft—weave.

Unless those colorful scamps and scalawags[19] who populate Jesus' parables were just as evil as we are, and evil in the same lazy, cowardly, and scheming ways. Unless those pure disciples themselves and those watercolor women—who so disconcertingly turned into The Christians overnight—were complex and selfish humans also, who lived in the material world, and whose errors and evils were not pretty but ugly, and had real consequences. If they were just like us, then Christ's words to them are addressed to us, in full and merciful knowledge—and we are lost. There is no place to hide.

---

[19] scamps and scalawags—rascals.

QUESTIONS TO CONSIDER

1. According to Annie Dillard, how is the nature of Jesus presented in Luke's Gospel?

2. How does the tone of Jesus' ministry change as he moves from Galilee to Jerusalem?

3. What does Dillard feel allows modern people to distance themselves from the message of the Gospel?

The Struggle over Icons

JOHN TAYLOR

There was a fierce conflict in the Byzantine Empire between those who reverenced sacred images (called icons) and those who wanted to destroy them. In his book Icon Painting, *art historian John Taylor describes the struggle between the iconophiles, who supported the use of icons, and their opponents, the iconoclasts.*

For the people of Constantinople,[1] there lay beyond their imperfect and corrupt world another, perfect and incorruptible, towards which they must constantly aspire. The state, with all its shortcomings, was, nevertheless, thought to be a model of the ideal state of heaven. Greeks considered that Christ's heaven upon earth ceased outside the boundaries of the Empire. Life on earth was a struggle against unseen forces, both divine and devilish, continuously tempting and never **satiated**.[2] Unable to reach across the gulf that separated the real world from the ideal, men enlisted as mediators entities which were thought to partake of both earth and heaven: they made use of saints, holy men, relics, and icons.

Each of these entities was a source of miracles, of mercy and guidance. If a man felt himself overcome by unseen forces, or if he fell ill, or his business was faltering, he would turn to such a mediator for its capacity to invoke divine power.

The Christian Empire was vast and contained converts from many different religions. Old Testament prohibitions upon image-worship were not forgotten by the Jews, and for the Bishops, conscious of the pagan ancestry of their flock, this tendency to ascribe miracles to images and relics was alarmingly akin to ancient practices. The distinction between worshipping an icon

---

[1] Constantinople—capital of the Byzantine Empire.
[2] **satiated**—satisfied.

for what it might represent, or worshipping it for itself; between seeing it as mediator, or as itself a worker of miracles, was too fine to be drawn by any but the highly educated. In 824 the Emperor Michael II complained to Lewis the Pious:

> They not only ask help of the above images, but many hanging linen cloths upon them, placed their children in them as they came out of the font, thus making them baptismal godfathers. . . . Some of the priests and clerks scraped the colors off the images, mixing them with the oblation[3] and wine, and after the celebration of mass, gave of this oblation to those who wished to communicate. Others put the Lord's Body into the hands of the images from which they caused those who wished to communicate to receive it.

From the **inception**[4] of the Christian State, many people were unhappy about the proliferation of images, and groups of iconoclasts were scattered about the Eastern Empire. However, when the state did move against images, the move was as much a political decision as a religious **imperative**.[5] Leo III, a general from the mountains of Isauria, in the east, came to power with the support of armies from Anatolia and Armenia, traditionally iconoclast. Their loyalty was vital to him, both to maintain his own power, and to protect the eastern borders of the Empire from Muslim invasion. His aim was not to attack the supremacy of Christ, but to lessen the authority of Christian establishments upon earth.

In 726, Leo III issued an edict banning representations. Subsequently, he moved cautiously towards the destruction of images. His caution did not lessen the impact of the ban. . . .

Leo's successor, Constantine V (741–75) imposed the ban more vigorously. In 765 the destruction of images began in earnest, and monasteries, the great refuge of iconophiles, came under attack. Religious houses were secularized, or turned into barracks and inns. The property of the monasteries was confiscated, and monks arrested, imprisoned, and exiled. Some of them died in prison. Others were exhibited in grotesque exhibitions in the Hippodrome[6]—the monks were paraded by the side of harlots, and forced to marry.

After the death of Leo IV in 780 there was a brief respite for the iconophiles during the regency of his wife, the Empress Irene. During her husband's lifetime she could do little, but on her accession to the throne she issued an **edict**[7] for liberty of

---

[3] oblation—offering; here the bread used with wine in the ritual of the Christian Mass.

[4] **inception**—beginning.

[5] **imperative**—necessity.

[6] Hippodrome—arena in which chariot races were held.

[7] **edict**—decree.

conscience, and gradually replaced icono-clast bishops with monks who had retained their love for icons. But the establishment was by now too strongly iconoclast to be soon won over, and the eastern boundaries of the Empire were still protected from Muslim **incursions**[8] by iconoclast armies. In 786 Irene's council in the Temple of the Holy Apostles, which aimed at restoring images, was broken up by troops, and so she moved the council to Nicaea. In 787, the seventh and last Ecumenical Council restored the worship of images, and Leontius explained the orthodox position to the meeting:

> I, worshipping the image of God, do not worship the material wood and colors, God forbid; but laying hold of the lifeless representation of Christ, I seem myself to lay hold of and to worship Christ through it . . . for the honor of the image passes on to the original and he who worships the image worships in it the person of Him who is therein depicted.

In spite of the intolerance with which Irene treated her opponents, the victory was a fragile one, and iconoclasm was soon reinstated.

In 815, Leo V reaffirmed the tenets of the first council of 754.[9] Leo had observed that while the iconophile emperors had tended to die in exile or in battle, all those emperors who had opposed images had died a natural death while still in power, and had been buried in imperial **sepulchers**.[10] Leo V drew his own conclu-sions. A decree of the council of 754 said: "We declare unanimously, in the name of the Holy Trinity, that there should be rejected and removed and cursed out of the Christian Church every likeness which is made out of any material whatever by the evil art of painters." The Eucharist was the only true image of Christ. The ascen-dancy of the iconophiles had been ended by two disastrous defeats inflicted on the Byzantine armies by the Bulgarians in 811 and 813, and with the death of the Bulgarian leader, Krum, in 814, Leo felt secure enough to launch his attack on images. Sacred ornaments were trampled underfoot, liturgical vessels turned to profane use, and churches scraped down and smeared with ashes because they contained holy images.

> And wherever there were venerable images of Christ or the Mother of God, or the saints, these were consigned to the flames or were gouged out or smeared over. If, on the other hand, there were pic-tures of trees or birds or senseless beasts and, in particular, satanic horse-races, hunts, theatrical and hippodrome scenes, these were preserved with honor and given greater luster.

---

[8] **incursions**—invasions, attacks.

[9] council of 754—Council of Hieria, which approved iconoclastic policies of Emperor Constantine V.

[10] **sepulchers**—tombs.

According to the *Life* of Stephen the Younger, the Church of the Holy Virgin at Blachernae in Constantinople was not only bereft of its magnificence, but covered in new paintings, and transformed into a "fruit store and aviary."[11]

John the Grammarian was particularly zealous in the cause of iconoclasm during this period. In 814 he gained admission to the libraries, and he and his helpers marked those passages amongst the books which favored iconoclasm. Once images had been condemned by the synod[12] of the following year, they tore holy vestments to shreds, and pictures and illuminated missals were burnt or broken up with axes. The icons were insulted by smearing them with cow dung and foul ointments.

> **Many great works of art were lost during the iconoclast period.**

It is to John's influence that late iconophile commentators attribute the iconoclasm of the Emperor Theophilus; John was regarded as a **necromancer**[13] and magician. After Theophilus' death in 842, however, his wife Theodora, who, like Irene before her, had always been a lover of icons, restored them more permanently. The Muslim threat in the East had abated for a while, the army was less powerful, and the people's superstition triumphed.

Many great works of art were lost during the iconoclast period. Nevertheless, the love of images never lost its hold, as can be seen in the complaint of Michael II, of 824, recorded above. A story is told about "Roman Mary," an icon sent out to sea by the Patriarch Germanus to save it from destruction by Leo III. It sailed upright for a night and a day until it reached the safety of Rome, where it was rescued from the water, and placed by the Pope in a church dedicated to St. Peter. There it remained, safe from harm, until Orthodoxy returned to Constantinople. Then the icon rattled and shook itself from its mountings and made its way down to the Tiber, and thence home to Constantinople.

Like "Roman Mary," such noble Byzantine ladies as Irene and Theodora concealed their icons until it was thought safe to profess their love for them. Long before Leo III, Constantia, sister of Constantine the Great, had been reproached by Eusebius[14] for asking him to send her an image of Christ. He replied that the "dignity and glory of God" cannot be painted, and although it would be possible to make an image of the "mortal flesh," such things are expressly forbidden by the law:

---

[11] aviary—enclosure for birds.

[12] synod—church council.

[13] **necromancer**—wizard, sorcerer.

[14] Eusebius—Christian bishop (c. 263–339? A.D.) who wrote a history of the Church (page 268).

Once, I do not know how, a woman brought me in her hands a picture of two men in the guise of philosophers, and let fall the statement that they were Paul and the Savior. I have no means of saying where she had had this from, or learned such a thing. With the view that neither she nor others might be given offence, I took it away from her and kept it in my house, as I thought it improper that such things ever be exhibited to others, lest we appear, like idol worshippers, to carry our God around in an image.

Before she came to power, Theodora hid her icons in her room, and kissed them in secret. The Emperor's jester, free to roam as he liked through the palace, stumbled upon her devotions, and enquired what she was doing. Her answer, that she was playing with dolls, he repeated to the Emperor, who immediately guessed how his wife had been occupied, and angrily taxed her with worshipping icons. This she denied, saying that the jester had seen nothing but the reflections of maids in a mirror. She ordered the jester to say no more about her activities to the Emperor, and thereafter, when he was asked whether Theodora had been playing with her dolls, he would place one hand to his lips, and the other on his behind, saying, "Quiet, Emperor, don't mention the dolls."

In spite of the edict of 843, which allowed the worship of icons, there was no great rush to restore the churches to their former glory. People preferred to move cautiously.

QUESTIONS TO CONSIDER

1. About what would extremists among supporters and opponents of icons have agreed?

2. What does the icon controversy indicate about Byzantine society?

3. Do you think that sacred images can serve a useful purpose in religious life? Why or why not?

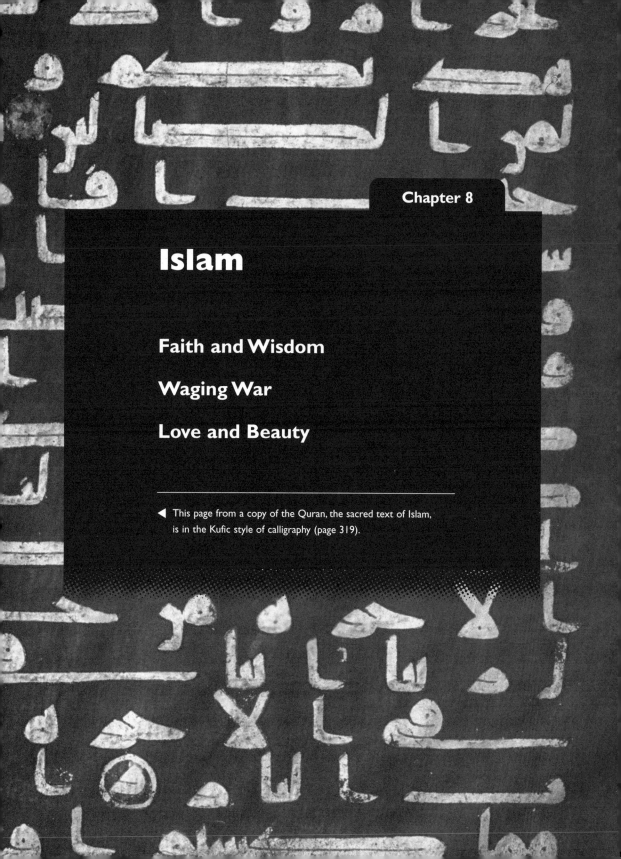

Chapter 8

Islam

Faith and Wisdom

Waging War

Love and Beauty

◀ This page from a copy of the Quran, the sacred text of Islam, is in the Kufic style of calligraphy (page 319).

The Teachings of Muhammad

The Quran, or Koran, is the sacred text of Islam. Muslims believe that it was revealed by God to the prophet Muhammad (570–632 A.D.). Divided into 114 suras, or chapters, the Quran includes prayer and theology, sacred and secular history, and civil and religious law.

In the name of God, the most merciful and compassionate.

Praise be to God, the Lord of the worlds; The most merciful, the compassionate; The king of the day of Judgment.

Thee do we worship, and of Thee do we beg assistance.

Direct us on the right way, the way of those to whom Thou has been gracious; not of those against whom Thou art angry, nor of those who go astray.

In the name of God, the most merciful and compassionate.

Praise the name of thy Lord, the Most High, Who hath created and completely formed His creatures: Who determineth them to various ends, and directeth them to attain the same, Who produceth the pastures for cattle, and afterwards rendereth the same dry stubble of a dusky hue.

God will enable thee to rehearse His revelations, and thou shalt not forget any part thereof, except what God shall please, for He knoweth that which is manifest,[1] and that which is hidden. And God will **facilitate**[2] unto thee the most easy way. Therefore **admonish**[3] thy people, if thy admonition shall be profitable unto them.

Whosoever feareth God, he will be admonished: but the most wretched unbeliever will turn away from it; who shall be cast to be broiled in the greater fire of hell, wherein he shall not die, neither shall he live.

Now hath he attained **felicity**[4] who is purified by faith, and who remembereth the name of his Lord, and prayeth. But ye prefer this present life: yet the life to come is better, and more durable.

---

[1] **manifest**—evident, clear.

[2] **facilitate**—make easy.

[3] **admonish**—caution, warn.

[4] **felicity**—happiness.

Verily[5] this is written in the ancient Books, the Books of Abraham and Moses.[6]

The Doctrine of One God

God! There is no God but Him; the Living, the Self-subsisting: neither slumber nor sleep seizeth Him; to Him belongeth whatsoever is in the heavens, and on earth. Who is he that can intercede with Him, but through His good pleasure? He knoweth that which is past, and that which is to come unto them, and they shall not comprehend anything of His knowledge, but so far as He pleaseth. His throne is extended over the heavens and the earth; and the preservation of both is no burden unto Him. He is the High, the Mighty.

Let there be no compulsion in religion. Now is right direction manifestly distinguished from deceit: whoever therefore shall deny Tagut[7] and believe in God, he shall surely take hold on a strong handle, which shall not be broken; God is He who heareth and seeth.

God is the patron of those who believe; He shall lead them out of darkness into light; but as to those who believe not, their patrons are Tagut; they shall lead them from the light into darkness; they shall be the companions of hell fire, they shall remain therein forever.

Alms to the Poor

Who is he that will lend unto God an acceptable loan? For God will double the same unto him, and he shall receive moreover an honorable reward.

Verily as to those who give alms, both men and women, and those who lend unto God an acceptable loan, He will double the same unto them; and they shall moreover receive an honorable reward.

And they who believe in God and His apostles, these are the men of **veracity**[8] and the witnesses in the presence of their Lord: they shall have their reward and their light. But as to those who believe not, and lie about God's signs; they shall be the companions of hell.

Know ye that this present life is only a play and a vain amusement; and worldly pomp, and the affectation of glory among you, and the multiplying of riches and children, are as the plants nourished by the rain, the springing up whereof delighteth the husbandmen;[9] then they wither, so that thou seest the same turn yellow, and at length they become dry stubble. But in the life to come will be a severe punishment for those who covet[10] worldly grandeur; and pardon from God, and favor for those who renounce it: for this present life is no other than a deceitful provision. Hasten with **emulation**[11] to obtain pardon from your Lord, and Paradise, the extent whereof equaleth the extent of heaven and earth, prepared for those who believe in

---

[5] verily—truly.

[6] Abraham and Moses—The Quran contains many references to biblical figures.

[7] Tagut—Satan.

[8] **veracity**—truthfulness.

[9] husbandmen—farmers.

[10] covet—desire.

[11] **emulation**—ambition.

God and His apostles. Such is the bounty of God; He will give the same unto whom He pleaseth: and God is endured with great bounty.

It is not righteousness that ye turn your faces in prayer towards the East and the West, but righteousness is of him who believeth in God and the last day, and the angels and the Scriptures, and the prophets; who giveth money for God's sake unto his kindred, and unto orphans, and the needy, and the wayfarer, and those who ask, and for the redemption of captives; who is constant in prayer, and giveth alms; and of those who perform their promises which they have made, and who behave themselves patiently in adversity, and hardships, and in time of violence: these are they who are true, and these are they who fear God.

The Devil threateneth you with poverty, and commandeth you filthy covetousness; but God promiseth you pardon from Himself and abundance: God is Bounteous and Wise. He giveth wisdom unto whom He pleaseth; and he unto whom wisdom is given, hath received much good: but none will consider it, except the wise of heart.

And whatever alms ye shall give, or whatever vow ye shall vow, verily God knoweth it; but the ungodly shall have none to help them. If ye make your alms to appear, it is well; but if ye conceal them, and give them unto the poor, this will be better for you, and will remove some of your sins: and God is well informed of that which ye do.

The guidance of them belongeth not unto thee [O Apostle]; but God guideth whom He pleaseth. The good that ye shall give in alms shall redound[12] unto yourselves; and ye shall not give unless out of desire of seeing the face of God. And what good thing ye shall give in alms, it shall be repaid you, and ye shall not be treated unjustly.

Alms unto the poor who are wholly employed in fighting for the religion of God, and cannot freely travel in the land; the ignorant man thinketh them rich, because of their modesty: thou shalt know them by this mark, they ask not men with **importunity**;[13] and what good ye shall give them in alms, verily God knoweth it.

They who distribute alms of their substance night and day, in private and in public, shall have their reward with the Lord; on them shall no fear come, neither shall they be grieved.

---

[12] redound—return as a consequence.

[13] **importunity**—strong, continual urging.

QUESTIONS TO CONSIDER

1. What are the most important characteristics of God as revealed in these passages from the Quran?

2. How is the importance of faith in God emphasized in the Quran?

3. What is meant by equating the giving of alms with making a loan to God?

4. How does the Quran guide the everyday conduct of Muslims?

Islamic Mysticism

RUMI

The Persian poet Jalal-al-Din (1207–1273) is known by his pen name Rumi. His poetry was strongly influenced by the Islamic mystical movement known as Sufism. His masterpiece, the long religious work known as the Mathnavi, is revered as "the Persian Quran."

The Man Who Fled from Azrael

One forenoon a freeborn nobleman arrived and ran into Solomon's hall of justice,[1] his countenance[2] pale with anguish and both lips blue. Then Solomon said, "Good sir, what is the matter?"

He replied, "Azrael[3] cast on me such a look, so full of wrath and hate."

"Come," said the king, "what boon do you desire now? Ask!" "O protector of my life," said he, "command the wind to bear me from here to India. Maybe, when thy slave is come thither he will save his life."

Solomon commanded the wind to bear him quickly over the water to the uttermost part of India. Next day, at the time of conference and meeting, Solomon said to Azrael: "Didst thou look with anger on that Moslem in order that he might wander as an exile far from his home?"

Azrael said, "When did I look on him angrily? I saw him as I passed by, and looked at him in astonishment, for God had commanded me, saying, 'Hark, today do thou take his spirit in India.' From wonder I said to myself, 'Even if he has a hundred wings, 'tis a far journey for him to be in India today.'"

The Elephant in the Dark House

The elephant was in a dark house: some Hindus[4] had brought it for exhibition.

In order to see it, many people were going, every one, into that darkness.

As seeing it with the eye was impossible, each one was feeling it in the dark with the palm of his hand.

---

[1] Solomon's hall of justice—Solomon was a king of ancient Israel renowned for his wisdom.

[2] countenance—face.

[3] Azrael—the angel of death.

[4] Hindus—people of India.

The hand of one fell on its trunk: he said, "This creature is like a waterpipe."

The hand of another touched its ear: to him it appeared to be like a fan.

Since another handled its leg, he said, "I found the elephant's shape to be like a pillar."

Another laid his hand on its back: he said, "Truly, this elephant was like a throne."

Similarly, when any one heard a description of the elephant, he understood it only in respect of the part that he had touched. If there had been a candle in each one's hand, the difference would have gone out of their words.

The Soul of Goodness in Things Evil

Fools take false coins because they are
 like the true.
If in the world no genuine minted coin
Were current, how would forgers pass
 the false?
Falsehood were nothing unless truth
 were there,
To make it specious. 'Tis the love
 of right
Lures men to wrong. Let poison but
 be mixed
With sugar, they will cram it into their
 mouths.
Oh, cry not that all creeds are vain!
 Some scent

Of truth they have, else they would
 not beguile.
Say not, "How utterly fantastical!"
No fancy in the world is all untrue.
Amidst the crowd of dervishes
 hides one,
One true fakir.[5] Search well and thou
 wilt find!

---

[5] dervishes . . . fakir—Dervishes are members of Islamic religious orders. A fakir is a Moslem holy man who lives by begging.

QUESTIONS TO CONSIDER

1. What is the moral of "The Man Who Fled from Azrael"?

2. A symbol is a concrete image that represents something abstract, such as an idea. What might the elephant in "The Elephant in the Dark House" symbolize?

3. A paradox is an apparently contradictory statement that points to a truth. What paradox does Rumi present in "The Soul of Goodness in Things Evil"?

Islamic Fables

Islamic tradition is rich in literature used to teach wisdom or morality. The first of the following fables, "The Mouse and the Cat," from the Arabic collection Kalila wa Dimna, *was originally told in India. The fables of the Persian writer Sadi (1184–1291) combine sincere piety, common sense, and a graceful style. The last three fables come from his most famous work, the* Gulistan *("Rose Garden").*

The Mouse and the Cat

The king asked the philosopher[1] to narrate a parable in which a man has many enemies who approach him from all sides and yet he manages to escape them.

The philosopher replied that **enmity**[2] is not always perpetual for sometimes hatred changes into love and love changes into hatred, as in the case of the mouse and the cat.

There was a banyan tree in one of the provinces. Living in a burrow under the tree was a mouse named Faridun and inhabiting a hole nearby was a cat called Rumi. This area was favored by hunters who came frequently to trap the animals. One day a hunter laid out his net near the tree and concealed it with branches and leaves. When the cat came out of his hole to search for food, he fell into the snare. The mouse, who had also come out of his burrow, saw the cat entangled in the net.

He looked around and, much to his distress, saw a weasel lurking in the background, ready to attack him; then he looked up and saw an owl perched on a tree, waiting to snatch him. The mouse was afraid that if he turned back, the weasel would kill him; if he climbed the tree, the owl would get him; and if he remained where he was, the cat would find a way to escape from the net and devour him.

Faridun thought for a while and decided that his best chance for survival was to make friends with the cat. He approached the cat and proposed an alliance: he would pretend to be an old friend of the cat and come closer, thereby warding off the weasel and the owl; after these two left, he would free the cat from the net. Rumi agreed to this arrangement. The mouse

---

[1] king . . . philosopher—In the frame narrative of *Kalila wa Dimna*, a king asks a philosopher to tell him stories that contain guidance for ruling.

[2] **enmity**—hostility.

went up to the cat and they embraced like old comrades, each asking the other how he felt. Then Faridun started gnawing at the ropes to free the cat. The owl and the weasel watched this phenomenal sight in astonishment and then departed.

After the weasel and the owl left, Faridun slowed his gnawing and left one rope intact. But upon seeing the hunter approach, he cut the last thread and ran quickly to his burrow. The cat sprang free from the net and climbed a tree. Thus traditional enemies, who had become friends in times of distress, parted **amicably**[3] forever.

The Padshah and the Slave
Sadi

A padshah[4] was in the same boat with a Persian slave who had never before been at sea and experienced the inconvenience of a vessel. He began to cry and to tremble to such a degree that he could not be pacified by kindness, so that at last the king became displeased as the matter could not be remedied. In that boat there happened to be a philosopher, who said: "With thy permission I shall quiet him." The padshah replied: "It will be a great favor." The philosopher ordered the slave to be thrown into the water so that he swallowed some of it, whereon he was caught and pulled by his hair to the boat, to the stern of which he clung with both his hands. Then he sat down in a corner and became quiet. This appeared strange to the king who knew not what wisdom there was in the proceeding and asked for it. The philosopher

replied: "Before he had tasted the calamity of being drowned, he knew not the safety of the boat; thus also a man does not appreciate the value of immunity from a misfortune until it has befallen him."

> O thou full man, barley-bread pleases
>   thee not.
> She is my sweetheart who appears
>   ugly to thee.
> To the huris[5] of paradise purgatory
>   seems hell.
> Ask the **denizens**[6] of hell. To them purgatory is paradise.

> There is a difference between him
>   whose friend is in his arms
> And him whose eyes of expectation are
>   upon the door.

Nushirvan the Just
Sadi

Someone had brought information to Nushirvan[7] the just that an enemy of his had been removed from this world by God the most high. He asked: "Hast thou heard anything about his intending to spare me?"

> There is no occasion for our rejoicing at
>   a foe's death
> Because our own life will also not last
>   for ever.

---

[3] **amicably**—peaceably.

[4] padshah—Persian ruler.

[5] huris—beautiful women who were among the delights of the Islamic paradise.

[6] **denizens**—inhabitants.

[7] Nushirvan—Khosru (died 579 A.D.), Persian king known as Nushirvan ("Of the immortal soul").

A Pious Child

Sadi

I remember, being in my childhood pious, rising in the night, addicted to devotion and abstinence.[8] One night I was sitting with my father, remaining awake and holding the beloved Quran[9] in my lap, whilst the people around us were asleep. I said: "Not one of these persons lifts up his head or makes a genuflection.[10] They are as fast asleep as if they were dead." He replied: "Darling of thy father, would that thou wert also asleep rather than **disparaging**[11] people."

The pretender sees no one but himself
Because he has the veil of conceit in
front.
If he were endowed with a God-
discerning eye
He would see that no one is weaker
than himself.

---

[8] abstinence—refraining from indulging some appetite, usually food.

[9] Quran—sacred text of Islam (page 296).

[10] genuflection—act of reverence performed by bending one knee.

[11] **disparaging**—speaking badly of, belittling.

QUESTIONS TO CONSIDER

1. If you were the king listening to the fable of "The Mouse and the Cat," what lesson would you draw?

2. How would you express the moral of "The Padshah and the Slave"?

3. In the literary strategy known as "irony of situation," what happens is not what is expected. How is this type of irony employed in "Nushirvan the Just" and in "A Pious Child"?

4. What is the tone of Sadi's fables?

5. In your opinion which of Sadi's fables teaches the most valuable lesson? Why?

The Nature of War

IBN KHALDUN

In 1375 a scholarly official named Ibn Khaldun (1332–1406) retired to a castle in North Africa and began writing a history of the world. He first wrote a lengthy introduction, the Muqaddimah, *in which he theorized about the nature of history and human society.*

It should be known that history is a discipline that has a great number of approaches. Its useful aspects are very many. Its goal is distinguished.

History makes us acquainted with the conditions of past nations as they are reflected in their national character. It makes us acquainted with the biographies of the prophets and with the **dynasties**[1] and policies of rulers. Whoever so desires may thus achieve the useful result of being able to imitate historical examples in religious and worldly matters.

The (writing of history) requires numerous sources and much varied knowledge. It also requires a good **speculative**[2] mind and thoroughness, which lead the historian to the truth and keep him from slips and errors. If he trusts historical information in its plain transmitted form and has no clear knowledge of the principles resulting from custom, the fundamental facts of politics, the nature of civilization, or the conditions governing human social organization; and if, furthermore, he does not evaluate remote or ancient material through comparison with near or contemporary material, he often cannot avoid stumbling and slipping and deviating from the path of truth. Historians, Quran[3] commentators and leading transmitters have committed frequent errors in the stories and events they reported. They accepted them in the plain transmitted form, without regard for its value. They did not check them with the principles underlying such historical situations, nor did they compare them with similar material. Also, they did not probe with the yardstick of philosophy,

---

[1] **dynasties**—successions of rulers from the same family.

[2] **speculative**—capable of creative thinking.

[3] Quran—sacred text of Islam (see page 296).

with the help of knowledge of the nature of things, or with the help of speculation and historical insight. Therefore, they strayed from the truth and found themselves lost in the desert of baseless assumptions and errors.

This is especially the case with figures, either of sums of money or of soldiers, whenever they occur in stories. They offer a good opportunity for false information and constitute a vehicle for nonsensical statements. They must be controlled and checked with the help of known fundamental facts.

For example, al-Mas'udi and many other historians report that Moses counted the army of the Israelites in the desert.[4] He had all those able to carry arms, especially those twenty years and older, pass muster. There turned out to be 600,000 or more. In this connection, al-Mas'udi forgets to take into consideration whether Egypt and Syria could possibly have held such a number of soldiers. Every realm may have as large a militia as it can hold and support, but no more. This fact is attested by well-known customs and familiar conditions. Moreover, an army of this size cannot march or fight as a unit. The whole available territory would be too small for it. If it were in battle formation, it would extend two, three, or more times beyond the field of vision. How, then, could two such parties fight with each other, or one battle formation gain the upper hand when one **flank**[5] does not know what the other flank

is doing! The situation at the present day testifies to the correctness of this statement. The past resembles the future more than one drop of water another. . . .

Whenever contemporaries speak about the dynastic armies of their own or recent times, and whenever they engage in discussions about Muslim or Christian soldiers, or when they get to figuring the tax revenues and the money spent by the government, the outlays of extravagant spenders, and the goods that rich and prosperous men have in stock, they are quite generally found to exaggerate, to go beyond the bounds of the ordinary, and to **succumb**[6] to the temptation of sensationalism. When the officials in charge are questioned about their armies, when the goods and assets of wealthy people are assessed, and when the outlays of extravagant spenders are looked at in ordinary light, the figures will be found to amount to a tenth of what those people have said. The reason is simple. It is the common desire for sensationalism, the ease with which one may just mention a higher figure, and the disregard of reviewers and critics. This leads to failure to exercise self-criticism about one's errors and intentions, to demand from oneself moderation and fairness in reporting, to reapply oneself to study and research. Such historians let

---

[4] Moses . . . the desert—In the Bible, the Israelites and their leader Moses wander in the desert of Sinai for 40 years after escaping from slavery in Egypt.

[5] **flank**—an army's extreme left or right side.

[6] **succumb**—give way, yield.

themselves go and made a feast of untrue statements. They procure for themselves entertaining stories in order to lead others away from the path of God. This is a bad enough business. . . .

Wars and the Methods of Waging War Practiced by the Various Nations

Wars and different kinds of fighting have always occurred in the world since God created it. The origin of war is the desire of certain human beings to take revenge on others. Each (party) is supported by the people sharing in its group feeling.[7] When they have sufficiently excited each other for the purpose and the two parties confront each other, one seeking revenge and the other trying to defend itself, there is war. It is something natural among human beings. No nation and no race (generation) is free from it.

The reason for such revenge is as a rule either jealousy and envy, or hostility, or zeal in behalf of God and His religion, or zeal in behalf of royal authority and the effort to found a kingdom.

The first (kind of war) usually occurs between neighboring tribes and competing families.

The second (kind)—war caused by hostility—is usually found among savage nations living in the desert, such as the Arabs, the Turks, the Turkomans, the Kurds, and similar peoples. They earn their **sustenance**[8] with their lances and their livelihood by depriving other people of their possessions. They declare war against those who defend their property against them. They have no further desire for rank and royal authority. Their minds and eyes are set only upon depriving other people of their possessions.

The third is the (kind) the religious law calls, the "holy war."

The fourth (kind), finally, is dynastic war against seceders[9] and those who refuse obedience.

These are the four kinds of war. The first two are unjust and lawless, the other two are holy and just wars.

Since the beginning of men's existence, war has been waged in the world in two ways. One is by advance in closed formation. The other is the technique of attack and withdrawal.

The advance in closed formation has been the technique of all the non-Arabs throughout their entire existence. The technique of attack and withdrawal has been that of the Arabs and of the Berbers of the Maghrib.[10]

Fighting in closed formation is more steady and fierce than fighting with the technique of attack and withdrawal. That is because in fighting in closed formation, the lines are orderly and evenly arranged, like arrows or like rows of worshippers at

---

[7] group feeling—sense of solidarity that ties a community together and enables it to compete with other communities. This concept is central to Khaldun's theory of human society.

[8] **sustenance**—needs for sustaining life.

[9] seceders—rebels.

[10] Berbers of the Maghrib—The Berbers are a people of North Africa. Maghrib ("West") is the Arabic term for North Africa.

prayers. People advanced in closed lines against the enemy. This makes for greater steadiness in assault and for better use of the proper tactics. It frightens the enemy more. A closed formation is like a long wall or a well-built castle which no one could hope to move.

It is obvious what great wisdom there is in requiring that the lines be kept steady and in forbidding anyone to fall back during an attack. Those who turn their backs to the enemy bring disorder into the line formation. They are guilty of the crime of causing a **rout**.[11] Fighting in closed formation was more important (than any other kind) in the opinion of Muhammad.[12]

Fighting with the technique of attack and withdrawal is not as fierce or as secure against the possibility of rout, as is fighting in closed formation, unless there is set up a steady line formation to the rear, to which the fighting men may fall back in attack and withdrawal throughout the fighting. Such a line formation would take the place of the closed formation. . . .

One of the techniques of the people who use the method of attack and withdrawal, is to set up, behind their armies, a (barricade) of solid objects and dumb animals to serve as a refuge for the cavalry during attack and withdrawal. It is intended to steady the fighters, so that they will fight more persistently and have a better chance of winning.

Those who fight in closed formation do the same, in order to increase their steadfastness and power. The Persians who fought in closed formation used to employ elephants in their wars. They made them carry wooden towers like castles, loaded with combatants, weapons, and flags. They disposed them in successive lines behind them in the thick of battle, as if they were fortresses. This fortified them psychologically and gave them added confidence. . . .

The Arabs and most other Bedouin nations[13] that move about and employ the technique of attack and withdrawal, dispose their camels and the pack animals carrying their litters[14] in lines to steady the fighting men. (Such lines) become for them a place to fall back upon. Every nation that follows this technique can be observed to be more steady in battle and to be better protected against being surprised and routed. This is a well-attested fact, but it has been altogether neglected by the contemporary dynasties. Instead, they dispose the pack animals carrying their baggage and large tents behind them, as a rear guard. These animals cannot take the place of elephants and camels. Therefore, the armies are exposed to the danger of being routed, and they are always ready to flee in combat.

At the beginning of Islam, all battles were fought in closed formation, although the Arabs knew only the technique of attack and withdrawal. Two things at the beginning of Islam caused them to (fight in closed formation). First, their enemies

---

[11] **rout**—defeat in which an army flees in disorder.

[12] Muhammad—founder of Islam (see page 296).

[13] Bedouin nations—desert-dwelling nomads.

[14] litters—couches on poles carried either by human bearers or by animals.

fought in closed formation, and they were thus forced to fight them in the same way. Second, they were willing to die in the holy war, because they wished to prove their endurance and were very firm in their belief. Now, the closed formation is the fighting technique most suitable for one willing to die.

When luxury penetrated the various dynasties, the use of the rally line behind the fighters was forgotten. This was because when they were Bedouins and lived in tents, they had many camels, and the women and children lived in camp with them. Then they achieved royal luxury and became used to living in palaces and in a sedentary[15] environment and they abandoned the ways of the desert and waste regions. At that time, they forgot the period of camels and litters, and it was difficult for them to use them. When they traveled, they left their women behind. Royal authority and luxury caused them to use tents both large and small. They restricted themselves to pack animals carrying baggage and tents. They used these things to form their (protective) line in war.

It was by no means sufficient. These things, unlike one's own family and property, do not inspire any willingness to die. People, therefore, have little endurance. The turmoil of the battle frightens them, and their lines crumble.

---

[15] sedentary—inactive.

QUESTIONS TO CONSIDER

1. What does Ibn Khaldun mean when he says, "The past resembles the future more than one drop of water another"?

2. How does Khaldun distinguish between just and unjust wars?

3. Khaldun observes, "closed formation is the fighting technique most suitable for one willing to die." What do you think he means?

4. What are some examples from American history of situations where the strength of a community's "group feeling" enabled it to succeed?

The Battle of Hittin

IBN AL-ATHIR

Islamic belief permitted jihad, or "holy war," to be waged against unbelievers or Muslim heretics. In the late 1180s Saladin (1137–1193), the sultan of Egypt, waged a jihad against the small Christian states that had been established in the Near East after the First Crusade in 1099. On July 4, 1187 he defeated the Christian forces at the Battle of Hittin (or Hattin), leading the way to the Muslim recapture of Jerusalem. This account of Hittin comes from the Arab historian Ibn al-Athir (1160–1233), who was living at the time of the events he describes.

While the reunited Franks[1] were on their way to Saffuriyya, Saladin called a council of his amirs.[2] Most of them advised him not to fight, but to weaken the enemy by repeated skirmishes and raids. Others however advised him to pillage the Frankish territories, and to give battle to any Frankish army that might appear in their path, "Because in the East people are cursing us, saying that we no longer fight the infidels[3] but have begun to fight Muslims instead. So we must do something to justify ourselves and silence our critics." But Saladin said: "My feeling is that we should confront all the enemy's forces with all the forces of Islam; for events do not turn out according to man's will and we do not know how long a life is

left to us, so it is foolish to **dissipate**[4] this concentration of troops without striking a tremendous blow in the Holy War." So on Thursday, 2 July 1187, the fifth day after we encamped at Uqhuwana, he struck camp and moved off up the hill outside Tiberias, leaving the city behind him. When he drew near to the Franks, however, there was no one to be seen, for they had not yet left their tents. So he went back down the hill with his army. At night he positioned troops where they would prevent the enemy from giving battle and then attacked Tiberias with

---

[1] Franks—Muslim term for their Christian opponents, many of whom came from France.

[2] amirs—chieftains.

[3] infidels—non-Muslims.

[4] **dissipate**—disperse, scatter.

a small force, breached the wall and took the city by storm during the night. . . .

When the Franks learned that Saladin had attacked Tiberias and taken it and everything in it, burning the houses and anything they could not remove, they met to take counsel. . . . The generals decided to advance and give battle to the Muslims, so they left the place where they had been encamped until now and advanced on the Muslim army. When Saladin received the news he ordered his army to withdraw from its position near Tiberias; his only reason for besieging Tiberias was to make the Franks abandon their position and offer battle. The Muslims went down to the water (of the lake).[5] The weather was blazingly hot and the Franks, who were suffering greatly from thirst, were prevented by the Muslims from reaching the water. They had drained all the local cisterns,[6] but could not turn back for fear of the Muslims. So they passed that night tormented with thirst. The Muslims for their part had lost their first fear of the enemy and were in high spirits, and spent the night inciting one another to battle. They could smell victory in the air, and the more they saw of the unexpectedly low morale of the Franks the more aggressive and daring they became; throughout the night the cries *Allah akbar* (God is great) and "there is no God but Allah" rose up to heaven. Meanwhile the Sultan was deploying the **vanguard**[7] of archers and distributing the arrows.

On Saturday, 4 July 1187, Saladin and the Muslims mounted their horses and advanced on the Franks. They too were mounted, and the two armies came to blows. The Franks were suffering badly from thirst, and had lost confidence. The battle raged furiously, both sides putting up a **tenacious**[8] resistance. The Muslim archers sent up clouds of arrows like thick swarms of locusts, killing many of the Frankish horses. The Franks, surrounding themselves with their infantry, tried to fight their way toward Tiberias in the hope of reaching water, but Saladin realized their objective and forestalled them by planting himself and his army in the way. He himself rode up and down the Muslim lines encouraging and restraining his troops where necessary. The whole army obeyed his commands and respected his prohibitions. One of his young mamluks[9] led a terrifying charge on the Franks and performed **prodigious**[10] feats of valor until he was overwhelmed by numbers and killed, when all the Muslims charged the enemy lines and almost broke through, slaying many Franks in the process. . . .

One of the volunteers had set fire to the dry grass that covered the ground; it took fire and the wind carried the heat and smoke down on to the enemy. They had to

---

[5] lake—the Lake of Tiberias or Sea of Galilee, a large body of fresh water in northern Palestine.

[6] cisterns—reservoirs for storing water.

[7] **vanguard**—forward part of an army.

[8] **tenacious**—stubborn.

[9] mamluks—Egyptian soldiers.

[10] **prodigious**—wonderful.

endure thirst, the summer's heat, the blazing fire and smoke and the fury of battle. The Franks lost heart and were on the verge of surrender, but seeing that the only way to save their lives was to defy death they made a series of charges that almost dislodged the Muslims from their position in spite of their numbers, had not the grace of God been with them. As each wave of attackers fell back they left their dead behind them; their numbers diminished rapidly, while the Muslims were all around them like a circle about its diameter. The surviving Franks made for a hill near Hittin, where they hoped to pitch their tents and defend themselves. They were vigorously attacked from all sides and prevented from pitching more than one tent, that of the King.[11] The Muslims captured their great cross, called the "True Cross," in which they say is a piece of the wood upon which, according to them, the Messiah[12] was crucified. This was one of the heaviest blows that could be inflicted on them and made their death and destruction certain. Large numbers of their cavalry and infantry were killed or captured. The King stayed on the hillside with five hundred of the most gallant and famous knights.

I was told that al-Malik al-Afdal, Saladin's son, said: "I was at my father Saladin's side during that battle, the first that I saw with my own eyes. The Frankish King had retreated to the hill with his band, and from there he led a furious charge against the Muslims facing him, forcing them back upon my father. I saw that he

was alarmed and distraught, and he tugged at his beard as he went forward crying: 'Away with the Devil's lie!' The Muslims turned to counter-attack and drove the Franks back up the hill. When I saw the Franks retreating before the Muslim onslaught I cried out for joy: 'We have conquered them!' But they returned to the charge with undiminished **ardor**[13] and drove our army back toward my father. His response was the same as before, and the Muslims counter-attacked and drove the Franks back to the hill. Again I cried: 'We have beaten them!' but my father turned to me and said: 'Be quiet; we shall not have beaten them until that tent falls!' As he spoke the tent fell, and the Sultan dismounted and **prostrated** himself[14] in thanks to God, weeping for joy." This was how the tent fell: the Franks had been suffering terribly from thirst during that charge, which they hoped would win them a way out of their distress, but the way of escape was blocked. They dismounted and sat down on the ground and the Muslims fell upon them, pulled down the King's tent and captured every one of them, including the King, his brother, and Prince Arnat of Karak, Islam's most hated enemy. They also took the ruler of Jubail, the son of Humphrey (of Toron), the Grand Master

---

[11] the King—Guy of Lusignan (died 1194), king of the Crusader state of Jerusalem.

[12] Messiah—Jesus.

[13] **ardor**—enthusiasm.

[14] **prostrated** himself—fell face down.

of the Templars, one of the Franks' greatest dignitaries, and a band of Templars and Hospitallers.[15] The number of dead and captured was so large that those who saw the slain could not believe that anyone could have been taken alive, and those who saw the prisoners could not believe that any had been killed. From the time of their first assault on Palestine in 1098 until now the Franks had never suffered such a defeat. . . .

A year later I crossed the battlefield, and saw the land all covered with their bones, which could be seen even from a distance, lying in heaps or scattered around. These were what was left after all the rest had been carried away by storms or by the wild beasts of these hills and valleys.

---

[15] Templars . . . Hospitallers—orders of Crusading knights.

QUESTIONS TO CONSIDER

1. What motivated the Muslim leaders to risk battle with the Crusaders?

2. How did the Muslims use weather and terrain to their advantage?

3. What attitude does Ibn al-Athir seem to have toward the Crusaders?

4. How is Saladin's character presented in this account?

5. Ibn al-Athir observes that the Muslim capture of the Christian relic of the True Cross from the Crusaders "made their death and destruction certain." Do you think he is ascribing supernatural powers to this relic or simply alluding to the impact of its loss on the Crusaders' morale? Explain.

Reflections on Love

The treatment of love in Islamic traditions ranges widely, from the bawdy stories and romantic tales of the Arabian Nights *to the religious love lyrics of Sufi mystics in which the poet finds divinity in the beloved. The first of the following works is from* The Dove's Necklace, *a treatise on love by Ibn Hazm (994–1064), who lived in the Islamic kingdom of Cordova in Spain. The second is a lyric by Maisuna, a desert-dwelling Bedouin Arab who became the wife of the Islamic ruler Muawiya (602–680).*

from *The Dove's Necklace*

Ibn Hazm

Every love-affair must necessarily have some original cause. I shall now begin with the most unlikely of all causes of love, so that the discourse may proceed in due order, starting as ever with the simplest and easiest example. Love indeed is sometimes caused by things so strange, that but for having myself observed them I would not have mentioned them at all.

Now here is an instance from my own experience. One day I visited our friend Abu 'l-Sari 'Ammar ibn Ziyad, the freedman[1] of al-Mu'aiyad, and found him deep in thought and much preoccupied. I asked him what was amiss; for a while he refused to explain, but then he said, "An extraordinary thing has happened to me, the like of which I have never heard."

"What is that?" I enquired.

"Last night," he answered, "I saw in a dream a young maiden, and on awaking I found that I had completely lost my heart to her, and that I was madly in love with her. Now I am in the most difficult straits possible, with this passion I have conceived for her."

He continued cast down and afflicted for more than a month; nothing would cheer him up, so profound was his emotion. At last I scolded him, saying, "It is a vast mistake to occupy your soul with something unreal, and to attach your fantasy to a nonexistent being. Do you know who she is?"

"No, by Allah!" he replied.

"Really," I went on, "you have very little judgment, and your **discretion**[2] must be

---

[1] freedman—freed slave.

[2] **discretion**—exercise of choice.

affected, if you are actually in love with a person whom you have never seen, someone moreover who was never created and does not exist in the world at all. If you had fallen for one of those pictures they paint on the walls of the public baths, I would have found it easier to excuse you."

So I continued, until at last by making a great effort he forgot his trouble.

The poet Yusuf ibn Harun, better known as al-Ramadi, was one day passing the Gate of the Perfumers at Cordova, a place where ladies were wont[3] to congregate, when he espied a young girl who, as he said, "entirely captured my heart, so that all my limbs were penetrated by the love of her." He therefore turned aside from going to the **mosque**[4] and set himself instead to following her, while she for her part set off towards the bridge, which she then crossed and came to the place known as al-Rabad. When she reached the mausolea[5] of the Banu Marwan, God have mercy on their souls, that are erected over their graves in the cemetery of al-Rabad, beyond the river, she observed him to have gone apart from the rest of the people and to be preoccupied solely with her.

She accordingly went up to him and said, "Why are you walking behind me?"

He told her how sorely smitten he was with her, and she replied, "Have done with that! Do not seek to expose me to shame; you have no prospect of achieving your purpose, and there is no way to gratifying your desire."

"I am satisfied merely to look at you," he countered.

"That is permitted to you," she replied.

Then he asked her, "My lady, are you a free woman, or are you a slave?"

"I am a slave," she answered.

"And what is your name?" he inquired.

"Khalwa," she told him.

"And to whom do you belong?" he asked next.

To this she retorted, "By Allah, you are likelier to know what inhabits the seventh heaven than the answer to that question. Seek not the impossible!"

"My lady," he begged, "where may I see you again?"

"Where you saw me today," she replied. "At the same hour, every Friday." Then she added, "Will you go off now, or shall I?"

"Do you go off, in Allah's protection!" he replied.

So she went off in the direction of the bridge; and he could not follow her, because she kept looking round to see if he was accompanying her or not. When she had passed the gate of the bridge he came after her, but could find no trace of her whatsoever.

"And by Allah," said Abu 'Umar (that is to say, Yusuf ibn Harun), recounting the story of his adventure, "I have frequented the Perfumers' Gate and al-Rabad the whole time from then till now, but I have never come upon any further news of her. I know not whether the heavens have devoured her, or whether the earth has

---

[3] wont—accustomed.

[4] **mosque**—Islamic house of worship.

[5] mausolea—tombs.

swallowed her up; and the feeling I have in my heart on her account is hotter than burning coals."

This is the Khalwa whose name he celebrates in his love lyrics.

Thereafter he had news of her after he journeyed to Saragossa for her sake, but that is a long story. . . .

One of the wonderful things that occur in Love is the way the lover submits to the beloved, and adjusts his own character by main force to that of his loved one. Often and often you will see a man stubborn by disposition, **intractable**,[6] jibbing[7] at all control, determined, arrogant, always ready to take umbrage;[8] yet no sooner let him sniff the soft air of love, plunge into its waves, and swim in its sea, than his stubbornness will have suddenly changed to **docility**,[9] his intractability to gentleness, his determination to easy-going, his arrogance to submission.

Sa'id ibn Mundhir ibn Sa'id, who used to lead the prayers in the cathedral mosque of Cordova during the days of al-Hakam al-Mustansir Bi'llah, God be merciful to his soul, had a slave-girl with whom he was deeply in love. He offered to manumit[10] and marry her, to which she scornfully replied—and I should mention that he had a fine long beard—"I think your beard is dreadfully long; trim it up, and then you shall have your wish." He thereupon laid a pair of scissors to his beard, until it looked somewhat more gallant; then he summoned witnesses, and invited them to testify that he had set the girl free. But when in due

course he proposed to her, she would not accept him.

Among those present was his brother Hakam ibn Mundhir, who promptly said to the assembled company, "Now I am going to propose marriage to her." He did so, and she consented; and he married her then and there. Sa'id acquiesced in this frightful insult, for all that he was a man known for his abstinence, piety and religious zeal. I myself met this same Sa'id; he was slain by the Berbers, on the day when they stormed and sacked Cordova. . . .

I have never seen anything to equal the helpfulness of women. They are far more forward than men in keeping love's secret, in counselling each other to be discreet, and in co-operating to conceal it whenever they happen to know of any such affair. I have never in my life known a woman to reveal the secret of a loving couple, without that she was hated, loathed and unanimously condemned by all her sisters. Old women excel young girls in this particular; the latter do sometimes disclose what they know out of jealousy (though that happens indeed rarely), whereas the former have despaired of further romances, and are therefore now anxious solely for the welfare of others. . . .

As for the reason why this instinct is so deeply rooted in women, I see no other

---

[6] **intractable**—stubborn.

[7] jibbing—balking, refusing.

[8] umbrage—offense.

[9] **docility**—manageability.

[10] manumit—set free.

explanation than that they have nothing else to fill their minds, except loving union and what brings it about, flirting and how it is done, intimacy and the various ways of achieving it. That is their sole occupation, and they were created for nothing else. Men on the other hand are divided in their interests; some seek to amass a fortune, some aspire to the company of kings, some pursue knowledge, some look after their families, some venture on **arduous**[11] journeys, some hunt, some ply diverse crafts, some go forth to the wars, some confront armed rebellions, some brave fearful perils, some cultivate the soil. All these different occupations diminish leisure, and divert men from the paths of idleness. . . .

Here is a story which I have often heard told concerning a certain Berber king. An Andalusian gentleman, finding himself in financial difficulties, had sold a female slave whom he loved passionately; she was bought by a man of the Berber country. The poor fellow who sold her never imagined that his heart would follow her in the way it did. When she reached her purchaser's home, her former owner almost expired. So he searched out the man to whom he had sold her and offered him all his possessions, and himself to boot, if he would restore her to him; but the Berber refused.

The Andalusian then besought the inhabitants of the town to prevail upon him; but not one of them came to his assistance. Almost out of his mind, he bethought himself of appealing to the king;

he therefore stood without the palace, and uttered a loud cry. The king, who was seated in a lofty chamber overlooking the courtyard, heard his shout and ordered him to be admitted. The Andalusian entered the royal presence, and standing before his Berber majesty he told his story, and implored and supplicated him to have compassion.

The king, much touched by his plight, commanded that the man who had bought the girl should be summoned to court. He duly came; and the king said, "This poor fellow is a stranger; you can see what a state he is in. I intercede with you personally on his behalf." But the purchaser refused, saying, "I am more deeply in love with her than he is, and I fear that if you return her to him I myself shall be standing here tomorrow imploring your aid, and in an even worse case." The king and all his courtiers offered him of their own riches to let her go; but he persisted in his refusal, pleading as his excuse the affection he bore her.

The audience having by now dragged on a long time, and there being no sign whatsoever that the purchaser would give way and consent, the king said to the Andalusian, "My good sir, I can do nothing more for you than this. I have striven to the utmost of my powers on your behalf; and you see how he excuses himself on the grounds that he loves her more than you do, and fears he may come to even greater evil than yourself. You had best endure patiently what Allah has decreed for you."

---

[11] **arduous**—difficult.

The Andalusian thereupon exclaimed, "Have you no means at all then of helping me?"

"Can I do anything more for you than entreat him, and offer him money?" the king answered.

The Andalusian, being in despair, bent himself double, and with his hands clutching his feet he threw himself down from the topmost height of the audience-chamber to the earth. The king cried out in alarm, and his slaves below ran to where the man was lying. It was his fate not to be greatly injured by the fall, and he was brought up to the king again.

"What did you intend by doing that?" the king said to him.

"O king," the man replied, "I cannot live any longer, now that I have lost her."

Then he would have thrown himself down a second time, but he was prevented.

"Allah is great!" the king thereupon exclaimed. "I have hit upon the just arbitrament[12] of this problem." Turning to the purchaser he said, "Good sir, do you claim that your love for the girl is greater than his, and do you state that you fear to come to the same pass as he is in?"

"Yes," replied the Berber.

"Very well," went on the king. "Your friend here has given us a clear indication of his love; he hurled himself down, and would have died, but that Almighty God preserved him. Now do you stand up and prove your love is true; cast yourself down from the topmost point of this **pavilion**,[13]

as your friend did. If you die, it will mean that your appointed time has come; if you live, you will have the better right to the girl, seeing that she is at present your property; and your companion in distress shall then go away. But if you refuse to jump, I will take the girl from you, whether you like it or not, and will hand her over to him."

At first the Berber held back, but then he said, "I will cast myself down." But when he came near the opening, and looked into the yawning void below him, he drew himself back again.

"By Allah," cried the king, "it shall be as I have said."

The man tried again, but shrunk away once more.

When he would not take the plunge, the king shouted to him, "Do not make sport of us! Ho, slaves, seize his hands and pitch him to the ground!"

The Berber, seeing the king thus resolved, exclaimed, "O king, I am content: let him have the girl."

The king replied, "Allah give thee a good **recompense**!"[14]

So saying, he bought the girl from him and gave her over to her former owner; and the two departed.

---

[12] arbitrament—settling of differences.

[13] **pavilion**—building.

[14] **recompense**—payment.

A Desert Cavalier

MAISUNA

The coarse cloth worn in the serenity of the desert
Is more precious to me than the luxurious robes of a queen;
I love the Bedouin's tent, caressed by the murmuring breeze,
   and standing amid boundless horizons,
More than the gilded halls of marble in all their royal splendor.
I feel more at ease with my simple crust,
Than with the delicacies of the court;
I prefer to rise early with the caravan,
Rather than be in the golden glare of the **sumptuous**[15] escort.
The barking of a watchdog keeping away strangers
Pleases me more than the sounds of the tambourine played by
   the court singers;
I prefer a desert **cavalier**,[16] generous and poor,
To a fat lout[17] in purple living behind closed doors.

---

[15] **sumptuous**—luxurious.

[16] **cavalier**—horseman.

[17] lout—coarse, clumsy person.

QUESTIONS TO CONSIDER

1. What characteristics of love does Ibn Hazm emphasize in these anecdotes from *The Dove's Necklace?*

2. What view of women does Ibn Hazm present?

3. What values does Maisuna contrast in her poem?

4. How do you think Maisuna would react to Ibn Hazm's characterization of Islamic women?

Islamic Art

Believing that creation of life belonged to God alone, Islam forbade the depiction of living beings. The effect of this was to foster excellence in nonfigurative art forms, such as Islamic calligraphy. Even when Islamic art did employ figures, as in manuscript illustrations, they were often incorporated into a nearly abstract design.

This Quran is written in the early, highly angular style of Islamic calligraphy known as Kufic. ▶

This sunburst design decorated an album produced around 1640 for the Mughal emperor Shah Jahan (page 69). ▶

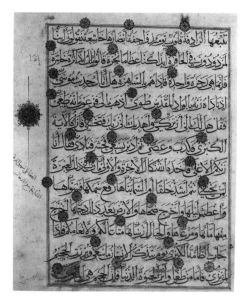

◀ Produced in Egypt in the mid-1300s, this Quran is an example of the Thuluth style of calligraphy.

▲
This illustration depicts a scene from one of the most famous
Islamic love stories, that of Layla and Majnun.

▲

This illustration from a manuscript of *Kalila wa Dimma* (page 301) shows a physician examining his patient.

This illustration of a crocus comes from a manual describing 500 medicinal plants and their uses. ▶

QUESTIONS TO CONSIDER

1. What do the examples of calligraphy convey about Islamic culture's attitude toward the written word, particularly the language of the Quran?

2. What qualities are conveyed by the sunburst design?

3. Did the painter of the illustration of Layla and Majnun seem to have been primarily interested in telling a story? Why or why not?

4. What can you infer about Islamic medicine from the illustrations of the physician and the flower?

The Arab Role in Islamic Civilization

J. S. BADEAU

In the hundred years after the death of Muhammad (570–682), the founder of Islam, Arab armies conquered a vast empire that stretched from the Atlantic Ocean to India. The civilization that eventually developed within these conquered lands was not exclusively Arabic but Islamic. J. S. Badeau discusses why this occurred and identifies the chief Arab contributions to this civilization.

The Arab conquest of the ancient world in the seventh and eighth centuries produced two momentous and enduring effects. The more immediate and dramatic was the creation of a new world state in the Mediterranean Basin and the Near East. The second effect, less rapid and **tumultuous**[1] but no less important, was the development of a new world culture within this state. The impact of both the conquest and the culture has deeply influenced the shape of modern times.

The Arab world state was launched as an imperial system with a rapidity seldom matched in history. Within a century of their appearance on the world scene, the Arabs held sway from the Pyrenees on the border of France to the Pamirs in Central Asia. Spain, North Africa, Egypt, the Byzantine territory south of the Taurus Mountains, and the Persian empire in the east were welded together into an imperial realm that rivaled that of Rome at its peak.

The new realm did not remain either imperial or Arab permanently, however. Stretching across 3,000 miles from east to west and embracing a great diversity of regions and peoples, it proved impossible to rule from a single seat of power by a single dynasty. For a little over a century the Arab conquerors were able to hold their subject lands together. After that, territories began to break away and non-Arab Muslims began to assert their right to a share in the rule of state and society. Spain, North Africa and, to a lesser extent, Egypt in the west struggled against imperial control and finally went their own ways. In the east, Persia grew in power until it came

---

[1] **tumultuous**—disorderly.

to be master of the eastern lands. By the time the Mongols of the thirteenth century overran the Muslim world, the original Arab empire had long since ceased to exist. In its place stood a bewildering array of petty states, regional powers, and contending dynasties, few of them ruled by Arabs.

The Arab empire of the first conquests was transformed into the Muslim world of the Middle Ages.

In effect, the Arab empire of the first conquests was transformed into the Muslim world of the Middle Ages. It was a *world* and not an empire—a political realm containing separate and often warring states, yet conscious of a common identity that distinguished it from other regions. It was *Muslim*, not solely Arab, built upon the community of faith rather than the exclusivism of racial and tribal bonds. As the Arab monopoly of power declined, Persians, Berbers, Seljuks, and other client peoples became the rulers and leaders of their own segments of a multiracial Muslim world.

It was within this Muslim setting that a new world culture, the second momentous result of the Arab conquest, was created. "Created" is the precise and proper term. For what happened was not the imposition of a foreign culture by invasion, not the same process that carried Western civilization to the East during the period of European colonialism. The Arab conquerors came with impressive military strength, but the culture of their desert home was simple and unsophisticated. Nothing in their culture, not even their language at the beginning, compared or competed with the classical and Hellenistic[2] heritage of the lands they overran. The distinctive and richly hued civilization that characterized the Muslim world at its height was formed "in situ."[3] It came into being within the new state, giving identity and character to the new order that resulted from the conquests of Islam as it spread among alien peoples. Its major components were at hand within the varied life and traditions of the subjugated people—classical literature, Hellenistic thought, Byzantine institutions, Roman law, Syriac scholarship, Persian art.

At first these resources were appropriated directly, with little reshaping. Before long, however, they were more selectively utilized, combined into novel patterns that served as both resource and stimulus to creative Muslim scholarship. The result was not simply a montage[4] of bits and pieces of disparate culture. It was a new creation with its own distinctive pattern, infused with a new spirit and expressing a new social order.

This development of a distinctly Islamic culture reached full stride about the time that the Arab leadership of the empire began to wane. At first the conquerors were chiefly absorbed in the tasks of consolidating their rule and buttressing[5] their position.

---

[2] Hellenistic—culture of the empire of Alexander the Great (356–323 B.C.), composed of Greek and Asian elements.

[3] in situ—at point of origin.

[4] montage—combination.

[5] buttressing—supporting.

The establishment of the new state, the maintenance of public order, the strengthening of military organization, and the collection of taxes were their major concerns. The daily business of government and administration was left to the existing bureaucracies. The Arab elite tended to live apart from their subjects, at first in military encampments and then in garrison cities.

This was obviously not a situation that stimulated much cultural absorption or creativity. Only when the conquest had settled into an accepted and permanent order and its exclusive monopoly of power had given way to a broader rule did the new culture develop rapidly. With the rise of the Abbasid dynasty in 750, convert Muslims and client peoples who were living on the fringes of the new society moved to its center, bringing with them their own heritage of culture and civilization.

In this setting the outstanding achievements of Muslim culture appeared. Arab literature reached its peak; the great codes of Canon Law[6] were formulated; philosophy, science, and medicine were taken over from the ancients and given new dimensions and content. Muslim civilization—rich, sophisticated, varied—became the mark of the societies of the Islamic world and took its place among the great cultural achievements of human history.

In the colorful tapestry of Muslim culture there are many threads of Arab weaving. In every field—literature, theology, philosophy, science, geography, architecture—there are notable Arab names and notable Arab achievements. But the Arab contribution goes far beyond the roles played by individual scholars and the significance of specific achievements. The **exigencies**[7] of history are as **nebulous**[8] as those of personal life; yet from the record it seems clear that the fact of an *Arab* conquest was definitive in determining the cultural development that followed. To their conquest of territory they brought constructive forces of their own, forces that set the stage for, and shaped the framework of, the civilization that finally emerged.

The first of these forces was the fact of empire itself. It might have been expected that the Arab invaders would be only desert raiders in the traditional pattern of the tribal **foray**,[9] content to plunder and then to vanish. But this was not so. The Arabs explained their conquests by saying they were made "in the path of God," *fi sabil Allah.* By this they meant that a new social order was to be established among men and that their conquest was to be the tool of its creation. The empire that resulted from the invasion was thus conceived as both a permanent and a self-perpetuating realm, not merely a collection of subjugated territories to be held together only so long as they could enrich their conquerors.

The fact and vision of empire created both the need and the setting for a new social and cultural order to express the

---

[6] Canon Law—Islamic religious law, the Shariah.

[7] **exigencies**—requirements of a situation.

[8] **nebulous**—cloudy, vague, uncertain.

[9] **foray**—raid, attack.

identity of the new realm. Those who had been Spaniards, Greeks, Egyptians, Syrians, and Persians, each with a separate history and tradition, were now subjects under one rule with a new, if as yet undefined, character. Inevitably, the creation of a new world state paved the way for the emergence of an imperial culture.

———————

The Arab conquerors themselves quickly responded to contact with the civilizations they overran.

———————

Within this new empire the diverse cultures and societies of the ancient world were shaken out of their regionalism and forced into new and fruitful interaction. The Arab conquerors themselves quickly responded to contact with the civilizations they overran. Once the initial absorption in conquest was relaxed, they "sat as pupils at the feet of the people they subdued—and what acquisitive pupils they proved to be," as Phillip K. Hitti has observed. Before the end of the first Arab dynasty, that of the Umayyads, classical works were being translated into Arabic, impressive buildings inspired by classical designs were being built, and Arab scholarship in grammar and literature, influenced by Greek patterns, began to flourish. By the time the Arabs lost their preeminence in rule, non-Arab materials had been established in the life and thought of the Islamic community.

At the same time, the diverse subject peoples shared in and absorbed one another's cultures. Barriers to travel through the Mediterranean and eastern lands were broken down, and subjects flocked from the provinces to the heart of empire, where they met and mingled in a new relationship. Moreover, their contact with Arabs produced many Muslim converts and many intermarriages. Inevitably the emerging Islamic order became both multicultural and intercultural, drawing on a prolific and varied stock of traditions to create a new civilization.

That this interaction resulted in an impressive civilization with a unique character was due in large part to the second force let loose by the Arabs in their conquest—the faith of Islam. The Arab invaders brought Islam with them. Islam was a decisive factor in the process of cultural creation, and Islam was basically and peculiarly an Arab achievement.

The significance of this becomes apparent when we remember how often foreign conquerors have been absorbed into the people they subjugated. Successive invaders of China (the Mongols and the Manchus, for example, ruled "the Heavenly Kingdom," but in the end they became Chinese in language and culture, almost indistinguishable from their subjects.)

This might have been so with the Arab invaders. Unfortified by a literate culture deeply rooted in history, confronted with civilizations much more sophisticated and rich than any they had known, they might have been expected to capitulate to the civilizations they overran, even while continuing to rule them. The result would have been either an indiscriminate synthesis of subject cultures, lacking distinctive character, or the fragmentation of the new realm into separate cultural components that shared nothing in common but imperial rule.

That the Arab conquest was Islamic as well as military prevented this kind of cultural formlessness. Once a territory had been subjugated, it became part of the "Abode of Islam" (dar al-Islam), a society under Muslim rule in which Muslims could practice their faith without hindrance. At the outset this did not mean that all the subject people, or even a majority, became Muslims. It did mean, however, that the Islamic way was to be the accepted institution of state and society.

Islam envisioned itself as an all-embracing framework of human life. No activity of the individual or community was alien to it. Its vision of God and man and society was definitive and rested upon divine authority —the "given" of human experience—which stood at the center and passed judgment on all that men might do. It is significant that, as Islam elaborated, it was Canon Law (Shari'ah) rather than theology that was most rigorously protected and applied. Men had to live within a Muslim society to be fully Muslim, not simply to profess Islamic beliefs in any society in which they might find themselves.

What shape and content Muslim society should have in the foreign world of the Arab conquests had to be worked out. In the new lands, the Arabs encountered conditions, problems, and materials that were unknown to the tribal life and that were often in apparent opposition to the unbending Islamic principles and obligations. In the interaction between these elements, it was the Islamic claim that had priority. Although Muslims might, and did, freely appropriate Greek, Byzantine, Hellenistic, Syriac, and Persian materials to construct their new civilization, the appropriation was under Islamic **auspices**[10] and was meant to serve Islamic purposes. On the surface Muslim culture might appear to be highly **eclectic**;[11] yet in fact and in substance it was selective and discriminating, including and excluding materials in terms of their compatibility with the nature and ends of an Islamic society.

Islam itself was influenced by this process. As a full-blown medieval intellectual system, it incorporated many elements of Neoplatonic philosophy, Aristotelian logic,[12] and Roman law—to name some major influences. Yet this did not alter the fact that in substance, in character, and in origin Islam was Arab. The initial vision of Islam was seen and given to the world by an Arab prophet. Its central emphasis on community was rooted in immemorial Arab tribal life. Its fundamental concepts were expressed in the vocabulary of Arab experience. Whatever non-Arab materials

---

[10] **auspices**—sponsorship.

[11] **eclectic**—composed of elements from different sources.

[12] Neoplatonic philosophy, Aristotelian logic—Founded by the Roman philosopher Plotinus (205?–270 A.D.), Neoplatonic philosophy blends the thought of the Greek philosopher Plato (page 233) with mysticism. The Greek philosopher Aristotle (384–322 B.C.) established a system of logic based on deductive reasoning and the use of the syllogism.

might be used in the elaboration of Islam as a system, the character of Islam as an Arab view of life and faith was never lost, and never could be. Arab rule could fade and Arab preeminence in the medieval Muslim world could recede, but the Arab impact on Islam could not be obliterated. By their faith the Arabs made an enduring and irradicable[13] contribution to both Islamic and world culture.

Closely related to the influence of an inclusive empire and an exclusive faith was a further contribution of Arabs to the rise of a new culture—their language. How inextricably Arabic **permeated**[14] the development of Muslim culture is shown by the fact that the system that finally evolved is still referred to as "Arab civilization" and "Arabic thought," despite the fact that many of its great cultural achievements did not take place under Arab auspices. Non-Arabs and even non-Muslims made important contributions, but they made them in the Arabic language, whatever their ethnic community.

That the language of the Arab invaders assumed this role may appear strange. The Mediterranean world was rich and old in its own classical tradition of language and literature. Greek, the most universal of the ancient tongues, still was used in Byzantine lands, and its classical literature was cherished. In comparison, the language of the conquering tribesmen of the desert seemed both alien and primitive. The Arabs had a tradition of oral poetry, but only one book—the Quran.[15] Their grammar was yet to be explored, and the canons of their literature remained to be

developed. The vocabulary of Arabic reflected the simple and limited experience of desert people and had yet to prove capable of expressing foreign ideas, abstract concepts, and the literary interests of a sophisticated society.

Yet Arabic overcame these handicaps and quickly became the dominant language of culture and scholarship in the rising Muslim world. It was able to do this partly because it was the language of both conquest and faith. Those who had business to do with Arabs or who sought to ingratiate themselves with their new rulers could not escape the use of Arabic. And no one could become a Muslim without some understanding of the Arabic language.

This fact of Islam as a vehicle for Arabic was preponderant. The Quran, source of all belief and piety, was in Arabic and could not be translated into any other tongue. Ritual prayers and public worship were in Arabic. Exegesis[16] of the Quran called forth some of the first Arab scholarship, and the fact that God had chosen Arabic as the language of revelation made the study of its grammar and usage a religious necessity.

Yet it was more than conquest and religion that raised Arabic to its preeminent place in Muslim culture. Despite its original character as a desert tongue, Arabic displayed a remarkable potential as a medium of sophisticated and complex communication. It had the strongly marked structure of Semitic languages, in which the

---

[13] irradicable—unerasable.

[14] **permeated**—spread throughout.

[15] the Quran—sacred text of Islam (page 296).

[16] exegesis—explanation.

parts of speech are closely and clearly related. It could create new words out of existing verbal forms, and its ability to compress shades of meaning into a single dramatic expression made it a vivid and exact language. Elaborated by its grammarians and stimulated by the challenge of new horizons, it became a superb tool for thought and scholarship.

The effects on culture of the dominance of Arabic were profound and enduring. Arabic provided the inclusive medium of communication that translated the political intermixture of diverse peoples into a commonly shared culture. As Latin did in medieval Europe and as English did in British India, Arabic in the new state overarched local languages and literature to create a new and universal intellectual realm where Persian philosophers, Arab theologians, Jewish and Christian physicians, and Indian mathematicians could not only speak a common language but also have a sense of sharing in a common intellectual order.

Moreover, the use of Arabic and the adoption of its alphabet by non-Arab Muslim languages formed a kind of cultural frontier that demarked the Muslim world from other civilizations. The traveler from Europe or the East knew at once as he passed through the Muslim world that he was in a different culture, one whose language and writing were not related to anything he had known. The same linguistic frontier turned the Muslim people themselves away from their own past cultures and gave them a sense of identity and an awareness of their difference from other people.

Arabic had a further effect on the growth of Islamic culture, although it is an elusive one and difficult to define. Today we are only beginning to understand and measure something of the relatedness of "medium and message," but we now know that the very form of a language shapes and gives character to the ideas expressed in it and to the minds that use it. The highly distinctive qualities of Arabic, the richness and content of its vocabulary, its particular mode of expressing an idea, and its propensity for meter and rhyme—all placed an imprint on scholarly productions and scholarly minds and hence on the "flavor" of the Islamic intellectual world. Thus the unique character of medieval Muslim culture is partly due to the fact that it did its work in Arabic. Like the contribution of Islam, the penetrating influence of language ensured the Arabness of the medieval world far beyond the period of Arab political rule.

QUESTIONS TO CONSIDER

1. Why did an Islamic rather than exclusively Arab culture develop within the empire conquered by the Arabs?

2. What were the most important Arab contributions to the development of Islamic civilization?

3. In your opinion, what is the most important element of Islamic civilization?

4. Should the United States perform a role today similar to that of the Arabs in the transmission of older cultures? Why or why not?

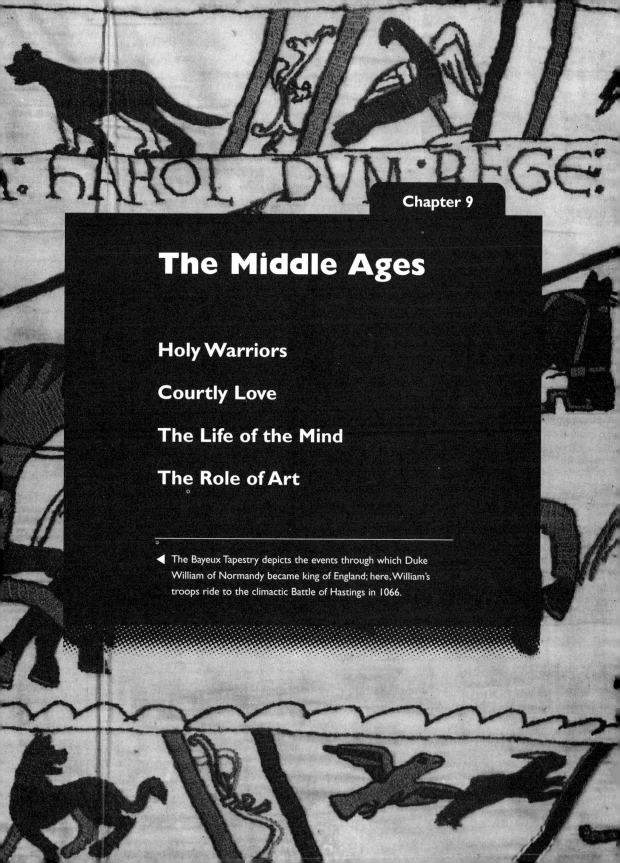

The Middle Ages

◀ The Bayeux Tapestry depicts the events through which Duke William of Normandy became king of England; here, William's troops ride to the climactic Battle of Hastings in 1066.

The Conquest of Jerusalem

FOUCHER

War in the Middle Ages was often inspired by religious faith. Beginning in 1095, the Crusades were a series of wars by Christian armies who believed that it was God's will that they force the Muslims from the Holy Land, although the area was sacred to Muslims as well. In this eyewitness account the French chronicler Foucher (or Fulcher) of Chartres (1058–c.1130) depicts the capture of Jerusalem in 1099 during the First Crusade.

The city itself is situated on hilly ground, with no streams, forests or springs except the spring of Siloah, which produces sufficient water at times and at other times runs dry. This tiny spring lies in the depths of a valley under Mt. Sion, beneath the course of the River Cedron that flows in winter through the Valley of Josaphat. Many cisterns amply filled with water abound in the city. If they are properly supervised they offer at all times an unfailing supply to all the inhabitants, both man and beast, except for the winter storms. The city is of adequate size, built in a circular shape, giving the appearance neither of smallness nor of pretentious magnitude.[1] On the west is the Tower of David and on either side a wall enclosing the city, which is hewn[2] solidly from its base to the middle and built of blocks of quarrystone fastened together with molten lead. Fortified with provisions, with only fifteen or twenty men inside to defend it, it can never be stormed by force by any army whatever.

In this city too there is a circular temple of the Lord, situated in the same spot where Solomon in earlier times built his second wonder.[3] Although it can in no sense be compared with that ancient plan, still it is a wonderfully constructed and very beautiful building. In the center there is a huge native rock, and where it is disfigured the temple itself is rather

---

[1] pretentious magnitude—showy greatness.

[2] hewn—shaped.

[3] circular temple ... second wonder—Housing the rock from which Muslims believe the Prophet Muhammad ascended to heaven, the mosque known as the Dome of the Rock (page 130) was built on the site of King Solomon's temple. Foucher calls it Solomon's "second wonder" because the king also built a great palace.

obstructed. I do not know why the Eternal allows the place to be occupied without destroying it utterly. . . . At sight of it, when the Franks[4] saw how difficult it was to storm, they were ordered by our leaders to make wooden ladders by means of which, when these were later on set against the wall, they mounted to the top in a powerful assault and, perhaps with the aid of God, attacked the city.

This done, on the following Sabbath at the command of the chiefs, with trumpets blaring in the clear morning light, in an amazing attack they assailed the city from all sides. When this had continued until the sixth hour of the day and still they were unable to enter over the ladders they had set up because they were too few, they dejectedly gave up the assault. Then a plan was devised and the engineers were ordered to build machines that could be moved up to the walls and, with God's help, thus achieve the result of their hopes. This was done. During this time there was no lack of bread or meat.

But as the location, as mentioned above, lacked water and rivers, our men and their beasts were greatly distressed for want of drinking water. Hence, under the compulsion of necessity, they searched for water far and wide and laboriously brought it for the siege in their leather skins, from a distance of four or five miles. Once the engines were ready, that is the battering rams and the mining devices, they prepared for the assault. Among other contrivances,[5] they fastened together a

tower made of small pieces of wood, because large timber was lacking. At night, at a given order, they carried it piece by piece to the most favorable point of the city. And so, in the morning, after preparing the catapults[6] and the other contraptions, they very quickly set it up, fitted together, not far from the wall. This erection they tied fast and bound with leather thongs on the outside, slowly moving it nearer the wall. Then a few daring soldiers at the sound of the trumpet mounted it, and from that position they immediately began to launch stones and arrows. In **retaliation**[7] against them the Saracens[8] proceeded to defend themselves similarly and with their slings hurled flaring brands soaked in oil and fat and fitted with small torches on the previously mentioned tower and the soldiers on it. Many therefore fighting in this manner on either side met ever-present death.

In that spot where Count Raymund and his men stood, at Mt. Sion, they made a vigorous assault with their engines. Elsewhere, where Duke Godefrey was, and Robert Count of Normandy, and Robert of Flanders,[9] the assault on the wall was more forceful. These were the tactics that day. On the following day, with trumpets

---

[4] Franks—the French.

[5] contrivances—mechanical devices.

[6] catapults—military devices for hurling large stones or other projectiles.

[7] **retaliation**—revenge.

[8] Saracens—Muslims.

[9] Count Raymund . . . Robert of Flanders—leaders of the First Crusade.

resounding, they repeated their actions with greater vigor, breaching[10] the wall in one place with battering rams. In front of the wall defenses two stakes hung, fastened with ropes, that the Saracens had prepared to stop the enemy rushing on them and showering stones. The tower was then moved up to the wall and the ropes that tied the bundles of wood were cut, and from the same wood the Franks fitted together a bridge that they cleverly extended and threw from the tower across the wall.

One stone citadel on the wall was now blazing away, over which our engineers had hurled burning firebrands. The fire was fed by the planks of timber, and the smoke and flame began to issue so that none of the citizen guards could stand there any longer. Presently therefore the Franks entered the city at midday, on the day dedicated to Venus,[11] with bugles blowing and all in an uproar and manfully attacking and crying "Help us, God," and raised a standard on the top of the wall. The heathens, utterly disgraced, all changed their bold stand into a scurrying flight through the alleyways of the city. The more quickly they fled, the more quickly were they driven into flight. Count Raymund, attacking on another side, was unaware of this, and his men too, until they saw the Saracens leap over the top of the wall in front of them. At sight of this, they rushed joyfully as fast as possible to the city and with the rest began to rout and slay the wicked enemy.

Then some Saracens, both Arabs and Ethiopians, fled into the citadel of David, others shut themselves in the temples of the Lord and of Solomon. In the halls of these temples they were fiercely attacked; there was nowhere for them to escape from our warriors. On the top of the temple of Solomon that they had climbed in their flight, many were pierced to death by their arrows and wildly hurled down from the wall. In this temple too almost 10,000 were **decapitated**.[12] If you had been there, you would have seen our feet bespattered to the soles with the blood of the slain. What is there to tell? Not a single life was spared. But they too spared neither women nor children. You would have seen an amazing sight when our squires and the poorest infantry troops, learning of the Saracens' cunning, slit the bellies even of the slain to extract from their bowels the bezants[13] that they had swallowed while alive. After a few days they piled up the bodies in a great heap and burned them in order to find the coins more easily among the burnt ashes.

Tancred[14] quickly entered the temple of the Lord and seized many gold and silver ornaments—a sinful theft—and precious stones. But atoning for this later on, he returned all of it to a holy place or bought it.

---

[10] breaching—making an opening.

[11] day dedicated to Venus—Friday.

[12] **decapitated**—beheaded.

[13] bezants—gold coins.

[14] Tancred—a Norman soldier.

Our soldiers now with swords drawn
    scour[15] the city.
They spare no one, they show no
    suppliant pity.
Like rotting fruit that falls lie strewn
    the dead,
Like acorns shaken from the oak,
    'tis said.

After such a massacre they entered the homes and took whatever they found there so that whoever first entered a house, whether rich or poor, in no way prevented anyone else, to their own loss, from seizing and keeping as their own whatever they found in home or palace. This gave a sense of mutual right of possession. The result was that many who were poor became wealthy.

Then, going to the sepulcher[16] of the Lord and His glorious temple, clerics and laity, chanting in a loud exulting voice the new hymn to the Lord, together joyously visited the sacred places so long yearned for, making offering and humble **supplications**.[17] O what an hour craved by us all! What a moment to be remembered beyond all others! What an incident above all others desired! Truly craved, since it had always been an object of yearning by all worshippers of the Catholic faith in their innermost yearning heart, that the place in which the Creator of all creatures, God made man, by His **manifold**[18] compassions for mankind, being born, dying, and being resurrected, conferred the gift

of new-born salvation, a place at last cleansed from the **contagion**[19] of the heathens dwelling therein, long defiled by their superstition, should be restored to its former prestige by the believers and the faithful. And truly memorable and rightly to be remembered, because whatever our Lord Jesus Christ, on earth a man dwelling with men, did and taught, was recalled and brought back to most glorious memory. . . .

---

[15] scour—search rapidly.

[16] sepulcher—tomb.

[17] **supplications**—requests, as in prayers.

[18] **manifold**—many and varied.

[19] **contagion**—evil influence.

QUESTIONS TO CONSIDER

1. In Foucher's account, expressions of piety are mixed with descriptions of slaughter or threat of warfare. What are your feelings about this juxtaposition?

2. What indications are there in Foucher's account that he was indeed an eyewitness to events in Jerusalem?

3. How does Foucher justify the Crusaders' slaughter of the inhabitants of Jerusalem?

4. What attitude does he have toward looting by the Crusaders?

Joan of Arc

Joan of Arc (1412–1431) was a young French peasant who claimed to hear heavenly voices directing her to rescue her country from English invaders. Joan inspired the French to resist, but was captured by her enemies, tried for witchcraft, and burned at the stake. The first document is a warning from Joan to the English leaders. The second is the statement of the charges against her at her trial.

Joan of Arc's Letter

King of England, and you Duke of Bedford, calling yourself **regent**[1] of France, you, William Pole, Count of Suffolk, John Talbot, and you Thomas Lord Scales, calling yourselves lieutenants of the said Duke of Bedford, do right in the King of Heaven's sight. Surrender to *The Maid*[2] sent hither by God the King of Heaven, the keys of all the good towns you have taken and laid waste in France. She comes in God's name to establish the Blood Royal, ready to make peace if you agree to abandon France and repay what you have taken. And you, archers, comrades in arms, gentles[3] and others, who are before the town of Orleans,[4] retire in God's name to your own country. If you do not, expect to hear tidings from *The Maid* who will shortly come upon you to your very great hurt. And to you, King of England, if you do not thus, I am *chef de guerre*,[5] and whenever I meet your followers in France, I will drive them out; if they will not obey, I will put them all to death. I am sent here in God's name, the King of Heaven, to drive you body for body out of all France. If they obey, I will show them mercy. Do not think otherwise; you will not withhold the kingdom of France from God, the King of Kings, Blessed Mary's Son. The King Charles, the true inheritor, will possess it,

---

[1] **regent**—governor.

[2] *The Maid*—Joan.

[3] gentles—gentlemen.

[4] Orleans—French city besieged by the English; Joan led her troops against the English, forcing them to abandon the siege.

[5] *chef de guerre*—commander of the war.

for God wills it, and has revealed it to him through *The Maid*, and he will enter Paris with a good company. If you do not believe these tidings from God and *The Maid*, wherever we find you we shall strike you and make a greater **tumult**[6] than France has heard for a thousand years. Know well that the King of Heaven will send a greater force to *The Maid* and her good men-at-arms than you in all your assaults can overcome: and by blows shall the favor of the God of Heaven be seen. You Duke of Bedford, *The Maid* prays and beseeches not to bring yourself to destruction. If you obey her, you may join her company, where the French shall do the fairest deed ever done for Christendom. Answer, if you desire peace in the city of Orleans; if not, bethink you of your great hurt soon. Written this Tuesday of Holy Week.

The Charges Against Joan

The said accused, not only in the present year, but from the time of her childhood, not only in your diocese and jurisdiction, but also in the neighboring and other parts of this kingdom, has performed, composed, mingled in and commanded many charms and superstitions; she has been **deified**,[7] permitted herself to be adored and venerated; she has called up demons and evil spirits, has consulted and frequented them, has had, made, and entered into pacts and treaties with them; she has similarly given counsel, aid and favor to others doing the same things, and has induced them to do the same or like things, saying, believing, maintaining, affirming, that so to do, to believe in them, to use such charms, divinations and superstitious proceedings was neither a sin nor a forbidden thing; but she has rather assured them that it is lawful, praiseworthy and **opportune**,[8] enticing into these evil ways and errors many people of different estate[9] and of either sex, in whose heart she imprinted these and like things. And in the accomplishment and perpetration of these crimes the said Jeanne has been taken and captured in the boundaries and limits of your diocese of Beauvais.

---

[6] **tumult**—disorderly commotion.

[7] **deified**—made into a god.

[8] **opportune**—suitable.

[9] estate—social class.

QUESTIONS TO CONSIDER

1. In her letter to the English, what authority did Joan invoke for her acts?

2. What words would you use to describe the tone of Joan's letter?

3. What indications are there in the charges against Joan that she did not view what she was doing as wrong?

The Rules of Love

ANDREAS CAPELLANUS

Often depicted in medieval songs, poetry, legends, and art, courtly love was a code of conduct among the nobility. Courtesy toward women was an important element in the knightly ideals of chivalry; but courtly love also meant that a man might worship from afar or express desire for a married woman, and that she might return his love. (How far this style of courtship typically led is uncertain.) The origins of courtly love are somewhat obscure, but in the 1100s Andreas Capellanus, a chaplain at a French court, established a set of rules. Legendary lovers who fit the courtly love model were Lancelot and Guinevere, shown in the illustration on page 339 from a French manuscript of the early 1200s.

Love is a certain inborn suffering derived from the sight of and excessive meditation upon the beauty of the opposite sex, which causes each one to wish above all things the embraces of the other and by common desire to carry out all of love's precepts in the other's embrace.

1 Marriage is no real excuse for not loving.

2 He who is not jealous cannot love.

3 No one can be bound by a double love.

4 It is well known that love is always increasing or decreasing.

5 That which a lover takes against the will of his beloved has no relish.

6 Boys do not love until they arrive at the age of maturity.

7 When one lover dies, a widowhood of two years is required of the survivor.

8 No one should be deprived of love without the very best of reasons.

9 No one can love unless he is impelled by the persuasion of love.

10 Love is always a stranger in the home of **avarice.**[1]

---

[1] **avarice**—greed.

Married to King Arthur, Queen Guinevere fell in love with his bravest knight, Sir Lancelot. The lovers are shown embracing in front of Galehaut, who acted as their go-between.

11 It is not proper to love any woman whom one would be ashamed to seek to marry.

12 A true lover does not desire to embrace in love anyone except his beloved.

13 When made public love rarely endures.

14 The easy attainment of love makes it of little value; difficulty of attainment makes it prized.

15 Every lover regularly turns pale in the presence of his beloved.

16 When a lover suddenly catches sight of his beloved his heart **palpitates.**[2]

17 A new love puts to flight an old one.

18 Good character alone makes any man worthy of love.

19 If love diminishes, it quickly fails and rarely revives.

20 A man in love is always apprehensive.

21 Real jealousy always increases the feeling of love.

22 Jealousy, and therefore love, are increased when one suspects his beloved.

23 He whom the thought of love **vexes**[3] eats and sleeps very little.

24 Every act of a lover ends in the thought of his beloved.

25 A true lover considers nothing good except what he thinks will please his beloved.

26 Love can deny nothing to love.

27 A lover can never have enough of the **solaces**[4] of his beloved.

28 A slight **presumption**[5] causes a lover to suspect his beloved.

---

[2] **palpitates**—beats rapidly.

[3] **vexes**—distresses.

[4] **solaces**—comforts.

[5] **presumption**—reason for believing.

29   A man who is vexed by too much passion usually does not love.

30   A true lover is constantly and without intermission possessed by the thought of his beloved.

31   Nothing forbids one woman being loved by two men or one man by two women.

QUESTIONS TO CONSIDER

1. According to the rules of courtly love, how, in general, should a lover treat a loved one?

2. Do these rules seem to you to outline a proper code of conduct? Why or why not?

3. How would you characterize someone who followed these rules?

4. Would these rules have been followed by the peasant class if they had known about them? Why or why not?

5. What is conveyed by the posture of Lancelot and Guinevere in the illustration?

from

La Vita Nuova

DANTE ALIGHIERI

Blending autobiographical prose and lyric poetry, La Vita Nuova ("The New Life") by the Italian poet Dante Alighieri (1265–1321) tells of his idealized love for Beatrice Portinari (1266–1290). Writing after her death, Dante comes to realize that his love for Beatrice was the beginning of his spiritual growth, preparing him for love of God. (The number nine, which Dante frequently mentions, is the square of three, a reference to the Trinity.)

Nine times the heaven of the light had revolved in its own movement since my birth and had almost returned to the same point when the woman whom my mind beholds in glory first appeared before my eyes. She was called Beatrice by many who did not know what it meant to call her this. She had lived in this world for the length of time in which the heaven of the fixed stars had circled one twelfth of a degree towards the East.[1] Thus she had not long passed the beginning of her ninth year when she appeared to me and I was almost at the end of mine when I beheld her. She was dressed in a very noble color, a **decorous**[2] and delicate crimson, tied with a girdle[3] and trimmed in a manner suited to her tender age. The moment I saw her I say in all truth that the vital spirit, which dwells in the inmost depths of the heart, began to tremble so violently that I felt the vibration alarmingly in all my pulses, even the weakest of them. As it trembled, it uttered these words: *Ecce deus fortior me, qui veniens domitiabitur mihi.*[4] At this point, the spirit of the senses which dwells on high in the place[5] to which all our sense perceptions are carried, was filled with amazement and, speaking especially to the spirits of vision, made this pronouncement: *Apparuit iam beatitudo vestra.*[6] Whereupon the natural

---

[1] heaven of the light . . . heaven of the fixed stars . . . the East—references to the apparent movements of the sun and stars around the earth in pre-Copernican astronomy.

[2] **decorous**—proper.

[3] girdle—a belt worn around the waist.

[4] *Ecce . . . mihi*—Behold a god more powerful than I who comes to rule over me.

[5] place—the brain.

[6] *Apparuit . . . vestra*—Now your source of joy has been revealed.

spirit, which dwells where our nourishment is digested, began to weep and, weeping, said: *Heu miser! quia frequenter impeditus ero deinceps*.[7] From then on indeed Love ruled over my soul, which was thus wedded to him early in life, and he began to acquire such assurance and mastery over me, owing to the power which my imagination gave him, that I was obliged to fulfil all his wishes perfectly. He often commanded me to go where perhaps I might see this angelic child and so, while I was still a boy, I often went in search of her; and I saw that in all her ways she was so praiseworthy and noble that indeed the words of the poet Homer[8] might have been said of her: "She did not seem the daughter of a mortal man, but of a god." Though her image, which was always present in my mind, **incited**[9] Love to dominate me, its influence was so noble that it never allowed Love to guide me without the faithful counsel of reason, in everything in which such counsel was useful to hear. But, since to dwell on the feelings and actions of such early years might appear to some to be fictitious, I will move on and, omitting many things which might be copied from the master-text from which the foregoing is derived, I come now to words inscribed in my memory under more important headings.

When exactly nine years had passed since this gracious being appeared to me, as I have described, it happened that on the last day of this intervening period this marvel appeared before me again, dressed in purest white, walking between two other women of distinguished **bearing**,[10] both older than herself. As they walked down the street she turned her eyes towards me where I stood in fear and trembling, and with her **ineffable**[11] courtesy, which is now rewarded in eternal life, she greeted me; and such was the virtue of her greeting that I seemed to experience the height of bliss. It was exactly the ninth hour of day when she gave me her sweet greeting. As this was the first time she had ever spoken to me, I was filled with such joy that, my senses reeling, I had to withdraw from the sight of others. So I returned to the loneliness of my room and began to think about this gracious person. As I thought of her I fell asleep and a marvelous vision appeared to me. In my room I seemed to see a cloud the color of fire, and in the cloud a lordly figure, frightening to behold, yet in himself, it seemed to me, he was filled with a marvelous joy. He said many things, of which I understood only a few; among them were the words: *Ego dominus tuus*.[12] In his arms I seemed to see a naked figure, sleeping, wrapped lightly in a crimson cloth. Gazing intently I saw it was she who had bestowed her greeting on me earlier that day. In one hand the standing figure

---

[7] *Heu miser! . . . deinceps*—Woe is me! for I shall often be impeded from now on.

[8] Homer—Greek epic poet (page 206).

[9] **incited**—provoked.

[10] **bearing**—manner.

[11] **ineffable**—not capable of being expressed.

[12] *Ego dominus tuus*—I am your Master.

held a fiery object, and he seemed to say, *Vide cor tuum.*[13] After a little while I thought he wakened her who slept and prevailed on her to eat the glowing object in his hand. Reluctantly and hesitantly she did so. A few moments later his happiness turned to bitter grief, and, weeping, he gathered the figure in his arms and together they seemed to ascend into the heavens. I felt such anguish at their departure that my light sleep was broken, and I awoke. . . .

From that vision onwards my natural spirit began to be **impeded**[14] in its functioning, for my soul was wholly given to thoughts of this most gracious person. In a short time I grew so frail and weak that many of my friends felt concern at my appearance. Many others, full of malicious curiosity, were doing their best to discover things about me which I particularly wished to conceal; and, perceiving the mischievous intent of their inquiries, in obedience to Love's will, who commanded me in accordance with the counsel of reason, I replied that it was Love who had reduced me to this state. I said this because I bore so many of Love's signs in my face

that they could not be hidden. And when they asked me "For whom has Love thus dealt with you?," I looked at them with a smile and said nothing.

---

[13] *Vide cor tuum*—Behold your heart.
[14] **impeded**—hindered.

QUESTIONS TO CONSIDER

1. Dante says that Beatrice caused him to tremble, that his soul commanded him to go where he might see her, that he experienced "the height of bliss," and that when she spoke to him, his senses reeled. How common are these symptoms of love in your opinion?

2. Though love dominated him, Dante says that it never guided him without the "counsel of reason." What does this imply about his attitude toward Beatrice?

3. What attributes does Dante admire in Beatrice?

4. How would you describe the love of Dante for Beatrice?

Women on Love

Medieval women wrote about different aspects of love. "The Nightingale, " a narrative poem by Marie de France (late 1100s), relates the story of a pair of lovers and a jealous husband that is firmly in the tradition of courtly love. A more practical side of love occupied the mind of Margery Brews when she wrote her "valentine" John Paston in February 1477. At issue was her dowry (the money or property a woman brings to her husband upon marriage). She wonders if John cares enough to marry her even with a rather small dowry. He did.

The Nightingale

MARIE DE FRANCE

The story I shall tell today
Was taken from a Breton lay
Called *Laüstic* in Brittany,[1]
Which, in proper French would be
Rossignol. They'd call the tale
In English lands *The Nightingale*.

There was, near Saint Malo, a town
Of some importance and renown.
Two barons who could well afford
Houses suited to a lord
Gave the city its good name
By their benevolence and fame.
Only one of them had married.
His wife was beautiful indeed
And courteous as she was fair,
A lady who was well aware

---

[1] Breton lay ... Brittany—A lay is a ballad. Brittany is a region of northwestern France that possesses its own Celtic language, Breton.

Of all that custom and rank required.
The younger baron was much admired,
Being, among his peers foremost
In valor, and a gracious host.
He never refused a tournament,[2]
And what he owned he gladly spent.
He loved his neighbor's wife. She knew
That all she heard of him was true,
And so she was inclined to be
Persuaded when she heard his plea.
Soon she had yielded all her heart
To his real merit and, in part,
Because he lived not far away.
Fearful that they might betray
The love that they had come to share,
They always took the greatest care
Not to let anyone detect
Anything that might be suspect.
And it was easy enough to hide;
Their houses were almost side by side
With nothing between the two at all
Except a single high stone wall.
The baron's wife need only go
And stand beside her bedroom window
Whenever she wished to see her friend.
They would talk for hours on end
Across the wall, and often threw
Presents through the window too.

They were much happier than before,
And would have asked for nothing more;
But lovers can't be satisfied
When love's true pleasure is denied.
The lady was watched too carefully
As soon as her friend was known to be
At home. But still they had the delight
Of seeing each other day or night

---

[2] tournament—medieval sport in which two groups of mounted men fought against each other with lances or swords.

And talking to their hearts' content.
The strictest guard could not prevent
The lady from looking out her window;
What she saw there no one could know.
Nothing came to interfere
With their true love until one year
In the season when the summer grows
Green in all the woods and meadows,
When birds to show their pleasure cling
To flower tops and sweetly sing.
Then those who were in love before
Do, in love's service, even more.
The baron, in truth, was all intent
On love; the messages he sent
Across the wall had such replies
From his lady's lips and from her eyes,
He knew that she felt just the same.
Now she very often came
To her window lighted by the moon,
Leaving her husband's side as soon
As she knew that he was fast asleep.
Wrapped in a cloak, she went to keep
Watch with her lover, sure that he
Would be waiting for her faithfully.
To see each other was, despite
Their endless longing, great delight.
She went so often and remained
So long, her husband soon complained,
Insisting that she must reply
To where she went at night and why.
"I'll tell you, my lord," the lady answered;
"Anyone who has ever heard
The nightingale singing will admit
No joy on Earth compares with it.
That music just outside my window
Gives me such pleasure that I know
I cannot go to sleep until
The sweet voice in the night is still."

The baron only answered her
With a malicious raging laughter.
He wrought[3] a plan that could not fail
To overcome the nightingale.
The household servants all were set
To making traps of cord or net;
Then, throughout the orchard, these
Were fixed to hazel and chestnut trees,
And all the branches rimmed with glue
So that the bird could not slip through.
It was not long before they brought
The nightingale who had been caught
Alive. The baron, well content,
Took the bird to his wife's apartment.
"Where are you lady? Come talk to me!"
He cried, "I've something for you to see!
Look! Here is the bird whose song
Has kept you from your sleep so long.
Your nights will be more peaceful when
He can't awaken you again!"

She heard with sorrow and with dread
Everything her husband said,
Then asked him for the bird, and he
Killed it out of cruelty;
Vile,[4] with his two hands he wrung
Its neck, and when he finished, flung
The body at his wife. The red
Drops of blood ran down and spread
Over the bodice[5] of her dress.
He left her alone with her distress.
Weeping, she held the bird and thought
With bitter rage of those who brought
The nightingale to death, betrayed
By all the hidden traps they laid.
"Alas!" she cried, "They have destroyed
The one great pleasure I enjoyed.

---

[3] wrought—crafted.

[4] vile—wicked.

[5] bodice—the portion of a woman's dress above the waist.

Now I can no longer go
And see my love outside my window
At night the way I used to do!
One thing certainly is true:
He'll think that I no longer care.
Somehow he must be made aware
Of what has happened. It will be clear
Then why I cannot appear."

And so she began at once to write
On a piece of gold-embroidered samite.[6]
When it couldn't hold another word
She wrapped it around the little bird.
Then she called someone in her service
Whom she could entrust with this,
Bidding him take without delay
Her message to the chevalier.[7]
Thus he came to understand
Everything, just as she planned.
The servant brought the little-bird;
And when the chevalier had heard
All that he so grieved to know,
His courteous answer was not slow.
He ordered made a little case,
Not of iron or any base
Metal, but fine gold embossed
With jewels—he did not count the cost.
The cover was not too long or wide.
He placed the nightingale inside
And had the casket sealed with care;
He carried it with him everywhere.

Stories like this can't be controlled,
And it was very promptly told.
Breton poets rhymed the tale,
Calling it *The Nightingale.*

---

[6] samite—heavy silk fabric.

[7] chevalier—knight or nobleman.

"Valentine" to John Paston

Margery Brews

Right worshipful and well-beloved Valentine, in my most humble wise[8] I recommend me unto you, &c. And heartily I thank you for the letter which that you sent me by John Beckerton, whereby I understand and know that you be purposed to come to Topcroft[9] in short time, and without any errand or matter but only to have a conclusion of the matter betwixt my father and you. I would be most glad of any creature alive so that the matter might grow to effect. And there as you say, an[10] you come and find the matter no more toward than you did aforetime you would no more put my father and my lady my mother to no cost nor business for that cause a good while after, which causes my heart to be full heavy; and that if you come and the matter take to none effect, then should I be much more sorry and full of heaviness.

And as for myself, I have done and understand in the matter that[11] I can or may, as God knows. And I let you plainly understand that my father will no more money part withal in that behalf but one hundred pounds and fifty marks,[12] which is right far from the accomplishment of your desire. Wherefore, if that you could be content with that good,[13] and my poor person, I would be the merriest maiden on ground. And if you think not yourself so satisfied, or that you might have much more good, as I have understood by you afore, good, true, and loving Valentine, that you take no such labor upon you as to come more for that matter; but let it pass, and never more to be spoken of, as I may be your true lover and bedewoman[14] during my life.

No more unto you at this time, but Almighty Jesus preserve you both body and soul, &c.

By Your Valentine,
Margery Brews

---

[8] wise—way.

[9] Topcroft—Margery's home.

[10] an—if.

[11] that—all that.

[12] marks—English coins.

[13] good—that sum as a dowry.

[14] bedewoman—woman who prays for another (using her rosary beads).

QUESTIONS TO CONSIDER

1. How does the story told in "The Nightingale" illustrate the tradition of courtly love?

3. What do you think Marie de France means when she says, "Stories like this can't be controlled"?

3. What has prompted Margery Brews's letter?

4. If John is not satisfied by the size of her dowry, what does she suggest is the alternative?

5. How would you describe the tone of Margery's letter?

Faith and Reason

The discovery in the Middle Ages of the writings of the Greek philosopher Aristotle began to reawaken critical thought. Among the thinkers who tried to reconcile faith and reason was Peter Abelard (1079–1142), who in his work Sic et Non ("Yes and No") presented opposing points of view on 158 questions. A powerful and influential abbot, Bernard of Clairvaux (1090–1153), who thought that faith was "above reason," was scandalized by Abelard's teachings. In his letters, Bernard defended the Church from the threat of these new ideas.

from *Sic et Non*
Peter Abelard

There are many seeming contradictions and even obscurities in the innumerable writings of the church fathers.[1] Our respect for their authority should not stand in the way of an effort on our part to come at the truth. The obscurity and contradictions in ancient writings may be explained upon many grounds, and may be discussed without **impugning**[2] the good faith and insight of the fathers. A writer may use different terms to mean the same thing, in order to avoid a monotonous repetition of the same word. Common, vague words may be employed in order that the common people may understand; and sometimes a writer sacrifices perfect accuracy in the interest of a clear general statement. Poetical, figurative language is often obscure and vague.

Not infrequently **apocryphal**[3] works are attributed to the saints. Then, even the best authors often introduce the erroneous views of others and leave the reader to distinguish between the true and the false. Sometime, as Augustine[4] confesses in his own case, the fathers ventured to rely upon the opinions of others.

Doubtless the fathers might err; even Peter,[5] the prince of the apostles, fell into error; what wonder that the saints do not always show themselves inspired? The fathers did not themselves believe that

---

[1] church fathers—a group of important theologians who defined the orthodox tradition of early Christianity (page 270).

[2] **impugning**—attacking as questionable or false.

[3] **apocryphal**—of questionable authenticity.

[4] Augustine—bishop and theologian (354–430 A.D.).

[5] Peter—chief among Jesus' followers and first head of the Christian church (died 67? A.D.).

they, or their companions, were always right. Augustine found himself mistaken in some cases and did not hesitate to retract his errors. He warns his admirers not to look upon his letters as they would upon the Scriptures, but to accept only those things which, upon examination, they find to be true.

All writings belonging to this class are to be read with full freedom to criticize, and with no obligation to accept unquestioningly; otherwise the way would be blocked to all discussion, and **posterity**[6] be deprived of the excellent intellectual exercise of debating difficult questions of language and presentation. But an explicit exception must be made in the case of the Old and New Testaments. In the Scriptures, when anything strikes us as absurd, we may not say that the writer erred, but that the scribe made a blunder in copying the manuscripts, or that there is an error in interpretation, or that the passage is not understood. The fathers make a very careful distinction between the Scriptures and later works. They advocate a discriminating, not to say suspicious, use of the writings of their own contemporaries.

In view of these considerations, I have ventured to bring together various dicta[7] of the holy fathers, as they came to mind, and to formulate certain questions which were suggested by the seeming contradictions in the statements. These questions ought to serve to excite tender readers to a zealous inquiry into truth and so sharpen their wits. The master key of knowledge is,

indeed, a persistent and frequent questioning. Aristotle, the most clear-sighted of all the philosophers, was desirous above all things else to arouse this questioning spirit, for in his *Categories* he exhorts a student as follows: "It may well be difficult to reach a positive conclusion in these matters unless they be frequently discussed. It is by no means fruitless to be doubtful on particular points." By doubting we come to examine, and by examining we reach the truth.

> Should human faith be based upon reason, or no?
> Is God one, or no?
> Is God a substance, or no?
> Does the first Psalm refer to Christ, or no?
> Is sin pleasing to God, or no?
> Is God the author of evil, or no?
> Is God all-powerful, or no?
> Can God be resisted, or no?
> Has God free will, or no?
> Was the first man persuaded to sin by the devil, or no?
> Was Adam saved, or no?
> Did all the apostles have wives except John, or no?
> Are the flesh and blood of Christ in very truth and essence present in the sacrament of the altar, or no?
> Do we sometimes sin unwillingly, or no?

---

[6] **posterity**—future generations.

[7] dicta—plural of *dictum*, authoritative pronouncement.

Does God punish the same sin both here and in the future, or no?

Is it worse to sin openly than secretly, or no?

from *Letters*
Bernard of Clairvaux

Master Peter Abelard is a monk without a rule,[8] a prelate[9] without responsibility. . . . He speaks **iniquity**[10] openly. He corrupts the integrity of the faith and the chastity of the Church. He oversteps the landmarks placed by our Fathers in discussing and writing about faith, the sacraments, and the Holy Trinity; he changes each thing according to his pleasure, adding to it or taking from it. In his books and in his works he shows himself to be a fabricator[11] of falsehood, a coiner of perverse dogmas,[12] proving himself a **heretic**[13] not so much by his error as by his obstinate defense of error. He is a man who does not know his limitations, making void the virtue of the cross by the cleverness of his words. Nothing in heaven or on earth is hidden from him, except himself. . . . He has defiled the Church; he has infected with his own blight the minds of simple people. He tries to explore with his reason what the devout mind grasps at once with a vigorous faith. Faith believes, it does not dispute. But this man, apparently holding God suspect, will not believe anything until he has first examined it with his reason. When the Prophet says, "Unless you believe, you shall not understand," this man decries willing faith as **levity**,[14] misusing that testimony of Solomon:[15] "He that is hasty to believe is light of head." Let him therefore blame the Blessed Virgin Mary for quickly believing the angel when he announced to her that she should conceive and bring forth a son. Let him also blame him who, while on the verge of death, believed those words of One who was also dying: "This day thou shalt be with me in Paradise."[16]

We have in France an old teacher turned into a new theologian, who in his early days amused himself with dialectics[17] and who now gives utterance to wild imaginations upon the Holy Scriptures. . . . I know not what there is in heaven above and in the earth beneath which he deigns to confess ignorance of: he raises his eyes to heaven and searches the deep things of God and . . .

---

[8] rule—regulations of a religious order.

[9] prelate—high-ranking member of the clergy.

[10] **iniquity**—wickedness, sin.

[11] fabricator—creator.

[12] perverse dogmas—corrupt principles or doctrines.

[13] **heretic**—person who dissents from orthodox religious teachings.

[14] **levity**—lack of seriousness; silliness.

[15] Solomon—king of ancient Israel famous for his wisdom.

[16] him . . . with me in Paradise"—One of the two thieves who was crucified with Jesus made an act of faith in him and was promised Paradise.

[17] dialectics—logical argumentation.

brings back unspeakable words which it is not lawful for a man to utter, while he is . . . prepared to give a reason for everything, even for those things which are above reason; he presumes against reason and against faith. For what is more against reason than by reason to attempt to transcend reason? And what is more against faith than to be unwilling to believe what reason cannot attain? . . .

And so he promises understanding to his hearers, even on those most sublime and sacred truths which are hidden in the very bosom of our holy faith; and he places degrees in the Trinity, modes in the Majesty, numbers in the Eternity. . . . Who does not shudder at such novel profanities of words and ideas?

QUESTIONS TO CONSIDER

1. According to Peter Abelard, how does one arrive at the truth?

2. Why do you think Abelard's approach to truth was unusual for the Middle Ages?

3. What exception does Abelard make to his rule that all writings must be examined criticallly?

4. Bernard of Clairvaux says, "Faith believes, it does not dispute." Abelard says, "By doubting we come to examine, and by examining we reach the truth." With which position do you agree? Why?

from

Scivias

HILDEGARD OF BINGEN

The youngest of ten children of a noble German family, Hildegard of Bingen (1098–1179) became a Benedictine nun at age fifteen and an abbess at age thirty-eight at the monastery of Disibodenberg. In 1141 she began to have visions, which she eventually recorded in Scivias, *an abbreviation of* Scito Vias Domini *("Know the ways of the Lord"). This is part of a preface (which she called "Declaration") to the descriptions of the visions themselves.*

It happened that, in the eleven hundred and forty-first year of the Incarnation[1] of the Son of God, Jesus Christ, when I was forty-two years and seven months old, Heaven was opened and a fiery light of exceeding brilliance came and **permeated**[2] my whole brain and inflamed my whole heart and my whole breast, not like a burning but like a warming flame, as the sun warms anything its rays touch. And immediately I knew the meaning of the exposition[3] of the Scriptures, namely the Psalter,[4] the Gospel, and the other catholic volumes of both the Old and the New Testaments, though I did not have the interpretation of the words of their texts or the division of the syllables or the knowledge of cases or tenses. But I had sensed in myself

wonderfully the power and mystery of secret and admirable visions from my childhood—that is, from the age of five— up to that time, as I do now. This, however, I showed no one except a few religious persons who were living in the same manner as I; but meanwhile, until the time when God by His grace wished it to be manifested, I concealed it in quiet silence. But the visions I saw I did not perceive in dreams, or sleep, or delirium, or by the eyes of the body, or by the ears of the outer self, or in hidden places, but I received them while awake and seeing with a pure

---

[1] Incarnation—becoming human.

[2] **permeated**—spread throughout.

[3] exposition—interpretation.

[4] Psalter—Book of Psalms in the Old Testament (page 21).

In this self-portrait, Hildegard depicted tongues of fire above her head.

the deep profundity of scriptural exposition; and, raising myself from illness by the strength I received, I brought this work to a close—though just barely—in ten years.

These visions took place and these words were written in the days of Henry, Archbishop of Mainz, and of Conrad, king of the Romans, and of Cuno, Abbot of Disibodenberg, under Pope Eugenius.

And I spoke and wrote these things not by the invention of my heart or that of any other person, but as by the secret mysteries of God I heard and received them in the heavenly places.

And again I heard a voice from Heaven saying to me, "Cry out, therefore, and write thus!"

---

[5] certain noble maiden . . . that man—Hildegard's close friends the nun Richardis of Stade and the monk Volmar of Disibodenberg.

mind and the eyes and ears of the inner self, in open places, as God willed it. How this might be is hard for mortal flesh to understand. . . .

But I, though I saw and heard these things, refused to write for a long time, through doubt and bad opinion and the diversity of human words, not with stubbornness but in the exercise of humility, until, laid low by the scourge of God, I fell upon a bed of sickness; then, compelled at last by many illnesses, and by the witness of a certain noble maiden of good conduct and of that man[5] whom I had secretly sought and found, as mentioned above, I set my hand to the writing. While I was doing it, I sensed, as I mentioned before,

QUESTIONS TO CONSIDER

1. Why does Hildegard want to make clear that she wasn't dreaming, sleeping, or delirious when she saw her visions?

2. Hildegard says that she "refused to write for a long time, through doubt and bad opinion." What do you think she means?

3. What do you think Hildegard was trying to represent in her self-portrait?

Medieval Drama

Much of the art of the Middle Ages served a religious purpose. Medieval European drama grew out of Christian services, particularly those of Christmas and Easter. In the 900s, the Bishop of Winchester in England gave instructions for enacting a bit of dialogue that was part of the Easter morning liturgy or ritual. Based on the Gospels, the dialogue is between the three women who visit the tomb of Jesus on Easter morning and the angel they encounter. Biblical dramas, often called mystery plays, were popular in Europe in the Middle Ages. They may take their name from the word mestier, meaning "trade," because they were often staged by craft guilds or unions. The stage directions are for the first scene of a play called Jeu d'Adam ("The Play of Adam") that was performed in front of church doors, probably in France in the 1100s.

The Easter Liturgy

While the third lesson is being chanted, let four brethren vest[1] themselves. Let one of these, vested in an alb,[2] enter as though to take part in the service, and let him approach the sepulcher[3] without attracting attention and sit there quietly with a palm in his hand. While the third respond is chanted, let the remaining three follow, and let them all, vested in copes,[4] bearing in their hands thuribles[5] with incense, and stepping delicately as those who seek something, approach the sepulcher. These things are done in imitation of the angel sitting in the monument, and the women with spices coming to anoint the body of Jesus. When therefore he who sits there beholds the three approach him like folk lost and seeking something, let him begin in a dulcet[6] voice of medium pitch to sing *Quem quaeritis* [Whom seek ye in the sepulcher, O Christian women?]. And when he has sung it to the end, let the three reply in unison *Ihesum Nazarenum* [Jesus of Nazareth, the crucified, O heavenly one]. So he, *Non est hic, surrexit sicut praedixerat. Ite, nuntiate quia surrexit a mortuis* [He is not here; He is risen, as He foretold. Go and announce that He is risen from the dead]. At the word of his bidding let those three

---

[1] vest—clothe.

[2] alb—a long, white robe.

[3] sepulcher—tomb.

[4] copes—long cloak-like vestments worn over an alb.

[5] thuribles—containers in which incense is burned.

[6] dulcet—pleasing to the ear.

This medieval illustration shows the three women encountering the angel at the tomb of Jesus.

demonstrate that the Lord has risen and is no longer wrapped therein, let them sing the anthem *Surrexit Dominus de sepulchro* [The Lord is risen from the sepulcher], and lay the cloth upon the altar. When the anthem is done, let the prior[7] sharing in their gladness at the triumph of our King, in that, having vanquished death, He rose again, begin the hymn *Te Deum laudamus* [We praise Thee, O God]. And this begun, all the bells chime out together.

Stage Directions for a Mystery Play

Let Paradise be set up in a somewhat lofty place; let there be put about it curtains and silken hangings, at such an height that those persons who shall be in Paradise can be seen from the shoulders upward; let there be planted sweet-smelling flowers and **foliage**;[8] let divers[9] trees be therein, and fruits hanging upon them, so that it may seem a most delectable place.

Then let the Savior come, clothed in a dalmatic,[10] and let Adam and Eve be set before him. Let Adam be clothed in a red tunic; Eve, however, in a woman's garment of white, and a white silken wimple;[11] and let them both stand before the Figure [*Figura*, that is, God]; but Adam a little nearer, with composed countenance; Eve,

turn to the choir and say *Alleluia! resurrexit Dominus!* [Alleluia! The Lord is risen!] This said, let the one, still sitting there and as if recalling them, say the anthem *Venite et videte locum* [Come and see the place]. And saying this, let him rise, and lift the veil, and show them the place bare of the cross, but only the cloths laid there in which the cross was wrapped. And when they have seen this, let them set down the thuribles which they bore in that same sepulchre, and take the cloth, and hold it up in the face of the clergy, and as if to

---

[7] prior—an officer in a monastery.

[8] **foliage**—leaves.

[9] divers—several.

[10] dalmatic—an open-sided liturgical vestment.

[11] wimple—a cloth wound round the head, framing the face, and extending under the chin.

however, with countenance a little more subdued. And let Adam himself be well instructed when he shall make his answers, lest in answering he be either too swift or too slow. Let not only Adam, but all the persons, be so instructed that they shall speak composedly and shall use such gestures as become the matter whereof they are speaking; and in uttering the verses, let them neither add a syllable nor take away, but let them pronounce all clearly; and let those things that are to be said be said in their due order. Whoever shall speak the name of Paradise, let him look back at it and point it out with his hand.

[The stage directions for the temptation scene read as follows:]

Then a serpent, cunningly put together, shall ascend along the trunk of the forbidden tree, unto which Eve shall approach her ear, as if hearkening unto its counsel.[12] Thereafter, Eve shall take the apple, and shall offer it unto Adam. . . . Then shall Adam eat a part of the apple; and having eaten it, he shall straightway take knowledge of his sin; and he shall bow himself down so that he cannot be seen of the people, and shall put off his goodly garments, and shall put on poor garments of fig-leaves sewn together; and manifesting exceeding great sorrow, he shall begin his lamentation.

[After the fall of man, Adam and Eve]

. . . shall be clean outside of Paradise, sad and confounded in appearance, they shall bow themselves to the ground, even unto their feet, and the Figure shall point to them with his hand, his face being turned toward Paradise; and the choir shall begin: "Behold Adam is become as one [of us]." And when this is ended, the Figure shall go back unto the church. Then shall Adam have a spade and Eve a mattock,[13] and they shall begin to till[14] the ground, and they shall sow wheat therein. After they shall have finished their sowing, they shall go and sit for a season in a certain place, as if wearied with their toil, and with tearful eyes shall they look back ofttimes at Paradise, beating their breasts. Meanwhile shall the Devil come and plant thorns and thistles in their tillage,[15] and then he shall depart. When Adam and Eve come to their tillage, and when they shall have beheld the thorns and thistles that have sprung up, stricken with grievous sorrow, they shall cast themselves down upon the ground; and remaining there, they shall beat their breasts and their thighs, manifesting their grief by their gestures; and Adam shall then begin his lamentation.

---

[12] hearkening to its counsel—listening attentively to its advice.

[13] spade . . . mattock—digging tools.

[14] till—cultivate.

[15] tillage—cultivated ground.

QUESTIONS TO CONSIDER

1. Why does the bishop observe that the three brethren playing the women should approach "like folk lost and seeking something"?

2. What common purposes would have been served by the enactment of the Easter Liturgy and the illustration of the women at the tomb?

3. What are the indications that the "director" is working with amateur actors?

4 The audience for a mystery play would have been very familiar with the theme of the biblical story. What, in your opinion, would have been the appeal of this particular performance?

Medieval Illustration

Much of medieval culture was based on books. Since they were produced by hand, these books were scarce and precious. Richly bound and ornamented with decorated capital letters, elaborate borders, and beautiful illustrations, these books were often works of art as well.

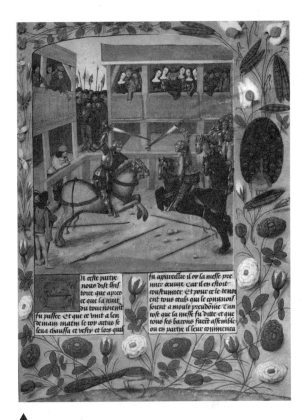

▲
Tournaments like the one shown in this illustration from an Arthurian romance were an exciting, expensive, and often dangerous entertainment for the nobility.

Members of the clergy, like the famous English historian Bede (673–735) shown here, were the intellectuals and educators of the Middle Ages.

This illustration of the Wife of Bath, a bold, jovial middle-class pilgrim in Geoffrey Chaucer's *Canterbury Tales*, comes from an edition produced about 1410.

▲

Depicting the hard life of the peasant, this illustration of the month of October comes from a prayer book created in the early 1400s for a French nobleman.

QUESTIONS TO CONSIDER

1. How does the border of the page from the Arthurian romance contrast with the illustration itself?

2. The illustration from the prayer book depicts one of the castles of the nobleman who commissioned it. What function would such an image serve?

3. Do you think the portrait of Bede depicts his actual appearance? Why or why not?

4. What do these illustrations tell you about the importance of the horse?

Chivalry and Courtly Love

BARBARA TUCHMAN

In her book A Distant Mirror: The Calamitous 14th Century, *historian Barbara Tuchman analyzes how chivalry developed, what its principles were, and how the life of a knight did or did not embody these principles. She also explores the odd societal duality between the ideals of courtly love and the belief that adultery was a sin.*

More than a code of manners in war and love, chivalry was a moral system, governing the whole of noble life. That it was about four parts in five illusion made it no less governing for all that. It developed at the same time as the great crusades of the 12th century as a code intended to fuse the religious and martial spirits and somehow bring the fighting man into accord with Christian theory. Since a knight's usual activities were as much at odds with Christian theory as a merchant's, a moral gloss was needed that would allow the Church to tolerate the warriors in good conscience and the warriors to pursue their own values in spiritual comfort. With the help of Benedictine thinkers, a code evolved that put the knight's sword arm in the service, theoretically, of justice, right,

piety, the Church, the widow, the orphan, and the oppressed. Knighthood was received in the name of the Trinity after a ceremony of purification, confession, communion. A saint's relic was usually embedded in the hilt of the knight's sword so that upon clasping it as he took his oath, he caused the vow to be registered in Heaven. Chivalry's famous celebrator Ramon Lull, a contemporary of St. Louis,[1] could now state as his thesis that "God and chivalry are in concord."

But, like business enterprise, chivalry could not be contained by the Church, and bursting through the pious veils, it developed its own principles. Prowess, that

---

[1] Ramon Lull . . . St. Louis—Lull (c. 1235–1315) was a Franciscan monk, mystic, and missionary to the Arabs. King Louis IX of France (1214–1270), or Saint Louis, led the Seventh Crusade; he was canonized in 1297.

combination of courage, strength, and skill that made a chevalier *preux*,[2] was the prime essential. Honor and loyalty, together with courtesy—meaning the kind of behavior that has since come to be called "chivalrous"—were the ideals, and so-called courtly love the presiding genius. Designed to make the knight more polite and to lift the tone of society, courtly love required its disciple to be in a chronically amorous condition, on the theory that he would thus be rendered more courteous, gay, and gallant, and society in consequence more joyous. Largesse[3] was the necessary accompaniment. An open-handed generosity in gifts and hospitality was the mark of a gentleman and had its practical value in attracting other knights to fight under the banner and bounty of the *grand seigneur*.[4] Over-celebrated by troubadours and chroniclers who depended on its flow, largesse led to reckless extravagance and careless bankruptcies.

Prowess was not mere talk, for the function of physical violence required real stamina. To fight on horseback or foot wearing 55 pounds of plate armor, to crash in collision with an opponent at full gallop while holding horizontal an eighteen-foot lance half the length of an average telephone pole, to give and receive blows with sword or battle-ax that could cleave a skull or slice off a limb at a stroke, to spend half of life in the saddle through all weathers and for days at a time, was not a weakling's work. Hardship and fear were part of it.

"Knights who are at the wars . . . are forever swallowing their fear," wrote the companion and biographer of Don Pero Niño, the "Unconquered Knight" of the late 14th century. "They expose themselves to every peril; they give up their bodies to the adventure of life in death. Moldy bread or biscuit, meat cooked or uncooked; today enough to eat and tomorrow nothing, little or no wine, water from a pond or a butt,[5] bad quarters, the shelter of a tent or branches, a bad bed, poor sleep with their armor still on their backs, burdened with iron, the enemy an arrow-shot off. 'Ware![6] Who goes there? To arms! To arms!' With the first drowsiness, an alarm; at dawn, the trumpet. 'To horse! To horse! Muster! Muster!' As lookouts, as sentinels, keeping watch by day and by night, fighting without cover, as foragers, as scouts, guard after guard, duty after duty. 'Here they come! Here! They are so many—No, not as many as that—This way—that—Come this side—Press them there—News! News! They come back hurt, they have prisoners—no, they bring none back. Let us go! Let us go! Give no ground! On!' Such is their calling."

> **"Knights who are at the wars . . . are forever swallowing their fear."**

---

[2] chevalier *preux*—knight gallant.

[3] largesse—generosity.

[4] *grand seigneur*—the lord under whom a knight served.

[5] butt—water cask.

[6] ware—beware.

. . . Loyalty, meaning the pledged word, was chivalry's fulcrum.[7] The extreme emphasis given to it derived from the time when a pledge between lord and vassal was the only form of government. A knight who broke his oath was charged with "treason" for betraying the order of knighthood. The concept of loyalty did not preclude treachery or the most **egregious**[8] trickery as long as no knightly oath was broken. When a party of armed knights gained entrance to a walled town by declaring themselves allies and then proceeded to slaughter the defenders, chivalry was evidently not violated, no oath having been made to the burghers.[9]

> *Fighting filled the noble's need of something to do, a way to exert himself.*

Chivalry was regarded as a universal order of all Christian knights, a transnational class moved by a single ideal, much as Marxism later regarded all workers of the world. It was a military guild in which all knights were theoretically brothers, although Froissart[10] excepted the Germans and Spaniards, who, he said, were too uncultivated to understand chivalry.

In the performance of his function, the knight must be prepared, as John of Salisbury wrote, "to shed your blood for your brethren"—he meant brethren in the universal sense—"and, if needs must, to lay down your life." Many were thus prepared, though perhaps more from sheer love of battle than concern for a cause. . . .

Fighting filled the noble's need of something to do, a way to exert himself. It was his substitute for work. His leisure time was spent chiefly in hunting, otherwise in games of chess, backgammon, and dice, in songs, dances, pageants, and other entertainments. Long winter evenings were occupied listening to the recital of **interminable**[11] verse epics. The sword offered the workless noble an activity with a purpose, one that could bring him honor, status, and, if he was lucky, gain. If no real conflict was at hand, he sought tournaments, the most exciting, expensive, ruinous, and delightful activity of the noble class, and paradoxically the most harmful to his true military function. Fighting in tournaments concentrated his skills and absorbed his interest in an increasingly formalized clash, leaving little thought for the tactics and strategy of real battle.

Originating in France and referred to by others as "French combat" *(conflictus Gallicus)*, tournaments started without rules or lists as an agreed-upon clash of opposing units. Though justified as training exercises, the impulse was the love of fighting. Becoming more regulated and mannered, they took two forms: jousts by

---

[7] fulcrum—pivotal support.

[8] **egregious**—offensive.

[9] burghers—townspeople.

[10] Froissart—French historian (1333?–c. 1400).

[11] **interminable**—endless.

individuals, and melees by groups of up to forty on a side, either *à plaisance* with blunted weapons or *à outrance* with no restraints, in which case participants might be severely wounded and not infrequently killed. Tournaments proliferated as the noble's primary occupation dwindled. Under the extended rule of monarchy, he had less need to protect his own fief,[12] while a class of professional ministers was gradually taking his place around the crown. The less he had to do, the more energy he spent in tournaments artificially re-enacting his role.

A tournament might last as long as a week and on great occasions two. Opening day was spent matching and seeding the players, followed by days set apart for jousts, for melees, for a rest day before the final tourney, all interspersed with feasting and parties. These occasions were the great sporting events of the time, attracting crowds of bourgeois spectators from rich merchants to common artisans, mountebanks,[13] food vendors, prostitutes, and pickpockets. About a hundred knights usually participated, each accompanied by two mounted squires, an armorer, and six servants in livery.[14] The knight had of course to equip himself with painted and gilded armor and crested helmet costing from 25 to 50 livres, with a war-horse costing from 25 to 100 livres in addition to his traveling palfrey,[15] and with banners and trappings and fine clothes. Though the expense could easily bankrupt him, he might also come away richer, for the loser in combat had to pay a ransom and the

winner was awarded his opponent's horse and armor, which he could sell back to him or to anyone. Gain was not recognized by chivalry, but it was present at tournaments.

Because of their extravagance, violence, and vainglory, tournaments were continually being denounced by popes and kings, from whom they drained money. In vain. When the Dominicans denounced them as a pagan circus, no one listened. When the formidable St. Bernard[16] thundered that anyone killed in a tournament would go to Hell, he spoke for once to deaf ears. Death in a tournament was officially considered the sin of suicide by the Church, besides jeopardizing family and tenantry without cause, but even threats of excommunication[17] had no effect. Although St. Louis condemned tournaments and Philip the Fair prohibited them during his wars, nothing could stop them permanently or dim the enthusiasm for them.

With brilliantly dressed spectators in the stands, flags and ribbons fluttering, the music of trumpets, the parade of combatants making their draped horses prance and champ on golden bridles, the glitter of harness and shields, the throwing of ladies' scarves and sleeves to their favorites, the bow of the heralds to the presiding prince

---

[12] fief—land held in exchange for military service by a medieval nobleman.

[13] mountebanks—quacks or frauds.

[14] livery—distinctive dress indicating that someone was in the service of a particular knight.

[15] palfrey—a saddle horse.

[16] St. Bernard—Bernard of Clairvaux (1090–1153), French abbot (page 350).

[17] excommunication—cutting off an individual from participation in the Christian church.

who proclaimed the rules, the cry of poursuivants[18] announcing their champions, the tournament was the peak of nobility's pride and delight in its own valor and beauty.

If tournaments were an acting-out of chivalry, courtly love was its dreamland. Courtly love was understood by its contemporaries to be love for its own sake, romantic love, true love, physical love, unassociated with property or family, and consequently focused on another man's wife, since only such an illicit liaison could have no other aim but love alone. (Love of a maiden was virtually ruled out since this would have raised dangerous problems, and besides, maidens of noble estate usually jumped from childhood to marriage with hardly an interval for romance.) The fact that courtly love idealized guilty love added one more complication to the maze through which medieval people threaded their lives. As formulated by chivalry, romance was pictured as extra-marital because love was considered irrelevant to marriage, was indeed discouraged in order not to get in the way of dynastic arrangements.

As its justification, courtly love was considered to ennoble a man, to improve him in every way. It would make him concerned to show an example of goodness,

> *As its justification, courtly love was considered to ennoble a man, to improve him in every way.*

to do his utmost to preserve honor, never letting dishonor touch himself or the lady he loved. On a lower scale, it would lead him to keep his teeth and nails clean, his clothes rich and well groomed, his conversation witty and amusing, his manners courteous to all, curbing arrogance and coarseness, never brawling in a lady's presence. Above all, it would make him more valiant, more preux; that was the basic premise. He would be inspired to greater prowess, would win more victories in tournaments, rise above himself in courage and daring, become, as Froissart said, "worth two men." Guided by this theory, woman's status improved, less for her own sake than as the inspirer of male glory, a higher function than being merely a sexual object, a breeder of children, or a conveyor of property.

The chivalric love affair moved from worship through declaration of passionate devotion, virtuous rejection by the lady, renewed wooing with oaths of eternal fealty, moans of approaching death from unsatisfied desire, heroic deeds of valor which won the lady's heart by prowess, consummation of the secret love, followed by endless adventures and subterfuges[19] to a tragic denouement.[20] . . .

"Melancholy, amorous and barbaric," these [romance] tales exalted adulterous love as the only true kind, while in the real

---

[18] poursuivants—followers or attendants.

[19] subterfuges—tricks.

[20] denouement—conclusion.

life of the same society adultery was a crime, not to mention a sin. If found out, it dishonored the lady and shamed the husband, a fellow knight. It was understood that he had the right to kill both unfaithful wife and lover.

Nothing fits in this canon. The gay, the elevating, the ennobling pursuit is founded upon sin and invites the dishonor it is supposed to avert. Courtly love was a greater tangle of irreconcilables even than usury.[21] It remained artificial, a literary convention, a fantasy (like modern pornography) more for purposes of discussion than for everyday practice.

The realities were more normal. As described by La Tour Landry, his amorous fellow knights were not overly concerned with loyalty and *courtoisie*. He tells how, when he used to ride abroad with his friends as a young man, they would beg ladies for their love and if this one did not accept they would try another, deceiving the ladies with fair words of blandishment[22] and swearing false oaths, "for in every place they would have their sport if they could." Many a gentlewoman was taken in by the "foul and great false oaths that false men use to swear to women." He tells how three ladies who were exchanging opinions of their lovers discovered that the senior Jean le Maingre, Sire de Boucicaut, was the favorite of each, he having made love to all, telling each he loved her best. When they taxed him with his falsity, he was in no way abashed, saying, "For at that time I spake with each of you, I loved her best that I spake with and thought truly the same."

* * *

. . . If the fiction of chivalry molded outward behavior to some extent, it did not, any more than other models that man has made for himself, transform human nature. Joinville's account of the crusaders at Damietta in 1249 shows the knights under St. Louis plunged in brutality, blasphemy, and debauchery. Teutonic knights in their annual forays against the unconverted natives of Lithuania conducted manhunts of the peasants for sport. Yet, if the code was but a veneer over violence, greed, and sensuality, it was nevertheless an ideal, as Christianity was an ideal, toward which man's reach, as usual, exceeded his grasp.

---

[21] usury—lending money at a very high rate of interest.

[22] blandishment—flattery.

QUESTIONS TO CONSIDER

1. What was the nature of the relationship between the Church and the knights?

2. What does Barbara Tuchman mean when she observes that "a knight's usual activities were as much at odds with Christian theory as a merchant's"?

3. What moral contradiction was the basis of courtly love?

4. What desirable social effects was courtly love supposed to produce?

Landscapes

What is a landscape? The Chinese name for such art, shan-shui, "mountain-water," conveys their taste for images of wild nature, with misty peaks and rushing streams. The Romans, who preferred the garden to the wilderness, painted realistic trees and flowers on the walls of their villas. These landscapes come from a variety of cultures and eras. As you examine them, reflect on these questions:

- *What attitudes toward nature do these landscapes suggest?*
- *What moods do they create?*
- *Do any of these landscapes seem to convey an idea of paradise? of hell?*

Herding Scene *(Africa)*
Created thousands of years ago when North Africa was not yet a desert, this rock art depicts a simple scene—women and children herd cattle outside circles symbolizing huts. ▶

▲

Hunting Scene (Egypt)
An Egyptian official and his family are shown hunting birds in the Nile marshes in this tomb painting.

Garden Scene (Rome)
This Roman wall painting uses aerial perspective—with details in the foreground depicted more sharply than those in the background—to heighten its realism. ▶

Abu'l Hasan
Squirrels in a Plane Tree *(India)*
Carefully observed studies of animals were a favorite subject of the painters of Mughal India.

Sesshu
Landscape *(Japan)*
The vigorous brushstrokes used by the Buddhist monk Sesshu to create his landscapes suggest calligraphy.

◀ **Li Cheng**
A Solitary Temple amid Clearing Peaks (China)
To show human beings and nature in harmony was the principal goal of Chinese landscape painting.

The Unicorn at the Fountain
(France/Flanders)
This tapestry is the second of a series of seven narrating the hunt of the unicorn and depicts the legendary beast surrounded by hunters beside a woodland fountain. ▶

▲

Albrecht Dürer
View of Arco *(Germany)*
Dürer's watercolors, like this one of an Italian hill
fortress painted in 1495, are the earliest examples in
European art of landscape for its own sake—not as
a detail of a larger work.

El Greco
View of Toledo *(Spain)*
Born in Crete, El Greco ("the Greek") settled in Spain,
where he created this stark portrait—his only true
landscape—of the austere spirit of his adopted city. ▶

▲

Théodore Rousseau
Under the Birches (France)
For 19th-century painters such as Rousseau, images of unspoiled landscapes like this one were cherished reminders of a long-lost pre-industrial world.

George Inness

The Lackawanna Valley (*United States*)

Ironically, this glimpse of serene rural America was commissioned by a railroad company to advertise its expanding service.

▲

Berthe Morisot
The Harbor at Lorient (France)
Her treatment of light and her evident brushwork mark Morisot as
an Impressionist.

▲

Paul Cézanne

Mont Sainte-Victoire with Viaduct (France)

Cézanne painted this landscape from a variety of perspectives during his career.

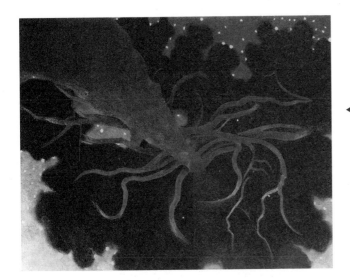

◀ **Georgia O'Keeffe**
The Lawrence Tree *(United States)*
Painted as though seen from below,
this image of a tree and a night sky
takes on a bizarre, abstract quality.

Max Ernst
The Eye of Silence *(Germany)*
The strange forms in this painting
by a Surrealist artist suggest the
landscape of a nightmare. ▶

Chapter 10

The Renaissance

Challenges to Tradition

The Art of Ruling

New Worlds

Experiments with Form

 The Gonzagas of Mantua, one of the noble Italian families whose patronage of the arts helped shape Renaissance culture, are shown here in a painting by Andrea Mantegna (1431–1506).

The Humanist Vision

PICO DELLA MIRANDOLA

In the 1300s, a revival of learning began based on the rediscovery of Greek and Roman civilization. This intellectual movement, called humanism, took shape in the cities of northern Italy and then spread throughout Europe, stimulating and shaping the culture of the 1400s and 1500s, a period referred to as the Renaissance ("Rebirth"). Humanism challenged medieval tradition with a new vision of the central importance and unlimited potential of human beings. The humanist vision is reflected in the Oration on the Dignity of Man *by the Italian humanist Pico della Mirandola (1463–1494).*

I have read in the records of the Arabians, reverend Fathers, that Abdala the Saracen, when questioned as to what on this stage of the world, as it were, could be seen most worthy of wonder, replied: "There is nothing to be seen more wonderful than man." In agreement with this opinion is the saying of Hermes Trismegistus: "A great miracle, Asclepius,[1] is man." But when I weighed the reason for these **maxims**,[2] the many grounds for the excellence of human nature reported by many men failed to satisfy me that man is the intermediary between creatures, the intimate of the gods, the king of the lower beings, by the acuteness of his senses, by the discernment of his reason, and by the light of his intelligence the interpreter of nature, the interval between fixed eternity and fleeting time, and (as the Persians say) the bond, nay,

rather, the marriage song of the world, on David's testimony[3] but little lower than the angels.

Admittedly great though these reasons be, they are not the principal grounds, that is, those which may rightfully claim for themselves the privilege of the highest admiration. For why should we not admire more the angels themselves and the blessed choirs of heaven? At last it seems to me I have come to understand why man is the most fortunate of creatures and consequently worthy of all admiration and what precisely is that rank which is his lot in the universal chain of Being—a rank to be envied not only by brutes but even by the

---

[1] Hermes Trismegistus . . . Asclepius—Hermes Trismegistus was the legendary author of certain works of philosophy and magic; Asclepius was a legendary Greek physician.

[2] **maxims**—expressions of general truths.

[3] David's testimony—in Psalm 8 (page 21).

stars and by minds beyond this world. It is a matter past faith and a wondrous one. Why should it not be? For it is on this very account that man is rightly called and judged a great miracle and a wonderful creature indeed.

But hear, Fathers, exactly what this rank is and, as friendly **auditors**,[4] conformably to your kindness, do me this favor. God the Father, the supreme Architect, had already built this cosmic home we behold, the most sacred temple of His godhead, by the laws of His mysterious wisdom. The region above the heavens He had adorned with Intelligences, the heavenly spheres He had quickened with eternal souls, and the excrementary and filthy parts of the lower world He had filled with a multitude of animals of every kind. But, when the work was finished, the Craftsman kept wishing that there were someone to ponder the plan of so great a work, to love its beauty, and to wonder at its vastness. Therefore, when everything was done (as Moses and Timaeus[5] bear witness), He finally took thought concerning the creation of man. But there was not among His **archetypes**[6] that from which He could fashion a new offspring, nor was there in His treasure houses anything which He might bestow on His new son as an inheritance, nor was there in the seats of all the world a place where the latter might sit to contemplate the universe. All was now complete; all things had been assigned to the highest, the middle, and the lowest orders. But in its final creation it was not the part of the Father's power to fail as though

exhausted. It was not the part of His wisdom to waver in a needful matter through poverty of counsel. It was not the part of His kindly love that he who was to praise God's divine generosity in regard to others should be compelled to condemn it in regard to himself.

At last the best of artisans ordained that that creature to whom He had been able to give nothing proper to himself should have joint possession of whatever had been peculiar to each of the different kinds of being. He therefore took man as a creature of **indeterminate**[7] nature and, assigning him a place in the middle of the world, addressed him thus: "Neither a fixed abode nor a form that is thine alone nor any function peculiar to thyself have we given thee, Adam, to the end that according to thy longing and according to thy judgment thou mayest have and possess what abode, what form, and what functions thou thyself shalt desire. The nature of all other beings is limited and constrained within the bounds of laws prescribed by Us. Thou, constrained by no limits, in accordance with thine own free will, in whose hand We have placed thee, shalt ordain for thyself the limits of thy nature. We have set thee at the world's center that thou mayest from thence more easily observe whatever is in the world.

---

[4] **auditors**—listeners.

[5] Moses and Timaeus—two accounts of creation: the first is the biblical story in Genesis (attributed to Moses); the second is from the *Timaeus*, one of the dialogues of the Greek philosopher Plato.

[6] **archetypes**—models.

[7] **indeterminate**—not fixed.

We have made thee neither of heaven nor of earth, neither mortal nor immortal, so that with freedom of choice and with honor, as though the maker and molder of thyself, thou mayest fashion thyself in whatever shape thou shalt prefer. Thou shalt have the power to **degenerate**[8] into the lower forms of life, which are brutish. Thou shalt have the power, out of thy soul's judgment, to be reborn into the higher forms, which are divine."

O supreme generosity of God the Father, O highest and most marvelous felicity of man! To him it is granted to have whatever he chooses, to be whatever he wills. Beasts as soon as they are born (so says Lucilius) bring with them from their mother's womb all they will ever possess. Spiritual beings, either from the beginning or soon thereafter, become what they are to be for ever and ever. On man when he came into life the Father conferred the seeds of all kinds and the germs of every way of life. Whatever seeds each man cultivates will grow to maturity and bear in him their own fruit. If they be vegetative, he will be like a plant. If sensitive, he will become brutish. If rational, he will grow into a heavenly being. If intellectual, he will be an angel and the son of God. And if, happy in the lot of no created thing, he withdraws into the center of his own unity, his spirit, made one with God, in the solitary darkness of God, who is set above all things, shall surpass them all. Who would not admire this our **chameleon**?[9] Or who could more greatly admire aught else

whatever? It is man who Asclepius of Athens, arguing from his **mutability**[10] of character and from his self-transforming nature, on just grounds says was symbolized by Proteus[11] in the mysteries. Hence those **metamorphoses**[12] renowned among the Hebrews and the Pythagoreans.

---

[8] **degenerate**—decline in quality.

[9] **chameleon**—lizard that changes color to blend in with its environment.

[10] **mutability**—changeableness.

[11] Proteus—in Greek mythology, a sea god who could change his shape.

[12] **metamorphoses**—complete changes of appearance.

QUESTIONS TO CONSIDER

1. Why are human beings "the most fortunate of creatures"?

2. One of Pico della Mirandola's goals was to reconcile Greek philosophy and Christianity. How is this reflected in his *Oration*?

3. What is Pico's tone?

4. Do you agree with Pico that the changeableness of human nature is a good thing? Why or why not?

Reforming the Church

MARTIN LUTHER

The Renaissance belief in the ability of humans to control their own destiny was a challenge to the authority of the Church. A far more specific threat appeared when a German monk, Martin Luther (1483–1546), drew up a list of his criticisms of the Church and nailed them to the door of a church at Wittenburg in 1517, beginning a process that led to the Protestant Reformation. Observations by Luther were collected in the Table Talk, *a record of some of his notable sayings gathered from the journals of people who knew him.*

All the works of God are beyond human comprehension and description, so human reason cannot comprehend them; faith only grasps them without human power or aid. No mortal creature can comprehend God in his majesty, and therefore did he come before us in the simplest manner, and was made man, in sin, death, and weakness.

In all things, even in the least creatures, and in their parts, God's almighty power and wonderful works clearly shine. For what man, no matter how powerful, wise, and holy, can make out of one fig a fig-tree, or another fig? or, out of one cherry-stone, a cherry, or a cherry-tree? or what man can know how God creates and preserves all things, and makes them grow?

Because as the everlasting, merciful God, through his Word and Sacraments, talks and deals with us, all other creatures excluded, not of temporal things which pertain to this vanishing life, and which in the beginning he provided richly for us, but as to where we shall go when we depart from here, and gives unto us his Son for a Savior, delivering us from sin and death, and purchasing for us everlasting righteousness, life, and salvation, therefore it is most certain, that we do not die away like the beasts that have no understanding; but so many of us . . . shall through him be raised again to life everlasting at the last day, and the ungodly to everlasting destruction.

As lately I lay very sick, so sick that I thought I should have left this world, I had many thoughts and musings in my weakness. Ah! thought I, what may eternity be? What joys may it have? However, I know for certain, that this eternity is ours; through Christ it is given and prepared for us, if we can but believe.

He that goes from the gospel to the law,[1] thinking to be saved by good works,[2] falls as uneasily as he who falls from the true service of God to idolatry; for, without Christ, all is idolatry and fictitious imaginings of God, whether of the Turkish Quran,[3] of the pope's decrees, or Moses' laws; if a man think thereby to be justified and saved before God, he is undone.

The gospel preaches nothing of the merit of works; he that says the gospel requires works for salvation, I say, flat and plain, is a liar.

Nothing that is properly good proceeds out of the works of the law, unless grace be present; for what we are forced to do, goes not from the heart, nor is acceptable.

A Capuchin says: wear a grey coat and a hood, a rope round thy body, and sandals on thy feet. A Cordelier[4] says: put on a black hood; an ordinary papist[5] says: do this or that work, hear mass, pray, fast, give alms, etc. But a true Christian says: I am justified and saved only by faith in Christ, without any works or merits of my own; compare these together, and judge which is the true righteousness.

I have often been resolved to live uprightly, and to lead a true godly life, and to set everything aside that would hinder this, but it was far from being put in execution; even as it was with Peter,[6] when he swore he would lay down his life for Christ.

I will not lie or **dissemble**[7] before my God, but will freely confess, I am not able to effect that good which I intend, but await the happy hour when God shall be pleased to meet me with his grace.

A Christian's worshiping is not the external, hypocritical mask that our friars wear, when they chastise their bodies, torment and make themselves faint, with **ostentatious**[8] fasting, watching, singing, wearing hair shirts, scourging themselves, etc. Such worshiping God does not desire.

Great is the strength of the divine Word. In the epistle to the Hebrews,[9] it is called "a two-edged sword." But we have neglected and scorned the pure and clear Word, and have drunk not of the fresh and

---

[1] the law—the regulations of the Church.

[2] good works—religious activities such as pilgrimages that were promoted by the Church as ways to gain salvation.

[3] Quran—the sacred text of Islam (page 296), which Luther associates with the Ottoman Turks, the Islamic people most familiar to Europeans.

[4] Capuchin . . . Cordelier—members of branches of the Franciscan religious order.

[5] papist—member of the Roman Catholic Church.

[6] Peter—follower of Jesus who after his master's arrest repeatedly denied knowing him.

[7] **dissemble**—misrepresent.

[8] **ostentatious**—showy.

[9] epistle to the Hebrews—one of the letters of Paul from the New Testament.

cool spring; we are gone from the clear fountain to the foul puddle, and drunk its filthy water; that is, we have **sedulously**[10] read old writers and teachers, who went about with speculative[11] reasonings, like the monks and friars.

No greater mischief can happen to a Christian people than to have God's word taken from them, or falsified, so that they no longer have it pure and clear. God grant that we and our descendants not witness such a calamity.

The ungodly papists prefer the authority of the church far above God's Word; a blasphemy abominable and not to be endured; void of all shame and piety, they spit in God's face. Truly, God's patience is exceeding great, in that they are not destroyed; but so it always has been.

How does it happen that the popes pretend that they form the Church, when, all the while, they are bitter enemies of the Church, and have no knowledge, certainly no comprehension, of the holy gospel? Pope, cardinals, bishops, not a soul of them has read the Bible; it is a book unknown to them. They are a pack of guzzling, gluttonous wretches, rich, wallowing in wealth and laziness, resting secure in their power, and never, for a moment, thinking of accomplishing God's will.

Kings and princes coin money only out of metals, but the pope coins money out of everything—indulgences, ceremonies, dispensations, pardons;[12] all fish come to

his net. Only baptism escapes him, for children came into the world without clothes to be stolen, or teeth to be drawn.

A gentleman being at the point of death, a monk from the next convent came to see what he could pick up, and said to the gentleman: Sir, will you give so and so to our monastery? The dying man unable to speak, replied by a nod of the head: whereupon the monk, turning to the gentleman's son, said: You see, your father makes us this bequest. The son said to the father: Sir, is it your pleasure that I kick this monk down the stairs? The dying man nodded as before, and the son immediately drove the monk out of doors.

The papists took the **invocation**[13] of saints from the pagans, who divided God into numberless images and idols, and ordained to each its particular office and work. . . .

The invocation of saints is a most abominable blindness and heresy; yet the papists will not give it up. The pope's greatest profit arises from the dead; for the calling on dead saints brings him infinite sums of money and riches, far more than he gets from the living. . . .

---

[10] **sedulously**—persistently.

[11] speculative—theoretical.

[12] indulgences . . . pardons—various types of spiritual privileges or religious rituals offered by the Church for fees.

[13] **invocation**—calling on for aid.

In Popedom they make priests, not to preach and teach God's Word, but only to celebrate mass, and to roam about with the sacrament. For, when a bishop **ordains**[14] a man, he says: Take the power to celebrate mass, and to offer it for the living and the dead. But we ordain priests according to the command of Christ and St. Paul, namely, to preach the pure gospel and God's Word. The papists in their ordinations make no mention of preaching and teaching God's Word, therefore their consecrating and ordaining is false and wrong, for all worshiping which is not ordained of God, or erected by God's Word and command, is worthless, yea, mere idolatry.

The pope and his crew can in no way endure the idea of reformation; the mere word creates more alarm at Rome than thunderbolts from heaven or the day of judgment. A cardinal said the other day: Let them eat, and drink, and do what they will; but as to reforming us, we think that is a vain idea; we will not endure it. Neither will we Protestants be satisfied, though they administer the sacrament in both kinds, and permit priests to marry;[15] we will also have the doctrine of the faith pure and unfalsified, and the righteousness that justifies and saves before God, and which expels and drives away all idolatry and false-worshiping; with these gone and banished, the foundation on which Popedom is built also falls.

The chief cause that I fell out with the pope was this: the pope boasted that he was the head of the church, and condemned all that would not be under his power and authority; for he said, although Christ is the head of the church, yet, notwithstanding, there must be a corporal head of the church upon earth. With this I could have been content, had he but taught the gospel pure and clear, and not introduced human inventions and lies in its stead. Further, he took upon him power, rule, and authority over the Christian church, and over the Holy Scriptures, the Word of God; no man must presume to **expound**[16] the Scriptures, but only he, and according to his ridiculous conceits; this was not to be endured. They who, against God's word, boast of the church's authority, are mere idiots.

---

[14] **ordains**—confers priesthood on.

[15] administer the sacraments . . . and permit priests to marry—Protestants insisted that all Christians, not just priests, should be able to drink the Communion wine and that priests should be allowed to marry.

[16] **expound**—explain.

QUESTIONS TO CONSIDER

1. What can you infer about Luther's character and personality from these writings?

2. What were Luther's views on faith versus good works?

3. Why did Luther attack the papacy and clergy?

4. In your opinion, which was Luther's more serious challenge to medieval tradition—his opposition to good works or his attacks on the papacy? Explain.

from

The Prince

NICCOLÒ MACHIAVELLI

What qualities do successful rulers have? How do they keep or lose power? Are honesty and generosity advantages or disadvantages? Is it better to be feared or loved? Renaissance thinkers were intrigued by such questions. The most famous—or notorious—Renaissance study of the art of ruling was The Prince *by Niccolò Machiavelli (1469–1527).*

It remains now to consider the manner in which a prince should conduct himself toward his subjects and his friends. I know that many writers have treated this topic, so that I am somewhat hesitant in taking it up in my turn lest I appear **presumptuous**,[1] especially because in what I shall have to say, I shall depart from rules which other writers have laid down. Since it is my intention to write something which may be of real utility to anyone who can comprehend it, it has appeared to me more urgent to penetrate to the effective reality of these matters than to rest content with mere constructions of the imagination. For many writers have constructed imaginary republics and principalities which have never been seen nor known actually to exist. But so wide is the separation between the way men actually live and the way that they ought to live, that anyone who turns his attention from what is actually done to what ought to be done, studies his own ruin rather than his preservation. Any man who wishes to make a profession of goodness in every department of conduct, must inevitably come to ruin among so many men who are not good. Therefore a ruler who wishes to preserve his power must learn to be able not to be good, and to use this knowledge or not use it as necessity may dictate.

Setting aside therefore all vain imaginings about what a prince ought to be and centering our discussion on things as they really are, I submit that all men, and especially princes by their high position, when

---

[1] **presumptuous**—bold.

discussion of their merit arises, are measured according to certain qualities the possession or reputation for which earns them either praise or censure. Thus it is that one is thought liberal, another miserly—using this word in the Tuscan sense, because "avaro" in our language still indicates one who wants to acquire possessions by plunder, while we call one "misero"[2] who abstains too much from the use of what he possesses—another is held to be a benefactor, another a plunderer; one cruel, another compassionate; one faithless to his word, another faithful; one effeminate and lacking in spirit, another full of spirit to the point of rashness; one man is considered courteous, another haughty; one **lascivious**,[3] another chaste; one, of single intention, another crafty and conniving; one **obstinate**,[4] another amenable; one grave, another light-hearted; one religious, another unbelieving and so forth. Everyone would of course hold that it would be a most **laudable**[5] thing in a prince to be possessed of all the favorable qualities enumerated above, but all of these cannot be possessed at once, nor observed in their entirety, for the conditions of human life do not permit this. A prince must therefore be prudent enough to know how to avoid any **derogatory**[6] reputation for those qualities which might lead him to lose his power, and to be on his guard against those qualities which do carry this danger, in so far as he finds it possible. And if he cannot avoid them, he can tolerate them in himself without too much concern for consequences.

Even more, however, he must not draw back from incurring a reputation for those vices without which his position cannot be maintained without difficulty; the reason is that, when the entire matter is considered carefully, certain qualities which appear to be virtues, when practiced will lead to his ruin; while the pursuit of others, which seem to be vices, will insure his own security and the stability of his position.

I shall begin then with the first of the above mentioned qualities, agreeing that it would indeed be most advantageous to be considered liberal; nevertheless, liberality, if exercised in such a way that you come to be held a free-spending man, may do you harm. This quality, if exercised as a virtue—as it ought to be—will not be obvious, and hence will not prevent your being accused of its contrary. If one wishes to keep up a name for liberality among men, one must not omit any kind of lavish display; however, if he indulges in such display, it will consume all his resources. In the end, he will be forced to place **exorbitant**[7] burdens upon his people, to resort to excessive taxes and have recourse to such other expedients as may increase revenue in order to maintain this reputation. This mode of conduct

---

[2] Tuscan sense . . . "misero"—Machiavelli is using the distinction between two words in the Tuscan dialect of Italian to differentiate between a greedy person and a miser.

[3] **lascivious**—lustful.

[4] **obstinate**—stubborn.

[5] **laudable**—praiseworthy.

[6] **derogatory**—bringing discredit.

[7] **exorbitant**—excessive.

will soon begin to earn him the hatred of his subjects, and general contempt when he reaches the point of impoverishment. In addition, his liberality will have benefited few, while offending many. As a consequence, he will be vulnerable at many points and the first real peril will prove a disaster. And, to fill up the measure of this irony, if the prince, realizing these dangers, tries to withdraw from such a position, he will immediately be marked down as a miser.

Since a prince cannot exercise this virtue of liberality without danger to himself, except by **ostentation**,[8] he ought not to be concerned about being thought a miser. With the passage of time, he will gradually acquire a reputation for liberality, when it is seen that by cautious expenditure his revenues always are sufficient to his needs, that he is always prepared to repel anyone who attacks him, and that he can carry through his undertakings without imposing exorbitant burdens on his people. All those from whom he takes nothing will deem him liberal, and they will be numerous; all those to whom he gives nothing will think him miserly, but they will be few. . . .

Coming down now to the other qualities mentioned above, I submit that every prince ought to want to be considered compassionate rather than cruel. At the same time, he must avoid an ill-advised use of compassion. Cesare Borgia[9] was thought cruel; nevertheless, that cruelty of his had restored the Romagna,[10] united it, brought it peace and reduced it to obedience. If one considers the matter carefully, it will be seen that he was in fact much more compassionate than were the Florentines who, in order to avoid being thought cruel, permitted Pistoia to be destroyed.[11] Therefore, a prince ought not to permit a reputation for cruelty to disturb him, if it is the price of keeping his subjects united and obedient. By making examples of a few, he will prove in the end more compassionate than those who, through excess of compassion, permit disorders to arise, which prove in turn the source of murders and violence. For the latter outrages inevitably arouse the entire community, while those few executions which the prince may impose harm only certain persons in particular. . . .

From this circumstance, an argument arises: whether it is better to be loved rather than feared, or the opposite. The answer is that one would like to be both one and the other; but since they are difficult to combine, it is more secure to be feared than loved, when one of the two must be surrendered. For it may be said of men in general, that they are ingrates,[12] fickle, deceivers, evaders of danger, desirous of gain. So long as you are doing good for

---

[8] **ostentation**—showiness, display.

[9] Cesare Borgia—Italian politician and military leader (1476–1507); the model for a ruler in *The Prince*.

[10] Romagna—a former province of the Papal States, a large district in Italy ruled by the popes.

[11] Florentines . . . Pistoia to be destroyed—Florence failed to suppress factionalism in Pistoia before it led to bloody riots.

[12] ingrates—ungrateful people.

any of them they are all yours, offering you their blood, goods, lives, children, when any real necessity for doing so is remote, but turning away when such need draws near, as I have remarked. The prince who relies wholly on their words, and takes no other precautions, will come to ruin. Friendships gained at a price and not founded on greatness and nobility of soul, are indeed purchased but never possessed; and in times of need cannot be drawn upon. Men are less concerned about giving offense to one who goes about making himself loved than to one who makes himself feared; love is a bond of obligation which men—sad creatures that they are—break on the first occasion touching their own interests; but fear binds by a threat of punishment which never relaxes. Still, the prince should take care to make himself feared in due measure; though he merits not love, he should avoid being hated. His position is strongest when he is feared but not hated. And he will establish such a relationship if he does not despoil[13] his subjects of their goods and keeps his hands off their women. Even when it is necessary for him to proceed against the blood-kin of anyone, he must make it clear that he does so only for manifest cause and with **commensurate**[14] justification. Above all, let him keep his hands off others' property, because men forget the death of their own fathers more readily than the loss of their patrimonies.[15] Moreover, pretexts for seizing another's property are never lacking; and one who begins to live by plunder, never fails to find a reason for seizing another's property. Justifications for taking a life, however, present themselves more rarely and are much less convincing. . . .

Everyone understands well enough how praiseworthy it is in a prince to keep his word, to live with integrity and not by **guile**.[16] Nevertheless, the experience of our times teaches us that those princes have achieved great things who have looked upon the keeping of one's word as a matter of little moment and have understood how, by their guile, to twist men's minds; and in the end have surpassed those who have rested their power upon faithfulness.

You ought to understand therefore that there are two ways of fighting, the one by the laws, the other with force. The first is proper to men, the second to beasts; but since in many instances the first is not enough, it is necessary to have recourse to the second. A prince, consequently, must understand how to use the manner proper to the beast as well as that proper to man. This truth has been taught to princes by the writers of ancient times covertly. Thus they described how Achilles and many other of those princes of ancient times were sent to be brought up by the centaur Chiron[17] and educated under his tutelage. To have as teacher a creature half man and

---

[13] despoil—rob.

[14] **commensurate**—corresponding in importance.

[15] patrimonies—inheritances.

[16] **guile**—trickery.

[17] Chiron—in Greek mythology, a creature half man and half horse who taught the hero Achilles and others.

half beast means nothing else than that a prince must know how to use the one nature and the other, and that without the one, the other cannot endure.

Since, then, a prince must of necessity know how to use the bestial nature, he should take as his models from among beasts the fox and the lion; for the lion does not defend himself from traps, and the fox does not defend himself from the wolves. One must therefore be a fox to scent out the traps and a lion to ward off the wolves. Those who act simply the lion do not understand the implications of their own actions. A prudent prince cannot—nor ought he—observe faith when such observance may turn against himself, and when the reasons which led him to pledge it have lost their force. If all men were good, this **precept**[18] would not be valid;

but since they are sorry creatures and would not keep faith with you, no obligation binds you to observe it toward them.

---

[18] **precept**—rule of conduct.

QUESTIONS TO CONSIDER

1. How does Niccolò Machiavelli distinguish his study of the art of ruling from that of earlier writers?

2. Machiavelli observes that anyone who attempts to be entirely good among people who are not good "must inevitably come to ruin." Do you agree or disagree? Explain.

3. Machiavelli says that "men are less concerned about giving offense to one who goes about making himself loved than to one who makes himself feared.... [F]ear binds by a threat of punishment which never relaxes." Is this good advice for someone in authority? Why or why not?

4. What opinions does Machiavelli have of the ruled, that is, human beings in general?

The Sultan's Court

OGIER GHISELIN DE BUSBECQ

One of the most successful rulers of the Renaissance period was the Turkish sultan Suleiman I (1494–1566), under whom the Ottoman empire reached its height. This account of the Ottoman regime was written by Ogier Ghiselin de Busbecq (1522–1590), a Flemish nobleman who served as Austrian ambassador to Suleiman's court.

The Sultan's hall was crowded with people, among whom were several officers of high rank. Besides these there were all the troopers of the Imperial guard, and a large force of Janissaries,[1] but there was not in all that great assembly a single man who owed his position to anything save his valor and his merit. No distinction is attached to birth among the Turks; the respect to be paid to a man is measured by the position he holds in the public service. There is no fighting for precedence; a man's place is marked out by the duties he discharges. . . . It is by merit that men rise in the service, a system which ensures that posts should only be assigned to the competent. . . . Those who receive the highest offices from the Sultan are for the most part the sons of shepherds or herdsmen, and so far from being ashamed of their parentage, they actually glory in it, and consider it a matter of

boasting that they owe nothing to the accident of birth; for they do not believe that high qualities are either natural or hereditary, nor do they think that they can be handed down from father to son, but that they are partly the gift of God, and partly the result of good training, great industry, and unwearied zeal. . . . Among the Turks, therefore, honors, high posts, and judgeships are the rewards of great ability and good service. . . .

Suleiman had a son by a concubine[2] who came from the Crimea. . . . His name was Mustafa, and at the time of which I am speaking he was young, vigorous, and of high repute as a soldier. But Suleiman had also several other children, by a Russian woman. . . . To the latter he was so much

---

[1] Janissaries—Ottoman troops that lived by a strict code that included absolute obedience and celibacy.

[2] concubine—a secondary wife.

attached that he placed her in the position of wife, and assigned her a dowry.[3] . . .

Mustafa's high qualities and matured years marked him out, to the soldiers who loved, and the people who supported him, as the successor of his father, who was now in the decline of life. On the other hand, his step-mother, by throwing the claim of a lawful wife onto the balance, was doing her utmost to counterbalance his personal merits and his rights as eldest son, with a view to obtaining the throne for her own children. In this intrigue, she received the advice and assistance of Rustem,[4] whose fortunes were inseparably linked with hers by his marriage with a daughter she had had by Suleiman. . . .

Inasmuch as Rustem was chief Vizier, he had no difficulty in influencing his master's mind. The Turks, accordingly, are convinced that it was by the **calumnies**[5] of Rustem and the spells of Roxelana, who was in ill repute as a practitioner of sorcery, that the Sultan was so estranged from his son as to entertain the design of getting rid of him. A few believe that Mustafa, being aware of the plans, determined to anticipate them, and thus engaged in designs against his father's throne and person. The sons of Turkish Sultans are in the most wretched position in the world, for, as soon as one of them succeeds his father, the rest are doomed to certain death. The Turk can endure no rival to the throne, and, indeed, the conduct of the Janissaries renders it impossible for the new Sultan to spare his brothers; for if one of them survives, the Janissaries are forever asking generous favors. If these are refused, the cry is heard, "Long live the brother!" "God preserve the brother!"—a tolerably broad hint that they intend to place him on the throne. So that the Turkish Sultans are compelled to celebrate their succession by staining their hands with the blood of their nearest relatives. . . .

Being at war with Shah Tahmasp, Shah of the Persians, [Suleiman] had sent Rustem against him as a commander-in-chief of his armies. Just as he was about to enter Persian territory, Rustem suddenly halted, and hurried off **dispatches**[6] to Suleiman, informing him that affairs were in a very critical state; that treason was **rife**;[7] that the soldiers had been tampered with, and cared for no one but Mustafa; . . . and he must come at once if he wished to preserve his throne. Suleiman was seriously alarmed by these dispatches. He immediately hurried to the army, sent a letter to summon Mustafa to his presence, inviting him to clear himself of those crimes of which he was suspected. . . .

There was great uneasiness among the soldiers, when Mustafa arrived. He was brought to his father's tent, and there everything **betokened**[8] peace. But there were in the tent certain mutes[9]—a favorite kind of servant among the Turks—strong

---

[3] dowry—gift of property from a man to a woman on marriage.

[4] Rustem—Rustem was Suleiman's chief Vizier, or prime minister.

[5] **calumnies**—false statements intended to injure someone's reputation.

[6] **dispatches**—written messages sent in haste.

[7] **rife**—widespread.

[8] **betokened**—gave evidence of.

[9] mutes—persons chosen as servants because they cannot speak.

and sturdy fellows, who had been appointed as his executioners. As soon as he entered the inner tent, they threw themselves upon him, and endeavored to put the fatal noose around his neck. Mustafa, being a man of considerable strength, made a stout defense and fought—not only for his life, but also for the throne; there being no doubt that if he escaped from his executioners and threw himself among the Janissaries, the news of this outrage on their beloved prince would cause such pity and indignation, that they would not only protect him, but also proclaim him Sultan. Suleiman felt how critical the matter was, being only separated by the linen hangings of his tent from the stage on which this tragedy was being enacted. When he found that there was an unexpected delay in the execution of his scheme, he thrust out his head from the chamber of his tent, and glared on the mutes with fierce and threatening eyes; at the same time, with signs full of hideous meaning, he sternly **rebuked**[10] their slackness. Hereon the mutes, gaining fresh strength from the terror he inspired, threw Mustafa down, got the bowstring round his neck, and strangled him. Shortly afterwards they laid his body on a rug in front of the tent, that the Janissaries might see the man they had desired as their Sultan. . . .

Meanwhile, Roxelana, not content with removing Mustafa from her path, was compassing the death of the only son he had left, who was still a child; for she did not consider that she and her children were free from danger, so long as his offspring survived. Some pretext, however, she thought

necessary, in order to furnish a reason for the murder, but this was not hard to find. Information was brought to Suleiman that, whenever his grandson appeared in public, the boys of Ghemlik[11]—where he was being educated—shouted out, "God save the Prince, and may he long survive his father"; and that the meaning of these cries was to point him out as his grandsire's future successor, and his father's avenger. Moreover, he was bidden to remember that the Janissaries would be sure to support the son of Mustafa, so that the father's death had in no way secured the peace of the throne and realm. . . .

Suleiman was easily convinced by these arguments to sign the death-warrant of his grandson. He commissioned Ibrahim Pasha to go to the Ghemlik with all speed, and put the innocent child to death.

---

[10] **rebuked**—expressed sharp disapproval.

[11] Ghemlik—a town in northwest Turkey.

QUESTIONS TO CONSIDER

1. Why did officials of the Ottoman court often boast of their humble birth?

2. How did the way in which officials of the Ottoman government advanced in position differ from the way in which sons of the sultan succeeded to the throne?

3. Who seemed to have had the most power in Turkey at this time—the sultan, his family, his courtiers, or the Janissaries?

The Americas

The Renaissance was a period of exploration. Impelled by curiosity, greed, desire for adventure, and missionary zeal, Europeans ventured across the Atlantic to "that other world which has been discovered in our century," as the French essayist Michel de Montaigne (1533–1592) describes the Americas. In his essay "On Cannibals," Montaigne gives an account of the simple culture of the Indians of Brazil. A sharply contrasting glimpse of the highly sophisticated Aztec civilization comes from the eyewitness narrative of the Spanish conquest of Mexico by Bernal Díaz del Castillo (c. 1492–1581). Díaz describes the palace of the Aztec ruler Montezuma, or Moctezuma (1470–1520).

from *On Cannibals*
Michel de Montaigne

I had with me for a long time a man who had lived for ten or twelve years in that other world which has been discovered in our century, in the place where Villegaignon landed, and which he called Antarctic France.[1] This discovery of a boundless country seems worthy of consideration. . . .

This man I had was a simple, crude fellow—a character fit to bear true witness; for clever people observe more things and more curiously, but they interpret them; and to lend weight and conviction to their interpretation, they cannot help altering history a little. . . . Besides this, he at various times brought sailors and merchants, whom he had known on that trip, to see

me. So I content myself with his information, without inquiring what the cosmographers[2] say about it. . . .

Now, to return to my subject, I think there is nothing barbarous and savage in that nation, from what I have been told, except that each man calls barbarism whatever is not his own practice; for indeed it seems we have no other test of truth and reason than the example and pattern of the opinions and customs of the country we live in. *There* is always the perfect religion, the perfect government, the perfect and accomplished manners in all things. Those people are wild, just as we call wild the

---

[1] Villegaignon . . . Antarctic France—In the 1500s, French adventurer Nicholas Durand de Villegaignon founded a colony in Brazil. *Antarctic* here simply means "south."

[2] cosmographers—geographers, mapmakers.

fruits that Nature has produced by herself and in her normal course; whereas really it is those that we have changed artificially and led astray from the common order, that we should rather call wild. The former retain alive and vigorous their genuine, their most useful and natural, virtues and properties, which we have **debased**[3] in the latter in adapting them to gratify our corrupted taste. . . .

These nations, then, seem to me barbarous in this sense, that they have been fashioned very little by the human mind, and are still very close to their original naturalness. The laws of nature still rule them, very little corrupted by ours; and they are in such a state of purity that I am sometimes vexed that they were unknown earlier, in the days when there were men able to judge them better than we. . . .

Their buildings are very long, with a capacity of two or three hundred souls; they are covered with the bark of great trees, the strips reaching to the ground at one end and supporting and leaning on one another at the top, in the manner of some of our barns, whose covering hangs down to the ground and acts as a side. They have wood so hard that they cut with it and make of it their swords and grills to cook their food. Their beds are of a cotton weave, hung from the roof like those in our ships, each man having his own; for the wives sleep apart from their husbands.

They get up with the sun, and eat immediately upon rising, to last them through the day; for they take no other meal than that one. . . . Their drink is made of some root, and is of the color of our claret wines. They drink it only lukewarm. . . . In place of bread they use a certain white substance like preserved coriander.[4] I have tried it; it tastes sweet and a little flat.

The whole day is spent in dancing. The younger men go to hunt animals with bows. Some of the women busy themselves meanwhile with warming their drink, which is their chief duty. Some one of the old men, in the morning before they begin to eat, preaches to the whole barnful in common, walking from one end to the other, and repeating one single sentence several times until he has completed the circuit (for the buildings are fully a hundred paces long). He recommends to them only two things: valor against the enemy and love for their wives. . . .

They have some sort of priests and prophets, but they rarely appear before the people, having their home in the mountains. On their arrival there is a great feast and solemn assembly of several villages—each barn, as I have described it, makes up a village, and they are about one French league[5] from each other. The prophet speaks to them in public, exhorting them to virtue and their duty; but their whole ethical science contains only these two articles: resoluteness[6] in war and affection for their wives. . . .

---

[3] **debased**—lowered in quality.

[4] coriander—an herb of the parsley family. Both its fruit and leafy shoots are used for food.

[5] league—three miles.

[6] resoluteness—determination.

They have their wars with the nations beyond the mountains, further inland, to which they go quite naked, with no other arms than bows or wooden swords ending in a sharp point, in the manner of the tongues of our boar spears. It is astonishing what firmness they show in their combats, which never end but in slaughter and bloodshed; for as to **routs**[7] and terror, they know nothing of either.

Each man brings back as his trophy the head of the enemy he has killed, and sets it up at the entrance to his dwelling. After they have treated their prisoners well for a long time with all the hospitality they can think of, each man who has a prisoner calls a great assembly of his acquaintances. He ties a rope to one of the prisoner's arms, by the end of which he holds him, a few steps away, for fear of being hurt, and gives his dearest friend the other arm to hold in the same way; and these two, in the presence of the whole assembly, kill him with their swords. This done, they roast him and eat him in common and send some pieces to their absent friends. . . .

I am not sorry that we notice the barbarous horror of such acts, but I am heartily sorry that, judging their faults rightly, we should be so blind to our own. I think there is more barbarity in eating a man alive than in eating him dead; and in tearing by tortures and the rack[8] a body still full of feeling, in roasting a man bit by bit, in having him bitten and mangled by dogs and swine (as we have not only read

but seen within fresh memory, not among ancient enemies, but among neighbors and fellow citizens, and what is worse, on the **pretext**[9] of piety and religion), than in roasting and eating him after he is dead. . . .

So we may well call these people barbarians, in respect to the rules of reason, but not in respect to ourselves, who surpass them in every kind of barbarity. . . .

Three of these men, ignorant of the price they will pay some day, in loss of repose and happiness, for gaining knowledge of the corruptions of this side of the ocean; ignorant also of the fact that of this intercourse will come their ruin (which I suppose is already well advanced: poor wretches, to let themselves be tricked by the desire for new things, and to have left the serenity of their own sky to come and see ours!)— three of these men were at Rouen, at the time the late King Charles IX was there. The king talked to them for a long time; they were shown our ways, our splendor, the aspect of a fine city. After that, someone asked their opinion, and wanted to know what they had found most amazing. They mentioned three things, of which I have forgotten the third, and I am very sorry for it; but I still remember two of them. They said that in the first place they thought it very strange that so many grown men, bearded, strong, and armed, who were around the king (it is likely that they were talking about the Swiss of his guard) should

---

[7] **routs**—defeats in which an army retreats in disorder.

[8] **rack**—an instrument of torture which stretched a victim's body painfully.

[9] **pretext**—excuse.

submit to obey a child,[10] and that one of them was not chosen to command instead. Second (they have a way in their language of speaking of men as halves of one another), they had noticed that there were among us men full and gorged with all sorts of good things, and that their other halves were beggars at their doors, **emaciated**[11] with hunger and poverty; and they thought it strange that these needy halves could endure such an injustice, and did not take the others by the throat, or set fire to their houses.

I had a very long talk with one of them; but I had an interpreter who followed my meaning so badly, and who was so hindered by his stupidity in taking in my ideas, that I could get hardly any satisfaction from the man. When I asked him what profit he gained from his superior position among his people (for he was a captain, and our sailors called him king), he told me that it was to march foremost in war. How many men followed him? He pointed to a piece of ground, to signify as many as such a space could hold; it might have been four or five thousand men. Did all his authority expire with the war? He said that this much remained, that when he visited the villages dependent on him, they made paths for him through the underbrush by which he might pass quite comfortably.

All this is not too bad—but what's the use? They don't wear breeches.[12]

from *The Conquest of New Spain*
Bernal Díaz

Above 300 kinds of dishes were served up for Montezuma's dinner from his kitchen, underneath which were placed pans of porcelain filled with fire, to keep them warm. Three hundred dishes of various kinds were served up for him alone, and above 1,000 for the persons in waiting. He sometimes, but very seldom, accompanied by the chief officers of his household, ordered the dinner himself, and desired that the best dishes and various kinds of birds should be called over to him. . . .

About this time a celebrated cacique,[13] whom we called Tapia, was Montezuma's chief **steward**:[14] he kept an account of the whole of Montezuma's revenue, in large books of paper which the Mexicans call *Amatl*. A whole house was filled with such large books of accounts.

Montezuma had also two arsenals filled with arms of every description, of which many were ornamented with gold and precious stones. These arms consisted in shields of different sizes, sabers, and a species of broadsword, which is wielded with both hands, the edge furnished with flint stones, so extremely sharp that they cut much

---

[10] child—Charles IX became king at the age of ten.

[11] **emaciated**—abnormally thin.

[12] breeches—trousers.

[13] cacique—in Mexico, a chief.

[14] **steward**—manager of a household.

better than our Spanish swords; further, lances of greater length than ours, with spikes at their end, full one fathom[15] in length, likewise furnished with several sharp flint stones. The spikes are so very sharp and hard that they will pierce the strongest shield, and cut like a razor; so that the Mexicans even shave themselves with these stones. . . .

I will now, however, turn to another subject, and rather acquaint my readers with the skillful arts practiced among the Mexicans: among which I will first mention the sculptors, and the gold and silversmiths, who were clever in working and smelting gold, and would have astonished the most celebrated of our Spanish goldsmiths. . . .

The powerful Montezuma had also a number of dancers and clowns: some danced on stilts, tumbled, and performed a variety of other antics for the monarch's entertainment: a whole quarter of the city was inhabited by these performers, and their only occupation consisted in such like performances. Lastly, Montezuma had in his service great numbers of stonecutters, masons, and carpenters, who were solely employed in the royal palaces. Above all, I must not forget to mention here his gardens for the culture of flowers, trees, and vegetables, of which there were various kinds. In these gardens were also numerous baths, wells, basins, and ponds full of **limpid**[16] water, which regularly ebbed and flowed. All this was enlivened by endless varieties of small birds, which sang among the trees. Also the plantations of medical plants and vegetables are well worthy of our notice: these were kept in proper order by a large body of gardeners. All the baths, wells, ponds, and buildings were substantially constructed of stonework, as also the theaters where the singers and dancers performed. There were upon the whole so many remarkable things for my observation in these gardens and throughout the whole town, that I can scarcely find words to express the astonishment I felt at the pomp and splendor of the Mexican monarch.

---

[15] one fathom—six feet.

[16] **limpid**—clear.

QUESTIONS TO CONSIDER

1. How would you define *barbarian?*

2. What is Michel de Montaigne's central point about culture?

3. What attitude does Montaigne take toward the culture of the Indians of Brazil?

4. What barbarism do the Brazilian Indians observe in France?

5. How does Díaz's purpose differ from Montaigne's purpose?

6. What do these two documents indicate about the variety of Native American cultures?

The Indies

Europeans were not the only ones who ventured to distant lands. In the early 1400s the emperor of China sent out seven enormous fleets under the command of a palace official, Zheng He (1371–1435). Not only did the ships sail around Southeast Asia, but they also went to places as far away as India, Arabia, and East Africa. This account is by Ma Huan, who sailed on three of Zheng He's voyages. Meanwhile, the Portuguese were exploring Africa's west coast. Vasco da Gama (c. 1469–1524) journeyed around the southern tip of Africa and through the Indian Ocean and dropped anchor at the Indian seaport of Calicut, ninety-one years after Zheng He's expedition reached there. Da Gama did not receive the welcome he had anticipated, according to the account from the log of a sailor who was on the voyage.

from *The Overall Survey of the Ocean's Shores*
Ma Huan

The Country of Manlajia[1]

From Zhan City[2] you go due south, and after traveling for eight days with a fair wind the ship comes to Longya strait,[3] after entering the strait you travel west; and you can reach this place in two days.

Formerly this place was not designated a "country"; and because the sea hereabouts was named "Five Islands," the place was in consequence named "Five Islands." There was no king of the country; and it was controlled only by a chief. This territory was subordinate to the jurisdiction of Xian Luo,[4] it paid an annual tribute of forty *liang* of gold; and if it were not paid, then Xian Luo would send men to attack it.

In the seventh year[5] of the Yongle period, the Emperor ordered the principal envoy, the grand eunuch[6] Zheng He, and others to assume command (of the treasure-ships), and to take the imperial edicts and to bestow upon this chief two silver seals, a hat, a belt and a robe. Zheng He set up a stone tablet and raised the place to a city; and it was subsequently called the "country of Manlajia." Thereafter Xian Luo did not dare to invade it.

---

[1] Manlajia—Malacca, a port on the west coast of the Malay Peninsula.

[2] Zhan City—a city in Vietnam.

[3] Longya strait—the Singapore Strait.

[4] Xian Luo—Thailand.

[5] seventh year—1409.

[6] eunuch—castrated male serving as a palace official.

The chief, having received the favor of being made king, conducted his wife and son, and went to the court at the capital[7] to return thanks and to present tribute of local products. The court also granted him a sea-going ship, so that he might return to his country and protect his land. . . .

Whenever the treasure-ships of the Central Country[8] arrived there, they at once erected a line of stockading, like a city-wall, and set up towers for the watchdrums at four gates; at night they had patrols of police carrying bells; inside, again, they erected a second stockade, like a small city-wall, within which they constructed warehouses and granaries; and all the money and provisions were stored in them. The ships which had gone to various countries returned to this place and assembled; they marshaled the foreign goods and loaded them in the ships; then waited till the south wind was perfectly favorable. In the middle decade of the fifth moon they put to sea and returned home.

Moreover, the king of the country made a selection of local products, conducted his wife and son, brought his chiefs, boarded a ship and followed the treasure-ships; and he attended at court and presented tribute. . . .

The Country of Sumendala[9]

The country of Sumendala is exactly the same country as that formerly named Xuwendana. This place is indeed the principal center of the Western Ocean. . . .

The king of the country of Sumendala had previously been raided by the "tattooed-face king" of Naguer; and in the fighting he received a poisoned arrow in the body and died. He had one son, who was young and unable to avenge his father's death. The king's wife made a vow before the people, saying "If there is anyone who can avenge my husband's death and recover his land, I am willing to marry him and to share with him the management of the country's affairs." When she finished speaking, a fisherman belonging to the place was fired with determination, and said "I can avenge him."

Thereupon he took command of an army and at once put the "tattooed-face king" to flight in battle; and later he avenged the former king's death when the "tattooed-face king" was killed. The people of the latter submitted and did not dare to carry on hostilities.

Whereupon the wife of the former king, failing not to carry out her previous vow, forthwith married the fisherman. He was styled "the old king," and in such things as the affairs of the royal household and the taxation of the land, everybody accepted the old king's decisions. In the seventh year of the Yongle period the old king, in fulfillment of his duty, brought tribute of local products, and was enriched by the kindness of Heaven;[10] and in the tenth year of the Yongle period he returned to his country.

---

[7] the capital—Nanjing.

[8] Central Country—China.

[9] Sumendala—place on the north coast of Sumatra.

[10] brought tribute . . . kindness of Heaven—He brought goods to Nanjing and was rewarded by the emperor.

When the son of the former king had grown up, he secretly plotted with the chiefs, murdered his adoptive father the fisherman, **usurped**[11] his position, and ruled the kingdom.

The fisherman had a son by his principal wife; his name was Suganla; he took command of his people, and they fled away, taking their families; and, after erecting a stockade in the neighboring mountains, from time to time he led his men in **incursions**[12] to take revenge on his father's enemies. In the thirteenth year of the Yongle period the principal envoy, the grand eunuch Zheng He, and others, commanding a large fleet of treasure-ships, arrived there; they dispatched soldiers who captured Suganla; and he went to the capital; and was publicly executed. The king's son was grateful for the imperial kindness, and constantly presented tribute of local products to the court. . . .

The Country of Guli[13]

This is the great country of the Western Ocean.[14] . . .

In the fifth year of the Yongle period the court ordered the principal envoy, the grand eunuch Zheng He, and others to deliver an imperial mandate to the king of this country and to bestow on him a patent[15] conferring a title of honor, and the grant of a silver seal, also to promote all the chiefs and award them hats and belts of various grades.

So Zheng He went there in command of a large fleet of treasure-ships, and he erected a tablet with a pavilion over it and set up a stone which said, "Though the journey from this country to the Central Country is more than a hundred thousand *li*,[16] yet the people are very similar, happy and prosperous, with identical customs. We have here engraved a stone, a perpetual declaration for ten thousand ages."

The king of the country is a Nankun[17] man; he is a firm believer in the Buddhist religion[18] and he venerates the elephant and the ox.

The population of the country includes five classes, the Muslim people, the Nankun people, the Zhedi people, the Geling people, and the Mugua people. . . .

The Country of Hulumosi[19]

Setting sail from the country of Guli, you go towards the north-west; and you can reach this place after traveling with a fair wind for twenty-five days. The capital lies beside the sea and up against the mountains.

Foreign ships from every place and foreign merchants traveling by land all come to this country to attend the market

---

[11] **usurped**—seized by force.

[12] **incursions**—attacks, raids.

[13] Guli—Calicut, a port on India's southwest coast.

[14] Western Ocean—Indian Ocean.

[15] patent—official document granting certain rights.

[16] *li*—approximately a third of a mile.

[17] Nankun—upper class.

[18] Buddhist religion—The king was actually a Hindu.

[19] Hulumosi—Hormuz, an island at the mouth of the Persian Gulf.

and trade; hence the people of the country are all rich. . . .

The king of this country, too, took a ship and loaded it with lions, *qilin*,[20] horses, pearls, precious stones, and other things, also a memorial to the throne written on a golden leaf, and he sent his chiefs and other men, who accompanied the treasure-ships dispatched by the Emperor, which were returning from the Western Ocean; and they went to the capital and presented tribute.

from *A Journal of the First Voyage of Vasco da Gama*

On Sunday [May 20, 1498] we found ourselves close to some mountains, and when we were near enough for the pilot to recognize them he told us that they were above Calicut, and that this was the country we desired to go to. . . .

On the following day [some] . . . boats came again alongside, when the captain-major sent one of the [crew] . . . to Calicut, and those with whom [the crew-member] went took him to two Moors[21] from Tunis, who could speak Castilian and Genoese.[22] The first greeting that he received was in these words: "May the Devil take thee! What brought you hither?" They asked what he sought so far away from home, and he told them that we came in search of Christians and of spices. . . .

On Tuesday [May 29] the captain got ready the following things to be sent to the king, viz., twelve pieces of *lambel*,[23] four scarlet hoods, six hats, four strings of coral,

a case containing six wash-hand basins, a case of sugar, two casks of oil, and two of honey. And as it is the custom not to send anything to the king without the knowledge of the Moor, his [agent], and of the [governor], the captain informed them of his intention. They came, and when they saw the present they laughed at it, saying that it was not a thing to offer to a king, that the poorest merchant from Mecca,[24] or any other part of India, gave more, and that if he wanted to make a present it should be in gold, as the king would not accept such things. When the captain heard this he grew sad, and said that he had brought no gold, that, moreover, he was no merchant, but an ambassador; and that if King Camolim would not accept these things he would send them back to the ships. Upon this they declared that they would not forward his presents, nor consent to his forwarding them himself. When they had gone there came certain Moorish merchants, and they all depreciated[25] the present which the captain desired to be sent to the king.

When the captain saw that they were determined not to forward his present, he said that as they would not allow him to send his present to the palace he would go to speak to the king, and would then return to the ships. They approved of this. . . .

---

[20] *qilin*—giraffe.

[21] Moors—Muslims from North Africa.

[22] Castilian . . . Genoese—Spanish and Italian.

[23] *lambel*—striped cloth.

[24] Mecca—city in Arabia.

[25] depreciated—belittled.

The king then said that [the captain] had told him that he came from a very rich kingdom, and yet had brought him nothing; that he had also told him that he was the bearer of a letter, which had not yet been delivered. To this the captain rejoined[26] that he had brought nothing, because the object of his voyage was merely to make discoveries, but that when other ships came he would then see what they brought him; as to the letter, it was true that he had brought one, and would deliver it immediately.

The king then asked what it was he had come to discover: stones or men? If he came to discover men, as he said, why had he brought nothing?

The king then asked what kind of merchandise was to be found in his country. The captain said there was much corn, cloth, iron, bronze, and many other things. . . . The king said . . . he might . . . land his merchandise, and sell it to the best advantage.

Five days afterwards [on June 7] the captain sent word to the king that, although he had landed his merchandise as he had been ordered, the Moors only came to depreciate it. The Moors no longer visited the house where the merchandise was, but they bore us no good will, and when one of us landed they spat on the ground, saying: "Portugal, Portugal." Indeed from the very first they had sought means to take and kill us.

. . . We were well aware that the Moors of the place, who were merchants from Mecca and elsewhere, and who knew us, could ill digest us. They had told the king that we were thieves, and that if once we navigated to his country, no more ships from Mecca, nor from Quambaye,[27] nor from Imgros,[28] nor from any other part, would visit him. They added that he would derive no profit from this [trade with Portugal] as we had nothing to give, but would rather take away, and that thus his country would be ruined. They moreover, offered rich bribes to the king to capture and kill us, so that we should not return to Portugal.

---

[26] rejoined—answered.

[27] Quambaye—city in western India.

[28] Imgros—possibly the Strait of Hormuz, which separates the Persian Gulf from the Arabian Sea.

QUESTIONS TO CONSIDER

1. What seems to have been the motive of Zheng He's voyages—discovery? trade? diplomacy?

2. Zheng He's treasure ships gathered so much that the Chinese had to build a stockade with police patrols to store the goods. Why might other countries have given tribute to China?

3. What did the Portuguese crew member mean when he said that "we came in search of Christians and of spices"?

4. Why did the merchants from Mecca say that the Portuguese goods were of little value and offer the king bribes to kill the Portuguese?

Renaissance Sonnets

Developed by the Italian poet Francesco Petrarca (1304–1374), or Petrarch, the sonnet is a verse form of fourteen lines. It is composed of an eight-line stanza, the octave, and a six-line stanza, the sestet. The octave states a theme or a problem that is developed or resolved in the sestet. Petrarch wrote a long sequence of sonnets exploring his feelings for his beloved, Laura. Very popular throughout Europe during the Renaissance, the sonnet form was altered by the English poet and dramatist William Shakespeare (1564–1616) into an arrangement of three four-line stanzas and a final couplet. The following sonnets are by Petrarch, the French poet Pierre de Ronsard (1524–1585), Shakespeare, the Spanish poet Francisco de Quevedo (1580–1645), and the Mexican poet Sor Juana Inès de la Cruz (1651–1695). Their themes—the briefness of life and the changes produced by age—were common in Renaissance poetry.

The Eyes I Spoke of Once

FRANCESCO PETRARCA

The eyes I spoke of once in words that burn,
the arms and hands and feet and lovely face
that took me from myself for such a space
of time and marked me out from other men;

the waving hair of unmixed gold that shone,
the smile that flashed with the angelic rays
that used to make this earth a paradise,
are now a little dust, all feeling gone;

and yet I live, grief and **disdain**[1] to me,
left where the light I cherished never shows,
in fragile bark[2] on the tempestuous[3] sea.

---

[1] **disdain**—scorn.

[2] bark—boat.

[3] tempestous—stormy.

Here let my loving song come to a close,
the vein of my accustomed art is dry,
and this, my lyre,[4] turned at last to tears.

Of His Old Lady's Old Age

PIERRE DE RONSARD

When you are very old, at evening
You'll sit and spin beside the fire, and say,
Humming my songs, "Ah well, ah well-a-day!
When I was young, of me did Ronsard sing."
None of your maidens that doth hear the thing,
Albeit[5] with her weary task foredone,[6]
But wakens at my name, and calls you one
Blest, to be held in long remembering.

I shall be low beneath the earth, and laid
On sleep, a phantom in the myrtle shade,
While you beside the fire, a grandame gray;
My love, your pride, remember and regret;
Ah, love me, love! We may be happy yet,
And gather roses, while 'tis called today.

Sonnet 73

WILLIAM SHAKESPEARE

That time of year thou mayst in me behold
When yellow leaves, or none, or few, do hang
Upon those boughs which shake against the cold,
Bare ruined choirs[7] where late the sweet birds sang.

---

[4] lyre—stringed instrument symbolizing poetic inspiration.

[5] albeit—although.

[6] foredone—exhausted.

[7] choirs—parts of a church where the singers are.

In me thou see'st the twilight of such day
As after sunset fadeth in the west,
Which by and by black night doth take away,
Death's second self, that seals up all in rest.
In me thou see'st the glowing of such fire,
That on the ashes of his youth doth lie
As the deathbed whereon it must expire,
Consumed with that which it was nourished by.
This thou perceivest, which makes thy love more strong.
To love that well which thou must leave ere long.

Life's Brevity

FRANCISCO DE QUEVEDO

Ah, what of life! Does no one answer me?
Ye days of yore,[8] that I have lived, draw near;
My times has Fortune swallowed, the severe,
The hours, my madness hides, my lunacy.
I know that health and years from me did flee,
But how and where they fled does not appear.
Life fails me, the already lived is here,
And I am haunted by calamity.
Yesterday's gone, Tomorrow does not delay,
Today is going, in a breath does pass,
I am a Was, Shall be, Is, sore bestead.[9]
In Tomorrow, Today and Yesterday
Joined, swaddling clothes[10] and shroud, I am, alas,
Now naught but a succession of the dead.

---

[8] yore—long ago.

[9] bestead—situated.

[10] swaddling clothes—infant garments.

Sonnet on a Portrait

SOR JUANA INÈS DE LA CRUZ

These lying pigments facing you,
with every charm brush can supply
set up false premises of color
to lead astray the unwary eye.

Here, against ghastly tolls of time,
bland flattery has staked a claim,
defying the power of passing years
to wipe out memory and name.

And here, in this hollow artifice—
frail blossom hanging on the wind,
vain pleading in a foolish cause,

poor shield against what fate has wrought—
all efforts fail and in the end
a body goes to dust, to shade, to nought.

QUESTIONS TO CONSIDER

1. What does the metaphor in the sestet of Petrarch's sonnet convey about his grief?

2. In Ronsard's sonnet, what might the reference to pride in line 12 mean?

3. To what does the speaker in Shakespeare's sonnet compare his old age?

4. What is the tone of "Life's Brevity"?

5. What does Sor Juana think of her portrait, and how do her thoughts fit the theme of the briefness of life?

Renaissance Paintings

Humanism changed the ways people thought about themselves. It also changed the way sculptors, architects, and artists thought about their work. Beginning in Italy, Renaissance artists experimented with new techniques, such as perspective, a method of giving the appearance of depth and volume to objects depicted on a flat surface. The painters of northern Europe were responsible for an equally important technical innovation, the use of oil paints, which allowed them to capture surface textures and effects of light with extraordinary realism. The following paintings by Italian and Northern Renaissance artists exhibit these experiments with form.

▲

In *Tribute Money* by Masaccio (1401?–1428), which tells a story from Matthew's Gospel, depth is achieved by the use of atmospheric perspective in which the mountains merge with the gray sky.

 St. James Led to His Execution by Andrea Mantegna (1431–1506) is unusual in that it is painted from the perspective of a viewer standing below the scene and looking up.

In *The School of Athens*, his homage to the great thinkers of the past, Raphael (1483–1520) used perspective to create a huge architectural space to contain his figures.

▼

▲

The distorted perspective of *Self-Portrait in a Convex Mirror* by Parmigianino (1503–1540) is an extreme example of the late Renaissance style known as Mannerism.

The Annunciation by Jan van Eyck (1390–1441) displays the subtle treatment of light and naturalistic definition of detail made possible by oil paints, an innovation for which he is traditionally given credit. ▶

◀ The objects rendered with such careful detail in *The French Ambassadors* by Hans Holbein the Younger (c. 1497–1543) display the varied interests of the Renaissance—science, the arts, exploration.

Adoration of the Magi by Albrecht Dürer (1471–1528) displays the Renaissance taste for realism in the three-dimensional treatment of the arches and the rich detail of the gifts presented to the infant Jesus. ▶

▲

In *The Fall of Icarus*, Flemish painter Pieter Breugel (c. 1525–1569) presents a Greek myth in a very realistically detailed northern European setting.

QUESTIONS TO CONSIDER

1. What does the enthusiasm for artistic techniques such as perspective and oil painting, which permit highly realistic effects, convey about the culture of the Renaissance?

2. In your opinion, which of these paintings seems to reflect most completely the ideals of Renaissance humanism?

3. Which painting seems to reflect these ideals least?

4. Why do you think Hans Holbein included objects that indicated his subjects' interests and achievements in his portrait *The French Ambassadors*?

5. If you could have commissioned a portrait from either Holbein or Parmigianino, which artist would you have chosen and why?

Chinese and European Voyages

DAME VERONICA WEDGWOOD

In the 1400s and 1500s, both Asians and Europeans were using sea power in an effort to extend their influence over large portions of the globe. In her book The Spoils of Time, *British historian Veronica Wedgwood describes Chinese, Portuguese, and Spanish voyages.*

The Chinese emperors in the fifteenth century extended their suzerainty[1] across Tibet to the mountain frontiers of India, south to Cambodia, Siam, and Burma, the Indies and Ceylon. Their ships not only protected their long coastline, but also established their control of the sea. Chinese shipping at its height is said to have comprised twenty-seven hundred coast guard vessels, four hundred armed transports, and at least as many ships, especially designed for long exploratory voyages, not to mention thousands of small craft for the coastal traffic. These Chinese ships were the ultimate development of the Chinese junk.[2] More solid and seaworthy than Western ships of the same period, their structural rigidity made them especially useful in shallow coastal waters, while their rigging enabled them to take every advantage of the wind and even to sail into it if necessary.

The Emperor Yung Lo[3] (reigned 1403–24) initiated a series of expeditions to establish Chinese naval preeminence. The measures taken by Hung Wu to protect the Silk Road[4] from disturbance by nomadic raiders had been nullified by the conquests of Timur,[5] and this may have been the reason why Yung Lo, and his Admiral Cheng Ho,[6] thought it wise to make known the greatness of China on sea routes hitherto dominated by Arabs and Indians.

---

[1] suzerainty—the domain of a nation that controls another nation in international affairs.

[2] junk—a flat-bottomed ship with sails.

[3] Yung Lo—the Chinese emperor in Ma Huan's account (page 400).

[4] Hung Wu . . . Silk Road—Chinese emperor Hung Wu (1328–1398) founded the Ming Dynasty. The Silk Road was an ancient trade route between China and the Mediterranean Sea.

[5] Timur—another name for Tamerlane (1336?–1405), conqueror of southern and western Asia and ruler of Samarkand.

[6] Admiral Cheng Ho—Admiral Zheng He in Ma Huan's account.

The great nine-masted "treasure ships" were said to be over 400 feet long and 185 feet wide. Each carried a year's supply of grain and had tubs for growing vegetables on the lower decks. Sixty-two of them sailed on the first expedition (1405), accompanied by over two hundred smaller vessels. Admiral Cheng Ho, who in course of time led seven such voyages, was of mixed Arab-Mongol origin and had begun his career as a palace official. Ambassador as well as admiral, representing the most powerful empire in the world, he opened the way for Chinese trade to Malaya, the East Indies and Ceylon, India and the Persian Gulf, the East African coast and the Red Sea. He expected the rulers on whose coasts he touched to acknowledge the supremacy of China. Some who refused—notably the King of Ceylon—were carried off as prisoners. But many states (once even Mecca[7]) sent a tribute of gold and jewels or strange beasts for the imperial menagerie—a rhinoceros, a zebra, and a giraffe. The expeditions were also accompanied by astronomers, cartographers, and geographers to record and chart them.

Whatever their ultimate purpose, the voyages came to an end after 1432. The Emperor Yung Lo's successor was involved with wars in Mongolia, where the tribes were on the move. The capital was shifted back to Peking; frontier forces were increased and the Wall[8] fully manned. These measures held back the barbarians for the next two centuries, while the naval power of China was confined to patrolling the coast. Arab traders, relieved of serious competition, made their base in Malacca, monopolized the trade of the whole region, and converted the islanders to Islam.

While Cheng Ho and his great ships explored the Indian Ocean, the Persian Gulf, and the Red Sea, the small and far inferior vessels of the seafaring Italian and Portuguese ventured far out into the Atlantic or sailed southward down the west coast of Africa into those regions whence few had ever returned. Already in the fourteenth century the Genoese had touched on the Canary Islands, known to ancient geographers but long-forgotten. The Portuguese, who landed there in 1340, saw at once that they were an excellent base for their further exploration of the African coast, but the Pope awarded them to Castile.[9]

In 1419 the Portuguese found and immediately colonized the thickly forested islands which they called Madeira (the Portuguese for "wood"); here they planted vineyards, set up sawmills driven by the waterpower of the plentiful streams, and were soon exporting timber and wine. Encouraged, they ventured farther into the ocean and reached the Azores, where they introduced another profitable crop, the sugarcane. More important, and more dangerous, were their recurrent expeditions down the west coast of Africa in search of gold.

---

[7] Mecca—city in Arabia, holiest site in Islamic world.

[8] the Wall—the Great Wall of China, a 1,500-mile-long fortification across northern China.

[9] Castile—former kingdom of Spain.

These expeditions began in 1420, but it was not until 1434 that Gil Eanes rounded Cape Bojador[10]—beyond which, according to legend, all ships would be lost in fog or boiled at the equator. Nuño Tristao reached Senegal in 1443 and thereafter the Portuguese traded with the African kingdoms of the coast, whence they returned with cargoes of gold dust and slaves. At about this time too they surmounted the dangers of the homeward voyage, on which earlier explorers had been lost, battling against the prevalent contrary winds. They had, by this time, developed the ships known as caravels, small, solidly built, maneuverable, which, with two or three masts and lateen sail, could haul close to the wind. Besides, their sea captains discovered a better route: they sailed westward across the Atlantic until they encountered southerly and easterly currents, which carried them quickly home.

> *Prince Henry's interest in exploration was enhanced by a fervent desire to spread the Catholic faith.*

The man behind these ventures was the Infante[11] of Portugal, the King's brother, known to the English-speaking world as Prince Henry the Navigator. (His mother was an English princess.) He was not himself a navigator, but he saw to it that his captains were equipped with the best instruments and knowledge available. His principal seat at Sagres, near Cape St. Vincent, was admirably placed for collecting, from the many ships that came and went, information about winds and currents. He had been credited with setting up something like a college for the study of mathematics and astronomy; it was more like an information center, with charts regularly revised and data recorded and made available.

Prince Henry's interest in exploration was enhanced by a fervent desire to spread the Catholic faith. He was not himself much interested in gold and was opposed to slave-raiding and unnecessary violence. "My Lord Infante will not permit further hurt to be done to any [natives], because he hopes that, mixing with Christians they may without difficulty be converted to our faith." So wrote the Venetian sea captain Cadamosto, who in 1455–56 led a Portuguese expedition to explore Gambia and Senegal. Cadamosto was impressed by the power and authority of the native chiefs, observed with interest the many villages of grass huts, the hippopotami and the elephants. He walked freely among the friendly people and was amused when they rubbed his hands with moistened fingers to see if his white skin was paint.

Shortly before Cadamosto's voyage Constantinople had fallen to the Ottoman Turks.[12] The effect on the commerce of the Mediterranean was not at first disastrous:

---

[10] Cape Bojador—spit of land extending into the Atlantic from present-day Western Sahara, southwest of Morocco.

[11] Infante—a son of a Spanish or Portuguese king other than the heir to the throne.

[12] Constantinople . . . Ottoman Turks—Constantinople, capital of the Byzantine Empire, was captured by the Ottoman Turks in 1453.

the Turks were anxious to keep open the trade routes, from which they gathered considerable revenues. The Venetians preserved much of their trade by treaties and tribute. The Portuguese were not involved; even Barcelona, the richest port in Spain, mistress of the western Mediterranean, was not seriously affected until the Ottomans conquered North Africa and cut off trade with Egypt.

Some years after Prince Henry's death in 1460, the Portuguese established a trading post on the Gold Coast (Ghana) for collecting bullion and slaves. In 1489 Diogo Cão explored the Congo estuary. Three years later Bartolomeu Dias rounded the Cape of Good Hope but was driven back by storms. At last, in 1497, Vasco da Gama circumnavigated Africa, touched on Mozambique, and put into Mombasa in the hope of getting advice from Arab traders about crossing the Indian Ocean. Jealous, they gave him none; he sailed in spite of them, reached Calicut on the coast of Malabar, and returned to Lisbon in triumph. He had found a **feasible**[13] route to India which bypassed alike the Arab middlemen and the Venetians. The Pope accordingly bestowed on the King of Portugal, Manoel the Fortunate, the title Lord of the Conquest, Navigation and Commerce of India, Ethiopia, Arabia and Persia. (In the following century, Luís de Camões was to celebrate Vasco da Gama's voyage in his poem *The Lusiads*, one of the greatest of European epics.)

Five years earlier, the discovery of a more direct route to Asia had been claimed on behalf of Spain by Christopher Columbus. Columbus may have been born in Genoa, but nothing certain is known of his origins and he seems deliberately to have made a mystery of them. He was a man of genius of the most difficult kind— a visionary, at once **tenacious**[14] and quarrelsome. But he was an experienced seaman and outstanding navigator who had sailed on several of the Portuguese African voyages and was convinced that the shortest way to Asia lay westward across the Atlantic.

The spherical shape of the earth was well known in classical antiquity; knowledge of it, supported by the experience of seamen and the authority of Ptolemy,[15] had never been wholly lost and was not questioned by any geographers in the time of Columbus. Ptolemy, however, who had greatly overestimated the extent of China, was the source of much error as to the size of the Atlantic, which was generally assumed to be the only great ocean in the world. At least two geographers at the time of Columbus had suggested that the distance between Europe and China by sea was not much above five thousand miles. Columbus deceived himself into the even shorter estimate of thirty-five hundred miles. When he sought authority and financial help for his venture he could not get it: the King of Portugal, the King of Aragon and his wife (the Queen of Castile),

---

[13] **feasible**—workable.

[14] **tenacious**—persistent.

[15] Ptolemy—astronomer and geographer (2nd century A.D.) who theorized that all the heavenly bodies revolved around a spherical earth.

the kings of England and France—all took expert advice and all refused. Indomitably persistent, he again approached Queen Isabella. Her marriage to Ferdinand of Aragon had united Spain, and when Columbus appealed to her for the second time she was encamped with her husband before the walls of Granada, the last Moorish stronghold, awaiting its inevitable surrender. After nearly eight hundred years Spanish soil would be free from the infidel.[16] In the **euphoria**[17] of the moment the Queen gave Columbus his chance.

He set sail on 3 August 1492 and landed on 12 October on what he took to be an island off the coast of Asia (in fact, one of the Bahamas). A fortnight later, further exploration brought him, as he thought, to a peninsula of mainland China. In April he was back in Spain, bringing with him some of the natives, samples of many plants which he believed to be oriental spices, together with gold ornaments and other curiosities. The grateful monarchs who received him at Barcelona bestowed on him the title of Admiral of the Ocean Sea and Governor of the Islands That He Has Discovered in the Indies.

The Portuguese, who for the last half century had disputed with the Spaniards for possession of the nearer Atlantic islands, now hastily agreed to a division of the potential spoils. The Pope fixed a line of demarcation about 1,175 miles west of the Azores; discoveries to the east of it belonged to Portugal; to the west of it to Spain (Treaty of Tordesillas, 1494). Through this agreement, when Pedro Cabral

discovered the mainland of Brazil in 1500 it fell to the share of Portugal.

Columbus made three further voyages to confirm his discovery. On the second he found and named the Virgin Islands, touched on Puerto Rico and Jamaica, and explored the southern coast of Cuba. On the third (1498–1500) he reached the mainland of South America, in the extreme west of Venezuela, the Paria Peninsula. On the fourth he explored the coasts of Costa Rica, Nicaragua, Honduras, and Panama. He recognized by this time that he had found a "new world," a great region hitherto unknown to geographers, but he stubbornly believed it to be a part of the immense continent of Asia.

As he grew older he became convinced that the prophecies in the Book of Esdras[18] concerned him and his God-given mission. In his last sad years he was distressed by his dismissal from his governorship and by criticism and disputes. With the death of Queen Isabella he lost his most active supporter, although Ferdinand treated him generously. He was disillusioned by the growing certainty of the geographers that his discoveries had nothing to do with India or Asia. He died in 1506, still convinced that he had found what he set out to find, yet before his death the Florentine Amerigo Vespucci had explored the coast of Brazil as far south as the Rìo de la Plata and

---

[16] Granada . . . infidel—In the early 700s, Muslim invaders from Africa (called Moors) conquered much of Spain, establishing a number of kingdoms; the last of these, Granada, was reconquered by the Spanish in 1492.

[17] **euphoria**—exaltation.

[18] Book of Esdras—either of two biblical books in a Greek translation corresponding to the books of Ezra and Nehemiah.

established beyond doubt the existence of the new continent. Only a year after Columbus died, in 1507, a German geographer, Martin Waldseemuller, in a new map of the world, named the new continent America in honor of Vespucci.

The stature of Columbus is not diminished by his error. He pioneered the Atlantic crossing, proved that it could be done, showed the way to others, and made (while rejecting it) the discovery which doubled the size and changed the balance of the known world.

In 1519 Ferdinand Magellan, a Portuguese in the service of the Spanish monarchy, sailed down the coast of South America, through the straits which bear his name, into the unknown vast ocean he called the Pacific. After fearful sufferings from lack of food and water, he reached the island of Cebu in the Philippines, where he offered to help the King in a tribal war and was killed. His most experienced pilot, Juan Sebastian Eleano, took command of the reduced and battered fleet, completed the circumnavigation, and brought back the *Vitoria*, the one surviving ship, with a cargo of spices and sandalwood to Seville in September 1527. This was the first circumnavigation of the globe; great credit must go to Eleano for bringing the *Vitoria* safely home, but he could hardly have done so without the example and the master plans of Magellan. On his return he was, not unnaturally, apt to emphasize his own achievement, but the glory of the first great circumnavigation belongs rightly to Magellan.

The survivors were given a royal welcome by the young King of Spain, Charles, grandson and heir of Ferdinand and Isabella and sovereign of territories scattered over half the globe.

The lives of Europeans, princes and peasants, capitalists and craftsmen, in every profession, in every country, would be changed: their agriculture, their diet, their trade, their hopes, their opportunities—all in course of time would be altered by the great unknown continent with its **myriad**[19] islands, the New World which now lay open to them.

> *The stature of Columbus is not diminished by his error.*

---

[19] **myriad**—innumerable.

QUESTIONS TO CONSIDER

1. What things enabled the Chinese, Spanish, and Portuguese to successfully extend their influence?

2. Scholars have speculated on how the world would have been different had the Chinese extended their voyages to what is now America, which they seemed capable of doing. How would the world have been different in your opinion?

3. How did Henry the Navigator advance European exploration?

4. What kind of individual was Christopher Columbus?

Chapter 11

The Seventeenth and Eighteenth Centuries

The Scientific Method

Social Satire

The Limits of Progress

◀ In *Canvassing for Votes*, a painting from his series satirizing the corrupt British election process, William Hogarth (1697–1764) depicts a farmer being bribed for his vote outside an inn.

Science and Religion

GALILEO GALILEI

Medieval thought was based on appeals to ancient authorities, such as the Bible or Greek and Roman writers. In the 17th century, some thinkers began to challenge this practice, seeking to establish a scientific method based on observation of nature and controlled experiments. Among the most important of these thinkers was Galileo Galilei (1564–1642), an Italian physicist, mathematician, and astronomer. Based on his observations with the newly invented telescope, Galileo became convinced that the Polish astronomer Nicholas Copernicus (1473–1543) had been correct in his theory that the planets orbit the sun rather than the earth. In 1615 Galileo defended scientific methods of inquiry in a published letter to the Grand Duchess of Tuscany.

Some years ago, as Your Serene Highness well knows, I discovered in the heavens many things that had not been seen before our own age. The novelty of these things, as well as some consequences which followed from them in contradiction to the physical notions commonly held among academic philosophers, stirred up against me no small number of professors—as if I had placed these things in the sky with my own hands in order to upset nature and overturn the sciences. . . .

Showing a greater fondness for their own opinions than for truth, they sought to deny and disprove the new things which, if they had cared to look for themselves, their own senses would have demonstrated to them. To this end they hurled various charges and published numerous writings filled with vain arguments, and they made the grave mistake of sprinkling these with passages taken from places in the Bible which they had failed to understand properly, and which were ill suited to their purposes.

Persisting in their original resolve to destroy me and everything mine by any means they can think of, these men are aware of my views in astronomy and philosophy. They know that as to the arrangement of the parts of the universe, I hold the sun to be situated motionless in the center of the revolution of the celestial orbs while the earth rotates on its axis and revolves about the sun. They know also that I support this position not only by refuting the arguments of Ptolemy and Aristotle,[1] but by producing many counter-arguments; in particular, some which relate to physical effects whose causes can perhaps be assigned in no other way. In addition there are astronomical arguments derived from many things in my new celestial discoveries that plainly **confute**[2] the Ptolemaic system while admirably agreeing with and confirming the contrary hypothesis. Possibly because they are disturbed by the known truth of other propositions of mine which differ from those commonly held, and therefore mistrusting their defense so long as they confine themselves to the field of philosophy, these men have resolved to fabricate a shield for their **fallacies**[3] out of the mantle of pretended religion and the authority of the Bible. These they apply, with little judgment, to the refutation of arguments that they do not understand and have not even listened to.

First they have endeavored to spread the opinion that such propositions in general are contrary to the Bible and are consequently damnable and heretical. . . . Next, becoming bolder, . . . they began scattering rumors among the people that before long this doctrine would be condemned by the supreme authority.[4] They know, too, that official condemnation would not only suppress the two propositions which I have mentioned, but would render damnable all other astronomical and physical statements and observations that have any necessary relation or connection with these. . . .

To this end they make a shield of their hypocritical zeal for religion. They go about invoking the Bible, which they would have minister to their deceitful purposes. Contrary to the sense of the Bible and the intention of the holy Fathers,[5] if I am not mistaken, they would extend such authorities until even in purely physical matters— where faith is not involved—they would have us altogether abandon reason and the evidence of our senses in favor of some biblical passage, though under the surface meaning of its words this passage may contain a different sense.

I hope to show that I proceed with much greater piety than they do, when I argue not against condemning this book, but against condemning it in the way they suggest—that is, without understanding it, weighing it, or so much as reading it. . . .

The reason produced for condemning the opinion that the earth moves and the sun stands still is that in many places in the Bible one may read that the sun moves and the earth stands still. Since the Bible cannot err, it follows as a necessary consequence that anyone takes an erroneous and heretical position who maintains that the sun is **inherently**[6] motionless and the earth movable.

---

[1] Ptolemy . . . Aristotle—Ptolemy was a Greek astronomer (2nd century A.D.) who mistakenly thought the sun and planets revolved around the earth. Aristotle (384—322 B.C.) was a Greek philosopher.

[2] **confute**—disprove.

[3] **fallacies**—false arguments.

[4] supreme authority—the pope.

[5] holy Fathers—Fathers of the Church (page 270).

[6] **inherently**—by nature.

With regard to this argument, I think in the first place that it is very pious to say and prudent to affirm that the holy Bible can never speak untruth—whenever its true meaning is understood. But I believe nobody will deny that it is often very **abstruse**,[7] and may say things which are quite different from what its bare words signify. Hence in expounding the Bible if one were always to confine oneself to the unadorned grammatical meaning, one might fall into error. Not only contradictions and propositions far from true might thus be made to appear in the Bible, but even grave heresies and follies. Thus it would be necessary to assign to God feet, hands, and eyes, as well as **corporeal**[8] and human affections, such as anger, repentance, hatred, and sometimes even the forgetting of things past and ignorance of those to come. These propositions uttered by the Holy Ghost were set down in that manner by the sacred scribes[9] in order to accommodate them to the capacities of the common people, who are rude and unlearned. . . .

This being granted, I think that in discussions of physical problems we ought to begin not from the authority of scriptural passages but from sense-experiences and necessary demonstrations; for the holy Bible and the phenomena of nature proceed alike from the divine Word, the former as the dictate of the Holy Ghost and the latter as the observant executrix[10] of God's commands. It is necessary for the Bible, in order to be accommodated to the understanding of every man, to speak many things which appear to differ from the absolute truth so far as the bare meaning of the words is concerned. But Nature, on the other hand, is inexorable and immutable;[11] she never transgresses the laws imposed upon her, or cares a whit[12] whether her abstruse reasons and methods of operation are understandable to men. For that reason it appears that nothing physical which sense-experience sets before our eyes, or which necessary demonstrations prove to us, ought to be called in question (much less condemned) upon the testimony of biblical passages which may have some different meaning beneath their words. For the Bible is not chained in every expression to conditions as strict as those which govern all physical effects; nor is God any less excellently revealed in Nature's actions than in the sacred statements of the Bible.

---

[7] **abstruse**—hard to understand.

[8] **corporeal**—bodily.

[9] Holy Ghost . . . sacred scribes—The Holy Spirit, in Christian belief, inspired those who wrote the Bible.

[10] executrix—Nature (viewed here as female, hence *executrix*) carries out God's commands.

[11] inexorable and immutable—unyielding and unchanging.

[12] whit—tiniest amount.

QUESTIONS TO CONSIDER

1. Why was there such resistance to Galileo's findings?

2. Why did Galileo feel that science should not be based solely on the authority of the Bible?

3. In attempting to answer questions about nature, Galileo said we should use "sense-experiences and necessary demonstrations." What did he mean by this?

Idols and False Notions

FRANCIS BACON

Francis Bacon (1561–1626) was an English government official and philosopher. In Novum Organon *("New Method of Investigation"), he describes types of false notions that prevent human beings from discovering objective truth and sets forth the goals of science.*

XIX

There are and can be only two ways of searching into and discovering truth. The one flies from the senses and particulars to the most general **axioms**,[1] and from these principles, the truth of which it takes for settled and immovable, proceeds to judgment and to the discovery of middle axioms. And this way is now in fashion. The other derives axioms from the senses and particulars, rising by a gradual and unbroken ascent, so that it arrives at the most general axioms last of all. This is the true way, but as yet untried.

XXIV

It cannot be that axioms established by argumentation should **avail**[2] for the discovery of new works, since the subtlety of nature is greater many times over than the subtlety of argument. But axioms duly and orderly formed from particulars easily discover the way to new particulars, and thus render sciences active.

XXXVI

One method of delivery alone remains to us which is simply this: we must lead men to the particulars themselves, and their series and order; while men on their side must force themselves for a while to lay their notions by and begin to familiarize themselves with facts.

XXXVII

The doctrine of those who have denied that certainty could be attained at all has some agreement with my way of proceeding at the first setting out; but they end in being infinitely separated and opposed. For the holders of that doctrine assert simply that nothing can be known. I also assert that not much can be known in nature by the way which is now in use. But then they go on to destroy the authority of the senses and

---

[1] **axioms**—propositions assumed without proof for the purpose of studying the consequences that follow from them.

[2] **avail**—be of value.

understanding; whereas I proceed to devise and supply helps for the same.

XXXVIII

The idols and false notions which are now in possession of the human understanding, and have taken deep root therein, not only so beset men's minds that truth can hardly find entrance, but even after entrance is obtained, they will again in the very instauration[3] of the sciences meet and trouble us, unless men being forewarned of the danger fortify themselves as far as may be against their assaults.

XXXIX

There are four classes of Idols which beset men's minds. To these for distinction's sake I have assigned names, calling the first class *Idols of the Tribe*; the second, *Idols of the Cave*; the third, *Idols of the Market Place*; the fourth, *Idols of the Theater*.

XLI

The Idols of the Tribe have their foundation in human nature itself, and in the tribe or race of men. For it is a false assertion that the sense of man is the measure of things. On the contrary, all perceptions as well of the sense as of the mind are according to the measure of the individual and not according to the measure of the universe. And the human understanding is like a false mirror, which, receiving rays irregularly, distorts and discolors the nature of things by mingling its own nature with it.

XLII

The Idols of the Cave are the idols of the individual man. For everyone (besides the errors common to human nature in general) has a cave or den of his own, which **refracts**[4] and discolors the light of nature,

owing either to his own proper and peculiar nature; or to his education and conversation with others; or to the reading of books, and the authority of those whom he esteems and admires; or to the differences of impressions, accordingly as they take place in a mind preoccupied and predisposed or in a mind indifferent and settled; or the like. So that the spirit of man (according as it is meted out to different individuals) is in fact a thing variable and full of **perturbation**,[5] and governed as it were by chance. Whence it was well observed by Heraclitus[6] that men look for sciences in their own lesser worlds, and not in the greater or common world.

XLIII

There are also Idols formed by the . . . association of men with each other, which I call Idols of the Market Place, on account of the commerce and consort of men there. For it is by discourse that men associate, and words are imposed according to the apprehension of the vulgar.[7] And therefore the ill and unfit choice of words wonderfully obstructs the understanding. Nor do the definitions or explanations wherewith in some things learned men are wont[8] to guard and defend themselves, by any means set the matter right. But words plainly force and overrule the understanding, and throw all into confusion, and lead men

---

[3] instauration—establishment.

[4] **refracts**—bends.

[5] **perturbation**—agitation.

[6] Heraclitus—Greek philosopher (c. 540–c. 470 B.C.).

[7] apprehension of the vulgar—understanding of the common people.

[8] wont—accustomed.

away into numberless empty controversies and idle fancies.

XLIV

Lastly, there are Idols which have immigrated into men's minds from the various dogmas of philosophies, and also from wrong laws of demonstration. These I call Idols of the Theater, because in my judgment all the received systems are but so many stage plays, representing worlds of their own creation after an unreal and scenic fashion. Nor is it only of the systems now in vogue, or only of the ancient sects and philosophies, that I speak; for many more plays of the same kind may yet be composed and in like artificial manner set forth; seeing that errors the most widely different have nevertheless causes for the most part alike. Neither again do I mean this only of entire systems, but also of many principles and axioms in science, which by tradition, **credulity,**[9] and negligence have come to be received.

LXXXI

Again there is another great and powerful cause why the sciences have made but little progress, which is this. It is not possible to run a course aright when the goal itself has not been rightly placed. Now the true and lawful goal of the sciences is none other than this: that human life be endowed with new discoveries and powers. But of this the great majority have no feeling, but are merely hireling[10] and professorial; except when it occasionally happens that some workman of acuter wit and covetous of honor applies himself to a new invention, which he mostly does at the expense of his fortunes. But in general, so far are men from proposing to themselves to augment the mass of arts and sciences, that from the mass already at hand they neither take nor look for anything more than what they may turn to use in their lectures, or to gain, or to reputation, or to some similar advantage. And if any one out of all the multitude court science with honest affection and for her own sake, yet even with him the object will be found to be rather the variety of contemplations and doctrines than the severe and rigid search after truth. And if by chance there be one who seeks after truth in earnest, yet even he will propose to himself such a kind of truth as shall yield satisfaction to the mind and understanding in rendering causes for things long since discovered, and not the truth which shall lead to new assurance of works and new light of axioms. If then the end of the sciences has not as yet been well placed, it is not strange that men have erred as to the means.

---

[9] **credulity**—tendency to believe too readily.

[10] hireling—mercenary or grasping.

QUESTIONS TO CONSIDER

1. In Bacon's view, what was wrong with the approach to science in his time and what was the remedy?

2. Which of the four categories of "idols" described by Bacon resulted from basing science solely on ancient authorities such as the Bible or Greek and Roman writers?

3. Would Bacon see the Nobel Prizes as useful in encouraging what he saw as the true goals of science? Why or why not?

from

Tartuffe

MOLIÈRE

Satire is an artistic technique that uses humor—gentle or bitter—to expose universal human failings or specific social ills. It was a major facet of 17th- and 18th-century culture. The French comic playwright Molière (1622–1673) used satire to ridicule the follies and vices represented by various human types—the miser, the hypochondriac, the social climber. In his comedy Tartuffe, *the title character is a religious hypocrite who has insinuated himself into Orgon's household, where almost everyone but Orgon sees through him. Before the following scene from Act 2, Orgon tells his daughter Mariane that he wishes her to marry Tartuffe, an idea that appalls both Mariane and her maid Dorine. In love with Valère, Mariane is baffled as to how to avoid agreeing to her father's strong wish.*

Valère. Madam, I've just received some wondrous news
   Regarding which I'd like to hear your views.
Mariane. What news?
Valère. You're marrying Tartuffe.
Mariane. I find
   That Father does have such a match in mind.
Valère. Your father, Madam . . .
Mariane. . . . has just this minute said
   That it's Tartuffe he wishes me to wed.
Valère. Can he be serious?
Mariane. Oh, indeed he can;
   He's clearly set his heart upon the plan.
Valère. And what position do you propose to take, Madam?
Mariane. Why—I don't know.
Valère. For heaven's sake—
   You don't know?
Mariane. No.
Valère. Well, well!

Mariane. Advise me, do.

Valère. Marry the man. That's my advice to you.

Mariane. That's your advice?

Valère. Yes.

Mariane. Truly?

Valère. Oh, absolutely.

You couldn't choose more wisely, more astutely.

Mariane. Thanks for this counsel; I'll follow it, of course.

Valère. Do, do; I'm sure 'twill cost you no remorse.

Mariane. To give it didn't cause your heart to break.

Valère. I gave it, Madam, only for your sake.

Mariane. And it's for your sake that I take it, Sir.

Dorine (*withdrawing to the rear of the stage*).

Let's see which fool will prove the stubborner.

Valère. So! I am nothing to you, and it was flat

Deception when you . . .

Mariane. Please, enough of that.

You've told me plainly that I should agree

To wed the man my father's chosen for me,

And since you've deigned to counsel me so wisely,

I promise, Sir, to do as you advise me.

Valère. Ah, no, 'twas not by me that you were swayed.

No, your decision was already made;

Though now, to save appearances, you protest

That you're betraying me at my behest.[1]

Mariane. Just as you say.

Valère. Quite so. And I now see

That you were never truly in love with me.

Mariane. Alas, you're free to think so if you choose.

Valère. I choose to think so, and here's a bit of news:

You've spurned my hand, but I know where to turn

For kinder treatment, as you shall quickly learn.

Mariane. I'm sure you do. Your noble qualities

Inspire affection . . .

Valère. Forget my qualities, please.

They don't inspire you overmuch, I find.

But there's another lady I have in mind

---

[1] behest—command.

Whose sweet and generous nature will not scorn
To compensate me for the loss I've borne.

Mariane. I'm no great loss, and I'm sure that you'll transfer
Your heart quite painlessly from me to her.

Valère. I'll do my best to take it in my stride.
The pain I feel at being cast aside
Time and forgetfulness may put an end to.
Or if I can't forget, I shall pretend to.
No self-respecting person is expected
To go on loving once he's been rejected.

Mariane. Now, that's a fine, high-minded sentiment.

Valère. One to which any sane man would assent.
Would you prefer it if I pined away
In hopeless passion till my dying day?
Am I to yield you to a rival's arms
And not console myself with other charms?

Mariane. Go then: console yourself; don't hesitate.
I wish you to; indeed, I cannot wait.

Valère. You wish me to?

Mariane. Yes.

Valère. That's the final straw.
Madame, farewell. Your wish shall be my law.

(He starts to leave, and then returns: this repeatedly.)

Mariane. Splendid.

Valère *(coming back again)*. This breach, remember, is of your making;
It's you who've driven me to the step I'm taking.

Mariane. Of course.

Valère *(coming back again)*. Remember, too, that I am merely
Following your example.

Mariane. I see that clearly.

Valère. Enough. I'll go and do your bidding, then.

Mariane. Good.

Valère *(coming back again)*. You shall never see my face again.

Mariane. Excellent.

Valère *(walking to the door, then turning about)*. Yes?

Mariane. What?

Valère. What's that? What did you say?

Mariane. Nothing. You're dreaming.

Valère. Ah. Well, I'm on my way.

Farewell, *Madame. (He moves slowly away.)*

Mariane. Farewell.

Dorine *(to Mariane).* If you ask me,

Both of you are as mad as mad can be.

Do stop this nonsense, now. I've only let you

Squabble so long to see where it would get you.

Whoa there, Monsieur Valère!

(She goes and seizes Valère by the arm; he makes a great show of resistance.)

Valère. What's this, Dorine?

Dorine. Come here.

Valère. No, no, my heart's too full of **spleen**.[2]

Don't hold me back; her wish must be obeyed.

Dorine. Stop!

Valère. It's too late now; my decision's made.

Dorine. Oh, pooh!

Mariane *(aside).* He hates the sight of me, that's plain.

I'll go, and so deliver him from pain.

Dorine *(leaving Valère, running after Mariane).*

And now *you* run away! Come back.

Mariane. No, no.

Nothing you say will keep me here. Let go!

Valère. *(aside).* She cannot bear my presence, I perceive.

To spare her further torment, I shall leave.

Dorine *(leaving Mariane, running after Valère).*

Again! You'll not escape, Sir; don't you try it.

Come here, you two. Stop fussing and be quiet.

(She takes Valère by the hand, then Mariane, and draws them together.)

Valère *(to Dorine).* What do you want of me?

Mariane *(to Dorine).* What is the point of this?

Dorine. We're going to have a little **armistice**.[3] *(to Valère.)*

Now, weren't you silly to get so overheated?

Valère. Didn't you see how badly I was treated?

Dorine *(to Mariane).* Aren't you a simpleton, to have lost your head?

Mariane. Didn't you hear the hateful things he said?

Dorine *(to Valère).* You're both great fools. Her sole desire, Valère,

---

[2] **spleen**—ill humor, spite.

[3] **armistice**—truce, cease-fire.

Is to be yours in marriage. To that I'll swear.

(To Mariane.)

He loves you only, and he wants no wife

But you, Mariane. On that I'll stake my life.

Mariane *(to Valère)*. Then why you advised me so, I cannot see.

Valère *(to Mariane)*. On such a question, why ask advice of *me*?

Dorine. Oh, you're impossible. Give me your hands, you two.

(To Valère)

    Yours first.

Valère *(giving Dorine his hand)*. But why?

Dorine *(to Mariane)*.   And now a hand from you.

Mariane *(also giving Dorine her hand)*. What are you doing?

Dorine. There: a perfect fit.

    You suit each other better than you'll admit.

(Valère and Mariane hold hands for some time without looking at each other.)

Valère *(turning toward Mariane)*. Ah, come, don't be so haughty. Give a man

    A look of kindness, won't you, Mariane?

(Mariane turns toward Valère and smiles.)

Dorine. I tell you, lovers are completely mad!

Valère *(to Mariane)*. Now come, confess that you were very bad

    To hurt my feelings as you did just now.

    I have a just complaint, you must allow.

Mariane. *You* must allow that you were most unpleasant . . .

Dorine. Let's table that discussion for the present;

    Your father has a plan which must be stopped.

Mariane. Advise us, then, what means must we adopt?

Dorine. We'll use all manner of means, and all at once.

(To Mariane)

    Your father's **addled**;[4] he's acting like a dunce.

    Therefore you'd better humor the old fossil.

    Pretend to yield to him, be sweet and **docile**,[5]

    And then postpone, as often as necessary,

    The day on which you have agreed to marry.

---

[4] **addled**—confused, foolish.

[5] **docile**—easy to manage.

You'll thus gain time, and time will turn the trick.
Sometimes, for instance, you'll be taken sick,
And that will seem good reason for delay;
Or some bad omen will make you change the day—
You'll dream of muddy water, or you'll pass
A dead man's hearse, or break a looking-glass.
If all else fails, no man can marry you
Unless you take his ring and say "I do."
But now, let's separate. If they should find
Us talking here, our plot might be **divined**.[6]

(To Valère.)

Go to your friends, and tell them what's occurred,
And have them urge her father to keep his word.
Meanwhile, we'll stir her brother into action,
And get Elmire,[7] as well, to join our faction.
Good-bye.

Valère *(to Mariane)*. Though each of us will do his best,
It's your true heart on which my hopes shall rest.

Mariane *(to Valère)*. Regardless of what Father may decide,
None but Valère shall claim me as his bride.

Valère. Oh, how those words content me! Come what will . . .

Dorine. Oh, lovers, lovers! Their tongues are never still.
Be off, now.

Valère *(turning to go, then turning back)*. One last word . . .

Dorine. No time to chat:
You leave by this door; and you leave by that.

(Dorine pushes them, by the shoulders, toward opposing doors.)

Curtain

---

[6] **divined**—discovered.

[7] Elmire—Orgon's wife and Mariane's stepmother.

QUESTIONS TO CONSIDER

1. What is being satirized in this scene?

2. What begins the argument between Valère and Mariane?

3. Throughout most of the scene, what is the tone of the two lovers' advice to one another?

4. What function does the maid Dorine excercise in this scene?

from

Pride and Prejudice

JANE AUSTEN

Like Molière (page 428), English novelist Jane Austen (1775–1817) had a sharp eye for human weaknesses, particularly vanity. Her novel Pride and Prejudice *concerns the Bennet family—Mr. and Mrs. Bennet and their five daughters—who live at Longbourn in Hertfordshire. Mrs. Bennet's chief concern is getting her daughters suitably married. Because the Bennets have no son, the laws governing inheritance in England at this time will result in most of Mr. Bennet's property passing at his death to a cousin, Mr. Collins, a smug, silly young clergyman who is their nearest male heir. He has been encouraged to marry by his benefactor Lady Catherine de Bourgh. His first efforts to do so are described here.*

Mr. Collins was not a sensible man, and the deficiency of Nature had been but little assisted by education or society; the greatest part of his life having been spent under the guidance of an illiterate and miserly father; and though he belonged to one of the universities, he had merely kept the necessary terms, without forming at it any useful acquaintance. The subjection in which his father had brought him up had given him originally great humility of manner; but it was now a good deal counteracted by the self-conceit of a weak head, living in retirement, and the consequential feelings of early and unexpected prosperity. A fortunate chance had recommended him to Lady Catherine de Bourgh when the living of Hunsford[1] was vacant; and the respect which he felt for her high rank, and his veneration for her as his patroness, mingling with a very good opinion of himself, of his authority as a clergyman, and his right as a rector, made him altogether a mixture of pride and **obsequiousness**,[2] self-importance and humility.

Having now a good house and very sufficient income, he intended to marry; and in seeking a reconciliation with the Longbourn family he had a wife in view, as he meant to choose one of the daughters,

---

[1] living of Hunsford—The position of the local clergyman of the Church of England was known as a "living," and in Mr. Collins's case, this living was bestowed by the wealthy Lady Catherine.

[2] **obsequiousness**—servility or submissiveness.

if he found them as handsome and **amiable**[3] as they were represented by common report. This was his plan of amends—of atonement—for inheriting their father's estate; and he thought it an excellent one, full of eligibility and suitableness, and excessively generous and disinterested on his own part.

His plan did not vary on seeing them. Miss Bennet's[4] lovely face confirmed his views, and established all his strictest notions of what was due to seniority; and for the first evening *she* was his settled choice. The next morning, however, made an alteration; for in a quarter of an hour's tête-à-tête[5] with Mrs. Bennet before breakfast, a conversation beginning with his parsonage-house, and leading naturally to the **avowal**[6] of his hopes, that a mistress for it might be found at Longbourn, produced from her, amid very complaisant smiles and general encouragement, a caution against the very Jane he had fixed on. "As to her *younger* daughters, she could not take upon her to say—she could not positively answer—but she did not *know* of any prepossession;—her *eldest* daughter, she must just mention—she felt it **incumbent**[7] on her to hint, was likely to be very soon engaged."

Mr. Collins had only to change from Jane to Elizabeth—and it was soon done—done while Mrs. Bennet was stirring the fire. Elizabeth, equally next to Jane in birth and beauty, succeeded her, of course.

Mrs. Bennet treasured up the hint, and trusted that she might soon have two daughters married; and the man whom she could not bear to speak of the day before was now high in her good graces. . . .

The next day opened a new scene at Longbourn. Mr. Collins made his declaration[8] in form. Having resolved to do it without loss of time, as his leave of absence extended only to the following Saturday, and having no feelings of **diffidence**[9] to make it distressing to himself even at the moment, he set about it in a very orderly manner, with all the observances, which he supposed a regular part of the business. On finding Mrs. Bennet, Elizabeth, and one of the younger girls together, soon after breakfast, he addressed the mother in these words: "May I hope, madam, for your interest with your fair daughter Elizabeth, when I solicit for the honor of a private audience[10] with her in the course of this morning?"

Before Elizabeth had time for anything but a blush of surprise, Mrs. Bennet instantly answered, "Oh dear!—Yes—certainly. I am sure Lizzy will be very happy—I am sure she can have no objection. Come, Kitty, I want you upstairs." And, gathering her work together, she was hastening away, when Elizabeth called out,

---

[3] **amiable**—pleasant, agreeable.

[4] Miss Bennet—the Bennets' eldest daughter, Jane.

[5] tête-à-tête—private talk.

[6] **avowal**—frank admission.

[7] **incumbent**—imposed as a duty.

[8] declaration—proposal of marriage to Elizabeth Bennet.

[9] **diffidence**—shyness, lack of confidence.

[10] private audience—Mr. Collins wants to speak with Elizabeth alone.

"Dear madam, do not go. I beg you will not go. Mr. Collins must excuse me. He can have nothing to say to me that anybody need not hear. I am going away myself."

"No, no, nonsense, Lizzy. I desire you will stay where you are." And upon Elizabeth's seeming really, with vexed and embarrassed looks, about to escape, she added, "Lizzy, I insist upon your staying and hearing Mr. Collins."

Elizabeth would not oppose such an injunction[11]—and a moment's consideration making her also sensible that it would be wisest to get it over as soon and as quietly as possible, she sat down again, and tried to conceal, by incessant employment, the feelings which were divided between distress and diversion. Mrs. Bennet and Kitty walked off, and as soon as they were gone Mr. Collins began.

"Believe me, my dear Miss Elizabeth, that your modesty, so far from doing you any disservice, rather adds to your other perfections. You would have been less amiable in my eyes had there *not* been this little unwillingness; but allow me to assure you, that I have your respected mother's permission for this address. You can hardly doubt the **purport**[12] of my discourse, however your natural delicacy may lead you to **dissemble**;[13] my attentions have been too marked to be mistaken. Almost as soon as I entered the house, I singled you out as the companion of my future life. But before I am run away with by my feelings on this subject, perhaps it would be advisable for me to state my reasons for marrying—and,

moreover, for coming into Hertfordshire with the design of selecting a wife, as I certainly did."

The idea of Mr. Collins, with all his solemn composure, being run away with by his feelings, made Elizabeth so near laughing, that she could not use the short pause he allowed in any attempt to stop him farther, and he continued—

"My reasons for marrying are, first, that I think it a right thing for every clergyman in easy circumstances (like myself) to set the example of matrimony in his parish; secondly, that I am convinced it will add very greatly to my happiness; and thirdly—which perhaps I ought to have mentioned earlier, that it is the particular advice and recommendation of the very noble lady whom I have the honor of calling patroness. Twice has she condescended to give me her opinion (unasked too!) on this subject; and it was but the very Saturday night before I left Hunsford—between our pools at quadrille,[14] while Mrs. Jenkinson was arranging Miss de Bourgh's footstool, that she said, 'Mr. Collins, you must marry. A clergyman like you must marry.—Choose properly, choose a gentlewoman for *my* sake; and for your *own*, let her be an active, useful sort of person, not brought up high, but able to make a small income go a good way. This is my advice. Find such a woman as soon as you can, bring her to Hunsford, and I will visit her.' Allow me,

---

[11] injunction—order.

[12] **purport**—intention.

[13] **dissemble**—disguise one's feelings.

[14] quadrille—card game played by four people.

by the way, to observe, my fair cousin, that I do not reckon the notice and kindness of Lady Catherine de Bourgh as among the least of the advantages in my power to offer. You will find her manners beyond anything I can describe; and your wit and vivacity, I think, must be acceptable to her, especially when tempered with the silence and respect which her rank will inevitably excite. Thus much for my general intention in favor of matrimony; it remains to be told why my views were directed to Longbourn instead of my own neighborhood, where I assure you there are many amiable young women. But the fact is, that being, as I am, to inherit this estate after the death of your honored father (who, however, may live many years longer), I could not satisfy myself without resolving to choose a wife from among his daughters, that the loss to them might be as little as possible, when the melancholy event takes place—which, however, as I have already said, may not be for several years. This has been my motive, my fair cousin, and I flatter myself it will not sink me in your esteem. And now nothing remains for me but to assure you in the most animated language of the violence of my affection. To fortune I am perfectly indifferent, and shall make no demand of that nature on your father, since I am well aware that it could not be complied with; and that one thousand pounds in the 4 per cents,[15] which will not be yours till after your mother's decease, is all that you may ever be entitled to. On that head, therefore, I shall be uniformly silent; and you may assure yourself that no ungenerous reproach shall ever pass my lips when we are married."

It was absolutely necessary to interrupt him now.

"You are too hasty, sir," she cried. "You forget that I have made no answer. Let me do it without further loss of time. Accept my thanks for the compliment you are paying me. I am very sensible of the honor of your proposals, but it is impossible for me to do otherwise than decline them."

"I am not now to learn," replied Mr. Collins, with a formal wave of the hand, "that it is usual with young ladies to reject the addresses of the man whom they secretly mean to accept, when he first applies for their favor; and that sometimes the refusal is repeated a second or even a third time. I am therefore by no means discouraged by what you have just said, and shall hope to lead you to the altar ere long."

"Upon my word, sir," cried Elizabeth, "your hope is rather an extraordinary one after my declaration. I do assure you that I am not one of those young ladies (if such young ladies there are) who are so daring as to risk their happiness on the chance of being asked a second time. I am perfectly serious in my refusal. You could not make *me* happy, and I am convinced that I am the last woman in the world who would make *you* so. Nay, were your friend Lady Catherine to know me, I am persuaded she would find me in every respect ill qualified for the situation."

---

[15] in the 4 per cents—paying 4 percent per year.

"Were it certain that Lady Catherine would think so," said Mr. Collins very gravely—"but I cannot imagine that her ladyship would at all disapprove of you. And you may be certain that when I have the honor of seeing her again, I shall speak in the highest terms of your modesty, economy, and other amiable qualifications."

"Indeed, Mr. Collins, all praise of me will be unnecessary. You must give me leave to judge for myself, and pay me the compliment of believing what I say. I wish you very happy and very rich, and by refusing your hand, do all in my power to prevent your being otherwise. In making me the offer, you must have satisfied the delicacy of your feelings with regard to my family, and may take possession of Longbourn estate whenever it falls without any self-reproach. This matter may be considered, therefore, as finally settled." And rising as she thus spoke, she would have quitted the room, had not Mr. Collins thus addressed her:

"When I do myself the honor of speaking to you next on the subject, I shall hope to receive a more favorable answer than you have now given me; though I am far from accusing you of cruelty at present, because I know it to be the established custom of your sex to reject a man on the first application, and perhaps you have even now said as much to encourage my suit as would be consistent with the true delicacy of the female character."

"Really, Mr. Collins," cried Elizabeth with some warmth, "you puzzle me exceedingly. If what I have hitherto said can appear to you in the form of encouragement, I know not how to express my refusal in such a way as may convince you of its being one."

"You must give me leave to flatter myself, my dear cousin, that your refusal of my addresses is merely words of course. My reasons for believing it are briefly these:—It does not appear to me that my hand is unworthy your acceptance, or that the establishment I can offer would be any other than highly desirable. My situation in life, my connections with the family of de Bourgh, and my relationship to your own, are circumstances highly in my favor; and you should take it into further consideration, that in spite of your manifold attractions, it is by no means certain that another offer of marriage may ever be made you. Your portion[16] is unhappily so small, that it will in all likelihood undo the effects of your loveliness and amiable qualifications. As I must therefore conclude that you are not serious in your rejection of me, I shall choose to attribute it to your wish of increasing my love by suspense, according to the usual practice of elegant females."

"I do assure you, sir, that I have no pretensions whatever to that kind of elegance which consists in tormenting a respectable man. I would rather be paid the compliment of being believed sincere. I thank you again and again for the honor you have done me in your proposals, but

---

[16] portion—a woman's dowry; that is, the money or property her husband receives from her family when she marries.

to accept them is absolutely impossible. My feelings in every respect forbid it. Can I speak plainer? Do not consider me now as an elegant female, intending to plague you, but as a rational creature, speaking the truth from her heart."

"You are uniformly charming!" cried he, with an air of awkward gallantry; "and I am persuaded that when sanctioned by the express authority of both your excellent parents, my proposals will not fail of being acceptable."

To such perseverance in wilful self-deception Elizabeth would make no reply, and immediately and in silence withdrew; determined, that if he persisted in considering her repeated refusals as flattering encouragement, to apply to her father, whose negative might be uttered in such a manner as must be decisive, and whose behavior at least could not be mistaken for the affectation and coquetry[17] of an elegant female.

---

[17] affectation and coquetry—artificiality and flirtatiousness.

QUESTIONS TO CONSIDER

1. The narrator describes Mr. Collins as a "mixture of pride and obsequiousness, self-importance and humility." How are his pride and self-importance demonstrated here?

2. Mr. Collins assures Elizabeth of "the violence of my affection" and his "indifference" to fortune. How has he demonstrated just the opposite?

3. How does Mr. Collins insult Elizabeth?

4. What is your chief impression of Elizabeth?

5. Does the tone of this satire of Mr. Collins strike you as gentle or bitter? Explain.

Satirical Art

Satire was a technique employed in the visual arts as well as literature. William Hogarth (1697–1764) was an English painter and graphic artist who became famous for his satirical engravings in such series as The Rake's Progress *and* Marriage à la Mode. *Several of Hogarth's engravings appear below and on the facing page. Francisco de Goya (1746–1828) was a Spanish painter and etcher who attacked folly, superstition, and brutality in such series as* Los Caprichos *("Caprices") and* Desastres de la Guerra *("Disasters of War"). Etchings from* Los Caprichos *appear on pages 442 and 443.*

▲

In the second engraving from *Marriage à la Mode*, Hogarth shows the newly married couple already bored with one another. Holding a bunch of unpaid bills, their servant raises his eyes anxiously to heaven.

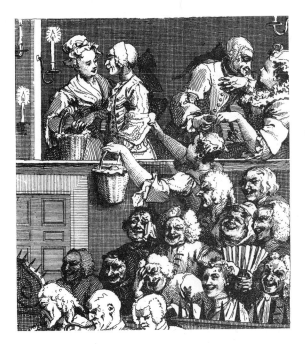

 In *The Laughing Audience*, Hogarth observes the crowd at a theater—including those paying no attention to the performance. (The spikes in the foreground were to protect actors from unruly spectators.)

Hogarth's *The Bench* shows English judges wearing their traditional garb of wigs and robes.

Goya's strange etching *The Sleep of Reason Produces Monsters* has been interpreted as an image of the dangers of the unfettered artistic imagination.

▲

In *Who Is More Bored?*, Goya shows a couple going through the motions of courtship with little enthusiasm on either side.

In Goya's *Till Death*, an old woman is shown adorning herself for her birthday while younger men (possible suitors?) look on. ▶

QUESTIONS TO CONSIDER

1. What does his engraving from *Marriage à la Mode* suggest about Hogarth's view of marriage?

2. What do you think Hogarth is satirizing in *The Laughing Audience*?

3. Why might judges who had seen *The Bench* have been annoyed with Hogarth?

4. Do you agree with Goya that the irrational side of human nature poses dangers for the artist? Why or why not?

5. What views of courtship are expressed in Goya's *Who Is More Bored?* and *Till Death*?

The Doctrine of Optimism

ALEXANDER POPE

In the late 17th and 18th centuries, a broad cultural movement known as the Enlightenment developed in Europe. Influenced by the revolution in science, the Enlightenment saw reason as the supreme authority in thought and action. Enlightenment thinkers believed the universe itself has a rational order, leading some to the doctrine of optimism—that human beings occupy "the best of all possible worlds." In An Essay on Man, *the English poet Alexander Pope (1688–1744) sums up the case for optimism.*

See, through this air, this ocean, and this earth,
All matter quick, and bursting into birth.
Above, how high progressive life may go?
Around how wide? how deep extend below?
Vast chain of being![1] which from God began,
Natures ethereal,[2] human, angel, man,
Beast, bird, fish, insect! what no eye can see,
No glass[3] can reach! from infinite to thee!
From thee to nothing!—On superior powers
Were we to press inferior might on ours;
Or in the full creation leave a void,
Where one step broken, the great scale's destroyed:

---

[1] chain of being—theory that each creature formed a link in a great chain leading from inanimate objects to God.
[2] ethereal—heavenly.
[3] glass—lens, such as that of a telescope or microscope.

From nature's chain whatever link you strike,
Tenth, or ten thousandth, breaks the chain alike.
And if each system in gradation roll,
Alike essential to th' amazing whole;
The least confusion but in one, not all
That system only, but the whole must fall.
Let earth unbalanced from her orbit fly,
Planets and suns run lawless through the sky;
Let ruling angels from their spheres be hurled,
Being on being wrecked, and world on world;
Heavens whole foundations to their center nod,
And nature trembles to the throne of God.
All this dread order break—For whom? For thee?
Vile worm!—O madness! pride! impiety!
What if the foot, ordained the dust to tread,
Or hand to toil, aspired to be the head?
What if the head, the eye or ear, repined[4]
To serve mere engines to the ruling mind?
Just as absurd, for any part to claim
To be another, in this general frame:
Just as absurd, to mourn the tasks or pains,
The great directing mind of all ordains.
All are but parts of one stupendous[5] whole:
Whose body Nature is, and God the soul.
That, changed through all and yet in all the same,
Great in the earth as in th' ethereal frame,
Warms in the sun, refreshes in the breeze,
Glows in the stars, and blossoms in the trees,
Lives through all life, extends through all extent,
Spreads undivided, operates unspent,
Breathes in our soul, informs our mortal part,
As full, as perfect, in a hair, as heart,
As full, as perfect, in vile[6] man that mourns,

---

[4] repined—yearned.

[5] stupendous—enormous.

[6] vile—lowly.

As the rapt seraph[7] that adores and burns;
To Him no high, no low, no great, no small;
He fills, he bounds, connects, and equals all.
Cease then, nor Order Imperfection name:
Our proper bliss depends on what we blame.
Know thy own Point. This kind, this due degree
Of blindness, weakness, Heaven bestows on thee.
Submit—in this, or any other sphere,
Secure to be as blest as thou canst bear.
Safe in the hand of one disposing Power,
Or in the natal, or the mortal hour.[8]
All nature is but art, unknown to thee;
All chance, direction which thou canst not see;
All discord, harmony not understood;
All partial evil, universal good:
And spite of pride, in erring Reason's spite,
One truth is clear; "Whatever is, is right."

---

[7] rapt seraph—enraptured angel.

[8] natal . . . mortal hour—birth and death.

QUESTIONS TO CONSIDER

1. What is Pope's vision of the natural world?

2. In Pope's view, what will happen if even the slightest change is made in the order of nature?

3. Pope observes, "Whatever is, is right." Would this view be likely to produce a just society? Why or why not?

from

Candide

VOLTAIRE

In his novel Candide, *the French writer Voltaire (1694–1778) satirizes Enlightenment faith in "the best of all possible worlds." Chapter 1 introduces the naive hero Candide and the other inhabitants of the castle where he lives; in Chapter 5, Candide, his former tutor Dr. Pangloss, and Jacques, a kindly member of the persecuted Protestant sect of the Anabaptists, sail for Lisbon.*

Chapter 1

How Candide was brought up in a noble castle and how he was expelled from the same

In the castle of the Baron Thunder-ten-tronckh in Westphalia[1] there lived a youth, endowed by Nature with the most gentle manners. His face proclaimed his soul. His judgment was quite honest and he was extremely simple-minded; and this was the reason, I think, that he was named Candide. Old servants in the house suspected that he was the son of the Baron's sister and of a good honest gentleman in the neighborhood, whom this young lady would never marry because he could only prove seventy-one quarterings,[2] and the rest of his genealogical tree was lost, owing to the ravages of time.

The Baron was one of the most powerful lords in Westphalia, for his castle possessed a door and windows. His Great Hall was even decorated with a piece of tapestry. The dogs in his stable-yard made up a pack of hounds when necessary; his grooms were his huntsmen; the village curate was his Grand Almoner.[3] They all called him "My Lord," and laughed at his jokes.

The Baroness weighed about three hundred and fifty pounds, was therefore greatly respected, and did the honors of the house with a dignity which rendered her still more respectable. Her daughter Cunégonde, aged seventeen, was rosy-

---

[1] Westphalia—western German province.

[2] quarterings—a reference to the four quarters of a coat of arms, each quarter displaying the arms of different branches of a family.

[3] curate . . . Grand Almoner—a curate is a local priest. The Grand Almoner was an official who distributed charity at a royal court.

cheeked, fresh, plump and tempting. The Baron's son appeared in every respect worthy of his father. The tutor Pangloss was the oracle of the house, and little Candide followed his lessons with all the candor of his age and character.

Pangloss taught metaphysico-theologo-cosmolonigology.[4] He proved admirably that there is no effect without a cause and that in this best of all possible worlds, My Lord the Baron's castle was the best of castles and his wife the best of all possible Baronesses.

"'Tis demonstrated," said he, "that things cannot be otherwise; for, since everything is made for an end, everything is necessarily for the best end. Observe that noses were made to wear spectacles; and so we have spectacles. Legs were visibly instituted to be breeched, and we have breeches. Stones were formed to be quarried and to build castles; and My Lord has a very noble castle; the greatest Baron in the province should have the best house; and as pigs were made to be eaten, we eat pork all the year round; consequently, those who have asserted that all is well talk nonsense; they ought to have said that all is for the best."

Candide listened attentively and believed innocently; for he thought Mademoiselle Cunégonde extremely beautiful, although he was never bold enough to tell her so. He decided that after the happiness of being born Baron of Thunder-ten-tronckh, the second degree of happiness was to be Mademoiselle Cunégonde; the third, to see her every day; and the fourth to listen to Doctor Pangloss, the greatest philosopher of the province and consequently of the whole world.

One day when Cunégonde was walking near the castle, in a little wood they called The Park, she observed Doctor Pangloss in the bushes, giving a lesson in experimental physics to her mother's waiting maid, a very pretty and docile brunette. Mademoiselle Cunégonde had a great inclination for science and watched breathlessly the reiterated experiments she witnessed; she observed clearly the Doctor's sufficient reason, the effects and the causes, and returned home very much excited, **pensive**,[5] filled with the desire of learning, reflecting that she might be the sufficient reason of young Candide and that he might be her own.

On her way back to the castle she met Candide and blushed; Candide also blushed. She bade him good-morning in a hesitating voice; Candide replied without knowing what he was saying. Next day, when they left the table after dinner, Cunégonde and Candide found themselves behind a screen; Cunégonde dropped her handkerchief, Candide picked it up; she innocently held his hand; the young man innocently kissed the young lady's hand with remarkable vivacity, tenderness and grace; their lips met, their eyes sparkled, their knees trembled, their hands wandered. Baron Thunder-ten-tronckh passed near the screen, and, observing this cause

---

[4] metaphyisico-theologo-cosmolonigology—Voltaire is satirizing German Enlightenment philosophy.
[5] **pensive**—thoughtful.

and effect, expelled Candide from the castle by kicking him in the backside frequently and hard. Cunégonde swooned; to recover her senses, the Baroness slapped her in the face; and all was in **consternation**[6] in the noblest and most agreeable of all possible castles.

Chapter 5
Storm, shipwreck, earthquake, and what happened to Dr. Pangloss, to Candide and the Anabaptist Jacques

Half the enfeebled passengers, suffering from that inconceivable anguish which the rolling of a ship causes in the nerves and in all the humors of bodies shaken in contrary directions, did not retain strength enough even to trouble about the danger. The other half screamed and prayed; the sails were ripped, the masts broken, the vessel leaking. Those worked who could, no one cooperated, no one commanded. The Anabaptist tried to help a little in the ship-handling; he was on the main deck; a furious sailor struck him violently and stretched him on the deck; but the blow he delivered gave him so violent a shock that he fell headfirst out of the ship. He remained hanging and clinging to part of the broken mast. The good Jacques ran to his aid, helped him to climb back, and from the effort he made was flung into the sea in full view of the sailor, who allowed him to drown without condescending even to look at him. Candide came up, saw his benefactor reappear for a moment and then be engulfed for ever. He tried to throw himself after him into the sea; he was prevented by the philosopher Pangloss, who proved to him that the Lisbon roads[7] had been expressly created for the Anabaptist to be drowned in them. While he was proving this *a priori*,[8] the vessel sank, and every one perished except Pangloss, Candide and the brutal sailor who had drowned the virtuous Anabaptist; the blackguard[9] swam successfully to the shore and Pangloss and Candide were carried there on a plank.

When they had recovered a little, they walked toward Lisbon; they had a little money by which they hoped to be saved from hunger after having escaped the storm. Weeping the death of their benefactor, they had scarcely set foot in the town when they felt the earth tremble under their feet; the sea rose in foaming masses in the port and smashed the ships which rode at anchor. Whirlwinds of flame and ashes covered the streets and squares; the houses collapsed, the roofs were thrown upon the foundations, and the foundations were scattered; thirty thousand inhabitants of every age and sex were crushed under the ruins.[10] Whistling and swearing, the sailor said: "There'll be something to pick up here."

"What can be the sufficient reason for this phenomenon?" said Pangloss.

---

[6] **consternation**—confusion.

[7] roads—sheltered anchorage for ships near shore; roadstead.

[8] *a priori*—by deductive rather than inductive reasoning.

[9] blackguard—scoundrel, meaning the sailor.

[10] thirty thousand . . . under the ruins—The Lisbon earthquake, which occurred in 1755 and killed tens of thousands, greatly weakened Enlightenment belief in a rational world order.

"It is the Last Day!" cried Candide.

The sailor immediately ran among the debris, dared death to find money, found it, seized it, got drunk, and having slept off his wine, bought the favors of the first woman of easy virtue he met on the ruins of the houses and among the dead and dying. Pangloss, however, pulled him by the sleeve. "My friend," said he, "this is not well, you are disregarding universal reason, you choose the wrong occasion."

"Bloody Hell!" he retorted, "I am a sailor and I was born in Batavia; four times have I stamped on the crucifix[11] during four voyages to Japan; you have found the right man for your universal reason!"

Candide had been hurt by some falling rocks; he lay in the street covered with debris. He said to Pangloss: "Alas! Get me a little wine and oil; I am dying."

"This earthquake is not a new thing," replied Pangloss. "The town of Lima felt the same shocks in America last year; similar causes produce similar effects; there must certainly be a train of sulphur underground from Lima to Lisbon."

"Nothing is more probable," replied Candide; "but, for God's sake, a little oil and wine."

"What do you mean, probable?" replied the philosopher; "I maintain that it is proved."

Candide lost consciousness, and Pangloss brought him a little water from a neighboring fountain.

Next day they found a little food as they wandered among the ruins and regained a little strength. Afterwards they worked like others to help the inhabitants who had escaped death. Some citizens they had assisted gave them as good a dinner as could be expected in such a disaster; true, it was a dreary meal; the hosts watered their bread with their tears, but Pangloss consoled them by assuring them that things could not be otherwise. "For," said he, "all this is for the best; for, if there is a volcano at Lisbon, it cannot be anywhere else; for it is impossible that things should not be where they are; for all is well."

A little man in black, a familiar of the Inquisition,[12] who sat beside him, politely took up the conversation, and said: "Apparently, you do not believe in original sin; for, if everything is for the best, there was neither fall nor punishment."

"I most humbly beg your excellency's pardon," replied Pangloss still more politely, "for the fall of man and the curse necessarily entered into the best of all possible worlds."

"Then you do not believe in free will?" said the familiar. "Your excellency will pardon me," said Pangloss; "free will can exist with absolute necessity; for it was necessary that we should be free; for in short, limited will . . ."

Pangloss was in the middle of his phrase when the familiar nodded to his armed attendant who was pouring out port or Oporto wine for him.

---

[11] stamped on the crucifix—practice performed by Dutch merchants to prove they were not Portuguese Catholics, who were not allowed in Japan.

[12] familiar of the Inquisition—official of the Roman Catholic court that tried heretics (those who dissented from orthodox Catholic teachings), as well as non-believers such as Jews and Muslims.

Chapter 6

How a splendid auto-da-fé was held to prevent earthquakes, and how Candide was flogged

After the earthquake which destroyed three-quarters of Lisbon, the wise men of that country could discover no more efficacious way of preventing total ruin than by giving the people a splendid *auto-da-fé*.[13] It was decided by the university of Coimbre that the sight of several persons being slowly burned in great ceremony is an infallible secret for preventing earthquakes. Consequently they had arrested a Biscayan convicted of having married his fellow-godmother, and two Portuguese who, when eating a chicken, had thrown away the bacon.[14] After dinner they came and bound Dr. Pangloss and his disciple Candide, one because he had spoken and the other because he had listened with an air of **approbation**.[15] They were both carried separately to extremely cool apartments, where there was never any discomfort from the sun; a week afterwards each was dressed in a sanbenito and their heads were ornamented with paper mitres[16] Candide's mitre and sanbenito were painted with flames upside down and with devils who had neither tails nor claws; but Pangloss's devils had claws and tails, and his flames were upright.[17]

Dressed in this manner they marched in procession and listened to a most pathetic sermon, followed by lovely plain song music. Candide was flogged in time to the music, while the singing went on; the Biscayan and the two men who had not wanted to eat the bacon were burned, and Pangloss was hanged, although this is not the usual practice. The very same day, the earth shook again with a terrible clamor.

Candide, terrified, dumbfounded, bewildered, covered with blood, quivering from head to foot, said to himself: "If this is the best of all possible worlds, what are the others? . . ."

---

[13] *auto-da-fé*—literally, "act of the faith," a burning of a heretic at the stake.

[14] thrown away the bacon—They were assumed to be Jews because they did not eat pork.

[15] **approbation**—approval.

[16] sanbenito . . . mitres—garments worn by victims at an *auto-da-fé*.

[17] flames upside down . . . upright—Candide's dress signifies repentance; Pangloss's signifies refusal to repent, and therefore damnation.

QUESTIONS TO CONSIDER

1. What is wrong with Dr. Pangloss's style of reasoning—for example, "noses were made to wear spectacles; and so we have spectacles"?

2. How does Pangloss explain the earthquake in Lisbon?

3. In your opinion, is satire effective in reforming society? Why or why not?

Government by Consent

JOHN LOCKE

Defined by formulas such as Pope's "Whatever is, is right," the Enlightenment had little interest in democratic ideas. An exception was the English political philosopher John Locke (1632–1704). In his Second Treatise on Civil Government, he argued that human beings were "by nature all free, equal, and independent," and that consequently government must be based on consent. Locke's theories had an important influence on the ideas of those who shaped the American Revolution.

Of the State of Nature

To understand political power aright, and derive it from its original, we must consider what estate all men are naturally in, and that is, a state of perfect freedom to order their actions, and dispose of their possessions and persons as they think fit, within the bounds of the law of Nature, without asking leave or depending upon the will of any other man.

A state also of equality, wherein all the power and **jurisdiction**[1] is **reciprocal**,[2] no one having more than another, there being nothing more evident than that creatures of the same species and rank, promiscuously[3] born to all the same advantages of Nature, and the use of the same faculties, should also be equal one amongst another, without subordination or subjection, unless the lord

and master of them all should, by any manifest declaration of his will, set one above another, and confer on him, by an evident and clear appointment, an undoubted right to dominion and sovereignty. . . .

Of Property

Whether we consider natural reason, which tells us that men, being once born, have a right to their preservation, and consequently to meat and drink and such other things as Nature affords for their subsistence, or "revelation," which gives us an account of those grants God made of the world to Adam, and to Noah and his

---

[1] **jurisdiction**—authority.
[2] **reciprocal**—mutual.
[3] promiscuously—without discriminations of rank.

sons,[4] it is very clear that God, as King David[5] says (Psalm cxv. 16), "has given the earth to the children of men," given it to mankind in common. But, this being supposed, it seems to some a very great difficulty how anyone should ever come to have a property in anything, I will not content myself to answer, that, if it be difficult to make out "property" upon a **supposition**[6] that God gave the world to Adam and his posterity in common, it is impossible that any man but one universal monarch should have any "property" upon a supposition that God gave the world to Adam and his heirs in succession, exclusive of all the rest of his posterity; but I shall endeavor to show how men might come to have a property in several parts of that which God gave to mankind in common, and that without any express **compact**[7] of all the commoners.

God, who hath given the world to men in common, hath also given them reason to make use of it to the best advantage of life and convenience. The earth and all that is therein is given to men for the support and comfort of their being. And though all the fruits it naturally produces, and beasts it feeds, belong to mankind in common, as they are produced by the spontaneous hand of Nature, and nobody has originally a private dominion exclusive of the rest of mankind in any of them, as they are thus in their natural state, yet being given for the use of men, there must of necessity be a means to appropriate them some way or other before they can be of any use, or at all beneficial, to any particular men. The fruit or venison[8] which nourishes the wild Indian, who knows no enclosure,[9] and is still a tenant in common, must be his, and so his—i.e., a part of him, that another can no longer have any right to it before it can do him any good for the support of his life.

Though the earth and all inferior creatures be common to all men, yet every man has a "property" in his own "person." This nobody has any right to but himself. The "labor" of his body and the "work" of his hands, we may say, are properly his. Whatsoever, then, he removes out of the state that Nature hath provided and left it in, he hath mixed his labor with it, and joined to it something that is his own, and thereby makes it his property. It being by him removed from the common state Nature placed it in, it hath by this labor something **annexed**[10] to it that excludes the common right of other men. For this "labor" being the unquestionable property of the laborer, no man but he can have a right to what that is once joined to, at least where there is enough, and as good left in common for others. . . .

---

[4] grants . . . Noah and his sons—In the biblical Book of Genesis, God gives dominion over the earth to Adam, the first man; after the Flood, God renews this grant to Noah and his family.

[5] David—king of ancient Israel to whom many of the Psalms in the Bible are attributed.

[6] **supposition**—assumption.

[7] **compact**—agreement.

[8] venison—meat of the deer.

[9] enclosure—act of turning common land into private holdings.

[10] **annexed**—attached as a consequence.

Of the Beginning of Political Societies

Men being, as has been said, by nature all free, equal, and independent, no one can be put out of this estate and subjected to the political power of another without his own consent, which is done by agreeing with other men, to join and unite a community for their comfortable, safe, and peaceable living, one amongst another, in a secure enjoyment of their properties, and a greater security against any that are not of it. This any number of men may do, because it injures not the freedom of the rest; they are left, as they were, in the liberty of the state of Nature. When any number of men have so consented to make one community or government, they are thereby presently incorporated, and make one body politic,[11] wherein the majority have a right to act and conclude the rest.

For, when any number of men have, by the consent of every individual, made a community, they have thereby made that community one body, with a power to act as one body, which is only by the will and determination of the majority. For that which acts any community, being only the consent of the individuals of it, and it being one body, must move one way, it is necessary the body should move that way whither the greater force carries it, which is the consent of the majority, or else it is impossible it should act or continue one body, one community, which the consent of every individual that united into it agreed that it should; and so everyone is bound by that consent to be concluded by the majority. And therefore we see that in assemblies empowered to act by positive laws where no number is set by that positive law which empowers them, the act of the majority passes for the act of the whole, and of course determines as having, by the law of Nature and reason, the power of the whole.

And thus every man, by consenting with others to make one body politic under one government, puts himself under an obligation to everyone of that society to submit to the determination of the majority, and to be concluded by it; or else this original compact, whereby he with others incorporates into one society, would signify nothing, and be no compact if he be left free and under no other ties than he was in before in the state of Nature. For what appearance would there be of any compact? What new engagement if he were no farther tied by any decrees of the society than he himself thought fit and did actually consent to? This would be still as great a liberty as he himself had before his compact, or anyone else in the state of Nature, who may submit himself and consent to any acts of it if he thinks fit.

For if the consent of the majority shall not in reason be received as the act of the whole, and conclude every individual, nothing but the consent of every individual can make anything to be the act of the whole, which, considering the infirmities

---

[11] body politic—political unit formed by individuals under a government.

of health and avocations[12] of business, which in a number though much less than that of a commonwealth, will necessarily keep many away from the public assembly; and the variety of opinions and contrariety[13] of interests which unavoidably happen in all collections of men, it is next impossible ever to be had. . . .

Whosoever, therefore, out of a state of Nature unite into a community, must be understood to give up all the power necessary to the ends for which they unite into society to the majority of the community, unless they expressly agreed in any number greater than the majority. And this is done by barely agreeing to unite into one political society, which is all the compact that is, or needs be, between the individuals that enter into or make up a commonwealth. And thus, that which begins and actually constitutes any political society is nothing but the consent of any number of freemen capable of majority, to unite and incorporate into such a society. And this is that, and that only, which did or could give beginning to any lawful government in the world. . . .

---

[12] avocations—customary work.

[13] contrariety—conflict.

QUESTIONS TO CONSIDER

1. What is "the state of nature"?

2. What are John Locke's views on property?

3. Why would a slave-owner have been opposed to Locke's ideas on property rights?

4. Why must the majority rule?

from

A Vindication of the Rights of Woman

MARY WOLLSTONECRAFT

When John Locke wrote of men being by nature free and equal, he meant men; he did not think of women, for women were not eligible to serve in the English Parliament, could not vote, and were rarely well educated. Mary Wollstonecraft (1759–1797) was the daughter of an abusive alcoholic father. She had a daughter out of wedlock; the father of the child abandoned her; she had to support herself, and she twice tried to commit suicide. Small wonder that in 1792 she published an appeal for greater independence for women. (A vindication is a defense.) Although she was later married happily to William Godwin, she died ten days after the birth of her second daughter.

To account for, and excuse the tyranny of man, many ingenious arguments have been brought forward to prove, that the two sexes, in the acquirement of virtue, ought to aim at attaining a very different character: or, to speak explicitly, women are not allowed to have sufficient strength of mind to acquire what really deserves the name of virtue. Yet it should seem, allowing them to have souls, that there is but one way appointed by providence to lead *mankind* to either virtue or happiness.

If then women are not a swarm of ephemeron[1] triflers, why should they be kept in ignorance under the **specious**[2]

name of innocence? Men complain, and with reason, of the follies and caprices of our sex, when they do not keenly satirize our headstrong passions and groveling vices. Behold, I should answer, the natural effect of ignorance! The mind will ever be unstable that has only prejudices to rest on, and the current will run with destructive fury when there are no barriers to break its force. Women are told from their infancy, and taught by the example of their mothers, that a little knowledge of human

---

[1] ephemeron—short-lived.
[2] **specious**—deceptively attractive.

weakness, justly termed cunning, softness of temper, *outward* obedience, and a scrupulous attention to a puerile kind of propriety,[3] will obtain for them the protection of man; and should they be beautiful, every thing else is needless, for at least twenty years of their lives. . . .

The most perfect education, in my opinion is, such an exercise of the understanding as is best calculated to strengthen the body and form the heart. Or, in other words, to enable the individual to attain such habits of virtue as will render it independent. In fact, it is a farce to call any being virtuous whose virtues do not result from the exercise of its own reason. This was Rousseau's opinion respecting men.[4] I extend it to women, and confidently assert, that they have been drawn out of their sphere by false refinement, and not by an endeavor to acquire masculine qualities. Still the regal homage which they receive is so intoxicating, that till the manners of the times are changed, and formed on more reasonable principles, it may be impossible to convince them, that the illegitimate power, which they obtain by degrading themselves, is a curse, and that they must return to nature and equality, if they wish to secure the placid satisfaction that unsophisticated affections impart. But for this epoch we must wait—wait, perhaps, till kings and nobles, enlightened by reason, and, preferring the real dignity of man to childish state, throw off their gaudy hereditary trappings; and if then women do not resign the arbitrary power of beauty, they will prove that they have *less* mind than man. . . .

Many are the causes that, in the present corrupt state of society, contribute to enslave women by cramping their understandings and sharpening their senses. One, perhaps, that silently does more mischief than all the rest, is their disregard of order.

To do every thing in an orderly manner, is a most important **precept**,[5] which women, who, generally speaking, receive only a disorderly kind of education, seldom attend to with that degree of exactness that men, who from their infancy are broken into method, observe. This negligent kind of guesswork, for what other **epithet**[6] can be used to point out the random exertions of a sort of instinctive common sense, never brought to the test of reason? prevents their generalizing matters of fact, so they do today what they did yesterday, merely because they did it yesterday. . . .

Women are, therefore, to be considered either as moral beings, or so weak that they must be entirely subjected to the superior faculties of men.

Let us examine this question. Rousseau declares, that a woman should never, for a moment feel herself independent, that she should be governed by fear to exercise her *natural* cunning, and made a coquettish[7] slave in order to render her a more alluring

---

[3] puerile . . . propriety—childish correctness.

[4] Rousseau's opinion . . . men—Jean Jacques Rousseau (1712–1778), French philosopher.

[5] **precept**—rule of action or behavior.

[6] **epithet**—descriptive expression.

[7] coquettish—flirtatious.

object of desire, a sweeter companion to man, whenever he chooses to relax himself. He carries the arguments, which he pretends to draw from the indications of nature, still further, and **insinuates**[8] that truth and fortitude, the corner stones of all human virtue, shall be cultivated with certain restrictions, because with respect to the female character, obedience is the grand lesson which ought to be impressed with unrelenting rigor.

What nonsense! When will a great man arise with sufficient strength of mind to puff away the fumes which pride and sensuality have thus spread over the subject! If women are by nature inferior to men, their virtues must be the same in quality, if not in degree, or virtue is a relative idea; consequently, their conduct should be founded on the same principles and have the same aim.

Connected with man as daughters, wives, and mothers, their moral character may be estimated by their manner of fulfilling those simple duties; but the end, the grand end of their exertions should be to unfold their own faculties, and acquire the dignity of conscious virtue. They may try to render their road pleasant; but ought never to forget, in common with man, that life yields not the **felicity**[9] which can satisfy an immortal soul. I do not mean to insinuate, that either sex should be so lost, in abstract reflections or distant views, as to forget the affections and duties that lie before them, and are in truth, the means

appointed to produce the fruit of life; on the contrary, I would warmly recommend them, even while I assert, that they afford most satisfaction when they are considered in their true subordinate light.

. . . But what have women to do in society? I may be asked, but to loiter with easy grace; surely you would not condemn them to suckle fools and chronicle small beer![10] No. Women might certainly study the art of healing, and be physicians as well as nurses.

How much more respectable is the woman who earns her bread by fulfilling any duty, than the most accomplished beauty!—beauty did I say?—so sensible am I of the beauty of moral loveliness, or the harmonious propriety that attunes the passions of a well-regulated mind, that I blush at making the comparison; yet I sigh to think how few women aim at attaining this respectability by withdrawing from the giddy whirl of pleasure, or the **indolent**[11] calm that stupefies the good sort of women it sucks in.

Proud of their weakness, however, they must always be protected, guarded from care, and all the rough toils that dignify the mind. If this be the fiat[12] of fate, if

---

[8] **insinuates**—hints.

[9] **felicity**—happiness.

[10] suckle fools and chronicle small beer—trivial domestic occupations, an allusion to an ironic praise of woman by Iago in Shakespeare's *Othello*.

[11] **indolent**—lazy.

[12] fiat—command.

they will make themselves insignificant and contemptible, sweetly to waste "life away," let them not expect to be valued when their beauty fades, for it is the fate of the fairest flowers to be admired and pulled to pieces by the careless hand that plucked them. In how many ways do I wish, from the purest benevolence, to impress this truth on my sex; yet I fear that they will not listen to a truth that dear bought experience has brought home to many an agitated bosom, nor willingly resign the privileges of rank and sex for the privileges of humanity, to which those have no claim who do not discharge its duties.

Those writers are particularly useful, in my opinion, who make man feel for man, independent of the station he fills, or the drapery of factitious[13] sentiments. I then would fain[14] convince reasonable men of the importance of some of my remarks, and prevail on them to weigh dispassionately the whole tenor of my observations. I appeal to their understandings; and, as a fellow-creature, claim, in the name of my sex, some interest in their hearts. I entreat them to assist to emancipate their companion, to make her a *help meet* for them!

Would men but generously snap our chains, and be content with rational fellowship instead of slavish obedience, they would find us more observant daughters, more affectionate sisters, more faithful wives, more reasonable mothers—in a word, better citizens. We should then love

them with true affection, because we should learn to respect ourselves; and the peace of mind of a worthy man would not be interrupted by the idle vanity of his wife, nor the babes sent to nestle in a strange bosom, having never found a home in their mother's.[15]

---

[13] factitious—artificial.

[14] fain—eagerly.

[15] sent to nestle . . . mother's—given to a nurse to be cared for.

QUESTIONS TO CONSIDER

1. In Wollstonecraft's view, how are the lessons that young girls are being taught different from what she argues is appropriate education for them?

2. What reforms does Wollstonecraft advocate?

3. Wollstonecraft says it is "the fate of the fairest flowers to be admired and pulled to pieces by the careless hand that plucked them." What does she mean?

4. What does Wollstonecraft claim will be the result if men would treat women as equals?

Economic Theories

If the Enlightenment was not animated by democratic ideals, it still applied reason to social questions. As the Industrial Revolution began in the late 1700s, two economists produced very influential studies that came to radically different conclusions about the direction in which human society was headed. In The Wealth of Nations, *Scottish economist Adam Smith (1723–1790) presented a positive view of the economic benefits of industrialization. In* Essay on the Principle of Population, *English economist Thomas Malthus (1766–1834) argued that unchecked population growth would only increase human misery.*

from *The Wealth of Nations*
Adam Smith

All the improvements in machinery, however, have by no means been the inventions of those who had occasion to use the machines. Many improvements have been made by the ingenuity of the makers of the machines, when to make them became the business of a peculiar trade; and some by that of those who are called philosophers or men of speculation,[1] whose trade it is not to do any thing, but to observe every thing; and who, upon that account, are often capable of combining together the powers of the most distant and dissimilar objects. In the progress of society, philosophy or speculation becomes, like every other employment, the principal or sole trade and occupation of a particular class of citizens. Like every other employment too, it is subdivided into a great number of different branches, each of which affords occupation to a peculiar tribe or class of philosophers; and this subdivision of employment in philosophy, as well as in every other business, improves dexterity,[2] and saves time. Each individual becomes more expert in his own peculiar branch, more work is done upon the whole, and the quantity of science is considerably increased by it.

It is the great multiplication of the productions of all the different arts, in consequence of the division of labor, which occasions,[3] in a well-governed society, that universal opulence[4] which extends itself to

---

[1] philosophers or men of speculation—Smith means primarily scientists and inventors.

[2] **dexterity**—skill in physical movement, or mental skill.

[3] occasions—causes.

[4] **opulence**—wealth.

the lowest ranks of the people. Every workman has a great quantity of his own work to dispose of beyond what he himself has occasion for; and every other workman being exactly in the same situation, he is enabled to exchange a great quantity of his own goods for a great quantity, or, what comes to the same thing, for the price of a great quantity of theirs. He supplies them abundantly with what they have occasion for, and they accommodate him as amply with what he has occasion for, and a general plenty diffuses itself through all the different ranks of the society.

Observe the accommodation of the most common artificer[5] or day-laborer in a civilized and thriving country, and you will perceive that the number of people of whose industry a part, though but a small part, has been employed in procuring him this accommodation, exceeds all computation. The woolen coat, for example, which covers the day-laborer, as coarse and tough as it may appear, is the produce of the joint labor of a great multitude of workmen. The shepherd, the sorter of the wool, the wool-comber or carder, the dyer, the scribbler, the spinner, the weaver, the fuller, the dresser, with many others, must all join their different arts in order to complete even this homely production. How many merchants and carriers, besides, must have been employed in transporting the materials from some of those workmen to others who often live in a very distant part of the country! How much commerce and navigation in particular, how many

ship-builders, sailors, sail-makers, ropemakers, must have been employed in order to bring together the different drugs made use of by the dyer, which often come from the remotest corners of the world! What a variety of labor too is necessary in order to produce the tools of the meanest[6] of those workmen! To say nothing of such complicated machines as the ship of the sailor, the mill of the fuller, or even the loom of the weaver, let us consider only what a variety of labor is requisite in order to form that very simple machine, the shears with which the shepherd clips the wool. The miner, the builder of the furnace for smelting the ore, the feller of the timber, the burner of the charcoal to be made use of in the smeltinghouse, the brick-maker, the bricklayer, the workmen who attend the furnace, the millwright, the forger, the smith, must all of them join their different arts in order to produce them. Were we to examine, in the same manner, all the different parts of his dress and household furniture, the coarse linen shirt which he wears next his skin, the shoes which cover his feet, the bed which he lies on, and all the different parts which compose it, the kitchen-grate at which he prepares his victuals,[7] the coals which he makes use of for that purpose, dug from the bowels of the earth, and brought to him perhaps by a long sea and a long land carriage, all the other utensils

---

[5] artificer—skilled worker or craftsperson.

[6] meanest—lowest in wealth or social class.

[7] victuals—food.

of his kitchen, all the furniture of his table, the knives and forks, the earthen or pewter plates upon which he serves up and divides his victuals, the different hands employed in preparing his bread and his beer, the glass window which lets in the heat and the light, and keeps out the wind and the rain, with all the knowledge and art requisite for preparing that beautiful and happy invention, without which these northern parts of the world could scarce have afforded a very comfortable habitation, together with the tools of all the different workmen employed in producing those different conveniences; if we examine, I say, all these things, and consider what a variety of labor is employed about each of them, we shall be sensible that without the assistance and co-operation of many thousands, the very meanest person in a civilized country could not be provided, even according to, what we very falsely imagine, the easy and simple manner in which he is commonly accommodated. Compared, indeed, with the more extravagant luxury of the great, his accommodation must no doubt appear extremely simple and easy; and yet it may be true, perhaps, that the accommodation of an European prince does not always so much exceed that of an industrious and **frugal**[8] peasant, as the accommodation of the latter exceeds that of many an African king, the absolute master of the lives and liberties of ten thousand naked savages.

Essay on the Principle of Population
Thomas Malthus

The principal object of the present essay is to examine the effects of the constant tendency of all animated life to increase beyond the nourishment prepared for it.

It is observed by Dr. Franklin,[9] that there is no bound to the prolific nature of plants or animals, but what is made by their crowding and interfering with each other's means of **subsistence**.[10] . . .

This is incontrovertibly true. Through the animal and vegetable kingdoms, nature has scattered the seeds of life abroad with the most profuse and liberal hand; but has been comparatively sparing in the room and the nourishment necessary to rear them. The germs of existence contained in this earth, if they could freely develop themselves, would fill millions of worlds in the course of a few thousand years. Necessity, that imperious, all-pervading law of nature, restrains them within the prescribed bounds. The race of plants and the race of animals shrink under this great restrictive law; and man cannot by any efforts of reason escape from it.

In plants and irrational animals, the view of the subject is simple. They are all

---

[8] **frugal**—thrifty.

[9] Dr. Franklin—Benjamin Franklin (1706–1790), American statesman, scientist, and inventor.

[10] **subsistence**—means of support.

impelled by a powerful instinct to the increase of their species; and this instinct is interrupted by no doubts about providing for their offspring. Wherever therefore there is liberty, the power of increase is exerted; and the superabundant effects are repressed afterwards by want of room and nourishment.

The effects of this check on man are more complicated. Impelled to the increase of his species by an equally powerful instinct, reason interrupts his career, and asks him whether he may not bring beings into the world, for whom he cannot provide the means of support. If he attend to this natural suggestion, the restriction too frequently produces vice. If he hears it not, the human race will be constantly endeavoring to increase beyond the means of subsistence. But as, by that law of our nature which makes food necessary to the life of man, population can never actually increase beyond the lowest nourishment capable of supporting it, a strong check on population, from the difficulty of acquiring food, must be constantly in operation. . . .

The ultimate check to population appears then to be a want of food, arising necessarily from the different ratios according to which population and food increase. But this ultimate check is never the immediate check, except in cases of actual famine.

The immediate check may be stated to consist in all those customs, and all those diseases, which seem to be generated by a scarcity of the means of subsistence; and all those causes, independent of this scarcity, whether of a moral or physical nature, which tend prematurely to weaken and destroy the human frame.

These checks to population, which are constantly operating with more or less force in every society, and keep down the number to the level of the means of subsistence, may be classed under two general heads—the preventive, and the positive checks.

The preventive check, as far as it is voluntary, is peculiar to man, and arises from that distinctive superiority in his reasoning faculties, which enables him to calculate distant consequences. The checks to the indefinite increase of plants and irrational animals are all either positive, or if preventive, involuntary. But man cannot look around him, and see the distress which frequently presses upon those who have large families; he cannot contemplate his present possessions or earnings, which he now nearly consumes himself, and calculate the amount of each share, when with very little addition they must be divided, perhaps, among seven or eight, without feeling a doubt whether, if he follow the bent of his inclinations, he may be able to support the offspring which he will probably bring into the world. In a state of equality, if such can exist, this would be the simple question. In the present state of society other considerations occur. Will he not lower his rank in life, and be obliged to give up in great measure his former habits? Does any mode of employment present itself by which he may reasonably hope to maintain a family?

Will he not at any rate subject himself to greater difficulties, and more severe labor, than in his single state? Will he not be unable to transmit to his children the same advantages of education and improvement that he had himself possessed? Does he even feel secure that, should he have a large family, his utmost exertions can save them from rags and **squalid**[11] poverty, and their consequent **degradation**[12] in the community? And may he not be reduced to the grating necessity of forfeiting his independence, and of being obliged to the sparing hand of Charity for support?

---

[11] **squalid**—filthy and disgusting.
[12] **degradation**—lowering in dignity or estimation.

1. What role does Adam Smith give to "men of speculation" in the division of labor?

2. What is the basic benefit of the division of labor in industrialized society?

3. What part does reason play in checking population, according to Malthus?

4. What other checks does Malthus mention?

5. Are Malthus's concerns still relevant today? Why or why not?

Life and Death among the Very Poor

OLWEN H. HUFTON

In the following passage from an essay on poverty in the 1700s, British historian Olwen H. Hufton describes the lives of poor women and children.

In any society in the 18th century, women of the working classes were expected to work to support themselves both when single and married: "Consider, my dear girl," runs *A Present for a Serving Maid* (1743) "that you have no portions[1] and endeavor to supply the deficiencies of fortune by mind. You cannot expect to marry in such a manner as neither of you shall have occasion to work and none but a fool will take a wife whose bread must be earned solely by his labor and who will contribute nothing towards it herself."

In fact they had no option but to do so. Generally speaking female employment fitted into three main categories. The first, restricted to the unmarried, was domestic service, perhaps the most highly sought-after employment by the unmarried girl because it made her independent of the family and she needed little skill or tuition—though Irish women in London and the Savoyardes[2] in Paris were considered too barbaric to perform even the most **menial**[3] tasks in the home.

Secondly, domestic industry of several kinds which could be carried out either by the unmarried or the married but which, in the latter case especially, was of crucial significance to the family economy. The commonest forms of this were, of course, spinning wool or cotton and the manufacture of lace. The first might or might not form part of an integrated family manufacture—the children helping in the initial stages of washing and carding the raw

---

[1] portions—dowries, money or property given to a woman's husband at marriage.

[2] Savoyardes—women from a mountainous region of southeastern France.

[3] **menial**—degrading.

material, the women in spinning, the men in weaving. In this case the woman was not paid a wage as such: rather was the whole family awarded a single sum for the completed cloth and the family, it should be remembered, was up to the end of the period the commonest unit of production.

. . . Domestic industry was essentially for women *at home* and herein lay much of its value. The baby could lie in the cradle and the smallest children play on the floor whilst the mother kept to her wheel or attended to her lace bobbins. If she fell behind in her tasks they could be completed late into the night, whilst the children slept. But changes were taking place which were to threaten the continuance of this situation—at least as far as spinning was concerned. For the distribution of the raw material and collection of the finished product an elaborate network of traveling merchants was involved, a lengthy and irregular process. Little wonder that spinning was the first process to be subject to industrial change, an important point, for no changes were to disrupt more the family economy. They were to take the spinner out of the house and destroy the family as a unit of production and hence to render employment in some cases very difficult for married women. Early town factories in England in fact accorded preference to the unmarried.

By far the commonest kind of female labor throughout the world at this time was simply the lowest kind of heavy and distasteful tasks such as load carrying.

Nothing in fact was too menial. They carried soil, heavy vegetables to market, water, coal—anything. The terraces cut into the steep mountain hillsides of Spain, France and Italy were kept watered by thousands of women who daily made the steep ascent with buckets—in the Auvergne[4] it was estimated that the climb could take anything up to three hours and often they performed as many as three a day. The Scottish miners employed their wives as "fremd[5] bearers" to carry coal from the face. The mines at this period had no winding gear and the women had to climb with their burden up a spiral staircase winding around the walls of the shaft. Sometimes the return journey could take up to four hours. The man was of course paid a single wage and if unmarried, had to find a girl to act as his beast of burden to whom he paid a part of his earnings. Irish women, unable to sew or clean who found their way to London acted as load carriers or helped their husbands work as navvies.[6] Elsewhere women found employment as rag sorters, cinder sifters, refuse collectors, assistants to masons and bricklayers and so on.

Easily the most mobile section of the population in their search for work, women, especially unmarried ones, would travel many miles in the hope of finding employment. Annually women from North Wales left their homes to work on the fruit

---

[4] Auvergne—a highland region in central France.

[5] fremd—Scottish dialect word meaning "not kin."

[6] navvies—manual laborers, originally employed digging navigation canals.

harvest in Middlesex; carrying a load on their backs into the London markets and sometimes walking anything up to fifteen miles a day during the fruit season. Moreover they had walked from Wales. One must imagine the wives and daughters of the poor condemned to a lifetime of drudgery in an attempt to keep themselves and their offspring fed. Women enclosed in tiny airless rooms, pouring over lace bobbins, working late into the night by the light of candles until their eyes would serve them no more. Blindness was the likeliest fate of the lacemaker. Even those who worked at home and delivered the fruit of their labors to a wandering merchant could not afford to be irregular in their production of work. Washing and mending, cooking and cleaning had to be done afterwards and childbirth had to be accomplished with the minimum of disruption. It is not surprising that they were old women by their late twenties.

The question of child labor was perhaps of even greater importance than that of female labor. The wage of the average working man was enough for his personal upkeep and perhaps, if his wife was employed, for that of two young children. Keen social observers were quick to point out that real trouble started for families with the advent of the third child. This consideration alone entitled the silk and diamond workers of Antwerp to some slight relief, but the situation was too common for the funds of public assistance to allow help to every man in this state.

The advent of child labor has often been depicted as the outstanding evil of the factory system and of the tragic plight of many children in the early factories there can be no doubt. But to approach the question from this angle is to view it with 20th century eyes, for life was hard for the children of laboring men in all European countries in the 18th century. They were expected to become self-supporting as soon as possible so as to relieve the strain on the family budget. Indeed, the children of the poor were committed as soon as they left the cradle to an unremitting struggle for survival in a hostile world. . . .

The annals of the poor, though numerous, [do not] often throw much light on how economic questions conditioned the attitude of a man and wife to each other and their children or how the family coped with the failure of the wage of the working man or woman to keep pace with rising costs, a problem felt most nearly in the home and in one's immediate relationships. It meant that one lived daily from hand to mouth without provision for old age, sickness, incapacity to work, or disasters such as harvest failure or even the arrival of a baby. It affected one's attitude toward one's aged parents and made one's own advancing years something to fear; it presented the working man with the demoralizing experience of toiling all day only to return home with a pittance inadequate for the decent maintenance of his family; it made

One must imagine the wives and daughters of the poor condemned to a lifetime of drudgery.

theft and violence, drunkenness, vagabondage[7] and prostitution constant features of this society and understandably so, for it was only too easy to cross the narrow boundary between poverty and destitution.[8] It needed only some everyday occurrence, a sickness of the main earner, his death, the drying up of domestic industry, the birth of a third or fourth child, to plunge the family into difficulties from which recovery was almost impossible. The ease with which the boundary between poverty and destitution could be crossed provided the century with its most cogent social problems. The sick or crippled who could earn nothing and the aged who were enfeebled might form a relatively small part of the population but the same could not be said of the family that could not manage because of its restricted earning capacity. In France probably something like a third of the population teetered on the fringes of destitution whilst something like a tenth had already crossed that boundary, and an extensive survey made by the French government in 1791 revealed that young children spelt disaster for the family economy. The **corollary**[9] of this was that in many areas begging children plagued the street

Any visitor to a European city in the 18th century would expect to be besieged by hordes of children.

crying for alms, begging bread, serving as decoys for pickpockets or as little tinkers peddling pins and ribbons. "Babies" a sub-delegate of the Auvergne moaned, "have scarcely left the cradle before they are taught how to beg so as not to be a burden to their families." In Paris groups of children made a poor living by selling bundles of firewood or working for rag and bone merchants. Elsewhere they acted as water carriers, sellers of flowers or melons or anything that they could gather together by their own labor and sell for a few pence.

The "mudlarks" of London, scavenger children making a living from tidal refuse,[10] Andersen's little match girl[11] who died frozen in the streets are as much 18th- as 19th-century figures and there is nothing picturesque about them. Far more often in non-industrial societies they made out by begging and semi-criminal practices. Any visitor to a European city in the 18th century would expect to be besieged by hordes of children, forming packs and loitering on street corners to plague the passer-by for alms, tugging at his coat sleeves, dogging his footsteps in tireless pursuit until they received a coin for their exertions. Long before adolescence they had learnt the tricks of the begging trade to perfection and had nothing to learn from the Brechtian-type

---

[7] vagabondage—tramp's or hobo's wandering life.

[8] destitution—extreme poverty.

[9] **corollary**—consequence.

[10] tidal refuse—debris washed in on the tide.

[11] Andersen's little match girl—a reference to Hans Christian Andersen's tale about a beggar girl who sold matches on the street.

beggar.[12] They knew how to hang around the doors of churches, the largest houses, the market stalls, the best bread shops where their demands might arouse some pity; how to tote their smaller brothers and sisters from door to door with long and pathetic tales of misfortunes and parental cruelty. Their parents aided them and encouraged them in deceit. They hired them out for the day to women who wanted to elicit pity and charity by the appearance of a large family or to tinkers who could thus urge unwanted wares upon the public in the name of charity. Thousands of children hovered on the fringe of criminality. . . . It was all too easy for a little girl to make a slow and steady progression from petty beggar to petty thief to part-time prostitute. Deformed by rickets and vitamin deficiency diseases, the begging children became the great fear of administrators. Would they ever take to a steady job or would they become so demoralized that living on their wits would become an ingrained habit? Small wonder that anyone who created work for children was regarded not with horror as an exploiter of the weak, but as a benefactor whose reward in heaven would be great, or that this was the great age of the charity school.

For poor children there was no age of innocence, only one of learning to make one's way in the world of the economically under-privileged, and there was no escape route: nothing by which one could guarantee that one's children would ever do any better. Hogarth's contrast between the idle apprentice who ended on the gallows and the industrious one who became lord mayor of London[13] was a myth of the comfortable classes who saw, and hence believed in, the depravity[14] of the poor.

---

[12] Brechtian-type beggar—a reference to *The Threepenny Opera* (1928) by Bertold Brecht and Kurt Weill, which depicts a criminal underworld. It is a version of an earlier work, *The Beggar's Opera* by British dramatist John Gay (1685–1732).

[13] Hogarth's contrast . . . lord mayor of London—English graphic artist William Hogarth (page 440) produced two series of engravings contrasting the fates of idle and industrious apprentices.

[14] depravity—wickedness.

QUESTIONS TO CONSIDER

1. What was the effect on married women when domestic industry began to be replaced by factory work in the 18th century?

2. What type of labor was most commonly undertaken by women at this time?

3. How did the 18th-century poor view child labor?

4. What might cause a family "to cross the narrow boundary between poverty and destitution"?

5. Why might middle-class people in the 18th century like to believe in "rags-to-riches" stories?

Chapter 12

The Nineteenth Century

The Lure of Fantasy

Lessons from Nature

Social Struggle

The Purpose of Art

 Work by English painter Ford Madox Brown (1821–1893) offers a glimpse of representative types of the British class system, from the idle rich to the poor.

Legends in Poetry

The Romantic Era of the late 18th and early 19th centuries was marked by cultural revolt against both the Enlightenment emphasis on reason and the dehumanizing impact of the Industrial Revolution. Romantic writers were drawn to tales of fantasy in old ballads and legends. The German poet Johann Wolfgang von Goethe (1749–1832) wrote of the Erl-King, an evil goblin of the Black Forest. Another German poet, Heinrich Heine (1797–1856), popularized the legend of the Loreley, a maiden haunting a rock in the Rhine River, who lures sailors to destruction.

The Erl-King

JOHANN WOLFGANG VON GOETHE

O who rides by night thro' the woodland so wild?
It is the fond father embracing his child;
And close the boy nestles within his loved arm.
To hold himself fast and to keep himself warm.

"O father, see yonder! see yonder!" he says;
"My boy, upon what dost thou fearfully gaze?"
"O, 'tis the Erl-King with his crown and his shroud."
"No, my son, it is but a dark wreath of the cloud."

(The Erl-King speaks)
"O come and go with me, thou loveliest child;
By many a gay sport shall thy time be **beguiled**;[1]
My mother keeps for thee full many a fair toy,
And many a fine flower shall she pluck for my boy."

---

[1] **beguiled**—charmed.

"O father, my father, and did you not hear
The Erl-King whisper so low in my ear?"
"Be still, my heart's darling—my child, be at ease;
It was but the wild blast as it sung thro' the trees."

Erl-King
"O wilt thou go with me, thou loveliest boy?
My daughter shall tend thee with care and with joy;
She shall bear thee so lightly thro' wet and thro' wild,
And press thee, and kiss thee, and sing to my child."

"O father, my father, and saw you not plain
The Erl-King's pale daughter glide past thro' the rain?"
"O yes, my loved treasure, I knew it full soon;
It was the gray willow that danced to the moon."

Erl-King
"O come and go with me, no longer delay,
Or else, silly child, I will drag thee away."
"O father, O father! now, now, keep your hold,
The Erl-King has seized me—his grasp is so cold!"

Sore trembled the father; he spurr'd thro' the wild,
Clasping close to his bosom his shuddering child;
He reaches his dwelling in doubt and in dread,
But, clasp'd to his bosom, the infant was dead.

The Loreley

HEINRICH HEINE

I cannot explain the sadness
That's fallen on my breast.
An old, old fable haunts me,
And will not let me rest.

The air grows cool in the twilight,
And softly the Rhine flows on;
The peak of a mountain sparkles
Beneath the setting sun.

More lovely than a vision,
A girl sits high up there;
Her golden jewelry glistens,
She combs her golden hair.

With a comb of gold she combs it,
And sings an evensong;
The wonderful melody reaches
A boat, as it sails along.

The boatman hears, with an anguish
More wild than was ever known;
He's blind to the rocks around him;
His eyes are for her alone.

—At last the waves devoured
The boat, and the boatman's cry;
And this she did with her singing,
The golden Loreley.

QUESTIONS TO CONSIDER

1. What elements are common to the figures of the Erl-King and the Loreley?

2. What mood does Goethe create in "The Erl-King"?

3. What do you think the Loreley represents for Heine?

4. Why would an interest in the fantastic have been an attractive alternative to the industrialization of society?

Visionary Images

Like the literature of the Romantic Era, much visual art in the 19th century reflected an interest in fantasy. The subjects of these works of art are all derived from myth and legend.

▲
Based on Alfred, Lord Tennyson's poem, *The Lady of Shalott* by English painter J. W. Waterhouse (1847–1917) depicts a young woman in the legend of King Arthur who dies because Sir Lancelot does not return her love.

A practitioner of the 19th century's new visual art, English photographer Julia Margaret Cameron (1815–1879) portrays in *Enid* a character from Tennyson's *Idylls of the King*, a series of poems based on Arthurian legend. ▶

The Ladies' Lament by English painter Elizabeth Siddal (1829–1862) was inspired by the famous Scottish ballad "Sir Patrick Spens," in which women wait in vain on the beach for the return of their shipwrecked men. ▼

In *Orpheus*, French painter Gustave Moreau (1826–1898) grimly concludes the Greek myth of the wondrous musician torn to pieces by maddened worshippers of the god Dionysus, showing a girl recovering Orpheus's head and lyre. ▶

▲

Swiss artist Arnold Böcklin (1827–1901), who often depicted mythological subjects and dream worlds, simply called this painting "a picture for dreaming over"; a dealer titled it *The Isle of the Dead*.

QUESTIONS TO CONSIDER

1. Which of these images elicits the greatest emotional response in you?

2. Both Waterhouse's painting *The Lady of Shalott* and Julia Margaret Cameron's photograph *Enid* are based on the legend of King Arthur. Why do you think the Arthurian stories held such interest for artists of the 19th century?

3. What do these images convey about the spirit of the 19th century?

Nature's Savagery

ALFRED, LORD TENNYSON

Romanticism found both a healing power and an elevating sublimity in nature. Later in the 19th century, a poet sought lessons in nature, but drew very different conclusions, as the following poems show. Alfred, Lord Tennyson (1809–1892) composed In Memoriam, *a series of 131 separate but related poems, after the early death of his friend Arthur Hallam in 1833. The poems chronicle Tennyson's grief, despair, and thoughts on immortality.*

55

The wish, that of the living whole
   No life may fail beyond the grave,
   Derives it not from what we have
The likest God within the soul?[1]

Are God and Nature then at strife,
   That Nature lends such evil dreams?
   So careful of the type she seems,
So careless of the single life;

That I, considering everywhere
   Her secret meaning in her deeds,
   And finding that of fifty seeds,
She often brings but one to bear,

---

[1] The likest God within the soul—the spark of divinity in man.

I falter where I firmly trod,
    And falling with my weight of cares
    Upon the great world's altar-stairs
That slope thro' darkness up to God,

I stretch lame hands of faith, and grope,
    And gather dust and chaff,[2] and call
    To what I feel is Lord of all,
And faintly trust the larger hope.

56

"So careful of the type"? but no.
    From scarped[3] cliff and quarried stone
    She cries, "A thousand types are gone:
I care for nothing, all shall go.

"Thou makest thine appeal to me:
    I bring to life, I bring to death:
    The spirit does but mean the breath:
I know no more." And he, shall he,

Man, her last work, who seem'd so fair,
    Such splendid purpose in his eyes,
    Who roll'd the psalm to wintry skies,
Who built him fanes[4] of fruitless prayer,

Who trusted God was love indeed
    And love Creation's final law—
    Tho' Nature, red in tooth and claw
With ravine,[5] shriek'd against his creed—

---

[2] chaff—straw.

[3] scarped—steep.

[4] fanes—places of worship.

[5] ravine—prey.

Who loved, who suffer'd countless ills,
    Who battled for the True, the just,
    Be blown about the desert dust,
Or seal'd within the iron hills?

No more? A monster then, a dream,
    A discord. Dragons of the prime,[6]
    That tare[7] each other in their slime,
Were mellow music match'd with him.

O life as futile, then, as frail!
    O for thy voice to soothe and bless!
    What hope of answer, or **redress**?[8]
Behind the veil, behind the veil.

---

[6] Dragons of the prime—reptiles from long ago, such as dinosaurs.

[7] tare—archaic form of tore.

[8] **redress**—remedy.

QUESTIONS TO CONSIDER

1. In poem 55, the speaker observes of nature, "So careful of the type she seems, So careless of the single life." What does this mean?

2. What contradiction does the speaker probe in stanzas 2–5 of poem 56?

3. What spiritual lessons does Tennyson derive from his observation of nature?

4. Do you think it is possible to derive spiritual lessons from nature? Why or why not?

Survival of the Fittest

CHARLES DARWIN

In the early 1830s the English naturalist Charles Darwin (1809–1882) participated in a lengthy scientific voyage aboard HMS Beagle. His observations eventually led him to propose the theory of evolution, the idea that species of plants and animals arise by means of a process of natural selection, which he set forth in On the Origin of Species (1859).

Before entering on the subject of this chapter, I must make a few preliminary remarks, to show how the struggle for existence bears on Natural Selection. It has been seen in the last chapter that amongst organic beings in a state of nature there is some individual variability: indeed I am not aware that this has ever been disputed. It is immaterial for us whether a multitude of doubtful forms be called species[1] or sub-species or varieties; what rank, for instance, the two or three hundred doubtful forms of British plants are entitled to hold, if the existence of any well-marked varieties be admitted. But the mere existence of individual variability and of some few well-marked varieties, though necessary as the foundation for the work, helps us but little in understanding how species arise in nature. How have all those exquisite adaptations of one part of the organization to another part, and to the conditions of life, and of one organic being to another being, been perfected? "We see these beautiful co-adaptations most plainly in the woodpecker and the mistletoe; and only a little less plainly in the humblest **parasite**[2] which clings to the hairs of a **quadruped**[3] or feathers of a bird; in the structure of the beetle which dives through the water: in the plumed seed which is wafted by the gentlest breeze; in short, we see beautiful adaptations everywhere and in every part of the organic world.

Again, it may be asked, how is it that varieties, which I have called **incipient**[4]

---

[1] species—the basic category in the biological classification of organisms, composed of individuals able to breed with one another but not with individuals of another species.

[2] **parasite**—an organism that lives on or inside of another organism, feeding on its host.

[3] **quadruped**—an animal with four feet.

[4] **incipient**—beginning to exist or appear.

species, become ultimately converted into good and distinct species, which in most cases obviously differ from each other far more than do the varieties of the same species? How do those groups of species, which constitute what are called distinct genera,[5] and which differ from each other more than do the species of the same genus, arise? All these results, as we shall more fully see in the next chapter, follow from the struggle for life. Owing to this struggle, variations, however slight, and from whatever cause proceeding, if they be in any degree profitable to the individuals of a species, in their infinitely complex relations to other organic beings and to their physical conditions of life, will tend to the preservation of such individuals, and will generally be inherited by the offspring. The offspring, also, will thus have a better chance of surviving, for, of the many individuals of any species which are periodically born, but a small number can survive. I have called this principle, by which each slight variation, if useful, is preserved, by the term Natural Selection, in order to mark its relation to man's power of selection. But the expression often used by Mr. Herbert Spencer[6] of the Survival of the Fittest is more accurate, and is sometimes equally convenient. We have seen that man by selection can certainly produce great results, and can adapt organic beings to his own uses, through the accumulation of slight but useful variations, given to him by the hand of Nature. But Natural Selection, as we shall hereafter see, is a power incessantly ready for action, and is as immeasurably superior to man's feeble efforts, as the works of Nature are to those of Art.

Nothing is easier than to admit in words the truth of the universal struggle for life, or more difficult—at least I have found it so—than constantly to bear this conclusion in mind. Yet unless it be thoroughly ingrained in the mind, the whole economy of nature, with every fact on distribution, rarity, abundance, extinction, and variation, will be dimly seen or quite misunderstood. We behold the face of nature bright with gladness, we often see superabundance of food; we do not see or we forget, that the birds which are idly singing round us mostly live on insects or seeds, and are thus constantly destroying life; or we forget how largely these songsters, or their eggs, or their nestlings, are destroyed by birds and beasts of prey; we do not always bear in mind, that, though food may be now superabundant, it is not so at all seasons of each recurring year. . . .

A struggle for existence inevitably follows from the high rate at which all organic beings tend to increase. Every being, which during its natural lifetime produces several eggs or seeds, must suffer destruction during some period of its life, and during some season or occasional year, otherwise, on the principle of geometrical increase, its numbers would quickly become so **inordinately**[7] great that no country could

---

[5] genera—plural of *genus*. In the biological classification of organisms, a genus is a subdivision of a family, and itself contains more than one species.

[6] Herbert Spencer—English philosopher (1820–1903) who applied the study of the natural sciences to philosophy.

[7] **inordinately**—exceeding reasonable limits.

support the product. Hence, as more individuals are produced than can possibly survive, there must in every case be a struggle for existence, either one individual with another of the same species, or with the individuals of distinct species, or with the physical conditions of life. It is the doctrine of Malthus[8] applied with manifold force to the whole animal and vegetable kingdoms; for in this case there can be no artificial increase of food, and no **prudential**[9] restraint from marriage. Although some species may be now increasing, more or less rapidly, in numbers, all cannot do so, for the world would not hold them. . . .

How will the struggle for existence, briefly discussed in the last chapter, act in regard to variation? Can the principle of selection, which we have seen is so potent in the hands of man, apply under nature? I think we shall see that it can act most efficiently. . . .

We shall best understand the probable course of natural selection by taking the case of a country undergoing some slight physical change, for instance, of climate. The proportional numbers of its inhabitants will almost immediately undergo a change, and some species will probably become extinct. We may conclude, from what we have seen of the intimate and complex manner in which the inhabitants of each country are bound together, that any change in the numerical proportions of the inhabitants, independently of the change of climate itself, would seriously affect the others. If the country were open on its borders, new forms would certainly immigrate, and this would likewise seriously disturb the relations of some of the former inhabitants. Let it be remembered how powerful the influence of a single introduced tree or mammal has been shown to be. But in the case of an island, or of a country partly surrounded by barriers, into which new and better adapted forms could not freely enter, we should then have places in the economy of nature which would assuredly be better filled up, if some of the original inhabitants were in some manner modified; for, had the area been open to immigration, these same places would have been seized on by intruders. In such cases, slight modifications, which in any way favored the individuals of any species, by better adapting them to their altered conditions, would tend to be preserved; and natural selection would have free scope for the work of improvement. . . .

As man can produce, and certainly has produced, a great result by his methodical and unconscious means of selection, what may not natural selection effect? Man can act only on external and visible characters: Nature, if I may be allowed to personify the natural preservation or survival of the fittest, cares nothing for appearances, except in so far as they are useful to any being. She can act on every internal organ, on every shade of constitutional difference, on the whole machinery of life. Man selects only for his own good: Nature only for that of the being which she tends. Every selected

---

[8] Malthus—English economist (1766–1834) who studied population growth (page 462).

[9] **prudential**—cautious.

character is fully exercised by her, as is implied by the fact of their selection. Man keeps the natives of many climates in the same country; he seldom exercises each selected character in some peculiar and fitting manner; he feeds a long and a short beaked pigeon on the same food; he does not exercise a long-backed or long-legged quadruped in any peculiar manner; he exposes sheep with long and short wool to the same climate. He does not allow the most vigorous males to struggle for the females. He does not rigidly destroy all inferior animals, but protects during each varying season, as far as lies in his power, all his productions. He often begins his selection by some half-monstrous form; or at least by some modification prominent enough to catch the eye or to be plainly useful to him. Under nature, the slightest differences of structure or constitution may well turn the nicely-balanced scale in the struggle for life, and so be preserved. How fleeting are the wishes and efforts of man! how short his time! and consequently how poor will be his results, compared with those accumulated by Nature during whole geological periods! Can we wonder, then, that Nature's productions should be far "truer" in character than man's productions; that they should be infinitely better adapted to the most complex conditions of life, and should plainly bear the stamp of far higher workmanship?

In order to make it clear how, as I believe, natural selection acts, I must beg permission to give one or two imaginary illustrations. Let us take the case of a wolf, which preys on various animals, securing some by craft, some by strength, and some by fleetness; and let us suppose that the fleetest prey, a deer for instance, had from any change in the country increased in numbers, or that other prey had decreased in numbers, during that season of the year when the wolf was hardest pressed for food. Under such circumstances the swiftest and slimmest wolves would have the best chance of surviving, and so be preserved or selected—provided always that they retained strength to master their prey at this or some other period of the year, when they were compelled to prey on other animals. I can see no more reason to doubt that this would be the result, than that man should be able to improve the fleetness of his greyhounds by careful and methodical selection, or by that kind of unconscious selection which follows from each man trying to keep the best dogs without any thought of modifying the breed.

QUESTIONS TO CONSIDER

1. What does Charles Darwin say is the cause of variations in species?

2. Which phrase seems a better description of Darwin's idea—natural selection or survival of the fittest? Why?

3. How does the example of the wolf help to explain Darwin's theory?

from

Communist Manifesto

KARL MARX AND FRIEDRICH ENGELS

The 19th century witnessed a variety of attempts to help oppressed groups, including antislavery movements, women's rights movements, and labor unions. By the mid-1800s, the adverse effects of industrialization on workers prompted radical reform proposals, such as socialism, which urged government control of factories. In 1848 German socialists Karl Marx (1818–1883) and Friedrich Engels (1820–1895) outlined even more radical proposals in a pamphlet, the Communist Manifesto. *Under Communism all economic resources— land, mineral wealth, factories, transportation, and business—would be owned by the people.*

The history of all hitherto existing society is the history of class struggles.

Freeman and slave, patrician and plebeian, lord and serf, guildmaster and journeyman, in a word, oppressor and oppressed, stood in constant opposition to one another, carried on an uninterrupted, now hidden, now open fight, a fight that each time ended, either in a revolutionary reconstitution of society at large, or in the common ruin of the contending classes.

In the earlier epochs of history, we find almost everywhere a complicated arrangement of society into various orders, a manifold gradation of social rank. In ancient Rome we have patricians, knights, plebeians, slaves; in the Middle Ages, feudal lords, vassals, guildmasters, journeymen, apprentices, serfs; in almost all of these classes, again, subordinate gradations.

The modern **bourgeois**[1] society that has sprouted from the ruins of feudal society, has not done away with class **antagonisms.**[2] It has but established new classes, new conditions of oppression, new forms of struggle in place of the old ones.

Our epoch, the epoch of the bourgeoisie, possesses, however, this distinctive feature: It has simplified the class antagonisms. Society as a whole is more and more splitting up into two great hostile camps into

[1] **bourgeois**—middle class; in Marxist theory, a member of the property-owning class, or a capitalist.

[2] **antagonisms**—hostilities.

two great classes directly facing each other—bourgeoisie and **proletariat**.[3] . . .

The immediate aim of the Communists is the same as that of all the other proletarian parties; formation of the proletariat into a class, overthrow of bourgeois supremacy, conquest of political power by the proletariat. . . .

The distinguishing feature of Communism is not the **abolition**[4] of property generally, but the abolition of bourgeois property. But modern bourgeois private property is the final and most complete expression of the system of producing and appropriating products that is based on class antagonisms, on the exploitation of the many by the few.

In this sense, the theory of the Communists may be summed up in the single sentence: abolition of private property.

We Communists have been reproached with the desire of abolishing the right of personally acquiring property as the fruit of man's own labor, which property is alleged to be the groundwork of all personal freedom, activity and independence.

Hard-won, self-acquired, self-earned property! Do you mean the property of the petty artisan and of the small peasant, a form of property that preceded the bourgeois form? There is no need to abolish that; the development of industry has to a great extent already destroyed it, and is still destroying it daily.

Or do you mean modern bourgeois private property?

But does wage-labor create any property for the laborer? Not a bit. It creates **capital**,[5]

i.e., that kind of property which exploits wage-labor and which cannot increase except upon condition of begetting a new supply of wage-labor for fresh exploitation. Property, in its present form, is based on the antagonism of capital and wage-labor. Let us examine both sides of this antagonism.

To be a capitalist, is to have not only a purely personal, but a social status in production. Capital is a collective product, and only by the united action of many members, nay, in the last resort, only by the united action of all members of society, can it be set in motion.

Capital is therefore not a personal, it is a social, power.

When, therefore, capital is converted into common property, into the property of all members of society, personal property is not thereby transformed into social property. It is only the social character of the property that is changed. It loses its class character.

Let us now take wage-labor.

The average price of wage-labor is the minimum wage, *i.e.*, that quantum[6] of the means of subsistence which is absolutely requisite to keep the laborer in bare existence as a laborer. What, therefore, the wage-laborer appropriates by means of his labor, merely suffices to prolong and reproduce a bare existence. We by no means

---

[3] **proletariat**—workers who earn their living by selling their labor.

[4] **abolition**—elimination.

[5] **capital**—property invested to make a profit.

[6] quantum—amount.

intend to abolish this personal appropriation of the products of labor, an appropriation that is made for the maintenance and reproduction of human life, and that leaves no surplus wherewith to command the labor of others. All that we want to do away with is the miserable character of this appropriation, under which the laborer lives merely to increase capital, and is allowed to live only insofar as the interest of the ruling class requires it.

In bourgeois society, living labor is but a means to increase accumulated labor. In Communist society, accumulated labor is but a means to widen, to enrich, to promote the existence of the laborer.

In bourgeois society, therefore, the past dominates the present; in Communist society, the present dominates the past. In bourgeois society capital is independent and has individuality, while the living person is dependent and has no individuality.

And the abolition of this state of things is called by the bourgeois, abolition of individuality and freedom! And rightly so. The abolition of bourgeois individuality, bourgeois independence, and bourgeois freedom is undoubtedly aimed at.

By freedom is meant, under the present bourgeois conditions of production, free trade, free selling and buying.

But if selling and buying disappears, free selling and buying disappears also. This talk about free selling and buying, and all the other "brave words" of our bourgeois about freedom in general, have a meaning, if any, only in contrast with restricted selling and buying, with the **fettered**[7] traders of the Middle Ages, but have no meaning when opposed to the Communist abolition of buying and selling, of the bourgeois conditions of production, and of the bourgeoisie itself.

You are horrified at our intending to do away with private property. But in your existing society, private property is already done away with for nine-tenths of the population; its existence for the few is solely due to its non-existence in the hands of those nine-tenths. You reproach us, therefore, with intending to do away with a form of property, the necessary condition for whose existence is the non-existence of any property for the immense majority of society.

In a word, you reproach us with intending to do away with your property. Precisely so; that is just what we intend.

From the moment when labor can no longer be converted into capital, money, or rent, into a social power capable of being monopolized, *i.e.*, from the moment when individual property can no longer be transformed into bourgeois property, into capital, from that moment, you say, individuality vanishes.

You must, therefore, confess that by "individual" you mean no other person than the bourgeois, than the middle class owner of property. This person must, indeed, be swept out of the way, and made impossible. . . .

But you Communists would introduce community of women, screams the whole bourgeoisie in chorus.

---

[7] **fettered**—restrained.

The bourgeois sees his wife as a mere instrument of production. He hears that the instruments of production are to be exploited in common, and, naturally, can come to no other conclusion that the lot of being common to all will likewise fall to the woman.

He has not even a suspicion that the real point aimed at is to do away with the status of women as mere instruments of production.

For the rest, nothing is more ridiculous than the virtuous indignation of our bourgeois at the community of women which, they pretend, is to be openly and officially established by the Communists. The Communists have no need to introduce community of women; it has existed almost from time immemorial.

Our bourgeois, not content with having the wives and daughters of their proletarians at their disposal, not to speak of common prostitutes, take the greatest pleasure in seducing each other's wives.

Bourgeois marriage is in reality a system of wives in common and thus, at the most, what the Communists might possibly be reproached with is that they desire to introduce, in substitution for a hypocritically concealed, an openly legalized community of women. For the rest, it is self-evident, that the abolition of the present system of production must bring with it the abolition of the community of women springing from that system, *i.e.*, of prostitution both public and private.

The Communists are further reproached with desiring to abolish countries and nationality.

The workingmen have no country. We cannot take from them what they have not got. Since the proletariat must first of all acquire political supremacy, must rise to be the leading class of the nation, must constitute itself *the* nation, it is, so far, itself national, though not in the bourgeois sense of the word.

National differences and antagonisms between peoples are vanishing gradually from day to day, owing to the development of the bourgeoisie, to freedom of commerce, to the world market, to uniformity in the mode of production and in the conditions of life corresponding thereto.

The supremacy of the proletariat will cause them to vanish still faster. United action, of the leading civilized countries at least, is one of the first conditions for the emancipation of the proletariat.

In proportion as the exploitation of one individual by another is put an end to, the exploitation of one nation by another will also be put an end to. In proportion as the antagonism between classes within the nation vanishes, the hostility of one nation to another will come to an end. . . .

"Undoubtedly," it will be said, "religion, moral, philosophical and juridical ideas have been modified in the course of historical development. But religion, morality, philosophy, political science, and law, constantly survived this change.

"There are, besides, eternal truths, such as Freedom, Justice, etc., that are common to all states of society. But Communism abolishes eternal truths, it abolishes all religion, and all morality, instead of constituting them on a new basis; it therefore acts in contradiction to all past historical experience."

What does this accusation reduce itself to? The history of all past society has consisted in the development of class antagonisms, antagonisms that assumed different forms at different epochs.

But whatever form they may have taken, one fact is common to all past ages, *viz.*, the exploitation of one part of society by the other. No wonder, then, that the social consciousness of past ages, despite all the multiplicity and variety it displays, moves within certain common forms, or general ideas, which cannot completely vanish except with the total disappearance of class antagonisms.

The Communist revolution is the most radical rupture with traditional property relations; no wonder that its development involves the most radical rupture with traditional ideas. . . .

The Communists disdain to conceal their views and aims. They openly declare that their ends can be attained only by the forcible overthrow of all existing social conditions. Let the ruling classes tremble at a Communist revolution. The proletarians have nothing to lose but their chains. They have a world to win.

Workingmen of all countries, unite!

QUESTIONS TO CONSIDER

1. What is the Communists' basic goal? Why do they want to accomplish this?

2. The *Communist Manifesto* observes, "In bourgeois society . . . the past dominates the present; in Communist society, the present dominates the past." What does this mean?

3. The *Communist Manifesto* argues that by creating a world market, capitalism is reducing hostilities between nations. Do you agree that the growth of a world market lessens the possibility of international conflicts? Why or why not?

4. In actuality, Communist governments have been marked by extreme repression, corruption, and lackluster economies. In your opinion, why didn't the *Communist Manifesto* foresee any of these problems?

Declaration of Sentiments and Resolutions

ELIZABETH CADY STANTON AND LUCRETIA MOTT

In 1848, the same year that the Communist Manifesto *appeared, Elizabeth Cady Stanton (1815–1902) and Lucretia Mott (1783–1880) led the first Women's Rights Convention in Seneca Falls, New York. The convention passed this "Declaration of Sentiments and Resolutions."*

When, in the course of human events, it becomes necessary for one portion of the family of man to assume among the people of the earth a position different from that which they have hitherto occupied, but one to which the laws of nature and of nature's God entitle them, a decent respect to the opinions of mankind requires that they should declare the causes that impel them to such a course.

We hold these truths to be self-evident: that all men and women are created equal; that they are endowed by their Creator with certain **inalienable**[1] rights; that among these are life, liberty, and the pursuit of happiness; that to secure these rights governments are instituted, deriving their just powers from the consent of the governed. Whenever any form of government becomes destructive of these ends, it is the right of those who suffer from it to refuse allegiance to it, and to insist upon the institution of a new government, laying its foundation on such principles, and organizing its powers in such form, as to them shall seem most likely to effect their safety and happiness. Prudence, indeed, will dictate that governments long established should not be changed for light and **transient**[2] causes; and accordingly all experience hath shown that mankind are more disposed to suffer while evils are sufferable, than to right themselves by abolishing the forms to which they are accustomed. But when a long train of abuses and usurpations,[3] pursuing invariably the same object, evinces a design to reduce them under absolute despotism, it is their duty

---

[1] **inalienable**—not capable of being lost.

[2] **transient**—short-lived, temporary.

[3] usurpations—wrongful seizures.

to throw off such government, and to provide new guards for their future security. Such has been the patient sufferance of the women under this government, and such is now the necessity which constrains them to demand the equal station to which they are entitled.

The history of mankind is a history of repeated injuries and usurpations on the part of man toward woman, having in direct object the establishment of an absolute tyranny over her. To prove this, let facts be submitted to a **candid**[4] world.

He has never permitted her to exercise her inalienable right to the elective franchise.[5]

He has compelled her to submit to laws, in the formation of which she had no voice.

He has withheld from her rights which are given to the most ignorant and degraded men—both natives and foreigners.

Having deprived her of this first right of a citizen, the elective franchise, thereby leaving her without representation in the halls of legislation, he has oppressed her on all sides.

He has made her, if married, in the eye of the law, civilly dead.

He has taken from her all right in property, even to the wages she earns.

He has made her, morally, an irresponsible being, as she can commit many crimes with **impunity**,[6] provided they be done in the presence of her husband. In the covenant of marriage, she is compelled to promise obedience to her husband, he becoming, to all intents and purposes, her master—the law giving him power to deprive her of her liberty, and to administer chastisement.

He has so framed the laws of divorce, as to what shall be the proper causes, and in case of separation, to whom the guardianship of the children shall be given, as to be wholly regardless of the happiness of women—the law, in all cases, going upon a false supposition of the supremacy of man, and giving all power into his hands.

After depriving her of all rights as a married woman, if single, and the owner of property, he has taxed her to support a government which recognizes her only when her property can be made profitable to it.

He has monopolized nearly all the profitable employments, and from those she is permitted to follow, she receives but a scanty **remuneration**.[7] He closes against her all the avenues to wealth and distinction which he considers most honorable to himself. As a teacher of theology, medicine, or law, she is not known.

He has denied her the facilities for obtaining a thorough education, all colleges being closed against her.

He allows her in Church, as well as State, but a subordinate position, claiming Apostolic authority[8] for her exclusion from the ministry, and, with some exceptions, from any public participation in the affairs of the Church.

He has created a false public sentiment by giving to the world a different code of morals for men and women, by which

---

[4] **candid**—honest, impartial.

[5] elective franchise—the right to vote.

[6] **impunity**—freedom from punishment.

[7] **remuneration**—payment.

[8] Apostolic authority—The Apostles of Jesus were all males.

moral delinquencies which exclude women from society, are not only tolerated, but deemed of little account in man.

He has usurped the prerogative of Jehovah himself, claiming it as his right to assign for her a sphere of action, when that belongs to her conscience and to her God.

He has endeavored, in every way that he could, to destroy her confidence in her own powers, to lessen her self-respect and to make her willing to lead a dependent and **abject**[9] life.

Now, in view of this entire disfranchisement of one-half the people of this country, their social and religious degradation—in view of the unjust laws above mentioned, and because women do feel themselves aggrieved, oppressed, and fraudulently deprived of their most sacred rights, we insist that they have immediate admission to all the rights and privileges which belong to them as citizens of the United States.

In entering upon the great work before us, we anticipate no small amount of misconception, misrepresentation, and ridicule; but we shall use every instrumentality within our power to effect our object. We shall employ agents, circulate tracts, petition the State and National legislatures, and endeavor to enlist the pulpit and the press in our behalf. We hope this Convention will be followed by a series of Conventions embracing every part of the country.

Resolutions

Whereas, The great precept of nature is conceded to be, that "man shall pursue his own true and substantial happiness." Blackstone in his *Commentaries*[10] remarks, that this law of Nature being coeval[11] with mankind, and dictated by God himself, is of course superior in obligation to any other. It is binding over all the globe, in all countries and at all times; no human laws are of any validity if contrary to this, and such of them as are valid, derive all their force, and all their validity, and all their authority, mediately and immediately[12] from this original; therefore,

Resolved, That all laws which prevent woman from occupying such a station in society as her conscience shall dictate, or which place her in a position inferior to that of man, are contrary to the great precept of nature, and therefore of no force or authority.

Resolved, That woman is man's equal—was intended to be so by the Creator, and the highest good of the race demands that she should be recognized as such.

Resolved, That the women of this country ought to be enlightened in regard to the laws under which they live, that they may no longer publish their degradation by declaring themselves satisfied with their present position, nor their ignorance, by asserting that they have all the rights they want.

---

[9] **abject**—miserable.

[10] Blackstone in his *Commentaries*—Sir William Blackstone's *Commentaries on the Laws of England* (1769) is a classic account of English law.

[11] coeval—of the same age.

[12] mediately and immediately—indirectly and directly.

Resolved, That inasmuch as man, while claiming for himself intellectual superiority, does accord to woman moral superiority, it is preeminently his duty to encourage her to speak and teach, as she has an opportunity, in all religious assemblies.

Resolved, That the same amount of virtue, delicacy, and refinement of behavior that is required of woman in the social state, should also be required of man, and the same **transgressions**[13] should be visited with equal severity on both man and woman.

Resolved, That the objection of indelicacy and impropriety, which is so often brought against woman when she addresses a public audience, comes with a very ill-grace from those who encourage, by their attendance, her appearance on the stage, in the concert, or in feats of the circus.

Resolved, That woman has too long rested satisfied in the circumscribed limits which corrupt customs and a perverted application of the Scriptures have marked out for her, and that it is time she should move in the enlarged sphere which her great Creator has assigned her.

Resolved, That it is the duty of the women of this country to secure to themselves their sacred right to the elective franchise.

Resolved, That the equality of human rights results necessarily from the fact of the identity of the race in capabilities and responsibilities.

Resolved, That the speedy success of our cause depends upon the zealous and untiring efforts of both men and women, for the overthrow of the monopoly of the pulpit, and for the securing to women an equal participation with men in the various trades, professions, and commerce.

Resolved, therefore, That, being invested by the creator with the same capabilities, and the same consciousness of responsibility for their exercise, it is demonstrably the right and duty of woman, equally with man, to promote every righteous cause by every righteous means; and especially in regard to the great subjects of morals and religion, it is self-evidently her right to participate with her brother in teaching them, both in private and in public, by writing and by speaking, by any instrumentalities proper to be used, and in any assemblies proper to be held; and this being a self-evident truth growing out of the divinely implanted principles of human nature, any custom or authority adverse to it, whether modern or wearing the **hoary**[14] sanction of antiquity, is to be regarded as a self-evident falsehood, and at war with mankind.

---

[13] **transgressions**—misdeeds.

[14] **hoary**—ancient.

QUESTIONS TO CONSIDER

1. Much of the wording of the "Declaration of Sentiments" is identical to the Declaration of Independence. Why do you think this was done?

2. What can you infer is the reason for the sixth resolution about "the objection of indelicacy and impropriety"?

3. In the United States, women received the right to vote in 1920 with the ratification of the 19th Amendment to the Constitution, 72 years after Seneca Falls. What can you conclude from this?

The Future of South America

SIMÓN BOLÍVAR

Spain had created a world empire in the 1500s; by the 1800s her power was in decline. Simón Bolívar (1783–1830), who was born to a wealthy Creole family in Caracas, Venezuela, burned with a passion to free South America from Spanish rule. Eventually he and others were successful in ousting the Spanish from the northern regions of South America. "The Jamaica Letter" was written in 1815 to "an English gentleman," probably the governor of Jamaica, during Bolívar's exile there.

With what a feeling of gratitude I read that passage in your letter in which you say to me: "I hope that the success which then followed Spanish arms may now turn in favor of their adversaries, the badly oppressed people of South America." I take this hope as a prediction, if it is justice that determines man's contests. Success will crown our efforts, because the destiny of America has been **irrevocably**[1] decided; the tie that bound her to Spain has been severed. Only a concept maintained that tie and kept the parts of that immense monarchy together. That which formerly bound them now divides them. The hatred that the Peninsula[2] inspired in us is greater than the ocean between us. It would be easier to have the two continents meet than to reconcile the spirits of the two countries. The habit of obedience; a community of interest,

of understanding, of religion; mutual goodwill; a tender regard for the birthplace and good name of our forefathers; in short, all that gave rise to our hopes, came to us from Spain. As a result there was born a principle of **affinity**[3] that seemed eternal, notwithstanding the misbehavior of our rulers which weakened that sympathy, or, rather, that bond enforced by the domination of their rule. At present the contrary attitude persists: we are threatened with the fear of death, dishonor, and every harm; there is nothing we have not suffered at the hands of that unnatural step-mother—

---

[1] **irrevocably**—unalterably.

[2] Peninsula—the Iberian Peninsula, made up of Spain and Portugal.

[3] **affinity**—feeling of kinship.

Spain. The veil has been torn asunder. We have already seen the light, and it is not our desire to be thrust back into darkness. . . .

We are a young people. We inhabit a world apart, separated by broad seas. We are young in the ways of almost all the arts and sciences, although, in a certain manner, we are old in the ways of civilized society. . . . But we scarcely retain a vestige[4] of what once was; we are, moreover, neither Indian nor European, but a species midway between the legitimate proprietors of this country and the Spanish usurpers.[5] In short, though Americans by birth we derive our rights from Europe, and we have to assert these rights against the rights of the natives, and at the same time we must defend ourselves against the invaders. This places us in a most extraordinary and involved situation. . . .

The role of the inhabitants of the American hemisphere has for centuries been purely passive. Politically they were non-existent. We are still in a position lower than slavery, and therefore it is more difficult for us to rise to the enjoyment of freedom. Permit me these digressions in order to establish the issue. States are slaves because of either the nature or the misuse of their constitutions; a people is therefore enslaved when the government, by its nature or its vices, infringes on and usurps the rights of the citizen or subject. Applying these principles, we find that America was denied not only its freedom but even an active and effective tyranny.

Let me explain. Under absolutism[6] there are no recognized limits to the exercise of governmental powers. The will of the great sultan, khan, bey, and other despotic[7] rulers is the supreme law, carried out more or less arbitrarily by the lesser pashas, khans, and satraps of Turkey and Persia, who have an organized system of oppression in which inferiors participate according to the authority vested in them. To them is entrusted the administration of civil, military, political, religious, and tax matters. But, after all is said and done, the rulers of Isfahan are Persians; the viziers of the Grand Turk are Turks; and the sultans of Tartary are Tartars. . . .

How different is our situation! We have been harassed by a conduct which has not only deprived us of our rights but has kept us in a sort of permanent infancy with regard to public affairs. If we could at least have managed our domestic affairs and our internal administration, we could have acquainted ourselves with the processes and mechanics of public affairs. . . .

Americans today, and perhaps to a greater extent than ever before, who live within the Spanish system occupy a position in society no better than that of serfs destined for labor, or at best they have no more status than that of mere consumers. Yet even this status is surrounded with

---

[4] vestige—trace.

[5] usurpers—those who seize the rights of others by force.

[6] absolutism—a form of government in which a single ruler has all the power.

[7] despotic—tyrannical.

galling[8] restrictions, such as being forbidden to grow European crops, or to store products which are royal monopolies, or to establish factories of a type the Peninsula itself does not possess. To this add the exclusive trading privileges, even in articles of prime necessity, and the barriers between American provinces, designed to prevent all exchange of trade, traffic, and understanding. In short, do you wish to know what our future held?—simply the cultivation of the fields of indigo, grain, coffee, sugar cane, cacao, and cotton; cattle raising on the broad plains; hunting wild game in the jungles; digging in the earth to mine its gold—but even these limitations could never satisfy the greed of Spain.

So negative was our existence that I can find nothing comparable in any other civilized society, examine as I may the entire history of time and the politics of all nations. Is it not an outrage and a violation of human rights to expect a land so splendidly endowed, so vast, rich, and populous, to remain merely passive?

As I have just explained, we were cut off and, as it were, removed from the world in relation to the science of government and administration of the state. We were never viceroys or governors, save in the rarest of instances; seldom archbishops and bishops; diplomats never; as military men, only subordinates; as nobles, without royal privileges. In brief, we were neither magistrates nor financiers and seldom merchants—all in flagrant contradiction to our institutions. . . .

It is harder, Montesquieu[9] has written, to release a nation from servitude than to enslave a free nation. This truth is proven by the annals[10] of all times, which reveal that most free nations have been put under the yoke, but very few enslaved nations have recovered their liberty. Despite the convictions of history, South Americans have made efforts to obtain liberal, even perfect, institutions, doubtless out of that instinct to aspire to the greatest possible happiness, which, common to all men, is bound to follow in civil societies founded on the principles of justice, liberty, and equality. But are we capable of maintaining in proper balance the difficult charge of a republic? Is it conceivable that a newly emancipated people can soar to the heights of liberty, and, unlike Icarus, neither have its wings melt[11] nor fall into an abyss? Such a marvel is inconceivable and without precedent. There is no reasonable probability to bolster our hopes.

More than anyone, I desire to see America[12] fashioned into the greatest nation in the world, greatest not so much by virtue of her area and wealth as by her freedom and glory. Although I seek perfection for the government of my country, I cannot persuade myself that the New World can,

---

[8] galling—irritating.

[9] Montesquieu—French political philosopher (1689–1755).

[10] annals—records of events.

[11] Icarus . . . wings melt—Greek myth of a boy who flies on artificial wings made of feathers held together with wax. He rashly soars too near the sun, the wax melts, and he falls into the sea and drowns.

[12] America—Bolívar means South America.

at the moment, be organized as a great republic. Since it is impossible, I dare not desire it; yet much less do I desire to have all America a monarchy because this plan is not only impracticable but also impossible. Wrongs now existing could not be righted, and our emancipation would be fruitless. The American states need the care of paternal governments to heal the sores and wounds of despotism and war. . . .

From the foregoing, we can draw these conclusions: The American provinces are fighting for their freedom, and they will ultimately succeed. Some provinces as a matter of course will form federal and some central republics; the larger areas will inevitably establish monarchies, some of which will fare so badly that they will disintegrate in either present or future revolutions. To consolidate a great monarchy will be no easy task, but it will be utterly impossible to consolidate a great republic.

It is a **grandiose**[13] idea to think of consolidating the New World into a single nation, united by pacts into a single bond. It is reasoned that, as these parts have a common origin, language, customs, and religion, they ought to have a single government to permit the newly formed states to unite in a confederation. But this is not possible. . . .

When success is not assured, when the state is weak, and when results are distantly seen, all men hesitate; opinion is divided, passions rage, and the enemy fans these passions in order to win an easy victory

because of them. As soon as we are strong and under the guidance of a liberal nation which will lend us her protection, we will achieve accord in cultivating the virtues and talents that lead to glory. Then will we march majestically toward that great prosperity for which South America is destined.

---

[13] **grandiose**—overly ambitious.

QUESTIONS TO CONSIDER

1. What, according to Simón Bolívar, were some reasons for such deep hatred between South America and Spain?

2. Why did Bolívar believe that Spain would ultimately have to give up South America?

3. Bolívar, quoting the French political philosopher Montesquieu, observes, "It is harder . . . to release a nation from servitude than to enslave a free nation." Do you agree with this view? Why or why not?

Imperialism

European nations had been acquiring empires since the 1500s, but the scramble for colonies intensified in the late 1800s. In the 19th century, this policy of one nation extending its rule over another became known as imperialism. *Differing views on British imperialism are reflected in the following passages from speeches by British statesmen William Ewart Gladstone (1809–1898) and Joseph Chamberlain (1836–1914). Among the victims of British expansion in South Africa were the Ndebele people. The memoir of Ndansi Kumalo, one of the Ndebele, tells of their fate.*

---

from a Speech by William Ewart Gladstone

I join issue[1] with the Prime Minister upon that subject, and I affirm that nothing can be more fundamentally unsound, more practically ruinous, than the establishment of Roman analogies for the guidance of British policy.[2]

What, gentlemen, was Rome? Rome was indeed an imperial state, you may tell me—I know not, I cannot read the counsels of Providence—a state having a mission to subdue the world; but a state whose very basis it was to deny the equal rights, to proscribe[3] the independent existence, of other nations. That, gentlemen, was the Roman idea. It has been partially and not ill described in three lines of a translation from Virgil by our great poet Dryden,[4] which run as follows:

O Rome! 'tis thine alone with awful
    sway
To rule mankind, and make the world
    obey,
Disposing peace and war thine own
    majestic way.

We are told to fall back upon this example. No doubt the word "Empire" was qualified with the word "Liberty." But what did the two words "Liberty" and "Empire" mean in a Roman mouth? They meant simply this—"Liberty for ourselves, Empire over the rest of mankind."

---

[1] join issue—disagree.

[2] Roman analogies ... British policy—Gladstone opposed using comparisons drawn from the Roman Empire in shaping England's foreign policy.

[3] proscribe—forbid.

[4] Virgil ... Dryden—English poet John Dryden (1631–1700) translated the works of the Roman poet Virgil (70–19 B.C.).

I do not think, gentlemen, that this ministry, or any other ministry, is going to place us in the position of Rome. What I object to is the revival of the idea—I care not how feebly, I care not even how, from a philosophic or historic point of view, how ridiculous the attempt at this revival may be. I say it indicates an intention—I say it indicates a frame of mind, and that frame of mind, unfortunately, I find, has been consistent with the policy of which I have given you some illustrations—the policy of denying to others the rights that we claim ourselves. No doubt, gentlemen, Rome may have had its work to do, and Rome did its work. But modern times have brought a different state of things. Modern times have established a sisterhood of nations, equal, independent; each of them built up under that legitimate defence which public law affords to every nation, living within its own borders, and seeking to perform its own affairs; but if one thing more than another has been **detestable**[5] to Europe, it has been the appearance upon the stage from time to time of men who, even in the times of the Christian civiliza-tion, have been thought to aim at universal dominion. It was this aggressive **disposition**[6] on the part of Louis XIV,[7] King of France, that led your forefathers, gentlemen, freely to spend their blood and treasure in a cause not immediately their own, and to struggle against the method of policy which, having Paris for its center seemed to aim at an universal monarchy.

from a Speech by Joseph Chamberlain

We must look this matter in the face, and must recognize that in order that we may have more employment to give we must create more demand. (Hear, hear.) Give me the demand for more goods and then I will undertake to give plenty of employment in making the goods; and the only thing, in my opinion, that the Government can do in order to meet this great difficulty that we are considering, is so to arrange its policy that every inducement shall be given to the demand; that new markets shall be created, and that old markets shall be effectually developed. (Cheers.) You are aware that some of my opponents please themselves occasionally by finding names for me (laughter)—and among other names lately they have been calling me a Jingo.[8] (Laughter.) I am no more a Jingo than you are. (Hear, hear.) But for the reasons and arguments I have put before you tonight I am convinced that it is a necessity as well as a duty for us to uphold the **dominion**[9] and empire which we now possess. (Loud cheers.) For these reasons, among others, I would never lose the hold which we now have over our great Indian dependency[10]— (hear, hear)—by far the greatest and most

---

[5] **detestable**—hateful.

[6] **disposition**—tendency.

[7] Louis XIV—Louis XIV (1638–1715) sought supremacy in Europe though warfare.

[8] Jingo—supporter of an aggressive foreign policy.

[9] **dominion**—rule.

[10] Indian dependency—India was a British colony in the 19th century.

valuable of all the customers we have or ever shall have in this country. For the same reasons I approve of the continued occupation of Egypt; and for the same reasons I have urged upon this Government, and upon previous Governments, the necessity for using every legitimate opportunity to extend our influence and control in that great African continent which is now being opened up to civilization and to commerce; and, lastly, it is for the same reasons that I hold that our navy should be strengthened—(loud cheers)—until its supremacy is so assured that we cannot be shaken in any of the possessions which we hold or may hold hereafter.

Believe me, if in any one of the places to which I have referred any change took place which deprived us of that control and influence of which I have been speaking, the first to suffer would be the workingmen of this country. Then, indeed, we should see a distress which would not be temporary, but which would be chronic, and we should find that England was entirely unable to support the enormous population which is now maintained by the aid of her foreign trade. If the workingmen of this country understand, as I believe they do—I am one of those who have had good reason through my life to rely upon their intelligence and shrewdness—if they understand their own interests, they will never lend any countenance to the doctrines of those politicians who never lose an opportunity of pouring contempt and abuse upon the brave Englishmen,

who, even at this moment, in all parts of the world are carving out new dominions for Britain, and are opening up fresh markets for British commerce, and laying out fresh fields for British labor. (Applause.)

from *Memoir of Ndansi Kumalo*

We were terribly upset and very angry at the coming of the white men. . . . Lobengula[11] had no war in his heart: he had always protected the white men and been good to them. If he had meant war, would he have sent our regiments far away to the north at this moment? As far as I know the trouble began in this way. Gandani, a chief who was sent out, reported that some of the Mashona[12] had taken the king's cattle; some regiments were detailed to follow and recover them. They followed the Mashona to Ziminto's people. Gandani had strict instructions not to molest the white people established in certain parts and to confine himself to the people who had taken the cattle. The commander was given a letter which he had to produce to the Europeans and tell them what the object of the party was. But the members of the party were restless and went without reporting to the white people and killed a lot of Mashonas. The pioneers were very angry and said, "You have trespassed into our part." They went with the letter, but only after they had killed some people, and the white men said, "You have done

[11] Lobengula—King Lobengula of the Ndebele had signed an agreement with England in 1888 that guaranteed there would be no English settlers on Ndebele land.

[12] Mashona—people whom the Ndebele had conquered.

wrong, you should have brought the letter first and then we should have given you permission to follow the cattle." The commander received orders from the white people to get out, and up to a certain point which he could not possibly reach in the time allowed. A force followed them up and they defended themselves. When the pioneers turned out there was a fight at Shangani and at Bembezi. . . .

The next news was that the white people had entered Bulawayo; the King's kraal[13] had been burnt down and the King had fled. Of the cattle very few were recovered; most fell into the hands of the white people. Only a very small portion were found and brought to Shangani where the King was, and we went there to give him any assistance we could. . . . Three of our leaders mounted their horses and followed up the King and he wanted to know where his cattle were; they said they had fallen into the hands of the whites, only a few were left. He said, "Go back and bring them along." But they did not go back again; the white forces had occupied Bulawayo and they went into the Matoppos. Then the white people came to where we were living and sent word round that all chiefs and warriors should go into Bulawayo and discuss peace, for the King had gone and they wanted to make peace. . . . The white people said, "Now that your King has deserted you, we occupy your country. Do you submit to us?" What could we do? "If you are sincere, come back and bring in all your arms, guns, and spears." We did so. . . .

So we surrendered to the white people and were told to go back to our homes and live our usual lives and attend to our crops. But the white men sent native police who did **abominable**[14] things; they were cruel and assaulted a lot of our people and helped themselves to our cattle and goats. These policemen were not our own people; anybody was made a policeman. We were treated like slaves. They came and were overbearing and we were ordered to carry their clothes and bundles. They interfered with our wives and our daughters and molested them. In fact, the treatment we received was intolerable. We thought it best to fight and die rather than bear it. How the rebellion started I do not know; there was no organization, it was like a fire that suddenly flames up. We had been flogged by native police and then they rubbed salt water in the wounds. There was much bitterness because so many of our cattle were branded and taken away from us; we had no property, nothing we could call our own. We said, "It is no good living under such conditions; death would be better— let us fight." Our King gone, we had submitted to the white people and they ill-treated us until we became desperate and tried to make an end of it all. We knew that we had very little chance because their weapons were so much superior to ours. But we meant to fight to the last, feeling that even if we could not beat them we might at least kill a few of them and so have some sort of revenge.

---

[13] Bulawayo . . . kraal—Bulawayo was Lobengula's capital. A kraal is a village.

[14] **abominable**—very hateful.

I fought in the rebellion. We used to look out for valleys where the white men were likely to approach. We took cover behind rocks and trees and tried to ambush them. We were forced by the nature of our weapons not to expose ourselves. I had a gun, a breech-loader. They—the white men—fought us with big guns and Maxims[15] and rifles.

I remember a fight in the Matoppos when we charged the white men. There were some hundreds of us; the white men also were as many. We charged them at close quarters: we thought we had a good chance to kill them but the Maxims were too much for us. We drove them off at the first charge, but they returned and formed up again. We made a second charge, but they were too strong for us. I cannot say how many white people were killed, but we think it was quite a lot. . . . Many of our people were killed in this fight: I saw four of my cousins shot. One was shot in the jaw and the whole of his face was blown away—like this—and he died. One was hit between the eyes; another here, in the shoulder; another had part of his ear shot off. We made many charges but each time we were beaten off, until at last the white men packed up and retreated. But for the Maxims, it would have been different. . . .

So peace was made. Many of our people had been killed, and now we began to die of starvation; and then came the rinderpest[16] and the cattle that were still left to us perished. We could not help thinking that all these dreadful things were brought by the white people. We struggled, and the Government helped us with grain; and by degrees we managed to get crops and pulled through. Our cattle were practically wiped out, but a few were left and from them we slowly bred up our herds again. We were offered work in the mines and farms to earn money and so were able to buy back some cattle. At first, of course, we were not used to going out to work, but advice was given that the chief should advise the young people to go out to work, and gradually they went. At first we received a good price for our cattle and sheep and goats. Then the tax came. It was 10s. a year. Soon the Government said, "That is too little, you must contribute more; you must pay £1."[17] We did so. Then those who took more than one wife were taxed; 10s. for each additional wife. The tax is heavy, but that is not all. We are also taxed for our dogs; 5s. for a dog. Then we were told we were living on private land; the owners wanted rent in addition to the Government tax; some 10s., some £1, some £2 a year. . . .

Would I like to have the old days back? Well, the white men have brought some good things. For a start, they brought us European implements—plows; we can buy European clothes, which are an advance. The Government has arranged for education and through that, when our children grow up, they may rise in status. We want them to be educated and civilized and make better citizens. Even in our own time there were troubles, there was much fighting

---

[15] Maxims—early machine guns.
[16] rinderpest—cattle disease.
[17] 10s. . . . £1—ten shillings . . . one pound.

and many innocent people were killed. It is infinitely better to have peace instead of war, and our treatment generally by the officials is better than it was at first. But, under the white people, we still have our troubles. Economic conditions are telling on us very severely. We are on land where the rainfall is scanty, and things will not grow well. In our own time we could pick our own country, but now all the best land has been taken by the white people. We get hardly any price for our cattle; we find it hard to meet our money obligations. If we have crops to spare we get very little for them; we find it difficult to make ends meet and wages are very low. When I view the position, I see that our rainfall has diminished, we have suffered drought and have poor crops and we do not see any hope of improvement, but all the same our taxes do not diminish. We see no prosperous days ahead of us. There is one thing we think an injustice. When we have plenty of grain the prices are very low, but the moment we are short of grain and we have to buy from Europeans at once the price is high. If when we have hard times and find it difficult to meet our obligations some of these burdens were taken off us it would gladden our hearts. As it is, if we do raise anything, it is never our own: all, or most of it, goes back in taxation. We can never save any money. If we could, we could help ourselves: we could build ourselves better houses; we could buy modern means of traveling about, a cart, or donkeys or mules.

As to my own life, I have had twelve wives altogether, five died and seven are alive. I have twenty-six children alive, five have died. Of my sons five are married and are all at work farming; three young children go to school. I hope the younger children will all go to school. I think it is a good thing to go to school.

There are five schools in our district. Quite a number of people are Christians, but I am too old to change my ways. In our religion we believe that when anybody dies the spirit remains and we often make offerings to the spirits to keep them good-tempered. But now the making of offerings is dying out rapidly, for every member of the family should be present, but the children are Christians and refuse to come, so the spirit-worship is dying out. A good many of our children go to the mines in the Union,[18] for the wages are better there. Unfortunately a large number do not come back at all. And some send money to their people—others do not. Some men have even deserted their families, their wives, and children. If they cannot go by train they walk long distances.

---

[18] Union—Union of South Africa.

QUESTIONS TO CONSIDER

1. What did Gladstone see as the essence of imperialism?

2. How did Gladstone feel nations should relate to one another?

3. What were Chamberlain's main arguments in favor of imperialism?

4. What arguments for and against imperialism were made by Kumalo?

from

What Is Art?

LEO TOLSTOY

What purpose should art serve? Russian novelist Leo Tolstoy (1828–1910), best known for War and Peace *and* Anna Karenina, *expressed a vision of art rooted in religion.*

In order to define art correctly it is necessary first of all to cease to consider it as means to pleasure, and to consider it as one of the conditions of human life. Viewing it in this way we cannot fail to observe that art is one of the means of **intercourse**[1] between man and man.

Every work of art causes the receiver to enter into a certain kind of relationship both with him who produced or is producing the art, and with all those who, simultaneously, previously, or subsequently, receive the same artistic impression.

Speech transmitting the thoughts and experiences of men serves as a means of union among them, and art serves a similar purpose. The peculiarity of this latter means of intercourse, distinguishing it from intercourse by means of words, consists in this, that whereas by words a man transmits his thoughts to another, by art he transmits his feelings. . . .

The feelings with which the artist infects others may be most various—very strong or very weak, very important or very insignificant, very bad or very good: feelings of love of one's country, self-devotion and submission to fate or to God expressed in a drama, raptures of lovers described in a novel, feelings of voluptuousness expressed in a picture, courage expressed in a triumphal march, merriment evoked by a dance, humor evoked by a funny story, the feeling of quietness transmitted by an evening landscape or by a lullaby, or the feeling of admiration evoked by a beautiful arabesque[2]—it is all art.

---

[1] **intercourse**—communication.

[2] arabesque—Arabesque can refer to an ornamental style of art, a fanciful musical composition, or a posture in ballet.

If only the spectators or auditors are infected by the feelings which the author has felt, it is art.

To evoke in oneself a feeling one has once experienced and having evoked it in oneself then by means of movements, lines, colors, sounds, or forms expressed in words, so to transmit that feeling that others experience the same feeling—this is the activity of art.

Art is a human activity consisting in this, that one man consciously by means of certain external signs, hands on to others feelings he has lived through, and that others are infected by these feelings and also experience them.

Art is not, as the metaphysicians[3] say, the manifestation of some mysterious Idea of beauty or God; it is not, as the aesthetic physiologists[4] say, a game in which man lets off his excess of stored-up energy; it is not the expression of man's emotions by external signs; it is not the production of pleasing objects; and, above all, it is not pleasure; but it is a means of union among men joining them together in the same feelings, and indispensable for the life and progress towards well-being of individuals and of humanity.

As every man, thanks to man's capacity to express thoughts by words, may know all that has been done for him in the realms of thought by all humanity before his day, and can in the present, thanks to this capacity to understand the thoughts of others, become a sharer in their activity and also himself hand on to his contemporaries and descendants the thoughts he has assimilated from others as well as those that have arisen in himself; so, thanks to man's capacity to be infected with the feelings of others by means of art, all that is being lived through by his contemporaries is accessible to him, as well as the feelings experienced by men thousands of years ago, and he has also the possibility of transmitting his own feelings to others.

If people lacked the capacity to receive the thoughts conceived by men who preceded them and to pass on to others their own thoughts, men would be like wild beasts, or like Kaspar Hauser.[5]

And if men lacked this other capacity of being infected by art, people might be almost more savage still, and above all more separated from, and more hostile to, one another.

And therefore the activity of art is a most important one, as important as the activity of speech itself and as generally diffused.

As speech does not act on us only in sermons, orations, or books, but in all those remarks by which we interchange thoughts and experiences with one another, so also art in the wide sense of the word permeates our whole life, but it is only to

---

[3] metaphysicians—those versed in metaphysics, a branch of philosophy that deals with the nature of reality.

[4] aesthetic physiologists—The English philosopher Herbert Spencer (1820–1903) theorized that aesthetic activities such as the arts served the physiological function of relieving the body of stored-up sensory and emotional energies.

[5] Kaspar Hauser—young man (1812?–1833) who mysteriously appeared in Nuremburg, Germany, at the age of about sixteen and, although of normal intelligence, seemed to have had no previous human contact.

some of its manifestations that we apply the term in the limited sense of the word.

We are accustomed to understand art to be only what we hear and see in theatres, concerts, and exhibitions; together with buildings, statues, poems, and novels. . . . But all this is but the smallest part of the art by which we communicate with one another in life. All human life is filled with works of art of every kind—from cradle-song, jest, **mimicry**,[6] the ornamentation of houses, dress, and utensils, to church services, buildings, monuments, and triumphal processions. It is all artistic activity. So that by art, in the limited sense of the word, we do not mean all human activity transmitting feelings but only that part which we for some reason select from it and to which we attach special importance.

This special importance has always been given by men to that part of this activity which transmits feelings flowing from their religious perception, and this small part they have specifically called art, attaching to it the full meaning of the word.

That was how men of old—Socrates, Plato, and Aristotle[7]—looked on art. Thus did the Hebrew prophets and the ancient Christians regard art. Thus it was, and still is, understood by the Mohammedans, and thus it still is understood by religious folk among our own peasantry.

Some teachers of mankind—such as Plato in his *Republic*, and people like the primitive Christians, the strict Mohammedans and the Buddhists—have gone so far as to **repudiate**[8] all art.

People viewing art in this way (in contradiction to the prevalent view of today which regards any art as good if only it affords pleasure) held and hold that art (as contrasted with speech, which need not be listened to) is so highly dangerous in its power to infect people against their wills, that mankind will lose far less by banishing all art than by tolerating each and every art.

Evidently such people were wrong in repudiating all art, for they denied what cannot be denied—one of the indispensable means of communication without which mankind could not exist. But not less wrong are the people of civilized European society of our class and day in favoring any art if it but serves beauty, that is, gives people pleasure.

Formerly people feared lest among works of art there might chance to be some causing corruption, and they prohibited art altogether. Now they only fear lest they should be deprived of any enjoyment art can afford, and they patronize any art. And I think the last error is much grosser than the first and that its consequences are far more harmful. . . .

The assertion that art may be good art and at the same time incomprehensible to a

---

[6] **mimicry**—imitation of speech, behavior, etc.

[7] Socrates, Plato, and Aristotle—ancient Greek philosophers.

[8] **repudiate**—reject completely.

great number of people, is extremely unjust, and its consequences are ruinous to art itself; but at the same time it is so common and has so eaten into our conceptions, that it is impossible to make sufficiently clear its whole absurdity.

Nothing is more common than to hear it said of reputed works of art that they are very good but very difficult to understand. We are quite used to such assertions, and yet to say that a work of art is good but incomprehensible to the majority of men, is the same as saying of some kind of food that it is very good but most people can't eat it. The majority of men may not like rotten cheese or **putrefying**[9] grouse, dishes esteemed by people with perverted tastes; but bread and fruit are only good when they are such as please the majority of men. And it is the same with art. Perverted art may not please the majority of men, but good art always pleases every one. . . .

Moreover it cannot be said that the majority of people lack the taste to esteem the highest works of art. The majority always have understood and still understand what we also recognize as being the very best art: the epic of Genesis, the Gospel parables, folk-legends, fairy-tales, and folk-songs are understood by all. How can it be that the majority has suddenly lost its capacity to understand what is high in our art? . . .

Art is differentiated from activity of the understanding, which demands preparation and a certain sequence of knowledge (so that one cannot learn trigonometry

before knowing geometry), by the fact that it acts on people independently of their state of development and education, that the charm of a picture, of sounds, or of forms, infects any man whatever his plane of development.

The business of art lies just in this: to make that understood and felt which in the form of an argument might be incomprehensible and inaccessible. Usually it seems to the recipient of a truly artistic impression that he knew the thing before, but had been unable to express it.

And such has always been the nature of good, supreme art; the *Iliad*, the *Odyssey*; the stories of Isaac, Jacob, and Joseph; the Hebrew prophets, the psalms, the Gospel parables; the story of Sakya Muni and the hymns of the Vedas,[10] all transmit very exalted feelings and are nevertheless quite comprehensible now to us, educated or uneducated, just as they were comprehensible to the men of those times, long ago, who were even less educated than our laborers. People talk about incomprehensibility; but if art is the transmission of feelings flowing from man's religious perception, how can a feeling be incomprehensible which is founded on religion, that is, on man's relation to God? Such art should be, and has actually always been, comprehensible to everybody, because every man's relation to God is one and the same. This is why the churches and the

---

[9] **putrefying**—rotting.
[10] Sakya Muni . . . Vedas—Sakya Muni is the Indian religious teacher known as the Buddha (page 50). The Vedas are ancient Indian religious poetry.

images in them were always comprehensible to every one. The hindrance to an understanding of the best and highest feelings (as is said in the Gospel) lies not at all in deficiency of development or learning, but on the contrary in false development and false learning. A good and lofty work of art may be incomprehensible, but not to simple, unperverted, peasant laborers (what is highest is understood by them)—it may be and often is unintelligible to **erudite**,[11] perverted people destitute of religion. And this continually occurs in our society in which the highest feelings are simply not understood. For instance, I know people who consider themselves most refined, and who say that they do not understand the poetry of love of one's neighbor, of self-sacrifice, or of chastity. . . .

Art cannot be incomprehensible to the great masses only because it is very good— as artists of our day are fond of telling us. Rather we are bound to conclude that this art is unintelligible to the great masses only because it is very bad art, or even is not art at all. So that the favorite argument (naively accepted by the cultured crowd), that in order to feel art one has first to understand it (which really only means habituate oneself to it), is the truest indication that what we are asked to understand by such a method is either very bad, exclusive art, or is not art at all.

---

[11] **erudite**—learned or scholarly.

QUESTIONS TO CONSIDER

1. According to Tolstoy, what is the basic purpose of art?

2. Tolstoy completely rejects the idea of art as a "means to pleasure." Do you agree? Why or why not?

3. Tolstoy mentions certain people who have wanted "to repudiate all art." Who were they and why did they want to do this?

4. Do you agree with Tolstoy that the greatest art must be comprehensible to all? Why or why not?

5. What do *you* think is the purpose of art?

Romanticism and Realism

During the first half of the 19th century, Romanticism dominated the visual arts. To Romantic artists, depicting the humble peasant at work in a rural landscape was a way of rejecting the ills of the Industrial Revolution, celebrating Nature, and glorifying a rapidly disappearing way of life. Developing in the mid-1800s in opposition to Romanticism, Realism attempted to portray things as they are. Less inclined to idealize workers, Realist painters often showed the bitterness and drudgery of their lives.

▲
In his etching *The Early Plowman*, English artist Samuel Palmer (1805–1881) presents a very Romantic vision of a farmer and his oxen at sunrise.

French painter Gustave Courbet (1819–1877) described the elderly laborer in his harshly realistic painting *The Stonebreakers* as "an old machine grown stiff with service and age." ▶

▲

Rosa Bonheur (1822–1899), the most famous woman artist of the mid-1800s, was famous for her powerful studies of animals, such as those who dominate her painting *Plowing in the Nivernais: The Dressing of Vines*.

QUESTIONS TO CONSIDER

1. Samuel Palmer and Rosa Bonheur depict basically the same subject. How do their treatments differ?

2. What attitude does Gustave Courbet seem to have had toward his subjects in *The Stonebreakers?*

Impressionism and Post-Impressionism

The term Impressionism was coined by a critic to describe the work of a group of French painters who began exhibiting together in the 1870s. Abandoning Realism's concern with presenting a convincing illusion by accurately reproducing surface detail, the Impressionists used frankly artificial techniques to create fleeting effects of light. Developing out of Impressionism in the 1880s and 1890s, Post-Impressionism moved still further away from the illusion of reality toward increasingly abstract patterns.

▲

Showing workers under the glass and iron shed of a Paris railroad station, *Gare St. Lazare* by French impressionist painter Claude Monet (1840–1926) is one of ten views he painted of this scene.

In *Farm Women at Work* by Georges Seurat (1859–1891), the artist's feathery brush strokes, the angles of the women's backs, and the rows of plants all display an emphasis on form. ▶

In *The Pool of London*, French painter André Derain (1880–1954) used strong angles and short brush strokes to portray the vigor and life of commerce on the river. ▼

QUESTIONS TO CONSIDER

1. What are the dominant images in Claude Monet's painting, and what do they imply about the role of the worker?

2. What does Georges Seurat indicate about the nature of work and the workers?

3. What tone did André Derain give to his portrayal of work?

Darwin's Delay

STEPHEN JAY GOULD

In this essay, biologist and historian of science Stephen Jay Gould examines the possible reasons for English naturalist Charles Darwin's delay in publishing his views on natural selection and evolution (page 481).

Few events inspire more speculation than long and unexplained pauses in the activities of famous people. Rossini crowned a brilliant operatic career with *William Tell* and then wrote almost nothing for the next thirty-five years. Dorothy Sayers abandoned Lord Peter Wimsey[1] at the height of his popularity and turned instead to God. Charles Darwin developed a radical theory of evolution in 1838 and published it twenty-one years later only because A.R. Wallace[2] was about to scoop him.

Five years with nature aboard the *Beagle* destroyed Darwin's faith in the fixity of species. In July, 1837, shortly after the voyage, he started his first notebook on "transmutation."[3] Already convinced that evolution had occurred, Darwin sought a theory to explain its mechanism. After much preliminary speculation and a few unsuccessful hypotheses, he achieved his central insight while reading an apparently unrelated work for recreation. Darwin later wrote in his autobiography:

In October 1838 . . . I happened to read for amusement Malthus on Population,[4] and being well prepared to appreciate the struggle for existence which everywhere goes on from long continued observation of the habits of animals and plants, it at once struck me that under these circumstances favorable variations would tend to be preserved and unfavorable ones to be destroyed. The result of this would be the formation of new species.

Darwin had long appreciated the importance of artificial selection practiced by animal breeders. But until Malthus's

---

[1] Lord Peter Wimsey—fictional detective in several novels and stories by Dorothy Sayers (1893–1957).

[2] A. R. Wallace—British naturalist (1823–1913) whose work on evolution was similar to Darwin's.

[3] transmutation—transformation; here, of species.

[4] Malthus on Population—*Essay on the Principle of Population* by English economist Thomas Malthus (page 462).

vision of struggle and crowding catalyzed[5] his thoughts, he had not been able to identify an agent for natural selection. If all creatures produced far more offspring than could possibly survive, then natural selection would direct evolution under the simple assumption that survivors, on the average, are better adapted to prevailing conditions of life.

Why then did he wait for more than twenty years to publish his theory?

Darwin knew what he had achieved. We cannot attribute his delay to any lack of appreciation for the magnitude of his accomplishment. In 1842 and again in 1844 he wrote out preliminary sketches of his theory and its implications. He also left strict instructions with his wife to publish these alone of his manuscripts if he should die before writing his major work.

Why then did he wait for more than twenty years to publish his theory? True, the pace of our lives today has accelerated so rapidly—leaving among its victims the art of conversation and the game of baseball—that we may mistake a normal period of the past for a large slice of eternity. But the span of a man's life is a constant measuring stick; twenty years is still half a normal career—a large chunk of life even by the most deliberate Victorian standards.

Conventional scientific biography is a remarkably misleading source of information about great thinkers. It tends to depict them as simple, rational machines pursuing their insights with steadfast devotion, under the drive of an internal mechanism subject to no influence but the constraints of objective data. Thus, Darwin waited twenty years—so the usual argument runs—simply because he had not completed his work. He was satisfied with his theory, but theory is cheap. He was determined not to publish until he had amassed an overwhelming **dossier**[6] of data in its support, and this took time.

But Darwin's activities during the twenty years in question display the inadequacy of this traditional view. In particular, he devoted eight full years to writing four large volumes on the taxonomy and natural history of barnacles.[7] Before this single fact, the traditionalists can only offer pap something like: Darwin felt that he had to understand species thoroughly before proclaiming how they change; this he could do only by working out for himself the classification of a difficult group of organisms—but not for eight years, and not while he sat on the most revolutionary notion in the history of biology. Darwin's own assessment of the four volumes stands in his autobiography.

> Besides discovering several new and remarkable forms, I made out the homologies of the various parts . . . and I proved the existence in certain genera of minute males complemental to and parasitic on the hermaphrodites. . . . Nevertheless, I doubt whether the work

---

[5] catalyzed—changed.

[6] **dossier**—a collection of papers giving detailed information about a person or subject.

[7] taxonomy . . . barnacles—classification of a knid of shellfish.

was worth the consumption of so much time.

So complex an issue as the motivation for Darwin's delay has no simple resolution, but I feel sure of one thing: the negative effect of fear must have played at least as great a role as the positive need for additional documentation. Of what, then, was Darwin afraid?

When Darwin achieved his Malthusian insight, he was twenty-nine years old. He held no professional position, but he had acquired the admiration of his colleagues for his astute work aboard the *Beagle*. He was not about to compromise a promising career by promulgating a heresy[8] that he could not prove.

What then was his heresy? A belief in evolution itself is the obvious answer. Yet this cannot be a major part of the solution; for, contrary to popular belief, evolution was a very common heresy during the first half of the nineteenth century. It was widely and openly discussed, opposed, to be sure, by a large majority, but admitted or at least considered by most of the great naturalists.

An extraordinary pair of Darwin's early notebooks may contain the answer. . . . These so-called M and N notebooks were written in 1838 and 1839, while Darwin was compiling the transmutation notebooks that formed the basis for his sketches of 1842 and 1844. They contain his thoughts on philosophy, esthetics,[9] psychology, and anthropology. On rereading them in 1856, Darwin described them as "full of metaphysics on morals." They include many statements showing that he **espoused**[10] but

feared to expose something he perceived as far more heretical than evolution itself: philosophical materialism—the postulate[11] that matter is the stuff of all existence and that all mental and spiritual phenomena are its by-products. No notion could be more upsetting to the deepest traditions of Western thought than the statement that mind—however complex and powerful—is simply a product of brain. Consider, for example, John Milton's[12] vision of mind as separate from and superior to the body that it inhabits for a time (*Il Penseroso*, 1633).

> Or let my lamp, at midnight hour,
> Be seen in some high lonely tower,
> Where I may oft outwatch the Bear,
> With thrice-great Hermes,[13] or unsphere
> The spirit of Plato, to unfold
> What worlds or what vast regions hold
> The immortal mind that hath forsook
> Her mansion in this fleshly nook.

The notebooks prove that Darwin was interested in philosophy and aware of its implications. He knew that the primary feature distinguishing his theory from all other evolutionary doctrines was its uncompromising philosophical materialism. Other evolutionists spoke of vital forces, directed history, organic striving,

---

[8] promulgating a heresy—spreading a false doctrine.

[9] esthetics—philosophy of art; also *aesthetics*.

[10] **espoused**—supported.

[11] postulate—basic principle.

[12] John Milton—English poet (1608–1674).

[13] the Bear . . . Hermes—The Bear is the constellation of Ursa Major, the Great Bear. Hermes Trismegistus was the legendary author of certain works of philosophy and magic.

and the essential irreducibility of mind—a **panoply**[14] of concepts that traditional Christianity could accept in compromise, for they permitted a Christian God to work by evolution instead of creation. Darwin spoke only of random variation and natural selection.

In the notebooks Darwin resolutely applied his materialistic theory of evolution to all phenomena of life, including what he termed "the citadel itself"—the human mind. And if mind has no real existence beyond the brain, can God be anything more than an illusion invented by an illusion? In one of his transmutation notebooks, he wrote:

> Love of the deity effect of organization, oh you materialist! . . . Why is thought being a secretion of brain, more wonderful than gravity a property of matter? It is our arrogance, our admiration of ourselves.

This belief was so heretical that Darwin even sidestepped it in *The Origin of Species* (1859), where he ventured only the cryptic comment that "light will be thrown on the origin of man and his history." He gave vent to his beliefs, only when he could hide them no longer, in the *Descent of Man* (1871) and *The Expression of the Emotions in Man and Animals* (1872). A. R. Wallace, the codiscoverer of natural selection, could never bring himself to apply it to the human mind, which he viewed as the only divine contribution to the history of life. Yet Darwin cut through 2,000 years of philosophy and religion in the most remarkable epigram of the M notebook:

Plato says in *Phaedo* that our "imaginary ideas" arise from the preexistence of the soul, are not derivable from experience—read monkeys for preexistence.

In his commentary on the M and N notebooks, Gruber labels materialism as "at that time more outrageous than evolution." He documents the persecution of materialistic beliefs during the late eighteenth and early nineteenth century and concludes:

> In virtually every branch of knowledge, repressive methods were used: lectures were proscribed, publication was hampered, professorships were denied, fierce invective and ridicule appeared in the press. Scholars and scientists learned the lesson and responded to the pressures on them. The ones with unpopular ideas sometimes recanted, published anonymously, presented their ideas in weakened forms, or delayed publication for many years.

Darwin had experienced a direct example as an undergraduate at the University of Edinburgh in 1827. His friend W. A. Browne read a paper with a materialistic perspective on life and mind before the Plinian Society. After much debate, all references to Browne's paper, including the record (from the previous meeting) of his intention to deliver it, were expunged[15]

---

[14] **panoply**—array.
[15] expunged—erased.

from the minutes. Darwin learned his lesson, for he wrote in the M notebook:

> To avoid stating how far, I believe, in Materialism, say, only that emotions, instincts, degrees of talent, which are hereditary are so because brain of child resembles parent stock.

The most ardent materialists of the nineteenth century, Marx and Engels,[16] were quick to recognize what Darwin had accomplished and to exploit its radical content. In 1869, Marx wrote to Engels about Darwin's *Origin*:

> Although it is developed in the crude English style, this is the book which contains the basis in natural history for our view.

Marx later offered to dedicate volume 2 of *Das Kapital* to Darwin, but Darwin gently declined, stating that he did not want to imply approval of a work he had not read. (I have seen Darwin's copy of volume I in his library at Down House. It is inscribed by Marx who calls himself a "sincere admirer" of Darwin. Its pages are uncut. Darwin was no devotee of the German language.)

Darwin was, indeed, a gentle revolutionary. Not only did he delay his work for so long, but he also **assiduously**[17] avoided any public statement about the philosophical implications of his theory. In 1880, he wrote to Karl Marx:

> It seems to me (rightly or wrongly) that direct arguments against Christianity and Theism hardly have any effect on the public; and that freedom of thought will best be promoted by that gradual enlightening of human understanding which follows the progress of science. I have therefore always avoided writing about religion and have confined myself to science.

Yet the content of his work was so disruptive to traditional Western thought that we have yet to encompass it all. Arthur Koestler's campaign against Darwin, for example, rests upon a reluctance to accept Darwin's materialism and an ardent desire once again to invest living matter with some special property (see *The Ghost in the Machine* or *The Case of the Midwife Toad*). This, I confess, I do not understand. Wonder and knowledge are both to be cherished. Shall we appreciate any less the beauty of nature because its harmony is unplanned? And shall the potential of mind cease to inspire our awe and fear because several billion neurons reside in our skulls?

---

[16] Marx and Engels—Karl Marx and Friedrich Engels, German socialists who produced the *Communist Manifesto* (page 485). Marx was also the author of *Das Kapital* ("Capital"), a large-scale work of economic analysis.

[17] **assiduously**—persistently.

QUESTIONS TO CONSIDER

1. How did the population theory of Malthus influence Darwin's thinking on evolution?

2. Why did Darwin's belief that mind is simply a product of the brain seem heretical?

3. Why does Stephen Jay Gould call Darwin "a gentle revolutionary"?

Forms and Motives of European Imperialism

J. M. ROBERTS

Between 1500 and 1900 the nations of Europe acquired control over much of the rest of the world. Sometimes this control was direct, in the form of colonies. European domination also took several indirect forms, as British historian J. M. Roberts points out in his Concise History of the World.

Though Europeans in the nineteenth century went in for empire-building even more vigorously than before, European world power in that era was not just a matter of running up the flag over new territories. It presented many different threats to the non-European world, some all the more disturbing because less direct than simple military or political takeover. In many places the arrival of European or American traders, prospectors and financiers led to economic concessions by formally independent local rulers which in fact, though not in name, soon tied their subjects to the wheels of the western chariot, whether this was intended or not. The shape of life in Malaysia was quite altered when Europeans brought the rubber plant there from South America, so creating a new industry on which many of the inhabitants were soon dependent for a living. Mining operations could give a country new political importance; the rulers of Morocco found that their country was being interfered with and squabbled over by Europeans as soon as it was suspected that there were minerals to be found there.

Interference with the internal government of formally independent states could go a long way without getting as far as outright **annexation**.[1] Since the sixteenth century, when they were first negotiated with the Ottoman Turks,[2] "Capitulations" had often been made with non-Christian powers in order to ensure security and

---

[1] **annexation**—takeover.

[2] Ottoman Turks—rulers of an empire that in the late 1400s and early 1500s controlled a large part of the eastern Mediterranean (page 392).

privileges for resident Europeans. They entitled them to exemption from local law-courts and to appear instead before special officials or tribunals manned by European judges, and so to escape the operation of the native law. In China in the later nineteenth century Europeans and Americans lived in special areas—"concessions," as they were called—in cities where they did business, and the governments of these areas was responsible not to the Chinese authorities but to the foreigners. Sometimes they had western garrisons and police, too. Such arrangements weakened the prestige of the local rulers in the eyes of their own people. With some rulers Europeans also negotiated treaties which gave them control over their foreign policy. Altogether, a large and vague zone of practical interference in the affairs of many non-European states stretched a long way beyond the formal boundaries of empire.

Finally, there was also another, more subtle form of domination which the European civilization of the nineteenth century began to exercise more and more as time passed. In many places it was to outlive more overt forms of imperial rule. This was the domination of western ideas and ways—of European civilization in the deepest sense. It is very hard to define this precisely except in individual instances. Over huge areas of the world millions of people went on living undisturbed within patterns of behavior and belief quite alien to the civilization we call western or European. To overlook this would be silly. Nonetheless, nationalism and nationality

were western ideas which were to be taken up enthusiastically and to have enormous success in Asia and Africa; so were the ideas of science and technology and the notions of progress attached to them, as well as western notions of law, economics, religion, politics, government and a hundred and one other things. Even if they at first only affected a few—the educated elites of the non-European societies—in the end they bit deeply into the old ways of doing things and had effects far beyond these narrow circles.

All these currents of the age of imperial expansion played upon different parts of the world in different ways. Broadly speaking, the direct acquisition of new territory was most marked in Africa and the Pacific islands, while the more indirect forms of western domination spread in the Asia of the old empires. It is only a rough guide, but a useful one.

The variety of ways in which Europeans came to exercise power over other peoples makes it tempting to over-simplify their motives. Ever since the fifteenth century one of them, clearly, was the hope of economic gain. Men had always eagerly sought new places to trade and make money, new resources in land, minerals or labor, or just opportunities for straightforward theft. In the nineteenth century, many of these possibilities became more attractive still as the European demand for raw materials from other parts of the world grew with industrialization. But it is not necessary to govern another part of the world in order to do business there and many businessmen actually preferred to operate out of reach of European law and order. What is more, even when imperialist nations competed most vigorously to acquire new territory, their officials and politicians were often very disinclined to take on new colonies, knowing that they cost money to govern and protect and that there was no guarantee that they would pay for themselves in the end.

_____

No country had more money invested abroad in 1900 than Great Britain.

_____

Nor does a search for places in which to invest at good returns explain why people should want new possessions. No country had more money invested abroad in 1900 than Great Britain. Yet though she had the largest empire in the world, British investors had not put money into it on anything like the scale of their investments in the United States and South America, which offered much better returns than most of Africa. Though there was a rough coincidence in time between expansion in the free-enterprise economies of Europe and North America and the building of new empires, and though individual businessmen sometimes tried to interest governments in taking on new colonies in which they had a special interest, the belief that capitalism by itself explains an imperialist "wave" does not fit all the facts.

In practice, the mixture of motives and purposes in any one part of the world differed strongly from that in another, as different governments listened in different degree to different special interests—those of soldiers, humanitarians, missionaries, crackpots and settlers, as well as those of businessmen. They also listened in varying degree to public opinion. In many countries, the last age of imperialism was also one in which attention was beginning to be paid to what mass electorate wanted for the first time. Those electorates were more likely to read newspapers than a few years earlier, and journalists picked (as they still do) on issues which could be easily dramatized and turned into good "copy"; imperialism provided many. As a result, statesmen who did not themselves really believe in imperial expansion sometimes went along with the popular tide, or what appeared to be one. Even in that most undemocratic of imperialist countries, Russia, the government seems to have felt that imperial advance would help to rally support behind the regime.

The last complication is that much of the story of imperialism is a story of different degrees of resistance to it, or of difficulty in pursuing it. Imperialism was a matter of opening doors, but sometimes the door was locked, or there was someone on the other side pushing it to keep it closed, while behind other doors there was no resistance at all. When the new empires expanded, they often faced very different opportunities. European settlers overseas soon found this out. Some of them had gone to parts of the world new to Europeans—Australia, New Zealand, Pacific islands, East Africa—and thus played a part in the great imperialist advance. Yet, in the first place, not all nations were equally represented among them; the biggest settler populations were all to be found in the colonies of one imperialist country, Great Britain (emigrants from other European countries tended to go to the United States, or South America). Secondly, although what they found on arrival might vary much from place to place, it was never an old, highly developed civilization, a once-great empire or a major religion such as might be found in India or China; the settlers found little to admire or respect. Nor were there usually big native populations. White settlers therefore could set about making lives for themselves with much greater freedom than the rulers of other British possessions, who had to confront much more complex local conditions. As for non-settler colonies, European states were often tempted to expand because of the difficulty of establishing settled and orderly frontiers if they did not take a hand in the affairs of the peoples who lived on them. Russians in Central Asia and British in India both thought themselves in this position, whether rightly or not.

As for the established great powers of the non-European world, the Ottoman empire in both western Asia and in Europe was already in serious difficulties in 1800. These worsened as the century went on. The Turks seemed no longer able to govern properly their subject peoples, some of whom were likely to ask European states for help. Further east, the once great empire of Persia was under pressure (especially from Russia) and was internally divided and weak. Further east still, the Moghul empire[3] was a shadow of that of the seventeenth century, one Indian state after

another seemed unable to provide itself with stable government, and even the once powerful Chinese empire was looking feeble by the early nineteenth century. There was nothing in an Indonesia dominated by the Dutch or in a south-east Asia slipping out of the control of its Chinese overlords to provide firm native resistance to the dominant and aggressive civilization of Europe. Elsewhere in the world, in Africa and the Pacific islands, even more backward communities faced white imperialists. All that had protected many such places for so long from foreign domination were the simple, but formidable obstacles of climate, distance and disease. But the nineteenth century brought ways of overcoming these.

---

[3] Moghul empire—empire established in northern India in the early 1500s by Muslim invaders from Central Asia (page 65).

QUESTIONS TO CONSIDER

1. Why would the special arrangements negotiated by the European nations tend to weaken the prestige of local governments in the eyes of their own people?

2. In your opinion, which of the indirect forms of European domination described by J. M. Roberts would have the most significant long-term effects?

3. What evidence does Roberts offer that economic gain was not the sole factor in European imperialism?

Linking Cultures

City Life

Civilization, as its root civil *suggests, is related to city life. The development of human culture started to accelerate when the first true cities appeared in southern Mesopotamia about 3500 B.C. Today human life is defined more and more by urbanization. As you examine the following scenes of city life from a variety of cultures and eras, reflect on these questions:*

- *What attitudes toward city life are reflected in these images?*
- *What elements reappear in these images?*
- *What definition of* civilized *can you derive from these images?*

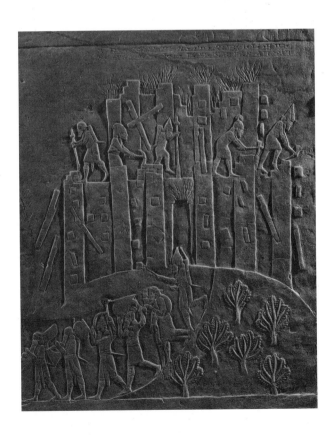

Relief showing the capture of a city *(Assyria)*
Flames sprout from the roofs of a captured city as Assyrian soldiers tear down its walls. ▶

◀ **Painting of Akbar**
building Fatephur Sikri (India)
The Moghul emperor Akbar is shown here inspecting the
building of his magnificent capital, Fatephur Sikri, which he
founded in 1569 and abandoned 15 years later.

Chang Tse-tuan
Scroll painting of town (China)
This portion of a scroll painting from the 1100s shows the
people of a river town participating in a festival.

▼

◀ *Interior of Kabuki theater* *(Japan)*
In the 1600s, the emergence of an urban middle class in Japan is reflected in the popularity of a new form of entertainment, Kabuki drama.

▲
Triumphal Procession from Arch of Titus *(Rome)*
Processions by successful generals displaying the spoils of victory (such as this booty from the capture of Jerusalem in 70 A.D.) were an important feature of civic life in imperial Rome.

▲

Tower of London from medieval manuscript *(France)*

This view from the early 1400s of the Tower of London, a combination of prison, fortress, and royal residence, shows London Bridge in the background topped with shops and houses.

Pieter Bruegel

Children's Games *(Holland)*

Bruegel uses this panoramic view of children at play in the streets of a town to satirize the follies of their elders. ▶

Canaletto

The Pier, Seen from the Basin of San Marco *(Italy)*

Canaletto's picturesque views of his native Venice were prized by English travelers who, in the fashion of modern tourists, wanted a souvenir of their trip.

▼

▲

Gustave Doré *Over London—By Rail* *(France)*
A grim vision of the impact of the Industrial Revolution is captured in Doré's depiction
of a London slum in the late 1800s.

▲

Henri de Toulouse-Lautrec
At the Moulin Rouge (France)
Lautrec was a sharp, disillusioned observer of the night life
of Paris in the late 1800s.

▲

Emile Otto Hoppé
A Boy Runs Along Fleet Street
Looking toward St. Paul's cathedral, this photograph
of London shows busy Fleet Street, center of
British journalism.

▲

Georgia O'Keeffe *East River from the Shelton* (United States)
Defined by the elements of nature, O'Keeffe's image of New York anticipates her later
abstract landscapes of the American Southwest.

▲

Diego Rivera

The Great City of Tenochtitlán (Mexico)

Rivera celebrates the grandeur of the Aztec capital in this mural painting.

◀ **Fernand Léger**
Construction Workers *(France)*
Leger's early career as a Cubist shows in
the geometric quality of this painting of
construction workers.

Cindy Sherman
Untitled Film Still #21 *(United States)*
Sherman's photograph of herself as a young
secretary in New York City is part of a
series in which she appears in a variety of
familiar types from the movies.
▼

Chapter 13

The Early Twentieth Century

The Horrors of War

Shadows and Masks

The Strength of the State

Cultural Limits

◄ *A ruined tank—a weapon first used in World War I—lies beside a road in the ravaged terrain of the Western Front (page 541).*

A Lost Generation

VERA BRITTAIN

World War I (1914–1918) decimated a generation of young men, set huge political and social changes in motion, and shattered the idealism and belief in progress that had characterized 19th-century values. English writer Vera Brittain (1893?–1970) had just been accepted at Oxford University when the war started. In her memoir Testament of Youth, *she describes the atmosphere in Buxton, her hometown in northern England, when the war broke out.*

When the Great War broke out, it came to me not as a superlative tragedy, but as an interruption of the most exasperating kind to my personal plans. . . .

It would not, I think, be possible for any present-day girl of the same age even to imagine how abysmally[1] ignorant, how romantically idealistic, and how utterly unsophisticated my more sensitive contemporaries and I were at that time. The **naiveties**[2] of the diary which I began to write consistently soon after leaving school, and kept up until more than half way through the War, must be read in order to be believed. My "Reflective Record, 1913," is endorsed on its title page with the following comprehensive aspirations:

"To extend love, to promote thought, to lighten suffering, to combat indifference, to inspire activity."

"To know everything of something and something of everything."

My diary for August 3rd, 1914, contains a most incongruous[3] mixture of war and tennis.

The day was Bank Holiday, and a tennis tournament had been arranged at the Buxton Club. I had promised to play with my discouraged but still faithful suitor, and did not in the least want to forgo the amusement that I knew this partnership would afford me—particularly as the events reported in the newspapers seemed too incredible to be taken quite seriously.

---

[1] abysmally—badly.

[2] **naiveties**—simplicities.

[3] incongruous—inconsistent.

"I do not know," I wrote in my diary, "how we all managed to play tennis so calmly and take quite an interest in the result. I suppose it is because we all know so little of the real meaning of war that we are so indifferent. B. and I had to owe 30. It was good handicapping as we had a very close game with everybody." . . .

After that[4] events moved, even in Buxton, very quickly. The German cousins of some local acquaintances left the town in a panic. My parents rushed over in the car to familiar shops in Macclesfield and Leek, where they laid in stores of cheese, bacon, and butter under the generally shared impression that by next week we might all be besieged by the Germans. Wild rumors circulated from mouth to mouth; they were more plentiful than the newspapers, over which a free fight broke out on the station platform every time a batch came by train from London or Manchester. Our elderly cook, who had three Reservist sons, dissolved into continuous tears and was too much upset to prepare the meals with her usual competence; her young daughter-in-law, who had had a baby only the previous Friday, became hysterical and had to be forcibly restrained from getting up and following her husband to the station. One or two Buxton girls were hurriedly married to officers summoned to unknown destinations. Pandemonium[5] swept over the town. Holiday trippers wrestled with one another for the *Daily Mail*; habitually quiet and respectable citizens struggled like wolves for the provisions in the food-shops, and vented upon the distracted assistants their dismay at learning that all prices had suddenly gone up.

My diary for those few days reflects *The Times* in its most **pontifical**[6] mood. "Germany has broken treaty after treaty, and disregarded every honorable tie with other nations. . . . Germany has destroyed the tottering hopes of peace. . . . The great fear is that our bungling Government will declare England's neutrality. . . . If we at this critical juncture refuse to help our friend France, we should be guilty of the grossest treachery."

I prefer to think that my real sentiments were more truly represented by an entry written nearly a month later after the fabulously optimistic reports of the Battle of Le Cateau. I had been over to Newcastle-under-Lyme to visit the family dentist, and afterwards sat for an hour in a tree-shadowed walk called The Brampton and meditated on the War. It was one of those shimmering autumn days when every leaf and flower seems to **scintillate**[7] with light, and I found it "very hard to believe that not far away men were being slain ruthlessly, and their poor disfigured bodies heaped together and crowded in ghastly indiscrimination into quickly provided common graves as though they were nameless vermin. . . . It is impossible," I concluded, "to find any satisfaction in the thought of 25,000 slaughtered Germans, left to mutilation and decay; the

---

[4] After that—August 4, when England entered the war.

[5] pandemonium—complete confusion.

[6] **pontifical**—pompous or dogmatic.

[7] **scintillate**—sparkle.

destruction of men as though beasts, whether they be English, French, German, or anything else, seems a crime to the whole march of civilization." . . .

Brittain saw her fiancé Roland Leighton off to war in March 1915. After a year at Oxford, she served throughout the rest of the war as a V.A.D., a nurse in the Voluntary Aide Department. On December 23, 1915, she received word that Roland had died of wounds. Her brother Edward was wounded in 1916; in 1917, two other close friends, Victor and Geoffrey, were killed.

"Never in my life have I been so absolutely filthy as I get on duty here," I wrote to my mother on December 5th in answer to her request for a description of my work.

"Sister A.[8] has six wards and there is no V.A.D. in the next-door one, only an orderly, so neither she nor he spend very much time in here. Consequently I am Sister, V.A.D. and orderly all in one (somebody said the other day that no one less than God Almighty could give a correct definition of the job of a V.A.D.!) and after, quite apart from the nursing, I have stoked the stove all night, done two or three rounds of bed-pans and kept the kettles going and prepared feeds on exceedingly black Beatrice oil-stoves and refilled them from the steam kettles, literally wallowing in paraffin,[9] all the time, I feel as if I had been dragged through the gutter! Possibly acute surgical is the heaviest kind of work

there is, but acute medical is, I think, more wearing than anything else on earth. You are kept on the go the whole time and in the end there seems nothing definite to show for it—except that one or two people are still alive who might otherwise have been dead."

The rest of my letter referred to the effect, upon ourselves, of the new offensive at Cambrai.

"The hospital is very heavy now—as heavy as when I came; the fighting is continuing very long this year, and the convoys keep coming down, two or three a night. . . . Sometimes in the middle of the night we have to turn people out of bed and make them sleep on the floor to make room for more seriously ill ones that have come down from the line. We have heaps of gassed cases at present who came in a day or two ago; there are 10 in this ward alone. I wish those people who write so glibly about this being a holy War, and the orators who talk so much about going on no matter how long the War lasts and what it may mean, could see a case—to say nothing of 10 cases—of mustard gas in its early stages— could see the poor things burnt and blistered all over with great mustard-colored suppurating[10] blisters, with blind eyes— sometimes temporarily, sometimes permanently—all sticky and stuck together, and always fighting for breath, with voices a mere whisper, saying that their throats are closing and they know they will choke. The only thing one can say is that such

---

[8] Sister A.—"Sister" is the title of a head nurse.

[9] paraffin—kerosene.

[10] suppurating—discharging pus.

severe cases don't last long; either they die soon or else improve—usually the former; they certainly never reach England in the state we have them here, and yet people persist in saying that God made the War, when there are such inventions of the Devil about ." . . .

In April 1918, Brittain returned to England to take care of her parents, who were then in London. Her brother was on the Italian front.

For some time now, my apprehensions for Edward's safety had been lulled by the long quiescence of the Italian front, which had seemed a haven of peace in contrast to our own raging vortex.[11] Repeatedly, during the German offensive, I had thanked God and the Italians who fled at Caporetto[12] that Edward was out of it, and rejoiced that the worst I had to fear from this particular push was the comparatively trivial danger that threatened myself. But now I felt the familiar stirrings of the old tense fear which had been such a persistent companion throughout the War, and my alarm was increased when Edward asked me a week or two later to send him "a funny cat from Liberty's[13]. . . to alleviate tragedy with comedy." On Sunday morning, June 16th, I opened the *Observer*, which appeared to be chiefly concerned with the new offensive—for the moment at a standstill—in the Noyon-Montdidier sector of the Western Front, and instantly saw at the head of a column the paragraph for which I had looked so long and so fearfully:

"ITALIAN FRONT ABLAZE
GUN DUELS FROM MOUNTAIN TO SEA
BAD OPENING OF AN OFFENSIVE"

The following Italian official *communiqué* was issued yesterday:

"From dawn this morning the fire of the enemy's artillery, strongly countered by our own, was intensified from the Lagerina Valley to the sea. On the Asiago Plateau, to the east of the Brenta and on the middle Piave, the artillery struggle has assumed and maintains a character of extreme violence."

A day or two later, more details were published of the fighting in Italy, and I learnt that the Sherwood Foresters[14] had been involved in the "show" on the Plateau. After that I made no pretense at doing anything but wander restlessly round Kensington or up and down the flat, and, though my father retired glumly to bed every evening at nine o'clock, I gave up writing the semi-fictitious record which I had begun of my life in France. Somehow I couldn't bring myself even to wrap up the *Spectator* and *Saturday Review* that I sent every week to Italy, and they remained in my bedroom, silent yet eloquent witnesses to the dread which my father and I, determinedly conversing on commonplace topics, each refused to put into words.

---

[11] vortex—violent activity.

[12] German offensive . . . Caporetto—The last great German offensive of the War began in March 1918. Caporetto was a battle in Italy in 1917.

[13] Liberty's—a London department store.

[14] Sherwood Foresters—Edward Brittain's regiment.

By the following Saturday we had still heard nothing of Edward. The interval usually allowed for news of casualties after a battle was seldom so long as this, and I began, with an artificial sense of lightness unaccompanied by real conviction, to think that there was perhaps, after all, no news to come. I had just announced to my father, as we sat over tea in the dining-room, that I really must do up Edward's papers and take them to the post office before it closed for the week-end, when there came the sudden loud clattering at the front-door knocker that always meant a telegram.

For a moment I thought that my legs would not carry me, but they behaved quite normally as I got up and went to the door. I knew what was in the telegram— I had known for a week—but because the persistent hopefulness of the human heart refuses to allow intuitive certainty to per-suade the reason of that which it knows, I opened and read it in a tearing anguish of suspense.

"Regret to inform you Captain E.H. Brittain M.C. killed in action Italy June 15th."

"No answer," I told the boy mechani-cally, and handed the telegram to my father, who had followed me into the hall. As we went back into the dining-room I saw, as though I had never seen them before, the bowl of blue delphiniums on the table; their intense color, vivid, ethereal, seemed too radiant for earthly flowers.

Then I remembered that we should have to go down to Purley and tell the news to my mother. . . .

Long after [father] had gone to bed and the world had grown silent, I crept into the dining-room to be alone with Edward's portrait. Carefully closing the door, I turned on the light and looked at the pale, pictured face, so dignified, so steadfast, so tragically mature. He had been through so much—far, far more than those beloved friends who had died at an earlier stage of the interminable War, leaving him alone to mourn their loss. Fate might have allowed him the little, sorry compensation of survival, the chance to make his lovely music in honor of their memory. It seemed indeed the last irony that he should have been killed by the countrymen of Fritz Kreisler[15] the violinist whom of all others he had most greatly admired.

And suddenly, as I remembered all the dear afternoons and evenings when I had followed him on the piano as he played his violin, the sad, searching eyes of the portrait were more than I could bear, and falling on my knees before it I began to cry "Edward! Oh, Edward!" in dazed repetition, as though my persistent crying and calling would somehow bring him back. . . .

Vera signed on for nursing duty in London, where she sorrowfully observed Armistice Day celebrations.

When the sound of victorious guns burst over London at 11 A.M. on November 11th, 1918, the men and women who

---

[15] Fritz Kreisler—Austrian violinist (1875–1962).

looked incredulously into each other's faces did not cry jubilantly: "We've won the War!" They only said: "The War is over."

From Millbank I heard the maroons[16] crash with terrifying clearness, and, like a sleeper who is determined to go on dreaming after being told to wake up, I went on automatically washing the dressing bowls in the annex outside my hut. Deeply buried beneath my consciousness there stirred the vague memory of a letter that I had written to Roland in those legendary days when I was still at Oxford, and could spend my Sundays in thinking of him while the organ echoed grandly through New College Chapel. It had been a warm May evening, when all the city was sweet with the scent of wallflowers and lilac, and I had walked back to Micklem Hall after hearing an Occasional Oratorio by Handel, which described the mustering of troops for battle, the lament for the fallen and the triumphant return of the victors.

"As I listened," I told him, "to the organ swelling forth into a final triumphant burst in the song of victory, after the solemn and mournful dirge over the dead, I thought with what mockery and irony the jubilant celebrations which will hail the coming of peace will fall upon the ears of those to whom their best will never return, upon whose sorrow victory is built, who have paid with their mourning for the others' joy. I wonder if I shall be one of those who take a happy part in the triumph—or if I shall listen to the merriment with a heart that breaks and ears that try to keep out the mirthful sounds."

And as I dried the bowls I thought: "It's come too late for me. Somehow I knew, even at Oxford, that it would. Why couldn't it have ended rationally, as it might have ended, in 1916, instead of all that trumpet-blowing against a negotiated peace, and the ferocious talk of secure civilians about marching to Berlin? It's come five months too late—or is it three years? It might have ended last June, and let Edward, at least, be saved! Only five months—it's such a little time, when Roland died nearly three years ago." . . .

Late that evening, when supper was over, a group of elated V.A.D.s who were anxious to walk through Westminster and Whitehall to Buckingham Palace prevailed upon me to join them. Outside the Admiralty a crazy group of convalescent Tommies[17] were collecting specimens of different uniforms and bundling their wearers into flagstrewn taxis; with a shout they seized two of my companions and disappeared into the clamorous crowd, waving flags and shaking rattles. Wherever we went a burst of enthusiastic cheering greeted our Red Cross uniform, and complete strangers adorned with wound stripes rushed up and shook me warmly by the hand. After the long, long blackness, it seemed like a fairy-tale to see the street lamps shining[18] through the chill November gloom.

---

[16] maroons—fireworks that sound like cannon.

[17] Tommies—British soldiers.

[18] long blackness . . . street lamps shining—There had been a wartime blackout in England.

I detached myself from the others and walked slowly up Whitehall, with my heart sinking in a sudden cold dismay. Already this was a different world from the one that I had known during four life-long years, a world in which people would be light-hearted and forgetful, in which themselves and their careers and their amusements would blot out political ideals and great national issues. And in that brightly lit, alien world I should have no part. All those with whom I had really been intimate were gone; not one remained to share with me the heights and the depths of my memories. As the years went by and youth departed and remembrance grew dim, a deeper and ever deeper darkness would cover the young men who were once my contemporaries.

For the time I realized, with all that full realization meant, how completely everything that had hitherto made up my life had vanished with Edward and Roland, with Victor and Geoffrey. The War was over; a new age was beginning; but the dead were dead and would never return.

QUESTIONS TO CONSIDER

1. Vera Brittain says that her diary was at first naive. What does she mean?

2. Brittain wishes that enthusiastic supporters of the war could see its hideous impact on soldiers who had been gassed. Do you think this would have changed their views? Why or why not?

3. Which do you think was harder on Brittain, her nursing work or anxiety and grief over her fiancé, brother, and friends?

4. If Brittain had been a member of a committee to create a proposal for a memorial for those who had served in World War I, what kind of memorial might she have proposed?

No Man's Land

HENRI BARBUSSE

Much of the fighting in World War I took place in Belgium and northeastern France, "the Western Front." Here both sides had constructed vast systems of fortified trenches flanking a devastated strip of terrain known as "No Man's Land." Attacking soldiers had to cross this wilderness of shell craters and barbed wire raked by deadly machine-gun fire. French writer Henri Barbusse (1873–1935), who was an infantryman and stretcher-bearer, based his novel Under Fire *on a diary he kept during the war. Here the soldiers are preparing to advance across No Man's Land. Bertrand is the corporal in charge.*

We are ready. The men marshal themselves, still silently, their blankets crosswise, the helmet-strap on the chin, leaning on their rifles. I look at their pale, contracted, and reflective faces. They are not soldiers, they are men. They are not adventurers, or warriors, or made for human slaughter, neither butchers nor cattle. They are laborers and artisans whom one recognizes in their uniforms. They are civilians uprooted, and they are ready. They await the signal for death or murder; but you may see, looking at their faces between the vertical gleams of their bayonets, that they are simply men.

Each one knows that he is going to take his head, his chest, his belly, his whole body, and all naked, up to the rifles pointed forward, to the shells, to the bombs piled and ready, and above all to the methodical and almost infallible machine-guns—to all that is waiting for him yonder and is now so frightfully silent—before he reaches the other soldiers that he must kill. They are not careless of their lives, like brigands,[1] nor blinded by passion like savages. In spite of the doctrines with which they have been cultivated they are not inflamed. They are above instinctive excesses. They are not drunk, either physically or morally. It is in full consciousness, as in full health and full strength, that they are massed there to hurl themselves once more into that sort of madman's part imposed on all men by the madness of the human race.

[1] brigands—bandits.

One sees the thought and the fear and the farewell that there is in their silence, their stillness, in the mask of tranquillity which unnaturally grips their faces. They are not the kind of hero one thinks of, but their sacrifice has greater worth than they who have not seen them will ever be able to understand.

They are waiting; a waiting that extends and seems eternal. Now and then one or another starts a little when a bullet, fired from the other side, skims the forward embankment that shields us and plunges into the flabby flesh of the rear wall. . . .

A man arrives running, and speaks to Bertrand, and then Bertrand turns to us—

"Up you go," he says, "it's our turn."

All move at once. We put our feet on the steps made by the sappers,[2] raise ourselves, elbow to elbow, beyond the shelter of the trench, and climb on to the **parapet**.[3]

Bertrand is out on the sloping ground. He covers us with a quick glance, and when we are all there he says, *"Allons,[4] forward!"*

Our voices have a curious resonance. The start has been made very quickly, unexpectedly almost, as in a dream. There is no whistling sound in the air. Among the vast uproar of the guns we discern very clearly this surprising silence of bullets around us—

We descend over the rough and slippery ground with **involuntary**[5] gestures, helping ourselves sometimes with the rifle. . . . On all sides the slope is covered by men who, like us, are bent on the descent. On the right the outline is defined of a company

that is reaching the ravine by Trench 97— an old German work in ruins. We cross our wire by openings. Still no one fires on us. Some awkward ones who have made false steps are getting up again. We form up on the farther side of the entanglements and then set ourselves to topple down the slope rather faster—there is an instinctive acceleration in the movement. Several bullets arrive at last among us. Bertrand shouts to us to reserve our bombs and wait till the last moment.

But the sound of his voice is carried away. Abruptly, across all the width of the opposite slope, lurid flames burst forth that strike the air with terrible detonations. In line from left to right fires emerge from the sky and explosions from the ground. It is a frightful curtain which divides us from the world, which divides us from the past and from the future. We stop, fixed to the ground, **stupefied**[6] by the sudden host that thunders from every side; then a simultaneous effort uplifts our mass again and throws it swiftly forward. We stumble and impede each other in the great waves of smoke. With harsh crashes and whirlwinds of pulverized earth, towards the profundity[7] into which we hurl ourselves pell-mell, we see craters opened here and there, side by side, and merging in each other. Then one knows no longer where the discharges

---

[2] sappers—military engineers who construct trenches and fortifications.

[3] **parapet**—the earthen embankment built above the trenches to protect the men from attack.

[4] *Allons*—Let's go!

[5] **involuntary**—unconscious.

[6] **stupefied**—amazed or stunned.

[7] profundity—depth.

fall. Volleys are let loose so monstrously resounding that one feels himself annihilated by the mere sound of the downpoured thunder of these great constellations of destruction that form in the sky. One sees and one feels the fragments passing close to one's head with their hiss of red-hot iron plunged in water. The blast of one explosion so burns my hands, that I let my rifle fall. I pick it up again, reeling, and set off in the tawny-gleaming tempest with lowered head, lashed by spirits of dust and soot in a crushing downpour like volcanic lava. The stridor[8] of the bursting shells hurts your ears, beats you on the neck, goes through your temples, and you cannot endure it without a cry. The gusts of death drive us on, lift us up, rock us to and fro. We leap, and do not know whither we go. Our eyes are blinking and weeping and obscured. The view before us is blocked by a flashing avalanche that fills space.

It is the barrage fire. We have to go through that whirlwind of fire and those fearful showers that vertically fall. We are passing through. We are through it, by chance. Here and there I have seen forms that spun round and were lifted up and laid down, illumined by a brief reflection from over yonder. I have glimpsed strange faces that uttered some sort of cry—you could see them without hearing them in the roar of annihilation. A brasier[9] full of red and black masses huge and furious fell about me, excavating the ground, tearing it from under my feet, throwing me aside like a bouncing toy. I remember that I strode over a smoldering corpse, quite black, with a tissue of rosy blood shriveling on him; and I remember, too, that the skirts of the great-coat flying next to me had caught fire, and left a trail of smoke behind. On our right, all along Trench 97, our glances were drawn and dazzled by a rank of frightful flames, closely crowded against each other like men.

Forward!

Now, we are nearly running. I see some who fall solidly flat, face forward, and others who founder meekly, as though they would sit down on the ground. We step aside abruptly to avoid the prostrate dead, quiet and rigid, or else offensive, and also— more perilous snares!—the wounded that hook on to you, struggling.

The International Trench! We are there. The wire entanglements have been torn up into long roots and creepers, thrown afar and coiled up swept away and piled in great drifts by the guns. Between these big bushes of rain-damped steel the ground is open and free.

The trench is not defended. The Germans have abandoned it, or else a first wave has already passed over it. Its interior bristles with rifles placed against the bank. In the bottom are scattered corpses. From the jumbled litter of the long trench, hands emerge that protrude from gray sleeves with red facings, and booted legs. In places the embankment is destroyed and its

---

[8] stridor—harsh sound.

[9] brasier—container for holding burning coals. Barbusse is referring to an exploding shell.

woodwork splintered—all the flank of the trench collapsed and fallen into an indescribable mixture. In other places, round pits are yawning. . . .

We have spread out in the trench. The lieutenant, who has jumped to the other side, is stooping and summoning us with signs and shouts—"Don't stay there; forward, forward!"

We climb the wall of the trench with the help of the sacks, of weapons, and of the backs that are piled up there. In the bottom of the ravine the soil is shot-churned, crowded with **jetsam**,[10] swarming with prostrate bodies. Some are motionless as blocks of wood; others move slowly or convulsively. The barrage fire continues to increase its infernal discharge behind us on the ground that we have crossed. But where we are at the foot of the rise it is a dead point for the artillery.

A short and uncertain calm follows. We are less deafened and look at each other. There is fever in the eyes, and the cheek-bones are blood-red. Our breathing snores and our hearts drum in our bodies.

In haste and confusion we recognize each other, as if we had met again face to face in a nightmare on the uttermost shores of death. Some hurried words are cast upon this glade in hell—"It's you!"—"Where's Cocon?"—"Don't know."—"Have you seen the captain?"—"No. "—"Going strong? "—"Yes."

The bottom of the ravine is crossed and the other slope rises opposite. We climb in Indian file by a stairway rough-hewn in the ground: "Look out!" The shout means that a soldier half-way up the steps has been struck in the loins by a shell-fragment; he falls with his arms forward, bareheaded, like the diving swimmer. We can see the shapeless silhouette of the mass as it plunges into the gulf. I can almost see the detail of his blown hair over the black profile of his face.

We debouch[11] upon the height. A great colorless emptiness is outspread before us. At first one can see nothing but a chalky and stony plain, yellow and gray to the limit of sight. No human wave is preceding ours; in front of us there is no living soul, but the ground is peopled with dead—recent corpses that still mimic agony or sleep, and old remains already bleached and scattered to the wind, half assimilated by the earth.

As soon as our pushing and jolted file emerges, two men close to me are hit, two shadows are hurled to the ground and roll under our feet, one with a sharp cry, and the other silently, as a felled ox. Another disappears with the caper of a lunatic, as if he had been snatched away. Instinctively we close up as we hustle forward—always forward—and the wound in our line closes of its own accord. The adjutant stops, raises his sword, lets it fall, and drops to his knees. His kneeling body slopes backward in jerks, his helmet drops on his heels, and he remains there, bareheaded, face to the sky. Hurriedly the rush of the rank has split open to respect his immobility.

---

[10] **jetsam**—discarded odds and ends.

[11] debouch—emerge.

But we cannot see the lieutenant. No more leaders, then—Hesitation checks the wave of humanity that begins to beat on the plateau. Above the trampling one hears the hoarse effort of our lungs. "Forward!" cries some soldier, and then all resume the onward race to perdition[12] with increasing speed.

"Where's Bertrand?" comes the laborious complaint of one of the foremost runners. "There! Here!" He had stooped in passing over a wounded man, but he leaves him quickly, and the man extends his arms toward him and seems to sob.

It is just at the moment when he rejoins us that we hear in front of us, coming from a sort of ground swelling, the crackle of a machine-gun. It is a moment of agony—more serious even than when we were passing through the flaming earthquake of the barrage. That familiar voice speaks to us across the plain, sharp and horrible. But we no longer stop. "Go on, go on!"

Our panting becomes hoarse groaning, yet still we hurl ourselves toward the horizon.

"The Boches![13] I see them!" a man says suddenly.

"Yes—their heads, there—above the trench—it's there, the trench that line. It's close. Ah, the hogs!"

We can indeed make out little round gray caps which rise and then drop on the ground level, fifty yards away, beyond a belt of dark earth, furrowed and humped. Encouraged they spring forward, they who now form the group where I am. So near the goal, so far unscathed, shall we not reach it? Yes, we will reach it! We make great strides and no longer hear anything. Each man plunges straight ahead, fascinated by the terrible trench, bent rigidly forward, almost incapable of turning his head to right or to left. I have a notion that many of us missed their footing and fell to the ground. I jump sideways to miss the suddenly erect bayonet of a toppling rifle. Quite close to me, Farfadet jostles me with his face bleeding, throws himself on Volpatte who is beside me and clings to him. Volpatte doubles up without slackening his rush and drags him along some paces, then shakes him off without looking at him and without knowing who he is, and shouts at him in a breaking voice almost choked with exertion: "Let me go, let me go, *nom de Dieu!*[14] They'll pick you up directly—don't worry."

The other man sinks to the ground, and his face, plastered with a scarlet mask and void of all expression, turns in every direction; while Volpatte, already in the distance, automatically repeats between his teeth, "Don't worry," with a steady forward gaze on the line.

A shower of bullets spurts around me, increasing the number of those who suddenly halt, who collapse slowly, defiant and gesticulating, of those who dive forward solidly with all the body's burden, of the shouts, deep, furious, and desperate, and even of that hollow and terrible gasp when a man's life goes bodily forth in a

---

[12] perdition—hell.

[13] Boches—offensive term for Germans; the word originated from the French *caboche*, "cabbage," "blockhead."

[14] *nom de Dieu!*—God's name!

breath. And we who are not yet stricken, we look ahead, we walk and we run, among the frolics of the death that strikes at random into our flesh.

The wire entanglements—and there is one stretch of them intact. We go along to where it has been gutted into a wide and deep opening. This is a colossal funnel-hole, formed of smaller funnels placed together, a fantastic volcanic crater, scooped there by the guns.

The sight of this convulsion is stupefying; truly it seems that it must have come from the center of the earth. Such a rending of virgin strata[15] puts new edge on our attacking fury, and none of us can keep from shouting with a solemn shake of the head even just now when words are but painfully torn from our throats—"Ah, Christ! Look what hell we've given 'em there! Ah, look!"

Driven as if by the wind, we mount or descend at the will of the hollows and the earthy mounds in the gigantic fissure dug and blackened and burned by furious flames. The soil clings to the feet and we tear them out angrily. The accouterments [16] and stuffs that cover the soft soil, the linen that is scattered about from sundered knapsacks, prevent us from sticking fast in it, and we are careful to plant our feet in this débris when we jump into the holes or climb the hillocks.

Behind us voices urge us—"Forward, boys, forward, *nom de Dieu!*"

"All the regiment is behind us!" they cry. We do not turn round to see, but the assurance electrifies our rush once more.

No more caps are visible behind the embankment of the trench we are nearing. Some German dead are crumbling in front of it, in pinnacled heaps or extended lines. We are there. The parapet takes definite and sinister shape and detail; the loopholes—we are **prodigiously**,[17] incredibly close!

Something falls in front of us. It is a bomb. With a kick Corporal Bertrand returns it so well that it rises and bursts just over the trench.

With that fortunate deed the squad reaches the trench.

Pépin has hurled himself flat on the ground and is involved with a corpse. He reaches the edge and plunges in—the first to enter. Fouillade, with great gestures and shouts, jumps into the pit almost at the same moment that Pépin rolls down it. Indistinctly I see—in the time of the lightning's flash—a whole row of black demons stooping and squatting for the descent, on the ridge of the embankment, on the edge of the dark ambush.

A terrible volley bursts point-blank in our faces, flinging in front of us a sudden row of flames the whole length of the earthen verge.[18] After the stunning shock we shake ourselves and burst into devilish laughter—the discharge has passed too high. And at once, with shouts and roars of salvation, we slide and roll and fall alive into the belly of the trench!

---

[15] virgin strata—undisturbed layers of earth.

[16] accouterments—equipment.

[17] **prodigiously**—extraordinarily.

[18] verge—edge.

QUESTIONS TO CONSIDER

1. What does the narrator mean when he observes that the French troops "are not soldiers, they are men"?

2. During the attack, what emotional reaction do the narrator and his fellow soldiers display toward wounded and dead comrades?

3. Do the narrator and his French comrades seem motivated by hatred for their German enemies? Why or why not?

Reflections on the Movies

In 1889, American inventor Thomas Edison (1847–1931) created the kinetescope, a kind of motion picture device that could be seen by one viewer only. In 1895, two French brothers, Louis Jean (1864–1948) and Auguste Marie Lumière (1862–1954), invented the cinematograph, which functioned as both camera and projector. At Aumont's, a Paris cafe, they showed ten short films, including Workers Leaving a Factory *and* The Sprinkler Sprinkled, *which were seen by Russian writer Maxim Gorky (1868–1936). In an article published in 1937, British-born director Alfred Hitchcock (1889–1980), one of the most famous filmmakers of the 20th century, discusses his methods.*

Lumière

Maxim Gorky

Last night I was in the Kingdom of Shadows.

If you only knew how strange it is to be there. It is a world without sound, without color. Everything there—the earth, the trees, the people, the water, and the air—is dipped in monotonous gray. Gray rays of the sun across the gray sky, gray eyes in gray faces, and the leaves of the trees are ashen gray. It is not life but its shadow, it is not motion but its soundless **specter**.[1]

Here I shall try to explain myself, lest I be suspected of madness or indulgence in symbolism. I was at Aumont's and saw Lumière's cinematograph—moving photography. The extraordinary impression it creates is so unique and complex that I

doubt my ability to describe it with all its **nuances**.[2] However, I shall try to convey its fundamentals.

When the lights go out in the room in which Lumière's invention is shown, there suddenly appears on the screen a large gray picture, "A Street in Paris"—shadows of a bad engraving. As you gaze at it, you see carriages, buildings and people in various poses, all frozen into immobility. All this is in gray, and the sky above is also gray— you anticipate nothing new in this all too familiar scene, for you have seen pictures of Paris streets more than once. But suddenly a strange flicker passes through the screen and the picture stirs to life.

---

[1] **specter**—ghost.
[2] **nuances**—fine shades of meaning.

Carriages coming from somewhere in the perspective of the picture are moving straight at you, into the darkness in which you sit; somewhere from afar people appear and loom larger as they come closer to you; in the foreground children are playing with a dog, bicyclists tear along, and pedestrians cross the street picking their way among the carriages. All this moves, teems with life and, upon approaching the edge of the screen, vanishes somewhere beyond it.

And all this in strange silence where no rumble of the wheels is heard, no sound of footsteps or of speech. Nothing. Not a single note of the intricate symphony that always accompanies the movements of people. Noiselessly, the ashen-gray foliage of the trees sways in the wind, and the gray silhouettes of the people, as though condemned to eternal silence and cruelly punished by being deprived of all the colors of life, glide noiselessly along the gray ground.

Their smiles are lifeless, even though their movements are full of living energy and are so swift as to be almost imperceptible. Their laughter is soundless, although you see the muscles contracting in their gray faces. Before you a life is surging, a life deprived of words and shorn of the living spectrum of colors—gray, the soundless, the bleak and dismal life.

It is terrifying to see, but it is the movement of shadows, only of shadows. Curses and ghosts, the evil spirits that have cast entire cities into eternal sleep, come to mind and you feel as though

Merlin's vicious trick[3] is being enacted before you. As though he had bewitched the entire street, he compressed its many-storied buildings from roof-tops to foundations to yard-like size. He dwarfed the people in corresponding proportion, robbing them of the power of speech and scraping together all the pigment of earth and sky into a monotonous gray color.

Under this guise he shoved his grotesque creation into a niche in the dark room of a restaurant. Suddenly something clicks, everything vanishes and a train appears on the screen. It speeds straight at you—watch out! It seems as though it will plunge into the darkness in which you sit, turning you into a ripped sack full of lacerated flesh and splintered bones, and crushing into dust and into broken fragments this hall and this building, so full of women, wine, music and vice.

But this, too, is but a train of shadows.

Noiselessly, the locomotive disappears beyond the edge of the screen. The train comes to a stop, and gray figures silently emerge from the cars, soundlessly greet their friends, laugh, walk, run, bustle, and . . . are gone. And here is another picture. Three men seated at the table, playing cards. Their faces are tense, their hands move swiftly. The cupidity[4] of the players is betrayed by the trembling fingers and by the twitching of their facial muscles. They play. . . . Suddenly, they break into laughter, and the waiter who has stopped at their table with beer, laughs too. They laugh

---

[3] Merlin's vicious trick—Merlin is a magician in the legends of King Arthur.

[4] cupidity—greed.

until their sides split but not a sound is heard. It seems as if these people have died and their shadows have been condemned to play cards in silence unto eternity. Another picture. A gardener watering flowers. The light gray stream of water, issuing from a hose, breaks into a fine spray. It falls upon the flowerbeds and upon the grass blades weighted down by the water. A boy enters, steps on the hose, and stops the stream. The gardener stares into the nozzle of the hose, whereupon the boy steps back and a stream of water hits the gardener in the face. You imagine the spray will reach you, and you want to shield yourself. But on the screen the gardener has already begun to chase the rascal all over the garden and having caught him, gives him a beating. But the beating is soundless, nor can you hear the gurgle of the water as it gushes from the hose left lying on the ground.

This mute, gray life finally begins to disturb and depress you. It seems as though it carries a warning, fraught with a vague but sinister meaning that makes your heart grow faint. You are forgetting where you are. Strange imaginings invade your mind and your consciousness begins to wane and grow dim. . . .

But suddenly, alongside of you, a gay chatter and a provoking laughter of a woman is heard . . . and you remember that you are at Aumont's, Charles Aumont's. . . . But why of all places should this remarkable invention of Lumière find its way and be demonstrated here, this invention which affirms once again the energy and the curiosity of the human mind, forever striving to solve and grasp all, and . . . while on the way to the solution of the mystery of life, incidentally builds Aumont's fortune? I do not yet see the scientific importance of Lumière's invention but, no doubt, it is there, and it could probably be applied to the general ends of science, that is, of bettering man's life and the developing of his mind. This is not to be found at Aumont's where vice alone is being encouraged and popularized. Why then at Aumont's, among the "victims of social needs" and among the loafers who here buy their kisses? Why here, of all places, are they showing this latest achievement of science? And soon probably Lumière's invention will be perfected, but in the spirit of Aumont-Toulon and Company.

Besides those pictures I have already mentioned, is featured "The Family Breakfast," an idyll[5] of three. A young couple with its chubby first-born is seated at the breakfast table. The two are so much in love, and are so charming, gay and happy, and the baby is so amusing. The picture creates a fine, felicitous impression. Has this family scene a place at Aumont's?

And here is still another. Women workers, in a thick, gay and laughing crowd, rush out of the factory gates into the street. This too is out of place at Aumont's. Why remind here of the possibility of a clean,

---

[5] idyll—simple and tranquil scene or event.

toiling life? This reminder is useless. Under the best of circumstances this picture will only painfully sting the woman who sells her kisses.

I am convinced that these pictures will soon be replaced by others of a genre more suited to the general tone of the "Concert Parisien." For example, they will show a picture titled: "As She Undresses," or "Madam at Her Bath," or "A Woman in Stockings." They could also depict a sordid squabble between a husband and wife and serve it to the public under the heading of "The Blessings of Family Life."

Yes, no doubt, this is how it will be done. The bucolic[6] and the idyll could not possibly find their place in Russia's markets thirsting for the **piquant**[7] and the extravagant. I also could suggest a few themes for development by means of a cinematograph and for the amusement of the market place. For instance: to impale a fashionable parasite upon a picket fence, as is the way of the Turks, photograph him, then show it.

It is not exactly piquant but quite edifying.

My Own Methods
Alfred Hitchcock

Many people think a film director does all his work in the studio, drilling the actors, making them do what he wants. That is not at all true of my own methods, and I can write only of my own methods. I like to have a film complete in my mind before I go on the floor. Sometimes the first idea one has of a film is of a vague pattern, a sort of haze with a certain shape. There is possibly a colorful opening developing into something more intimate; then, perhaps in the middle, a progression to a chase or some other adventure; and sometimes at the end the big shape of a climax, or maybe some twist or surprise. You see this hazy pattern, and then you have to find a narrative idea to suit it. Or a story may give you an idea first and you have to develop it into a pattern.

Imagine an example of a standard plot—let us say a conflict between love and duty. This idea was the origin of my first talkie, *Blackmail*. The hazy pattern one saw beforehand was duty—love—love versus duty—and finally either duty or love, one or the other. The whole middle section was built up on the theme of love versus duty, after duty and love had been introduced separately in turn. So I had first to put on the screen an episode expressing duty.

I showed the arrest of a criminal by Scotland Yard detectives,[8] and tried to make it as concrete and detailed as I could. You even saw the detectives take the man to the lavatory to wash his hands—nothing exciting, just the routine of duty. Then the young detective says he's going out that evening with his girl, and the sequence ends, pointing on from duty to love. Then you start

---

[6] bucolic—rustic.

[7] **piquant**—provocative.

[8] Scotland Yard detectives—members of the Criminal Investigation Department (CID) of the London police force.

showing the relationship between the detective and his girl: they are middle-class people. The love theme doesn't run smoothly; there is a quarrel and the girl goes off by herself, just because the young man has kept her waiting a few minutes. So your story starts; the girl falls in with the villain—he tries to seduce her and she kills him. Now you've got your problem prepared. Next morning, as soon as the detective is put on to the murder case, you have your conflict—love versus duty. The audience know that he will be trying to track down his own girl, who has done the murder, so you sustain their interest: they wonder what will happen next.

The blackmailer was really a subsidiary[9] theme. I wanted him to go through and expose the girl. That was my idea of how the story ought to end. I wanted the pursuit to be after the girl, not after the blackmailer. That would have brought the conflict on to a climax, with the young detective, ahead of the others, trying to push the girl out through a window to get her away, and the girl turning round and saying: "You can't do that—I must give myself up." Then the rest of the police arrive, misinterpret what he is doing, and say "Good man, you've got her," not knowing the relationship between them. Now the reason for the opening comes to light. You repeat every shot used first to illustrate the duty theme, only now it is the girl who is the criminal. The young man is there ostensibly[10] as a detective, but of course the audience know he is in love with the girl. The girl is locked up in her cell and the two detectives walk away, and the older one says, "Going out with your girl tonight?" The younger one shakes his head. "No. Not tonight."

That was the ending I wanted for *Blackmail*, but I had to change it for commercial reasons. The girl couldn't be left to face her fate. And that shows you how the films suffer from their own power of appealing to millions. They could often be subtler than they are, but their own popularity won't let them.

But to get back to the early work on a film. With the help of my wife, who does the technical continuity,[11] I plan out a script very carefully, hoping to follow it exactly, all the way through, when shooting starts. In fact, this working on the script is the real making of the film, for me. When I've done it, the film is finished already in my mind. Usually, too, I don't find it necessary to do more than supervise the editing myself.

Settings, of course, come into the preliminary plan, and usually I have fairly clear ideas about them; I was an art student before I took up with films. Sometimes I even think of backgrounds first. *The Man Who Knew Too Much* started like that; I looked in my mind's eye at snowy Alps and dingy London alleys, and threw characters into the middle of the contrast. Studio settings, however, are often a problem; one difficulty is that extreme effects—extremes of luxury or extremes of squalor—are much the easiest to register on the screen. If you

---

9 subsidiary—secondary.

10 **ostensibly**—apparently.

11 technical continuity—shooting script of a movie.

try to reproduce the average sitting-room in Golders Green or Streatham[12] it is apt to come out looking like nothing in particular, just nondescript. It is true that I have tried lately to get interiors giving a real lower-middle-class atmosphere—for instance, the Verlocs' living room in *Sabotage*[13]—but there's always a certain risk in giving your audience humdrum truth.

However, in time the script and the sets are finished somehow and we are ready to start shooting. One great problem that occurs at once, and keeps on occurring, is to get the players to adapt themselves to film technique. Many of them, of course, come from the stage; they are not cinema-minded at all. So, quite naturally, they like to play long scenes straight ahead. But if I have to shoot a long scene continuously I always feel I am losing grip on it, from a cinematic point of view. The camera, I feel, is simply standing there, *hoping* to catch something with a visual point to it. I want to put my film together on the screen, not simply to photograph something that has been put together already in the form of a long piece of stage acting. This is what gives an effect of life to a picture—the feeling that when you see it on the screen you are watching something that has been conceived and brought to birth directly in visual terms.

You can see an example of what I mean in *Sabotage*. Just before Verloc is killed there is a scene made up entirely of short pieces of film, separately photographed. This scene has to show how Verloc comes to be killed—how the thought of killing him

arises in Sylvia Sidney's[14] mind and connects itself with the carving knife she uses when they sit down to dinner. But the sympathy of the audience has to be kept with Sylvia Sidney; it must be clear that Verloc's death, finally, is an accident. So, as she serves at the table, you see her unconsciously serving vegetables with the carving knife, as though her hand were keeping hold of the knife of its own accord. The camera cuts from her hand to her eyes and back to her hand; then back to her eyes as she suddenly becomes aware of the knife, making its error. Then to a normal shot—the man unconcernedly eating; then back to the hand holding the knife. In an older style of acting Sylvia would have had to show the audience what was passing in her mind by exaggerated facial expression. But people today in real life often don't show their feelings in their faces: so the film treatment showed the audience her mind through her hand, through its unconscious grasp on the knife. Now the camera moves again to Verloc—back to the knife—back again to his face. You see him seeing the knife, realizing its implication. The tension between the two is built up with the knife as its focus.

Now when the camera has immersed the audience so closely in a scene such as this, it can't instantly become objective again. It must broaden the movement of

---

[12] Golders Green or Streatham—areas in greater London that were middle class at the time Hitchcock wrote.

[13] *Sabotage*—a 1936 film (based on Joseph Conrad's novel *The Secret Agent*) about a spy named Verloc.

[14] Sylvia Sidney—American actress (1910–1999) in *Sabotage*.

the scene without loosening the tension. Verloc gets up and walks round the table, coming so close to the camera that you feel, if you are sitting in the audience, almost as though you must move back to make room for him. Then the camera moves to Sylvia Sidney again, then returns to the subject—the knife.

So you gradually build up the psychological situation, piece by piece, using the camera to emphasize first one detail, then another. The point is to draw the audience right inside the situation instead of leaving them to watch it from outside, from a distance. And you can do this only by breaking the action up into details and cutting from one to the other, so that each detail is forced in turn on the attention of the audience and reveals its psychological meaning. If you played the whole scene straight through, and simply made a photographic record of it with the camera always in one position, you would lose your power over the audience. They would watch the scene without becoming really involved in it, and you would have no means of concentrating their attention on those particular visual details which make them feel what the characters are feeling.

One way of using the camera to give emphasis is the reaction shot. By the reaction shot I mean any close-up which illustrates an event by showing instantly the reaction to it of a person or a group. The door opens for someone to come in, and before showing who it is you cut to the expressions of the persons already in the room. Or, while one person is talking, you keep your camera on someone else who is listening. This over-running of one person's image with another person's voice is a method peculiar to the talkies; it is one of the devices which help the talkies to tell a story faster than a silent film could tell it, and faster than it could be told on the stage.

Or, again, you can use the camera to give emphasis whenever the attention of the audience has to be focused for a moment on a certain player. There is no need for him to raise his voice or move to the center of the stage or do anything dramatic. A close-up will do it all for him—will give him, so to speak, the stage all to himself.

I must say that in recent years I have come to make much less use of obvious camera devices. I have become more commercially-minded; afraid that anything at all subtle may be missed. I have learnt from experience how easily small touches are overlooked.

The film always has to deal in exaggerations. Its methods reflect the simple contrasts of black and white photography. One advantage of color is that it would give you more intermediate shades. I should never want to fill the screen with color: it ought to be used economically—to put new words into the screen's visual language when there's a need for them. You could start a color film with a boardroom scene: sombre paneling and furniture, the directors all in dark clothes and white collars. Then the chairman's wife comes in, wearing a red hat. She takes the attention of the audience at once, just because of that one note of color.

A journalist once asked me about distorted sound—a device I tried in *Blackmail* when the word "knife" hammers on the consciousness of the girl at breakfast on the morning after the murder. Again, I think this kind of effect may be justified. There have always been occasions when we have needed to show a phantasmagoria[15] of the mind in terms of visual imagery. So we may want to show someone's mental state by letting him listen to some sound—let us say church bells—and making them clang with distorted insistence in his head. But on the whole nowadays I try to tell a story in the simplest possible way, so that I can feel sure it will hold the attention of any audience and won't puzzle them.

I know there are critics who ask why lately I have made only thrillers. Am I satisfied, they say, with putting on the screen the equivalent merely of popular novelettes? Part of the answer is that I am out to get the best stories I can which will suit the film medium, and I have usually found it necessary to take a hand in writing them myself. There is a shortage of good writing for the screen. In this country[16] we can't usually afford to employ large writing staffs, so I have had to join in and become a writer myself. I choose crime stories because that is the kind of story I can write, or help to write, myself—the kind of story I can turn most easily into a successful film. It is the same with Charles Bennett, who has so often worked with me; he is essentially a writer of melodrama. I am ready to use other stories, but I can't find writers who will give them to me in a suitable form.

Sometimes I have been asked what films I should make if I were free to do exactly as I liked without having to think about the box-office. There are several examples I can give very easily. For one thing, I should like to make travel films with a personal element in them. Or I should like to do a verbatim of a celebrated trial. The Thompson-Bywaters case,[17] for instance. The cinema could reconstruct the whole story. Or there is the fire at sea possibility—that has never been tackled seriously on the screen. It might be too terrifying for some audiences, but it would make a great subject worthwhile.

British producers are often urged to make more films about characteristic phases of English life.

Why, they are asked, do we see so little of the English farmer or the English seaman? Or is there not plenty of good material in the great British industries—in mining or shipbuilding or steel? One difficulty here is that English audiences seem to take more interest in American life—I suppose because it has a novelty value. They are rather easily bored by everyday scenes in their own country. But I certainly should like to make a film of the Derby,[18] only it might not be quite in the popular class. It would be hard to invent a Derby story that

---

[15] phantasmagoria—disordered sequence of images as in a dream.

[16] this country—England.

[17] Thompson-Bywaters case—famous British murder case from the early 1920s.

[18] the Derby—England's most famous horse race.

play music

wasn't hackneyed, conventional. I would rather do it more as a documentary—a sort of pageant, an animated modern version of Frith's *Derby Day*.[19] I would show everything that goes on all round the course, but without a story.

Perhaps the average audience isn't ready for that, yet. Popular taste, all the same, does move; today you can put over scenes that would have been ruled out a few years ago. Particularly towards comedy, nowadays, there is a different attitude. You can get comedy out of your stars, and you used not to be allowed to do anything which might knock the glamor off them.

In 1926 I made a film called *Downhill*, from a play by Ivor Novello, who acted in the film himself, with Ian Hunter and Isabel Jeans. There was a sequence showing a quarrel between Hunter and Novello. It started as an ordinary fight; then they began throwing things at one another. They tried to pick up heavy pedestals to throw, and the pedestals bowled them over. In other words I made it comic. I even put Hunter into a morning coat and striped trousers because I felt that a man never looks so ridiculous as when he is well dressed and fighting. This whole scene was cut out; they said I was guying[20] Ivor Novello. It was ten years before its time.

I think public taste is turning to like comedy and drama more mixed up; and this is another move away from the conventions of the stage. In a play your divisions are much more rigid; you have a scene in one key—then curtain, and after an interval another scene starts. In a film

you keep your whole action flowing; you can have comedy and drama running together and weave them in and out. Audiences are much readier now than they used to be for sudden changes of mood; and this means more freedom for a director. The art of directing for the commercial market is to know just how far you can go. In many ways I am freer now to do what I want to do than I was a few years ago. I hope in time to have more freedom still— if audiences will give it to me.

---

[19] Frith's *Derby Day*—famous 19th-century painting by William Powell Frith (1819–1909) depicting the crowd attending the Derby.

[20] guying—making fun of.

QUESTIONS TO CONSIDER

1. Maxim Gorky says he will explain his experience lest he be "suspected of madness." Why might people think he was crazy?

2. Gorky's metaphor for films is "the Kingdom of Shadows." Why is this metaphor appropriate?

3. What did Gorky predict would happen to films, and what do you think of his glimpse into the future?

4. According to Alfred Hitchcock, what is the disadvantage of filming long scenes?

5. The reaction shot is still an often-used directorial device. How does such a shot produce suspense?

6. Hitchcock comments on changing public taste. Assume you are a director. What prediction can you make about how the preferences of film audiences might change in the next five years?

The Influence of Africa

In the 20th century, Africa's ancient traditions exerted a powerful influence on the modern cultures of both Africa itself and of Europe. The Negritude movement was founded in the mid-1930s by a group of young African writers who wanted to revolt against colonial values and rediscover the authentic content of African culture. One of the founders was Léopold Sédar Senghor (born 1906) of Senegal, who defined Negritude as "the sum total of all cultural values of Africa." In his poem "Prayer to the Masks," Senghor celebrated one of the central artifacts of African culture—the mask (page 146). The art of African masks also fascinated many modern European artists, who incorporated their bold patterns and stylized contours into their paintings and sculptures.

Prayer to the Masks

LÉOPOLD SÉDAR SENGHOR

Masks! O Masks!
Black mask red mask, you black and white masks
Masks with the four points from which the Spirit blows
I greet you in the silence!
And not you the last, lion-headed Ancestor
You guard this place forbidden to all laughter of woman, to every smile
    that fades
You give forth this air of eternity wherein I breathe the breath of my Fathers.
Masks with maskless faces, bereft[1] of every dimple as of every wrinkle
Who have fashioned this image, this face of mine leaning over the altar of
    white paper
In your image, hear me!
Behold, Africa of the empires is dying—it is the agony of a pitiable princess
And also Europe to whom we are bound by the navel.
Fix your immutable[2] eyes upon your children who are commanded

---

[1] bereft—deprived.

[2] immutable—unchanging.

Who give their lives like the poor man his last garment.

May we answer Present at the rebirth of the World

As the leaven[3] which is necessary to the white flour.

For who would teach rhythm to the dead world of machines and of cannons?

Who would raise the cry of joy to awaken the dead and the orphans at dawn?

Speak, who would restore the memory of life to the man with gutted hopes?

They call us the men of cotton, of coffee, of oil.

They call us the men of death.

We are the men of dance, whose feet regain vigor in striking the hard earth.

---

[3] leaven—yeast that makes bread dough rise.

▲
The bold outlines of this portrait of his wife by French artist Henri Matisse (1869–1954) suggest the influence of African masks.

African art influenced Cubists, who portrayed objects as arrangements of geometrical planes, as in this detail from *Les Demoiselles d'Avignon* ("Girls of Avignon") by Spanish painter Pablo Picasso (1881–1973). ▶

▲
The influence of African sculpture can be seen in the elongated contours of *Head of Woman* by Italian artist Amedeo Modigliani (1884–1920).

Figure, by Latvian-born sculptor Jacques Lipschitz (1891–1973), has the abstract quality of some African masks.
▼

QUESTIONS TO CONSIDER

1. What do the masks symbolize in Léopold Sédar Senghor's poem, and why are they important?

2. Examine the African masks on pages 146–148. Why do you think traditional African art exerted such a strong influence on European artists of the early 20th century?

The Rise of Hitler

LILO LINKE

Political and social changes after the end of World War I contributed to the rise of Fascism in Europe. Authoritarian, nationalistic, and racist, Fascist governments suppressed opposition through censorship and terrorism. In the mid-1930s, the National Socialist (or Nazi) Party, under the leadership of Adolf Hitler (1889–1945), seized total control of the German government. Although she was unsympathetic to the Nazis, German journalist Lilo Linke recognized the extraordinary power of Hitler's appeal. The Germans had been humiliated at the end of World War I, and he promised that Germany would once again be a world power. In her autobiography, Restless Days, *she describes Hitler's impact at a Nazi rally.*

At this moment the whole audience rose from their seats, most of them with wild cheers—from the back, behind an S.A.[1] man who carried a large swastika flag, and a drumming and blowing and dinning band, a procession of S.A. men and Hitler Youth marched towards the platform. I enjoyed the right to remain seated as a member of the press. When they were half-way through the hall, the curtain draped behind the platform opened and Hitler, wearing a dark suit, stepped forward to the decorated desk. The audience howled with enthusiastic madness, lifting their right arms in the Fascist salute.

Hitler stood unmoved. At last, when the crowd was already hoarse with shouting, he made a commanding gesture to silence them, and slowly obeying, they grew calmer, as a dog called to order by its master after wild play, lies down, exhaustedly snarling.

For an hour and a half Hitler spoke, every few minutes interrupted by fanatic acclamations which grew into a frenzy after such phrases as:

"Today the world treats us like outcasts. But they will respect us again when we show them our good old German sword, flashing high above our heads!"

Or: "Pacifism is the contemptible religion of the weak; a real man is not afraid of defending his rights by force."

[1] S.A.—Nazi storm troopers, who were especially chosen to carry out assault operations.

Or: "Those foreign blood-suckers, those degenerate asphalt-democrats, those cunning Jews, those whining pacifists, those corrupted November criminals[2]—we'll knock them all down with our fists without pardoning a single one of them."

He thrust his chin forward. His voice, hammering the phrases with an obsessed energy, became husky and shrill and began to squeak more and more frequently. His whole face was covered with sweat; a greasy tress[3] kept on falling on his forehead, however often he pushed it back.

Speaking with a stern face, he crossed his arms over his breast—the imposing attitude of one who stood under his own supreme control. But a moment later a force bursting out of him flung them into the air, where they **implored**,[4] threatened, accused, condemned, assisted by his hands and fists. Later, exhausted, he crossed them on his back and began to march a few steps to and fro along the front of the platform, a lion behind the bars of his cage, waiting for the moment when the door will be opened to jump on the terror-stricken enemy.

The audience was breathlessly under his spell. This man expressed their thoughts, their feelings, their hopes; a new prophet had arisen—many saw in him already another Christ, who predicted the end of their sufferings and had the power to lead them into the promised land if they were only prepared to follow him.

Every word he said was true. They had won the war—yes. Been deprived of the reward for their heroism by a number of traitors—yes. Had suffered **incessantly**[5]

ever since—yes. Been enslaved, suppressed, exploited—yes, yes, yes. But the day had arrived when they would free and revenge themselves—yes.

A single question as to reason or proof or possibility would have shattered the whole argument, but nobody asked it—the majority because they had begun to think with their blood, which condemns all logic, and the others because they sat amazed, despairing, and hopeless in a small boat tossed about by the foaming waves of emotional uproar which surrounded it.

---

[2] November criminals—German officials who had surrendered to the Allies in November 1918 at the end of World War I.

[3] tress—lock of hair.

[4] **implored**—pleaded.

[5] **incessantly**—without pause.

QUESTIONS TO CONSIDER

1. How did the staging of the rally add to the audience's response?

2. Which of Hitler's words do you think had the most emotional appeal?

3. Lilo Linke observes that under Hitler's spell most of his audience began "to think with their blood." How would this contribute to the strength of Nazi control of Germany?

Buchenwald Prisoners

MARGARET BOURKE-WHITE

When the Nazis took power in Germany, they began a campaign for "racial purity." With the coming of World War II, this campaign became the Holocaust, the systematic murder of millions of people throughout Europe, including Jews, Russians, Poles, Gypsies, the aged, the handicapped, homosexuals, and "traitors" who opposed Nazi rule. The extermination program was methodically carried out in concentration camps established in the areas controlled by the Nazis. American photographer Margaret Bourke-White (1906–1971) was present when the Buchenwald concentration camp was liberated in the spring of 1945.

QUESTIONS TO CONSIDER

1. What emotions are depicted on the faces of these Buchenwald inmates?

2. What does this photograph convey about the Nazi regime?

3. In your opinion, what was a greater factor in the horrors of the Holocaust—Nazi racism or the totalitarianism of the Nazi regime?

Requiem 1935–1940

ANNA AKHMATOVA

The repressive methods of Nazism were also practiced by the Communist government of Russia under the dictatorial rule of Joseph Stalin (1879–1953). Stalin became general secretary of the Communist Party in Russia in 1922, and in the 1930s totally controlled Russia, largely through purging the government and the army of anyone who opposed him. "Requiem 1935–1940," a cycle of poems by Russian poet Anna Akhmatova (1889–1966), was inspired by the arrest and exile of her son during the Stalinist purges. The entire poem was not published until some years after Stalin's death.

No, not under the vault of another sky,
not under the shelter of other wings.
I was with my people then,
there where my people were doomed to be.
1961

Instead of a Foreword

During the terrible years of Yezhovschina[1] I spent seventeen months in
the prison queues[2] in Leningrad. One day someone recognized me. Then
a woman with lips blue with cold who was standing behind me, and of
course had never heard of my name, came out of the numbness which
affected us all and whispered in my ear (we all spoke in whispers there):
"Can you describe this?"
I said, "I can!"
Then something resembling a smile slipped over what had once
    been her face.
1 April 1957 Leningrad

---

[1] Yezhovschina—head of Stalin's secret police in the late 1930s.
[2] queues—lines of visitors waiting to see prisoners.

Dedication

The mountains bend before this grief,
the great river does not flow,
but the prison locks are strong
and behind them the convicts' holes
and a deathly sadness.
For someone the fresh wind blows,
for someone the sunset basks . . .
We don't know, we are the same everywhere;
we only hear the repellent clank of keys,
the heavy steps of the soldiers.
We rose as though to early mass,[3]
and went through the savage capital,
and we used to meet there, more lifeless than the dead,
the sun lower, the Neva[4] mistier,
but in the distance hope still sings.
Condemned . . . Immediately the tears start,
one woman, already isolated from everyone else,
as though her life had been wrenched from her heart,
as though she had been smashed flat on her back,
still, she walks on . . . staggers . . . alone . . .
Where now are the chance friends
of my two hellish years?
What do they see in the Siberian blizzard,
what comes to them in the moon's circle?
I send them my farewell greeting.
March 1940

Introduction

It was a time when only the dead
smiled, happy in their peace.
And Leningrad dangled like a useless pendant
at the side of its prisons.
A time when, tortured out of their minds,
the convicted walked in regiments,
and the steam whistles sang

---

[3] mass—Christian religious service.
[4] Neva—river that flows through Petersburg (then Leningrad).

their short parting song.
Stars of death stood over us,
and innocent Russia squirmed
under the bloody boots,
under wheels of Black Marias.[5]

I

They took you away at dawn,
I walked after you as though you were being borne out,
the children were crying in the dark room,
the candle swam by the ikon-stand.[6]
The cold of the ikon on your lips.
Death sweat on your brow . . . Do not forget!
I will howl by the Kremlin towers
like the wives of the Streltsy.[7]
1935

2

The quiet Don[8] flows quietly,
the yellow moon goes into the house,

goes in with its cap askew,
the yellow moon sees the shadow.

This woman is sick,
this woman is alone,

husband in the grave, son in prison,
pray for me.

3

No, this is not me—someone else suffers.
I couldn't stand this: let black drapes
cover what happened,
and let them take away the street lights . . . Night.

---

[5] Black Marias—the patrol wagons that took prisoners to jail.

[6] ikon-stand—holder for religious images, or ikons.

[7] Kremlin . . . Streltsy—The Kremlin is the ancient citadel of Moscow that houses many of the most important offices of the Russian government. The Streltsy were soldiers organized about 1550 by Russian ruler Ivan the Terrible; Peter the Great finally disbanded them in 1698, executing 800.

[8] Don—river of western Russia.

4

If I could show you, the mocker,
everybody's favorite,
happy sinner of Tsarskoe Selo,[9]
how your life will turn out:
you will stand at Kresty[10]
three hundredth in the line with your prison parcel,
and set fire to the new year ice
with your hot tears.
There the prison poplar sways,
silence—and how many
innocent lives are ending there . . .

5

For seventeen months I have been screaming,
calling you home.
I flung myself at the executioner's feet.
You are my son and my terror.
Everything is confused for ever,
and I can no longer tell
beast from man,
and how long I must wait for the execution.
Only the dusty flowers,
the clank of censers, and tracks
leading from somewhere to nowhere.
An enormous star
looks me straight in the eye
and threatens swift destruction.

6

Weightless weeks fly by,
I will never grasp what happened.
How the white nights[11] looked
at you, my son, in prison,
how they look again
with the burning eye of the hawk,

---

[9] Tsarskoe Selo—Russian village where Akhmatova had lived in her youth.

[10] Kresty—a prison in Leningrad; the name (meaning "crosses") refers to the shape of the building.

[11] white nights—in northern Russia the sun never totally sets during the summer.

they speak of your tall cross,
they speak of death.
1939

7

Verdict
The stone word fell
on my still living breast.
Never mind, I was prepared,
somehow I'll come to terms with it.

Today I have much work to do:
I must finally kill my memory,

I must, so my soul can turn to stone,
I must learn to live again.

Or else . . . The hot summer rustle,
like holiday time outside my window.
I have felt this coming for a long time,
this bright day and the empty house.
Summer 1939

8

To Death
You will come anyway—so why not now?
I am waiting for you—it's very difficult for me.
I have put out the light and opened the door
to you, so simple and wonderful.
Assume any shape you like,
burst in as a poison gas shell,
or creep up like a burglar with a heavy weight,
or poison me with typhus vapors.
Or come with a denunciation thought up by you
and known *ad nauseam*[12] to everyone,
so that I may see over the blue cap[13]
the janitor's fear-whitened face.
I don't care now. The Yenisey[14] rolls on,
the Pole star shines.

---

[12] *ad nauseam*—to a disgusting degree.

[13] blue cap—policeman.

[14] Yenisey—Siberian river.

And the blue luster of loving eyes
conceals the final horror.
19 August 1939

9

Already madness has covered
half my soul with its wing,
and gives me strong liquor to drink,
and lures me to the black valley.

I realized that I must
hand victory to it,
as I listened to my delirium,
already alien to me.

It will not allow me to take
anything away with me
(however I beseech it,
however I pester it with prayer):
not the terrible eyes of my son,
the rock-like suffering,
not the day when the storm came,
not the prison visiting hour,

nor the sweet coolness of hands,
nor the uproar of the lime trees' shadows,
nor the distant, light sound—
the comfort of last words.
4 May 1940

10

Crucifixion[15]
"Weep not for Me, Mother,
in the grave I have life."

I

The choir of angels glorified the great hour,
the heavens melted in flames.
He said to His Father: "Why hast Thou forsaken Me?"
and to His Mother: "Oh, weep not for Me . . ."

---

[15] Crucifixion—Akhmatova alludes to the death of Jesus on the Cross. Mary Magdalene was one of the followers of Jesus; "the disciple whom He loved" was St. John.

II

Mary Magdalene smote her breast and wept,
the disciple whom He loved turned to stone,
but where the Mother stood in silence
nobody even dared look.
1940

Epilogue

I

I found out how faces droop,
how terror looks out from under the eyelids,
how suffering carves on cheeks
hard pages of cuneiform,[16]
how curls ash-blonde and black
turn silver overnight,
a smile fades on submissive lips,
fear trembles in a dry laugh.
I pray not for myself alone,
but for everyone who stood with me,
in the cruel cold, in the July heat,
under the blind, red wall.

II

The hour of remembrance has drawn close again.
I see you, hear you, feel you.

The one they hardly dragged to the window,
the one who no longer treads this earth,

the one who shook her beautiful head,
and said: "Coming here is like coming home."

I would like to call them all by name,
but the list was taken away and I can't remember.

For them I have woven a wide shroud
from the humble words I heard among them.

I remember them always, everywhere,
I will never forget them, whatever comes.

---

[16] cuneiform—wedge-shaped script used in ancient Mesopotamia.

And if they gag my tormented mouth
with which one hundred million people cry,

then let them also remember me
on the eve of my remembrance day.

If they ever think of building
a memorial to me in this country,

I solemnly give my consent,
only with this condition: not to build it

near the sea where I was born;
my last tie with the sea is broken;

nor in Tsarsky Sad[17] by the hallowed stump
where an inconsolable shadow seeks me,

but here, where I stood three hundred hours,
and they never unbolted the door for me.

Since even in blessed death I am terrified
that I will forget the thundering of the Black Marias,

forget how the hateful door slammed,
how an old woman howled like a wounded beast.

And let the melting snow stream
like tears from my motionless, bronze eyelids,

let the prison dove call in the distance
and the boats go quietly on the Neva.
March 1940

---

[17] Tsarsky Sad—a place name; literally, "the Tsar's Garden."

QUESTIONS TO CONSIDER

1. What does the episode Anna Akhmatova describes in "Instead of a Foreword" indicate about her purpose in "Requiem 1935–1940"?

2. There are a number of references to Christianity in this poem. Does religion seem to provide consolation for Akhmatova? Why or why not?

3. In "Epilogue," where does Akhmatova ask that any memorial to her be erected? Why?

4. Do you think literature can be an effective protest against government repression? Why or why not?

5. What images in the poem convey the power of the Communist state?

from

Nineteen Eighty-Four

GEORGE ORWELL

The novel Nineteen Eighty-Four *by English writer George Orwell (1903–1950) was inspired by the totalitarian governments of the 1930s and 1940s, particularly Stalinist Russia. Orwell's novel is perhaps the best-known example of a characteristic 20th-century literary form, the antiutopia or dystopia. This type of fiction depicts an imaginary society in which political, social, technological, environmental, or other forces have degraded human life. The famous opening of* Nineteen Eighty-Four *introduces Orwell's hero Winston Smith and the society in which he lives.*

It was a bright cold day in April, and the clocks were striking thirteen. Winston Smith, his chin nuzzled into his breast in an effort to escape the vile wind, slipped quickly through the glass doors of Victory Mansions, though not quickly enough to prevent a swirl of gritty dust from entering along with him.

The hallway smelt of boiled cabbage and old rag mats. At one end of it a colored poster, too large for indoor display, had been tacked to the wall. It depicted simply an enormous face, more than a meter wide: the face of a man of about forty-five, with a heavy black mustache and ruggedly handsome features. Winston made for the stairs. It was no use trying the lift.[1] Even at the best of times it was seldom working, and at present the electric current was cut off during daylight hours. It was part of the economy drive in preparation for Hate Week. The flat[2] was seven flights up, and Winston, who was thirty-nine and had a varicose ulcer above his right ankle, went slowly, resting several times on the way. On each landing, opposite the lift shaft, the poster with the enormous face gazed from the wall. It was one of those pictures which are so contrived that the eyes follow you about when you move. BIG BROTHER IS WATCHING YOU, the caption beneath it ran.

---

[1] lift—elevator.

[2] flat—apartment.

Inside the flat a fruity[3] voice was reading out a list of figures which had something to do with the production of pig iron. The voice came from an oblong metal plaque like a dulled mirror which formed part of the surface of the right-hand wall. Winston turned a switch and the voice sank somewhat, though the words were still distinguishable. The instrument (the telescreen, it was called) could be dimmed, but there was no way of shutting it off completely. He moved over to the window: a smallish, frail figure, the meagerness of his body merely emphasized by the blue overalls which were the uniform of the Party. His hair was very fair, his face naturally **sanguine**,[4] his skin roughened by coarse soap and blunt razor blades and the cold of the winter that had just ended.

Outside, even through the shut window pane, the world looked cold. Down in the street little eddies[5] of wind were whirling dust and torn paper into spirals, and though the sun was shining and the sky a harsh blue, there seemed to be no color in anything except the posters that were plastered everywhere. The black-mustachio'd face gazed down from every commanding corner. There was one on the house front immediately opposite. BIG BROTHER IS WATCHING YOU, the caption said, while the dark eyes looked deep into Winston's own. Down at street level another poster, torn at one corner, flapped fitfully in the wind, alternately covering and uncovering the single word INGSOC.[6] In the

far distance a helicopter skimmed down between the roofs, hovered for an instant like a bluebottle, and darted away again with a curving flight. It was the Police Patrol, snooping into people's windows. The patrols did not matter, however. Only the Thought Police mattered.

Behind Winston's back the voice from the telescreen was still babbling away about pig iron and the overfulfillment of the Ninth Three-Year Plan. The telescreen received and transmitted simultaneously. Any sound that Winston made, above the level of a very low whisper, would be picked up by it; moreover, so long as he remained within the field of vision which the metal plaque commanded, he could be seen as well as heard. There was of course no way of knowing whether you were being watched at any given moment. How often, or on what system, the Thought Police plugged in on any individual wire was guesswork. It was even conceivable that they watched everybody all the time. But at any rate they could plug in your wire whenever they wanted to. You had to live—did live, from habit that became instinct—in the assumption that every sound you made was overheard, and, except in darkness, every movement scrutinized.

Winston kept his back turned to the telescreen. It was safer; though, as he well

---

[3] fruity—overly sweet.

[4] **sanguine**—ruddy.

[5] eddies—whirling currents.

[6] INGSOC—acronym for English Socialism, imaginary political system of Orwell's dystopia.

knew, even a back can be revealing. A kilometer away the Ministry of Truth, his place of work, towered vast and white above the grimy landscape. This, he thought with a sort of vague distaste—this was London, chief city of Airstrip One, itself the third most populous of the provinces of Oceania. He tried to squeeze out some childhood memory that should tell him whether London had always been quite like this. Were there always these vistas of rotting nineteenth-century houses, their sides shored up with balks[7] of timber, their windows patched with cardboard and their roofs with corrugated iron, their crazy garden walls sagging in all directions? And the bombed sites where the plaster dust swirled in the air and the willow herb straggled over the heaps of rubble; and the places where the bombs had cleared a larger patch and there had sprung up sordid colonies of wooden dwellings like chicken houses? But it was no use, he could not remember: nothing remained of his childhood except a series of bright-lit tableaux,[8] occurring against no background and mostly unintelligible.

The Ministry of Truth—Minitrue, in Newspeak[9]—was startlingly different from any other object in sight. It was an enormous pyramidal structure of glittering white concrete, soaring up, terrace after terrace, three hundred meters into the air. From where Winston stood it was just possible to read, picked out on its white face in elegant lettering the three slogans of the Party:

WAR IS PEACE
FREEDOM IS SLAVERY
IGNORANCE IS STRENGTH.

The Ministry of Truth contained, it was said, three-thousand rooms above ground level, and corresponding **ramifications**[10] below. Scattered about London there were just three other buildings of similar appearance and size. So completely did they dwarf the surrounding architecture that from the roof of Victory Mansions you could see all four of them simultaneously. They were the homes of the four Ministries between which the entire apparatus of government was divided: the Ministry of Truth, which concerned itself with news, entertainment, education, and the fine arts; the Ministry of Peace, which concerned itself with war; the Ministry of Love, which maintained law and order, and the Ministry of Plenty, which was responsible for economic affairs. Their names, in Newspeak: Minitrue, Minipax, Miniluv, and Miniplenty.

The Ministry of Love was the really frightening one. There were no windows in it at all. Winston had never been inside the Ministry of Love, nor within half a kilometer of it. It was a place impossible to enter except on official business, and then only by penetrating through a maze of barbed-wire entanglements, steel doors, and hidden

---

[7] balks—heavy beams.

[8] tableaux—pictures.

[9] Newspeak—language of Orwell's imaginary society, designed to help the state control people's thoughts.

[10] **ramifications**—branches.

machine-gun nests. Even the streets leading up to its outer barriers were roamed by gorilla-faced guards in black uniforms, armed with jointed truncheons.[11] . . .

O'Brien, a goverment official, later explains to Smith the philosophy of power that underlies the society.

"The Party seeks power entirely for its own sake. We are not interested in the good of others; we are interested solely in power. Not wealth or luxury or long life or happiness; only power, pure power. What pure power means you will understand presently. We are different from all the **oligarchies**[12] of the past in that we know what we are doing. All the others, even those who resembled ourselves, were cowards and hypocrites. The German Nazis and the Russian Communists came very close to us in their methods, but they never had the courage to recognize their own motives. They pretended, perhaps they even believed, that they had seized power unwillingly and for a limited time, and that just round the corner there lay a paradise where human beings would be free and equal. We are not like that. We know that no one ever seizes power with the intention of relinquishing it. Power is not a means; it is an end. One does not establish a dictatorship in order to safeguard a revolution; one makes the revolution in order to establish the dictatorship. The object of persecution is persecution. The object of torture is torture. The object of

power is power. Now do you begin to understand me?"

Winston was struck, as he had been struck before, by the tiredness of O'Brien's face. It was strong and fleshy and brutal, it was full of intelligence and a sort of controlled passion before which he felt himself helpless; but it was tired. There were pouches under the eyes, the skin sagged from the cheekbones. O'Brien leaned over him, deliberately bringing the worn face nearer.

"You are thinking," he said, "that my face is old and tired. You are thinking that I talk of power, and yet I am not even able to prevent the decay of my own body. Can you not understand, Winston, that the individual is only a cell? The weariness of the cell is the vigor of the organism. Do you die when you cut your fingernails?"

He turned away from the bed and began strolling up and down again, one hand in his pocket.

"We are the priests of power," he said. "God is power. But at present power is only a word so far as you are concerned. It is time for you to gather some idea of what power means. The first thing you must realize is that power is collective. The individual only has power in so far as he ceases to be an individual. You know the Party slogan: 'Freedom is Slavery.' Has it ever occurred to you that it is reversible? Slavery is freedom. Alone—free—the human being is always defeated. It must be so, because every human being is doomed to die, which is the greatest of all failures. But if he can

---

[11] truncheons—clubs.

[12] **oligarchies**—states governed by a few people.

make complete, utter submission, if he can escape from his identity, if he can merge himself in the Party so that he is the Party, then he is all-powerful and immortal. The second thing for you to realize is that power is power over human beings. Over the body—but, above all, over the mind. Power over matter—external reality, as you would call it—is not important. Already our control over matter is absolute."

For a moment Winston ignored the dial. He made a violent effort to raise himself into a sitting position, and merely succeeded in wrenching his body painfully.

"But how can you control matter?" he burst out. "You don't even control the climate or the law of gravity. And there are disease, pain, death—"

O'Brien silenced him by a movement of the hand. "We control matter because we control the mind. Reality is inside the skull. You will learn by degrees, Winston. There is nothing that we could not do. Invisibility, levitation[13]—anything. I could float off this floor like a soap bubble if I wished to. I do not wish to, because the Party does not wish it. You must get rid of those nineteenth-century ideas about the laws of nature. We make the laws of nature."

"But you do not! You are not even masters of this planet. What about Eurasia and Eastasia? You have not conquered them yet."

"Unimportant. We shall conquer them when it suits us. And if we did not, what difference would it make? We can shut them out of existence. Oceania is the world."

"But the world itself is only a speck of dust. And man is tiny—helpless! How long has he been in existence? For millions of years the earth was uninhabited."

"Nonsense. The earth is as old as we are, no older. How could it be older? Nothing exists except through human consciousness."

"But the rocks are full of the bones of extinct animals—mammoths and mastodons and enormous reptiles which lived here long before man was ever heard of."

"Have you ever seen those bones, Winston? Of course not. Nineteenth-century biologists invented them. Before man there was nothing. After man, if he could come to an end, there would be nothing. Outside man there is nothing."

"But the whole universe is outside us. Look at the stars! Some of them are a million light-years away. They are out of our reach forever."

"What are the stars?" said O'Brien indifferently. "They are bits of fire a few kilometers away. We could reach them if we wanted to. Or we could blot them out. The earth is the center of the universe. The sun and the stars go round it."

Winston made another convulsive movement. This time he did not say anything. O'Brien continued as though answering a spoken objection:

"For certain purposes, of course, that is not true. When we navigate the ocean, or when we predict an eclipse, we often find

---

[13] levitation—floating in the air.

it convenient to assume that the earth goes round the sun and that the stars are millions upon millions of kilometers away. But what of it? Do you suppose it is beyond us to produce a dual system of astronomy? The stars can be near or distant, according as we need them. Do you suppose our mathematicians are unequal to that? Have you forgotten doublethink?"[14]

Winston shrank back upon the bed. Whatever he said, the swift answer crushed him like a bludgeon.[15] And yet he *knew*, he knew, that he was in the right. The belief that nothing exists outside your own mind—surely there must be some way of demonstrating that it was false. Had it not been exposed long ago as a fallacy? There was even a name for it, which he had forgotten. A faint smile twitched the corners of O'Brien's mouth as he looked down at him.

"I told you, Winston," he said, "that metaphysics[16] is not your strong point. The word you are trying to think of is solipsism. But you are mistaken. This is not solipsism. Collective solipsism, if you like. But that is a different thing; in fact, the opposite thing. All this is a digression," he added in a different tone. "The real power, the power we have to fight for night and day, is not power over things, but over men." He paused, and for a moment assumed again his air of a schoolmaster questioning a promising pupil: "How does one man assert his power over another, Winston?"

Winston thought, "By making him suffer," he said.

"Exactly. By making him suffer. Obedience is not enough. Unless he is suffering, how can you be sure that he is obeying your will and not his own? Power is in inflicting pain and humiliation. Power is in tearing human minds to pieces and putting them together again in new shapes of your own choosing. Do you begin to see, then, what kind of world we are creating? It is the exact opposite of the stupid **hedonistic**[17] Utopias that the old reformers imagined. A world of fear and treachery and torment, a world of trampling and being trampled upon, a world which will grow not less but *more* merciless as it refines itself. Progress in our world will be progress toward more pain. The old civilizations claimed that they were founded on love or justice. Ours is founded upon hatred. In our world there will be no emotions except fear, rage, triumph, and self-abasement. Everything else we shall destroy—everything. Already we are breaking down the habits of thought which have survived from before the Revolution. We have cut the links between child and parent, and between man and man, and between man and woman. No one dares trust a wife or a child or a friend any longer. But in the future there will be no wives and no friends. Children will be taken from their mothers at birth, as one takes eggs from a hen. The sex instinct

---

[14] doublethink—ability of people in Orwell's society to accept two contradictory ideas at the same time.

[15] bludgeon—club.

[16] metaphysics—branch of philosophy that examines the nature of reality.

[17] **hedonistic**—relating to the ethical doctrine holding that only what is pleasant is good.

will be eradicated. Procreation will be an annual formality like the renewal of a ration card. We shall abolish the orgasm. Our neurologists are at work upon it now. There will be no loyalty, except loyalty toward the Party. There will be no love, except the love of Big Brother. There will be no laughter, except the laugh of triumph over a defeated enemy. There will be no art, no literature, no science. When we are **omnipotent**[18] we shall have no more need of science. There will be no distinction between beauty and ugliness. There will be no curiosity, no enjoyment of the process of life. All competing pleasures will be destroyed. But always—do not forget this, Winston—always there will be the intoxication of power, constantly increasing and constantly growing subtler. Always, at every moment, there will be the thrill of victory, the sensation of trampling on an enemy who is helpless. If you want a picture of the future, imagine a boot stamping on a human face—forever."

---

[18] **omnipotent**—all-powerful.

QUESTIONS TO CONSIDER

1. What picture does George Orwell give of his imaginary society?

2. What can you infer is the reason everyone is constantly watched?

3. What is ironic about the appearance and function of the Ministry of Love?

4. How does O'Brien dismiss "facts" as Winston Smith knows them?

5. What is the basis of state power in *Nineteen Eighty Four?*

from

Civilization and Its Discontents

SIGMUND FREUD

Austrian psychoanalyst Sigmund Freud (1856–1939) was one of the most influential thinkers of the 20th century. He theorized that human behavior was largely shaped by irrational drives residing in an unconscious of which the individual is largely unaware and which reason can only partially control. Given this vision of human nature, what is the role of civilization? Do cultural limits impress a necessary order on society, or do they prevent people from being happy or reaching their full potential? Freud set forth his view in his book Civilization and Its Discontents.

One of the ideal demands . . . of civilized society . . . runs: "Thou shalt love thy neighbor as thyself." It is known throughout the world and is undoubtedly older than Christianity, which puts it forward as its proudest claim. Yet it is certainly not very old; even in historical times it was still strange to mankind. Let us adopt a naive attitude towards it, as though we were hearing it for the first time; we shall be unable then to suppress a feeling of surprise and bewilderment. Why should we do it? What good will it do us? But, above all, how shall we achieve it? How can it be possible? My love is something valuable to me which I ought not to throw away without reflection. It imposes duties on me for whose fulfilment I must be ready to make sacrifices. If I love someone, he must deserve it in some way. (I leave out of account the use he may be to me, and also his possible significance for me as a sexual object, for neither of these two kinds of relationship comes into question where the precept to love my neighbor is concerned.) He deserves it if he is so like me in important ways that I can love myself in him; and he deserves it if he is so much more perfect than myself that I can love my ideal of my own self in him. Again, I have to love him if he is my friend's son, since the pain my friend would feel if any harm came to him would be my pain too—I should have to share it. But if he is a stranger to me and if he cannot attract me by any worth of his own or any significance that he may already have acquired for my emotional life, it will be hard for me to love him. Indeed, I should be wrong to do so, for my love is valued by all my own people as a sign of my preferring them, and it is an injustice to them if I put a stranger on a par with them. But if I am to love him (with this universal love) merely because he, too, is an inhabitant of this earth, like an insect, an earth-worm or a grass-snake, then I fear that only a small **modicum**[1] of my love will fall to his share—not by any possibility as much as, by the judgment of my reason, I am entitled to retain for myself. What is the point of a precept enunciated with so much solemnity if its fulfilment cannot be recommended as reasonable?

On closer inspection, I find still further difficulties. Not merely is this stranger in general unworthy of my love; I must honestly confess that he has more claim to my hostility and even my hatred. He seems not to have the least trace of love for me and shows me not the slightest consideration. If it will do him any good he has no hesitation in injuring me, nor does he ask himself whether the amount of advantage he gains bears any proportion to the extent of the harm he does to me. Indeed, he need not even obtain an advantage; if he can satisfy any sort of desire by it, he thinks nothing of jeering at me, insulting me, slandering me and showing his superior power; and the more secure he feels and the more helpless I am, the more certainly I can expect him to behave like this to me. If he behaves differently, if he shows me

consideration and **forbearance**[2] as a stranger, I am ready to treat him in the same way, in any case and quite apart from any precept. Indeed, if this grandiose commandment had run "Love thy neighbor as thy neighbor loves thee," I should not take exception to it. And there is a second commandment, which seems to me even more incomprehensible and arouses still stronger opposition in me. It is "Love thine enemies." If I think it over, however, I see that I am wrong in treating it as a greater **imposition**.[3] At bottom it is the same thing. . . .

Now it is very probable that my neighbor, when he is **enjoined**[4] to love me as himself, will answer exactly as I have done and will repel me for the same reasons. I hope he will not have the same objective grounds for doing so, but he will have the same idea as I have. Even so, the behavior of human beings shows differences, which ethics, disregarding the fact that such differences are determined, classifies as "good" or "bad." So long as these undeniable differences have not been removed, obedience to high ethical demands **entails**[5] damage to the aims of civilization, for it puts a positive premium on being bad. One is irresistably reminded of an incident in the French Chamber when capital punishment was being debated. A member had been passionately supporting its abolition and his speech was being received with

---

[1] **modicum**—small amount.

[2] **forbearance**—tolerance.

[3] **imposition**—obligation.

[4] **enjoined**—ordered.

[5] **entails**—imposes.

tumultuous applause, when a voice from the hall called out: "Que messieurs les assassins commencement!"[6]

The element of truth behind all this, which people are so ready to disavow, is that men are not gentle creatures who want to be loved, and who at the most can defend themselves if they are attacked; they are, on the contrary, creatures among whose instinctual endowments is to be reckoned a powerful share of aggressiveness. As a result, their neighbor is for them not only a potential helper or sexual object, but also someone who tempts them to satisfy their aggressiveness on him, to exploit his capacity for work without compensation, to use him sexually without his consent, to seize his possessions, to humiliate him, to cause him pain, to torture and to kill him. *Homo homini lupus.*[7] Who, in the face of all his experience of life and of history, will have the courage to dispute this assertion? As a rule this cruel aggressiveness waits for some provocation or puts itself at the service of some other purpose, whose goal might also have been reached by milder measures. In circumstances that are favorable to it, when the mental counter-forces which ordinarily inhibit it are out of action, it also manifests itself spontaneously and reveals man as a savage beast to whom consideration towards his own kind is something alien. Anyone who calls to mind the atrocities committed during the racial migrations or the invasions of the Huns, or by the people known as Mongols under Jenghiz Khan and Tamerlane, or at the capture of Jerusalem by the pious Crusaders, or even, indeed, the horrors of the recent World War—anyone who calls these things to mind will have to bow humbly before the truth of this view.

The existence of this inclination to aggression, which we can detect in ourselves and justly assume to be present in others, is the factor which disturbs our relations with our neighbors and which forces civilization into such a high expenditure [of energy]. In consequence of this primary mutual hostility of human beings, civilized society is perpetually threatened with disintegration. The interest of work in common would not hold it together; instinctual passions are stronger than reasonable interests. Civilization has to use its utmost efforts in order to set limits to man's aggressive instincts and to hold the manifestations of them in check by psychical reaction-formations.[8] Hence, therefore, the use of methods intended to incite people into identifications and aim-inhibited relationships of love, hence the restriction upon sexual life, and hence too the ideal's commandment to love one's neighbor as oneself—a commandment which is really justified by the fact that nothing else runs so strongly counter to the original nature of man. In spite of every effort, these endeavors of civilization have not so far achieved very much. It hopes to prevent the crudest excesses of brutal violence by

---

[6] "Que messieurs . . . commencent!"—"It's the murderers who should make the first move!"

[7] *Homo homini lupus*—"Man is a wolf to man."

[8] reaction-formations—In Freudian theory, a reaction-formation is a conscious activity directly opposed to an unconscious tendency.

itself assuming the right to use violence against criminals, but the law is not able to lay hold of the more cautious and refined manifestations of human aggressiveness. The time comes when each one of us has to give up as illusions the expectations which, in his youth, he pinned upon his fellow-men, and when he may learn how much difficulty and pain has been added to his life by their ill-will. At the same time, it would be unfair to reproach civilization with trying to eliminate strife and competition from human activity. These things are undoubtedly indispensable. But opposition is not necessarily **enmity**;[9] it is merely misused and made an *occasion* for enmity. . . .

If civilization imposes such great sacrifices not only on man's sexuality but on his aggressivity, we can understand better why it is hard for him to be happy in that civilization. In fact, primitive man was better off in knowing no restrictions of instinct. To counterbalance this, his prospects of enjoying this happiness for any length of time were very slender. Civilized man has exchanged a portion of his possibilities of happiness for a portion of security. We must not forget, however, that in the **primal**[10] family only the head of it enjoyed this instinctual freedom; the rest lived in slavish suppression. In that primal period of civilization, the contrast between a minority who enjoyed the advantages of civilization and a majority who were robbed of those advantages was, therefore, carried to extremes. As regards the primitive peoples who exist today, careful researches have shown that their instinctual life is by no

means to be envied for its freedom. It is subject to restrictions of a different kind but perhaps of greater severity than those attaching to modern civilized man.

When we justly find fault with the present state of our civilization for so inadequately fulfilling our demands for a plan of life that shall make us happy, and for allowing the existence of so much suffering which could probably be avoided—when, with unsparing criticism, we try to uncover the roots of its imperfection, we are undoubtedly exercising a proper right and are not showing ourselves enemies of civilization. We may expect gradually to carry through such alterations in our civilization as will better satisfy our needs and will escape our criticisms. But perhaps we may also familiarize ourselves with the idea that there are difficulties attaching to the nature of civilization which will not yield to any attempt at reform.

---

[9] **enmity**—mutual hatred.

[10] **primal**—belonging to the earliest age; ancient.

QUESTIONS TO CONSIDER

1. Do you agree with Freud that human beings are naturally aggressive?

2. According to Freud, why is it so difficult to live by the Golden Rule?

3. Does Freud think civilization can be improved? Why or why not?

4. Do you think the 21st century will see more or fewer cultural restraints in American society? Explain.

Shakespeare's Sister

VIRGINIA WOOLF

*Speaking to women at Cambridge University, English novelist and essayist Virginia Woolf (1882–1941)
began by saying that "a woman must have money and a room of her own if she is to write fiction."
Woolf later analyzed the cultural attitudes that kept women from reaching their artistic potential in her
book-length essay* A Room of One's Own.

It was disappointing not to have brought
back in the evening some important statement, some authentic fact. Women are
poorer than men because—this or that.
Perhaps now it would be better to give up
seeking for the truth, and receiving on
one's head an avalanche of opinion hot as
lava, discolored as dish-water. It would be
better to draw the curtains; to shut out
distractions; to light the lamp; to narrow
the inquiry and to ask the historian, who
records not opinions but facts, to describe
under what conditions women lived, not
throughout the ages, but in England,
say in the time of Elizabeth.[1]

For it is a **perennial**[2] puzzle why no
woman wrote a word of that extraordinary
literature when every other man, it
seemed, was capable of song or sonnet.
What were the conditions in which women
lived, I asked myself; for fiction, imaginative work that it is, is not dropped like a
pebble upon the ground, as science may
be; fiction is like a spider's web, attached
ever so lightly perhaps, but still attached to
life at all four corners. Often the attachment
is scarcely perceptible; Shakespeare's plays,
for instance, seem to hang there complete
by themselves. But when the web is pulled
askew,[3] hooked up at the edge, torn in the
middle, one remembers that these webs
are not spun in midair by incorporeal[4]
creatures, but are the work of suffering
human beings, and are attached to grossly
material things, like health and money and
the houses we live in.

---

[1] Elizabeth—Queen Elizabeth I (1533–1603), who ruled
when the Renaissance in England was in full flower.

[2] **perennial**—continuing.

[3] **askew**—crooked.

[4] incorporeal—bodiless.

I went, therefore, to the shelf where the histories stand and took down one of the latest, Professor Trevelyan's *History of England*. Once more I looked up Women, found "position of," and turned to the pages indicated. "Wife-beating," I read, "was a recognized right of man, and was practiced without shame by high as well as low. . . . Similarly," the historian goes on, "the daughter who refused to marry the gentleman of her parents' choice was liable to be locked up, beaten, and flung about the room, without any shock being inflicted on public opinion. Marriage was not an affair of personal affection, but of family avarice, particularly in the 'chivalrous' upper classes. . . . Betrothal often took place while one or both of the parties was in the cradle, and marriage when they were scarcely out of the nurses' charge." That was about 1470, soon after Chaucer's time.[5] The next reference to the position of women is some two hundred years later, in the time of the Stuarts.[6] "It was still the exception for women of the upper and middle class to choose their own husbands, and when the husband had been assigned, he was lord and master, so far at least as law and custom could make him. Yet even so," Professor Trevelyan concludes, "neither Shakespeare's women nor those of authentic seventeenth-century memoirs, like the Verneys and the Hutchinsons, seem wanting in personality and character.". . . Certainly, if we consider it, Cleopatra must have had a way with her; Lady Macbeth, one would suppose, had a will of her own; Rosalind, one might conclude, was an attractive girl.[7] Professor Trevelyan is speaking no more

than the truth when he remarks that Shakespeare's women do not seem wanting in personality and character. Indeed, if woman had no existence save in the fiction written by men, one would imagine her a person of the utmost importance; very various; heroic and mean; splendid and **sordid**;[8] infinitely beautiful and hideous in the extreme; as great as a man, some think even greater. But this is woman in fiction. In fact, as Professor Trevelyan points out, she was locked up, beaten, and flung about the room.

A very queer, **composite**[9] being thus emerges. Imaginatively she is of the highest importance; practically she is completely insignificant. She pervades poetry from cover to cover; she is all but absent from history. She dominates the lives of kings and conquerors in fiction; in fact she was the slave of any boy whose parents forced a ring upon her finger. Some of the most inspired words, some of the most profound thoughts in literature fall from her lips; in real life she could hardly read, could scarcely spell, and was the property of her husband. . . .

It would have been extremely odd had one of them suddenly written the plays of Shakespeare, I concluded, and I thought of that old gentleman, who is dead now, but was a bishop, I think, who declared that it was impossible for any woman, past,

---

[5] Chaucer's time—English poet Geoffrey Chaucer died in 1400.

[6] Stuarts—dynasty that ruled England from 1603 to 1714.

[7] Cleopatra . . . attractive girl—Cleopatra is in Shakespeare's play *Antony and Cleopatra*; Lady Macbeth is in *Macbeth*; Rosalind is in *As You Like It*.

[8] **sordid**—morally low.

[9] **composite**—made up of various parts.

present, or to come, to have the genius of Shakespeare. He wrote to the papers about it. He also told a lady who applied to him for information that cats do not as a matter of fact go to heaven, though they have, he added, souls of a sort. How much thinking those old gentlemen used to save one! How the borders of ignorance shrank back at their approach! Cats do not go to heaven. Women cannot write the plays of Shakespeare.

Be that as it may, I could not help thinking, as I looked at the works of Shakespeare on the shelf, that the bishop was right at least in this; it would have been impossible, completely and entirely, for any woman to have written the plays of Shakespeare in the age of Shakespeare. Let me imagine, since facts are so hard to come by, what would have happened had Shakespeare had a wonderfully gifted sister, called Judith, let us say. Shakespeare himself went, very probably—his mother was an heiress—to the grammar school, where he may have learnt Latin—Ovid, Virgil, and Horace[10]—and the elements of grammar and logic. He was, it is well known, a wild boy who poached[11] rabbits, perhaps shot a deer, and had, rather sooner than he should have done, to marry a woman in the neighborhood, who bore him a child rather quicker than was right. That escapade sent him to seek his fortune in London. He had, it seemed, a taste for the theater; he began by holding horses at the stage door. Very soon he got work in the theater, became a successful actor, and lived at the hub of the universe, meeting everybody, knowing everybody, practicing his art on the boards, exercising his wits in the

streets, and even getting access to the palace of the queen. Meanwhile his extraordinarily gifted sister, let us suppose, remained at home. She was as adventurous, as imaginative, as agog to see the world as he was. But she was not sent to school. She had no chance of learning grammar and logic, let alone of reading Horace and Virgil. She picked up a book now and then, one of her brother's perhaps, and read a few pages. But then her parents came in and told her to mend the stockings or mind the stew and not moon about with books and papers. They would have spoken sharply but kindly, for they were substantial people who knew the conditions of life for a woman and loved their daughter—indeed, more likely than not she was the apple of her father's eye. Perhaps she scribbled some pages up in an apple loft on the sly, but was careful to hide them or set fire to them. Soon, however, before she was out of her teens, she was to be betrothed to the son of a neighboring wool-stapler.[12] She cried out that marriage was hateful to her, and for that she was severely beaten by her father. Then he ceased to scold her. He begged her instead not to hurt him, not to shame him in this matter of her marriage. He would give her a chain of beads or a fine petticoat, he said; and there were tears in his eyes. How could she disobey him? How could she break his heart? The force of her own gift alone drove her to it. She made up a small parcel of her belongings, let herself down by a rope one summer's night and

---

[10] Ovid, Virgil, and Horace—Roman poets.

[11] poached—hunted illegally.

[12] wool-stapler—wool-seller.

took the road to London. She was not seventeen. The birds that sang in the hedge were not more musical than she was. She had the quickest fancy, a gift like her brother's, for the tune of words. Like him, she had a taste for the theater. She stood at the stage door; she wanted to act, she said. Men laughed in her face. The manager—a fat, loose-lipped man—**guffawed**.[13] He bellowed something about poodles dancing and women acting—no woman, he said, could possibly be an actress. He hinted—you can imagine what. She could get no training in her craft. Could she even seek her dinner in a tavern or roam the streets at midnight? Yet her genius was for fiction and lusted to feed abundantly upon the lives of men and women and the study of their ways. At last—for she was very young, oddly like Shakespeare the poet in her face, with the same gray eyes and rounded brows—at last Nick Green the actor-manager took pity on her; she found herself with child by that gentleman and so—who shall measure the heat and violence of the poet's heart when caught and tangled in a woman's body?—killed herself one winter's night and lies buried at some crossroads where the omnibuses now stop outside the Elephant and Castle.[14]

That, more or less, is how the story would run, I think, if a woman in Shakespeare's day had had Shakespeare's genius. But for my part, I agree with the deceased bishop, if such he was—it is unthinkable that any woman in Shakespeare's day should have had Shakespeare's genius. For genius like Shakespeare's is not born among laboring, uneducated, servile people. It was not born in England among the Saxons and the Britons.[15] It is not born today among the working classes. How, then, could it have been born among women whose work began, according to Professor Trevelyan, almost before they were out of the nursery, who were forced to it by their parents and held to it by all the power of law and custom? Yet genius of a sort must have existed among women as it must have existed among the working classes. . . . Indeed, I would venture to guess that Anon, who wrote so many poems without signing them, was often a woman. It was a woman Edward FitzGerald,[16] I think, suggested who made the ballads and the folk songs, crooning them to her children, beguiling her spinning with them, or the length of the winter's night.

---

[13] **guffawed**—laughed loudly.

[14] Elephant and Castle—suicides were often buried at crossroads; Elephant and Castle is a common name for a tavern.

[15] Saxons and Britons—early Germanic and Celtic inhabitants of England.

[16] Edward FitzGerald—English poet (1809–1883); translator of *The Rubáiyát of Omar Khayyám*.

QUESTIONS TO CONSIDER

1. Does Woolf blame men for the fact that no woman could have succeeded as Shakespeare did?

2. Was the bishop's reasoning that "it was impossible for any woman, past, present, or to come, to have the genius of Shakespeare" the same as Woolf's reasoning? Why or why not?

3. Do you agree with Woolf's view about the limits that culture places on the development of genius? Why or why not?

from

The Great War and Modern Memory

PAUL FUSSELL

Among the many cultural legacies of World War I was the experience of trench warfare itself—alternatively dreary and terrifying—recalled by those who endured it. In his book The Great War and Modern Memory, *literary historian Paul Fussell writes of what life was like in the trenches.*

The idea of "the trenches" has been **assimilated**[1] so successfully by metaphor and myth ("Georgian[2] complacency died in the trenches") that it is not easy now to recover a feeling for the actualities. *Entrenched*, in an expression like *entrenched power*, has been a dead metaphor so long that we must bestir ourselves to recover its literal sense. It is time to take a tour.

From the winter of 1914 until the spring of 1918 the trench system was fixed, moving here and there a few hundred yards, moving on great occasions as much as a few miles. London stationers purveying maps felt secure in stocking "sheets of 'The Western Front' with a thick wavy black line drawn from North to South alongside which was printed 'British Line.'"

If one could have gotten high enough to look down at the whole line at once, one would have seen a series of multiple parallel excavations running for 400 miles down through Belgium and France, roughly in the shape of an S flattened at the sides and tipped to the left. . . .

Henri Barbusse estimates that the French front alone contained about 6,250 miles of trenches. Since the French occupied a little more than half the line, the total length of the numerous trenches occupied by the British must come to about 6,000 miles. We thus find over 12,000 miles of

---

[1] **assimilated**—absorbed.

[2] Georgian—referring to the culture of the immediate pre–World War I period.

trenches on the Allied side alone. When we add the trenches of the Central Powers, we arrive at a figure of about 25,000 miles, equal to a trench sufficient to circle the earth. . . .

The British trenches were wet, cold, smelly, and thoroughly squalid. Compared with the precise and thorough German works, they were decidedly amateur, reflecting a complacency about the British genius for improvisation. Because defense offered little opportunity for the display of pluck or swank, it was by implication derogated[3] in the officers' *Field Service Pocket Book*. One reason the British trench system was so haphazard and ramshackle was that it had originally taken form in accord with the official injunction: "The choice of a [defensive] position and its preparation must be made with a view to economizing the power expended on defense in order that the power of offense may be increased." And it was considered really useless to build solid fortifications anyway: "An occasional shell may strike and penetrate the parapet, but in the case of shrapnel the damage to the parapet will be trifling, while in the case of a shell filled with high explosive, the effect will be no worse on a thin parapet than on a thick one. It is, therefore, useless to spend time and labor on making a thick parapet simply to keep out shell." The repeatedly revived hopes for a general breakout and pursuit were another reason why the British trenches were so shabby. A typical soldier's view is George Coppard's:

The whole conduct of our trench warfare seemed to be based on the concept that we, the British, were not stopping in the trenches for long, but were tarrying awhile on the way to Berlin and that very soon we would be chasing Jerry[4] across country. The result, in the long term, meant that we lived a mean and impoverished sort of existence in lousy scratch holes.

In contrast, the German trenches, as the British discovered during the attack on the Somme,[5] were deep, clean, elaborate, and sometimes even comfortable. As Coppard found on the Somme, "Some of the [German] dugouts were thirty feet deep, with as many as sixteen bunk-beds, as well as door bells, water tanks with taps, and cupboards and mirrors." They also had boarded walls, floors, and ceilings; finished wooden staircases; electric light; real kitchens; and wallpaper and overstuffed furniture, the whole protected by steel outer doors. Foreign to the British style was a German dugout of the sort recalled by Ernst Jünger:

At Monchy . . . I was master of an underground dwelling approached by forty steps hewn in the solid chalk, so that even the heaviest

> **The British trenches were wet, cold, smelly, and thoroughly squalid.**

---

[3] derogated—belittled.

[4] Jerry—British slang for Germans, collectively.

[5] Somme—a river in northern France, the scene of huge battles in 1916 and 1918.

shells at this depth made no more than a pleasant rumble when we sat there over an interminable game of cards. In one wall I had a bed hewn out. . . . At its head hung an electric light so that I could read in comfort till I was sleepy. . . . The whole was shut off from the outer world by a dark-red-curtain with rod and rings. . . .

As these examples suggest, there were "national styles" in trenches as in other things. The French trenches were nasty, **cynical**,[6] efficient, and temporary. Kipling remembered the smell of delicious cooking emanating from some in Alsace. The English were amateur, vague, *ad hoc*,[7] and temporary. The German were efficient, clean, **pedantic**,[8] and permanent. Their occupants proposed to stay where they were. Normally the British troops rotated trench duty. After a week of "rest" behind the lines, a unit would move up—at night —to relieve a unit in the front-line trench. After three days to a week or more in that position, the unit would move back for a similar length of time to the support trench, and finally back to the reserve. Then it was time for a week of rest again. In the three lines of trenches the main business of the soldier was to exercise self-control while being shelled. As the poet Louis Simpson has accurately remembered:

> **The main business of the soldier was to exercise self-control while being shelled.**

Being shelled is the main work of an infantry soldier, which no one talks about. Everyone has his own way of going about it. In general, it means lying face down and contracting your body into as small a space as possible. In novels [The Naked and the Dead[9] is an example] you read about soldiers, at such moments, fouling themselves. The opposite is true. As all your parts are contracting, you are more likely to be constipated.

Simpson is recalling the Second War, but he might be recalling the First. While being shelled, the soldier either harbored in a dugout and hoped for something other than a direct hit or made himself as small as possible in a funk-hole. An unlucky sentry or two was supposed to be out in the open trench in all but the worst bombardments, watching through a periscope or loophole for signs of an attack. When only light shelling was in progress, people moved about the trenches freely, and we can get an idea of what life there was like if we posit[10] a typical twenty-four hours in a frontline trench.

The day began about an hour before first light, which often meant at about 4:30. This was the moment for the invariable ritual of morning stand-to (short for the archaic formal command for repelling

---

[6] **cynical**—contemptuous of accepted standards.

[7] *ad hoc*—informal, impromptu.

[8] **pedantic**—rigid, fussy.

[9] *The Naked and the Dead*—novel (1948) by American writer Norman Mailer based on his World War II experiences.

[10] posit—assume.

attack, "Stand to Arms"). Because dawn was the favorite time for launching attacks, at the order to stand-to everyone, officers, men, forward artillery observers, visitors, mounted the fire-step, weapon ready, and peered toward the German line. When it was almost full light and clear that the Germans were not going to attack that morning, everyone "stood down" and began preparing breakfast in small groups. The rations of tea, bread, and bacon, brought up in sandbags during the night, were broken out. The bacon was fried in mess-tin lids over small, and if possible smokeless, fires. If the men were lucky enough to be in a division whose commanding general permitted the issue of the dark and strong government rum, it was doled out from a jar with the traditional iron spoon, each man receiving about two tablespoonsful. Some put it into their tea, but most swallowed it straight. It was a precious thing, and serving it out was almost like a religious ceremonial, as David Jones recalls in *In Parenthesis*, where a corporal is performing the rite:

O have a care—don't spill the precious
O don't jog his hand—ministering; do take
care.
O please—give the poor bugger elbow room.

Larger quantities might be issued to stimulate troops for an assault, and one soldier remembers what the air smelled like during a British attack: "Pervading the air was the smell of rum and blood." In 1922 one medical officer deposed before a

parliamentary committee investigating the phenomenon of "shell shock": "Had it not been for the rum ration I do not think we should have won the war."

During the day the men cleaned weapons and repaired those parts of the trench damaged during the night. Or they wrote letters, deloused themselves, or slept. The officers inspected, encouraged, and strolled about looking **nonchalant**[11] to inspirit the men. They censored the men's letters and dealt with the quantities of official inquiries brought them daily by runner. How many pipe-fitters had they in their company? Reply immediately. How many hairdressers, chiropodists,[12] bicycle repairmen? Daily "returns" of the amount of ammunition and the quantity of trench stores had to be made. Reports of the nightly casualties had to be sent back. And letters of condolence, which as the war went on became form-letters of condolence, had to be written to the relatives of the killed and wounded. Men went to and fro on sentry duty or working parties, but no one showed himself above the trench. After evening stand-to, the real work began.

Most of it was above ground. Wiring parties repaired the wire in front of the position. Digging parties extended saps[13] toward the enemy. Carrying parties brought up not just rations and mail but the heavy engineering materials needed for the constant repair and improvement of

---

[11] **nonchalant**—relaxed, unexcited.

[12] chiropodists—foot doctors.

[13] saps—trenches extending toward a fortified position.

the trenches: timbers, A-frames, duckboards, stakes and wire, corrugated iron, sandbags, tarpaulins,[14] pumping equipment. Bombs and ammunition and flares were carried forward. All this ant-work was illuminated brightly from time to time by German flares and interrupted very frequently by machine gun or artillery fire. Meanwhile night patrols and raiding parties were busy in No Man's Land.[15] As morning approached, there was a nervous bustle to get the jobs done in time, to finish fitting the timbers, filling the sandbags, pounding in the stakes, and then returning mauls and picks and shovels to the Quartermaster Sergeant. By the time of stand-to, nothing human was visible above ground anywhere, but every day each side scrutinized the look of the other's line for significant changes wrought by night.

> *The men were not the only live things in the line.*

Flanders and Picardy have always been notorious for dampness. It is not the least of the ironies of the war for the British that their trenches should have been dug where the water-table was the highest and the annual rainfall the most copious. Their trenches were always wet and often flooded several feet deep. Thigh-boots or waders were issued as standard articles of uniform. Wilfred Owen writes his mother from the Somme at the beginning of 1917: "The waders are of course indispensable. In 2½ miles of trench which I waded yesterday there was not one inch of dry ground.

There is a mean depth of two feet of water." Pumps worked day and night but to little effect. Rumor held that the Germans not only could make it rain when they wanted it to—that is, all the time—but had contrived some shrewd technical method for conducting the water in their lines into the British positions—perhaps piping it underground. Ultimately there was no defense against the water but humor. "Water knee deep and up to the waist in places," one soldier notes in his diary. "Rumors of being relieved by the Grand Fleet." One doesn't want to dwell excessively on such discomforts, but here it will do no harm to try to imagine what, in these conditions, going to the latrine was like.

The men were not the only live things in the line. They were accompanied everywhere by their lice, which the professional delousers in rest positions behind the lines, with their steam vats for clothes and hot baths for troops, could do little to eliminate. The entry *lousy* in Eric Partridge's *Dictionary of Slang and Unconventional English* speaks volumes: "Contemptible; mean; filthy. . . . Standard English till 20th C, when, especially after the Great War, colloquial and used as a mere pejorative." *Lousy with*, meaning *full of*, was "originally military" and entered the colloquial word-hoard around 1915: "That ridge is lousy with Fritz."[16]

The famous rats also gave constant trouble. They were big and black, with

---

[14] tarpaulins—waterproof cloth sheet.

[15] No Man's Land—area between opposing trenches.

[16] Fritz—British slang for a German soldier.

wet, muddy hair. They fed largely on the flesh of cadavers[17] and on dead horses. One shot them with revolvers or coshed them to death with pick-handles. Their hunger, vigor, intelligence, and courage are recalled in numerous anecdotes. One officer notes from the Ypres Salient:[18] "We are fairly plagued with rats. They have eaten nearly everything in the mess, including the table-cloth and the operations orders! We borrowed a large cat and shut it up at night to exterminate them, and found the place empty next morning. The rats must have eaten it up, bones, fur, and all, and dragged it to their holes."

One can understand rats eating heartily there. It is harder to understand men doing so. The stench of rotten flesh was over everything, hardly repressed by the chloride of lime sprinkled on particularly offensive sites. Dead horses and dead men—and parts of both—were sometimes not buried for months and often simply became an element of parapets and trench walls. You could smell the front line miles before you could see it. Lingering pockets of gas added to the unappetizing atmosphere. Yet men ate three times a day, although what they ate reflected the usual gulf between the ideal and the actual. The propagandist George Adam announced with satisfaction that "the food of the army is based upon the conclusions of a committee, upon which sat several eminent scientists." The result, he asserted, is that the troops are "better fed than they are at home." Officially, each man got daily:

> 1¼ pounds fresh meat
>   (or 1 pound preserved meat),
> 1¼ pounds bread,
> 4 ounces bacon,
> 3 ounces cheese,
> 1¼ pound fresh vegetables
>   (or 2 ounces dried).

Together with small amounts of tea, sugar, and jam. But in the trenches there was very seldom fresh meat, not for eating, anyway; instead there was "Bully" (tinned corned-beef) or "Maconochie" (ma-con'-o-chie), a tinned meat-and-vegetable stew named after its manufacturer. If they did tend to grow tedious in the long run, both products were surprisingly good. The troops seemed to like the Maconochie best, but the Germans favored the British corned beef, seldom returning from a raid on the British lines without taking back as much as they could carry. On trench duty the British had as little fresh bread as fresh meat. "Pearl Biscuits" were the substitute. They reminded the men of dog biscuits, although, together with the Bully beef, they were popular with the French and Belgian urchins, who ran (or more often strolled) alongside the railway trains bringing troops up to the front, soliciting gifts by shouting, "Tom-mee! Bull-ee! Bee-skee!" When a company was out of the line, it fed better. It was then serviced by its company cookers—stoves on wheels—and often got something

---

[17] cadavers—dead bodies.

[18] Ypres Salient—Ypres is a town in Belgium in the region of Flanders and the scene of three major World War I battles. A salient is the area of a military defense that projects closest to the enemy.

approaching the official ration, as it might also in a particularly somnolent[19] part of the line, when hot food might come up at night in the large covered containers known as Dixies.

Clothing and equipment improved as the war went on, although at the outset there was a terrible dearth and improvisation. During the retreat from Mons, as Frank Richards testifies, "A lot of us had no caps: I was wearing a handkerchief knotted at the four corners—the only headgear I was to wear for some time." Crucial supplies had been omitted: "We had plenty of small-arm ammunition but no rifle-oil or rifle-rag to clean our rifles with. We used to cut pieces off our shirts . . . and some of us who had bought small tins of vaseline . . . for use on sore heels or chafed legs, used to grease our rifles with that." At the beginning line officers dressed very differently from the men. They wore riding boots or leather puttees;[20] melodramatically cut riding breeches; and flare-skirted tunics with Sam Browne belts. Discovering that this costume made them special targets in attacks (German gunners were instructed to fire first at the people with the thin knees), by the end they were dressing like the troops, wearing wrap puttees; straight trousers bloused below the knee; Other Ranks'

> *To be in the trenches was to experience an unreal, unforgettable enclosure and constraint, as well as a sense of being unoriented and lost.*

tunics with inconspicuous insignia,[21] no longer on the cuffs but on the shoulders; and Other Ranks' web belts and haversacks.[22] In 1914 both officers and men wore peaked caps, and it was rakish for officers to remove the grommet[23] for a "Gorblimey" effect. Steel helmets were introduced at the end of 1915, giving the troops, as Sassoon observed, "a Chinese look." Herbert Read found the helmets "the only poetic thing in the British Army, for they are primeval[24] in design and effect, like iron mushrooms." A perceptive observer could date corpses and skeletons lying on disused battlefields by their evolving dress. A month before the end of the war, Major P. H. Pilditch recalls, he

spent some time in the old No Man's Land of four years' duration. . . . it was a morbid but intensely interesting occupation tracing the various battles amongst the hundreds of skulls, bones and remains scattered thickly about. The progress of our successive attacks could be clearly seen from the types of equipment on the skeletons, soft cloth caps denoting the 1914 and early 1915 fighting, then respirators, then steel helmets marking attack in 1916. Also Australian slouch hats, used in the costly and abortive attack in 1916.

---

[19] somnolent—quiet, sleepy.

[20] puttees—leggings worn from ankle to knee.

[21] inconspicuous insignia—not easily seen badges.

[22] haversacks—bags for carrying supplies.

[23] grommet—fastener.

[24] primeval—suggesting early forms of life.

To be in the trenches was to experience an unreal, unforgettable enclosure and constraint, as well as a sense of being unoriented and lost. One saw two things only: the walls of an unlocalized, undifferentiated earth and the sky above. Fourteen years after the war J.R. Ackerley was wandering through an unfrequented part of a town in India. "The streets became narrower and narrower as I turned and turned," he writes, "until I felt I was back in the trenches, the houses upon either side being so much of the same color and substance as the rough ground between." That lost feeling is what struck Major Frank Isherwood, who writes his wife in December 1914: "The trenches are a labyrinth, I have already lost myself repeatedly. . . . you can't get out of them and walk about the country or see anything at all but two muddy walls on each side of you." What a survivor of the Salient remembers fifty years later are the walls of dirt and the ceiling of sky, and his eloquent optative[25] cry rises as if he were still imprisoned there: "To be out of this present, everpresent, eternally present misery, this stinking world of sticky, trickling earth ceilinged by a strip of threatening sky." As the only visible theater of variety, the sky becomes all-important. It was the sight of the sky, almost alone, that had the power to persuade a man that he was not already lost in a common grave.

---

[25] optative—expressing a wish or choice.

QUESTIONS TO CONSIDER

1. Based on this account, what do you think would have been the worst aspects to trench warfare?

2. What were the reasons for the differences between British and German trenches?

3. Why did the soldiers feel "an unreal, unforgettable enclosure and constraint"?

4. Do you think the experience of serving in the trenches would have strengthened an individual's view of the power of the state? Why or why not?

5. How were the limits imposed by culture reflected in the experience of the trenches?

Chapter 14

The Later Twentieth Century

The Atomic Age

Facing Absurdity

Struggles for Freedom

A World Without Borders

◀ *Running Fence* by the Bulgarian-born artist Christo (1935–) was
a curtain made of nylon panels erected in 1976 and spanning
twenty-four miles across Sonoma and Marin Counties in California.

At Ground Zero in Hiroshima

SHIZUKO YAMASAKI

On August 6, 1945, at the end of World War II, an American plane dropped an atom bomb on the Japanese city of Hiroshima. A blue-white fireball leveled most of the city, killing 60,000 people instantly; tens of thousands more died from the effects of radiation. In an account published in 1999, a survivor recalls the horrifying advent of the atomic age.

It was a very hot day. I came out of an air-raid shelter with my 2-year-old son, Atsunori, a little before 8. It was breakfast time, and we hurried back to our old wooden house. I was just about to hand him a bowl of rice when rays of a strange bluish and whitish color came in through the kitchen window, brushed my right cheek and hit Atsunori right in the eyes. I held him tight to my bosom as the house was lifted and moved by the blast.

The next moment I found myself crushed underneath the collapsed house. It was pitch dark and I couldn't move an inch with the roof, walls and rubble on my back. All I could think of was "I'm going to die here." Then something moved under my body. It was Atsunori, begging for help and crying with pain. I had to find a way out to save his life. If he died, I could not face my husband when he returned from the war. The mushroom cloud must have gone, and I saw a ray of sunlight coming through. All I could do was dig the ground with my hand and move like a snail toward the sunlight.

Covered with mud and blood, I pushed my son out, then came out of the fallen house to see a kind of Hiroshima I had never seen—a destroyed city much worse than a living hell. I saw people walking like ghosts with their skin peeled and hanging like seaweed, and there were charred bodies inside the burned trams.[1] Carrying Atsunori, whose body was slippery with blood, I rushed to the riverbank, where we spent three nights, surrounded by the injured and corpses. On the fourth day I stood up. Holding my son in my arms, I

---

[1] trams—streetcars.

managed to reach a village over the mountain where my father lived.

Soon after the blast, our hair began to fall out and Atsunori developed a serious nose-bleeding problem that continued for years to come. We stayed in Hiroshima in that hot summer to wait for the return of my husband. I wanted to make sure that he had a place to come back to. But there was no word from him even after the war was over. So I visited a former military office on Aug. 29 to ask about my husband. There I was informed that he had died of dengue fever[2] in Singapore on March 29. If only they had told us of his death, we could have been spared from the radiation and the hardship that followed.

After the blast, I made a living sewing and selling kimonos.[3] I later taught knitting and at times worked as a clerk. But the sufferings from the A-bomb never stopped. When he was in the fifth grade I noticed that something was terribly wrong with Atsunori's eyesight. He was becoming blind, and was diagnosed as having an "A-bomb" cataract.[4] Even after an operation, his eyesight remained weak. He had to attend the school for the blind and became a masseur. He and I worked hard, hoping to build a house one day.

That dream was short-lived. Atsunori began to have serious problems in the early '80s with walking and speaking. Doctors said it was due to a cerebellum[5]

disorder. His condition has been deteriorating ever since. As for myself, I have undergone about 10 operations starting in 1958. I am getting old, but I cannot die yet. How can I leave my son behind the way he is? Though almost 54 years have passed since the A-bomb was dropped over Hiroshima, I don't feel the war is over yet. The tragedy of Hiroshima hasn't ended. My son and I are living proof.

---

[2] dengue fever—an infectious fever of warm climates, usually contagious.

[3] kimonos—loose Japanese robes with wide sleeves.

[4] cataract—clouding of the lens of the eye.

[5] cerebellum—portion of the brain that controls balance and movement.

QUESTIONS TO CONSIDER

1. What effect is created by Shizuko Yamasaki's memories of Hiroshima immediately after the atomic bomb exploded?

2. In her account of the bombing of Hiroshima and its aftermath, does Yamasaki place any blame for her hardships? Explain.

3. What circumstances, if any, would justify the use of atomic weapons? Explain.

The Horses

EDWIN MUIR

The later 20th century has been haunted by the realization that with the advent of nuclear weapons humans had achieved the capacity to destroy their world. In the mid-1950s, a period of great tension between two nuclear superpowers, the United States and the Soviet Union, Scottish poet Edwin Muir (1887–1959) wrote "The Horses," in which he imagines the strange aftermath of a "seven days war that put the world to sleep."

Barely a twelvemonth after
The seven days war that put the world to sleep,
Late in the evening the strange horses came.
By then we had made our **covenant**[1] with silence,
But in the first few days it was so still
We listened to our breathing and were afraid.
On the second day
The radios failed; we turned the knobs; no answer.
On the third day a warship passed us, heading north,
Dead bodies piled on the deck. On the sixth day
A plane plunged over us into the sea. Thereafter
Nothing. The radios dumb;
And still they stand in corners of our kitchens,
And stand, perhaps, turned on, in a million rooms
All over the world. But now if they should speak,
If on a sudden they should speak again,
If on the stroke of noon a voice should speak,

---

[1] **covenant**—agreement.

We would not listen, we would not let it bring
That old bad world that swallowed its children quick
At one great gulp. We would not have it again.
Sometimes we think of the nations lying asleep,
Curled blindly in impenetrable sorrow,
And then the thought confounds us with its strangeness.
The tractors lie about our fields; at evening
They look like **dank**[2] sea-monsters couched and waiting.
We leave them where they are and let them rust:
"They'll **molder**[3] away and be like other **loam**."[4]
We make our oxen drag our rusty ploughs,
Long laid aside. We have gone back
Far past our fathers' land.

And then, that evening
Late in the summer the strange horses came.
We heard a distant tapping on the road,
A deepening drumming; it stopped, went on again
And at the corner changed to hollow thunder.
We saw the heads
Like a wild wave charging and were afraid.
We had sold our horses in our fathers' time
To buy new tractors. Now they were strange to us
As fabulous steeds[5] set on an ancient shield
Or illustrations in a book of knights.
We did not dare go near them. Yet they waited,
Stubborn and shy, as if they had been sent
By an old command to find our whereabouts
And that long-lost archaic[6] companionship.

---

[2] **dank**—damp and cold.
[3] **molder**—rot, decay.
[4] **loam**—dirt, earth.
[5] steeds—horses.
[6] archaic—ancient.

In the first moment we had never a thought
That they were creatures to be owned and used.
Among them were some half-a-dozen colts
Dropped in some wilderness of the broken world,
Yet new as if they had come from their own Eden.
Since then they have pulled our ploughs and borne our loads,
But that free servitude still can pierce our hearts.
Our life is changed; their coming our beginning.

QUESTIONS TO CONSIDER

1. How does the speaker evoke the horror of atomic war in the first half of "The Horses"?

2. What are the immediate effects of the war on the speaker's community?

3. How does the return of the horses affect the speaker's community?

Modern Fables

In the 20th century, the human condition often appeared baffling and even absurd. The works of many modern artists and philosophers were explorations of this seeming absurdity. Writers offered new interpretations of ancient stories as comments on the modern quest for meaning. In a passage from an essay, French writer Albert Camus (1913–1960) reflects on the Greek myth of Sisyphus, condemned to roll a huge rock up a hill in the underworld forever. In her poem "Eve to Her Daughters," Australian writer Judith Wright (1915–   ) extends the biblical story of Adam and Eve, imagining Eve explaining to her daughters what drives their father to struggle against the fate that has exiled them from paradise.

---

from *The Myth of Sisyphus*
Albert Camus

The gods had condemned Sisyphus to ceaselessly rolling a rock to the top of a mountain, whence the stone would fall back of its own weight. They had thought with some reason that there is no more dreadful punishment than futile and hopeless labor.

If one believes Homer,[1] Sisyphus was the wisest and most prudent of mortals. According to another tradition, however, he was disposed to practice the profession of **highwayman**.[2] I see no contradiction in this. Opinions differ as to the reasons why he became the futile laborer of the underworld. To begin with, he is accused of a certain **levity**[3] in regard to the gods. He stole their secrets. Aegina, the daughter of Aesopus, was carried off by Jupiter.[4] The father was shocked by that disappearance and complained to Sisyphus. He, who knew of the abduction, offered to tell about it on condition that Aesopus would give water to the citadel of Corinth. To the celestial thunderbolts he preferred the benediction of water. He was punished for this in the underworld. Homer tells us also that Sisyphus had put Death in chains. Pluto[5] could not endure the sight of his deserted, silent empire. He dispatched the

---

[1] Homer—Greek epic poet (page 206).

[2] **highwayman**—robber.

[3] **levity**—humor, irreverance.

[4] Aesopus . . . Jupiter—Aesopus was a river god; Jupiter, the sky god, used a thunderbolt as a weapon. (Camus uses the Roman names for the classical gods.)

[5] Pluto—god of the underworld and ruler of the dead.

god of war, who liberated Death from the hands of her conqueror.

It is said also that Sisyphus, being near to death, rashly wanted to test his wife's love. He ordered her to cast his unburied body into the middle of the public square. Sisyphus woke up in the underworld. And there, annoyed by an obedience so contrary to human love, he obtained from Pluto permission to return to earth in order to chastise his wife. But when he had seen again the face of this world, enjoyed water and sun, warm stones and the sea, he no longer wanted to go back to the infernal darkness. Recalls, signs of anger, warnings were of no avail. Many years more he lived facing the curve of the gulf, the sparkling sea, and the smiles of earth. A decree of the gods was necessary. Mercury[6] came and seized the impudent man by the collar and, snatching him from his joys, led him forcibly back to the underworld, where his rock was ready for him.

You have already grasped that Sisyphus is the absurd hero. He *is*, as much through his passions as through his torture. His scorn of the gods, his hatred of death, and his passion for life won him that unspeakable penalty in which the whole being is exerted toward accomplishing nothing. This is the price that must be paid for the passions of this earth. Nothing is told us about Sisyphus in the underworld. Myths are made for the imagination to breathe life into them. As for this myth, one sees merely the whole effort of a body straining to raise the huge stone, to roll it

and push it up a slope a hundred times over; one sees the face screwed up, the cheek tight against the stone, the shoulder bracing the clay-covered mass, the foot wedging it, the fresh start with arms outstretched, the wholly human security of two earth-clotted hands. At the very end of his long effort measured by skyless space and time without depth, the purpose is achieved. Then Sisyphus watches the stone rush down in a few moments toward that lower world whence he will have to push it up again toward the summit. He goes back down to the plain.

It is during that return, that pause, that Sisyphus interests me. A face that toils so close to stones is already stone itself! I see that man going back down with a heavy yet measured step toward the torment of which he will never know the end. That hour like a breathing-space which returns as surely as his suffering, that is the hour of consciousness. At each of those moments when he leaves the heights and gradually sinks toward the **lairs**[7] of the gods, he is superior to his fate. He is stronger than his rock.

If this myth is tragic, that is because its hero is conscious. Where would his torture be, indeed, if at every step the hope of succeeding upheld him? The workman of today works every day in his life at the same tasks, and this fate is no less absurd. But it is tragic only at the rare moments

---

[6] Mercury—messenger of the gods.

[7] **lairs**—retreats.

when it becomes conscious. Sisyphus, **proletarian**[8] of the gods, powerless and rebellious, knows the whole extent of his wretched condition: it is what he thinks of during his descent. The lucidity that was to constitute his torture at the same time crowns his victory. There is no fate that cannot be surmounted by scorn.

If the descent is thus sometimes performed in sorrow it can also take place in joy. This word is not too much. Again I fancy Sisyphus returning toward his rock, and the sorrow was in the beginning. When the images of earth cling too tightly to memory, when the call of happiness becomes too **insistent**,[9] it happens that melancholy rises in man's heart: this is the rock's victory, this is the rock itself. The boundless grief is too heavy to bear. These are our nights of Gethsemane.[10] But crushing truths perish from being acknowledged. Thus, Oedipus[11] at the outset obeys fate without knowing it. But from the moment he knows, his tragedy begins. Yet at the same moment, blind and desperate, he realizes that the only bond linking him to the world is the cool hand of a girl. Then a tremendous remark rings out: "Despite so many ordeals, my advanced age and the nobility of my soul make me conclude that all is well." Sophocles' Oedipus, like Dostoevsky's Kirilov,[12] thus gives the recipe for the absurd victory. Ancient wisdom confirms modern heroism.

One does not discover the absurd without being tempted to write a manual of happiness. "What! by such narrow ways—?" There is but one world, however.

Happiness and the absurd are two sons of the same earth. They are inseparable. It would be a mistake to say that happiness necessarily springs from the absurd discovery. It happens as well that the feeling of the absurd springs from happiness. "I conclude that all is well," says Oedipus, and that remark is sacred. It echoes in the wild and limited universe of man. It teaches that all is not, has not been, exhausted. It drives out of this world a god who had come into it with dissatisfaction and a preference for futile sufferings. It makes of fate a human matter, which must be settled among men.

All Sisyphus' silent joy is contained therein. His fate belongs to him. His rock is his thing. Likewise, the absurd man, when he contemplates his torment, silences all the idols. In the universe suddenly restored to its silence, the myriad wondering little voices of the earth rise up. Unconscious, secret calls, invitations from all the faces they are the necessary reverse and price of victory. There is no sun without shadow, and it is essential to know the night. The absurd man says yes and his effort will henceforth be unceasing. If there is a personal fate, there is no higher destiny, or at

---

[8] **proletarian**—worker, common laborer.

[9] **insistent**—emphatic.

[10] Gethsemane—garden near Jerusalem where Jesus suffered spiritual agony on the evening before he was crucified.

[11] Oedipus—In Greek myth, Oedipus, abandoned at birth, discovers too late that he has killed his father and married his mother.

[12] Sophocles' Oedipus . . . Kirilov—The Greek dramatist Sophocles (495?–406? B.C.) wrote a trilogy about Oedipus. Kirilov is a character in the novel *The Possessed* by Russian writer Fyodor Dostoevsky (1821–1881).

least there is but one which he concludes is inevitable and despicable. For the rest, he knows himself to be the master of his days. At that subtle moment when man glances backward over his life, Sisyphus returning toward his rock, in that slight pivoting he contemplates that series of unrelated actions which becomes his fate, created by him, combined under his memory's eye and soon sealed by his death. Thus, convinced of the wholly human origin of all that is human, a blind man eager to see who knows that the night has no end, he is still on the go. The rock is still rolling.

I leave Sisyphus at the foot of the mountain! One always finds one's burden again. But Sisyphus teaches the higher fidelity that **negates**[13] the gods and raises rocks. He too concludes that all is well. This universe henceforth without a master seems to him neither sterile nor futile. Each atom of that stone, each mineral flake of that nightfilled mountain, in itself forms a world. The struggle itself toward the heights is enough to fill a man's heart. One must imagine Sisyphus happy.

---

[13] **negates**—makes ineffective.

Eve to Her Daughters

JUDITH WRIGHT

It was not I who began it.
Turned out into draughty[14] caves,
hungry so often, having to work for our bread,
hearing the children whining,
I was nevertheless not unhappy.
Where Adam went I was fairly contented to go.
I adapted myself to the punishment: it was my life.

But Adam, you know . . . !
He kept on brooding over the insult,
over the trick They had played on us, over the scolding.
He had discovered a flaw in himself
and he had to make up for it.
Outside Eden the earth was imperfect,
the seasons changed, the game was fleet-footed,
he had to work for our living, and he didn't like it.
He even complained of my cooking
(it was hard to compete with Heaven).

So, he set to work.
The earth must be made a new Eden
with central heating, domesticated animals,
mechanical harvesters, combustion engines,
escalators, refrigerators,
and modern means of communication
and multiplied opportunities for safe investment
and higher education for Abel and Cain[15]
and the rest of the family.
You can see how his pride has been hurt.

In the process he had to unravel everything,
because he believed that mechanism
was the whole secret—he was always mechanical-minded.
He got to the very inside of the whole machine
exclaiming as he went, So this is how it works!
And now that I know how it works, why,

---

[14] draughty—windy.

[15] Abel and Cain—sons of Adam and Eve.

I must have invented it.
As for God and the Other, they cannot be demonstrated,
and what cannot be demonstrated
doesn't exist.
You see, he had always been jealous.

Yes, he got to the center
where nothing at all can be demonstrated.
And clearly he doesn't exist; but he refuses
to accept the conclusion.
You see, he was always an egotist.

It was warmer than this in the cave;
there was none of this fallout.
I would suggest, for the sake of the children,
that it's time you took over.

But you are my daughters, you inherit my own faults of character;
you are submissive, following Adam
even beyond existence.
Faults of character have their own logic
and it always works out.
I observed this with Abel and Cain.

Perhaps the whole elaborate fable
right from the beginning
is meant to demonstrate this; perhaps it's the whole secret.
Perhaps nothing exists but our faults?

But it's useless to make
such a suggestion to Adam.
He has turned himself into God,
who is faultless and doesn't exist.

QUESTIONS TO CONSIDER

1. Why do you think Albert Camus saw in Sisyphus an image of the human condition?

2. In what sense does Camus see Sisyphus as victorious?

3. Do you agree with Camus that, "One must imagine Sisyphus happy"? Why or why not?

4. In Judith Wright's poem, why might Adam's curiosity be a symbol for modern people?

5. Into what kind of dilemma has Adam got himself?

Satires of Bureaucracy

One aspect of the modern life that seems to offer particularly strong examples of absurdity is the bureaucratic world. Governments are often pictured as run by soulless officials enforcing foolish regulations in a dehumanized society. These short stories, "The Elephant" by Polish writer Slawomir Mrozek (1930–) and "The Censors" by Argentine writer Luisa Valenzuela (1938–), offer satirical views of modern bureaucratic absurdity.

The Elephant

Slawomir Mrozek

The director of the Zoological Gardens has shown himself to be an **upstart**.[1] He regarded his animals simply as stepping stones on the road of his own career. He was indifferent to the educational importance of his establishment. In his Zoo the giraffe had a short neck, the badger had no burrow and the whistlers,[2] having lost all interest, whistled rarely and with some reluctance. These shortcomings should not have been allowed, especially as the Zoo was often visited by parties of school-children.

The Zoo was in a provincial town, and it was short of some of the most important animals, among them the elephant. Three thousand rabbits were a poor substitute for the noble giant. However, as our country developed, the gaps were being filled in a well-planned manner. On the occasion of the anniversary of the liberation, on 22nd July, the Zoo was notified that it had at long last been **allocated**[3] an elephant. All the staff, who were devoted to their work, rejoiced at this news. All the greater was their surprise when they learnt that the director had sent a letter to Warsaw, renouncing the allocation and putting forward a plan for obtaining an elephant by more economic means.

"I, and all the staff," he had written, "are fully aware how heavy a burden falls upon the shoulders of Polish miners and foundry[4] men because of the elephant.

---

[1] **upstart**—a person who has risen rapidly; with an implication of excessive pride and lack of merit.

[2] whistlers—groundhogs or woodchucks.

[3] **allocated**—assigned.

[4] foundry—workplace where metal is cast.

Desirous of reducing our costs, I suggest that the elephant mentioned in your communication should be replaced by one of our own procurement.[5] We can make an elephant out of rubber, of the correct size, fill it with air and place it behind railings. It will be carefully painted the correct color and even on close inspection will be indistinguishable from the real animal. It is well known that the elephant is a sluggish animal and it does not run and jump about. In the notice on the railings we can state that this particular elephant is exceptionally sluggish. The money saved in this way can be turned to the purchase of a jet plane or the conservation of some church monument.

"Kindly note that both the idea and its execution are my modest contribution to the common task and struggle.

"I am, etc."

This communication must have reached a soulless official, who regarded his duties in a purely bureaucratic manner and did not examine the heart of the matter but, following only the directive about reduction of expenditure, accepted the director's plan. On hearing the Ministry's approval, the director issued instructions for the making of the rubber elephant.

The carcase[6] was to have been filled with air by two keepers blowing into it from opposite ends. To keep the operation secret the work was to be completed during the night because the people of the town, having heard that an elephant was joining the Zoo, were anxious to see it. The director insisted on haste also because he expected a bonus, should his idea turn out to be a success.

The two keepers locked themselves in a shed normally housing a workshop, and began to blow. After two hours of hard blowing they discovered that the rubber skin had risen only a few inches above the floor and its bulge in no way resembled an elephant. The night progressed. Outside, human voices were stilled and only the cry of the jackass interrupted the silence. Exhausted, the keepers stopped blowing and made sure that the air already inside the elephant should not escape. They were not young and were unaccustomed to this kind of work.

"If we go on at this rate," said one of them, "we shan't finish before the morning. And what am I to tell my Missus? She'll never believe me if I say that I spent the night blowing up an elephant."

"Quite right," agreed the second keeper. "Blowing up an elephant is not an everyday job. And it's all because our director is a leftist."[7]

They resumed their blowing, but after another half-an-hour they felt too tired to continue. The bulge on the floor was larger but still nothing like the shape of an elephant.

"It's getting harder all the time," said the first keeper.

"It's an uphill job, all right," agreed the second. "Let's have a little rest."

---

[5] procurement—obtaining.

[6] carcase—body; also *carcass.*

[7] leftist—When Mrozek wrote "The Elephant," Poland was run by a communist government.

While they were resting, one of them noticed a gas pipe ending in a valve. Could they not fill the elephant with gas? He suggested it to his mate.

They decided to try. They connected the elephant to the gas pipe, turned the valve, and to their joy in a few minutes there was a full-sized beast standing in the shed. It looked real: the enormous body, legs like columns, huge ears and the inevitable trunk. Driven by ambition the director had made sure of having in his Zoo a very large elephant indeed.

"First class," declared the keeper who had the idea of using gas. "Now we can go home."

In the morning the elephant was moved to a special run in a central position, next to the monkey cage. Placed in front of a large real rock it looked fierce and magnificent. A big notice proclaimed: "Particularly sluggish. Hardly moves."

Among the first visitors that morning was a party of children from the local school. The teacher in charge of them was planning to give them an object-lesson about the elephant. He halted the group in front of the animal and began:

"The elephant is a **herbivorous**[8] mammal. By means of its trunk it pulls out young trees and eats their leaves."

The children were looking at the elephant with enraptured admiration. They were waiting for it to pull out a young tree, but the beast stood still behind its railings.

". . . The elephant is a direct descendant of the now extinct mammoth. It's not sur-prising, therefore, that it's the largest living land animal."

The more conscientious pupils were making notes.

". . . Only the whale is heavier than the elephant, but then the whale lives in the sea. We can safely say that on land the elephant reigns supreme."

A slight breeze moved the branches of the trees in the Zoo.

". . . The weight of a fully grown elephant is between nine and thirteen thousand pounds."

At that moment the elephant shuddered and rose in the air. For a few seconds it swayed just above the ground but a gust of wind blew it upwards until its mighty silhouette was against the sky. For a short while people on the ground could still see the four circles of its feet, its bulging belly and the trunk, but soon, propelled by the wind, the elephant sailed above the fence and disappeared above the tree-tops. Astonished monkeys in the cage continued staring into the sky.

They found the elephant in the neighboring botanical gardens. It had landed on a cactus and punctured its rubber hide.

The schoolchildren who had witnessed the scene in the Zoo soon started neglecting their studies and turned into hooligans.[9] It is reported that they drink liquor and break windows. And they no longer believe in elephants.

---

[8] **herbivorous**—plant-eating.
[9] hooligans—hoodlums.

The Censors

Luisa Valenzuela

Poor Juan! One day they caught him with his guard down before he could even realize that what he had taken as a stroke of luck was really one of fate's dirty tricks. These things happen the minute you're careless and you let down your guard, as one often does. Juancito let happiness—a feeling you can't trust—get the better of him when he received from a confidential source Mariana's new address in Paris and he knew that she hadn't forgotten him. Without thinking twice, he sat down at his table and wrote her a letter. *The* letter that keeps his mind off his job during the day and won't let him sleep at night (what had he scrawled, what had he put on that sheet of paper he sent to Mariana?).

Juan knows there won't be a problem with the letter's contents, that it's **irreproachable**,[10] harmless. But what about the rest? He knows that they examine, sniff, feel, and read between the lines of each and every letter, and check its tiniest comma and most accidental stain. He knows that all letters pass from hand to hand and go through all sorts of tests in the huge censorship offices and that, in the end, very few continue on their way. Usually it takes months, even years, if there aren't any snags; all this time the freedom, maybe even the life, of both sender and receiver is in jeopardy. And that's why Juan's so down in the dumps; thinking that something might happen to Mariana because of his letters. Of all people, Mariana, who must finally feel safe there where she always dreamed she'd live. But he knows that the *Censor's Secret Command* operates all over the world and cashes in on the discount in air rates; there's nothing to stop them from going as far as that hidden Paris neighborhood, kidnapping Mariana, and returning to their cozy homes, certain of having fulfilled their noble mission.

Well, you've got to beat them to the punch, do what everyone tries to do: sabotage the machinery, throw sand in its gears, get to the bottom of the problem so as to stop it.

This was Juan's sound plan when he, like many others, applied for a censor's job—not because he had a calling or needed a job: no, he applied simply to intercept his own letter, a consoling but unoriginal idea. He was hired immediately, for each day more and more censors are needed and no one would bother to check on his references.

Ulterior motives couldn't be overlooked by the *Censorship Division*, but they needn't be too strict with those who applied. They knew how hard it would be for those poor guys to find the letter they wanted and even if they did, what's a letter or two when the new censor would snap up so many others? That's how Juan managed to join the *Post Office's Censorship Division*, with a certain goal in mind.

---

[10] **irreproachable**—not blameworthy.

The building had a festive air on the outside which contrasted with its inner staidness.[11] Little by little, Juan was absorbed by his job and he felt at peace since he was doing everything he could to get his letter for Mariana. He didn't even worry when, in his first month, he was sent to *Section K* where envelopes are very carefully screened for explosives.

It's true that on the third day, a fellow worker had his right hand blown off by a letter, but the division chief claimed it was sheer negligence on the victim's part. Juan and the other employees were allowed to go back to their work, albeit[12] feeling less secure. After work, one of them tried to organize a strike to demand higher wages for unhealthy work, but Juan didn't join in; after thinking it over, he reported him to his superiors and thus got promoted.

You don't form a habit by doing something once, he told himself as he left his boss's office. And when he was transferred to *Section J*, where letters are carefully checked for poison dust, he felt he had climbed a rung in the ladder.

By working hard, he quickly reached *Section E* where the work was more interesting, for he could now read and analyze the letters' contents. Here he could even hope to get hold of his letter which, judging by the time that had elapsed, had gone through the other sections and was probably floating around in this one.

Soon his work became so absorbing that his noble mission blurred in his mind.

Day after day he crossed out whole paragraphs in red ink, pitilessly chucking many letters into the censored basket. These were horrible days when he was shocked by the subtle and conniving ways employed by people to pass on **subversive**[13] messages; his instincts were so sharp that he found behind a simple "the weather's unsettled" or "prices continue to soar" the wavering hand of someone secretly scheming to overthrow the Government.

His zeal brought him swift promotion. We don't know if this made him happy. Very few letters reached him in *Section B*— only a handful passed the other hurdles— so he read them over and over again, passed them under a magnifying glass, searched for microprint with an electronic microscope, and tuned his sense of smell so that he was beat by the time he made it home. He'd barely manage to warm up his soup, eat some fruit, and fall into bed, satisfied with having done his duty. Only his darling mother worried, but she couldn't get him back on the right road. She'd say, though it wasn't always true: Lola called, she's at the bar with the girls, they miss you, they're waiting for you. Or else she'd leave a bottle of red wine on the table. But Juan wouldn't overdo it: any distraction could make him lose his edge and the perfect censor had to be alert, keen, attentive, and sharp to nab cheats. He had a truly patriotic task, both self-denying and uplifting.

---

[11] staidness—sedateness.

[12] albeit—although.

[13] **subversive**—intended to overthrow authority.

His basket for censored letters became the best fed as well as the most cunning basket in the whole *Censorship Division*. He was about to congratulate himself for having finally discovered his true mission, when his letter to Mariana reached his hands. Naturally, he censored it without regret. And just as naturally, he couldn't stop them from executing him the following morning, another victim of his devotion to his work.

QUESTIONS TO CONSIDER

1. What is Slawomir Mrozek satirizing in "The Elephant"?

2. What is absurd about Juan's actions in "The Censors"?

3. In your opinion, is satirical humor an effective weapon against bureaucratic oppression?

4. What are some current censorship issues that could profit from satire?

Reflections on Nonviolence

The history of the 20th century is a tragic catalogue of the use of force, including two world wars, dozens of regional wars, campaigns of genocide, and widespread political repression. In opposition to this brutality has been the courageous advocacy of nonviolence by such political leaders as Mohandas Gandhi (1869–1948) of India and Bernadette Devlin (1947–   ) of Northern Ireland. As a Hindu nationalist leader, Gandhi's campaign of passive resistance to British rule in India forced the British to grant independence in 1947. In Hind Swaraj *("Indian Home Rule"), Gandhi presents in dialogue form the main features of his doctrine of passive resistance. Devlin was one of the leaders of the "long march" from Northern Ireland's capital, Belfast, to the city of Londonderry ("Derry") 73 miles away. In her memoir,* The Price of My Soul, *she describes the march.*

from *Hind Swaraj*
Mohandas Gandhi

Reader.

Is there any historical evidence as to the success of what you have called soul-force or truth-force? No instance seems to have happened of any nation having risen through soul-force. I still think that the evil-doers will not cease doing evil without physical punishment.

Editor.

The poet Tulsidas[1] has said: "Of religion, pity, or love, is the root, as egotism of the body. Therefore, we should not abandon pity so long as we are alive." This appears to me to be a scientific truth. I believe in it as much as I believe in two and two being

four. The force of love is the same as the force of the soul or truth. We have evidence of its working at every step. The universe would disappear without the existence of that force. But you ask for historical evidence. It is, therefore, necessary to know what history means. The Gujarati[2] equivalent means: "It so happened." If that is the meaning of history, it is possible to give **copious**[3] evidence. But, if it means the doings of kings and emperors, there can be no evidence of soul-force or passive resistance in such history. You cannot expect silver ore in a tin mine. History, as

---

[1] Tulsidas—Hindu poet (1532–1623).

[2] Gujarati—the language of Gujarat, a region of western India.

[3] **copious**—plentiful.

we know it, is a record of the wars of the world, and so there is a proverb among Englishmen that a nation which has no history, that is, no wars, is a happy nation. How kings played, how they became enemies of one another, how they murdered one another, is found accurately recorded in history, and if this were all that had happened in the world, it would have been ended long ago. If the story of the universe had commenced with wars, not a man would have been found alive today. Those people who have been warred against have disappeared as, for instance, the natives of Australia of whom hardly a man was left alive by the intruders. Mark, please, that these natives did not use soul-force in self-defense, and it does not require much foresight to know that the Australians will share the same fate as their victims. "Those that take the sword shall perish by the sword." With us the proverb is that professional swimmers will find a watery grave.

The fact that there are so many men still alive in the world shows that it is based not on the force of arms but on the force of truth or love. Therefore, the greatest and most **unimpeachable**[4] evidence of the success of this force is to be found in the fact that, in spite of the wars of the world, it still lives on.

Thousands, indeed tens of thousands, depend for their existence on a very active working of this force. Little quarrels of millions of families in their daily lives disappear before the exercise of this force.

Hundreds of nations live in peace. History does not and cannot take note of this fact. History is really a record of every interruption of the even working of the force of love or of the soul. Two brothers quarrel; one of them repents and re-awakens the love that was lying dormant in him; the two again begin to live in peace; nobody takes note of this. But if the two brothers, through the intervention of solicitors[5] or some other reason take up arms or go to law—which is another form of the exhibition of brute force,—their doings would be immediately noticed in the press, they would be the talk of their neighbors and would probably go down to history. And what is true of families and communities is true of nations. There is no reason to believe that there is one law for families and another for nations. History, then, is a record of an interruption of the course of nature. Soul-force, being natural, is not noted in history.

Reader.

According to what you say, it is plain that instances of this kind of passive resistance are not to be found in history. It is necessary to understand this passive resistance more fully. It will be better, therefore, if you enlarge upon it.

Editor.

Passive resistance is a method of securing rights by personal suffering; it is the reverse of resistance by arms. When I

---

[4] **unimpeachable**—above suspicion.
[5] solicitors—lawyers.

refuse to do a thing that is **repugnant**[6] to my conscience, I use soul-force. For instance, the Government of the day has passed a law which is applicable to me. I do not like it. If by using violence I force the Government to repeal the law, I am employing what may be termed body-force. If I do not obey the law and accept the penalty for its breach, I use soul-force. It involves sacrifice of self.

Everybody admits that sacrifice of self is infinitely superior to sacrifice of others. Moreover, if this kind of force is used in a cause that is unjust, only the person using it suffers. He does not make others suffer for his mistakes. Men have before now done many things which were subsequently found to have been wrong. No man can claim that he is absolutely in the right or that a particular thing is wrong because he thinks so, but it is wrong for him so long as that is his deliberate judgment. It is therefore meet[7] that he should not do that which he knows to be wrong, and suffer the consequence whatever it may be. This is the key to the use of soul-force.

Reader.

You would then disregard laws—this is rank disloyalty. We have always been considered a law-abiding nation. You seem to be going even beyond the extremists.[8] They say that we must obey the laws that have been passed, but that if the laws be bad, we must drive out the law-givers even by force.

Editor.

Whether I go beyond them or whether I do not is a matter of no consequence to either of us. We simply want to find out what is right and to act accordingly. The real meaning of the statement that we are a law-abiding nation is that we are passive resisters. When we do not like certain laws, we do not break the heads of law-givers but we suffer and do not submit to the laws. That we should obey laws whether good or bad is a new-fangled notion. There was no such thing in former days. The people disregarded those laws they did not like and suffered the penalties for their breach. It is contrary to our manhood if we obey laws repugnant to our conscience. Such teaching is opposed to religion and means slavery. If the Government were to ask us to go about without any clothing, should we do so? If I were a passive resister, I would say to them that I would have nothing to do with their law. But we have so forgotten ourselves and become so compliant that we do not mind any degrading law.

A man who has realized his manhood, who fears only God, will fear no one else. Man-made laws are not necessarily binding on him. Even the Government does not expect any such thing from us. They do not say: "You must do such and such a thing," but they say: "If you do not do it, we will punish you." We are sunk so low that we fancy that it is our duty and our religion to do what the law lays down. If man will

---

[6] **repugnant**—offensive, objectionable.

[7] meet—appropriate.

[8] extremists—radicals.

only realize that it is unmanly to obey laws that are unjust, no man's tyranny will enslave him. This is the key to self-rule or home-rule.

It is a superstition and ungodly thing to believe that an act of a majority binds a minority. Many examples can be given in which acts of majorities will be found to have been wrong and those of minorities to have been right. All reforms owe their origin to the initiation of minorities in opposition to majorities. If among a band of robbers a knowledge of robbing is obligatory, is a pious man to accept the obligation? So long as the superstition that men should obey unjust laws exists, so long will their slavery exist. And a passive resister alone can remove such a superstition.

To use brute-force, to use gunpowder, is contrary to passive resistance, for it means that we want our opponent to do by force that which we desire but he does not. And if such a use of force is justifiable, surely he is entitled to do likewise by us. And so we should never come to an agreement. We may simply fancy, like the blind horse moving in a circle round a mill, that we are making progress. Those who believe that they are not bound to obey laws which are repugnant to their conscience have only the remedy of passive resistance open to them. Any other must lead to disaster.

Reader.

From what you say I deduce that passive resistance is a splendid weapon of the weak, but that when they are strong they may take up arms.

Editor.

This is gross ignorance. Passive resistance, that is, soul-force, is matchless. It is superior to the force of arms. How, then, can it be considered only a weapon of the weak? Physical-force men are strangers to the courage that is **requisite**[9] in a passive resister. Do you believe that a coward can ever disobey a law that he dislikes? Extremists are considered to be advocates of brute force. Why do they, then, talk about obeying laws? I do not blame them. They can say nothing else. When they succeed in driving out the English and they themselves become governors, they will want you and me to obey their laws. And that is a fitting thing for their constitution. But a passive resister will say he will not obey a law that is against his conscience, even though he may be blown to pieces at the mouth of a cannon.

What do you think? Wherein is courage required—in blowing others to pieces from behind a cannon, or with a smiling face to approach a cannon and be blown to pieces? Who is the true warrior—he who keeps death always as a bosom-friend, or he who controls the death of others? Believe me that a man devoid of courage and manhood can never be a passive resister.

This however, I will admit: that even a man weak in body is capable of offering this resistance. One man can offer it just as well as millions. Both men and women can indulge in it. It does not require the training of an army; it needs no jiu-jitsu.[10]

---

[9] **requisite**—necessary.

[10] jiu-jitsu—Japanese system of self-defense in which an opponent's strength is used against him.

Control over the mind is alone necessary, and when that is attained, man is free like the king of the forest and his very glance withers the enemy.

Passive resistance is an all-sided sword, it can be used anyhow; it blesses him who uses it and him against whom it is used. Without drawing a drop of blood it produces far-reaching results. It never rusts and cannot be stolen. Competition between passive resisters does not exhaust. The sword of passive resistance does not require a scabbard. It is strange indeed that you should consider such a weapon to be a weapon merely of the weak.

Reader.

You have said that passive resistance is a speciality of India. Have cannons never been used in India?

Editor.

Evidently, in your opinion, India means its few princes. To me it means its teeming millions on whom depends the existence of its princes and our own.

Kings will always use their kingly weapons. To use force is bred in them. They want to command, but those who have to obey commands do not want guns: and these are in a majority throughout the world. They have to learn either body-force or soul-force. Where they learn the former, both the rulers and the ruled become like so many madmen; but where they learn soul-force, the commands of the rulers do not go beyond the point of their

swords, for true men disregard unjust commands. Peasants have never been subdued by the sword, and never will be. They do not know the use of the sword, and they are not frightened by the use of it by others. That nation is great which rests its head upon death as its pillow. Those who defy death are free from all fear. For those who are laboring under the delusive charms of brute-force, this picture is not overdrawn. The fact is that, in India, the nation at large has generally used passive resistance in all departments of life. We cease to co-operate with our rulers when they displease us. This is passive resistance.

I remember an instance when, in a small principality, the villagers were offended by some command issued by the prince. The former immediately began vacating the village. The prince became nervous, apologized to his subjects and withdrew his command. Many such instances can be found in India. Real Home Rule is possible only where passive resistance is the guiding force of the people. Any other rule is foreign rule.

Reader.

Then you will say that it is not at all necessary for us to train the body?

Editor.

I will certainly not say any such thing. It is difficult to become a passive resister unless the body is trained. As a rule, the mind, residing in a body that has become weakened by pampering, is also weak, and where there is no strength of mind there can be no strength of soul. We shall have to improve our physique by getting rid of infant marriages and luxurious living. If I were to ask a man with a shattered body to face a cannon's mouth I should make a laughing-stock of myself.

Reader.

From what you say, then, it would appear that it is not a small thing to become a passive resister, and, if that is so, I should like you to explain how a man may become one.

Editor.

To become a passive resister is easy enough but it is also equally difficult. I have known a lad of fourteen years become a passive resister; I have known also sick people do likewise; and I have also known physically strong and otherwise happy people unable to take up passive resistance. After a great deal of experience it seems to me that those who want to become passive resisters for the service of the country have to observe perfect chastity, adopt poverty, follow truth, and cultivate fearlessness.

Chastity is one of the greatest disciplines without which the mind cannot attain requisite firmness. A man who is unchaste loses stamina, becomes emasculated and cowardly. He whose mind is given over to animal passions is not capable of any great effort. This can be proved by innumerable instances. What, then, is a married person to do is the question that arises naturally; and yet it need

not. When a husband and wife gratify the passions, it is no less an animal indulgence on that account. Such an indulgence, except for perpetuating the race, is strictly prohibited. But a passive resister has to avoid even that very limited indulgence because he can have no desire for progeny.[11] A married man, therefore, can observe perfect chastity. This subject is not capable of being treated at greater length. Several questions arise: How is one to carry one's wife with one, what are her rights, and other similar questions. Yet those who wish to take part in a great work are bound to solve these puzzles.

Just as there is necessity for chastity, so is there for poverty. **Pecuniary**[12] ambition and passive resistance cannot well go together. Those who have money are not expected to throw it away, but they *are* expected to be indifferent about it. They must be prepared to lose every penny rather than give up passive resistance.

Passive resistance has been described in the course of our discussion as truth-force. Truth, therefore, has necessarily to be followed and that at any cost. In this connection, academic questions such as whether a man may not lie in order to save a life, etc., arise, but these questions occur only to those who wish to justify lying. Those who want to follow truth every time are not placed in such a **quandary;**[13] and if they are, they are still saved from a false position.

---

[11] progeny—children.

[12] **pecuniary**—relating to money.

[13] **quandary**—puzzling situation, dilemma..

Passive resistance cannot proceed a step without fearlessness. Those alone can follow the path of passive resistance who are free from fear, whether as to their possessions, false honor, their relatives, the government, bodily injuries or death.

These observances are not to be abandoned in the belief that they are difficult. Nature has implanted in the human breast ability to cope with any difficulty or suffering that may come to man unprovoked. These qualities are worth having, even for those who do not wish to serve the country. Let there be no mistake, as those who want to train themselves in the use of arms are also obliged to have these qualities more or less. Everybody does not become a warrior for the wish. A would-be warrior will have to observe chastity and to be satisfied with poverty as his lot. A warrior without fearlessness cannot be conceived of. It may be thought that he would not need to be exactly truthful, but that quality follows real fearlessness. When a man abandons truth, he does so owing to fear in some shape or form. The above four attributes, then, need not frighten anyone. It may be as well here to note that a physical-force man has to have many other useless qualities which a passive resister never needs. And you will find that whatever extra effort a swordsman needs is due to lack of fearlessness. If he is an embodiment of the latter, the sword will drop from his hand that very moment. He does not need its support. One who is free from hatred requires no sword. A man with a stick suddenly came face to face with a lion and instinctively raised his weapon in self-

defense. The man saw that he had only prated[14] about fearlessness when there was none in him. That moment he dropped the stick and found himself free from all fear.

from *The Price of My Soul*
Bernadette Devlin

And then we came to Burntollet Bridge, and from lanes at each side of the road a curtain of bricks and boulders and bottles brought the march to a halt. From the lanes burst hordes of screaming people wielding planks of wood, bottles, laths, iron bars, crowbars, cudgels studded with nails, and they waded into the march. . . .

I was a very clever girl: cowardice makes you clever. Before this onslaught, our heads-down, arms-linked tactics were no use whatever, and people began to panic and run. Immediately my mind went back to Derry on October 5[15] and I remembered the uselessness of running. As I stood there I could see a great big lump of flatwood, like a plank out of an orange-box, getting nearer and nearer my face, and there were two great nails sticking out of it. By a quickreflex action, my hand reached my face before the wood did, and immediately two nails went into the back of my hand. Just after that I was struck on the back of the knees with this bit of wood which had failed to get me in the face, and fell to the ground. And then my brain began to tick. "Now, Bernadette," I said, "what is the best thing to do? If you leave your arms

---

[14] prated—babbled.

[15] October 5—an earlier march.

and legs out, they'll be broken. You can have your skull cracked, or your face destroyed." So I rolled up in a ball on the road, tucked my knees in, tucked my elbows in, and covered my face with one hand and the crown of my head with the other. Through my fingers, I could see legs standing round me: about six people were busily involved in trying to beat me into the ground, and I could feel dull thuds landing on my back and head. Finally these men muttered something **incoherent**[16] about leaving that one, and tore off across the fields after somebody else.

When everything was quiet, and five seconds had gone by without my feeling anything, I decided it was time to take my head up. I had a wee peer round, ducked again as a passing Paisleyite[17] threw a swipe[18] at me, and then got up. What had been a march was a shambles. . . .

As we approached Derry, we were met by the Radical Students' Alliance who had come out to meet us. They stood to attention, singing the "Internationale"[19] with us, as we went past, then fell in to form the end of the march. They were the only people who did this: other supporters joining us forced their way into our ranks, but the Radical Students paid this homage to those of us who had come all the way from Belfast. The police had promised us more trouble before we reached the city center, and as we drew level with the first houses, Eamonn McCann[20] got up on a chair to call through a megaphone: "Remember we have marched seventy-three miles. Please don't let violence mar the end of the march.

If you're attacked, just keep marching." The march went by, Eamonn was left there all on his own, and a wee Paisleyite ran out and thumped him; so Eamonn, of course, took to his heels and ran and found the rest of the march again. We came abreast of Altnagelvin Hospital, and all our people who could hobble out, hobbled into the front rows with their bandages, and so, two thousand strong, we rounded the corner and came down the hill to the walled city of Derry.

A bonfire was waiting for us in Irish Street, to burn such of our banners as had survived Burntollet Bridge. Again the march was met by a rain of stones, bricks, bottles, burning sticks from the bonfire, and petrol bombs. Fortunately the Paisleyites were very bad at making petrol bombs—most of the ones they threw simply didn't materialize. I could feel stones bouncing off my head, leaving me apparently undamaged, and I saw four hit Michael Farrell before he fell: he carries his blood-stained coat around with him to this day for the prestige of it. Farther down the road a squad of Paisleyites had got into a quarry behind the houses and were lobbing stones over the roofs. The police advised us to wait until the enemy ran out

---

[16] **incoherent**—unclear.

[17] Paisleyite—member of an extreme Protestant group led by the Rev. Ian Paisley.

[18] swipe—punch.

[19] "Internationale"—a French revolutionary workers' song composed in 1871.

[20] Eamonn McCann—another civil-rights leader.

of ammunition, and this looked like being a long wait, for they had ammunition there for the next ten years. The marchers stood in against the houses to avoid the stones, which were coming flying over into the middle of the street, and overshooting to break windows in the houses opposite. Every time there was a lull, a few more marchers sprinted to safety, and bit by bit we all got past.

That was the last danger: now we were in Derry, and the people lined the streets and cheered. They'd put up a platform in Guildhall Square, and they wanted all of us on it at once: every time a few more were dragged up one side, several fell off at the other side. But the people wanted to hear something from all of us. That was when I called Derry "the capital city of injustice"—grand phrase: it flashed all over Ireland. It was impossible to describe the atmosphere, but it must have been

like that on V-Day:[21] the war was over and we had won; we hadn't lifted a finger, but we'd won.

---

[21] V-Day—end of World War II.

QUESTIONS TO CONSIDER

1. What does Gandhi take as proof that the world is based on the force of truth or love?

2. Gandhi observes, "It is a superstition and ungodly thing to believe that an act of a majority binds a minority." Do you agree? Why or why not?

3. How would you describe the tone of Bernadette Devlin's account of her participation in passive resistance?

4. What made the marchers to Derry effective passive resisters?

5. In what types of situations do you think that passive resistance would work most effectively? In what situations might it not work?

Programs for Change

Political repression was widespread in the 20th century. In South Africa after World War II, an official policy of racial segregation known as apartheid was established, involving severe political, legal, and economic discrimination against nonwhites. In 1955 a black civil rights organization, the African National Congress, joined with three other groups to adopt a manifesto known as the "Freedom Charter" that outlined a program of change. After a long struggle the apartheid laws were repealed by the South African Parliament in 1991. In 1988 widespread protests began in Burma (now Myanmar) against repressive military rule. Aung San Suu Kyi (1945–   ), the leader of the pro-democracy movement, was held under house arrest in Burma from 1989 to 1995. Her essay "Freedom from Fear" was published in 1991.

Freedom Charter
African National Congress

We, the people of South Africa, declare for all our country and the world to know:

—that South Africa belongs to all who live in it, black and white, and that no government can justly claim authority unless it is based on the will of the people;

—that our people have been robbed of their birthright to land, liberty and peace by a form of government founded on injustice and inequality;

—that our country will never be prosperous and free until all our people live in brotherhood, enjoying equal rights and opportunities;

—that only a democratic state, based on the will of all the people, can secure to all their birthright without distinction of color, race, sex, or belief;

And therefore, we the people of South Africa, black and white together—equal countrymen and brothers—adopt this Freedom Charter. And we pledge ourselves to strive together, sparing neither strength nor courage, until the democratic changes set out here have been won.

The people shall govern!

Every man and woman shall have the right to vote and to stand as a candidate for all bodies which make laws;

All people shall be entitled to take part in the administration of the country;

The rights of the people shall be the same, regardless of race, color, or sex;

All bodies of minority rule, advisory boards, councils and authorities shall be replaced by democratic organs of self-government.

All national groups shall have equal rights!

There shall be equal status in the bodies of state, in the courts and in the schools for all national groups and races;

All people shall have equal rights to use their own languages and to develop their own folk culture and customs;

All national groups shall be protected by law against insults to their race and national pride.

The preaching and practice of national, race or color discrimination and contempt shall be a punishable crime;

The people shall share in the country's wealth!

All apartheid laws and practices shall be set aside.

The people shall share in the country's wealth!

The national wealth of our country, the heritage of all South Africans, shall be restored to the people.

The mineral wealth beneath the soil, the banks and monopoly industry shall be

transferred to the ownership of the people as a whole.

All other industry and trade shall be controlled to assist the well-being of the people;

All people shall have equal rights to trade where they choose, to manufacture and to enter all trades, crafts and professions.

The land shall be shared among those who work it!

Restrictions of land ownership on a racial basis shall be ended, and all the land redivided amongst those who work it, to banish famine and land hunger;

The state shall help the peasants with implements, seeds, tractors and dams to save the soil and assist the tillers.[1]

Freedom of movement shall be guaranteed to all who work on the land;

All shall have the right to occupy land wherever they choose.

People shall not be robbed of their cattle, and forced labor and farm prisons shall be abolished.

All shall be equal before the law!

No one shall be imprisoned, deported or restricted without a fair trial;

No one shall be condemned by the order of any government official;

The courts shall be representative of all the people;

---

[1] tillers—farmers.

Imprisonment shall be only for serious crimes against the people; and shall aim at re-education, not vengeance;

The police force and army shall be open to all on an equal basis and shall be the helpers and protectors of the people;

All laws which discriminate on grounds of race, color or belief shall be repealed.

All shall enjoy human rights!

The law shall guarantee to all their rights to organize, to meet together, to punish, to preach, to worship and to educate their children;

The privacy of the house from police raids shall be protected by law;

All shall be free to travel without restriction from countryside to town, from province to province and from South Africa abroad;

Pass Laws,[2] permits, and all other laws restricting these freedoms, shall be abolished.

There shall be work and security!

All who work shall be free to form unions, to elect their officers and to make wage agreements with their employers;

The state shall recognize the right and duty of all to work, and to draw full unemployment benefits;

Men and women of all races shall receive equal pay for equal work;

There shall be a forty-hour working week, a national minimum wage, paid annual leave, and sick leave for all workers, and maternity leave on full pay for all working mothers;

Miners, domestic workers, farm workers, and all civil servants shall have the same rights as all others who work;

Child labor, compound labor, the tot system[3] and contract labor shall be abolished.

The doors of learning and of culture shall be opened!

The government shall discover, develop and encourage national talent for the enhancement of our cultural life;

All the cultural treasures of mankind shall be open to all, by free exchange of books, ideas and contact with other lands;

The aim of education shall be to teach the youth to love their people and their culture, to honor human brotherhood, liberty and peace;

Education shall be free, compulsory, universal and equal for all children;

Higher education and technical training shall be opened to all by means of state allowances and scholarships awarded on the basis of merit;

Adult illiteracy shall be ended by a mass state education plan;

Teachers shall have all the rights of other citizens;

The color bar in cultural life, in sport and in education shall be abolished.

---

[2] Pass Laws—Under apartheid, black people were required to carry an identification card, or "pass," and produce it on demand, or be subject to arrest.

[3] tot system—Under apartheid law, whites used "tots," small portions of liquor, to pay black workers, who were themselves forbidden to make or get liquor.

There shall be houses, security, and comfort!

All people shall have the rights to live where they choose, to be decently housed, and to bring up their families in comfort and security;

Unused housing space shall be made available to the people;

Rent and prices shall be lowered, food plentiful and no one shall go hungry;

A preventative health scheme shall be run by the state;

Free medical care and hospitalization shall be provided for all, with special care for mothers and young children;

Slums shall be demolished, and new suburbs built where all have transport, roads, lighting, playing fields, crèches[4] and social centers;

The aged, the orphans, the disabled and the sick shall be cared for by the state;

Rest, leisure and recreation shall be the right of all;

Fenced locations[5] and ghettoes shall be abolished, and laws which break up families shall be repealed;

South Africa shall be a fully independent state, which represents the rights and sovereignty of nations.

There shall be peace and friendship!

South Africa shall strive to maintain world peace and the settlement of all international disputes by negotiation—not war;

Peace and friendship amongst all our people shall be secured by upholding the equal rights, opportunities and status of all;

The people of the protectorates—Basutoland, Bechuanaland and Swaziland[6]—shall be free to decide for themselves their own future;

The rights of all the peoples of Africa to independence and self-government shall be recognized, and shall be the basis of close cooperation;

Let all who love their people and their country now say, as we say here:

"These freedoms we will fight for, side by side, throughout our lives, until we have won our liberty."

Freedom from Fear
Aung San Suu Kyi

It is not power that corrupts but fear. Fear of losing power corrupts those who wield it and fear of the scourge of power corrupts those who are subject to it. Most Burmese are familiar with the four *a-gati*, the four kinds of corruption. *Chanda-gati*, corruption induced by desire, is deviation from the right path in pursuit of bribes or for the sake of those one loves. *Dosa-gati* is taking the wrong path to spite those against whom one bears ill will, and *moga-gati* is aberration due to ignorance. But perhaps the worst of the four is *bhaya-gati*, for not only does *bhaya*, fear, stifle and slowly destroy all sense of right and wrong, it so

---

[4] crèches—day nurseries.

[5] locations—areas where blacks were required to live under apartheid.

[6] Basutoland, Bechuanaland and Swaziland—Basutoland and Bechuanaland became the independent countries of Botswana and Lesotho in 1966; Swaziland became independent in 1968.

often lies at the root of the other three kinds of corruption.

Just as *chanda-gati*, when not the result of sheer **avarice**,[7] can be caused by fear of want or fear of losing the goodwill of those one loves, so fear of being surpassed, humiliated or injured in some way can provide the impetus for ill will. And it would be difficult to dispel ignorance unless there is freedom to pursue the truth unfettered by fear. With so close a relationship between fear and corruption it is little wonder that in any society where fear is rife corruption in all forms becomes deeply entrenched.

Public dissatisfaction with economic hardships has been seen as the chief cause of the movement for democracy in Burma, sparked off by the student demonstrations in 1988. It is true that years of incoherent policies, inept official measures, burgeoning inflation and falling real income had turned the country into an economic shambles. But it was more than the difficulties of eking out a barely acceptable standard of living that had eroded the patience of a traditionally good-natured, **quiescent**[8] people—it was also the humiliation of a way of life disfigured by corruption and fear. The students were protesting not just against the death of their comrades but against the denial of their right to life by a totalitarian regime which deprived the present of meaningfulness and held out no hope for the future. And because the students' protests articulated the frustrations of the people at large, the demonstrations quickly grew into a nationwide movement. Some of its keenest supporters were businessmen who had developed the skills and the contacts necessary not only to survive but to prosper within the system. But their affluence offered them no genuine sense of security or fulfilment, and they could not but see that if they and their fellow citizens, regardless of economic status, were to achieve a worthwhile existence, an accountable administration was at least a necessary if not a sufficient condition. The people of Burma had wearied of a precarious state of passive apprehension where they were "as water in the cupped hands" of the powers that be.

> Emerald cool we may be
> As water in cupped hands
> But oh that we might be
> As splinters of glass
> In cupped hands.

Glass splinters, the smallest with its sharp, glinting power to defend itself against hands that try to crush, could be seen as a vivid symbol of the spark of courage that is an essential attribute of those who would free themselves from the grip of oppression. Bogyoke Aung San[9] regarded himself as a revolutionary and searched tirelessly for answers to the problems that beset Burma during her times of trial. He exhorted the people to develop courage: "Don't just depend on the

---

[7] **avarice**—greed.

[8] **quiescent**—peaceful.

[9] Bogyoke Aung San—Burmese political leader and the author's father. He was assassinated in 1947.

courage and **intrepidity**[10] of others. Each and every one of you must make sacrifices to become a hero possessed of courage and intrepidity. Then only shall we all be able to enjoy true freedom."

The effort necessary to remain uncorrupted in an environment where fear is an integral part of everyday existence is not immediately apparent to those fortunate enough to live in states governed by the rule of law. Just laws do not merely prevent corruption by meting out impartial punishment to offenders. They also help to create a society in which people can fulfil the basic requirements necessary for the preservation of human dignity without recourse to corrupt practices. Where there are no such laws, the burden of upholding the principles of justice and common decency falls on the ordinary people. It is the cumulative effect on their sustained effort and steady endurance which will change a nation where reason and conscience are warped by fear into one where legal rules exist to promote man's desire for harmony and justice while restraining the less desirable destructive traits in his nature.

In an age when immense technological advances have created lethal weapons which could be, and are, used by the powerful and the unprincipled to dominate the weak and the helpless, there is a compelling need for a closer relationship between politics and ethics at both the national and international levels. The Universal Declaration of Human Rights of the United Nations proclaims that "every individual and every organ of society" should strive to promote the basic rights and freedoms to which all human beings regardless of race, nationality or religion are entitled. But as long as there are governments whose authority is founded on **coercion**[11] rather than on the mandate of the people, and interest groups which place short-term profits above long-term peace and prosperity, concerted international action to protect and promote human rights will remain at best a partially realized struggle. There will continue to be arenas of struggle where victims of oppression have to draw on their own inner resources to defend their inalienable rights as members of the human family.

The **quintessential**[12] revolution is that of the spirit, born of an intellectual conviction of the need for change in those mental attitudes and values which shape the course of a nation's development. A revolution which aims merely at changing official policies and institutions with a view to an improvement in material conditions has little chance of genuine success. Without a revolution of the spirit, the forces which produced the iniquities of the old order would continue to be operative, posing a constant threat to the process of reform and regeneration. It is not enough merely to call for freedom, democracy and human rights. There has to be a united determination to persevere in the struggle, to make

---

[10] **intrepidity**—fearlessness.

[11] **coercion**—force.

[12] **quintessential**—purest.

sacrifices in the name of enduring truths, to resist the corrupting influences of desire, ill will, ignorance and fear.

Saints, it has been said, are the sinners who go on trying. So free men are the oppressed who go on trying and who in the process make themselves fit to bear the responsibilities and to uphold the disciplines which will maintain a free society. Among the basic freedoms to which men aspire that their lives might be full and uncramped, freedom from fear stands out as both a means and an end. A people who would build a nation in which strong, democratic institutions are firmly established as a guarantee against state-induced power must first learn to liberate their own minds from **apathy**[13] and fear.

Always one to practice what he preached, Aung San himself constantly demonstrated courage—not just the physical sort but the kind that enabled him to speak the truth, to stand by his word, to accept criticism, to admit his faults, to correct his mistakes, to respect the opposition, to parley[14] with the enemy and to let people be the judge of his worthiness as a leader. It is for such moral courage that he will always be loved and respected in Burma— not merely as a warrior hero but as the inspiration and conscience of the nation. The words used by Jawaharlal Nehru to describe Mahatma Gandhi[15] could well be applied to Aung San: "The essence of his teaching was fearlessness and truth, and action allied to these, always keeping the welfare of the masses in view."

Gandhi, that great apostle of non-violence, and Aung San, the founder of a national army, were very different personalities, but as there is an inevitable sameness about the challenges of authoritarian rule anywhere at any time, so there is a similarity in the intrinsic qualities of those who rise up to meet the challenge. Nehru, who considered the instillation of courage in the people of India one of Gandhi's greatest achievements, was a political modernist, but as he assessed the needs for a twentieth-century movement for independence, he found himself looking back to the philosophy of ancient India: "The greatest gift for an individual or a nation . . . was *abhaya*, fearlessness, not merely bodily courage but absence of fear from the mind."

Fearlessness may be a gift but perhaps more precious is the courage acquired through endeavor, courage that comes from cultivating the habit of refusing to let fear dictate one's actions, courage that could be described as "grace under pressure"— grace which is renewed repeatedly in the face of harsh, unremitting pressure.

Within a system which denies the existence of basic human rights, fear tends to be the order of the day. Fear of imprisonment, fear of torture, fear of death, fear of losing friends, family, property or means of

---

[13] **apathy**—inaction.

[14] parley—negotiate.

[15] Nehru . . . Gandhi—Nehru (1889–1964) was the first prime minister of India after independence in 1948; Gandhi (1869–1948) was an Indian nationalist who led the country's independence movement (page 613).

livelihood, fear of poverty, fear of isolation, fear of failure. A most **insidious**[16] form of fear is that which masquerades as common sense or even wisdom, condemning as foolish, reckless, insignificant or futile the small, daily acts of courage which help to preserve man's self-respect and inherent human dignity. It is not easy for a people conditioned by fear under the iron rule of the principle that might is right to free themselves from the enervating miasma[17] of fear. Yet even under the most crushing state machinery courage rises up again and again, for fear is not the natural state of civilized man.

The wellspring of courage and endurance in the face of unbridled power is generally a firm belief in the sanctity of ethical principles combined with a historical sense that despite all set-backs the condition of man is set on an ultimate course for both spiritual and material advancement. It is his capacity for self-improvement and self-redemption which most distinguishes man from the mere brute. At the root of human responsibility is the concept of perfection, the urge to achieve it, the intelligence to find a path towards it, and the will to follow that path if not to the end at least the distance needed to rise above individual limitations and environmental impediments. It is man's vision of a world fit for rational, civilized humanity which leads him to dare and to suffer to build societies free from want and fear. Concepts such as truth, justice and compassion cannot be dismissed as trite when these are often the only bulwarks which stand against ruthless power.

---

[16] **insidious**—treacherous.

[17] enervating miasma—weakening atmosphere.

QUESTIONS TO CONSIDER

1. What inferences can you make from the Freedom Charter about how apartheid laws were enforced?

2. Many of the changes proposed by the Freedom Charter deal with issues that are debated in the United States today. Which of these changes would you think would be most controversial?

3. Suu Kyi says that a "revolution of the spirit" is needed to guarantee the success of a revolution. What part does courage play in this spiritual revolution?

4. According to Suu Kyi, what happens when political power changes but there is no spiritual revolution?

5. Think of some instance of corruption or political oppression that you know of or have read about. Was fear at the root of it, as Suu Kyi says?

from

Cities of Salt

ABDELRAHMAN MUNIF

Since the Industrial Revolution, technology has been drawing the peoples of the world ever closer. When different cultures meet, misunderstandings are almost certain to result. The following passage from Cities of Salt *by Arab novelist Abdelrahman Munif (1933–   ) deals with the period when oil was discovered in Saudi Arabia. Miteb al-Hathal, a Bedouin, is puzzled and distressed at the mysterious behavior of three Americans, who claim to be searching for water. In reality, they are petroleum engineers.*

They were busy all day long. They went places no one dreamed of going. They collected unthinkable things. They had a piece of iron—no one knew what it was or what they did with it—and when they returned in the evening they brought with them bags of sand and pieces of rock. Once they brought tamarisk and wormwood branches, and bunches of clover. They broke the branches in a strange way and attached pieces of paper on which they had written **obscure**[1] things. That was not all: they placed wooden markers and iron poles everywhere they went, and wrote on them, and wrote things no one understood on the sheets of paper they carried with them everywhere. The markers were hidden or moved around whenever they went away—the boys of the wadi[2] moved and gathered up some of the markers, and the grown-ups did nothing to stop them. When Fawaz[3] showed up with some of the iron poles after he had been tending the sheep, his father scrutinized them carefully and a little fearfully. He knocked them on a rock, knocked them against the other and listened to them for a long time, then he said that they must not be brought near the fire.

And the water. Where was the water and how could they find it? Did the government know where they were and what they were doing? When Miteb al-Hathal

---

[1] **obscure**—unclear.
[2] wadi—Wadi al-Uyoun, a desert oasis.
[3] Fawaz—Miteb's son.

asked him, Ibn Rashed said that they had a certificate from the emir[4] and had been his guests for a week. When Miteb asked the two guides, they said that the emir had sent them and that was why they had come.

Miteb al-Hathal grew more pessimistic with every passing day; his fears mounted and his curses were more frequent. He came to talk about nothing else. If all the men joined him in discussing the problem, not all of them agreed with him, but because of his age and social standing they let him think and swear as he pleased.

He sensed that something terrible was about to happen. He did not know what it was or when it would happen, and he took no comfort in the explanations offered him from all sides. The very sight of the foreigners and their constant activity all day, the instruments they carried around, the bags of sand and stones they had amassed after writing in their notebooks and drawing symbols on them, the discussions that lasted from sundown until after supper and the writing that followed, the damned questions they asked about dialects, about tribes and their disputes, about religion and sects, about the routes, the winds, and the rainy seasons—all these caused Miteb's fear to grow day by day that they meant to harm the wadi and the people. The wadi's inhabitants, who at first viewed the three foreigners with scorn and laughed when they saw them carrying bags of sand and rock, grew more surprised when they discovered that the three knew a lot about religion, the desert, the bedouin's life, and

the tribes. The [Islamic] profession of faith [the foreigners] repeated whenever they asked, and their scriptural citations, moved many people of the wadi to wonder among themselves if these were jinn,[5] because people like them who knew all those things and spoke Arabic yet never prayed were not Muslims and could not be normal humans.

---

[4] emir—local Arab ruler.

[5] jinn—supernatural beings.

QUESTIONS TO CONSIDER

1. Why do the Bedouins suspect that the American engineers might be supernatural beings?

2. Imagine the Americans tell Miteb al-Hathal they are looking for oil. Would this information convey much to him? Why or why not?

3. Why do you think Miteb cautions his son not to bring the engineers' poles near the fire?

4. What does this episode suggest about the problems of contact between cultures?

Looking at Language

Even though technology has changed how we communicate, we still use language. Different views of the role of language in a rapidly changing world are presented in a poem by Chinese writer Bei Dao (1949–   ) and a speech by Colombian writer Gabriel García Márquez (1928–   ) at the First International Congress of the Spanish Language in 1997.

Language

BEI DAO

many languages
fly around the world
producing sparks when they collide
sometimes of hate
sometimes of love

reason's mansion
collapses without a sound
baskets woven of thoughts
as flimsy as bamboo splints
are filled with blind toadstools

the beasts on the cliff
run past, trampling the flowers
a dandelion grows secretly
in a certain corner
the wind has carried away its seeds

many languages
fly around the world
the production of languages
can neither increase nor decrease
mankind's silent suffering

Words Are in a Hurry, Get Out of the Way

Gabriel García Márquez

When I was 12 I was almost run down by a bicycle. A passing priest saved me by shouting, "Watch out!" The cyclist fell to the ground. Without stopping, the priest called to me, "Did you see the power of the word?" I learned it that day. And we know now that ever since the time of Christ the Mayans had known it too, and with so much clarity they even had a special god of words. That power has never been as great as it is today. Humankind will enter the third millennium under the sway of words. It is not true that images are replacing them or can ever eradicate them.

On the contrary, images empower them; the world has never seen the vast number of far-reaching, strong-willed, authoritative words that exists today in the Babel[1] of contemporary life. Words invented, abused or sacralized[2] by the press, throw-away books, billboards; words spoken and sung on radio, on television, in the movies, on the phone, over loudspeakers; words screamed out in graffiti scrawled on public walls or whispered into an ear in the dark of love. No: silence is the great loser. Things now have so many names in so many tongues that it is difficult to find out what they are called in any of them. Languages run free, scatter, mix and become confused with one another as they race toward the **ineluctable**[3] destiny of a single, world-wide speech.

Spanish has to be prepared to play a major role in this future without frontiers. It is a historic right. Not because of the kind of economic domination other languages have enjoyed, but because of its vitality, dynamic creativity and vast cultural experience, its rapid, powerful expansion within its own territory covering 19 million square kilometers, with 400 million inhabitants at century's end.

A teacher of Hispanic literature in the United States has said, and with good reason, that he spends most of his class time acting as an interpreter among Latin Americans from different countries. It is worth noting that the verb *pasar* has 54 distinct meanings, while in the republic of Ecuador there are 105 names for the male sex organ, though the word "condolent,"[4] which is self-explanatory and sorely needed, has not yet been invented.

A young French journalist has expressed his astonishment at the poetic treasures he discovers everywhere in our domestic life. A young boy kept awake by the intermittent bleating of a lamb says, "It sounds like a lighthouse." A foodseller in a market in La Guajira, Colombia, refuses to drink a lemon balm tea because she claims it tastes like Good Friday. And Don Sebastián de Covarrubias, in his memorable dictionary, changed the gender of a noun when he

---

[1] Babel—allusion to a story in the Bible of a tower intended to reach heaven. Its builders were unable to complete it because God caused them to speak many languages.

[2] sacralized—made holy.

[3] **ineluctable**—unavoidable.

[4] condolent—sympathetic.

wrote in his own hand that yellow was "la color" of lovers. How often have we had coffee that tastes of window, bread that tastes of corner, cherries that taste of kiss?

These are solid proofs of the intelligence of a language that for some time has been bursting at the seams. Our contribution, however, should not be to force it back inside its skin but to free it from normative restraints and allow it to enter the 21st century with all the ease of a man walking into his own house. And in that sense, I will presume to suggest to this learned audience that we simplify our grammar before our grammar simplifies us. Let us humanize its rules, and accept from our **indigenous**[5] languages—to which we owe so much already—the great, enriching lessons they can teach us; assimilate with speed and efficiency technical and scientific neologisms[6] before they seep in, undigested; negotiate in good faith with the barbaric gerund, the endemic *que*, the parasitic *de que*, and give back to the present subjunctive the splendor of its dactyls:[7] *váyamos* instead of *vayamos* [we may go], *cántemos* instead of *cantemos* [we may sing], or the harmonious *muéramos* [we may die] instead of the sinister *muramos*.

Let us discard orthography,[8] the terror of all human beings from birth; bury the archaic silent "h," sign a peace treaty between the "g" and the "j," and bring more rationality to written accent marks, since no one, after all, will ever mistake *lagrima* [he weeps] for *lágrima* [tear] or confuse *revólver* [revolver] with *revolver*

[to stir up]. And what about our indistinguishable "b" and "v," brought to us by our Spanish forebears as if they were two separate consonants with one always left over?

These are random questions, of course, like bottles tossed into the sea in the hope they reach the god of words. Unless it turns out that the **effrontery**[9] of the questions makes both him and us regret that the providential bicycle in my 12th year did not run me down in time.

---

[5] **indigenous**—native.

[6] neoligisms—new words or expressions.

[7] dactyls—metrical feet consisting of one accented syllable followed by two unaccented ones.

[8] orthography—spelling.

[9] **effrontery**—boldness.

QUESTIONS TO CONSIDER

1. Bei Dao describes languages "producing sparks when they collide." What do you think he means?

2. Is Bei Dao's view of language finally positive or negative? Explain your answer.

3. Gabriel García Márquez thinks there will be a "single, worldwide speech." Do you agree? Why or why not?

4. Although Márquez gives examples of changes he would like to see in Spanish, he doesn't say how these changes would be accomplished. If you were going to make deliberate changes in any language, how would you go about it?

Reflections on Cultural Contact

As the world's peoples become linked through the media, migration, and leisure travel, cultural contacts multiply. What responsibilities do we have to other cultures? Is the growing global influence of American culture a good or bad thing? These questions are explored in a poem by Canadian Anishanabe writer Marie Baker Annharte (1942–   ) and an essay by Salman Rushdie (1947–   ), who was born in India and now lives in England.

An Account of Tourist Terrorism

MARIE BAKER ANNHARTE

History is just used pampers on the
grave of Sitting Bull[1] at Yankton but
because of crushed beer cans, obvious
Lakota[2] visitors to this historic site
know what is under the earth, the lake,
the black cook who died the same day.
McLaughlin[3] buried both in the fort
with quicklime to foul up those Mobridge
businessmen's rendezvous with the right
bones to connect to make one skeleton.
What is history and what did happen
is a deeper question than tourists

---

[1] Sitting Bull—Sioux chief whose warriors defeated a force of U.S. cavalry at the Battle of the Little Bighorn in 1876. Sitting Bull eventually settled on the Standing Rock Reservation, was killed there, and is buried near Mobridge, South Dakota.

[2] Lakota—one of the largest groups of Sioux peoples.

[3] McLaughlin—James McLaughlin was the agent at the Standing Rock Reservation when Sitting Bull was killed.

dumping dollars in an empty memorial.
The words not written on the plaque or
between the lines are ghostwritten graffiti.
Glow in the dark instructions if you dare
to landfill history, deposit postcards,
return artifacts, souvenirs and the clutter
of plastic tomahawks buried in our minds.
Indian raids are nothing in comparison.
Tourist terrorism is ceremony without fuss,
and who takes the bother stops **desecration**.[4]

---

[4] **desecration**—defilement.

Rethinking the War on American Culture

Salman Rushdie

A couple of years ago a British literary festival staged a public debate on the motion that "it is the duty of every European to resist American culture." Along with two American journalists (one of whom was Sidney Blumenthal, now more famous as a Clinton aide and impeachment witness), I opposed the motion. I'm happy to report that we won, capturing roughly 60 percent of the audience's vote.

But it was an odd sort of victory. My American co-panelists were surprised by the strength of the audience's anti-Americanism—after all, 40 percent of the crowd had voted for the motion. Sidney, noting that "American culture" as represented by American armed forces had liberated Europe from Nazism not all that many years ago, was puzzled by the audience's apparent lack of gratitude. And there was a residual feeling that the case for "resistance" was actually pretty strong.

Since that day, the debate about cultural globalization and its military-political sidekick, intervention, has continued to intensify, and anti-American sentiment is, if anything, on the increase. In most people's heads, globalization has come to mean the worldwide triumph of Nike, the Gap and MTV. Confusingly, we want these goods and services when we behave as consumers, but with our cultural hats on we have begun to **deplore**[5] their omnipresence.

On the merits of intervention, even greater confusion reigns. We don't seem to know if we want a world policeman or not. If the "international community," which

these days is little more than a euphemism for the United States, fails to intervene promptly in Rwanda, Bosnia, Kosovo, it is **excoriated**[6] for that failure. Elsewhere, it is criticized just as vehemently when it does intervene: when American bombs fall on Iraq, or when American agents assist in the capture of the Kurdish leader Abdullah Ocalan.

Clearly, those of us who shelter under the pax Americana[7] are deeply ambiguous[8] about it, and the United States will no doubt continue to be surprised by the level of the world's ingratitude. The globalizing power of American culture is opposed by an improbable alliance that includes everyone from cultural-relativist liberals to hard-line fundamentalists, with all manner of pluralists and individualists, to say nothing of flag-waving nationalists and splintering sectarians,[9] in between.

Much ecological concern is presently being expressed about the crisis in biodiversity, the possibility that a fifth or more of the earth's species of living forms may soon become extinct. To some, globalization is an equivalent social catastrophe with equally alarming implications for the survival of true cultural diversity, of the world's precious localness: the Indianness of India, the Frenchness of France.

Amid this din of global defensiveness, little thought is given to some of the most important questions raised by a

---

[5] **deplore**—lament.

[6] **excoriated**—criticized severely.

[7] pax Americana—"American peace," a reference to current status of the United States as the dominant global superpower.

[8] ambiguous—difficult to understand.

[9] sectarians—members of a sect.

phenomenon that, like it or not, isn't going away any time soon.

For instance: do cultures actually exist as separate, pure, defensible entities? Is not mélange,[10] adulteration, impurity, pick'n'mix at the heart of the idea of the modern, and hasn't it been that way for most of this all-shook-up century? Doesn't the idea of pure cultures, in urgent need of being kept free from alien contamination, lead us inexorably toward apartheid, toward ethnic cleansing, toward the gas chamber?

Or, to put it another way: are there other universals besides international conglomerates and the interests of superpowers? And if by chance there were a universal value that might, for the sake of argument, be called "freedom," whose enemies—tyranny, bigotry, intolerance, fanaticism—were the enemies of us all; and if this "freedom" were discovered to exist in greater quantity in the countries of the West than anywhere else on earth; and if, in the world as it actually exists, rather than in some unattainable Utopia, the authority of the United States were the best current guarantor of that "freedom," then might it not follow that to oppose the spread of American culture would be to take up arms against the wrong foe?

By agreeing on what we are against, we discover what we are for. André Malraux[11] believed that the third millennium must be the age of religion. I would say rather that it must be the age in which we finally grow out of our need for religion. But to cease to believe in our gods is not the same thing as commencing to believe in nothing.

There are fundamental freedoms to fight for, and it will not do to doom the terrorized women of Afghanistan or of the circumcision-happy lands of Africa by calling their oppression their "culture."

And of course it is America's duty not to abuse its pre-eminence, and it is our right to criticize such abuses when they happen—when, for example, innocent factories in Sudan are bombed, or Iraqi civilians pointlessly killed.

But perhaps we, too, need to rethink our easy condemnations. Sneakers, burgers, blue jeans and music videos aren't the enemy. If the young people of Iran now insist on rock concerts, who are we to criticize their cultural contamination? Out there are real tyrants to defeat. Let's keep our eyes on the prize.

---

[10] mélange—mixture.

[11] André Malraux—French writer (1901–1976).

QUESTIONS TO CONSIDER

1. What does Marie Baker Annharte mean by "tourist terrorism"?

2. What does her reference to "plastic tomahawks" tell you about the sacred site?

3. Why does Salman Rushdie support the idea of a global blending of cultures?

4. Should Americans oppose some cultural practices in other parts of the world? For example, should Americans actively support women's suffrage in those countries whose governments oppose it?

5. Which elements of American culture would you like to see contribute to world civilization? Which would you prefer not to export?

Art Across Borders

Like languages, art crosses borders between cultures and periods. One of the characteristics of late 20th-century art is a reworking of traditional subjects and styles into something new. Each of the following works reflects a reinterpretation of cultural forms—with varying degrees of reverence.

▲

Commissioned to design a new entrance for the Louvre Museum in Paris, Chinese-born architect I. M. Pei (1917–   ) reinterpreted the ancient form of the pyramid in a modern structure of steel and glass.

◀ The work of American theatrical designer and director Julie Taymor (1952–), for such works as the fantasy *Juan Darien*, draws on theatrical and artistic traditions from many cultures and expresses a vision of a world theater.

Erected by Chinese students in Beijing's Tiananmen Square during pro-democracy demonstrations in 1989, the so-called "Freedom Goddess" was inspired by America's Statue of Liberty. ▶

▲
Designed by American architect Charles Moore (1925–1993) for the Italian American community of New Orleans, the Piazza d'Italia makes a playful use of the forms of classical Roman architecture.

QUESTIONS TO CONSIDER

1. Does the Piazza d'Italia seem to you to be an inviting place? Why or why not?

2. I. M. Pei's design for the entrance to the Louvre was extremely controversial when it was first built. Why do you think this might have been so?

3. What does the erection in Tiananmen Square of a statue based on an American symbol suggest to you?

4. What qualities are conveyed by Julie Taymor's design for *Juan Darien*?

from

Post-modern Humanism

VACLAV HAVEL

Czech playwright Vaclav Havel (1936–   ) was a political dissident who spent many years in jail under his country's repressive communist regime. After the fall of the communist government in 1989, Havel was the first freely elected president of Czechoslovakia. The country has since divided into two nations, the Czech Republic and Slovakia. On July 4, 1994, Havel spoke at Independence Hall in Philadelphia.

There are good reasons for suggesting that the modern age has ended. Many things indicate that we are going through a transitional period, when it seems that something is on the way out and something else is painfully being born. It is as if something were crumbling, decaying and exhausting itself, while something else, still indistinct, were arising from the rubble.

The distinguishing features of transitional periods are a mixing and blending of cultures and a plurality or parallelism of intellectual and spiritual worlds. These are periods when all consistent value systems collapse, when cultures distant in time and space are discovered or rediscovered. New meaning is gradually born from the encounter, or the intersection, of many different elements.

Today, this state of mind, or of the human world, is called post-modernism. For me, a symbol of that state is a Bedouin mounted on a camel and clad in traditional robes under which he is wearing jeans, with a transistor radio in his hands and an ad for Coca-Cola on the camel's back.

I am not ridiculing this, nor am I shedding an intellectual tear over the commercial expansion of the West that destroys alien cultures. I see it as a typical expression of this multicultural era, a signal that an **amalgamation**[1] of cultures is taking place. I see it as proof that something is being born, that we are in a phase when one age is succeeding another, when everything is

---

[1] **amalgamation**—merger.

possible. Yes, everything is possible because our civilization does not have its own spirit, its own **esthetic**.[2]

This is related to the crisis, or to the transformation, of science as the basis of the modern conception of the world. The dizzying development of science, with its unconditional faith in objective reality and complete dependency on general and rationally knowable laws, led to the birth of modern technological civilization. It is the first civilization that spans the entire globe and binds together all societies, submitting them to a common global destiny. . . .

The world of our experiences seems chaotic, confusing. Experts can explain anything in the objective world to us, yet we understand our own lives less and less. We live in the post-modern world, where everything is possible and almost nothing is certain.

This state of affairs has its social and political consequences. The planetary civilization to which we all belong confronts us with global challenges. We stand helpless before them because our civilization has essentially globalized only the surface of our lives. But our inner self continues to have a life of its own. And the fewer answers the era of rational knowledge provides to the basic questions of human being, the more deeply it would seem that people, behind its back as it were, cling to the ancient certainties of their tribe. . . .

In searching for the most natural source for the creation of a new world order, we usually look to an area that is the traditional

foundation of modern justice and a great achievement of the modern age: to a set of values that were first declared in this building. I am referring to the respect for the unique human being and his or her liberties and inalienable rights, and the principle that all power derives from the people. I am referring to the fundamental ideas of modern democracy. Even these ideas are not enough. We must go farther and deeper.

Today, we are in a different place and facing a different situation, one to which classically modern solutions do not give a satisfactory response. After all, the very principle of inalienable human rights, conferred on man by the Creator, grew out of the typically modern notion that man—as a being capable of knowing nature and the world—was the pinnacle of creation and lord of the world.

This modern anthropocentrism[3] inevitably meant that He who allegedly endowed man with his inalienable rights began to disappear from the world: He was so far beyond the grasp of modern science that He was gradually pushed in to a sphere of privacy of sorts, if not directly into a sphere of private fancy—that is, to a place where public obligations no longer apply. The existence of a higher authority than man himself simply began to get in the way of human aspirations.

The idea of human rights and freedoms must be an integral part of any meaningful

---

[2] **esthetic**—sense of beauty.

[3] anthropocentrism—the idea that humans are the center of the universe.

world order. Yet I think it must be anchored in a different place, and in a different way, than has been the case so far.

Paradoxically, inspiration for the renewal of this lost integrity can once again be found in science. In a science that is new—post-modern—a science producing ideas that in a certain sense allow it to transcend its own limits. I will give two examples.

The "anthropic cosmological principle" brings us to an idea, perhaps as old as humanity itself; that we are not at all just an accidental **anomaly**,[4] the microscopic **caprice**[5] of a tiny particle whirling in the endless depths of the universe. Instead, we are mysteriously connected to the universe, we are mirrored in it, just as the entire evolution of the universe is mirrored in us.

The moment it begins to appear that we are deeply connected to the entire universe, science reaches the outer limits of its own powers.

With the "anthropic cosmological principle," science has found itself on the border between science and myth. In that, however, science has returned, in a roundabout way, to man, and offers him his lost integrity. It does so by anchoring him once more in the cosmos.

The second example is the "Gaia hypothesis." This theory brings together proof that the dense network of mutual interactions between the organic and inorganic portions of the Earth's surface form a single system, a kind of mega-organism, a living planet, Gaia named after an ancient goddess recognizable as an archetype of the Earth Mother in perhaps all religions.

According to the Gaia hypothesis, we are parts of a greater whole. Our destiny is not dependent merely on what we do for ourselves but also on what we do for Gaia as a whole. If we endanger her, she will dispense with us in the interests of a higher value—life itself.

What makes the "anthropic principle" and the "Gaia hypothesis" so inspiring? One simple thing: Both remind us of what we have long suspected, of what we have long projected into our forgotten myths and what perhaps has always lain dormant within us as archetypes. That is, the awareness of our being anchored in the Earth and the universe, the awareness that we are not here alone nor for ourselves alone but that we are an integral part of higher, mysterious entities against whom it is not advisable to blaspheme.

This forgotten awareness is encoded in all religions. All cultures anticipate it in various forms. It is one of the things that form the basis of man's understanding of himself, of his place in the world and ultimately of the world as such. . . .

It follows that, in today's multicultural world, the truly reliable path to peaceful co-existence and creative cooperation must start from what is at the root of all cultures and what lies infinitely deeper in human hearts and minds than political opinion,

---

[4] **anomaly**—something that is peculiar or not normal.
[5] **caprice**—whim.

convictions, **antipathies**[6] or sympathies: it must be rooted in self-transcendence.

The Declaration of Independence, adopted 218 years ago in this building, states that the Creator gave man the right to liberty. It seems man can realize that liberty only if he does not forget the One who endowed him with it.

---

[6] **antipathies**—strong feelings of dislike.

QUESTIONS TO CONSIDER

1. What two ideas, according to Vaclav Havel, have replaced anthropocentrism?

2. What is one example of the way the Gaia hypothesis works?

3. Havel says that the path to peace lies in self-transcendence. What people or groups of people in the world seem to have achieved this? What has been the result so far?

4. How might self-transcendence help to reverse the growing gap between the rich and the poor of the world?

Texts

2 *The Epic of Gilgamesh* translated by N.K. Sandars (Penguin Classics 1960, second revised edition 1972). Copyright © N.K. Sanders 1960, 1964, 1972. Reproduced by permission of Penguin Books Ltd. **5** "The Harper's Song for Inherkhawy" from *Echoes of Egyptian Voices: An Anthology of Ancient Egyptian Poetry,* translated by John L. Foster. Copyright © 1992 by John L. Foster. Reprinted by permission of the author. **7** From Genesis, Chapters 2–3, from *The New English Bible.* Copyright © 1961, 1970, 1989 by Oxford University Press, Inc. and Cambridge University Press, Inc. Used by permission of Oxford University Press, Inc. **13** "The Negative Confession" from *Ancient Egyptian Literature: A Book of Readings* by Miriam Lichtheim. Copyright © 1973–1980 Regents of the University of California. Reprinted by permission of the Regents of the University of California and the University of California Press. **24** "Egyptian Hymns and Prayers," from *Ancient Near Eastern Texts Relating to the Old Testament* trans. by John A. Wilson. Copyright © 1969 by Princeton University Press. Reprinted by permission of Princeton University Press. **27** "The Sister as Matchmaker" from *Most Ancient Verse,* selected and translated by Thorkild Jacobsen and John A. Wilson, 1963. Reprinted by permission of The University of Chicago Press. **28** "I was simply off to see Nefrus my friend" from *Love Songs of the New Kingdom* translated from the Ancient Egyptian by John L. Foster and illustrated with hieroglyphs drawn by John L. Foster. Copyright © 1969, 1970, 1971, 1972, 1973, 1974 by John L. Foster. Reprinted by permission of the University of Texas Press. **35** From "Life, Death, and Destiny," from *Ancient Iraq* by Georges Roux, 1964. **39** From "Education" from *The Splendor That Was Egypt* by Margaret A. Murray. Reprinted with permission of St. Martin's Press, LLC. **43** From *The Gifts of the Jews* by Tom Cahill. Copyright © 1998 by Tom Cahill. Used by permission of Doubleday, a division of Random House Inc. **50** From "The Sermon at Benares" from *Buddhist Texts Through the Ages,* Edward Conze, editor. (Oxford: Bruno Cassirer Publishers Ltd., 1954). **53** From *The Bhagavad Gita* translated by Juan Mascaró (Penguin Books, 1962). Copyright © Juan Mascaró, 1962. Reproduced by permission of Penguin Books Ltd. **61** From "Tales of the Ten Princes: Dandin" from *The Wonder That Was India* by Arthur L. Basham, 1954. Reprinted by permission of Macmillan Publishers Ltd. **63** "What She Said: to Her Girl Friend, and What Her Girl Friend Said in Reply," from *Poems of Love and War* edited by A. K. Ramanujan, Copyright © 1985 Columbia University Press. Reprinted with the permission of the publisher. **72** Excerpts from "The Great Tradition" from *India: Art and Culture 1300-1900* by Stuart Cary Welch, copyright © 1985 by The Metropolitan Museum of Art. Reprinted courtesy of The Metropolitan Museum of Art. **80** Reprinted with the permission of Simon & Schuster, Inc. from *The Analects of Confucius,* translated by Arthur Waley. Copyright © 1938 by George Allen & Unwin Ltd. Also reprinted by permission of the Estate of Arthur Waley. **81** From *Tao Te Ching* by Lao Tzu translated by John C.H. Wu. Copyright © 1961 St. John's University Press, New York. Reprinted by arrangement with Shambhala Publications, Inc., 300 Massachusetts Ave., Boston, MA 02115. **82** From *Chaung Tzu* translated by Burton Watson. Copyright © 1994 Columbia University Press. Reprinted with the permission of the publisher. **82** From "Selections from Chuang-tzu" from *Three Ways of Thought in Ancient China* by Arthur Waley. Reprinted by permission of The Estate of Arthur Waley. **84, 85** From "The Moral Power of the Ruler" and "The Deep Significance of the Spring and Autumn Annals" from *Sources of Chinese Tradition* edited by William Theodore de Bary, Wing-tsit Chan and Burton Watson. Copyright © 1960 Columbia University Press. Reprinted with the permission of the publisher. **86** "Tokugawa Hidetada, Laws Governing the Military Households" from *Sources of Japanese Tradition* edited William Theodore de Bary, Donald Keene et al. Copyright © 1958 Columbia University Press. Reprinted with the permission of the publisher. **89** From "The Chinese Civil Service Examinations, Matteo Ricci, Journals," from *China in the Sixteenth Century,* by Matthew Ricci, translated by Louis J. Gallagher, S. J. Copyright © 1942, 1953 and renewed 1970 by Louis J. Gallagher. Reprinted by permission of Random House, Inc. **91** Excerpted with permission from *Japan: A Documentary History* by David J. Lu (Armonk, NY and London, M. E. Sharpe, 1997), pp. 258-261. Reprinted by permission of the author. **94** "The Ballad of Mulan" from *The Temple and Other Poems,* translated by Arthur Waley, 1923. Reprinted by permission of The Estate of Arthur Waley. **97** "The Death of Atsumori" translated by Arthur Waley from *Anthology of Japanese Literature* edited by Donald Keene. Copyright © 1955 by Grove Press, Inc. Used by permission of Grove/Atlantic, Inc. **99** From "Lessons for Women" by Pan Chao translated by Nancy Lee Swann from *The Columbia Anthology of Traditional Chinese Literature,* Victor H. Mair, Editor. Copyright © Gest Oriental Library and East Asian Collections, Princeton University. Reprinted by permission. **103** From "The Diary of Murasaki Shikibu" by Murasaki Shikibu Nikki translated by Annie Shepley Omori and Kochi Doi. First edition pubished 1935. Copyright © 1935 Kenkyusha Co. Reprinted 1992 by Kenkyusha Publishing Co., Ltd. Reprinted by permission the publisher. **104** From *The Pillow Book of Sei Shōnagon* translated by Ivan Morris. Copyright © 1967 Columbia University Press and Ivan Morris. Reprinted with the permission of Columbia University Press and Oxford University Press. **109, 110** "In the Quiet Night" and "A Sigh from a Staircase of Jade" by Li Po and "Remembering My Brothers on a Moonlight Night" and "A Night Abroad" by Tu Fu from "The Jade

Mountain" from *The Chinese Translations* by Witter Bynner. This edition copyright © 1978 by The Witter Bynner Foundation. Translation copyright © 1944 by Witter Bynner. Translation copyright renewed © 1972 by Dorothy Chauvenet and Paul Horgan. Reprinted by permission of Farrar, Straus and Giroux, LLC. **110, 111** "Clouds," "The Poor Man's Child," "Darkness," and "In a Wide Wasteland" from *An Introduction to Haiku* by Harold G. Henderson. Copyright © 1958 by Harold G. Henderson. Used by permission of Doubleday, a division of Random House, Inc. **114** From "Introduction: Chinese Literature and Its Characteristics" from *An Introduction to Chinese Literature* by Liu Wu-Chi, 1966. Reprinted by permission of Indiana University Press. **120** From "The Japanese Appreciation of Nature" by Yuriko Saito from *Aesthetics in Perspective* by Kathleen M. Higgins. Copyright © 1996 by Harcourt Brace & Company. Reprinted by permission of Oxford University Press and Yuriko Saito. **144** "The Ancestors" from *Les Pygmes de la grande Sylve Quest Equatoriale* by P. Trilles. English version by Ulli Beier first published by Cambridge University Press in *African Poetry*. Copyright © 1971. Reprinted by permission of Professor Ulli Beier. **153** From *Sundiata* by D. T. Niane, translated by G. D. Picket. (Longman Drumbeat, 1965). **162** "Letters to the King of Portugal" from *The African Past* by Basil Davidson. Copyright © 1964 by Basil Davidson. Reprinted by permission of Curtis Brown, Ltd. **168** From "The Mask, Masking, and Masquerade Arts in Africa" by Herbert M. Cole in *I Am Not Myself: The Art of African Masquerade*. Copyright © 1985 Herbert M. Cole. Reprinted by permission of the UCLA Fowler Museum of Cultural History and Dr. Herbert M. Cole. **174** Excerpts from *Popol Vuh: The Sacred Book of the Ancient Quiché Maya* by Adrian Recinos, translated by Delia Goetz and Sylvanus G. Morley, 1950. Reprinted by permission of the University of Oklahoma Press. **179** "Song of the Sky Loom" adapted by Brian Swann from Herbert J. Spinden *Songs of the Tewa* (1933) and included in Brian Swann, *Wearing the Morning Star* (Random House, 1996). Reprinted by permission of the author. **180** "I Have Killed the Deer" from *Hollering Sun*. Copyright © by Nancy Wood, 1972, Simon & Schuster. All rights reserved. Reprinted by permission of the author. **191** "On certain laws the Incas had in their government," Chapter XIII from *Royal Commentaries Of The Incas And General History Of Peru* by Garcilaso de la Vega, translated by Harold V. Livermore, Copyright © 1966. By permission of the University of Texas Press. **194** From *Broken Spears* by Miguel Leon-Portilla. Copyright © 1962, 1990 by Miguel Leon-Portilla. Expanded and Updated Edition copyright © 1992 by Miguel Leon-Portilla. Reprinted by permission of Beacon Press, Boston. **198** "The End of the World: The Buffalo Go," Kiowa (adapted) from *American Indian Mythology* by Alice Marriott. Copyright © 1968 by Alice Marriott and Carol K. Rachlin. Reprinted by permission of HarperCollins Publishers, Inc. **200** From "The Rise of the Aztecs" from *Seeds of Change: A Quincentennial Commemoration* edited by Herman J. Viola and Carolyn Margolis; copyright © 1991 by the Smithsonian Institution. Used by permission of the publisher. **206** From *The Iliad* by Homer, translated by Robert Fagles. Translation copyright © 1990 by Robert Fagles. Introduction and Notes Copyright © 1990 by Bernard Knox. Used by permission of Viking Penguin, a division of Penguin Putnam Inc. **211** From *The Trojan Women* by Euripides from *Three Greek Plays: Prometheus Bound, Agamemnon and The Trojan Women* by Edith Hamilton, translator. Copyright 1937 by W.W. Norton & Company, Inc., renewed © 1965 by Doris Fielding Reid. Reprinted by permission of W.W. Norton & Company, Inc. **218–221** "To Anaktoria," "To an Uneducated Woman," "Klëis," "Age and Light," "Her Wealth," "On Herself," "Of the Sensual World," and "Repose" from *Sappho and the Greek Lyric Poets* by Willis Barnstone. Copyright © 1962, 1988 by Willis Barnstone. Reprinted by permission of Schocken Books, distributed by Pantheon Books, a division of Random House, Inc. **225** From *The History of the Peloponnesian War* by Thucydides, translated by Rex Warner, (Penguin Classics, 1954), Copyright © Rex Warner, 1954. Reproduced by permission of Penguin Books Ltd. **238** From *On the Nature of the Universe by Lucretius,* translated by R.E. Latham (Penguin Classics, 1951). Copyright © R. E. Latham, 1951. Reproduced by permission of Penguin Books Ltd. **239, 240** "Book One, 11" and "Book Two, 10" from *The Odes of Horace* translated by Helen Rowe Henze. Copyright © by permission of the University of Oklahoma Press. **241** From "The Greek Mind" from *The Greeks* by H.D.F. Kitto (Penguin Books, 1951, revised edition, 1957). Copyright © H.D.F. Kitto, 1951, 1957. Reproduced by permission of Penguin Books Ltd. **245** From "The Social Status of Women in Republican Rome" from *Pandora's Daughters: The Role and Status of Women in Greek and Roman Antiquity* by Eva Cantarella, trans. by Maureen B. Fant, pp. 55-61, 1987. Reprinted by permission of The Johns Hopkins University Press. **266, 268** "To Emperor Trajan" and "Trajan to Pliny" from *Latin Literature In Translation* by Kevin Guinagh and Alfred P. Dorjahn. Copyright © 1966 Kevin J. Guinagh, Ph D. Reprinted by permission of the Estate of Kevin J. Guinagh. (David McKay Co., 1966). **268** "Christian Martyrs" reprinted by permission of the publishers and the Loeb Classical Library from *Eusebius: The Ecclesiastical History, Volume I,* translated by Kirsopp Lake, Cambridge, Mass.: Harvard University Press, 1926. **270** From Saint Jerome's "The Christian and the Classics," from F. A. Wright's translation of *Select Letters of St. Jerome* (New York: G. P. Putnam's Sons, 1933). **275** "Empress Theodora Speaks Her Mind" reprinted by permission of the publishers and the Loeb Classical Library. *Procopius: The Persian War, Volume 1,* translated by H.B. Dewing, Cambridge, Mass.: Harvard University Press, 1914. **281** "On an Icon of the Virgin" by Manuel Philes, from *The Penguin Book of Greek Verse*, edited and translated by Constantine

1989 by Peter Theroux. Reprinted by permission of Random House, Inc. **632** "Language" by Bei Dao from *August Sleepwalker.* Copyright © 1988 by Bei Dao. Reprinted by permission of New Directions Publishing Corp. **633** "Words Are in a Hurry, Get Out of the Way" by Gabriel Garcia-Márquez from *The New York Times,* Op-Ed, Sunday, August 3, 1997. Copyright © 1997 by the New York Times Co. Reprinted by permission. **635** "An Account of Tourist Terrorism," by Marie Annharte Baker, as appeared in *Gatherings: The En'owkin Journal of First North American People, Vol 2.* Reprinted by permission of the author. **637** "Rethinking the War on American Culture" by Salman Rushdie from *The New York Times,* Op-Ed, March 5, 1999. Copyright © 1999 by the New York Times Co. Reprinted by permission. **642** "The New Measure of Man" by Vaclav Havel from *The New York Times,* July 8, 1994. Copyright © 1994 by the New York Times, Co. Reprinted by permission.

Illustrations

Position of illustration on a page is indicated by these abbreviations: (T) top, (C) center, (B) bottom, (L) left, (R) right.

xviii–1 Alinari/Art Resource, NY. **11** CORBIS/Gianni Dagli Orti. **14** CORBIS/Bettmann. **18** CORBIS/Gianni Dagli Orti. **19T** © Copyright The British Museum. **19CL** Erich Lessing/Art Resource, NY. **19BR** CORBIS/Bettmann. **20TR** CORBIS/Gianni Dagli Orti. **20BL** CORBIS/Roger Wood. **48–49** Art Resource, NY. **51** The Seattle Art Museum, Eugene Fuller Memorial Collection. **54** Nataraja: Shiva as King of Dance. South India, Chola Period, 11th century. Bronze, H. 111.5 cm. © The Cleveland Museum of Art, 1999. Purchase from the J.H. Wade Fund, 1930.331. **69** The Bodleian Library, University of Oxford, MS Ouseley add. 171, fol. 4r. **70L** Akbar Receives Mirza 'Aziz Koka, 1602. Cincinnati Art Museum, Gift of John J. Emery. **70R** Courtesy of the Freer Gallery of Art, Smithsonian Institution, Washington, D.C. **71** Tiers/Monkmeyer Press. **78–79** CORBIS/Burstein Collection. **112** The Metropolitan Museum of Art, Rogers Fund, 1936. **113** Du Jin, Chinese, active c. 1465-1505, Ming dynasty. *The Poet Lin Bu Wandering in the Moonlight.* Hanging scroll, ink and slight color on paper, H. 156.5. © The Cleveland Museum of Art, 1999, John L. Severance Fund, 1954.582. **124** CORBIS/Dagli Orti. **125T** CORBIS/ Richard T. Nowitz. **125B** CORBIS/ Marilyn Bridges. **126TL** CORBIS/ Richard A. Cooke. **126BR** CORBIS/Robert Holmes. **127** CORBIS/© Werner Forman. **128** CORBIS/Michael T. Sedam. **129T** © Robert Frerck/ Odyssey/Chicago. **129B** Panini, Giovanni Paolo, *Interior of the Pantheon, Rome,* Samuel H. Kress Collection, Photograph © 1999 Board of Trustees, National Gallery of Art, Washington, c. 1734. **130T** CORBIS/© Werner Forman. **130B** © I. Perlman, Stock Boston. **131** Alinari/Art Resource, NY. **132**

CORBIS/David Samuel Robbins. **133T** CORBIS/G.E. Kidder Smith. **133B** CORBIS/Patrick Ward. **134–135** © Copyright The British Museum. **146** Werner Forman/Art Resource, NY. **147TR** The Metropolitan Museum of Art, The Michael C. Rockefeller Collection, Bequest of Nelson A. Rockefeller, 1979. (1979.206.294). **147BL** © Copyright The British Museum. **148L** © Copyright The British Museum. **148R** The Metropolitan Museum of Art, The Michael C. Rockefeller Memorial Collection, Bequest of Nelson A. Rockefeller, 1979. (1979.206.229). **165** © Copyright The British Museum. **166TL** Plaque with multiple figures, mid 16th to 17th century Edo peoples, Benin Kingdom, Nigeria Copper alloy 46 cm. Photograph by Franko Khoury, image no. 82–5–3, National Museum of African Art. **166BR** Werner Forman/Art Resource, NY. **167** CORBIS/© Werner Forman. **172–173** CORBIS/Richard A. Cooke. **186L** Ohio Historical Society. **186R** Courtesy Arizona State Museum. **187TL** CORBIS/Dagli Orti. **187TR** CORBIS/© Werner Forman. **187B** Negative No. 326848. Photo by K. Perkins and J. Beckett. Courtesy Department of Library Resources, American Museum of Natural History. **188TL** Negative No. 3730(2). Photo by K. Perkins and J. Beckett. Courtesy Department of Library Services, American Museum of Natural History. **188R** CORBIS/Jonathan Blair. **204–205** Alinari/Art Resource, NY. **222L** Nimatallah/Art Resource, NY. **222R** CORBIS/Gianni Dagli Orti. **223T** CORBIS/ Gianni Dagli Orti. **223BL** CORBIS/Paul Almasy. **223BR** The Metropolitan Museum of Art, The Walter C. Baker Collection, 1972. (1972.118.95). **224L** CORBIS/Araldo de Luca. **224R** CORBIS/Mimmo Jodice. **250** The Metropolitan Museum of Art, Carnarvon Collection, Gift of Edward S. Harkness, 1926. (26.7.1394). **251TL** The Metropolitan Museum of Art, The Howard Mansfield Collection, Rogers Fund, 1936. (JP 2650) **251BR** Victoria and Albert Museum/ Art Resource. **252L** CORBIS/ Bettmann. **252R** CORBIS/© Werner Forman. **253** The Metropolitan Museum of Art, Gift of Edward S. Harkness, 1918. (18.9.2). **254** CORBIS/Francis G. Mayer. **255L** Werner Forman/Art Resource, NY. **255R** Leonardo da Vinci, *Ginevra de' Benci* (obverse), Alisa Mellon Bruce Fund, Photograph © 1999 Board of Trustees, National Gallery of Art, Washington, 1974. **256L** William Hogarth, *The Shrimp Girl,* by permission of National Gallery Company Limited, London. **256R** Cameron, Julia Margaret, *George Frederick Watts.* By courtesy of the National Portrait Gallery. **257** Murillo, Bartolomé Esteban, *Two Women at a Window,* Widener Collection, Photograph © 1999 Board of Trustees, National Gallery of Art, Washington, c. 1655/1660. **258T** Alinari/Art Resource, NY. **258B** Tate Gallery, London/Art Resource, NY. **259** Tate Gallery, London/Art Resource, NY. **260–261** Alinari/Art Resource, NY. **276** Alinari/Art Resource, NY. **279** Scala/Art Resource, NY. **280L** Scala/Art Resource, NY. **280R** *Madonna Enthroned,* Andrew W. Mellon Collection, Photograph © 1999 Board of Trustees, National Gallery of Art,

Washington; Panel, 32 x 19 ½". **281** Scala/Art Resource, NY. **294–295** Giraudon/Art Resource, NY. **319** CORBIS/© Werner Forman. **320T** The Metropolitan Museum of Art, Purchase, Rogers Fund and The Kevorkian Foundation Gift, 1955. (55.121.10.39). **320B** Courtesy of the Freer Gallery of Art, Smithsonian Institution, Washington, D.C. **321** Courtesy of the Freer Gallery of Art, Smithsonian Institution, Washington, D.C. **322L** Giraudon/Art Resource, NY. **322R** Courtesy of the Freer Gallery of Art, Smithsonian Institution, Washington, D.C. **330–331** Alinari/Art Resource, NY. **339** The Pierpont Morgan Library/Art Resource, NY. **355** Erich Lessing/Art Resource, NY. **357** The Granger Collection. New York. **360L** The Bodleian Library, University of Oxford, MS Douce, 383 f.16. **360R** British Library Add. Ms. 39943, fol. 2. **361L** This item is reproduced by permission of The Huntington Library, San Marino, California. Ellesmere Chaucer, "The Wife of Bath," 26 C9 f.72r. **361R** Giraudon/Art Resource, NY. **368** Alinari/Art Resource, NY. **369T** © Copyright The British Museum. **369B** Museo Nazionale Romano, Rome/Art Resource, NY. **370T** By Permission of the British Library, Photo No. 1003384.011. **370B** "The Seattle Art Museum," Eugene Fuller Memorial Collection. **371L** The Nelson-Atkins Museum of Art, Kansas City, Missouri (Purchase: Nelson Trust). **371R** The Metropolitan Museum of Art, The Cloisters Collection, Gift of John D. Rockefeller, Jr., 1937. (37.80.2). **372L** Erich Lessing/Art Resource, NY. **372R** The Metropolitan Museum of Art, The H.O. Havemeyer Collection, Bequest of Mrs. H.O. Havemeyer, 1929. (29.100.6). **373** Pierre-Étienne-Théodore Rousseau, *Under the Birches, Evening* (1933.37), The Toledo Museum of Art, Gift of Arthur J. Secor. **374** Inness, George, *The Lackawanna Valley*, Gift of Mrs. Huttleston Rogers, Photograph © 1999 Board of Trustees, National Gallery of Art, Washington, c. 1856. **375** Morisot, Berthe, *The Harbor at Lorient*, Ailsa Mellon Bruce Collection, Photograph © 1999 Board of Trustees, National Gallery of Art, Washington, c. 1869. **376** Cézanne, Paul, *Mont Sainte–Victoire with Viaduct*, Philadelphia Museum of Art: George W. Elkins Collection. **377T** WADSWORTH ATHENEUM, HARTFORD. The Ella Gallup Sumner and Mary Catlin Sumner Collection Fund. **377B** Max Ernst, *The Eye of Silence*, 1943-44. Oil on canvas, 42 1/2 x 55 ½". Washington University Gallery of Art, St. Louis. University purchase, Kende Sale Fund, 1946. **378–379** Alinari/Art Resource, NY. **409** Alinari/Art Resource, NY. **410T** Scala/Art Resource, NY. **410B** Scala/Art Resource, NY. **411L** Kunsthistorisches Musem, Vienna. **411R** Eyck, Jan van, *The Annunciation,* Andrew W. Mellon Collection, Photograph © 1999 Board of Trustees, National Gallery of Art, Washington, c. 1435/1436. **412T** CORBIS/National Gallery Collection. **412B** Alinari/Art Resource, NY. **413** Pieter Bruegel. *Fall of Icarus.* c. 1555(?). Panel transferred to canvas, 29 x 44 1/8". Musées Royaux des Beaux-Arts, Brussels. **420-421** Hogarth, William, *An Election:*

Canvassing for Votes, c. 1754, By courtesy of the Trustees of Sir John Soane's Museum. **440** Hogarth, William, *Marriage à la Mode,* Plate II, (Breakfast Scene), Philadelphia Museum of Art: Gift of Boies Penrose. **441T** Hogarth, William, *The Laughing Audience,* Philadelphia Museum of Art: Gift of Carl Zigrosser. **441B** CORBIS. **442** The Metropolitan Museum of Art, Gift of M. Knoedler and Co., 1918. [18.64(43)]. **443L** CORBIS/Burstein Collection. **443R** CORBIS/Burstein Collection. **470–471** Ford Madox Brown, *Work.* © Manchester City Art Galleries. **475** Tate Gallery, London/Art Resource, NY. **476TR** The Metropolitan Museum of Art, David Hunter McAlpin Fund, 1952. (52.524.3.3) **476CL** Tate Gallery, London/Art Resource, NY. **476BR** Alinari/Art Resource, NY. **477** The Metropolitan Museum of Art, Reisinger Fund, 1926. (26.90). **509** Palmer, Samuel, *The Early Plowman.* **510T** Foto Marburg/Art Resource, NY. **510B** Giraudon/Art Resource, NY. **511** Fogg Art Museum, Harvard University. Maurice Wertheim Bequest. **512T** Photograph by David Heald © The Solomon R. Guggenheim Foundation, New York. **512B** Tate Gallery, London/Art Resource, NY. **522** Erich Lessing/Art Resource, NY. **523T** V&A Picture Library. **523B** © Copyright The British Museum. **524T** The Granger Collection. New York. **524B** Alinari/Art Resource, NY. **525** By Permission of the British Library, Photo No. 1006801.21. **526T** CORBIS/Francis G. Mayer. **526B** Scala/Art Resource, NY. **527** By Permission of the British Library. **528L** CORBIS/ Francis G. Mayer. **528R** CORBIS/E.O. Hoppé. **529** Copyright © 2000 The Georgia O'Keeffe Foundation/ Artists Rights Society (ARS), New York. New Jersey State Museum Collection. Purchased by the Friends of the New Jersey State Museum with a gift from Mary Lea Johnson. FA 1972.229. **530** CenterSchalkwijk/Art Resource, NY. **531T** Alinari/Art Resource, NY. **531B** Courtesy Cindy Sherman and Metro Pictures. **532–533** Library of Congress. **558L** CORBIS/Archivo Iconografico, S.A. **558R** Picasso, Pablo. *Les Demoiselles d'Avignon.* Paris (June–July 1907). Oil on canvas, 8' x 7' 8" (243.9 x 233.7 cm). The Museum of Modern Art, New York. Acquired through the Lillie P. Bliss Bequest. Photograph © 1999 The Museum of Modern Art, New York. **559L** CORBIS/ Burstein Collection. **559R** Lipchitz, Jacques. *Figure,* 1926–30. Bronze (cast 1937). The Museum of Modern Art, New York. Van Gogh Purchase Fund. Photograph © The Museum of Modern Art, New York. **562** Margaret Bourke-White/Life Magazine. © Time Inc. **594-595** CORBIS/Morton Beebe, S.F. **639** CORBIS/ Richard List. **640T** © Joan Marcus. **640B** REUTERS/CORBIS-BETTMANN. **641** Courtesy of the Louisiana Office of Tourism. Photo by Charles N. Fisher.

Every effort has been made to secure complete rights and permissions for each selection presented herein. Updated acknowledgements, if needed, will appear in subsequent printings.

Index of Authors, Artists and Titles